New approaches to economic life

Economic restructuring:
unemployment and the social division of labour

New approaches to economic life

Economic restructuring:
unemployment and the social division
of labour

editors
Bryan Roberts, Ruth Finnegan, Duncan Gallie

Manchester University Press

Published by Manchester University Press
Oxford Road, Manchester M13 9PL, UK
and 51 Washington Street, Dover,
New Hampshire 03820, USA

British Library cataloguing in publication data
New approaches to economic life – economic
  restructuring : unemployment and the social
  division of labour.
  1. Industrial sociology
  I. Roberts, Bryan   II. Finnegan, Ruth
  III. Gallie, Duncan   IV. Manchester Conference
  on Local Labour markets : 1983.
  306'.36   HD6955

Library of Congress cataloging in publication data

New approaches to economic life.
  Papers presented at the Manchester Conference on Local
  Labour Markets, held in December 1983 at the University
  of Manchester.
  Bibliography : p. 531
  1. Labor supply – Congresses. 2. Occupations – Congresses.
  3. Unemployment – Congresses. 4. Households – Economic aspects –
  Congresses. 5. Informal sector (Economics) – Congresses.
  I. Roberts, Bryan.   II. Finnegan, Ruth.   III. Gallie, Duncan.
  IV. Manchester Conference on Local Labour Markets (1983 : University
  of Manchester)

  HD5701.3.N49   1984   331.12   84-19371

  ISBN 0-7190-1098-5
  ISBN 0-7190-1731-9 (pbk.)

Photoset by E. B. Photosetting Ltd.,
Woodend Avenue, Liverpool L24 9JL
Printed in Great Britain by
Unwin Brothers Limited, The Gresham Press, Old Woking, Surrey

Contents

List of tables

Acknowledgements

This volume is based on the proceedings of the Manchester Conference on Local Labour Markets, funded by the Economic and Social Research Council.

Chapter 6, by John Goldthorpe, appeared in the volume *Order and conflict in contemporary capitalism: study in the political economy of Western European nations,* © Social Science Research Council (USA) 1984, ed. J. Goldthorpe, and is reproduced by kind permission of Oxford University Press.

Chapter 24 originally appeared in *Consommation, Revue de Socio-Economie,* ed. Dunod, no. 4, 1983 and is reproduced by kind permission of the Centre de Recherche pour l'Étude et l'Observation des Conditions de Vie, Paris. This article was translated by Dr A. Gordon Kinder.

Research for chapter 2 was supported by the College of Agriculture and Life Sciences, the University of Wisconsin-Madison, Hatch Project no. 2549. Computational work was supported by a grant to the Centre for Demography and Ecology, University of Wisconsin-Madison, from the Centre of Population, the National Institute of Child Health and Human Development (HD-05876).

L. Murgatroyd and J. Urry would like to thank the Department of Employment, the Manpower Services Commission, Mr R. H. Kelsall of Enterprise Lancaster and others for providing them with information, and to Mr M. Lee for assistance in processing it. The work for chapter 3 was financed by the Human Geography Committee, SSRC. This is an abbreviated version of chapter 3, L. Murgatroyd *et al.*, 1984. The authors take sole responsibility for the views expressed in this article.

Chapter 5 summarises views developed during a long period of study by the Labour Studies Group of macro and micro behaviour in the labour market. The group's current research is funded by the ESRC.

Versions of chapter 9 have appeared in *La Ricerca Folklorica* (Milan no. 7, 1983), special issue 'Cultura populare e cultura di massa', ed. A.

Signorelli; and in *Les économies non officielles*, eds. E. Archambault and X. Greffe (Paris, Editions la Découverte, 1984).

V. Beechey and T. Perkins would like to thank Simon Frith, Duncan Gallie and Stephen Wood for their comments on the paper which now forms chapter 13 of this volume, and Pamela Jackson for the typing.

The research for chapter 20 was funded by grants from the SSRC which the authors are glad to acknowledge.

The research for chapter 21 was funded by the SSRC (award no. G00230004). A longer version of this paper was originally produced for the SSRC Research Workshop on Employment and Unemployment, 11 November 1983 at the Department of Employment. It was tabled at the Manchester Local Labour Markets Workshop. The authors would like to acknowledge the continual close involvement in the study of their postgraduate student, Derek Walsgrove.

Chapter 22 is reproduced by kind permission of Macmillan Press Ltd and the British Sociological Association from the volume *Restructuring Capital*, eds. H. Newby and C. Vogler, 1985.

Chapter 23 is based on research carried out by R. Martin and J. S. Wallace. The authors wish to thank the Department for financing the research project from which this paper was derived. The views expressed are those of the authors and do not necessarily reflect those of the Department.

Notes on contributors

Veronica Beechey
Attached to the Department of Science, Open University. She is currently researching on part-time employment in the Coventry labour market. She has completed an EOC/ESRC research project on gender and employment.

Colin Bell
Professor of Sociology at the University of Aston. His most recent publications are *Social Researching*, Routledge, 1984 (with Helen Roberts) and *Fathers, Childbirth and Work*, EOC 1983 (with Lorna McKee and Karen Priestley).

Bob Blackburn
Head of Sociological Research in the Department of Applied Economics at Cambridge and Fellow of Clare College. He has been a Nuffield Foundation Fellow at the University of Lausanne and Fellow at the Netherlands Institute of Advanced Study. He is author of *Union Character and Social Class*, and joint author of *Perceptions of Work* (with Huw Beynon), *The Working Class in the Labour Market* (with Michael Mann) and, with the present authors, *Social Stratification and Occupations, White-Collar Work* and *White-Collar Unionism*.

Anne-Marie Bostyn and Daniel Wight
Research associates on an ESRC funded project, 'Work and non-work in a small Scottish Lowlands town' which was headed by Dr R. Turner and ran from June 1982 to October 1983. They are both currently working on PhDs (using data collected in the small town studied) in the Department of Social Anthropology, University of Edinburgh.

Glynis Breakwell
BA (Leics), MSc (Strath), MA (Oxon), PhD (Bristol). Currently lecturer in Social Psychology at the University of Surrey and conducting research on

the attitudes of young people to the new technologies at work. The research reported in this chapter was carried out when Dr Breakwell was Prize Fellow in Social Psychology at Nuffield College, Oxford where the ESRC project on young people in and out of work was based. Dr Breakwell's central research interests are social identity, ideology and social change.

Richard Brown

Professor of Sociology, University of Durham, since 1982. Studied history at Cambridge and personnel management at the London School of Economics. Researched and lectured in sociology at the University of Leicester (1959–66) and in Durham (since 1966). Has undertaken research and written extensively in the sociology of work and industry, including studies of women hosiery workers, of shipbuilding workers, and of local labour markets.

Cambridge Labour Studies Group

This group is made up of Jill Rubery, Frank Wilkinson, Roger Tarling and Christine Craig and works at the Department of Applied Economics, University of Cambridge.

Roy Carr-Hill PhD

Senior Research Fellow, Centre for Health Economics, University of York.

John Davis

Professor of Social Anthropology at the University of Kent. He has worked mostly in Italy and in Libya and is preparing a book on local politics in the revolutionary Libyan state.

Ruth Finnegan

Reader in Comparative Social Institutions at the Open University, and Social Anthropology member of the ESRC Social Affairs Committee. Her earlier research included field work in Sierra Leone and work on the comparative sociology of oral literature, orality and literacy. She is currently contributing to the third level Open University Sociology Course 'Work and society' and doing research on local musical activities and groups in Milton Keynes.

Colin Fraser

University Lecturer in Social Psychology, Social and Political Sciences Committee, University of Cambridge and Fellow of Churchill College.

Duncan Gallie

Reader in Sociology, University of Warwick until 1985, then Fellow of Nuffield College, Oxford. He is engaged on a comparison of unemployment and family relationships in the Coventry and Rouen labour markets, funded by CNRS/ESRC.

Jonathan I. Gershuny
Professor of Sociology, University of Bath. Formerly Research Associate at the Science Policy Research Unit, University of Sussex. Author of *Social Innovation and the Division of Labour.*

John Goldthorpe
Fellow of Nuffield College, Oxford. His research includes the Oxford Mobility studies and the Affluent Worker studies. He is the author (with C. Llewellyn and C. Payne) of *Social Mobility and Class Structure in Modern Britain.*

Chris Harris
Reader in Sociology, University College of Swansea; published works include *The Family and Social Change* (1965) (with C. Rosser) *The Family* (1969), *Fundamental Concepts and the Sociological Enterprise* (1980) and *The Family and Industrial Society* (1983).

Richard Jenkins
Lecturer in the Department of Sociology and Social Anthropology, University College, Swansea. He was Research Fellow at the ESRC Research Unit on Ethnic Relations at Aston until 1983. He has done research on the transition from school to work in Belfast and on racism and job recruitment in the West Midlands labour market. His publications include *Lads, Citizens and Ordinary Kids.*

Ray Jobling
University Lecturer in Sociology, Faculty of Economics and Politics, University of Cambridge, and Fellow of St John's College.

R. M. Lee
Senior Research Officer at the University College of Swansea. His research interests – besides the study of redundancy – include the family and the sociology of religion. He received his doctorate from Edinburgh University for a study of inter-religious marriage in Northern Ireland and he has been involved in two large-scale surveys of Roman Catholics in England and Wales.

Gordon Marshall
Teaches in the Department of Sociology, University of Essex, and is co-director of the ESRC project 'Economic stagflation and social change'.

Catherine Marsh
University Lecturer in Social and Psychological Research Methods, Social and Political Sciences Committee, University of Cambridge, and Fellow of Newnham College.

Roderick Martin
Professor of Industrial Sociology, Imperial College, University of London. Until recently Fellow and Tutor in Politics and Sociology, Trinity College, Oxford (1969–84). Most recent publications on industrial relations and technological change (*New Technology and Industrial Relations in Fleet Street*, OUP, 1981), union government, (*Ballots and Trade Union Democracy*, Basil Blackwell, 1984, with Roger Undy) and unemployment, (*Working Women in Recession*, OUP, 1984, with Judith Wallace).

Lorna McKee
District Health Education Officer for Kidderminster and District Health Authority. She studied at Trinity College Dublin and York University. She has worked in social research on family and health issues and is joint editor with Margaret O'Brien of *The Father Figure* (Tavistock, 1982).

Ian D. Miles
Research Associate, Science Policy Research Unit, University of Sussex. He is currently researching 'Adaptation to unemployment?' funded by Joseph Rowntree Trust.

Lydia Morris
PhD (London) Lecturer in Sociology, University of Durham. She has carried out fieldwork in Puerto Rico, Mexico City and South London and was research officer in the Department of Sociology and Anthropology, University College Swansea.

Linda G. Murgatroyd
BA (Cambridge), DPhil (Oxford), Research Officer, Lancaster Regionalism Group, 1980–1. Currently government statistician, Department of Employment. Author of various papers on gender and stratification. Joint author of *Localities, Class and Gender*.

Howard Newby
Professor of Sociology, and Director of the Survey Archives at the University of Essex. He is currently co-directing an ESRC research project on 'Economic stagflation and social change'.

Iain Noble
Honorary Research Fellow in the Department of Sociological Studies, University of Sheffield. He was previously a graduate student of the University of Essex, Lecturer in Sociology at the University of Reading and Social Survey Officer at OPCS. He was Research Officer on the After Redundancy Project. He is co-author of *The Privately Rented Sector* (HMSO, 1982).

R. E. Pahl

Professor of Sociology at the University of Kent at Canterbury. He has done empirical research on Hertfordshire villages, managers and directors in British industry as well as unemployed workers in Medway and the Isle of Sheppey. His most recent book is *Division of Labour* (Blackwell, 1984). Professor Pahl has been a member of the University Grants Committee Social Studies Sub-Committee since 1979.

Ken Prandy

Senior Research Officer in the Department of Applied Economics at Cambridge and Fellow of Fitzwilliam College. He is author of *Professional Employees* and, with the present authors, joint author of *Social Stratification and Occupations, White-Collar Work* and *White-Collar Unionism*.

Bryan Roberts

Professor of Sociology, University of Manchester. He is currently researching on labour markets in urban Mexico.

Ceridwen Roberts

She has worked in the Economic and Social Division of the Department of Employment since 1978 having formerly taught Industrial Sociology at Trent Polytechnic. After five years in the Social Science Branch where she was responsible for initiating and running a programme of research advice on women in the labour market, she has now moved to a post in the recently created Employment Market Research Unit and works in labour market issues more generally.

David Rose

Senior Lecturer in Sociology, University of Essex. He is a co-ordinator of the ESRC seminars on stratification, and co-director of the ESRC research project 'Economic stagflation and social change'.

Sandy Stewart

Senior Research Officer in the Department of Applied Economics at Cambridge. He has twice been Visiting Fellow at the Australian National University and was Drapers' Visiting Lecturer at the University of Tasmania. With the present authors he is joint author of *Social Stratification and Occupations, White-Collar Work* and *White-Collar Unionism*.

Joachim Singelmann

Research Officer, Population Division of the United Nations, New York. Visiting Professor, University of Duisburg 1983–4. Author of *From Agriculture to Services* (Sage).

Marta Tienda
Assistant Professor of Sociology, University of Wisconsin, USA.

Robert Turner
Recently appointed as Lecturer in Physics at Nottingham University. Previously an Honorary Fellow and Research Fellow at the Department of Social Anthropology, Edinburgh University. He has conducted extensive fieldwork in Lowland Scotland, and publications include 'Models of good government' (1980) in ASA Monograph *Structure of Folk Models*, Holy and Stuchlik (eds.) London, Academic Press.

John Urry
MA, PhD (Cambridge). Lecturer in Sociology, University of Lancaster 1970–81. Senior Lecturer from 1981, Head of Department from 1983. Author/joint author of *Reference Groups and the Theory of Revolution*, *Social Theory as Science, The Anatomy of Capitalist Societies, Capital, Labour and Middle Classes, Localities, Class and Gender.* Co-ordinator Lancaster Regionalism Group.

Carolyn Vogler
Research Associate, Department of Sociology, University of Essex. She is researching on the ESRC project 'Economic stagflation and social change'.

Sylvia Walby
Lecturer in Sociology, University of Lancaster. She has done extensive research on gender and employment for the EOC/ESRC.

Roger Waldinger
He is Associate Professor of Sociology, City College, City University New York. He is currently researching 'Immigrant enterprise and youth employment'.

Alan Walker
Senior Lecturer in Social Policy at the University of Sheffield. He was previously Research Officer and Senior Research Officer at the University of Essex and the National Children's Bureau. His main research interests are in the fields of employment and unemployment, social gerontology, poverty and inequality, public expenditure and the social services. He is author of *Unqualified and Underemployed* (Macmillan, 1981), *Social Planning* (Robertson/Blackwell, 1984), editor of *Public Expenditure and Social Policy* (Heinemann, 1982) and *Community Care* (Robertson/Blackwell, 1982) and co-editor of *Disability in Britain* (Robertson, 1981).

Claire Wallace

Research Fellow at the University of Kent. From 1980–4 she has been work-ing on an ESRC sponsored project with Professor Ray Pahl entitled 'The social and political implications of household work strategies'. At present she is funded by the Joseph Rowntree Memorial Trust and is still at the University of Kent examining the effects of youth unemployment upon the transition to marriage and parenthood.

Sandra Wallman

Social anthropologist with a background in Development Studies. Now Senior Research Fellow at London School of Economics and director of a multidisciplinary programme of research into *Resource Options for Economy and Identity in the Inner City*. This programme builds on work begun in the ESRC's Research Unit on Ethnic Relations at the University of Bristol (1975–80) and continues to be financed by the ESRC.

Robin Ward

He is the Deputy Director of Research Unit on Ethnic Relations and is also attached to the Management Studies Centre of the University of Aston. He has researched on housing and race, and is currently undertaking a large scale project on ethnic business.

Peter Warr

Professor and Director of ESRC Social and Applied Psychology Unit at University of Sheffield.

John Westergaard

Professor of Sociological Studies at Sheffield University since 1975. Educated in Denmark and at the London School of Economics, he began his career as a research worker on social aspects of town planning at University College London; was successively Assistant Lecturer, Lecturer, Senior Lecturer and Reader in Sociology at LSE from 1956 to 1975, and also served till 1975 as part-time Deputy Director of the Centre for Urban Studies, UCL. His early research focused on urban development, and his work since the mid-1960s on class structure, including *Class in a Capitalist Society* (1975).

Introduction

The present volume results from the interest of the Economic and Social Research Council and its Social Affairs Committee in sponsoring research to examine how important features of the economy, such as the labour market and attitudes to work, are shaped by the values and strategies of individuals and the nature of their social relationships. The papers in the present volume were given in a conference in December 1983 which was part of an ESRC research initiative on the social dimensions of economic activity. This concern with the interpenetration of social and economic structure has been given urgency by contemporary changes in employment opportunities that result from recession and technological innovation. These changes have significantly altered the life chances of households and communities. Familiar jobs have been removed and others created that require new types of skills and often recruit different categories of worker than in the past, such as women workers rather than men. A situation of high unemployment, accompanied by the permanent disappearance of jobs in many traditional sectors of employment, inevitably focuses attention on the immediate social problems attending loss of work and of an accustomed style of life. In this volume, however, we will also look to the future, and to the long-term implications of the current restructuring of the British and other national economies.

It is likely that we are moving into a future where the way people live their lives is much less determined by the type of paid work that they do than has been the case in the past. The amount of the lifespan spent working is diminishing. Moreover, the likelihood that people will pursue stable work careers in any one job may also be decreasing. Further, the range of possibilities open to people outside of paid employment or domestic work has increased both through a greater range of leisure activities and through the 'labour saving' devices that have substituted for much household drudgery. Though the economic motivation to work in order to earn and achieve a high level of consumption is likely to remain strong, the lifestyles and aspirations of a family may in the future be less determined by the occupational status of the male head of household. Not only are males less likely to have stable work careers than in the past, characterising a household by a male's occupational status is less accurate when increasing numbers of married women work. This emerging situation makes it imperative to examine how individuals and communities interpret current economic changes, since their responses, as either consumers or suppliers of labour and as entrepreneurs, are likely to be less predictable than in the past.

Antecedents

The original concern of the then Sociology and Social Anthropology Committees of the ESRC was to encourage research on economic activity at the local level. The aim was to study the economic strategies of individuals and households as contributing factors in the overall pattern of economic change. The first workshops, organised by Ray Pahl, were thus entitled 'Local labour markets and stagflation'. This focus on people, their relationships and activities was intended to provide an alternative to the 'view from above' provided by studies of national class and employment structures. It was also intended that their focus should contrast sharply with that of the debates over the changing nature of the British class system that had dominated the economic sociology of much of the post-war period in Britain. The questions that we wished to pursue concerned the extent to which people could shape their environment despite the limiting conditions of national and international economic trends – the extent, then, that people were active agents in, rather than passive respondents to, macro-economic forces. We will outline why we felt that a fresh direction in research was necessary, first by considering the historical context and then, in a subsequent section, by looking briefly at the theoretical issues concerning how local practices and cultures affect economic behaviour.

With hindsight, we can see that the earlier research agenda, focusing on such issues as the changing characteristics of the working class or increased affluence, had been shaped by the especially dramatic impact on Britain of rapid international economic growth in the post-war period. One aspect of this was the unification of world markets under American economic leadership. The countries of the advanced capitalist world, including Britain, adopted similar models of economic growth based on the expansion of consumer markets. The state became an engine of growth promoting economic centralisation through direct investment and planning and intervening to ameliorate the socially disruptive consequences of economic change.

Observers of this period moved beyond a simple charting of these economic and political trends to propose a theory of social change. As Goldthorpe points out, this theory was based on the idea of 'industrial society', seen as a general type to which all societies were converging and which marked the end of the old bases of social cleavage, such as regional loyalties or class conflict between propertied and propertyless. Thus, a major claim was the convergence in the stratification systems of the major industrial societies (Lipset and Bendix, 1959). Status in society was viewed as being increasingly determined by occupation, with the emergence of a highly differentiated occupational structure reducing the polarisation between owners and workers. These occupations, it was argued, were held in similar prestige in all advanced industrial countries. In most western countries, in fact, there were substantial amounts of occupational mobility as sons improved on their fathers' occupations. This convergence in occupational mobility was produced by the rapid shift of all western economies away from manual and industrial occupations to white-collar and service occupations. The immense growth in post-war productivity, following on technological innovation, meant that less people could produce more, but the servicing of industry, including the distribution and sale of its goods, opened up new, 'cleaner', job opportunities. The increasing role of the state in managing the economy and in providing for citizen welfare also required new white-collar manpower.

One of the assumptions of the theory of industrial society was that economic rewards would increasingly be allocated according to individual merit and educational qualification, rather than depend on birth or on whom one knew. Another was that local community relationships would have a decreasing significance as a result of increased geographical and occupational mobility (see Nisbet, 1959). Moreover, the expansion of the cities, slum clearance and the building of the suburbs were all seen to reinforce these trends, breaking up the old communities, splitting elderly parents from their adult children and ending long-standing social relationships. In this same period, increases in real salary levels led to changes in consumption patterns based on the generalised use of an increasing range of standardised consumer goods, including the private car. These social trends were seen as breaking down local allegiances and the particularities of local cultures and as making way for a universal culture, that of industrial society in which lifestyles and consumption patterns were determined by a person's educational and income level.

These issues set the research agenda even for those who did not accept that major inequalities and substantial conflicts of class interest had been eliminated by the coming of industrial society. Thus, even the research critical of the notion of industrial society tended not to question the trend towards a homogeneous market economy with national and culturally similar status systems in which local particularities had little significance. Instead, debate focused on whether the trend was as beneficial as was claimed, showing, for example, that children from poor homes continued to suffer educational disadvantages despite the increase in equality of opportunity in education.

However, by the end of the 1970s, there was increasing reason to question the assumption of a unilinear trend towards homogeneity of lifestyles and interests. The questions came from two main sources. First were the doubts about the prospects of unlimited growth that the oil crisis of the mid-seventies brought to the forefront. In Britain's case, despite our oil resources, these doubts were reinforced by a growing awareness of the long-term nature of our economic weakness and the fact that we were falling well behind our continental partners in the European community in terms of national product and standard of living. The possibility was thus open that instead of continuous economic progress, we could actually 'underdevelop' as a nation. Indeed regional inequalities became more evident in this period. Also, as Urry and Murgatroyd point out, intra-regional inequalities sharpened, contrasting economically stagnant big cities with the more prosperous smaller towns on their periphery. Regional and sub-regional identities, instead of becoming a less relevant source of political cleavage, as the theory of industrial society would argue, became along with other particular loyalties, such as religion or ethnicity, a more important one.

Second, the direction of technological change, based upon computerisation, threatened to displace jobs without bringing innovations that would create substantial numbers of employment opportunities. Indeed, it was feared that new job opportunities would be unevenly distributed geographically and in terms of the skills required. Thus, highly skilled jobs would concentrate in already prosperous regions, while those demanding low levels of skill would concentrate in areas where local labour was abundant and cheap. These trends suggested that we were about to enter a period of increasing social and economic heterogeneity in which life chances, attitudes and aspirations would differ according to the local pattern of economic change.

There were further reasons for seeing the study of local variations and of the strategies that people adopt to cope with them as an important means of understanding national trends. One possibility was that economic decline would increasingly localise relationships and put greater stress on people fending for themselves. Unemployment and the dearth of new job opportunities result in lower levels of residential mobility, both within and between economic regions. Furthermore, the strain placed on the welfare system to accommodate not only the unemployed, but the increasing population of the elderly, re-emphasises the significance of the community in providing care. Caring networks and other forms of voluntary help thus seemed an important focus of research and policy concern. Technological change also potentially enhanced the self-sufficiency of the household, creating possibilities of family and community self-help that might offset the negative consequences of the new technology for jobs. Thus, modern consumer technology made possible more home-based self-entertainment, released time from domestic drudgery and enabled people to provide services, such as home improvements, that otherwise would have been bought on the market.

The labour market, household economic strategies and the 'informal economy'

Concentrating on locality and on social and economic heterogeneity raises the research problem of linking findings at this level to the broader structural changes taking place in society. We need to identify national processes of change that may be producing social and economic heterogeneity. Also, we need to identify the salient characteristics of localities that result from and influence these processes and affect the life chances of the inhabitants. Finally, we need to explore the resources available to local people to meet these changes. Thus Sandra Wallman, for example, contrasts structure, or the framework of social, economic or conceptual options provided by the housing and labour market, and organisation, or the pattern of choices made from amongst the options.

One starting point is provided by those theoretical perspectives that question the assumption that the trend in modern capitalist economies is towards economic homogeneity, perfect markets and individualised economic behaviour and show, instead, that social and economic heterogeneity can survive, and even be reinforced, in these economies. Such a perspective is the concept of dual labour markets as used by a group of American economists to analyse labour market segmentation in the United States (Edwards, Reich and Gordon, 1982). Basically, this segmentation consists in the separation of what they call a primary labour market, made up of skilled and relatively highly rewarded jobs, from a secondary labour market of semi- and unskilled jobs whose pay and conditions of work were markedly less favourable than jobs in the primary sector.

From their perspective, segmentation occurs mainly between jobs in enterprises that form part of large-scale corporations with an oligopolistic market position and those in smaller-scale enterprises employing mainly unskilled labour on routine tasks and operating in a highly competitive market situation. In the corporate or 'core' sector of the economy, high productivity and market dominance enable firms to offer reasonably good pay and working conditions. Also, their complex organisational structures are suited to a stable, even unionised, labour force socialised into the working practices of the firm. In contrast, in the peripheral sector of small firms, the possibility of directly supervising labour, the routine nature of the tasks which can rapidly be learned by new entrants and the pressure to reduce labour costs, mean that employers have little incentive to retain workers through offering good pay or conditions of work. This sector is thus characterised by low pay and high turnover. Under these conditions, segmented labour forces will tend to have different social characteristics, with the primary labour market being mainly the preserve of full-time, unionised male employees belonging to high status ethnic groups, while the secondary labour market tended to be disproportionately filled by women or lower status ethnic groups, such as blacks, Puerto Ricans or Mexicans.

Dual labour markets theory is an analysis of historical trends in the relation between capital and labour, identifying a stage in which the basis for rapid economic growth is a diversified system of control in the labour process resulting in divisions among workers and differences in working practices and arrangements. It provides one means of understanding the fragmentation of the working class, its political volatility and the 'consensus' politics of the post-war period (see Newby, Vogler and Marshall). It also suggests future trends, seeing an increasing erosion of the position of workers through techno-logical changes that routinise much 'primary' sector labour. This trend, coupled with economic recession, and the displacement of employment to cheap labour countries is seen to reduce the advantages and bargaining power of primary sector workers and result in high and relatively permanent levels of unemployment. A major hypothesis of this approach is that the struggle to create the conditions of economic growth will, in all advanced capitalist countries, be displaced from the workplace to the political arena, as the different parties seek institutional changes or state intervention to offset the negative consequences of recession. The politicising of economic change is also pronounced since the supply of secondary labour is undermined by political movements that have extended public welfare provision and increased the rights of all classes of workers. It is to the political consequences of such trends that Goldthorpe addresses himself in his paper.

The hypothesis of dual labour markets is generally useful in drawing atten-tion to possible inherent sources of imperfection in the workings of the labour market and to ways in which such imperfections affect households and com-munities. Thus, the increasing importance of women's work could indicate, from a dual labour markets perspective, an increase in the secondary work sector and the replacement of full-time male workers by a casualised female part-time labour force. Likewise, the place of ethnic minorities in the British economic structure needs also to be examined in terms of labour market segmentation to see whether a possible root of ethnic conflict is the segmentation of ethnic minorities into secondary jobs.

Another way in which the study of the labour market helps us to under-stand the basis of social and economic heterogeneity is through the careful study of its local characteristics. The concept of the local labour market focuses attention on the consequences for community and family relation-ships of localised patterns of economic change, such as the decline in employ-ment in traditional industries, increasing employment in service industries and the increasing importance of women's part-time work. This emphasis on the particular attributes of labour markets contrasts with the use of the concept in economics as a model to explore the extent to which labour moves freely around the economy so that the demand for needed work skills is supplied at the appropriate price. From this economics perspective, the labour market is seen as a mechanism for sorting and differentiating workers through objective criteria, rewarding skills in short supply.

However, there are a series of reasons for supposing that the labour market rarely operates in anything like a perfect way. Blackburn and Mann (1978) in their study of the Peterborough labour market had indicated the various kinds of imperfections that were an integral part of any labour market. First, information about available job opportunities and the wages attached to them is unlikely to be widespread among those interested in seeking work or changing jobs. Further, there is so little skill differentiation among most jobs on offer that it is unlikely that any neat fit can be made between the job qualifications of a job seeker and the skill requisites of a job. These two factors make it difficult for employers to use objective impersonal criteria for job selection. Instead, those recruiting workers are likely to use such general and impressionistic criteria as the applicant's seriousness of purpose and suitability, as vouchsafed by his or her marital status, physical appearance, manner of speech or, importantly, the fact that other employees can 'speak for' the applicant.

The focus on local labour markets is thus intended to draw attention to the way in which change in industrial structure affects the nature of community, as well as enabling us to understand better the resistances to change that derive from existing links between work and residence. Historically and in certain locations, such as mining and textile townships, the job recruitment process creates a strong link between work and residence and between work relationships and community relationships. An aim of research is thus to explore the nature of the link between work and community under contemporary conditions, in which people live and work in different places and even 'local' employment depends on externally controlled enterprises or on government. The analysis of local labour markets also raises the general issue of the extent to which economic behaviour is culturally variable, shaped by assumptions of what makes for a 'good' worker or a desirable job. To the extent that these assumptions depend on local cultures and conditions, then the generality of economic theories of market behaviour is circumscribed. Local labour markets are another way, then, to study alternative economic rationalities and their significance in producing, in Britain, heterogeneous responses to economic change.

One such alternative rationality that we thought merited attention was that based on people's social relationships. The fostering of social relationships, whether in the household or in the community, and their use to obtain needed resources, including a desired style of life, must necessarily affect economic activity. Indeed, a desired style of life is itself a social and cultural construct based on values learnt at home, in the community and at work and often depending upon sharing activities with others. This social context can affect the supply of labour through workers' preferences for jobs or the value that they place on work as against leisure. It affects the demand for labour through promoting, or not, entrepreneurial activity and the particular strategies adopted by entrepreneurs. Social relationships also affect the pattern of consumption and aspirations for consumer goods, as when status in a community is measured by the amount of goods and services purchased, or, alternatively, strong community or kinship norms limit social and economic differentiation based on individual or household accumulation. A further consideration is the numbers of dependents that have to be maintained and the social resources available to do so, including those prepared to work without pay as well as those who can supplement household income through part- or full-time work.

The issues here relate to long-standing theoretical debates about the applicability of market-based notions of exchange to situations in which social and economic relationships cannot easily be disentangled (and these include most economic activities even in modern industrial societies). Of relevance are the issues arising from the debate between formalists and substantivists in economic anthropology to which we return below. Equally relevant is the discussion of the extent to which kinship and like relationships involve 'sharing without reckoning' (Bloch, 1973). They thus provide a source of economic assistance without being subject to market calculations of the value of the exchanges (often involving labour or the loans of cash and material). One of the first ways in which we thought to explore social and economic strategies at the household and community level was through the analysis of the 'informal economy'. The term has been used in a variety of ways to refer to different types of activity, often referring to illegal activities such as pilfering from an employer or doing a job without declaring it for tax purposes. Our early discussions revealed disagreement about the utility of the concept and over the extent to which it referred to an identifiable sector of economic activity. Indeed, there is not a single paper in the present volume that uses the term for analysis and where it is used, its function is to illustrate the dangers of reifying the differences between the economic strategies of households and communities. We discuss it here partly to fill in the context of our present research concerns, but mainly because the issues identified with the concept remain, to our mind, basic to understanding the rationale of much of the research reported here.

The term informal economy has been used to refer to a sector of economic activity that operates according to principles sufficiently different to that of the formal or recorded economy to possess a dynamic that can be seen as relatively independent of the fluctuations of that economy. These principles can include factors such as an economic rationality among participants that places greater value on the use of available labour or on the intrinsic satisfaction of work than on profit maximisation. Also, the informal economy has often been defined to include activities that escape, or are not easily covered by state regulation, avoiding certain legal obligations such as health and safety regulations, tax and insurance. The emphasis on these differences was designed to demonstrate that the informal economy could flourish alongside the formal economy because it is not subject to the same constraints.

Our interest in this use of the concept came from research in the under-developed world on the ways in which people coped with the uneven nature of economic change. The Dutch anthropologist Boeke (1953) used the term 'economic and social dualism' to describe the situation of colonial Indonesia in which highly modern plantation enterprises coexisted with traditional peasant farming practices. Boeke was concerned to explain why it was that modern economic theory, with its emphasis on the economic subject seeking to fulfil unlimited wants within a money economy, was not appropriate for understanding economic development or for designing the policies that would maximise such development. He emphasised the importance of traditional culture and of the difference in rationality between that culture and that of the capitalist enterprise. The reason why work was valued and the import-ance of monetary gain were, for example, different in the two cultures. Peasant farmers gave priority to the social needs of the community – its festivals, religious services and customary law – and work and production were aimed at fulfilling these.

Boeke's critique of modern economic theory was that it was culture bound. It provided an accurate description of economic behaviour only when that behaviour was sustained by an appropriate social structure, for example through laws that individualised property rights and through value systems, fostered by religion, education or the media, which rewarded individual competition and acquisition. This argument was taken further by Clifford Geertz's (1963) distinction between the bazaar and firm economy, based on field work in Indonesia, but subsequently extended to North Africa. Geertz elaborated further the idea that economic activity is essentially a cultural phenomenon, depending for its efficacy on implicit as well as institutionalised understandings about norms and goals. Thus Geertz (1979) demonstrated the 'efficiency' of the economic practices of the bazaar based on the rationality of investing time to create relationships of trust and understanding that would enable sellers and buyers to minimise their risks in an environ-ment where the product or service was not a standard one. This line of analysis provided a means to understand the vitality of apparently traditional economic practices in the midst of economic development – a vitality based on local cultures, kinship and friendship relationships and on goods and services that were insufficiently standardised to be profitably provided by the large firm.

This was the sense in which the analysis of the informal economy was used to understand how people survived within the modern urban economies of underdeveloped countries. In these economies, it was clear that there were insufficient formal job opportunities to cater for the migrant and native population seeking work. However, observers noted that despite the apparent lack of formal opportunities, there was a considerable entrepreneurial vitality present amongst the poorest segments of the population (Lloyd, 1979; Roberts, 1973). Self-employment and small-scale enterprise abounded in these cities and, through the combined efforts of household members, the poor seemed to make out. Keith Hart (1973) coined the term 'informal income opportunities' to describe the sector of economic activity that existed outside of the formally organised economy. He demonstrated that there was no lack of entrepreneurial skills available among low-income populations. Indeed, it was with the thought of tapping this talent and putting its energies to even more productive use that the ILO, in a series of labour market studies, drew the attention of governments and international organisations to the need to provide credit and technical assistance to the small-scale informal sector as an alternative development strategy to that of fostering large-scale high technology production (see Moser, 1978, for a critique of this strategy).

A common theme of studies of the informal economy in the underdeveloped situation was the way in which household labour and wider communal relationships provided the essential means of survival for the self-employed or the small-scale enterprise. Thus, fellow villagers or co-religionists worked long hours for small return. In this situation, entrepreneurs often used profits to diversify and create new job opportunities rather than to invest in labour-replacing capital goods. The economic rationality of this sector was thus sufficiently different to that of the modern sector to protect it from the competition of the latter. However, observers also noted that this difference of rationality also created opportunities for the modern sector to exploit the informal sector either directly or indirectly. On this point the analysis of the dual labour markets theorists coincided with that of those interested in informal economic strategies. Thus modern sector firms not wishing to invest large sums in production lines for products for which there was a shifting demand might 'put-out' such products to the informal sector, providing the materials and paying by the piece. Also, some commentators argued that the availability of cheap services and goods provided by the informal sector could be viewed as generally cheapening the cost of urban living and thus benefiting those working in the formal sector (Portes, 1982).

These themes are relevant to modern Britain because they focus attention on the household and on its wider social relations as basic elements in survival in times of economic change and uncertainty. They also serve to counter a widespread misunderstanding as to the significance of social relationships and of their family and community context. Terms such as community have tended to be identified with cooperative, anti-individualistic social structures which disappear as a consequence of modern economic change, the basis, for example, of a traditional working class and its economic and political behaviour. However, in modern Britain there is still a considerable interconnection of social and economic relationships locally or extra-locally (a basic meaning of community). Also, interconnection does *not* imply harmony, solidarity or the absence of economic individualism or of diverse individual strategies of survival. It is more useful for research purposes to see social relations within families or communities as resources whose use may foster co-operative, competitive or individualistic economic (and political) behaviour. The outcome depends on the framework of opportunities and the range of social resources available. This context will differ between localities and will change with time; but there is no reason to suppose that the change is unidirectional promoting, for example, greater political or economic individualism. Studies of English history provide some support for this case, as do anthropological studies of small, highly interconnected, but far from harmonious communities (MacFarlane, 1979; Lewis, 1951). This is also the theme of Pahl's (1974) account of individual and communal strategies of welfare during the urbanisation of the underdeveloped world and that of nineteenth-century Britain.

Research on underdevelopment also suggested some of the long-term and possibly negative consequences of an over-reliance on individual initiative and self-help not only for economic behaviour, but also for politics and for the administration of welfare. Thus, the vitality of the informal economics of Third World cities also meant children working long hours and not studying, shanty towns and conditions of work akin to the sweatshops of the early industrial revolution. Such urban conditions have also been associated with non-elected authoritarian governments intent on reserving resources to promote rapid economic growth, rather than using them to meet the welfare demands of the mass of the population. However, it could also be argued that the development of an 'informal' economy through do-it-yourself activities and exchanges with kin and neighbours could offset a decline in income opportunities in the formal sector. Moreover, the quality of life might also be improved by these means, making households and communities less dependent on outside agencies and more self-reliant. The caring capacity of the community, for example, in terms of looking after the aged or the infirm, might increase the more people were bound together within a more informally based economy.

Recent research, some of which is reported in this volume, has suggested that the informal economy is a relatively unimportant phenomenon in this country in the sense of a distinct economic sector comparable to some of those described for developing countries. Pahl and Wallace's article stresses many of the reasons why this should be so. A developed welfare state and effective economic regulation provide little scope, outside the 'black economy', for the informal economic practices, or for the extreme exploitation of family and non-family labour that are characteristic of underdeveloped economies. Moreover, recession has meant the taking-out of economic resources via redundancies and a lower level of economic activity from those places that have been hardest hit, reducing income opportunities, even informal ones. Indeed, the vibrancy of the informal economy in underdeveloped countries was reported in a period in which considerable economic growth was taking place and where, consequently, the informal economy could expand through the 'trickle down' of resources, from those employed in the high income

sectors of the economy. Moreover, the scope of do-it-yourself and neigh-
bourly exchange is necessarily limited in complex economies in which there
are high standards of housing and social and economic infrastructure. As
Pahl and Wallace and Gershuny and Miles indicate, the cost of do-it-yourself
practices is often considerable, involving the purchase of expensive equipment
or parts. Thus, the poorest families and the unemployed are unlikely to
participate effectively in such activities.

Despite its limitations, the concept of the informal economy has served
the purpose of drawing attention to (a) the possible dangers to our political
and social structure if dualistic economic strategies are fostered to cheapen
labour costs, (b) the economic significance of the household and of the various
ways in which household members contribute their labour and (c) the
possibilities of households and communities organising their own activities
to substitute for goods or services bought on the market or provided by the
state, thus affecting consumption patterns and, ultimately, the industrial and
service structure that meets the changing pattern of individual and collective
demand.

Finally, then, the earlier concept of the informal economy as a separable
and, as it were, autonomous economic sector has turned out to be unproductive for the study of contemporary Britain, as have ideas of a set of
different sub-economies (the black economy, the domestic economy and the
communal economy, for instance) between which people could move at will.
Certain specific theories related to the concept of the informal economy are
also now in question, particularly the somewhat optimistic view that by
moving between the different sub-economies in our society people could
somehow keep up their standard of living, even in times of unemployment,
so that as the official economy contracted, the informal economy or one of
its sub-varieties like 'black' or 'domestic', would expand to fill the gap. Such
ideas now turn out to be too simple and are not supported by the research
reported in this volume. The basic realities, however, that stimulated the
interest in the informal economy in the first place still remain to challenge
social scientists: the existence of a whole series of economic activities (in the
broad sense of that term) which do not fall easily within the definitions and
analysis of traditional economics or get measured by government – the
activities that tend to fall outside the market place or outside the official
or 'blue' economy (as Davis calls it). As will be clear in several of the papers
in this volume, social scientists are now turning their attention to many such
activities – domestic work, self-provisioning, 'invisible' economic rewards,
various unofficial enterprises (such as those described by Turner *et al.* in
Cauldmoss, for example), household strategies, voluntary unpaid work in
the local community or elsewhere – all forms of economic activities or
relationships which are in a general way informal or unofficial – even though
the *term* 'the informal economy' is now no longer regarded as sufficiently
exact or unproblematic to provide, in itself, a clear guide to their analysis.

The approach in this volume

This volume claims to present 'new approaches to economic life'. We will end with a brief explanation of our title, with its chosen dual reference first, to the new challenges which people and institutions face in the changing economic patterns of the contemporary world; and second, to the new ways of analysing these now being developed by social scientists.

First, it is undeniable that economic changes in the western world, both current and in prospect, are presenting us with new challenges and that there are, in consequence, a new range of phenomena to which social scientists must now address themselves. No longer can we continue, for example, in the unspoken assumption that full employment is the 'normal' state, that the relation between occupations is the one we learned about in the classic social science texts, and that the somehow natural pattern – beyond a few marginal exceptions – is for men to earn outside the home and women to housekeep within it.

Part of the interest of the research in this volume, then, is the way people have adapted to – indeed, in a measure brought about – these changes: how they have approached the current challenges. Thus there are discussions of the arguably increasingly important area of part-time work, of the significance of occupational change, of women's role and experience in the labour market, of the economic strategies taken up by householders as a whole in the current recession (no longer necessarily depending on a sole male earner): all topics which in the past might have seemed of less than central interest in the social scientific study of economic life. It is the changing economic patterns around us, too, which have made us aware of the importance in our economic experience not just of the employer/employee relationship, but also of local and regional heterogeneity, of unemployment and the approaches that people adopt to this (a topic taken up particularly in Section Five, but also running through many of the other discussions), and the possible implications for the social division of labour within households (discussed especially in Section Six). Allied to this is the question of whether and how far people's ideas about work and non-work are changing. This is another element in our current economic situation about which it is essential for us to know, whether such ideas are to be interpreted as the result of economic change or as themselves a constraint on current and future economic developments.

The first objective of this volume, therefore, is to give some account from recent social scientific research in sociology, social psychology, social anthropology and social economics (among others) of the nature and significance of emerging patterns in economic life which would have received relatively little attention a decade ago: new approaches in our experience of unemployment, occupational restructuring and the changing divisions of labour within society. The main focus of this research is Britain, but some comparative perspective is introduced not only by a couple of reports on comparable patterns elsewhere in the western world (notably Singelmann on occupational change in the US, as well as the discussion of recent French research in the paper by Barrère-Maurisson *et al.*), but also through the implicit and often iluminating comparative insights brought by the social anthropologists who have applied their experience of other cultures to the study, here, of their own (notably in the papers by Jenkins, Wallman, Turner *et al.* and Davis).

These accounts of recent research, be it noted, go beyond mere description of new patterns of economic life, for they perforce introduce many current *controversies* about the nature and significance of these patterns. What are the implications for now and the future of current economic restructuring? (See especially Sections One and Two.) What are the constraints and opportunities provided in local sub-cultures, in ethnic networks, in family patterns, and how do these affect economic activities? Do we really know about the effects of unemployment on individuals, localities, the nation? Does it 'cause crime', for example, or mental ill-health, or a loss of identity? All simple-sounding and often-asked questions, but ones raising many problems of investigation and interpretation (see especially the papers by Carr-Hill, Warr and Section Seven generally). The papers in this volume may not be able to provide clear-cut answers, but they do present an up-to-date account of recent work on such issues, question some simplistic assumptions, and, equally important, give some indication of the current questions and controversies on a series of topics of major importance within our contemporary experience.

There is also the second sense in which the papers in this volume can be called new: their academic orientation to the study of economic life. Many of the older academic orthodoxies have lately come under challenge, both in regard to the appropriate boundaries of the separate social science disciplines and in previously unquestioned assumptions about what should be taken as of *central* significance within economic activity and how it should be studied.

One of the chief features of these new approaches is their interdisciplinary nature. Not only are some of the older, taken-for-granted boundaries between disciplines being challenged, but much recent research is now drawing on insights from a number of disciplines, not just from one. The whole study of labour markets is one prominent example here. As already explained, recent work on local labour markets has involved challenging economists on what used to look like 'their own' ground, drawing attention to the importance of the many social and (in a sense) 'non-economic' factors which also profoundly influence people's economic behaviour, an expansion of interest which has drawn on insights from social anthropology, social history, sociology and political science to supplement those of traditional economics. As Craig *et al.* put it in their plea for, and demonstration of, the virtues of drawing on ideas from several disciplines, 'We believe that segmentation in the social sciences has been one of the greatest obstacles to real under-standing'. Another example is to be found in the opening paper by Gershuny and Miles which challenges the established economic model with its implicit view of 'the social sphere as a mere appendage of the economic'; instead, they draw together work in economics, sociology and social psychology to try to construct a 'new social economics' to provide more illuminating tools for understanding current economic patterns and the major issues for the future.

Similarly, there are now challenges from many sides to the older orthodoxy within economic sociology with its long concentration on the patterns of official employment (especially full-time male employment in large-scale industrial organisations) as somehow the heart of the matter, the 'typical' economic activity of industrial society. For by now, as Richard Brown put it elsewhere, 'What were the predominant characteristics of employment in the early 1960s and what was problematic about work then, are no longer an adequate agenda for research on work in the 1980s' (Brown, 1984). Other academic moves, too, have added to this new look. The feminist challenge within social science, the many studies of aspects of the so-called 'informal economy', or wider perspectives on the nature of work *outside* official employment by social historians, as well as by the social anthropologists who have recently been paying more attention to research on their own cultures, have all led to the opening up of new topics for academic curiosity. Among these are – to mention just some – the ways of 'getting by' outside formal employment, productive if unofficial economic activity along personal or group networks, women's (and indeed men's) work within the household, and the whole area of economic activity outside the officially recorded economy (the 'blue economy' as it is called in Davis' paper). Some of these areas for research, many would argue, were actually there all along (not just a result of the economic recession, for example), but they were somehow missed because of influential academic models which tended to define them out of the accepted issues for research.

This volume is not intended to provide a new and united conceptual framework. It represents new approaches in the plural, and there is no single new orthodoxy to guide our analysis nor are 'interdisciplinary projects' necessarily claimed to be the only – or even the best – answer to all our questions. What was striking, however, in the conference discussion was a new preparedness to consider research across a range of disciplines and to question once taken-for-granted assumptions. This is a trend which runs through many of the papers in this collection and, it will be clear, has resulted – and no doubt will result in the future – in a fresh light on the nature of economic activity.

Running parallel with this widening of disciplinary boundaries in the social scientific study of economic life has been what can also be seen as a greater integration of the field. The number of research topics which once

looked marginal or merely the concern of special interest groups have somehow become central to the study of economic life. Studies of women provide
one obvious example. Once assumed to be a specialist topic for those with a
personal concern for such matters, or, alternatively as something to be
pursued in the 'social problem' context of women's 'dual role', it now turns
out that research on women, whether as employees, as household members,
or as unpaid workers within society, is after all of central, not peripheral,
interest in the study of economic life, one that perhaps no longer needs to
be fought for. Indeed one of the most forcefully put points in the conference
discussion was the reiterated comment that the time is past for special studies
of 'women' as such – for a ghettoisation, as it were, of women's studies.
Rather the study of economic life must necessarily include some attention
to the constraints of gender (on *men* as well as on women) and consider
women *and* men in their economic roles within society and – related to this
– their domestic situations within the household.

A similar trend has taken place in work on the household. Once this seemed
the preserve of feminists or of 'family specialists' (somewhat looked down
upon, truth be told, by those working on topics of apparently more 'central'
significance such as employment). But as is clear from the work of researchers
such as Pahl, McKee and Bell, Morris, Turner *et al.*, Wallman, and others,
the economic strategies within households, or the potential economic or
psychological support provided within families in both prosperity and need
(of which unemployment is perhaps only the most striking example) may play
an important, even central, role in the way in which people respond to – and,
in turn, mould – our current economic situation. In the conference proceedings, reports on the changing roles in household maintenance, on the
significance of wider family networks, or on household work strategies were
taken as of central relevance to the understanding of class, mobility, the job
market or patterns of occupational change.

Up to a point the same is true of studies of 'ethnic groups', though the
trend here has not as yet gone so far. Once again, this is research often considered the preserve of specialists which is out on its own, only marginal to
mainstream research on economic patterns in our society. But it will be
obvious from the papers in Section Three that many of the features uncovered
in these studies are widespread in our society: the use of kinship, friendship
and minority group networks, for example, word-of-mouth recruitment processes, and the significance of locality. As Richard Jenkins reminded the conference in the oral discussion of Waldinger's paper perhaps we should see
many of the characteristics of 'ethnic'-run small businesses as typical not
so much of immigrant enterprise as of *small businesses as such*, perhaps to
be found equally among white small enterprises; put another way, a 'white'
small business too could be studied as a kind of ethnic enterprise with implications for our more general understanding of economic life. As the study
of women has led us to a greater understanding not just of women but of

the gender constraints on people's economic activity, so too perhaps the new trend will be for ethnic studies no longer to be just a separate specialism but a sphere of research much more widely relevant for the light it throws on economic activity *outside* as well as within the groups conventionally thought of as 'ethnic'. A start of this kind of approach can be discerned in Jenkins' own paper and gleaned from the many potentially more widely applicable points in his, Waldinger's and Ward's papers in this volume.

Unemployment is perhaps the most prominent example of a subject which has now come to occupy central ground in studies of economic life. Once thought of as marginal only, representing the untypical and unnatural aspects of economic life (even in a sense the negative of 'the economic'), studies of the nature and many possible implications of unemployment have become a major concern to scholars working on current social and economic patterns. No longer can full-time employment be taken as constituting the taken-for-granted field of study, for the other forms of economically relevant situations in which people find themselves – unemployment, part-time jobs, unpaid work of many kinds – have also moved to the centre of attention.

The significance of local and particular factors in economic behaviour is another theme touched on in several papers, and one that raised a certain amount of debate during the conference itself. One aspect of this was the methodological. Can what people are discovered to be doing or thinking in one small community in central Scotland, or after unemployment from a steelworks in one (or another) specific locality, or in two small areas in inner London really tell us anything significant about anywhere except those particular localities? The debate on such questions perhaps followed predictable lines: the well-worn pros and cons of different methods of data collection; the nature and relevance of 'typicality'; the significance – whatever the 'typicality' – of understanding the probably varied local patterns within the country as a whole and the illuminating questions such studies may raise for helping us to understand both patterned variety and local particularities; the difficulty of persuading government agencies to release funding for arguably uncumulative research; the interrelationship of 'macro' with 'micro' studies. An incisive challenge was thrown out by John Goldthorpe to the proponents of grass-roots case studies to demonstrate the contribution that they could make to understanding important structural determinants of economic behaviour, a question well worth pondering.

The Conference did not resolve these lasting questions. What was significant, though, was its concern to try to tackle these problems, an eagerness to explore the possibility of understanding economic life through a range of different approaches, participant observation as well as interviews and sample surveys, small-scale local studies as well as wide ranging analyses from secondary sources. This trend within many of the social sciences towards a more eclectic range of methods and materials – sociology, for example, turning once again to 'qualitative' locality-based studies, social anthropology adding greater appreciation of wider structural constraints to their locally-based micro studies – was reflected in the conference papers and discussion, with people prepared to consider both localised *and* more general studies as of potential relevance to their own questions, and as equally part of the overall field.

This was not just a negative, 'anything goes' mood. For one of the other common themes seemed to be a move away from an interest in abstract theoretical models as such, to a concern with the realities of the situation, with economic *life*, rather than economic *models*. There was, indeed, an interest in reaching new theoretical perspectives (often interdisciplinary) but the emphasis seemed to be strongly on an *empirically* as well as theoretically based understanding of economic life. To quote again from the paper by the Cambridge Labour Studies group stressing the 'detailed investigation of the historical phenomena and the way that industry operates in the real world . . . It is our view that this approach is both more scientific and more fruitful than the methodology of abstract *a priori* reasoning followed by attempts to assess how far reality approximates to the theoretical abstractions'. One of the empirical findings that seemed to be emerging from the studies reported or referred to in the conference, as well as from the antecedents discussed earlier, was the danger of making too-ready generalisations for the country as a whole – let alone for 'industrial society' generally – whether about the effects of unemployment or the attitudes to 'work'. Redundant steel workers in Sheffield turned out to differ from those in Port Talbot, the social isolation and lack of creative activity among unemployed young people in an area without traditional high unemployment reported in Breakwell's paper were *not* the same as those in the small community of Cauldmoss with its strong cross-kin and cross-group ties, and one part of the economic reality in so many cases seemed to be the *local* networks and opportunities.

The interest in local and particular studies thus leads back to the way in which once apparently marginal studies are becoming integrated with other forms of investigation in the general field of research on economic life (further reinforced by the more widespread re-awakening of interest in community and local studies represented in a number of recent works, e.g. Wild (1984)). So what once looked like little one-off local and particular studies, whether by social anthropologists, social psychologists or 'community studies' sociologists, have joined the more generalised approaches as equally part – debatable but relevant – of our understanding of the economic realities of our society.

Once upon a time a volume covering the varied topics of these papers would have seemed a disparate enterprise, the accidental conglomeration of a number of varied specialisms. Now, the contributions of scholars working in a number of fields – on gender constraints, households, local and ethnic experiences, or the varying forms of work, employment and non-employment

– are coming together to constitute a wider and, we would argue, more illuminating field of study than before, in accord with the new realities of economic life in the present and the future. The parameters of this field are as yet far from settled, and it will be clear from the many different approaches in the papers here that the boundaries, even the key definitions, are controversial; there is, to repeat, no new orthodoxy. But what did seem to be shared was a fresh look at economic patterns, a widening of earlier narrower definitions of the field to encompass not only new developments in our society but new approaches to studying these, bringing together insights across disciplines and once-specialist interests into one field of study. Above all, there was the awareness that the study of economic life necessarily encompasses the many *social* determinants of economic activities. Even to understand the significance of jobs and non-jobs in our society, we have to go beyond the purely economic in the narrow sense, and consider the range of factors which play a part in people's economic lives, not only the overall economic and occupational structures (though this is one very real aspect), but also the constraints and opportunities presented through gender, ethnic affiliation, family, locality, socially sanctioned divisions of labour, moral categories, personally expressed social representations, and sense of identity – in short a whole set of socially constructed values relating to economic life as it is in practice carried on within our society.

Section one

Directions of occupational change

This first section introduces the changes in occupational structure which provide the context for understanding the changing patterns of individual and household economic activity. The general nature of the trend is clear: there has been a general shift of employment from extractive industries and manufacturing industries to the service sector of the economy. Within all sectors, jobs are increasingly 'white collar' with substantial increases in higher status categories such as the professional, technical and managerial ones. This is the basis for the high rates of occupational mobility which were reported in the post-war period in all advanced capitalist countries. (There is, however, little evidence that children with fathers in unskilled or semi-skilled jobs improved their chances of obtaining professional, technical or managerial work relative to children of professional and managerial fathers.) Even in the United States, often thought of as the free enterprise economy *par excellence*, the most rapid source of employment growth in recent decades has been that of state employment, suggesting that those who identified the growth in state employment as a peculiarly British vice were overhasty in their diagnoses of our economic stagnation.

More significant, however, is the emphasis in the papers by Gershuny and Miles and by Singelmann and Tienda that to talk of a trend to a 'service economy' is misleading since it obscures marked differences between the services in their occupational composition, their dependence on political currents and on whether they are offered to consumers or producers. The increasing importance of the services implies, they show, an increasingly differentiated employment structure, both within industrial sectors and between them. The increase in the service sector of employment reflects two fundamental components of modern economic growth. First is a substantial change in the organisation of economic activity in which services such as marketing, technical expertise, transport, finance and even education and welfare, become an integral part of modern productive activities, some of them expanding within firms while others are provided externally by specialised agencies. Modern technology raises the productivity of the individual worker, but it also depends upon higher levels of skill and an increasing range of ancillary services. Also, as Urry and Murgatroyd argue, this process involves a centralisation of economic activity that makes local jobs and the mix of local employment opportunities dependent on external investment decisions, on industrial restructuring and consolidation and on service provision. Second, in the advanced capitalist countries, increased productivity has raised average incomes and shortened average work-time, thus providing both the means and the leisure for people to consume a wider range of goods and participate in a wider range of activities outside of formal work.

Gershuny and Miles argue that there is, consequently, more latitude for households to determine the range of their consumption. Also, the particular choices made will have considerable significance for the distribution of employment, as when certain types of marketed services (and the employment associated with them) fall into disuse and are replaced by people purchasing consumer durables, such as home entertainment devices, sports and do-it-yourself equipment. In this context, lifestyle becomes a more variable and significant determinant of economic activity than has been the case in the past. Their case for a social economics is thus not simply the need to take social factors into account in economic analysis, but is based on what they see as a fundamental historical change in economic behaviour. Echoing points made in other sections and with reference to Marie Jahoda's (1982) categories of experience, they show, however, that formal work retains a considerable significance for social identity despite, or perhaps because of, the increasing importance of 'leisure-based' consumption activities outside of formal work.

The consequence of these patterns of occupational change for social stratification and politics is taken up in the papers by Murgatroyd and Urry and by Newby, Vogler, Rose and Marshall. Murgatroyd and Urry demonstrate how contemporary economic change necessarily contributes to an increasing intra-regional social and economic heterogeneity, pointing to the need for comparative studies of how localities are currently being restructured. They show, in detail, how macro-economic processes work themselves out at the local level, leading to new patterns of employment not only by industrial sector, but by gender. The outcomes are shaped, however, by the history of a locality's industrial and political development, suggesting a variation in the impact of economic change concealed by focusing on national trends. In their case, the emergence of a diverse employment pattern has worked against a strong or coherent political response to counter the marginalisation of the local economy.

Newby, Vogler, Rose and Marshall take up this latter theme at the national level, basing themselves on an extensive review of the debate on the working class in Britain. They challenge the assumption that there is any longer an identity of interest among workers arising from a common relation to production. Instead, they argue that there is an increasing individualisation of interests as households strive to maximise pay and consumption in a situation in which social relationships are less interconnected, and solidarity less important in achieving economic security. The trend to privatisation that they identify is not a retreat, however, into narrow family concerns, but an indication of the extent to which the changing nature of occupations and the achievement of such citizen rights, as a minimum standard of welfare, have undermined the old basis of solidarity. Their argument is open-ended, raising issues for research and challenging the assumption that declining economic opportunities must necessarily increase working-class consciousness and organisation. It thus has significance for one of Singelmann and Tienda's most interesting findings – that there is a slowing-down in the creation of 'better' jobs after the mid-seventies. This trend, which is likely to be stronger in Britain, means that the sense of improvement over the previous generation that may have underpinned much of the optimism and politics of the post-war period is unlikely to be sustained in the next generation – a generation whose jobs will at best be the same as that of their parents.

1 *J. I. Gershuny, I. D. Miles*

Towards a new social economics

This paper describes work in progress by the TASC (Technology and Social Change) group at the Science Policy Research Unit at the University of Sussex. We are pursuing a number of related lines of research in the area that may broadly be described as 'social economics'; we seek to relate technological innovation, ways of life and social relations (in the household as well as in the wider political arena) to such 'economic' affairs as labour markets, industrial structure and long-term development processes.

The purpose of the group

Conventional economics now seems less useful than once it did. Many eminent economists (for example, Scitovsky, Galbraith, Hirsch and Thurow) consider that it does not provide appropriate tools for understanding the current economic crisis, or major issues for the future, such as the balance between different sorts of work and leisure. It gives us few explicit insights into the likely effects of new technologies on economic prospects, let alone into their possible implications for future patterns of social organisation. Its focus of concern may be seen as too narrow, so that it rigidly addresses a confined range of variables. And it is inclined to view social affairs as a mere appendage of, or obstacle to, the working out of economic processes. Current changes in the structure of our economies make the established post-war economic models look increasingly inadequate; we need, in Thurow's phase, to begin 'rebuilding the foundations of economics' (Thurow, 1983: 218).

The TASC group sees its work as relevant to this enterprise. It is concerned with the development of theory *and* empirical analysis concerning the inter-relations between the processes of *development of the productive system*, and the processes of *change in styles of life* – a contribution to a new social economics. We shall not, however, present a systematically argued exposition of a grand new paradigm. Rather, we shall provide a set of notes and ideographs describing some examples of our methods and of the results of our research into current patterns of socio-economic change, together with an outline of the sort of theoretical structure which we hope will eventually emerge from the work of our group and others.

The first example of our research programme focuses on changing economic structures. Drawing on a study which set out to understand the emergence of, and prospects for, the 'service economy', we argue that a new conceptualisation of 'services' and of economic sectors is overdue, and suggest how such an approach can help us map out changes in industrial structures, employment and consumption. Our second example of research draws on studies which are intended to contribute to an analysis of possible futures for work. Again we suggest that the term 'work' requires redefinition, and demonstrate how time-budget data can be of value in explicating shifts in the boundaries of formal and informal work. Not all work is contained within the formal economy, and furthermore, even formal employment has extra-economic functions for workers. The final section of this paper outlines a social accounting structure which relates together changes in the formal and informal economies, so as to portray innovations in economic production and ways of life. While this accounting framework may not in itself constitute the 'new foundations of economics' which Thurow pleads for, it should nevertheless contribute to a fundamental reassessment of historical and future trends in socio-economic organisation.

The changing structure of the formal economy

The 'three sector' model of economic development is practically a cliché of social science. This model proposes that at first economies are dominated by 'primary' (farming, mining) production, employment and consumption; subsequently by 'secondary' (manufacturing) activities; and finally by the tertiary (service) sector. New sorts of technology, and new sorts of interconnection among the various stages of production and consumption, have however rendered this model increasingly unhelpful as an explanatory device. For example, the advent of information technology has undermined the complacent idea that jobs lost in manufacturing would be smoothly replaced by employment opportunities in the service sector.[1] The growth of services derives in large part from state expenditure, but now the continued expansion of this expenditure has been cast into doubt. It has been apparent, too, that among the most buoyant sectors of the economy are those which supply business services, and which may thus be contributing more to consumers' acquisition of material goods than their purchases of personal or social services. Attempts to extend the three sector model by adding on extra sectors ('quaternary, quinary', or 'the information sector') have achieved some popularity, but on closer inspection it is clear that they tend to raise more questions than they answer.[2]

A large part of the problem, in our view, derives from a certain conceptual slipperiness in the descriptions of the traditional 'sectors'. To be sure, they are usually initially described as referring to sets of industries that produce particular sorts of commodities. But then there are also 'service occupations', and accounts of the growth of white-collar employment are very often dovetailed together with descriptions of the rise of the service sector. Both economists and sociologists are inclined to slide between these alternatives. In the discussion of structural change in Daniel Bell's *The Coming of Post-industrial Society* (chapter 2), for example, the development of tertiary industries, which is elaborated upon in one context, is taken in another part of the same argument to imply the growth of white-collar employment, and elsewhere to rely on a growth of final consumption of services. (This is by no means an exceptional case: despite many sociologists' disagreements with Bell on the social and political nature of 'post-industrial society', his account of the rise of the service economy remains at least close to the conventional wisdom of the topic.)[3]

A similar logic might persuade us that the growth of a manufacturing industry in a particular region will necessarily lead to an increase in the proportion of manual jobs in that region. But these simple connections do not hold good. Manufacturing industries employ large and increasing numbers of white-collar workers, service industries employ manual workers. Tertiary sector firms are just as likely to supply their services to other firms as to final consumers. And those final consumers may, we shall argue, acquire their 'services' by buying goods.

For some purposes, notably for assessing the potential for incorporation of new technologies into service industries, it is necessary to break completely with the archaic notion of *the* service sector, which really derives from a period when the diverse activities encompassed under this heading were of sufficiently small scale that little was lost by treating them as a residual. It is certainly useful to disaggregate the sector into different branches supplying very different types of product, and typically organised in quite distinct ways, as does Singelmann in his classification of business, distributive, personal and collective services.[4] But neither this breakdown, nor the more detailed classification from the same or other sources, can be considered ideal for analysing the processes of socio-economic change. A more radical change in classificatory procedures is required.

Our solution, appropriate to our interest in the long-term evolution of economic and social structure, involves both a simplification of the three-sector model, and a considerable increase in its complexity. On one hand, we reduce the sectors to two groups by combining the primary and secondary classification, so as to yield a simple service/non-service dichotomy. On the other, we identify quite distinct meanings for the two groups, in each of four spheres: occupations, industries, products and functions.

The first three of these terms are in common usage. In the occupational sphere, the service/non-service dichotomy corresponds – roughly – to the non-manual/manual, white collar/blue collar distinction. In the example given in figure 1.1, the automobile engineer is a service worker in the occupational sphere, and the bus mechanic is a non-service worker in the occupational sphere. However, the automobile engineer is employed by a firm in the vehicle engineering (i.e. manufacturing) industry, and is thus to be considered a non-service worker in the industrial sphere. The bus mechanic is employed by a regional transport authority, and is therefore a service worker in the industrial sphere (since he or she is employed in a 'service industry').[5]

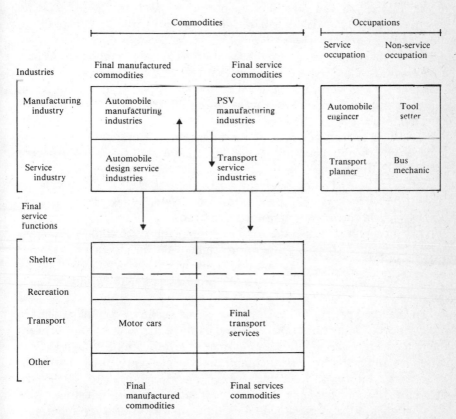

Figure 1.1 Commodities, functions, industries and occupations

The complexity increases when we consider the nature of the final product that results from these workers' labour. (A measure of ambiguity arises from using the term 'product' here, so we shall often replace it with 'commodity' – although strictly the latter term applies only to products that are offered for exchange in the market.) If the automobile engineer's employer is making public service vehicles (PSVs) such as buses, for sale to public transport under-takings, then the engineer's work is ultimately embodied in a final service (i.e. transport) to consumers. And a transport planner working for a firm providing consultancy services to the mining industry, is (probably) engaged in the production of a non-service final commodity.

The fourth sphere involves the 'final service function' (we discuss inter-mediate or 'producer' service functions below). This is concerned with the nature of the use to which the final consumer puts the commodities he or she purchases or otherwise acquires. Each of the categories of final function are in this sense 'services'. To continue with our example, both motor cars (non-service final commodities) and bus trips (service commodities) contribute to the final service function of 'transportation'. Whereas there are fairly broadly accepted classifications of occupations, industries and commodities, those of functions are less familiar, and we are aware that the very intro-duction of the term is liable to invite accusations of functional*ism* from some quarters. All we are in fact saying is that commodities do have their own 'use-values', and that similar use values may be supplied by very different commodities – both a car and a bus are useful for transportation; they both contribute to the same 'final service function'.

This fourth sphere is difficult to investigate at an empirical level; but the latest generation of national accounting systems are gradually moving towards the sort of 'functional' classification of final consumption that we are suggesting. The System of National Accounts used by the EEC involves a classification of household expenditures into different categories of use, and we have found this appropriate for our purposes – although it is unsubtle and fails to capture the full range of social functions which commodities may fulfil, or to address the question of the origin of the 'needs' that households experience. But perhaps these are questions which can be addressed afresh after first exploring how far we can make progress with these readily available data.

The changing pattern of development of the economy can be, at least in part, understood in terms of the changing nature of the relationships between the four spheres. This requires several lines of investigation. What is the mix of service and non-service final commodities which go to satisfy particular final service functions? How does this change over time, and why? What determines the changing mix of products from the various industries which are combined in particular final commodities? Likewise, what underpines the distribution of occupations employed by the particular industries?

This may sound a rather complex conceptual framework. It is in fact rather easy to use; and we have been able to apply it in the analysis of conventional National Accounts and other data for a wide range of EEC economies. In the following paragraphs, however, we shall not present our raw empirical material, but instead, ideographs depicting some of the patterns of change that we have observed.[6]

Our findings can be summarised in the form of *four processes of change* which hold generally for European economies during the 1970s (and also, though our research has concentrated on the latest decade, for the 1950s and 1960s). Consider a cross-tabulation of employment in particular occupations by employment in particular industries, in the manner of figure 1.2. For each industry there is a particular occupation that is in some sense *central*: for agriculture, farm workers; for mineral extraction, miners; for textiles, machine operators; for medical services, doctors and nurses, etc. Now order the two lists of occupational and industrial categories in such a way that the entries for those 'central' occupations in their appropriate industries fall on the top left to bottom right diagonal of the matrix.[7] We might fancifully imagine that at some (mythical) historical juncture, all employment was concentrated on this diagonal.

Myth apart, the currently observable pattern of change in the elements of this diagonal constitutes the first of our four processes of change. For most traditional industries, the proportion of employment concentrated in the 'central' occupation has been progressively decreasing. A growing proportion of occupational employment is spread among a wide range of specialised service, support and other occupations. This of course represents the *occupational division of labour*. There is nothing very surprising in this tendency; but what is perhaps less expected is the scale of this phenomenon, and its importance in the overall development of the distribution of occupational employment. The data for various European countries for the 1960s and 1970s suggest that the greatest proportion of the growth in 'service' (white-collar and non-production) occupations, is a consequence, not of a shift of employment from manufacturing to service industries, but rather of the growth of service occupational employment *within* each industry (Gershuny and Miles, 1983: 57–82). Occupational tertiarisation is certainly not the overwhelming consequence of the growth of the service industries that it appears to be in the three sector model.

Running partly contrary to the occupational division of labour is another process, which does not find a place in the classical economics textbooks. Alongside occupational disaggregation within industries, we may find the *second* of our processes of change, *occupational reconcentration* – the reaggregation of particular categories of occupational employment into new, highly specialised 'intermediate producer service industries'. These provide firms and institutions (for example, local government) with service or other functions on a subcontracting basis; these functions might under other circumstances be produced by these firms' and institutions' own salaried employees. So, to refer back to figure 1.2, we find cleaning and catering services being provided to factories, say, or hospitals, by specialised contracting firms, clerical services by text processing firms – also, perhaps increasingly in the future, we may find management and other technical functions (for example, repair and maintenance, data processing, etc.) provided in a similar manner.

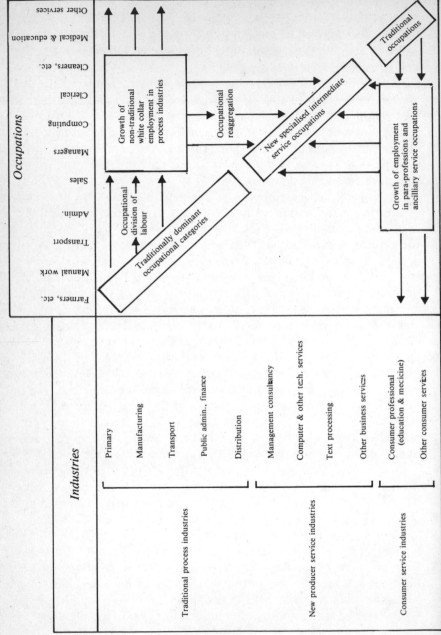

Figure 1.2 Occupational division of labour and producer services

Here is a growing part of the industrial service sector (the 'producer services'), which contributes in large degree to the output of non-service commodities.

The third of our processes of change relates to the sphere of 'final service functions'. Consider a set of final function categories which together group household expenditures into a fairly comprehensive set of applications. Figure 1.3 takes a set of nine such categories (food, shelter, domestic services, entertainment, transport, education, medicine, defence and other government services); all commodities purchased by consumers, or supplied to consumers by the state, may be assigned to one or other of these categories (in the manner

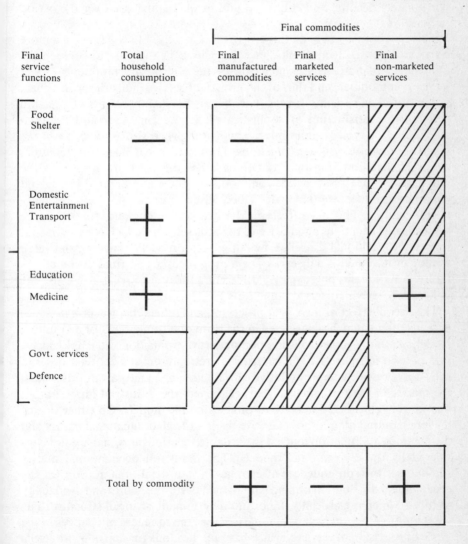

Figure 1.3 Final consumption, by commodity and function

outlined by figure 1.4). Taking first the total supply of commodities to each function, we find a quite regular pattern across Europe. The proportion of total consumption devoted to the more basic function decreases, and that devoted to the more sophisticated increases. Among those functions predominantly provided from disposable household income, food and shelter decline as a proportion of the total, and domestic, entertainment and transport service functions tend to increase. Among the functions predominantly provided by the state (or by other collective and quasi-compulsory means such as insurance), traditional government services and defence proportionately decline, and education and medicine increase over the period in question.

This is of course not at all surprising – it is merely 'Engel's Law' in a more elaborated form. Such results have been used in the past to provide the ultimate, demand-driven explanation of the rise of consumption of final service commodities, and thus of the growth of service industries. Our fourth process of change demonstrates that there is no such necessary connection between the satisfaction of sophisticated service functions and the consumption of service commodities. This is the process of *innovation in the mode of provision of service functions.* The increase in demand for domestic, entertainment and transport functions takes the form of growth in the purchases of, not final service commodities, but manufactured goods and materials – what we have described elsewhere as the 'self-servicing' phenomenon.[8] The net effect of the growth in demand for the more sophisticated functions and the trend towards self-servicing has been, in contrast to the traditional 'Engel's Law'/three sector model prediction, an overall decline of marketed final services as a proportion of all final demand. (As figure 1.3's ideograph suggests, different processses are at work for the collectively provided service functions.)[9]

The overall effect of these four processes, and others that we have no space here to outline, may be considered in the form of a framework, or accounting model, relating together consumption patterns, production and employment, summarised in figure 1.5. (The arrows here represent logical relations and need not necessarily imply exclusive causal relations.) One part of this model, the matrix in the top left-hand corner, covers the industrial input/output relationship considered in conventional economic models. On either side of the input/output matrix, however, are the industrial/occupational matrix and the commodity/function matrix; these depict relationships that are not considered by the conventional models. The industrial/occupational matrix summarises the consequences of changes in industrial organisation for the occupational distribution of paid employment – for the nature and availability of jobs – which is a crucially important determinant of social structure. The commodity/function matrix summarises the consequences of changes in the mode of provision of services, which have implications for unpaid work ('self-servicing'), leisure and other consumption activities. At both ends of the

Figure 1.4 Purposes of household and government final expenditure, classified by function and by the type of commodity

'Function' classification	'Commodity' classification			Reference in parentheses to classification of the European System of Integrated Economic Accounts (ESA)
	Primary and manufactured goods	Marketed services	Non-marketed services	
A. Food, drink, tobacco	Food, drink, tobacco (D1)	—	—	
B. Shelter, clothing	Rent, fuel and power, clothing and footwear (D2, D5)	Personal care and effects (D81)	Housing and community amenities (sewers etc) (G6)	Functions provided mainly by households ←
C. Domestic functions	Furniture, furnishings, appliances, utensils and repairs to these (D41 to D44)	Household operation and domestic services (D45, D46)	Social security and welfare services (G5)	
D. Entertainment	Equipment, accessories, and repairs to these, books etc. (D71, D75)	Entertainment, recreation, cultural, hotels, cafés, etc. packaged tours (D72, D83, D84)	Recreational culture and religious services (G7)	
E. Transport, communications	Personal transport equipment and operation (D61, D63)	Purchased transport and communications services (D65, D64)	Roads, waterways, communications and their administration subsidies (G8.3, G8.5, G8.7)	
F. Education	—	Purchased education (D74)	Public education (G5)	
G. Medical functions	Medical and pharmaceutical products and appliances (D51, D52)	Purchased medical services, medical insurance service charges (D53, D54, D55)	Public health services (G4)	Functions provided mainly by governments →
H. Other government functions	—	—	General public services, and economic services excluding transport and communications (G1, G8.1 to G8.4, G8.5)	
I. Defence	—	—	Defence (G2)	
J. Functions NES	Goods NES (D82)	Services NES (D85, D86)	Other public services NES (G9)	

ESA Classifications and Coding of the Purposes of Final Consumption of Households, ESA 1979 Table 7. (The same as Table 6.1, SNA, UN, New York 1968.)

ESA Classification and Coding of the Purposes of General Government, ESA 1979, Table 8. (The same as Table 5.3, SNA, New York, 1968.)

framework, then, are connections with the sorts of data and behaviour that economists have in the past largely ignored – time use, social structure and lifestyle patterns – but which are included among the concerns of the TASC group.

Before turning to our research on time use patterns, however, we should note that the model of change in the structure of the formal economy is useful for more than just historical analysis. The same structure can be used as a framework for considering the future implications of the current set of new technologies. A considerable part of our work over the last year has been devoted to thinking about the implications of the new information technologies; figure 1.6 summarises our view of the future implications of these technologies, taking as our starting point the analytical framework outlined in the previous paragraphs. (This is in fact only one among a range of possible scenarios; it is discussed, together with other issues, such as the role of social innovation in 'long waves', the impact of the growth of community-based service provision, and the importance of infrastructure choices, in pp. 231–68 of Gershuny and Miles, 1983, and in Miles, 1983 a.)

Work and non-work outside the 'economy'

Much of the research carried out in this group relates to the collection, production and analysis of data concerning the changing pattern of economic and non-economic activities outside the formal economy. The main methodology that we have employed has been the time-budget survey; a number of such surveys are now under analysis, giving us insight into lifestyles as far back as the 1930s, and as up-to-date as 1984.[8] During 1984 we hope to collect comparative data from a number of other European countries.

The analysis of these data is, however, less far advanced than that of the formal economy described above. We do have a clear picture of how the aggregate time use data will be integrated with the model of the formal economy – this will be briefly described in the final section of this paper. In the following paragraphs we will merely give a series of examples of some intermediate results of analysis, which demonstrate the range of issues that must concern us when we seek to use these data to cast light on the future of work and non-work.

Following on from our analysis of the formal economy, one issue of particular interest involves the relationship between change in the mode of provision of particular services (as evidenced by the shift from the purchase of final service commodities to that of goods related to the particular service function) and the amount of unpaid work that is being carried out. Does the 'self-servicing' trend lead to an absolute increase in the total amount of unpaid work, as households 'invest' in domestic capital goods and shift their labour resources into the increasingly productive 'informal' domestic sphere?

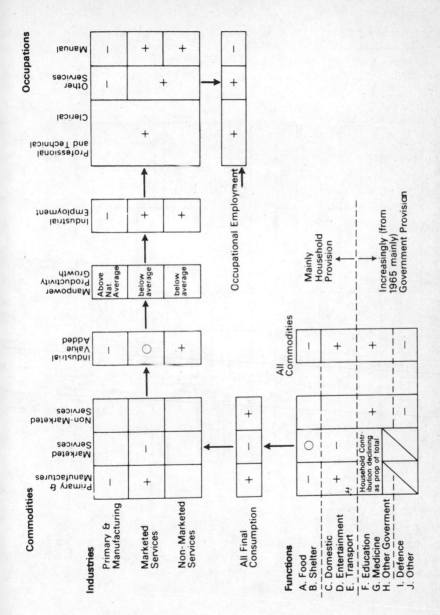

Figure 1.5 Summary of major changes, Europe 1959–80

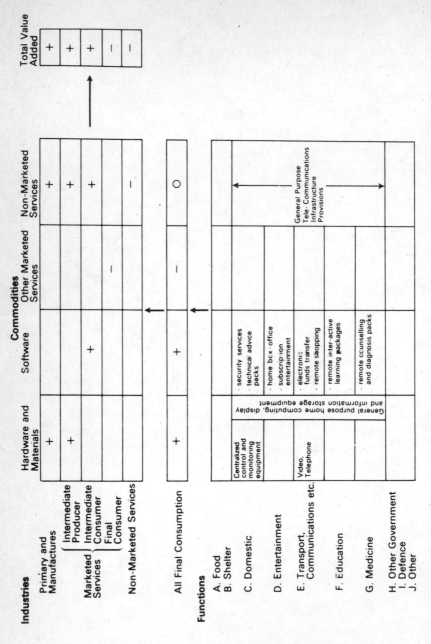

Figure 1.6 Change in distribution of consumption, output and employment, 1980s and 1990s

American researchers have put forward evidence suggestive of a small increase in domestic work in the USA between the 1930s and 1960s, and this result has become enshrined in the form of the oft-repeated assertion that domestic gadgets lead to an unnecessary proliferation of housework.

Our results challenge this proposition. As figure 1.7 makes clear, there appears to have been a small aggregate increase in the amount of domestic work in the UK between the 1930s and the 1960s (our estimates for this period are very similar to the American ones). But once we break down the aggregate by social class, the explanation becomes apparent: middle-class domestic work time is enormously increased over the period, as a result of the virtual disappearance of domestic servants. By contrast, through the 1950s, working-class households were beginning to receive the benefits of domestic equipment (and changing family size?), leading to a small fall in their domestic work total. And from the early 1960s, both social classes show a similar reduction in domestic work. Contrary to our initial guess, the increased productivity of domestic work led to a reduction in domestic work time, whether or not there has actually been an increase in the output of domestic work. [10]

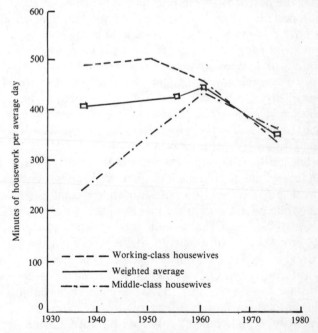

Figure 1.7 Housewives' domestic work (non-employed or part-time employed women).

The data in figure 1.7, of course, do not reflect *household* domestic work, but only *women's* domestic work. The sexual division of (formal and informal) labour forms another focus of concern, and time-budget data, in so far as they cover households as opposed to just individuals, provide a means for the investigation of this issue. Overwhelmingly, it is women who shoulder the burden of domestic work. We can look at the sexual division of labour in specific types of tasks by other types of survey instrument as well. Figure 1.8 illustrates an index of sexual specialisation in domestic work derived from combining information for a set of 'husband and wife pairs'. We score each pairing + 1 if the husband alone reports using a particular item of domestic technology during a given period, 0 if both husband and wife use it and − 1 if the wife alone uses it. The pattern of specialisation that emerges is quite clear and not at all unpredictable; we are currently trying to pinpoint the determinants and consequences of different household strategies for the sharing out of tasks, to plot past changes in the division of labour, and to speculate on its future development. [11]

We have seen a tendency for the overall amount of domestic work carried out to decline (and the average hours of formal work put in by men also declines), in spite of the apparent growth in importance of informal production of domestic service functions. One important issue which we need to address is the potential and implications of further developments in this direction, especially where the 'impact' of information technologies on existing service commodities is concerned. This raises the question of the potential demand for new modes of service provision in the UK, and what groups would gain and lose relatively most for such changes in service provision. (So, for example, women might have to take the burden of the greater part of new informal work activities, as they have had to do in many cases where public services have been reshaped into a 'community care' pattern; the erosion of traditional services is liable to penalise predominantly low-income latecomers to the new modes of provision.)

The current crisis of unemployment, and the widely touted prospect of continuing large-scale displacement of jobs, also raises questions about the future of work and the use of time outside of formal employment. Researchers outside the group have on occasion suggested that involvement in informal production activities might be a viable substitute for conventional jobs in the formal economy. [12] An important influence within the Science Policy Research Unit has been Professor Marie Jahoda, whose research on the social-psychological consequences of unemployment suggests a less sanguine conclusion. Jahoda's hypothesis is that involvement in a paid job carries with it (in addition to financial reward) access to five categories of experience (physical activity, social contact, collective purpose, a time structure, and social status) which are crucial to the maintenance of psychological integrity; and that it is the lack of these social relations that is in response to the persistence of psychological malaise among unemployed people over and above that which can be accounted for in terms of their economic hardship. [13] We have been involved in testing the Jahoda proposition, relying on the observation that though the five categories of experience are all necessarily provided by a paid job, they *may* also be provided in other contexts – including some forms of informal work. If Jahoda is correct, then those individuals who have no jobs, but access to the categories of experience from other sources, should show evidence of better psychological health than those who have no jobs and no alternative access to these experiences.

In the first of a series of studies testing this hypothesis, we carried out a survey of some three hundred unemployed and one hundred employed men in Brighton. The survey instrument covered a number of general and psychological health indicators, and for the unemployed men, the extent of involvement in a range of social, leisure and informal work activities, as well as a time-budget diary. From the interview questions on activity patterns and the time diaries we constructed two separate sets of indicators of access to the Jahoda categories – thus, for example, 'social contact' was indicated by answers to questions about one's range of social encounters, and also by the proportion of the diary day that was recorded as being spent with friends. From the sets of indicators we constructed two independent additive indices (one from the questionnaire data and one from the time diary evidence), by scoring each respondent one point wherever he had exceeded a certain level of access to each of the categories. (So an unemployed man with 'high' access to each of the categories would score five points in his index of access.)

Figure 1.9 shows the strong positive correlation between the two indices and the scores on the General Health Questionnaire.[14] This correlation remains highly significant even when such factors as age, socio-economic status, money problems, and length of time unemployed are taken into account. Those unemployed men with high access to the Jahoda categories show a state of health more similar to that of the employed sample than to that of those unemployed with no access to the Jahoda set – although still somewhat depressed. The Jahoda hypothesis itself clearly stands up very well to the test. But the fact that relatively few of the respondents had high levels of access to the categories, means that involvement in informal work, or other (non-work) activities providing the Jahoda set of experiences, cannot in general be expected to alleviate the adverse health and psychological consequences of unemployment.[15]

The time-budget data produced in this study show that unemployed men do tend to increase the amount of time devoted to domestic work rather dramatically following the loss of their jobs. However, this devotion of time to housework and shopping is not experienced as time well spent, and contributes little to the sense of access to the Jahoda categories. Increased domestic work seems more to reflect shortage of household equipment and money than any renegotiation of the domestic division of labour, in most cases – and we might add that this shortage of resources also largely inhibits unemployed people from profitable participation in the 'underground economy'. The relatively few men who did appear to be doing fairly well in terms of Jahoda's categories tended to do so by means of more social

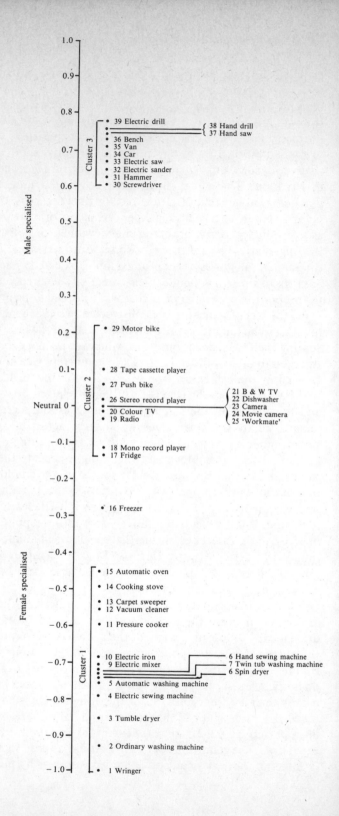

Figure 1.8
Task segregation –
detailed activity types

activities: sports, voluntary work, cultural pursuits and other forms of 'meaningful leisure'. Those who seemed to be doing worse spent much time in passive leisure, especially watching TV: hardly the ideal paradigm of the 'information society'!

The *possibility* of involvement in 'informal' economic activity, then, hardly constitutes the grounds for abandoning full employment as an important goal of economic and social policy – unless there are drastic changes in the opportunities available for constructive use of time out of formal employment, and the appropriate resources for people to make use of these opportunities. Given that those with high levels of access to such opportunities and resources did have better health and psychological adjustment, we are inclined to believe that the provision of facilities and social organisations which improve unemployed people's access to Jahoda's categories of experience – perhaps though their involvement in new informal collective institutions for the provision of social care – could be beneficial.

We are presently extending the empirical base of the above study so as to assess the circumstances of unemployed women and youth. And we have already amassed some evidence concerning the circumstances of housewives and retired people, whose position in respect of the five categories of experience appears to be quite distinctive.[16]

But one important part of our work – the development of a framework for the explanation of people's overall pattern of activities – is less far advanced. We have been involved in various causal modelling and analysis of variance exercises, with the aim of explaining the allocation of time between broad categories of activities; we can develop high levels of 'explanation' for some particular categories of activity – we can, for example, 'explain' 60 per cent–70 per cent of variance in paid and unpaid work time by a small set of demographic and social variables. But in general, for the whole set of activities which constitute a lifestyle, we have so far been less successful. We are now coming to the conclusion that the essentially linear approaches of most conventional statistical techniques are inappropriate to this problem. It may be that instead we should turn to a more structural approach, involving rule-based systems ('grammars') of modification and combination of (in our case) strings or sequences of activities. This work is now just starting, as we begin to analyse the structure of activities at particular times of day and particular parts of the week and year.[17]

A socio-economic accounting structure

As we suggested at the beginning of this paper, and have tried to demonstrate by the examples above, our aim is to develop an analytical structure which brings the 'economic' and the 'sociological' realms of discourse closer together than does most empirical research at present. At a high level of aggregation, we are now able to propose a social accounting structure which ties together certain aggregate statistics of the two realms. Figure 1.10 outlines the concepts used in this sort of accounting system.

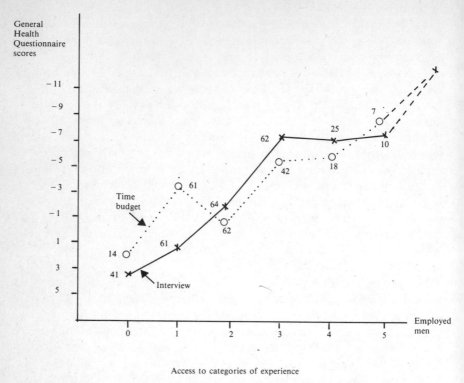

Access to categories of experience

Figure 1.9   Relations between access to categories of experience and
General Health Questionnaire scores

The left-hand side of this figure, relating the distribution of employment to the distribution of final consumption is derived by a straightforward process of multiplication of the matrices illustrated in figure 1.5. It demonstrates simply that the use of particular commodities to satisfy particular final functions must, at any one point of time, be associated with particular quantities of employment in particular occupations. The distributions at either end of our formal economy model – the distribution of occupational employment and the distribution of consumption – must also be associated with phenomena observable in our time budget data.

We know the economic occupations of our diary keepers, which means that we can say not only how many people are in a particular occupational category (which we know from our system of accounts for the formal economy) but also how much work time is devoted to these occupations (which we know from our time budget data). The problem that we shall face in interpreting these data concerns the reciprocal influences of occupation upon way of life, and of household type (and gender) on occupational careers and time use in formal employment: the accounting system directs us to some extremely interesting questions, but does not in itself provide us with the data or theories sufficient to answer them – this is one area where more detailed studies are necessary.

We can also associate the formal economy measures of consumption patterns with estimates of time spent in other categories of activity. We know what proportion of total household consumption is devoted to the 'food'· and 'shelter' functions from the formal accounting system; we also know how much unpaid domestic work time, cooking and cleaning, is devoted to them, from the time budgets; and from the same source we can estimate how much leisure and consumption time (eating, relaxing, personal care) is associated with these functions. In this way we can build up a very general set of accounts, which show the pattern of relationships between the society's overall distribution of final consumption, its distribution of paid jobs, and the distribution of its members' time among a comprehensive range of activities. Figure 11 is an example of such comprehensive sets of accounts, for the UK in the late 1970s. (Again the arrows in the framework do not necessarily represent exclusive casual paths: the question for research is not whether it is consumption that determines production or vice versa, but rather, what forms are taken by the mutual influences of the different parts of this system upon each other.)

We are interested in the processes by which this set of relationships change, and with the human consequences of such changes. We hope to answer questions such as: what are the employment consequences of technological and organisational changes in the mode of provision of services? Are paid work and unpaid work complements or substitutes for each other? What are the consequences of changes in the sexual distribution of domestic work for the demand for, and supply of, paid labour? What are the prospects for job sharing? What are the employment consequences of the new activity patterns which result from increase in leisure time? What are the consequences of such changes for physical and psychological welfare and social well-being? Not all of the answers to these questions can be found within our analytical framework – but many in principle can, and the framework provides important background information in terms of which to address the others.

The qualification 'in principle' is important. As we have already suggested, only part of this theoretical framework has yet been adequately elaborated. We have been able to go quite a long way towards understanding certain important processes of change in the formal economy at an aggregate level. Our analysis of macro-economic and sectoral data has reached the point that we can turn to the consideration of case studies of particular industries (we are at present working on the development of high technology producer service firms, and on the implications of information technology for a number

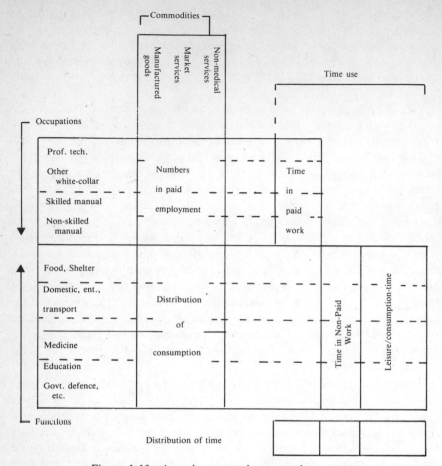

Figure 1.10 A socio-economic accounting system

of consumer service industries). This work will enable us to introduce some new institutional dimensions into our analysis: we shall, for example, be taking account of firm and organisation structure, government policies, and labour process/quality of working life issues. These will hardly be encompassed within the framework sketched in above, but nevertheless we would expect to be able to relate the dynamics of change in these areas to the processes that can be mapped out in the matrices.

By contrast, our understanding of the overall determinants of time use patterns is less advanced; the right-hand side of our matrix must be elaborated, as we suggested above, to take account of social differentiation (by age, stage in family life cycle, class etc.). In so far as time use patterns or lifestyle determines consumption patterns, this particular aspect of our research may yield important insights into the future of the formal economy; this will be among the main foci of our work in the coming years.

Figure 1.11 Consumption patterns, employment and time use – UK, late 1970s

	Goods	Marketed services	Non-marketed services	Total employment (by occupation)	% of all adults' time — All paid work time	All unpaid work time	Sleep (@ 8½ hrs)	Uncommitted time
Admin. prof. technical	9.4	4.7	9.6	23.7	3.9	6.6[1]		10.4[4]
Clerical	6.9	3.2	9.1	19.2	3.2	5.8[2]		24.3[5]
Sales	3.2	2.0	1.1	6.3	1.0			– [6]
Security, catering, cleaning	4.4	2.6	5.6	17.6	2.1	C.9[3]		
Transport	3.4	1.4	2.4	7.2	1.2			
Other manual	19.9	4.9	6.2	31.0	5.2	—		
Total employment (by commodity)	47.2	18.8	34.0	% of Jobs				
Distribution of all adult time					16.6 (30)	13.3 (22)	35.4 (59)	34.7 (58)

	Goods	Marketed services	Non-marketed services	Total household consumption
Total household consumption (by commodity)	50.0	21.3	28.8	% of Total household consumption
Food, shelter	31.1	0.6	0.8	32.5 (by function)
Domestic, entertainment transport	17.1	17.3	3.4	37.8
Education, medicine	6.3	2.1	12.3	14.7
Other govt., defence etc.	1.5	1.3	12.3	15.1

1 Cooking, odd jobs, gardening
2 Shopping, housework etc.
3 Childcare
4 Eating, personal care
5 Leisure activities
6 No sick in TB sample

Notes

1 Likewise, such technological change make it unlikely that later industrialising countries will follow closely in the tracks of earlier ones; it has, in any case, long been apparent that the service sectors of contemporary Third World countries are quite distinct from those of industrial countries either now or when they were at comparable levels of national income.

2 The most influential attempt to define an information sector and information occupations is that of Porat, 1977. According to his approach, large proportions of the labour force of most industrial countries are engaged in information work (more than one-third of the UK workforce according to OECD, 1981). But this covers everything from telephone repairs to scientific research, from computer programming to hosting radio chat shows. On the other hand, it excludes those working in the manufacture of informatics hardware, as opposed to those installing, maintaining and operating it. There is some logic in these classifications, but we do not believe that they provide a useful framework for the analysis of what are extremely diverse kinds of service activity.

3 Bell, 1973. The main focus of criticism of Bell's work has been his suggestion that the post-industrial society would be one in which the possession of knowledge would be both more important as a source of social power than ownership of wealth, and more equally and meritocratically distributed; see Miles, 1975.

4 We have found the Singelmann classification extremely useful when looking at service industries in terms of labour market and other economic segmentation approaches, for example: some services tend to approximate descriptions of the peripheral segment, others the corporate or state segments of the formal economy. Such descriptions may be quite helpful in considering such issues as the rate of diffusion of new technologies, worker influence on the labour process, or the political salience of different industries. As is often the case in social science, different classification systems may well be necessary for investigating different facets of the same phenomenon.

5 The concept of 'service occupation' which we are proposing is close to that of the 'non-production worker' used by Crum and Gudgin, 1977.

6 An extended discussion of the empirical results on which this is based is presented in Gershuny and Miles, 1983.

7 These central occupations are perhaps those that may be appropriately thought of as the 'production workers' in each industry, even though some of them are clearly producing services rather than goods. They will tend to be central workers, too, as that concept is used in labour market segmentation theories, but this will not invariably be the case and our use of the term here should be distinguished from the latter.

8 Gershuny, 1977.

9 Collective services are, of course, subject to different channels of demand articulation than are marketed services, and the expansion of collective services seems to be much more a matter of political processes. Lack of innovation in the provision of these services may be part of the explanation for the public acceptance of curbs on services and budgets: in which case, using new technologies so as to promote improvements in service quality here may be an option for their future.

10 See Gershuny, 1983 b.

11 For example, we have studies underway on the development of laundry services, and members of our group hope to research food preparation and other types of domestic work in more detail.

12 Among the more sympathetic versions of this argument we would include Heinze and Olk, 1982 and Robertson, 1982.

13   Jahoda, 1982.
14   The General Health Questionnaire is described in Banks *et al.*, 1980.
15   This study is described in Miles, 1983 b.
16   Henwood, 1983, Henwood and Miles (forthcoming).
17   Work now underway on recent time budgets is focusing on the instances of transition between different types of activity, and we plan to relate the data we are producing here to information about environmental constraints on activity patterns.

The process of occupational change in a service society: the case of the United States, 1960–80

Several recent studies which examined the relationship between the industrial structure and the nature of work (see e.g., Singelmann and Browning, 1980; Wright and Singelmann, 1982) argued that the industrial transformation of employment from a goods-producing economy to a service economy would have far-reaching consequences for the occupational structure and for the labour process. As these studies noted, a specification of the influence of the industrial transformation on changes in the occupational structure and the labour process is important for three reasons. First, the findings that the changing occupational structure was solely responsible for improvements in inter-generational mobility among US males during the post-war period require more knowledge about the ways by which the occupational structure itself changes (Hauser and Featherman, 1977; Featherman and Hauser, 1980; Hauser *et al.*, 1975 a, 1975 b). Second, such information would be useful for adjudicating the debate between post-industrial theory and the degradation thesis concerning the direction of change in the occupational structure and the labour process of a service society (Bell, 1973, 1976; Richta, 1969; Braverman, 1974; Edwards, 1979). Finally, the previous findings suggest that a slowdown or a completion of the industrial transformation may well have negative consequences for the occupational structure.

Although Wright and Singelmann (1982) found that the changes in the labour process within industries had a greater impact on the changing US class structure than did the industrial transformation, Singelmann and Browning (1980) showed that the industrial shifts were clearly the dominant factor for changes in the occupational structure during the 1960s. Moreover, the industrial transformation from a goods-producing to a service economy favoured the expansion of *desirable* class as well as occupational positions to a greater extent than did the changing class and occupational compositions within industrial sectors.

Those findings gain additional significance when evaluated against several assumptions predicting the future course of the industrial transformation.

The basic expectation was that the transformation from a goods-oriented economy to a service economy during the 1950s and 1960s was unlikely to continue at the same pace during the remainder of this century (Singelmann and Browning, 1980; Wright and Singelmann, 1982). Several reasons support this expectation. In the past, the increasing productivity of the extractive sector, especially agriculture, was the motor of the industrial transformation. These gains in productivity which were accomplished largely through labour-saving mechanisation released many workers for transformative and service industries in urban areas. But since the share of total employment engaged in agriculture declined to less than four per cent in 1970, further decreases in employment would have to be small and could exert only limited effects on the industrial or occupational structure.

Social services, on the other hand, had continuously expanded since 1920. Their growth was largely underwritten by the state through an extensive set of welfare policies. Even private social services, such as those rendered by physicians' and dentists' offices are influenced by state policies and are largely outside the market economy. Insurance programmes provide but one illustration of how state policies can influence employment in the private sector. But given the growing fiscal deficits of governments at all administrative levels, coupled with the increasing criticism of the welfare state, it seemed that any further expansion of social services would have to be on a much smaller scale relative to their rates of growth between 1950 and 1970 (see Browning and Singelmann, 1978). Although no clear expectations were formulated with respect to the employment trends of transformative industries and producer services, it seemed unlikely that their possible changes after 1970 would compensate for the greater stagnation of extractive industries and social services. Neither were distributive and personal services expected to change substantially after 1970.

If the tempo of the industrial transformation did slow down during the 1970s, and if it could be demonstrated that social services contributed to the upgrading of the occupational structure in the past more than any other industry sector,[1] it would seem that further improvements in the occupational structure at the rate observed in the past could only be achieved through changes in the occupational composition within industries of sufficient magnitude that they compensate for the favourable effects previously produced by the industrial transformation. A change of this magnitude in the intra-industry occupational composition is unlikely, however, given the negligible improvements in the occupational structure which resulted from past changes in the intra-industry occupational mix.

Thus, the general implication from the available empirical evidence for the 1960–70 decade is that the occupational structure would not show much further upgrading over the next decade, and that a downgrading of the occupational structure via the increased prevalence of low-status jobs cannot be ruled out. Much depends on the outcome of recent occupational change, such as the structural conditions for occupational mobility and for continued integration of women and minorities into the labour market.

Therefore, this paper proposes to evaluate the stated expectations about the industrial transformation and occupational change, and to identify the industrial location of occupational change during the 1970–80 decade. We believe, however, that the economic trends during the 1970s, in contrast to the previous two decades, are not linear but are characterised by a turn-around. Although it would be difficult – and for our purposes also not necessary – to pinpoint the exact date of that turn-around, the 1974–5 recession provides a useful benchmark. We argue that until the mid-decade recession the industrial transformation in the 1970s essentially continued along the trendline of the 1950s and 1960s. This means that the thirty years marked by the end of World War II until 1975 could be designated as the post-war period during which the US economy developed into a service economy.

Although some further growth of service employment can be expected, we think that for all the above-mentioned reasons, a marked slow-down in the rate of the expansion of service employment is probable. This slow-down, moreover, could be quite sharp when compared to the magnitude of the industrial transformation during the post-war period. We do not view this change, should it emerge, as a temporary result of cyclical forces related to the recent recession. Rather, we believe that the late 1970s represent the beginning of a new period characterised by the substantially lower rates of economic growth in advanced industrial societies, severe labour market problems, and growing opposition to the welfare state (see also Berger and Offe, 1982). In order to examine the expected differences between the early and late 1970s in terms of the industrial transformation, we conduct separate analyses for the 1970–5 and 1975–80 periods.

Data and methods

We base our empirical analyses on the Public Use Samples (PUS) of the 1960 and 1970 censuses, and the March Current Population Surveys (CPS) for the years 1970, 1975 and 1980. We decided against using the 1980 Public Use Microdata Sample (PUMS) for the analysis of occupational change during the 1970–80 intercensal period because the US Bureau of the Census extensively revised the occupational classification scheme, making time trend analyses problematic, even those conducted at a relatively high level of aggregation. Although a reasonable amount of comparability can be achieved using supplementary information provided by the Bureau, use of the 1980 PUMS increases the risk of confusing real changes in the occupational structure with artifactual change due to the new classification scheme. In contrast, no changes in the occupational classification were made in the CPS during the 1970–80 period.[2] For this reason, and because we wished to assess our hypothesis about the mid-1970s as a watershed between the fast-growth post-war period and the new slow-growth period, we relied exclusively on the CPS data for the most recent period. Our samples include all individuals aged sixteen or more who were employed at the time of the survey, but exclude the unemployed and military personnel.

Our method of analysis has been described extensively elsewhere (Singelmann and Browning, 1980; Singelmann and Tienda, 1979) and will not be elaborated in detail in the interest of brevity. However, a summary of the key aspects of the computation procedures should help the reader unfamiliar with shift-share analysis. This technique is analogous to standardisation and basically permits the decomposition of differences in occupational structures into three components. The first, denoted an *industry shift effect*, represents the change in the occupational structure between two points in time attributable to the transformation of the industry structure, once the effects of intercensal growth changes in the intra-industry occupational mix, and the interaction of industry and occupational shift effects have been eliminated. The second component, denoted the occupational *mix effect*, represents the changes in the occupational structure which result from changes in the intra-industry occupational composition (again net of the effects of growth and other components). Finally, the third component is an interaction effect which reflects the changes in the occupational structure arising from the joint influence of industry and occupational mix effects. The interaction effects are derived as a residual by subtracting the pure industry and occupational mix effects from the total net change for each occupational category during the period in question. All computations are based on a matrix of 407 cells comprised of thirty-seven detailed industry and eleven major occupational categories. The rationale for the thirty-seven industry scheme is elaborated at some length in Browning and Singelmann (1978).

Our analytic strategy consists of three phases. First we present a descriptive overview of industrial and occupational change in the United States between 1960 and 1980, making some note of the discrepancies in the occupational and industry classifications between the CPS and PUS sources. Subsequently, we compute three shift-share analyses for the 1960–70, 1970–5 and 1975–80 time periods to assess the relative magnitudes of the industry shift and occupational mix effects in accounting for changes in the occupational structure over the three time intervals. Finally, we locate the sources of occupational change in terms of major industry sectors to evaluate with greater precision how the changing nature of the service economy has impacted the occupational structure. This will also help us determine whether the importance of the industrial transformation of employment as the primary motor of occupational change shows signs of slowing down, while the relative importance of the intra-industry occupational mix increases its influence in modifying the occupational structure.

Industrial and occupational trends during the 1970s

Industries

According to the 1980 census data, the industrial transformation from goods-producing to service industries did not slow down much during the 1970s (see table 2.1). The change in the industrial structure during the most recent period, as measured by the index of dissimilarity, decreased only slightly to 6.00 from 6.35 during the 1960–70 decade. In both decades, social and producer services were the beneficiaries of the industrial transformation, although the location of the major structural decline changed from the extractive sector during the sixties to transformative industries during the seventies.

But an inspection of the data from the Current Population Surveys of 1970, 1975 and 1980 shows substantial differences in the industrial transformation between the early and late 1970s. Those data reveal that most of the structural changes during the 1970s took place between 1970 and 1975: the index of dissimilarity for this period is 5.05, as compared to 1.70 for the 1975–80 period. Further inspection of the changes in the industrial sectors shows that the relative decrease of transformative employment levelled off by 1975, and that most of the intercensal growth of social services took place in the first half of the 1970s. However, the social services sector requires further differentiation to interpret the significance of these changes. It appears that the long-term expansion of educational institutions has come to a halt, and that a contraction seems likely in the future. Not only do the 1975–80 data presage a slowdown – or even decline – in the growth of education employment, but so also do recent demographic changes towards smaller birth cohorts.

Medical services and hospitals registered the better part of their above-average growth during the early years of the decade as well, but both services continued their relative expansion, albeit at a slower pace, during the second half of the 1970s. We believe that the growth in medical services and hospitals during the 1970s partly results from the continued extension of medical coverage to formerly under-serviced population groups and from the additional demands for those services among the swelling numbers of elderly individuals.

Neither personal nor distributive services changed their relative levels of employment much during the 1970–80 period. However, the turn-around in retailing employment is noteworthy. For the first time in many decades, the growth of retailing employment did not keep pace with changes in total employment (Singelmann, 1978). The coverage of the United States with retailing outlets has apparently become so dense that a large part of new retail activities either represents replacements of older stores and/or shifts in the geographical locations of retail establishments. This change from expansion of the number of stores to upgrading and relocation is quite apparent in the marketing strategies of the large US retail corporations. Since

Table 2.1 Industrial structure of US employment, 1960–80

Sector and industry	Per cent in 1960	Per cent in 1970		Per cent in 1975	Per cent in 1980	
	PUS	PUS	CPS	CPS	CPS	PUS
A. *Extractive*	8.1	4.5	4.9	4.7	4.1	4.0
1. Agriculture	7.1	3.7	4.3	3.8	3.2	3.0
2. Mining	1.0	0.8	0.6	0.9	0.9	1.0
B. *Transformative*	35.7	33.8	34.1	29.3	29.6	29.7
3. Construction	6.2	5.9	5.7	5.5	5.9	5.9
4. Food	3.1	1.9	2.3	2.2	1.8	1.6
5. Textile	3.4	2.9	2.9	2.2	2.0	2.3
6. Metal	4.0	3.1	3.9	3.0	2.8	2.8
7. Machinery	7.9	7.9	8.7	6.8	7.4	7.6
8. Chemicals	1.8	1.6	1.9	1.5	1.6	1.5
9. Misc. manufacturing	7.9	8.8	7.2	6.8	6.7	6.6
10. Utilities	1.4	1.7	1.5	1.3	1.4	1.4
C. *Distributive services*	20.5	20.9	19.3	20.5	19.5	19.8
11. Transportation	4.4	3.7	3.7	3.7	3.6	3.6
12. Wholesale	3.6	4.1	3.3	3.9	3.9	4.2
13. Retail	12.5	13.1	12.3	12.9	12.0	12.0
D. *Producer services*	8.1	9.1	9.3	10.2	12.2	11.3
14. Communications	1.3	1.4	1.4	1.4	1.4	1.5
15. Banking	1.7	2.0	2.2	2.3	2.4	2.6
16. Insurance	1.8	1.7	1.8	1.9	1.8	2.0
17. Real estate	1.0	1.0	1.0	1.3	1.6	1.5
18. Engineering	0.3	0.4	0.3	0.4	0.6	0.6
19. Accounting	0.3	0.4	0.3	0.3	0.5	0.4
20. Misc. producer services	1.2	1.7	1.8	2.0	2.3	2.8
21. Legal services	0.5	0.5	0.5	0.6	0.7	0.8
E. *Social services*	16.4	21.7	21.1	23.9	24.2	24.7
22. Medical services	1.4	2.0	2.1	3.0	3.4	2.9
23. Hospitals	2.7	3.5	3.4	4.0	4.2	4.6
24. Education	5.5	8.0	8.2	9.2	8.8	8.7
25. Welfare	1.0	1.1	1.1	1.4	1.7	0.7
26. Non profit	0.4	0.4	0.4	0.5	0.4	0.4
27. Postal service	0.9	0.9	1.1	0.8	0.7	0.7
28. Public administration	4.3	4.5	4.6	4.7	4.6	5.3
29. Misc. social services	0.2	1.3	0.2	0.3	0.4	1.4
F. *Personal services*	11.4	10.1	11.3	11.1	11.0	9.9
30. Domestic services	3.1	1.6	2.9	2.2	1.5	0.7
31. Hotels	1.0	0.9	1.2	1.1	1.1	1.1
32. Eating and drinking	2.9	3.1	3.1	3.9	4.5	4.3
33. Repair services	1.5	1.4	1.3	1.3	1.5	1.4
34. Laundry	1.0	0.7	0.8	0.5	0.4	0.4
35. Barber and beauty	0.8	0.8	0.9	0.8	0.7	0.7
36. Entertainment	0.8	0.8	0.8	0.9	0.9	1.0
37. Misc. personal services	0.3	0.8	0.3	0.4	0.4	0.3
Total	100.2	100.1	100.0	99.7	100.3	99.7

Sources: PUS: Public Use Samples, Population Censuses 1960–80
         CPS: Current Population Survey, 1970–80
Note: Percentages may not add to 100.0 owing to rounding errors

the growth of retail trade in the past had fuelled the relative increase of the distributive sector, the changing trend in retail employment resulted in a slight decrease of distributive services.

Producer services are the only sector which grew fairly steadily during the entire 1970–80 period. The demand for these services is largely of an intermediate nature (see also Gershuny and Miles, 1983; and their contribution in this volume), for the they cater primarily to other businesses and less to individual consumers. A substantial part of producer services is not 'new' in its content but rather in its location; as a result of the continued division of labour, many producer services such as accounting, advertising or legal services, which were formerly carried out within the firm, became independent businesses to be subcontracted. But this reallocation of activities is only part of the explanation for the growth of producer services. Their expansion is also a reflection of the increased importance of financing and marketing which require the allocation of more resources to those tasks.

A closer examination of the data on table 2.1 shows that not all producer services expanded equally. The growth of this sector is largely concentrated in banking and real estate, reflecting the land speculation of the 1970s in the US and the deregulation of financial institutions, and in engineering, legal and miscellaneous producer services which are part and parcel of the new technological developments.

Occupations

The long-standing shift of the occupational structure from manual to white-collar occupations continued during the 1970s. While the white-collar occupations (professional, technical, managerial, clerical and sales workers) already outnumbered the manual and service occupations in 1970 (Singelmann and Browning, 1980), they accounted for more than one out of every two workers in 1980. Most importantly, the three highest status occupations of professional, technical and managerial workers continued to increase their share of employment. But the extent of that growth differs between the two data sets. Owing to the substantial changes in the occupational classification between the 1970 and 1980 population censuses, the 1980 census results show a sharp increase of managers and a substantial increase of professionals. The Current Population Survey, on the other hand, which did not change its occupational classification between 1970 and 1980, indicates a much smaller growth of managerial employment, and the rate of growth for professionals is also below that derived from census data.[3] Accordingly, while the census data suggest only a slight slowdown of occupational change from the 1960s to the 1970s (with indices of dissimilarity of 6.9 and 6.65, respectively), the slowdown is more pronounced when the CPS data are used (ID = 4.70).

Separate analyses of the early and late 1970s show, again, that the 1970–5 period was characterised by more occupational change (ID = 3.6) than the

Table 2.2 Occupational structure of US employment, 1960–80

Occupation	Per cent in 1960	Per cent in 1970		Per cent in 1975	Per cent in 1980	
	PUS	PUS	CPS	CPS	CPS	PUS
Professional	10.2	12.8	12.3	12.9	13.4	14.6
Technical	1.6	2.0	2.0	2.3	2.5	2.8
Farmer	4.1	1.8	2.2	1.8	1.5	1.3
Manager	8.7	8.3	10.5	10.5	11.1	10.9
Clerical	15.2	17.8	17.4	17.8	18.7	19.1
Sales	7.6	7.3	6.2	6.6	6.4	6.5
Craft	14.2	13.7	12.6	12.5	12.7	12.1
Operative	19.4	17.6	17.7	14.8	14.2	14.8
Service	11.7	13.0	13.0	14.6	13.9	12.6
Labourer	5.0	4.6	4.5	4.8	4.5	4.2
Farm labourer	2.4	1.2	1.6	1.4	1.1	0.9
Total	100.1	100.1	100.0	100.0	100.0	99.8

Sources: PUS: Public Use Samples, Population Censuses, 1960–80
CPS: Current Population Survey, 1970–80
Note: Percentages may not add to 100.0 owing to rounding errors

1975–80 period (ID = 2.4). Those results also indicate, however, that the slow-down of occupational change during the 1970s was not as pronounced as in the case of the industrial transformation. This suggests either that the importance of intra-industry occupational changes in accounting for changes in the occupational structure during the latter part of the 1970–80 decade became more important than those changes due to the industrial trans-formation, or that the effects of the industrial transformation and the intra-industry occupational distribution on occupational change reinforced each other more than was previously the case.

Closer examination of the changes in particular occupations reveals that the aggregate occupational change during the 1970–5 period resulted largely from the substantial decrease of operative workers, a shift which was not continued during the 1975–80 period. That pattern of change parallels the 1970–80 changes of transformative employment, which decreased sub-stantially during the early 1970s and remained stable after 1975.

The 1960–80 period was also characterised by important changes in the occupational composition of individual industries and sectors. The traditional configuration was that *one* type of occupation represented the dominant category for employment in a given industry. In the case of agriculture, for example, most persons used to be farmers; similarly, a plurality of workers in producer services had clerical occupations. Although that concentration of employment in one or two occupations has not disappeared, the continued division of labour has reduced the degree of that concentration. That trend also characterises occupational change in the US during the past two decades: within all industrial sectors, the traditionally predominant occupational category decreased its share of sectoral employment, and measures of the occupational differentiation within sectors show increased values during the 1960–80 period in each of the six cases. The most dramatic shift occurred in the extractive sector: while farmers accounted for one-half of total extractive employment in 1960, their share dropped to one-third by 1980. During the same time, the index of occupational differentiation increased by 23 per cent.[4] This intra-sectoral deconcentration of employment did not benefit all occupational categories alike, but was directed at the higher status categories of professional (except in the case of social services), technical and managerial occupations.

In sum, the overall occupational structure was affected by both the industrial transformation towards a service economy and by an increased division of labour within industrial sectors. The following section allows us to specify (with greater precision) the components of occupational change and their magnitude over the past twenty years.

The process of occupational change

Given the apparent slowdown in the pace of the industrial and occupational transformation during the second half of the 1970s, we decided to estimate the relative contributions of the industrial transformation and the intra-industry occupational composition separately for the 1970–5 and 1975–80 periods. Table 2.3 presents the results of the estimation procedure, together with a re-estimation of the components of occupational change during the 1960–70 period.

These results show that the process of occupational change during the 1970–75 period in many ways was a continuation of the previous decade. The industrial transformation contributed 63 per cent to total occupational change during the 1960s, and that proportion increased to 70 per cent during the 1970–75 period. In the second half of the 1970s, however, the slowdown of the industrial transformation reduced its impact on total occupational change to 41 per cent. Thus, the intra-industry occupational redistribution emerged as the primary source of change in the occupational structure, accounting for 60 per cent of total occupational change during the latter part of the 1970s. The aggregate interaction effect was negligible during the entire 1960–80 period.

Of special importance are the effects of the industrial transformation and the intra-industry occupational mix on the growth of the higher-status occupations (professional, technical and managerial workers), because their net expansion has a profound effect on the structural conditions for occupational mobility. The results show that the industrial transformation contributed 152 and 157 per cent, respectively, to the net growth of these occupational categories during the 1960–70 and 1970–5 periods, whereas the changes in the occupational composition within industries would have reduced employment in those higher status positions.

But as the intra-industry occupational recomposition became the major source of total occupational change during the late 1970s, it also contributed the major part (58 per cent) to the net growth of the highest status occupations. Particularly remarkable is the turn-around of the occupational shifts within industries with regard to professional and managerial workers

Table 2.3 Components of occupational change, 1960–80

| Occupation | Net shift | Components of net shift | | | Components of net shift % | | |
		Industry shift effect	Occupation shift effect	Interaction shift effect	Industry shift effect	Occupation shift effect	Interaction shift effect
1960–70							
Professional	19522.3	24201.0	127.9	− 4806.7	124.0	0.7	− 24.6
Technical	3255.4	2404.2	1799.3	− 948.1	73.9	55.3	− 29.1
Farmer	− 17027.3	− 14958.6	− 3987.3	1918.6	87.9	23.4	− 11.3
Manager	− 3489.8	2778.0	− 6227.4	− 40.4	− 79.6	178.1	1.2
Clerical	20090.0	8931.9	10125.8	1032.3	44.5	50.4	5.1
Sales	− 2218.7	2668.0	− 4728.7	− 158.0	− 120.3	213.1	7.1
Craft	− 3763.6	− 2282.8	− 876.2	− 604.6	60.7	23.3	16.1
Operative	− 13814.7	− 10138.1	− 3364.5	− 312.1	73.4	24.4	2.3
Service	9555.2	− 2607.8	7760.9	4402.1	− 27.3	81.2	46.1
Labourer	− 3146.1	− 2299.1	− 117.0	− 729.9	73.1	3.7	23.2
Farm labourer	− 8962.8	− 8696.8	− 512.6	246.7	97.0	5.7	− 2.8
Total	0.0	− 0.1	0.0	− 0.1			
1970–5							
Professional	53364.4	94847.8	− 33502.8	− 7980.5	177.7	− 62.8	− 15.0
Technical	31550.3	10743.0	22615.7	− 1808.4	34.1	71.7	− 5.7
Farmer	− 29439.2	− 22435.7	− 7973.8	970.3	76.2	27.1	− 3.3
Manager	− 143.3	27749.5	27579.3	− 313.4	− 19379.8	19244.1	218.7
Clerical	35306.4	31893.1	6317.0	− 2903.5	90.3	17.9	− 8.2
Sales	25755.0	27806.5	− 5245.7	3194.2	108.0	− 20.4	12.4
Craft	− 6102.0	− 58716.5	55916.6	− 3302.0	962.3	− 916.4	54.1
Operative	− 247413.9	− 140491.6	− 110292.8	3370.6	56.8	44.6	− 1.4
Service	131503.0	59201.6	63767.5	8534.1	45.0	48.5	6.5
Labourer	24999.3	− 14234.6	39414.1	− 180.3	− 56.9	157.7	− 0.7
Farm labourer	− 19380.9	− 16362.6	− 3436.4	418.1	84.4	17.7	− 2.2
Total	− 0.9	0.5	0.1	− 0.7			
1975–80							
Professional	43921.0	37581.6	6162.4	176.9	85.6	14.0	0.4
Technical	20206.0	9704.2	10404.0	97.8	48.0	51.5	0.5
Farmer	− 37543.8	− 25660.5	− 13863.9	1980.6	68.3	36.9	− 5.3
Manager	61130.8	3546.6	56487.5	1096.5	5.8	92.4	1.8
Clerical	81010.6	13331.0	69574.4	− 1895.0	16.5	85.9	− 2.3
Sales	− 15839.6	− 14850.0	− 3896.4	2906.8	93.8	24.6	− 18.4
Craft	17327.6	27219.1	− 8436.3	− 1455.3	157.1	− 48.7	− 8.4
Operative	− 58018.3	− 26018.6	− 36105.8	4105.9	44.8	62.2	− 7.1
Service	− 63152.9	5264.6	− 62365.9	− 6051.7	− 8.3	98.8	9.6
Labourer	− 23008.0	− 11057.3	− 9826.0	− 2124.8	48.1	42.7	9.2
Farm labourer	− 26032.6	− 19060.5	− 8134.0	1162.0	73.2	31.2	− 4.5
Total	0.8	0.1	0.0	− 0.2			

during the 1970s. During the early parts of the 1970s, the occupational mix effect tended to *reduce* the net growth of professionals and managers, but it substantially *increased* their growth during the latter part of the 1970s.

Among the manual occupations, only operative workers exhibit a consistent trend: employment in this category declined throughout the 1960–80 period, and both the industrial transformation and the intra-industry occupational composition contributed to that decrease. Once again, the industrial transformation was the more dominant factor for the decrease of operatives between 1960 and 1975, after with the occupational composition within industries became the major source of change.

Both factors also contributed to the decline of labourers and craftspersons during the 1960s, but their effects on net employment growth in those two occupational categories counteracted each other during the 1970s. Between 1970 and 1975, the industrial transformation tended to reduce the growth of crafts and unskilled manual positions, undoubtedly as a result of the decrease of transformative industries during that period. Within industries, on the other hand, there was a tendency to create those occupational positions at an above average rate. During the latter part of the 1970s, however, the industrial transformation favoured the growth of crafts occupations while the occupational changes within industries had a negative effect on employment in that category. Both components of change contributed to the net decline of labourer jobs during the latter part of the 1970s, as was the case during the 1960s. The main difference is that for the most recent period, the industrial transformation and the intra-industry occupational recomposition contributed about equally to the net decline of labourers, whereas previously the decrease of unskilled workers resulted largely from the industrial shift effect.

The industrial location of occupational change

The results of the previous two sections showed that the impact of the industrial transformation and total occupational change during the later part of the 1970s was substantially lower than between 1960 and 1975. A second major finding is that the occupational changes within industries, which had been overshadowed by the industrial transformation during earlier periods, became the major source of total occupational change during the late 1970s. Moreover, the occupational recomposition within industries also accounted for the major part of the net growth of high status occupations between 1975 and 1980.

This section completes the analysis by locating the components of occupational change within the industrial structure. In identifying the industrial location of occupational change, we also recalculated the components of occupational change as proportions of the *absolute size* of each occupational category at the beginning of a period rather than as *proportion of net change* in each category. Since some net changes are quite small, as was shown above, a larger relative contribution by either component to net change would affect the occupational category less than a smaller share of larger net shifts. Also, in the case of a large occupational category, many net shifts may not affect the growth of that occupational category any more than fewer shifts of a smaller occupational category.

The data in table 2.4, which present the results of this procedure, indicate the percentage by which the net growth (or decline) of an industrial sector during a given period changed the number of persons who were in an occupatinal category at the beginning of that period. Similarly, the data also indicate the change in each occupational category which is attributable to occupational changes within each industrial sector. The totals are the sum of the sectoral contributions. Accordingly, the first entry of 38.6 indicates the per cent by which the number of professionals in 1960 increased as a result of industry shifts in all sectors during the 1960–70 decade.

1960–70 occupational change

These data show that the net growth of social services had the largest impact on the employment of professionals, increasing their 1960 employment by 36 per cent. The results also indicate, however, that the growth of professional positions within social services failed to keep pace with the growth of employment in other occupational categories. Social services are the only sector where that situation prevailed, for the expansion of professional jobs outpaced the growth of total employment in all other industrial sectors. The negative effect of the occupational recomposition within social services does not necessarily imply, however, that professional positions in this sector have been downgraded, for the estimated effects refer to shifts net of the expected growth pattern. Negative shifts, in this case, only indicate a below average growth and not an absolute decline of professional positions in social services.

The expansion of social services was also important in accounting for the growth of employment of technical workers, increasing the number of workers in this category by 17.2 per cent. This positive effect was augmented by the occupational recomposition within that sector, which added another 8 per cent to the 1960 employment level of technical workers. The combined growth of social, producer, and distributive services during the 1960s increased the employment of managers by approximately 7 per cent, but this was more than offset by the substantial change in the occupational composition within distributive services which reduced the growth of managers during the 1960–70 period.

The decline of the transformative sector was the major reason for the decrease of crafts, and operative occupations. The shrinking manufacturing sector also contributed to the decrease of labourers, but the more important

Table 4 Disaggregation of percentage changes by industrial sectors 1960–80

Occupation	Total	Extractive	Trans-formative	Distributive services	Produce services	Social services	Personal services
1960–70							
Professional: industry shifts	38.6	−0.7	−0.9	0.1	2.8	36.2	1.0
occupation shifts	0.2	1.2	5.2	2.0	1.0	−9.7	0.6
Technical: industry shifts	24.8	−0.6	−2.6	−0.0	2.8	17.2	8.1
occupation shifts	18.6	2.6	5.3	1.8	4.2	8.0	−3.2
Farmer: industry shifts	−59.9	−59.9	—	—	—	—	—
occupation shifts	−16.0	−16.0	—	—	—	—	—
Manager: industry shifts	5.2	−0.5	−1.8	2.4	2.4	2.6	0.2
occupation shifts	−11.6	0.5	−0.3	−10.8	−1.7	3.7	−3.0
Clerical: industry shifts	9.6	−0.4	−1.5	0.7	3.9	6.9	−0.0
occupation shifts	10.9	0.8	1.4	4.4	−0.2	2.2	2.3
Sales: industry shifts	5.8	−0.1	−1.0	5.7	0.7	0.4	0.2
occupation shifts	−10.2	0.4	−2.7	−9.1	0.5	0.2	0.5
Craft: industry shifts	−2.6	−0.7	−3.8	−0.3	0.6	1.7	−0.3
occupation shifts	−1.0	1.0	−1.2	1.5	−0.0	−1.4	−0.9
Operative: industry shifts	−8.5	−1.4	−6.8	−0.7	0.3	0.6	−0.4
occupation shifts	−2.8	−1.0	−0.1	−0.3	−0.1	−0.4	−1.1
Service: industry shifts	−3.6	−0.1	−0.5	0.0	0.8	9.7	−13.5
occupation shifts	10.8	0.3	2.5	2.6	0.1	4.1	1.2
Labourer: industry shifts	−7.5	−2.5	−3.7	−0.5	0.3	1.0	−2.2
occupation shifts	−0.4	8.1	−14.6	5.5	−0.2	−0.5	1.2
Farm labourer: industry shifts	−59.9	−59.9	—	—	—	—	—
occupation shifts	−3.5	−3.5	—	—	—	—	—
1970–5							
Professional: industry shifts	9.8	0.2	−3.0	0.2	1.0	10.9	0.4
occupation shifts	−3.4	−0.2	0.6	0.9	0.2	−4.8	−0.2
Technical: industry shifts	7.0	−0.0	−6.3	0.1	1.7	10.1	1.3
occupation shifts	14.6	1.7	5.7	−0.1	2.7	5.3	−0.8
Farmer: industry shifts	−12.9	−12.9	—	—	—	—	—
occupation shifts	−4.6	−4.6	—	—	—	—	—
Manager: industry shifts	3.4	0.1	−3.0	2.6	1.8	0.8	1.0
occupation shifts	−3.3	0.4	0.2	2.0	2.1	4.8	2.0

	Total						
Sales: industry shifts	5.6	0.0	−1.6	4.9	2.1	0.1	0.1
occupation shifts	−1.1	−0.1	−1.1	−4.2	4.6	0.0	−0.4
Craft: industry shifts	−5.9	0.5	−8.0	0.8	0.4	0.6	−0.1
occupation shifts	5.6	0.4	5.0	0.4	−0.5	−1.1	1.4
Operative: industry shifts	−10.0	0.7	−11.4	0.9	0.1	0.3	−0.5
occupation shifts	−7.9	−0.4	−6.2	−0.5	0.3	−0.5	−0.6
Service: industry shifts	5.8	0.0	−0.6	0.1	0.6	6.4	−0.9
occupation shifts	6.2	−0.2	1.5	0.8	1.1	2.0	1.0
Labourer: industry shifts	−4.0	−0.4	−5.2	1.7	0.5	0.2	−0.8
occupation shifts	11.2	4.9	0.2	8.1	−0.9	−2.3	1.2
Farm labourer: industry shifts	−12.9	−12.9	—	—	—	—	—
occupation shifts	−2.7	−2.7	—	—	—	—	—
1975–80							
Professional: industry shifts	3.5	−0.1	0.5	0.2	2.9	0.4	0.0
occupation shifts	0.6	0.4	1.4	0.2	−0.6	−0.9	0.1
Technical: industry shifts	5.0	−0.2	1.0	−0.1	1.9	2.2	0.0
occupation shifts	5.3	−0.1	−2.4	0.3	1.8	3.8	1.8
Farmer: industry shifts	−16.6	−16.6	—	—	—	—	—
occupation shifts	−9.0	−9.0	—	—	—	—	—
Manager: industry shifts	0.4	−0.1	0.5	−2.1	1.5	−0.3	0.8
occupation shifts	6.4	0.2	1.7	0.4	0.6	2.0	1.4
Clerical: industry shifts	0.9	−0.1	0.3	−1.2	2.1	−0.3	0.1
occupation shifts	4.7	0.3	0.6	1.8	0.1	1.2	0.6
Sales: industry shifts	−2.7	−0.0	−0.1	−4.4	1.8	−0.0	0.0
occupation shifts	−0.7	−0.1	0.5	−2.0	0.8	−0.3	0.4
Craft: industry shifts	2.6	−0.1	2.3	−0.9	0.3	0.0	1.1
occupation shifts	−0.8	0.5	−1.8	1.2	0.0	−0.4	−0.3
Operative: industry shifts	−2.1	−0.1	−0.8	−1.1	0.3	0.0	−0.4
occupation shifts	−2.5	−0.0	0.7	−2.9	−0.4	0.2	−0.4
Service: industry shifts	3.4	0.0	−0.0	−0.2	0.9	1.3	1.5
occupation shifts	−5.1	0.0	−0.4	0.2	−0.7	−3.0	−1.2
Labourer: industry shifts	−2.8	−1.0	0.6	−1.9	0.4	−0.0	−0.8
occupation shifts	−2.5	1.7	−5.5	0.5	0.3	1.7	−1.3
Farm labourer: industry shifts	−16.6	−16.6	—	—	—	—	—
occupation shifts	−7.1	−7.1	—	—	—	—	—

influences explaining the decline of this occupation were the occupational shifts within transformative industries which strongly disfavoured the employment of labourers. Since this is the least-skilled occupational category for non-farm employment, the occupational shifts within the transformative sector point to a tendency of transformative employment to move towards higher-skilled positions.

1970–5 occupational change

A comparison of the 1960–70 results with the findings for the 1970–5 period shows many similarities. Although the various industrial and occupational shifts resulted in relatively smaller percentage changes for many categories during the 1970–5 period as compared to the 1960s, one must take into account that those shifts refer only to a five-year period and should be smaller by definition. Yet the industrial location of occupational change was little changed between 1960–70 and 1970–5. Again, the expansion of social services contributed most to the increase in professional employment, and it also increased the employment of technical workers by a substantial share. The below average growth of professional employment within social services represents a continuation of the trend begun during the 1960s.

We showed before that the employment of managers expanded in line with the growth of total employment during the 1970–5 period, because the positive net shifts due to the industrial transformation only barely outnumbered the negative net shifts of the intra-industry occupational composition. As in 1960–70, the service sectors continued to favour the employment of managers, and the decline of the transformative sector depressed their growth. The data for the occupational shifts within industries show that the overall negative occupational shifts for managers resulted primarily from the below average growth of managerial employment in distributive producer and personal services, although the negative shifts in the distributive sector were much reduced in comparison with those observed during the 1960s. The growth of social services during the early 1970s had little effect on the employment of managers, but the occupational composition within social services strongly favoured managerial employment. Without the occupational recomposition of social services, overall managerial employment would have registered a relative decrease during the early 1970s.

In comparison to the 1960s, the process of change in the manual occupations also remained fairly similar during the early 1970s, except that labourers in transformative industries changed more or less in accordance with the other occupations in this sector, in contrast to their decrease during the 1960s.

1975–80 occupational change

The changed pace of the industrial transformation and occupational recomposition during the latter 1970s also resulted in shifting industrial locations of changes in the occupational structure. As a result of the decreased rate of growth of social services, that sector no longer played a major role in the growth of occupational categories with the exception of technical workers. Although the rapid growth of producer services during the latter half of the 1970s benefited the employment of professionals, its influence remained far below that of social services during the 1960–75 period.

We pointed out earlier that the most significant change in the occupational structure during the 1975–80 period, as compared to the 1960–75 period, was the growth of managerial employment attributable to intra-industry occupational recomposition. This trend characterised all industrial sectors, with the above-average growth of managers being most important in the transformative sector and in social and personal services.

The net industry and occupational shifts during the 1975–80 period only slightly changed the manual occupations, compared to the magnitude of change which took place between 1960 and 1975. This is partly due to the absence of the employment decline in transformative activities which had characterised the earlier periods, but it also reflects relatively fewer changes of the intra-industry occupational composition. The major exception concerns labourers, whose employment in the transformative sector, as during the 1960s, did not keep pace with total transformative employment.

Discussion

The preceding analysis of the process of occupational change during the 1960–80 period showed that our expectations concerning the course of change during the 1970s were only partially borne out. In order to recapitulate, we set forth three specific expectations which were derived from earlier studies of industrial and occupational change (see Singelmann and Browning, 1980; Wright and Singelmann, 1982). First we argued that the industrial transformation from a goods to a service economy was nearing its completion. This expectation was based, among others, on the observation that the decline of the extractive sector, which had largely propelled this transformation in the past, had reduced extractive employment to such a low level that further reductions could only have minimal effects on the industrial transformation in the future. Moreover, the further expansion of social services has met increasing political resistance, thereby making a continuation of the past rates of growth improbable. In addition, the decline of the school-age population is contributing to a net reduction of employment in education. Our results showed that the pace of this transformation did slow down during the latter part of the 1970s. Specifically, during the 1975–80 period, social services and the transformative sectors held their share of total employment, but the structural shifts among the other three sectors were not sufficient to maintain the impact of the industrial transformation on occupational change which characterised the period from 1945 to 1975.

The second expectation concerned the pace of occupational change. We argued that once the industrial transformation nears its completion, it would cease being a major source of occupational change. Therefore, fewer changes in the occupational structure would be expected unless the changes in the intra-industry occupational composition increased sufficiently to compensate for the decreasing industrial effects. Our results, once again, showed a substantial decrease in the magnitude of occupational change during the late 1970s as compared to the 1960–75 period. That decrease, however, was less pronounced than the reduction in the pace of the industrial transformation precisely because the extent of intra-industry occupational composition increased between the early and late 1970s.

The third expectation concerned the direction of occupational change. Given the previous finding that the industrial transformation was mostly responsible for the changes in the occupational structure between 1960 and 1970, our expectation about its slower pace also implied that only little, if any, future occupational upgrading could be anticipated. In hypothesising this, we assumed that the effects of the industrial transformation would not be substituted by more favourable changes in the occupational composition within industries. The observed negative effects of the intra-industry occupational shifts on the growth of managerial employment even pointed to the possibility of a downgrading of the occupational structure, once the service economy had fully unfolded. Our results show, however, that this expectation so far has been incorrect. The highest status occupations (professional, technical and managerial workers) continued their post-war expansion during the late 1970s – albeit at a slower rate. This continued growth of high status occupations resulted largely from changes in the intra-industry occupational composition. Thus, while the occupational composition within industries was detrimental to the growth of high status occupations during the 1960s and early 1970s, the employment of high status workers within industries increased faster, on average, than total employment in these industries during the late 1970s. This turn-around of the relative importance of intra-industry occupational shifts on total occupational change is – if continued – of major importance, because it implies possibilities for future occupational upgrading even after the industrial transformation towards a service economy has been completed.

We noted at the outset of this paper that a disaggregation of occupational change should contribute new information which bears upon the conflicting predictions of post-industrial theory and the degradation thesis concerning the nature of work in a service society. The thrust of the argument made by post-industrialists (e.g. Bell, 1973, 1976; Richta, 1969; Fuchs, 1968; Touraine, 1969) is that post-industrial society will be characterised by a dominance of technological knowledge provided by the professional and technical class. This perspective predicts that an increasing number of persons will become professionals and technicians in order to meet the technological requirements of post-industrial society. Others (e.g. Moore, 1966) who focus on the relationship between economic development and the occupational structure make similar arguments for a continued upgrading of employment. Degradation theorists, on the other hand, have pointed to the effects of a continued division of labour which, in their view, destroys formerly complex work tasks, reduces workers' autonomy over their task completion, and decreases the skill demands for individual work positions.

The present data clearly cannot confirm or disprove the conflicting expectations of the two approaches. With respect to the degradation thesis, one must keep in mind that this approach addresses the qualifications of positions and not the qualifications of workers. In order to assess the possible extent of the degradation of work in a service society, one would need, for example, historical data for individual enterprises.

But even given the shortcomings of the data available for the present study, we find it difficult – despite our view that many analyses in the tradition of the degradation approach are very compelling (e.g. Stone, 1976) – to reconcile our results with the implications of the degradation thesis. Although the process of degradation might not be reflected in occupational statistics in the short run because degraded work positions could keep their occupational titles for some time, a shift *towards* the higher status occupations within industries appears to contradict the expectation about a general degradation of work positions, unless one assumes that the supply of highly qualified workers has the effect of creating additional high status positions. Even if one concedes that the best occupational structure of the current supply of labour does affect the structure of employment, it is questionable whether occupational upgrading would occur at a time when work positions are being degraded. We would like to offer, instead, another hypothesis for the observed pattern during the latter part of the 1970s.

Virtually all advanced western economies, including the United States, never solved their unemployment problem after the 1974–5 recessions, and the arrival of the world-wide economic downturn of the early 1980s resulted in depression-like rates of unemployment. It is possible that the increasing unemployment during the late 1970s had a disproportionately negative effect on the lower-status occupations consequently permitting the higher-status occupations to register above average gains. More generally, it may well be that the rise in productivity which occur as a result of economic recessions took more the form of elimination of work positions (mostly displacement for lower-status workers) that of a general downgrading throughout the workforce. This hypothesis will be difficult to test empirically with conventional labour force data, and we should also like to point out that the United States labour force did increase substantially during the 1975–80 period. But it may be well worth investigating whether the current conflict between labour and capital manifests itself mostly in the degradation of work positions, as it is conventionally understood, or if the crucial form of degradation today will mean the elimination of work opportunities.

In either case, however, our data point to important implications for the structural conditions of social mobility. To recapitulate, the findings of research on inter-generational occupational mobility (e.g. Featherman and Hauser, 1980; Hauser, *et al.*, 1975 a; 1975 b) showed that despite the many social and economic changes during the post-war period, the relative chances of mobility in the United States did not improve when the occupational structure was held constant. An upgrading of the occupational structure thus is of central importance for relative social mobility. Although the anticipated deterioration of the occupational structure did not take place during the 1970s, our results did point to a slowdown in the rate of occupational change in general, and in the growth of higher-status positions in particular.

Moreover, we argued that the mid-1970s represent the end of the post-war period which was characterised by high and sustained rates of economic growth, and that we are now at the beginning of a new period during which the economy will expand at much slower rates. This implies a likely continuation of the high rates of unemployment at least through the 1980s, and probably well into the 1990s, especially in many countries of the European community. Thus, if countries continue to have problems employing people – and the United States is no exception to this – changes in the occupational structure are but one structural parameter for relative occupational mobility, while the other parameter is the availability of work *per se*. If the son or daughter of a worker cannot find employment (and unemployment rates are related to educational attainment which in turn are related to social origin), improvements in the occupational structure of an insufficient number of jobs will do little for lifting the relative mobility chances of those children. Thus, although the transition towards a service economy created conditions which were favourable for social mobility, those conditions will not necessarily persist once a service economy is fully established.

Notes

1   Although Singelmann and Browning (1980) assumed that the upgrading of the occupational structure (i.e., the structural occupational shifts towards the higher status occupations) resulted from an expansion of producer and, foremost, social services, they did not estimate this effect empirically. A re-examination of the data does confirm their assumption about the extent to which the expansion of social services contributed to occupational upgrading: roughly 93 per cent of the net growth of professional employment and 69 per cent of the total industry shift in technical employment during the 1960s was due to the expansion of social services.

2   We did compute a shift share analyses for the 1970–80 period using both the PUMS and CPS data. While our results are quite similar, there were sufficient

differences for us to prefer using an exactly comparable classification for all three periods. These results are available upon request.

3 This difference between the two data sets results from the changes in the occupational classification system undertaken by the Bureau of the Census during the 1970s, which reclassified several occupations as managerial activities in 1980 which belonged to other occupational categories in 1970. This reclassification also affected professional occupations. In contrast, the occupational classification system used by the Current Population Survey remained unchanged over the 1970–80 period. We would also like to point to the greater sampling variability of the CPS in comparison to the census data.

4 We based our computation of occupational differentiation on the formula developed by Gibbs and Poston (1975).

$$OD = 1 - \frac{\Sigma X^2}{(\Sigma X)^2}$$

where X is the percentage of employed persons in each of the eleven occupational categories.

3 *Linda G. Murgatroyd, John Urry*

The class and gender restructuring of the Lancaster economy, 1950–80

1 Introduction

In this chapter we shall consider how one particular local economy within Britain has been reorganised over the past thirty years. We shall suggest that this reorganisation, reflected in the apparently simple changes in the relative size of manufacturing and service employment, is in fact the product of complex relationships between the underlying 'restructuring' of the various industrial sectors pertinent in the locality. Thus, industrial location and employment changes are not to be viewed as the consequence of certain general processes which are merely developed to a lesser or greater extent in any particular local economy. Any such economy must rather be seen as a specific conjuncture, in both time and space, of the particular forms of capitalist and state restructuring within manufacturing and service industries. As Massey argues, 'the social and economic structure of any given local area will be a complex result of the combination of that area's succession of roles within the series of wider, national and international, spatial divisions of labour' (Massey, 1978: 116).

There are three important implications of this 'structural' approach for the analysis of industrial location and employment change. First, it is necessary to investigate the changing forms of the spatial division of labour, especially the shift away from a high degree of regional specialisation, which are derived from new patterns of capital accumulation, including the internationalisation of capitalist accumulation (see Urry, 1984 b). Second, changes in the location of industry are not to be explained simply in terms of either 'economic' or 'political' factors. Location is rather to be understood in relation to those forms of economic restructuring within and between industrial sectors which are necessitated by the requirements of capital accumulation and state reorganisation. Moreover, relations between classes, and other social forces, particularly gender, also significantly affect patterns of economic restructuring, and the latter themselves influence social relations within particular localities to a substantial extent. Third, problems of uneven development cannot be analysed simply in terms of 'regions' and of regional growth or decline. With the growth of national and international branch circuits of capital there has been a decrease in the degree to which productive systems are centred upon a particular region (Massey, 1978, 1979). This has been related to the dispersal of new manufacturing employment on something of a 'periphery-centre' pattern and to some consequential decline in regional variations in unemployment and economic activity rates between the mid-1960s and the late 1970s (see Keeble, 1976: 71–85; and Dunford, Geddes and Perrons, 1981: 12–13). This homogenisation amongst the peripheral regions has also been partly reinforced by the growing concentration of the functions of conception and control within the south-east region of the UK (see Crum and Gudgin, 1977; Marquand, 1980). Similarly, in terms of industrial change, Fothergill and Gudgin conclude that 'there are much greater contrasts within any region than between the regions themselves' (1979: 157; more generally see Urry, 1981, 1983). One example of such contrasts may be seen in the North West Plannning Region in which Lancaster is situated. In 1966, this was one of only two regions said to possess a 'regional' industrial structure (see Fothergill and Gudgin, 1979: 170–72, 174–6). Yet even in this case there have been considerable intra-regional variations in patterns of employment and unemployment in the recent period.

In this chapter we shall consider these three points in some detail, in relationship to the de-industrialisation of the Lancaster sub-region, situated in the north of the North West Planning Region (north of Preston and Blackburn). (See Murgatroyd, 1981, for background details.) Lancaster has, like much of the rest of the UK, been 'de-industrialised' in recent years. However, this change in the pattern of employment, consisting of a shift out of manufacturing into both service employment and into unemployment and underemployment, results from a number of underlying processes whose impact varies greatly in different regions and localities. There is no simple 'de-industrialising' process by which national and sub-national economies develop, with one kind of economic activity automatically replacing another as dominant. To say that a local, regional or national economy has been 'de-industrialised' is, then, merely a way of *describing* certain shifts in the structure of employment – it does not provide any kind of explanation. Hence, although Britain as a whole has experienced 'de-industrialisation' in recent years, this in fact results from highly diverse processes, affecting different localities in different ways, depending upon their location within pre-existing and new forms of the spatial division of labour (see Urry, 1984 b for details).

2   The de-industrialisation of Lancaster

Between 1951 and 1977 there was a major reduction in manufacturing employment in the Lancaster economy, from around 17,000 to 9,000, with considerable job loss being recorded in all the industries with a substantial labour force. And at the same time there were major increases in many of the service industries such that the overall numbers increased by 5,000 between 1951 and 1977. However, this overall change has not occurred smoothly during this period. In the 1950s both manufacturing and service employment grew considerably, the former by 9.5 per cent and the latter by 13.2 per cent, both between 1952 and 1964 (Fulcher *et al.*, 1966: 2; unless otherwise stated all data between 1952 and 1964 comes from this source). Overall, there was an increase in the labour force of over 4,000, a rate of employment growth about equivalent to the UK average, but faster than the average for the North West Region. The North West Regional Council predicted that the Lancaster sub-region would be a future growth point of both population and employment. By 1981 they expected that the population would have grown to 140,000 (compared with 117,000 in 1961) with the development of new science-based industries and extensive office employment.

These optimistic predictions for the 1960s and 1970s were based in part on the experiences of the 1950s. Within manufacturing, employment in a number of industries grew considerably: textiles by 32.3 per cent (representing 1,349 employees), engineering by 56.5 per cent (360), clothing and footwear by 17 per cent (124), and floor coverings and coated fabrics etc. by 25 per cent (1,002) (all between 1952 and 1964). Moreover, these increases involved considerable new building and machinery. Lancaster in fact attracted new industrial building 7 per cent higher than one might have expected on the basis of the size and structure of the manufacturing sector (compared with the north-west as a whole which was 21 per cent lower than 'expected'; see Fulcher *et al.*, 1966: 10–11, 22). Certain categories of service employment also showed very substantial rates of employment growth: distribution 38 per cent, insurance, banking 35 per cent, professional services 42 per cent, and public administration 19 per cent. The strong demand for labour was met by considerable migration into the sub-region; between 1951 and 1964 there was net in-migration of 6,845 people (see Fulcher *et al.*, 1966: 34). Moreover, even with this migration the rate of unemployment remained very low – the June unemployment figures were lower than the national average in every year bar one between 1954 and 1963 (see Fulcher *et al.*, 1966: 38). This strong demand for labour was also reflected in considerable increases in female employment in the 1950s. The ratio of female/male employees increased from 57 per cent to 61 per cent, while the ratio for the north-west remained more or less constant (1952–64; see Fulcher *et al.*, 1966: 37). Finally, even as late as 1964 local employers maintained that because there was over-full employment they were unable to recruit the labour they required, and that labour had generally become much shorter in supply in recent years.

Over the next fifteen years this position was to alter quite dramatically. The significant feature of this period was the decline in manufacturing employment; at the beginning of the 1960s it accounted for about 35 per cent of the labour force, by 1971 this was down to 26 per cent, and by 1977 it had reached 20 per cent (Department of Employment, ER II). The proportion of service employment has risen accordingly – by 1977 it accounted for two-thirds of local employment (note that the economically active population remained fairly stable). However, this apparent stability conceals a number of divergent trends. Between 1951 and 1981 male employment fell by 5,820 and the male economic activity rate fell from 81.4 per cent to 71.9 per cent; while over the same period female employment rose by 5,400 (Census of Population, 1951, 1981). This change was also reflected in the increase in the ratio of female to male workers in the sub-region; by 1977 it had risen to 0.74, slightly higher than the mean for the north-west which has always had high female activity rates (Department of Employment). The general shift towards the service industries was related to the increased feminisation of the Lancaster labour force since the proportion of women employed in these industries tends to be high. However, there was also a shift *within* the service sector towards increased feminisation (10 per cent increase between 1971 and 1977).

Thus, up to the mid-1960s, Lancaster was a centre for investment with a considerable labour shortage. From 1965, though, this became less the case as investment took place elsewhere and the local unemployment rate rose above the national average. The male rate in particular has increased steeply, there being a growing gap between the national and local rates, except during the 1972–3 and 1978–9 upturns in economic activity.

We have so far merely described the shift in Lancaster's recent history. An obvious explanation of its de-industrialisation might simply be that it reflected the archaic industrial structure in the sub-region. However, Fothergill and Gudgin's shift-share analysis of sub-regional employment change between 1959 and 1975 suggests that this was not the case (see 1979, as well as 1981; and Keeble, 1976). Their analysis enables us to distinguish three components: first, employment change that would have resulted if local employment had changed at exactly the national rate (national); second, change which would have resulted if *each* of the industries in the area had changed its employment at the same rate as those industries had done nationally (structural); and third, the differential growth caused by industrial movement in and out of the sub-region and by indigenous performance (differential). When applied to the Lancaster sub-region the results are as shown in table 3.1.

Thus, we could have expected manufacturing to have increased by 2,100 (2,900–800) between 1959 and 1975. Indeed the structural component for Lancaster was more favourable than for any of the other sixty-one sub-regions in the UK. By the late 1950s the industrial structure of Lancaster was the most favourable in the UK. Fothergill and Gudgin note:

Expressed as a percentage of 1959 employment the worst sub-regional employment structure for *manufacturing* was North East Lancashire (-20.0%), reflecting its heavy dependence on the declining cotton industry, and the best was Lancaster (19.5%) . . . dominated by a handful of firms in growing industries.
(1979: 169; the map on p. 170 shows that only six sub-regions out of sixty-one had a structural component higher than even 10 per cent).

Table 3.1 Different components of manufacturing employment change in Lancaster, 1959–75

National	Structural		Differential		Actual
	Nos.	% 1959 employment	Nos.	% 1959 employment	Change
-800	$+2,900$	$+19.5\%$	$-5,400$	-36%	$-3,300$

(Fothergill and Gudgin, 1979: 210–14)

Hence, the explanation of the decline in manufacturing employment (3,300 between 1959–75) rests with the differential component, with the fact that existing firms failed to grow and to expand employment, with their closure or shrinkage, and with the failure to attract the potentially mobile employment being generated in the 1960s and early 1970s. Indeed, Fothergill and Gudgin also show that the structural component remained positive throughout the 1960s, only becoming slightly negative in 1971–5 (1979: 216). However, in the same decade the differential component remained strongly negative; this then breaks down further in the period 1966–71 as shown in table 3.2.

Table 3.2 Manufacturing employment in Lancaster, 1966–71

Differential component	Net industrial movement	Indigenous performance	
		Nos. employed	% 1966 employment
$-2,500$	0	$-2,500$	-17.1%

(Fothergill and Gudgin, 1979: 219)

In óther words, in this period of considerable industrial restructuring there were no industrial moves into the sub-region. The decline in manufacturing employment was attributable to the 'poor' performance of the firms and plants located in Lancaster, although the industrial structure over the period 1959–75 was, as we have seen, exceptionally favourable.

In the case of services the results were almost exactly the opposite of those for manufacturing employment, as can be seen in table 3.3. The negative structural component for service employment was the highest for any of the sub-regions in the UK. The considerable growth in service employment in Lancaster was thus accounted for in terms of a very favourable 'performance' of the service sector industries during the 1960s, the pattern here being the opposite of that in most of the neighbouring sub-regions (see the maps in Fothergill and Gudgin, 1979: 170–1).

Table 3.3   Service employment in Lancaster, 1959–71

National component	Structural component		Differential component		Actual change
	Nos.	% 1959 employment	Nos.	% 1959 employment	
+ 2,400	− 1,800	− 8%	+ 2,700	12.1%	+ 3,300

(Fothergill and Gudgin, 1979: 213)

Fothergill and Gudgin thus argue that there was enormous variation *within* regions, in particular with regard to the indigenous performance of existing plants, and that the main distinction in terms of employment change is between urban areas and semi-rural areas. It is in the former, and especially in the large conurbations, that manufacturing employment decline has been most marked. And it is in the less industrialised, semi-rural areas that the most substantial increases in both manufacturing employment and total employment were recorded (1979: 189). Thus, cities or localities like Lancaster in terms of its rural/urban characteristics showed very considerable growth of manufacturing employment in this period (between 16.3 per cent and 38.8 per cent), while Lancaster's declined by 22 per cent.

Two conclusions follow: first, according to Fothergill and Gudgin's analysis, Lancaster *should* have experienced some increases in manufacturing employment, given its industrial structure and the 'performance' of similar less heavily industrialised sub-regions. And second, it is necessary to undertake more detailed analysis in order to explain the 'indigenous performance' of particular sub-regions, and hence to demonstrate the complex, interrelated and spatially sigificant forms of capital restructuring involved here.

3   Lancaster and the restructuring of capital

Initially here we should note a significant increase in the numbers of establishments and enterprises, from fifty-eight manufacturing 'firms' in 1964 to 135 in 1979. There were very few small manufacturing firms in Lancaster in 1964, and this may have been connected with the tightness of the local labour market at the time; small firms found it hard to attract labour (Fulcher *et al.*, 1966), and the abundance of jobs may have lessened the attractiveness of self-employment. Even then, allowing for some under-reporting of smaller firms in 1964, there has been a substantial increase in the number of manufacturing firms in Lancaster, at the very same time that the sub-region has been de-industrialised and that manufacturing employment has dropped to about one-fifth. This increase is accounted for largely by the growth of small enterprises. Partly this has resulted from the efforts of the City Council to encourage the establishment and growth of such firms, not simply because this is the only alternative, but also because of the perceived problems caused by dependence on 'externally controlled' capital. This problem was graphically highlighted in 1980 when the closure of the Lansil works owned by British Celanese (part of Courtaulds) caused more jobs to be lost than had been created by small firms during the whole of the 1970s.

We have already noted the local concern with the issue of external control. The local planning department has noted: '. . . it is significant that a very high proportion of closures and redundancies declared during recent periods of recession have been in firms who are under external control, i.e. 'pruning the branches to encourage growth' (Lancaster City Council, 1977, Appendix III c). Two interesting trends can, though, be noted: first, an increase in the proportion of the labour force employed in 'externally controlled' enterprises over this period, but, second, a decline in the *proportion* of manufacturing firms that are in fact externally controlled (see Murgatroyd and Urry, 1983: Table IV). A further point to note here is that *all* large manufacturing firms in Lancaster are now externally controlled; while independent ownership is much more characteristic of the very small firms. Moreover, hardly any of the large plants were established by major multinationals; rather they were locally owned firms which were *acquired* by (or merged with) large companies based elsewhere. In other words, external takeovers have been far more important for the employment structure of Lancaster than have patterns of branch-plant migration (except in the 1940s and 1950s with the establishment of a fertiliser factory by ICI and of a refinery by Shell). Lancaster has not therefore developed as a typical branch-plant economy.

We will now consider briefly why industrial capital did not invest in this sub-region in the 1960s and 1970s. Already by the early '60s there were a number of identifiable features relevant to this:

1. The vulnerability of the economy because of the local dependence on a *small* number of important manufacturing sectors, namely, fertilisers, weaving, textiles, plastics and linoleum.
2. The domination of the manufacturing labour market by a few large firms – this generally lowers the rate of formation of new companies (see *Cambridge Economic Policy Review*, 1980: 23–4).
3. The low unemployment rate and the small size of the pool of labour which would mean both a failure to attract regional policy incentives and to effect

new plant in-migration.

4. The pattern of increasing external ownership of the economy so that even by 1964 the majority of workers in manufacturing were employed in plants that were externally controlled (see Fulcher *et al.*, 1966: 14).

5. The development of an active policy of restructuring during especially the later 1960s and early 1970s partly under the sway of British regional policy; this would weaken those local economies like Lancaster which were unsuccessful in attracting the new potentially mobile employment (much of which, of course, went abroad).

In order to explain the poor 'performance' in Lancaster, both in not attracting new accumulation and in failing to prevent *in situ* employment loss, we need to consider the distinctions made by Massey and Meegan (1982) between the different forms in which production is reorganised.

There are three: 'intensification', 'investment and technical change' and 'rationalisation'. The first is the process by which changes take place in order to increase the productivity of labour, but there is little, if any, loss of capacity and no investment in new forms of production. Such a reorganisation of production will generally entail less change in the distribution of employment than any of the other forms of reorganisation. In the second type, 'investment and technical change', there is heavy capital investment within new forms of production and as a result considerable job-loss, often highly unequally distributed. And in the third form, 'rationalisation', there is closure of capacity without any particularly new investment or change in technique. We shall show that Lancaster's manufacturing employment was concentrated in industries in which 'investment and technical change' and 'rationalisation' were to occur, rather than 'intensification' (for more detail, especially with regard to the statistics, see Murgatroyd and Urry, 1983).

First, then, we will consider linoleum, plastic floor coverings, leather cloth etc. (MLH 492); table 3.4 indicates the main changes here.

Table 3.4 Local and national employment in linoleum, plastic floor-coverings, leather cloth etc. industries

	1952	1964	1971	1973	1977
Lancaster TTWA	4,091	5,021	2,502	1,888	1,483
United Kingdom	13,800	13,800	13,500	16,000	14,300

(Fulcher *et al.*, 1966; and Department of Employment, various years, and unpublished data)

During the 1950s this was a relatively buoyant industrial sector with a 25 per cent increase in the local employed labour force. However, during the 1960s there was a sharp decline in employment. The effect of this on what had been the major company in Lancaster since the 1860s has been described as follows:

> The boom collapsed in the early 1960s, and the Mills [Williamsons] were forced into a defensive merger with a major rival: the merger led to considerable rationalisation, the disposal of surplus assets and the consolidation of both administration and production at the headquarters of the former rival [Nairns], in a government development area [Kirkcaldy].
>
> (Martin and Fryer, 1973: 168; names in brackets added.)

In fact, all floor-covering production was transferred to Kirkcaldy and the Lancaster plant mainly concentrated on PVC wall-coverings. Overall, the rate of decline of this sector has been far faster in Lancaster than in the UK as a whole. This is because of the dramatic decline in linoleum production and the development of plastic floor-coverings and cheap carpeting based on man-made fibres. Hence, there was a combination of two processes, in linoleum of rationalisation and the almost complete disappearance of manufacturing capacity, and of technical change and investment within plastic floor-coverings and carpet manufacture.

In the case of fertilisers (MLH 278) there was a similarly healthy employment pattern nationally, the number increasing from 18,000 to 22,000 between 1963 and 1970, and then declining to 19,000 (Census of Production). However, at the same time, there were enormous increases in net output, capital expenditure and productivity. In table 3.5 the contrast can be seen with the floor-coverings industry.

Table 3.5 Output, productivity and capital investment in floor-coverings* and fertilisers,* 1963–78

	Net output £m		Net output per head £		Total capital investment £m	
	Fertilisers	Floor-coverings	Fertilisers	Floor-coverings	Fertilisers	Floor-coverings
1963	36.7	33.0	2,041	1,644	10.1	3.5
1968	70.9	38.4	3,674	2,224	8.3	3.7
1970	81.6	47.4	3,708	2,530	16.1	4.4
1974	214.6	77.7	10,875	4,653	26.1	8.2
1978	366.2	117.0	19,312	8,963	71.2	n.a.

(Census of Production)
* 'Floor-coverings' refers to industries in MLH 492 of the 1968 Standard Industrial Classification; 'fertilisers' to MLH 278. Note changes in classification in 1969, 1973 and 1979

Both output and productivity in fertiliser production increased ten times over the period 1963–78, while capital investment increased nine times between 1968 and 1978 (all in money terms). The increases in productivity in fertilisers were greater than for any other branch of the chemicals industry between 1970 and 1975 (see COI 1978: 17). This capital investment was concentrated in the development of new, very large, low cost manufacturing plant – by the late 1960s there were six major plants in the UK (ICI at Avonmouth, Billingham, Immingham; Fisons at Avonmouth, Immingham; and Shell at Ince Marshes: see Warren, 1971, especially 194–200). As a result there was a 20 per cent reduction in the numbers of both establishments and enterprises between 1963 and 1978. Moreover, these enormous increases in output were achieved with little or no increase in total employment in the fertiliser industry. There was more or less constant national employment during the 1970s. Overall then the process of restructuring within the fertiliser industry was one of 'investment and technical change'. What then were the consequences for the Lancaster economy?

Local employment in this sector fell from 2,285 in 1952 to 624 in 1977 for two main reasons. First, ammonia production was itself abandoned from 1977 and concentrated in the larger plants, especially in the north-east. Secondly, the fertiliser made locally by ICI at Heysham (Nitrogel) could not compete with the new fertiliser (Nitran) which had been developed by ICI in the mid-1960s. The Heysham plant (in Lancaster TTWA) was disadvantaged in that its capacity was too small (500 tons per day as opposed to up to 1,500/200 tons at more modern plants) and because none of its main production capacity dates from later than 1962 (source: interview with management). Again we see both how capital accumulation in manufacturing industry did not occur in Lancaster in the past twenty years, and that this decline resulted from the development *elsewhere* of newer, cheaper manufacturing capacity. Even moderate-sized plants producing for a specific regional market (for example, the ESSO Plant at Warboys, Essex) were unable to compete with the major plants listed above (see Warren, 1971: 197–8).

In the case of the third major industry, man-made fibres, the production of this had begun in Lancaster in 1928 with the establishment of Cellulose Acetate Silk Co. Ltd (later known as Lansils). This was an era of considerable expansion in the production of cellulosic textile yarns in general so that by the end of 1929 Courtaulds had thirty-three competitors nationally. However, in the next thirty years, Courtaulds came to dominate the production of cellulose-based textile yarns (i.e. rayons). By 1962, for example, Lansils was the only other producer of cellulose acetate (see Monopolies Commission 1968: 15; Cowling, 1980: 81–92). However, even in the early 1950s, the market for rayon was being eroded by the development of synthetic fibres, especially nylon and then polyesters, and of improved cotton. Over the following twenty years, Courtaulds came to dominate production in all sections of the textile industry, except that of weaving which remained fragmented.

In 1978 there were 303 enterprises and 368 establishments in MLH 413, weaving of cotton, linen and man-made fibres (Census of Production). Courtaulds partly overcame this fragmentation by establishing their own weaving plants, for example, at Skelmersdale (see Knight, 1974, as well as Cowling, 1980: 291–3, which lists all major acquisitions 1963–74). Lansils was finally taken over by Courtaulds in 1973/4, having been owned by Chemstrand Ltd. (a subsidiary of Monsanto) from 1962 (see Monopolies Commission 1968: 15 and Appendix 7).

Two conclusions are important here. First, man-made fibres constituted a sector in which investment and technical change was particularly marked, especially in the period up to 1970 (see Ewing, 1972: chs. 4 and 5, on some of the main technical changes). This can be seen from table 3.6.

Table 3.6 Main developments in the UK man-made fibres industry, 1958–78

	Enterprises	Establishments	£m net output	£ per person	000 total employment	Total capital expenditure
1958	10	30	49.5	1,360	36.4	10.7
1963	7	26	108.8	2,918	37.3	11.7
1968	5	26	163.0	4,043	40.3	24.4
1970	9	26	172.8	4,014	43.1	41.4
1974	27	43	293.9	6,917	42.5	37.3
1978	24	36	297.3	8,538	34.8	27.3

(Census of Production)

Courtaulds itself was able to enlarge its monopoly position by moving into synthetics, and by vertical integration (see Counter-information Service Report 1974). The second point is that the effect of this in Lancaster was that Lansils closed in September 1980 after a long period of decline. Courtaulds said that this was due to substantial losses, but it was also partly due to the lack of updating or replacement of machinery since installation in 1952. More generally, the reorganisation of the textile industry, the mergers, acquisitions, technical changes, and new plants in development areas and abroad (see Counter-information Services, 1974: 15, 25–7, and Newbould, 1970: 35, on the 1967/8 merger boom) produced new accumulation away from the traditional Lancashire textile towns. The total number of textile workers in Lancaster area declined from 5,500 in 1964 to 1,800 in 1977 (Fulcher *et al.*, 1966, and Department of Employment).

To summarise, Lancaster benefited from the accumulation in manufacturing industry in the 1950s, and by the end of the decade had high representation in a number of growing industrial sectors. However, these were sectors that were to experience investment and technical change and rationalisation, particularly because of the increased centralisation of ownership. New plants were established elsewhere, while existing plants based on earlier technologies shed labour. Local branches of multi-plant companies were run down, as these companies restructured their production away from Lancaster. While the number of small manufacturing enterprises swelled during the later period, these did not provide sufficient employment to off-set the decline in the larger establishments. It is important to note that of those industries in which there was much less job loss in this period, two appear as 'intensifiers' between 1968 and 1973, according to Massey and Meegan (1982: 3). These are textile finishing (MLH 423), whose employment in Lancaster fell from 432 to 278 between 1971–7 and footwear (MLH 450) whose employment fell from 549 to 414 (Department of Employment).

We will now consider the reorganisation of the service industries in Lancaster (for general discussion, see Urry, 1984a; and Gershuny and Miles, 1983). Between 1951 and 1977 the numbers employed in them increased by 21 per cent (5,000) as compared with a 23 per cent increase nationally. This overall expansion conceals, though, a number of divergent trends. Between 1960 and 1979 employment in transport and communication declined by over one third, while that in professional and scientific services almost tripled (rising by 180 per cent). Other service industries maintained fairly steady levels of employment. In the relatively large size of the transport sector and the small numbers employed in financial services and government administration, Lancaster was fairly typical of the north-west as a whole. During the 1950s Lancaster had a lower proportion of people employed in professional and scientific services than was the national average (7.5 per cent compared with 7.9 per cent nationally), and in this also it resembled the average for the North West Region (see Marquand, 1980). However, during the 1960s and 1970s, the expansion of this sector resulted in strong local concentration of employment in these services. 24 per cent of the employed labour force in Lancaster were in this Industry Order (25) in 1977, compared with 16 per cent nationally.

Many of these shifts resulted not from changes in local markets or other indigenous factors, but from decisions taken at a national level, concerning (mainly) changes in the railway, education and health systems. As in the case of manufacturing industry, the domination of the transport and the professional and scientific services (Industry Order 25) by organisations which extended beyond the boundaries of Lancaster resulted in reorganisation which affected the locality to a disproportionate extent. While the 'market' for many of these services is local, in the sense that health and education authorities cater for those living within their boundaries, there has been a concentration in Lancaster of specialised areas of health care (e.g. mental hospitals, geriatrics), and of higher education which serve a population far wider than that permanently living in the travel-to-work area. Both employees and clients in these services are geographically mobile into the area in order to take up the jobs or services available in Lancaster (see Murgatroyd, 1981). There was thus an increasing local dependence on public sector employment in educational and health services. Not only has an increasing proportion of the local population come to depend directly on the state sector for employment, but also a great deal of employment in other services depends on the incomes generated by these sectors. As manufacturing employment declined, the economy of Lancaster has become increasingly dependent on the level and direction of state expenditure (this has been further shown by the designation of Heysham as the service centre for the Morecambe Bay Gas Field by British Gas).

There are some important effects of these processes on the gender distribution of employment in this economy. First of all, although only one quarter of Lancaster's employment was in manufacturing industries in 1971, yet almost one half of employed males remained in manual (non-agricultural) work. This was accounted for by the small number of women in manual work. Only 21 per cent of female employees were in manual occupations, whereas 31 per cent were in junior non-manual occupations, and a further 15 per cent each in personal service and intermediate non-manual occupations. Most of the local expansion of employment in the service industries was taken up by women. Thus, the marked sexual division of labour became even more pronounced over this period. There were at least twice as many men as women engaged in manufacturing employment, the numbers of both sexes declining in a steady manner over the period, with a small decline in the proportion of women. Numbers of both male and females employed in the service industries increased, but whereas in 1961 there were 127 males to every 100 females employed in this sector, the ratio had been reversed by 1977, with 116 females for every 100 males. Female employment in the service sector almost doubled during this period, while male employment increased less steadily and only slightly, overall. Women dominated clerical and service occupations whereas men dominated most manual occupations, both in Lancaster and in the whole country. The manual occupations in which significant numbers of women were engaged in Lancaster, making clothing, textiles or leather, were very much dominated by women. 90 per cent, 69 per cent and 83 per cent (respectively) of workers in these trades were female. These were also the only manual (non-servicing) occupational group which were predominantly female at the national level.

Thus the expansion of women's employment did not imply a greater similarity between the positions of men and of women in the local labour market, nor indeed in the division of labour more generally. A high degree of occupational segregation persisted in Lancaster, as we have seen. Far from women entering traditional domains of male activity, it was the feminised sectors that expanded. To some extent, the lack of alternative occupations for less-skilled males has meant that they have been forced to accept work of traditionally feminine types, or else provide their own employment, if they were to avoid unemployment. However, while there is no evidence that the types of work and the conditions of employment of women noticeably improved, and there was an increasing level of female unemployment as well as male, it is clear that the local labour market position did improve compared with that of men.

4 State policies and local politics

Thus, there has been a substantial shift in the character of this local economy over the past thirty years. It has changed from an economy which was dominated by a small number of private manufacturing employers, who were involved in numerous commodity and interpersonal linkages with the locality and with the surrounding textile-based region, and who mainly employed semi-skilled male workers. It has become an economy in which the state is the dominant employer and in which the fortunes of the small private employers depend upon the expansion or contraction of state expenditure, partly within the more feminised service sector. Hardly any substantial manufacturing establishments remain (two of the three biggest have now closed), and there are limited linkages with other locally based firms.

We will now consider three significant political aspects of these developments. First, why was Lancaster unable to attract the mobile new employment that was generated in those manufacturing industries undergoing technical change and making new investments in the 1960s and early 1970s? Second, what were the characteristic features of the economic and social relations in Lancaster? How far can these relations be described as those of 'paternalism'? And third, what have been the consequences of the changes in the ownership and the structure of employment upon the local social structure?

On the first question we should note that Lancaster is part of the North West Region, and this region has performed badly in employment terms over the recent period. Stillwell maintains that the north-west was among 'the least attractive regions in which to locate industry' (1968: 10; and see Fothergill and Gudgin, 1982). This meant that other regions attracted the mobile plants which made a major difference in employment terms. MacKay and Thomson suggest that the net gain for movement between 1945 and 1971 was equivalent to almost one quarter of 1960 manufacturing employment (1979: 241). This produced, for those less-favoured areas, cumulative disadvantage, as the age of the regions' capital stock got progressively older and less competitive with the new plant being established elsewhere. Lancaster should have been partly protected from this effect, given its relative expansion in the 1940s and '50s. However, this was not sustained, partly because the North West Region has not constituted an important force politically (in comparison with Scotland or South Wales, for example), and partly because Lancaster has had little chance of making effective representation on its own (it has maintained Intermediate Area Status). In each case, both regionally and locally, the weakness of the labour movement has helped beneficiaries of regional aid (apart from Merseyside). The labour movement never developed a regional basis here, by contrast, for example, with South Wales or the north-east of England. One crude indicator of this is given by the fact that the proportion of people voting Labour in Lancashire has generally been lower than in corresponding regions. (In 1974, 50.1 per cent in Lancashire voted Labour, compared with 59.4 per cent in the north-east.)

The local state has concentrated upon two policies: first, to attract new service employment within the public sector – hence the university and expanded hospital services – and second, to develop small manufacturing firms. The latter policy was developed in the early 1960s (after the closure of the Gillow furniture workshops following the takeover by Great Universal Stores); it was consolidated in the late 1960s and 1970s and did not change substantially, even when unemployment began to rise. Land and technical and financial assistance were made available and a 'seed-bed' experiment was set up to help very small firms to become established. Preference for these facilities were actively given to those small firms, with 'high quality' products, in technologically-based industries (Lancaster City Council, 1977). A substantial number of such firms were successfully brought to or started in Lancaster, using the facilities provided by the council and the university through *Enterprise Lancaster*, and also helped by the *Small Firms Club* initiated by the City Council. Large-scale manufacturing investments were less strongly encouraged by the local Council throughout the '60s and early '70s, and Lancaster's designation as an Intermediate Area during the era of Regional Policy after 1972 did not facilitate the attraction of large-scale capital during a period of massive industrial restructuring.

On the second and third questions above, we have already noted that the Lancaster sub-region has not had a strong labour movement, but contrary to commentators, this did not attract large flows of capital to the sub-region to profit from the quiescent labour force (by contrast with the inter-war period). It has been argued that the quiescence of the Lancaster labour force has resulted from the paternalist character of social relations both within workplaces and between the local firms and the city (see Martin and Fryer, 1973, on the firm of Wiliamsons; and see Urry, 1980, for some sceptical comments). Norris defines paternalism (of the sort once found in Lancaster) as existing where inequalities of economic and political power are 'stabilised through the legitimating ideology of traditionalism' (Norris, 1978: 471). He suggests that there are four components to such an ideology: 'gentlemanly ethic', 'personal dependence', 'localism', and a 'gift relationship'.

While traditional forms of paternalism clearly no longer existed by the 1960s and '70s, vestiges of these practices seem to be indicated by the responses of the local labour movement to the mass redundancies and plant closures which characterised 1980 and 1981. These events elicited fatalistic responses from the labour force and the only negotiations that took place were about the terms of redundancies, their necessity being accepted from the start. This can be seen by considering the closure of Courtaulds' cellulose-acetate Lansil works, previously a major source of local employment. Over the summer of 1980 there were a series of redundancies (120, 20, 11) before the announced closure of the works in September with a further 669 redundancies (source:

interview with shop stewards). This demoralised the labour force; it was felt that decisions were being taken over which they had no control and in which their actions would have no effect. There was little sympathy for the company, and indeed a belief that it did not 'care' for its employees. For example, it was thought that UK profits and hence the viability of UK plants were lower than they should have been because pulp imported from South Africa was given too high a transfer price for currency reasons (source: interview with shop stewards). However, this was not translated into a belief in the efficacy of industrial or political action; and in the end the workers from Lansils appeared grateful to accept the minimal redundancy payments paid out by Courtaulds. It is interesting to note that at the time of redundancy it was widely held that it was 'inevitable' that this plant should close, and that there was no alternative since it had lost £91,000 in the last financial year. Yet part of the reason why this was inevitable was that there had been no major updating or replacement of much of the machinery, some of which was forty years old! A year earlier it had been announced that Courtaulds were to build a new rayon producing plant 'somewhere in Europe' (*The Guardian*, 2 April 1979), and although this was apparently to produce viscose yarn (rather than cellulose acetate) it demonstrated that there was nothing inevitable about corporate restructuring and associated plant closures.

The main active response to such closures was also characterised by attitudes associated with paternalism, namely localism and personal dependence. The *Save Lancaster Campaign* was established by the Trades Council late in 1980, in the wake of several redundancy announcements and the emphasis of the campaign was firmly on the locality rather than on class politics. This campaign did not gain much active support even at this time, and it withered away after a few weeks. Most of those affected preferred either to depend on the provisions of the state and the efforts of the City Council, or to find individualistic solutions to unemployment. It may well be that the blossoming of small business during the 1970s was an accommo-dating local response to the decline in employment in older manufacturing firms. In addition, the existence of a large (traditional) petit bourgeoisie (the self-employed) probably undermined collectivist protests.

We have already mentioned two of the strongly localist responses to the industrial restructuring which has affected the Lancaster area, namely the *Save Lancaster Campaign*, and the City Council's initiatives to encourage the establishment of new small businesses whose local inter-linkages (and hence presumed local control) would be more marked than in the case of externally owned and controlled plants. Although there was considerable con-troversy within the labour movement about its involvement in such local initiatives it would seem that the forms of capitalist restructuring made it difficult for employers and city officials to resist the claims of labour (particularly male labour) to some say in future developments. Indeed, to some extent, it appears that the labour movement had more involvement in trying to 'save' the city's industry than have most other groupings, certainly more than the major transnational companies who happen to have one of their plants in the locality (except Unilever). Part of the efforts of the City Council have been directed to getting such companies to take some responsibility for the effects of their decisions. Yet, at the same time, the efforts of the local labour movement to preserve capitalist manufacturing activity in the locality clearly deflected labourist struggles away from the traditional issues of the wage-relation or the forms of capitalist control, concentrating them instead on presenting the city as a suitable site for private investment. To some extent the labour movement has also put its weight behind the 'small firms strategy'.

A number of other developments in local politics took place over this period. In particular, various 'oppositional fragments' have emerged, which have been concerned with struggles in the area of consumption as well as with production. Such issues as ecology, nuclear energy and weaponry, sexual politics, transport, leisure and the arts, have grown in importance locally, as the service sector has come to dominate the area's industry, many of those active in such 'fragments' being either employed in the service sector or unemployed. Particularly noticeable in Lancaster (as opposed to Morecambe/Heysham) has been the development of a strong set of cultural institutions (theatre, film theatre, dance, literature festival, community arts) which nevertheless receive low levels of local state funding. It is suggested that this low funding results from the domination of the local council by representatives of the Morecambe tourist industry. In 1984 this has become a major issue in local politics. Lancaster also is widely known for the strength of its local women's movement, which is at least partly connected with the structural shifts in industry and employment noted above.

5   Conclusion

We have tried to show how the Lancaster economy has been transformed as a consequence of its location within the changing forms of the spatial division of labour. During the period of post-war reconstruction, based on the expansion of national capital, Lancaster benefited and developed in a number of growing industrial sectors. But with the industrial restructuring of the 1960s and early '70s, a new, in part international, spatial division of labour developed under the influence of British regional policy. This new spatial division did not benefit Lancaster and indeed, since its capital was of a previous vintage, the effect of the new round of accumulation was to undermine those industries established within the previous round. The main expansion was in state service employment – and partly in private service employment. There was an increasing gap between the relatively skilled employment available in the service sector (especially that of the state) and

that relatively low skilled male employment available in the private manufacturing sector. The political composition of Lancaster in part interestingly
reflects this particular combination of forms under which the local economy
has been restructured.

From class structure to class action: British working-class politics in the 1980s

Privatisation and fatalism as responses to economic recession

With the sweeping general election victory of the Conservative Party in 1983, the 'debate on the working class' (Goldthorpe, 1972, 1979) might be said to have entered a new phase. In one sense, of course, we have been here before. During the 1950s a run of Conservative electoral successes re-shaped the research agenda of conventional academic social science by posing the question of whether this reflected a fundamental shift in the class structure of contemporary Britain. Psephological *post mortems* on the 1959 general election were quick to invest it with far-reaching significance and for a time there was a growing belief in the classlessness of a British society affected by the experience of post-war affluence and the growth of mass consumerism. Butler and Rose, for example, argued that 'The swing to the Conservatives cannot be dismissed as an ephemeral veering of the electoral breeze. Long-term factors were also involved. Traditional working-class attitudes had been eroded by the steady growth of prosperity' (1960: 15). This argument was also elaborated at greater length by Abrams and Rose in *Must Labour Lose?* As one of us has indicated elsewhere (Newby, 1982) it can be seen in retrospect that not only was research into social stratification and political sociology in Britain dominated by this problem for the next decade or more, but also that the terms in which it was to be considered were also set by these considerations.

In other words, a major preoccupation in British sociology during the 1960s was the impact of working-class affluence upon the 'traditional working-class attitudes' identified by Butler and Rose, not only in the specific case of the exploration of 'the *embourgeoisement* thesis' by Goldthorpe *et al.* in the *Affluent Worker* series (Goldthorpe *et al.*, 1968, 1969, 1970) but also in the lengthy preoccupation with studies of working-class 'images of society' and other aspects of social and political consciousness. Similarly, the debate within Labour Party politics stimulated by the writings of Crosland was echoed within studies of working-class Conservatism (Abrams and Rose, 1960; Nordlinger, 1967; McKenzie and Silver, 1967) or 'civic culture' (Almond and Verba, 1963) and thence into sociological studies of political attitudes and behaviour (e.g. Runciman, 1966; Parkin, 1967; Jessop, 1975; Newby, 1977). Lockwood's influential paper (1966) which arose directly out of concerns with working-class 'affluence' (see his comments in Bulmer, 1975) stimulated a considerable number of studies at the interface between social stratification, industrial sociology and occupational sociology and which explored, usually within a neo-Weberian framework, the relationship between certain structural features of a range of occupational groups and their social consciousness. Further work along these lines continued to appear well into the 1970s (e.g. Moorhouse, 1976; Roberts *et al.*, 1977; Davis, 1979). This is not to say that all or any of those engaged in this line of research accepted many of the popular beliefs about the consequences of 'affluence'. Indeed a sceptical view was almost unanimous. It was, rather, that the considerations which emerged from the 'age of affluence' tended to set the terms of the debate, even the research agenda, of a great deal of research on the British working class over the next two decades. If only by acting as a point of departure for this research it had a decisive influence on the issues which were examined and the ways in which it was conducted.

By 1983, however, the terms of this debate had shifted markedly. The Conservative electoral success has been achieved during a period not of universal affluence in the working class, but of deep economic recession and unemployment on a scale unknown since the 1930s. If 'affluence', 'privatisation' and 'instrumental collectivism' were the watchwords of this research theme during the 1960s and 1970s, then by the 1980s they were 'stagflation', 'fatalism' and 'authoritarian populism' (Hall, 1978). Nevertheless, if there is one lesson that sociologists have learned from the previous round of Conservative electoral victories it is that 'the veering of the electoral breeze' is, indeed, a poor basis on which to found a research agenda. By the time the *Affluent Worker* study was under way the Labour Party had been returned to power and thus the *embourgeoisement* thesis in its most restricted form was killed as a serious argument. It was what changing patterns of voting behaviour *signified* that provided a much more fertile area of sociological investigation and it is this – rather than the voting patterns of 1979 and 1983 *per se* – which is going to carry 'the debate on the working class' further forward.

The very different economic circumstances of the 1980s represent one reason why the analyses of the 1950s cannot be simply recycled and redeployed. But this is not the only reason. 'The working class', however it is defined, has undergone considerable change during the intervening period. Structurally, normatively and relationally the character of the working class – and, indeed, of the entire British class structure – has been considerably altered by processes which themselves have defined these changing economic circumstances. It is not the purpose of this paper to examine these in detail beyond a few schematic ciphers, but we refer here to recent discussions of how observed sectoral shifts in the occupational composition of British society have produced effects at the cultural, political and ideological levels. On the one hand there is a view emanating from theories of 'post-industrial society' (Bell, 1973; Touraine, 1974) which regards the labour process as becoming increasingly less proletarianised, requiring a higher proportion of workers with technical expertise and knowledge and demanding less monotonous routinisation. With the shift from a manufacturing to a service-based economy workers are regarded as having greater control over their conditions of work and greater freedom within work. Marxist theories (especially Braverman, 1974) have contained almost the opposite view. Here work is regarded as generally becoming more 'de-skilled', real technical expertise is being confined to a smaller proportion of the labour force, alienation is being intensified and proletarianisation is an endemic process. Both theories have been subject to searching criticisms (see, respectively, Kumar, 1978 and Wood, 1982), but each have, in their way, been grappling with different aspects of observed changes in the class structure.

As Wright and Singelmann (1978) have persuasively argued, in order to understand these conflicting claims it is necessary to decompose the relevant transformations in the class structure into three distinct components (see also Singelmann and Tienda in this volume). The first of these is what they term the 'industry shift effect', i.e., that part of the overall change in the class structure which is due to shifts in the labour force from industrial sectors with one distribution of classes into sectors with a different distribution of classes. Rapid 'de-industrialisation' and the growth of the service sectors has, indeed, brought about such a transformation in Britain in the last two decades (see Routh, 1980; Garnsey, 1978). The second component consists of the 'class composition effect' which concerns the transformation of class relations *within* industrial sectors. Both evidence and interpretations are quite divergent here, as recent debates over de-skilling and white-collar proletarianisation have demonstrated (Wood, 1982). The third component is the 'interaction effect', which is the result of simultaneous shifts in employment across industrial sectors with different class structures *and* shifts in the internal class structures of these sectors. Wright and Singelmann attach to this component a generally minor significance. However, Lee (1981) has implied that such interaction effects are part of *cyclical* shifts in capitalist production mediated via the social construction of the labour market. This alone points to the *sociological* significance of the recessionary 1980s, compared to the affluent 1950s, in developing an understanding of how the class structure has changed.

We would also, however, want to add two important contextual dimensions to Wright and Singelmann's overall schema. The first concerns the importance of gender relations which, as Garnsey (1978) has argued, constitute an integral component of changes in the class structure. Industry and class composition shifts both affect, and are in turn affected by, the sexual composition of the labour force, since the terms under which different categories of labour are available is an important factor influencing investment decisions as well as changes in the labour process; and conversely, these processes also have effects on the sexual composition of the labour force (Garnsey, 1978). Industry shift effects for example have been associated with a decline in male jobs in the manufacturing and production sectors; and a large increase in less skilled, low paid and often part-time female jobs in the service sector (Thatcher, 1979). Similarly with regard to changes in the labour process, Crompton (1979, 1980) has shown how the de-skilling of clerical work in the banking and insurance sectors has also been associated with its feminisation, so that women are largely restricted to the de-skilled tasks while men continue to be promoted through the internal clerical and administrative labour market.

The second contextual dimension is a geographical one, since industry shift effects are also part of a trend towards an increasingly international economy, involving direct investment by multinational companies as well as trade and international finance. Since the early 1970s, this has been associated with a restructuring of the division of labour on an international level. Multinational companies have been relocating the capital intensive stages of production and research and development to countries with the highest labour productivity and the best markets; and the labour intensive stages of production to Third World countries where labour is very cheap (Amin, 1976). This has been linked to the phenomenon of de-industrialisation in the advanced countries, although its precise effects are likely to vary, firstly according to the extent to which countries are dependent on the international sector and secondly according to a country's competitive position in the world market. Since Britain is particularly dependent on an advanced multinational sector and also relatively uncompetitive in relation to other states, international restructuring is more likely to result in higher levels of unemployment, especially in the traditional skilled and semi-skilled areas, which is not compensated for by new inward investment or an expanding state sector (Pratten, 1976; Holland, 1979).

Within Britain this is creating a much more diverse and uneven economic structure, in which differences between workers in different economic sectors (and thus also geographical localities) may well be increasing (Fothergill and Gudgin, 1979, 1982). Workers in the advanced multinational sector, for example, are now dependent on economic enterprises operating in rather different economic circumstances from those in the declining national and state sectors. These differences are in fact reflected in recent changes in the nature and organisation of collective action, which we discuss later.

During the 1960s, these effects were initially brought together within the empirical investigation of changes in the working class, through an analysis of the decline of 'traditional proletarian' work situations and the emergence of the privatised worker (Lockwood, 1966). During the more recent period of intense recession, the decline of all forms of manufacturing industry and the rise of white-collar employment has also been widely recognised as representing a crucial change in the class structure, although interpretations continue to vary (see, for example, Gorz, 1983; Abercrombie and Urry, 1983). Suffice to say at this point that 'the debate on the working class' can only be sustained by a recognition that 'the working class' has itself been considerably changed by the 'shift effects' outlined above.

Although we make these statements on the basis of *empirical observation*, they are, inevitably, laden with questions of *conceptual definition*. Thus questions of how, and in what ways, 'the working class' has changed quickly elide into the question of 'what is the working class?'. The sociological convention of the 1960s was to draw the crucial line at the manual/non-manual boundary (see Goldthorpe and Lockwood, 1963). The archetypal – indeed stereotypical – 'worker' was thus the 'traditional proletarian' in Lockwood's terms (1966) with the connotation that a decline in the representation of such 'male, manual and muscular' workers thereby constituted a decline of the working class *in toto*. Since it is precisely such 'traditional proletarian' industrial workers that have suffered the greatest decline in numbers in the recent recession (coal-mining, steel-making, heavy engineering, the docks, etc.) then this has undermined the apparent relevance of the concept of 'the working class' – the same conclusion as that arrived at in the 1950s, but by a very different route. Economic decline rather than economic growth is now seen as being responsible. This has led in turn to epitaphs for 'the working class' such as Gorz (1983) and to attempts to re-categorise labour (productive, non-productive, domestic, waged, state, private, etc.) in order to arrive at a more appropriate definition of 'work' and 'working class' to suit contemporary conditions (see Pahl, 1980, 1984; Pahl and Wallace, 1984).

The utility of operationalising class in terms of manual/non-manual occupations has accordingly been called into question both from within the pre-existing terms of the debate and from beyond – for example from writers concerned with sexual and ethnic divisions. Some writers (the most sophisticated of which is Bauman, 1982) have seized upon such difficulties in order to argue that the concept of class has had its day. Others have preferred to re-conceptualise class boundaries and class structure, particularly Marxist writers such as Poulantzas (1975), Carchedi (1977) and Wright (1978). In all cases there has been a recognition that recent changes demand a much greater complexity of categories than a simple manual/non-manual distinction will allow. There is much less confidence that the manual/non-manual boundary is any longer the most salient or meaningful distinction when it comes to analysing the effect of class location upon class action and consciousness. We shall return to this issue below.

These comments become more relevant when viewed in the light of research conducted during the 1960s and 1970s into the issue of working-class culture and consciousness. This work was in reality often little more than a series of case studies on particular occupational groups and local labour markets which tended to produce compatible but rather negative findings – namely, that structural location and social consciousness were not related in quite the straightforward way which has often been assumed and that, indeed, this social consciousness is neither highly developed nor particularly coherent among the majority of employees from whom data was gathered. That is to say that a number of studies (e.g. Blackburn and Mann, 1978; Davis, 1979; Roberts *et al.*, 1977; Cousins and Brown, 1975; Newby, 1977; Nichols and Armstrong, 1979) have concluded that workers do not possess well-defined and consistent images of society or of its class structure of any kind and that their social consciousness is at best accommodative and pragmatic (Mann, 1970), and at worst contradictory and ephemeral (but see the dissenting comments of Moorhouse, 1976 and Hill, 1981). This has tended to leave the study of working-class images of society, which had thrived from the *embourgeoisement* debate onwards, rather played out.

In view of these converging difficulties it is not surprising that Goldthorpe should comment that 'the debate on the working class has at the present time reached a serious impasse' (1979, p. 2). Goldthorpe comes to this conclusion via a review of three intellectual perspectives on the historical role of the working class, which he labels the 'liberals' the 'organicists' and the 'left'. Each has, in his view, projected its own socio-political goals on to the working class, producing 'wishful, rather than critical, thinking' and a tendency 'to assert that what was desired was already historically in train' (*ibid.*, p. 15). This is, perhaps, more widely recognised in the wake of the successive Conservative electoral victories. Our point here is a different, though by no means incompatible one: that the 'shift effects' that have occurred in the British working class over the last two decades have produced a degree of both objective and subjective opacity to the class structure which demands a fresh approach to 'the debate on the working class'. The main purpose of this paper is to explore this opacity at the subjective level – i.e. to outline our approach to the understanding of class *action* (or lack of it) in the face of severe recession. Before doing so, however, it is essential to sketch our approach to the broader issues of class structure at the subjective, objective and theoretical levels.

Neo-Weberian class analysis

We would share Goldthorpe's rejection of the Marxist theory of class as historical teleology – a gamble with the outcome of history which has not come off. There is simply no evidence to suggest that under advanced capitalism the working class (however this is defined) is necessarily the bearer of historical change. Attempts to find a revolutionary functional equivalent to the proletariat are, if anything, even less convincing (see, for example, the analysis of Gallie, 1978). Moreover, Marxism lacks a theory of action adequate to explain either the historical inevitability of the end-shift of the proletariat, from a class-in-itself to a revolutionary class-for-itself, or the current reluctance of the western working classes to initiate this. In fact, as Lockwood has convincingly demonstrated (1981), Marxists have 'theorised' the relationship between class structure and class conflict in ways which are either incompatible with their own basic premises, logically inconsistent or empirically implausible – where, indeed they have addressed this issue at all rather than simply resolving it by fiat.

For these reasons we would distance ourselves from those who have argued that class analysis must now proceed via the integration of structuralist accounts of place and position with the insights into process and agency gleaned from recent *Marxisant* analyses of the labour process (Wright, 1978). Instead we wish to adhere to Weber's alternative – and to us, more satisfactory – explanation of the relationship between ownership and production – the operation of the capitalist market. In our view it is the operation of the capitalist market which is the primary mechanism determining class processes. (For an elaboration of this argument see Marshall *et al.*, 1983.) Changes in the market necessitate the continuous reorganisation of capital and labour as capital moves from less to more profitable sectors and technologies. The ownership and control of profits, plant and investment has taken new and generally more complex forms. Labour, too, is constantly reorganised as a result of international and sectoral movements of capital and the adoption of new technologies and forms of work organisation. These changes in the direction of investment and the division of labour have had three important consequences from the point of view of the class structure. First, the ownership and control of capital has become more opaque, as pension funds, multinational corporations, and horizontally and vertically integrated cartels, companies and 'spheres of interest' have replaced the family proprietorship as the prevailing form of organisation (Scott, 1979). Secondly, sectoral shifts in the economy (industry shift effects) and in the reorganisation and restructuring of labour itself (class composition shift effects) have, on balance created a much more diverse and sectorally uneven economic structure, within which the differences between workers in different economic sectors are increasing. Thirdly, the shedding of 'surplus' labour during the current recession has reinforced labour market segmentation, in particular the boundary between those in relatively secure occupational or company careers and the unemployed or subemployed (Sinfield, 1980). We believe that the composite effect of these changes has been to render class processes increasingly opaque: the owners and controllers of capital are less concrete and more distant; the occupational structure has become increasingly complex; and the conventional distinction between manual and non-manual labour has become less salient both sociologically and among the population at large. The degree of ambiguity, ambivalence and contradiction which emerges from the literature on working-class images of society is not, therefore, merely cognitive mystification. It reflects many of the objective characteristics of the contemporary class structure.

In this way class conflicts have increasingly taken the form of sectional *distributional* conflicts. The class structure appears as an opaque hierarchy based on the distributional competition over scarce resources (see Hirsch, 1975; Saunders, 1983). We suspect that a lengthy period of inflation *and* recession during the 1970s has exacerbated, rather than diminished, the pecuniary attitudes to work and instrumental orientation to class organisations that was regarded as the hallmark of the privatised, affluent workers of the 1960s. Indeed, if one recognises that the impact of recession has been thrown principally onto the unemployed and the unwaged, and that those in work have experienced a substantial increase in real living standards (Marshall and Rose, 1983) then arguments about affluence and recession converge. In the distributional conficts which characterise the market situation of the working population, the lesson which has been learned from the ubiquity of capitalist social relations is that moral restraints upon acquisitiveness have no part to play and that one's market situation must be exploited to the full (Goldthorpe, 1978: 200–1). Thus rather than develop a revolutionary political and economic consciousness, class conflicts have come to assume an increasingly sectional nature. These statements are supported by two recent studies of industrial relations, both of which show a fundamental change in the nature of British trade unionism during the last ten years. In this period centralised industry bargaining between national trade union leaders and nationally organised employers has been almost completely replaced by sectional, decentralised single-employer bargaining on the basis of the market position of individual companies. This form of bargaining is also particularly characteristic of the advanced multinational sector, consisting of high wage industries, which tend to take the lead in pay bargaining (Brown, 1981; Daniel and Millward, 1983). These changes have also been associated with increasing regional and sub-regional disparities in employment and wages, since multi-employer bargaining tends to be concentrated in the declining regions, whereas company bargaining is more prevalent in the relatively buoyant south-east (Mellor, 1975; Fothergill and Gudgin, 1979, 1982).

Privatisation and working-class politics

At this stage our argument must perforce become highly speculative, since the empirical data to substantiate it is either not available or only patchy in its extent. We cannot, for example, determine whether the continuing acceptance of gross inequalities of income and wealth are best explained in cognitive or evaluative terms. During the 1960s Runciman (1966) claimed that perceptions of inequality were highly limited, but his interpretation has been increasingly called into question (see Barry, 1966; Gurney and Tierney, 1982). Alt (1979), for example, has argued that after two decades of incomes policy, media exposure and persistent stagflation, most people's perceptions of inequality are reasonably accurate, but that what is salient to them is *personal* well-being rather than comparisons with putative reference groups. Such egoism has affected voting behaviour by producing a decline in partisanship (Crewe, 1981) and thereby a decline in class-based political affiliation: the 1970s were a 'decade of de-alignment' (Sarlvik and Crewe, 1983). Thus recent psephological evidence has turned the *embourgeoisement* thesis on its head: affluence is necessary to make voters feel sufficiently well-off to support altruistic social policies, whereas recession prompts a defensive, hard-headed instrumentalism. Alt's summary of the evidence from studies of voting behaviour and opinion poll data is that the apparent intractability of Britain's persistent economic problems has led to increasing *fatalism* about their solution. This results not in a politics of protest, but in a politics of quiet disillusion, in which lack of partisanship or indifference to organised party politics is the most important feature. Such fatalism is, however, an informed fatalism: people are aware of widespread inequalities, but judge them to be unassailable. The economy – and, in broad outline, the class structure – are, like the weather, beyond human control.

Similar findings emerge from a recent study of work orientations (Sparrow, 1983) which discovered a mood of 'resigned realism' among British workers. Compared with workers in other advanced industrial societies, British workers were mainly motivated by the achievement of material success but were also characterised by a very high rate of failure to achieve their aspirations for personal autonomy through work. Finding their jobs boring, most people do not seek fulfilment through work, but elsewhere. As far as work itself is concerned an 'instrumental stoicism' predominates: again, the fatalism which lies behind these perceptions is not merely informed, but to a large extent experiential.

These perceptions of an intractable public world may, however, be contrasted with a more private, home-centred sphere over which individuals feel they can and do exert control. Moreover it is the nature of this private domain which may be as crucial for the formation of their social identities and their politics as the more public domain of work or production, which is perceived as exerting control over them. As Goldthorpe (1983) has argued, structural locations create sets or arrays of potential interests. Which of these potential interests, individuals or groups actually take as their 'own' then depends on how they see themselves in relation to other individuals or groups. Collective social identities thus form a crucial mediating link in the analysis of the relationship between social structure and social action, since interests depend for their realisation on the creation of such social identities. Typically, however, sociologists have assumed social identities arise primarily from the sphere of production (in particular from paid work) and have largely ignored the importance of changes in those non-work areas of life which may have become more salient as sources of social identity. As Mann has argued, capitalism is a somewhat diffuse economic system, involving not just production and factories, but also a sphere of civil society and a sphere of consumption. We would argue that recent changes both in the nature of local communities and in patterns of consumption are combining to produce increasingly privatised lifestyles and increasingly individualised home- or family-centred social identities based on them. For certain groups or classes, these privatised home- or family-centred social identities may now be more significant in mediating political interests than work- or production-based identities. Changes in non-work life may therefore be contributing towards a decline in the experience of class identity and solidarity outside work and in the community so that the recession has been associated not with the emergence of class struggle and class politics, but with a retreat from class politics into a privatised world within the home.

This suggests that privatised or individualised lifestyles are now coming to replace the traditional, close-knit, occupational and neighbourhood communities which used to be regarded by sociologists as an important factor reinforcing class consciousness (Bott, 1957; Gans, 1967; Young and Willmott, 1962; Hoggart, 1958; Jackson, 1973; Berger, 1960; Bell, 1968; Whyte, 1960; Seeley *et al.*, 1956; see also studies of 'affluent workers', Zweig, 1961; Goldthorpe and Lockwood, 1970). Hitherto, working-class families were thought to have been embedded in close-knit, overlapping social networks of relatives, neighbours, workmates and kin, with an associated social life (centred on the extended family and wider community) which was public, highly visible and hence subject to considerable local social control. We would argue that privatisation has indeed undermined the communal sociability which characterised such working-class communities, but we would not accept that the only factors responsible are those identified by sociologists in the 1960s, namely geographical mobility and affluence. We would, indeed, wish to disengage the consideration of privatisation from these two issues and to relate it to some of the broader structural changes that we have identified above. Before doing so, however, it is instructive to review this literature before further developing our own conception of the role of privatisation.

In the literature on working-class social change developed during the 1950s and 1960s, geograpical mobility was thought to reduce the degree of embeddedness of families in local communities by reducing the degree of overlap between social relations in different spheres of life. In Bott's (1957) model, for example, geographical mobility reduces the connectedness of a family's social networks. This, in turn, reduces the extent of the family's visibility to social scrutiny and hence its vulnerability to extra-familial controls. It is this that lies at the root of Goldthorpe *et al.*'s (1969) link between communal sociability and a collective political orientation. Conversely, Lipset

(1960) argued that working-class authoritarianism was associated with social isolation, low participation in voluntary associations, a low level of interest in national politics and a concern with the immediate and personal. Bott (1957) also argued that loose-knit social networks were associated with an increase in joint conjugal roles within the family – and, therefore, home-centredness (although not necessarily, as Oakley (1972, 1974) has argued, greater sexual equality). The precise effects of these changes were thought, however, to vary with social class. In the geographically mobile working class, loose-knit social networks resulted in privatisation in the sense of isolation and withdrawal from virtually all effective social relations outside the elementary family (Goldthorpe *et al.*, 1969; Berger, 1960; Gans, 1967). Thus privatisation took the form of *home-centredness*. In the geographically and/or socially mobile middle class, however, loose-knit social networks were established outside the home as a basis for associational activity. These tended to be segmented, or only loosely connected, and constituted *gesellschaftlich*, rather than *gemeinschaftlich*, relationships. Thus privatisation here took the form of *family-centredness*, rather than home-centredness (Bell, 1968; Whyte, 1960; Gans, 1967; Seeley *et al.*, 1956). Since most of these studies were concerned mainly with changes in kinship and/or descriptions of suburban lifestyles, however, the concept of privatisation was not linked to wider changes in, for example, work and politics (for exceptions see Zweig, 1961; Goldthorpe *et al.*, 1968 b, 1969). As a result there is disputed evidence about the precise nature of the relationship between changes in the work situation and privatisation (e.g. Goldthorpe *vs* Berger) and, subsequently, between the latter and political consciousness (e.g. Castells (1975) *vs* Saunders (1981)).

In the *Affluent Worker* studies (Zweig, 1961; Goldthorpe and Lockwood, 1970; Berger, 1960; Chinoy, 1955) privatisation was used to describe the emergence of a new stereotypical form of manual worker, in contrast to more 'traditional' types. The concept of privatisation was therefore used in a rather all-embracing way, specifically to link changes in the non-work family or community spheres of workers' lives to changes in their orientations to work and in their politics. In contrast with traditional proletarian workers, 'privatised' workers were thought to exhibit an instrumental work orientation; were devoted to a pattern of social life centred on, and largely restricted to, the home and the conjugal family rather than communal sociability outside the home; adopted a pecuniary image of society; and attributed status on the basis of conspicuous consumption. The social processes giving rise to privatisation however, were not specified as clearly as the ideal-typical actor – the privatised worker – so that privatisation as a process tended to be imputed on the basis of the contrast between two sociological stereotypes, namely 'traditional proletarian' and newly-affluent 'privatised' workers.

Because the causal mechanisms involved in privatisation were somewhat unclear this led to a divergence of interpretation over how this process could be explained. Goldthorpe *et al.* (1969) claim that changing work-orientations originate from changes in the family, especially those resulting from geographical mobility. In an analysis reminiscent of Bott (1957) they argued that geographical mobility produces changes in conjugal roles leading to a 'more companionate' – and thus inherently rewarding – marriage. This in turn produces a more instrumental orientation to work. In presenting this model, Goldthorpe *et al.* reversed the hitherto conventional model of home-centred workers (Chinoy, 1955; Berger, 1960) in which the direction of causation runs the opposite way. In the latter model it is the increasingly alienating character of work which causes workers to shift their central life interests to the non-work sphere, redefining achievement in terms of an advancement in the accumulation of personal possessions rather than increasing control over the work situation. In fact, neither of these alternatives have been thoroughly tested so that the causes of privatisation remain greatly under-researched. In so far as recent research has examined this issue it has called into question the typification of the 'traditional proletarian' worker (see Bulmer, 1975, *passim*; More, 1979) and thence the assumption that privatisation is a specifically recent, or emergent, social process. Other work has called into question the belief that geographical mobility leads to privatisation (Williams, 1983). For the remainder we must rely upon broader historical and contemporary treatments of the problem, where the concept of privatisation is invoked in order to describe changes in the structural differentiation of industrial society and as an ideology which accompanies such structural differentiation.

Shorter (1976), for example, has argued that with the emergence of capitalism and the spread of the market economy, formerly quasi-self-sufficient households become integrated into a network of economic relationships which serve to undermine traditional extended kinship and community controls. The family becomes an increasingly isolated, private sphere, separated from work and less embedded in the community in the sense that social relations in different institutional spheres become non-overlapping. The line between the public and the private world is redrawn (see Lasch, 1979; Sennett, 1977). As the family becomes separated in this way, it is transformed into an emotional unit, based on close affective relations, which are increasingly private and impermeable to wider community controls. For Shorter, therefore, modern society is characterised by a bifurcation into the 'public' sphere outside the family and a 'private' sphere which is family- and home-centred. This theme has been taken up by a number of other writers (e.g. Lasch, 1979; Sennett, 1977; Rainwater, 1966) who chart how the family has come to be idealised as a refuge from an impersonal, unpredictable and insecure world outside: a 'haven in a heartless world' (see also Davidoff *et al.*, 1976).

What these authors neglect to mention, however, is that privatisation, in the sense of a separation between a private domestic sphere and a public sphere outside it, emerges historically as part of the push for citizenship and political rights. Privatisation cannot therefore be regarded as a retreat from an already existing public sphere, since the 'domestic' actually emerges as a separate sphere alongside (rather than in response to) the creation of the public or political arena (Davidoff *et al.*, 1976; Davidoff and Hall, 1983). The breakdown of high levels of social integration at the local level is therefore associated not just with the emergence of relatively socially isolated private households, but also with a process of their cultural, political and economic integration into the nation state, particularly with the winning and exercising of citizenship rights. Although the arguments of Shorter, Sennett and Lasch remain somewhat open to reinterpretation, they do nevertheless provide us with at least a broad historical backdrop, against which to interpret empirical studies of family, kinship and community, in which the concept of privatisation is used very much more narrowly.

It is this broader historical analysis of privatisation which needs to be integrated into the narrower sociological focus that emerges from empirical studies of the family and community. The latter focuses much too narrowly on the family and communal sociability in isolation from work and politics, and thus over-emphasises the importance of geographical mobility in explaining the shift to privatisation. Studies of affluent workers, however, while including work and politics in their analyses, only do so in terms of workers' subjective consciousness (or 'orientations') to them. Both the family/community literature and the studies of affluent workers therefore overlook the importance of wider economic shift effects (such as those we have outlined earlier in this paper) in undermining the economic basis for occupational communities. In addition these studies overlooked the significance of successful working-class political struggles, firstly for citizenship and then for the welfare state, which, although highly partial in coverage, succeeded in removing much of the need for mutual self-help which lay at the basis of communal solidarity. As long as workers were exposed to the precariousness of life governed by market forces, neighbourhoods and local communities provided some meagre collective self-defence by acting as units of self-help – and in the process generating a sense of class identity which helped sustain the emergence of workers collective organisations. It is also worth emphasising that neighbourhoods based on communal solidarity were also established despite high levels of geographical mobility, thus casting some doubt on the extent to which geographical mobility in itself is sufficient to explain the more recent decline of communal solidarity. With the emergence of the welfare state, however, communal solidarity became less of a functional necessity so that neighbourhood communities have not been reconstituted, on the same basis. Perhaps the pattern demonstrated by Bell (1968) in the middle class has been extended to the working class, whereby aid continues within extended families, but community relationships became more status-based. The achievement of the welfare state has thus tended towards a process of individuation, so that people come to exist as individual citizens in civil society, with home or family based collective social identities, rather than the class-based identities generated and sustained by traditional patterns of working-class culture and community.

These changes in traditional patterns of working-class culture and community have also been reinforced during the post-war period by changes in consumption, which have similarly affected social identities and thus conceptions of political interest. As Moorhouse (1983) has argued, rising living standards have come to integrate people into the capitalist market economy as individual consumers, thus reducing the coherence of their experience of society as fundamentally class-divided. One particularly important feature of changes in consumption patterns (first noted by Zweig in 1961) and which is of crucial importance in the formation of social identities is home ownership. As Westergaard (1984) points out, recent growth in home ownership is particularly noticeable among the skilled working class. By 1981 over half of all households headed by skilled manual or junior non-manual workers owned or were buying their homes, as were more than one third of all semi-skilled households and about one quarter of all unskilled households. The broad effect (he argues) has been to produce a new dividing line between home owners and others, which is now affecting voting patterns. As Crewe (1983) found, 59 per cent of former Labour voters who bought their council houses switched to the Conservatives at the 1983 general election.

This link between changing patterns of consumption (especially home ownership) and politics also emerges clearly in recent studies by Edgell and Duke (n.d.) who argue that the working class is now politically fragmented by what they refer to as 'consumption sectoral cleavages'. Edgell and Duke argue that private market based consumption of housing and transport have now come to fragment the working class, undermining the strength and extent of working class support for the Labour Party's traditional policies of increasing state provision in housing and transport. Edgell and Duke show how both party alignment and variations in support for Labour's traditional policy of increasing state spending, are now more affected by how people consume housing and transport (i.e. their consumption locations) than they are by their class locations. As expected, those most dependent on state provision are most supportive of state spending in these areas and *vice versa*. The Labour Party thus appears to be representing a smaller and smaller minority rather than a clear majority of the working class. Post-war patterns of consumption (in particular housing) have thus served to integrate workers into capitalism as individuals, and in a directly economic (rather than simply ideological) way, providing them with a stake in the system of financial and property markets which in turn undermines their sense of class identity and hence their participation in class politics. This is supported by a number of recent empirical studies which show an ambivalence in working-class attitudes both to the welfare state and to the traditional policies of the Labour Party (Taylor-Gooby, 1982, 1983; Edgell and Duke, n.d.). As various authors have stressed (Goldthorpe, 1983; Mann, 1983; Westergaard, 1984) the British Labour Party has been relatively unsuccessful (compared with the Swedish Social Democrats for example) in constituting and mobilising class interests by presenting issues in class terms and reinforcing the formation of collectivities with shared class identities. Labour's housing policy, for example, fragments and divides rather than unifies the working class and Labour have similarly been unable to capture the partisanship of newly emergent collectivities such as women (Goldthorpe, 1983; Mann, 1983). This issue of organisational capacity is clearly a mediating influence between the broader structural changes which have occurred in the working class and the individualised response in terms of privatisation.

In summary, then, we would argue that sociologists have exaggerated the extent to which the sphere of production generally, and work in particular, does now provide workers with a clear sense of collective social identity which could form the basis for class action. For many people, work is now part of the world which is not regarded as amenable to either personal or collective control, and thus approached instrumentally and fatalistically. Such empirical findings as are available point to a combination of increasing sectionalism and increasing fatalism in the sphere of production. As Daniel (1975) argues these may well be causally related: the British economy is seen as unalterable precisely because of the high degree of sectionalism and lack of common identity and purpose between different groups of workers in different companies and different sectors of the economy. In the sphere of consumption similarly, post-war changes in patterns of working-class culture and community are tending towards a relative privatisation of individual households or families, which is in turn reinforced by patterns of private consumption, particularly of housing. Both in the sphere of production and in the sphere of consumption, groups of workers are coming to occupy increasingly diverse social positions (in terms of their potential interests) which traditional working-class organisations such as the Labour Party and the trade unions have failed to articulate or constitute in terms of collective class identities. These diverse potential interests have thus come to be mediated through non-class 'sectional' identities (in the sphere of production) and 'privatised' 'home'- or 'family'-centred identities (in the sphere of consumption) both of which are associated with increasing fatalism in relation to the structure of the wider economy. The problem of the Labour Party is thus precisely one of devising policies which are able to overcome diverse sectional and privatised identities, by generating a sense of collective class identity in the face of both trade union and consumption sectionalism.

Conclusions

In considering the relevance of privatisation to the analysis of contemporary class action in Britain, therefore, we need to distinguish between three issues.

1. To what extent can privatisation – in a *structural* sense – be considered to be a general *social process* brought about by the development of industrial and post-industrial capitalism? In order to establish the relevance of privatisation in this sense, it would be necessary to establish a general trend towards institutional and geographical non-coincidence as a feature of modern society. This would in turn be reflected empirically in the nature of social relations (e.g. loose-knit social networks, etc.).

2. To what extent does privatisation characterise the social *consciousness* of the contemporary population? This would be reflected empirically in such matters as central life interests being home-centred; the recognition of a domain of control which lies within the home in contradistinction to the world outside which is unpredictable and uncontrollable, an instrumental orientation towards social relations outside the home and/or family, etc.

3. To what extent does privatisation, in either a structural or a cultural sense (1. and 2. above), carry political connotations? This would be reflected empirically in a preference for 'personal politics'; political instrumentalism; a shift towards status, rather than class, consciousness, etc.

Whether or not there is a correspondence between these three issues pertaining to privatisation is an empirical question. It may be that under conditions of economic growth, full employment and relative economic security, privatisation is associated (as Goldthorpe *et al.* found) with instrumental collectivism. And it should not be forgotten that these conditions remain relevant, even during recession, for those who have remained in employment. What has changed, however, is the sense of advantage (and good fortune?) brought about by having remained in employment. Under these conditions, relatively socially-isolated, home-centred workers with low levels of active participation in collective organisations, such as the trade unions and Labour Party, may well seek to defend their personal lifestyles and thus, as in Lipset's model, be prepared to support certain kinds of authoritarian populism – if only on a pragmatic basis. We anticipate, then, that as the result of increasing privatisation, the restructuring of labour (industry and class composition shift effects) and extensive induced mobility (both social and geographical), sources of social identity are increasingly diffuse and less likely to be drawn from the 'traditional proletarian' sources of work and community. These complex processes reinforce the breakdown of class-based politics (or, more precisely, the working-class support for the Labour Party) and the growth of instrumental voting.

The restructuring of capital and labour; the class structure as an opaque hierarchy; distributional struggles of which instrumental collectivism is the epitome; privatisation of individuals and families; the fatalistic acceptance of structured inequality allied to an inability to conceive of an alternative – this is the skeletal structure of our argument. Of course, at this stage, most of this is mere speculation. However, we believe that it is possible to

generate sufficient evidence to substantiate at least parts of our general interpretation of social classes and distributional struggles in contemporary
Britain.

Section two

Labour markets in capitalist society

The central importance of the labour market in structuring life chances and in patterning social conflict has been long recognised by social theorists. However, the social analysis of the labour market has remained curiously primitive. The construction of theories of the operation of the labour market has been left largely to economists. Yet the explanatory adequacy of orthodox economic theories has become increasingly dubious. The social assumptions that underpin these models appear unrealistic in the light of the accumulating empirical evidence about the way in which employment opportunities are structured by firms and about the determinants of labour market participation and job acquisition.

There is clearly a need for a major reformulation of labour market theory, and, in different ways, this problem lies at the heart of the papers in this section. They address three fundamental issues. First, what type of theoretical framework should be adopted in analysing labour markets? Second, what are the major empirical determinants of labour market structure? Third, what are the principal directions in which the structure of labour markets may be changing with the recession?

The section begins with a critique of the underlying assumptions of orthodox neo-classical theory by the Cambridge Labour Studies Group. Rejecting the conception of a competitive labour market in which workers are paid according to their natural ability or their investment in training and education, they emphasise the ways in which institutions on both the demand and the supply sides discriminate between different types of workers. Labour markets, they suggest, are best conceptualised as divided into largely non-competing occupational groups and workers are allocated into such groups on the basis of criteria that have little to do with skill. While the post-war period of expansion may have weakened segmentation (largely through encouraging the growth of state welfare provision), the general tendency of the recession would appear to be to accentuate the labour market disadvantages of those that are already most heavily disadvantaged.

If the allocation and pricing of labour is determined not by universal laws of the market but by the specific configuration of institutions that have emerged through the process of historical development, then substantial variations may exist between societies in the way labour markets are organised. The paper by Goldthorpe addresses this issue directly. In sharp contrast to the theorists of industrialism, who anticipated a growing similarity between the advanced societies in the institutions regulating employment and the labour market, Goldthorpe suggests that structural divergence may well be occurring. Confronted by the constraints on the functioning of market mechanisms set by the growth of trade union power in the post-war era, the business and political elites of capitalist societies sought to resolve this dilemma in very different ways. Some moved towards an 'institutional transcendence' of pluralism – seeking to include the trade unions through corporatist arrangements. Others sought to undercut pluralism through expanding the sphere in which market forces and managerial authority could operate freely. This second, or 'dualistic' strategy relied heavily upon the recruitment of exceptionally vulnerable immigrant labour and upon the reorganisation of production through the extension of subcontracting and the use of temporary labour.

Finally, the third paper in this section examines the labour market at local level. The Cambridge Labour Studies Group's paper argues that issues about the operation and direction of change of labour markets cannot be resolved by theoretical fiat, but require detailed empirical investigation. The study by Harris and his colleagues of the labour market experiences and behaviour of redundant steel workers seeks to do precisely this, in the context of a specific local labour market. The authors' research points to the crucial importance of company policies in structuring local employment opportunities, and interestingly, much as Craig *et al.* anticipate, they find a marked tendency towards the casualisation of employment. Further, they indicate the limitations of rational models of job search and emphasise the way in which the relationship between individuals and the labour market is mediated by the nature of local social networks.

5   *Christine Craig, Jill Rubery, Roger Tarling, Frank Wilkinson*
(Labour Studies Group, Department of Applied Economics,
Cambridge)

Economic, social and political factors in the operation of the labour market

Introduction

This paper draws together the various ideas from our current and past research linked by some more speculative views of interrelationships. The intention is not to put forward a general theory of how labour markets operate but to develop a framework which permits the coherent discussion of economic, social and political aspects. This has proved necessary to develop a clearer understanding of observations derived from case study research and the analysis of macro-economic aggregates.

Economic theories ascribe certain roles to social and political forces which we find unacceptable. This applies to analyses both at micro- and macro-economic levels. For this reason, the paper begins with a brief presentation of economic orthodoxy as a starting point for arguing the need for a wider and more integrated view of labour markets. In developing this argument and subsequently our own view we have necessarily strayed into the subject area of other social science disciplines but we hope that those sympathetic to our argument will forgive us for the amateurism of this trespass.

We use our analysis to try to explain why we see the way forward to be through more collaboration within a common framework. In that context we are putting forward proposals for research areas for inclusion on our agenda for research which are neither exhaustive nor completely thought out. If the will for a more integrated approach is present among the academic community it is our belief that the benefits are potentially very large and the policy proposals derivative from such research would be far more appropriate for dealing with labour market problems.

Economic orthodoxy

The orthodox neo-classical theory of the operation of the labour market rests on the proposition that the worker is paid the value of his product – or more precisely the value of the marginal worker's product. This is brought about by the supposed existence of well-behaved production functions (where good behaviour is defined by diminished returns to factor inputs) and perfect labour markets (where perfection requires large numbers of capitalists and workers with equality of status within and between these groups). Given these pre-conditions, the equilibrium price of labour will be determined by the elasticity of its substitution for capital in the production process and its relative plentitude. Problems arising from differences in skill requirements and labour quality are resolved by supposing that labour productivity results partly from natural endowment and partly from investment in human capital. The market signals its demand for 'quality' labour, and labour adjusts itself by increasing human capital investment to raise its productivity and hence its price.

The abundant evidence of wide differences within occupational and other groups consisting of workers with apparently similar attributes, which would seem to contradict the central proposition of competitive theory that the prices of workers of a given level of skill tend to equality under the pressure of market forces, is dealt with in several ways. Marshall argued that although workers might seem equally endowed they are different in the degree of efficiency by which they apply their endowment. It is therefore suggested that the use of a standard measure – the efficiency wage – which allows adjustments for, for example, differences in the pace of work between individuals, would largely eliminate variations in individual earnings unexplained by differences in skill levels. Other explanations of such wage differences include the notion of the existence of non-pecuniary benefits which compensate for earnings differentials or of clauses in employment contracts which are implied – for example a trade-off between employment security and earnings levels.

Deviations of market conditions from 'perfection' also provide orthodox labour economists with explanations of why outcomes are different from their predictions. Market 'imperfections' are recognised to exist both 'in-market' (in the form of the monopoly power of labour and the monopsony power of capital), and 'out-market' in the form of non-competing groups. But such imperfections are considered to be of only marginal importance compared with the 'deep silent strong stream of the tendencies of normal distribution and exchange' (Marshall, 1952: 522).

Following Marshall's example, neo-classical economists have continued to assert that the competitive labour market (using their definition of competition) is the norm. This is also accepted by the majority of their critics within the profession and the debate as to the explanatory value of the orthodox paradigm is about the extent to which the real world has deviated from this norm. To test this, data sets are constructed representing the variables alleged to explain labour market behaviour and these data are manipulated by econometric methods and by the inclusion and exclusion of the variables according to the degree of fit that they manifest. However, the partial or even total failure of the data to provide strong support for the hypothesis does not necessarily cast doubt on its validity. As we have seen, economists are particularly adept at producing clever arguments as to why evidence which apparently contradicts their hypothesis in fact provides strong support.

But despite the enormous importance given to the market in conventional labour economics, there is no evidence that the atomistic labour market has *ever* been the general rule. The notion of the 'perfect' market is derived from utilitarian political philosophy rather than a consideration of how markets operate in reality. Labour markets have always been structured, and the higher the skill and status of the workers the more organised and protected their position: professional associations are the most powerful of trade unions and have always been with us. Moreover, those parts of the labour market where workers are continually thrown into competition with each other have generally been those typified by the lowest pay and the most degrading working conditions. There is no doubt that labour markets have become more organised. But this process cannot be regarded as a retreat from the neo-classical 'ideal market'. Rather it indicates a spread of organisation leading to a general structuring of occupational and industrial labour markets and the elimination, often by legislation, of the worst abuses of the sweated trades.

An alternative perspective

(a) *The point of departure*

As we understand it, neo-classical theory rests on three assertions: labour is a scarce resource, individuals are inherently unequal and they are free to compete for a wide range of jobs. In such circumstances, the market operates to allocate 'scarce means to alternate uses' and provides equality of opportunities; consequently, wage differentials measure the inequality of individuals in terms of the quantity and quality of their labour. It is our contention that none of these assertions are tenable. Labour is in more or less abundant supply, its usage is demand constrained and in terms of the requirements of the vast majority of jobs workers are intrinsically equal. In these circumstances the institutions on both the supply and demand side of the labour market operate in precisely the opposite way to that postulated by economic theory: they discriminate between claimants in the allocation of scarce good jobs and in the process generate wage differentials.

This paper explores in general terms the nature of labour markets concentrating in turn on the supply of labour, the demand for labour, and the interaction between supply and demand before discussing the implications of the alternative approach for an understanding of cyclical and trend developments.

Finally some consideration is given to methodology and some attempt is made to outline fruitful areas for research.

(b) *Labour supply*

In a capitalist system labour is inherently weak when compared with capital. Individual workers lack the means of production and the resources necessary to sustain themselves without the sale of labour. This power imbalance may be somewhat redressed if workers have access to resources from the domestic or other out-of-market sources or from the state. But generally such resources are not sufficient to allow workers to maintain a reasonable standard of life independently of the labour market. Therefore collective actions are more important than out-of-market resources in redressing the imbalance of power between capital and labour and these are organised in the domestic sector, in the market and at the level of the state. However the ability to counter the inherent superiority of capital varies between groups of workers by degrees determined by their access to out-market resources, education and training, by their role in domestic production and by the organisation of other groups of workers aimed at the exclusion of others. The consequent structuring of the potential labour supply at any one level – domestic, market and the state – may be offset or buttressed by organisation at another.

Organisation at the level of the family and the community allows the withdrawal of certain classes of workers from the labour market – particularly women and children – and provides alternative sources of subsistence and mutual support which strengthens the bargaining power of individual workers. Moreover the family provides resources for education and training which enhances the market value of individuals. In class terms, domestic and community organisation are sources of strength but at the same time they serve to sectionalise and fragment the working class. Patriarchy, which forms the basis for the organisation of the family, inherently weakens the position of women in domestic production. The unequal distribution of wealth between families and communities differentiates the labour force in terms of education and training. Moreover, out-of-market and in-market disadvantages are reinforcing. Women's domestic responsibilities, which inhibit labour market participation, and male dominance in the labour market, which ensures an inferior status, place women in a lower paid and easily exploitable category which is exacerbated by their partial dependence on family income for subsistence. The lack of out-of-market resources for education and training discriminates against the young from poor families and communities and the consequent low levels of pay reinforce their disadvantage.

Worker organisation in the labour market is also typified by the contradictory tendency towards collective action and sectionalism. Trade unions (here used to include professional associations and the more informal 'old boy' networks which create privileged access to classes of jobs) necessarily operate on the dual principle of representing the common interest of those within the union whilst protecting their areas of influence by policies of exclusion. This need is reinforced by the stratification of the labour force from the supply side which creates a pool of cheap labour posing a continuous threat to organised labour which further encourages demarcation and exclusion strategies. But paradoxically this, by denying access to jobs with decent pay and conditions, increases the desperation of the disadvantaged worker and consequently their potential threat to the well organised.

The state provides the third main force structuring the labour supply. Much of the state's activity can be interpreted as being in the interest of capital in ensuring the existence of a disciplined, trained and healthy labour force and in maintaining a reserve army of labour by the provision of social welfare. On the other hand the struggle between labour and capital at the level of the state has resulted in important gains for labour.

From the early nineteenth century the British state enacted legislation which laid down minimum conditions for the employment of labour and excluded certain classes of labour from the market; criminal and then civil law restrictions on trade union activities were removed and minimum wage legislation enacted. The state has also intervened directly into the struggle over the distribution of income by extending state provision into health, education and housing and social security. The introduction of state pensions, unemployment pay and sickness benefit ultimately replaced those provided by trade unions and friendly societies and no doubt more informal support from the family and the community. But the state system was more comprehensive and more efficient than the combination of provision by the market, charities, and intra-family and intra-community transfers it largely replaced and in particular extended provisions to those partially or totally excluded before because of their inability to pay.

Thus an important effect of the development of the floor of rights by the state was to benefit differentially workers in the lowest paid segments of the labour force. The lifting of legal constraints on collective industrial action and minimum wage legislation stood to benefit most those who individually were in the weakest bargaining position. The lowest paid were least able to provide for education and health in the market and when it was provided free by the state they stood to gain most. This is equally true of social welfare payments and moreover in Britain many of these benefits are flat rate and therefore are in proportionate terms a more important element in the income of the low paid. Thus one of the effects of extension of the welfare state has been to counteract effects of labour market segmentation. Social security has lifted the burden of poverty somewhat; education and improved health care have raised expectations.

However the extent to which the state counteracts segmentation in the labour market should not be exaggerated. The continued existence alongside the state system of private education with access based on the ability to pay but which is nevertheless heavily subsidised by the state ensures privileged access to enhanced job and earning opportunities. Such privilege is not confined to the ability to pay. The middle classes' greater knowledge of the system and awareness of the benefits of education and the health service places them in a stronger position than the working class to exploit the state system. Moreover their social training and articulateness make them more at ease when confronted with state officials particularly as the profession-alisation of state facilities means that the officials come from the middle classes.

The modern welfare state in Britain has also preserved the nineteenth-century distinction between the 'deserving' and 'undeserving' poor and the notion of 'less eligibility' for those in receipt of state financial support. Social welfare benefits are kept at a minimum so as to maintain the 'incentive' to work and a clear distinction is drawn between benefits which are secured as of right and others which are given at the discretion of the social security administration. National insurance provides entitlement by right of contri-butions made to sickness and unemployment pay, and although eligibility for the latter is impaired if workers quit their jobs voluntarily, contribute to their own dismissal or cannot prove they are genuinely seeking work (in such cases unemployment pay is suspended and social security payment is reduced by 40 per cent), payments are automatic after a short waiting period. However eligibility for contributory benefits expires after one year – the claimants are thrown onto social security where they join those in need but without rights to benefits established by contribution. Eligibility for non-contributory social security benefit is at the discretion of the administration; need has to be established by a test of means and those able to work are obliged to demonstrate how genuine is their search for work.

The operation of the British social security system also reflects the economic dependence of women on men and consequently their secondary role in the labour market. Until recently, married women were allowed to contract out of the national insurance scheme which meant they were not eligible for unemployment or sickness pay in their own right and were refused social security because they were adjudged to be financially dependent on their husbands. Since the mid-1970s the right to contract out of the national insurance scheme for women newly entering the labour market has been withdrawn and so many married women are now eligible for contributory benefits in their own right. However, much female employment is casual or part-time and therefore it is difficult for women to build up rights to benefits based on contribution. The inferior position of women is not confined to those who are married. In particular the growing number of female heads of single parent families are particularly disadvantaged. Domestic respon-sibility prevents them from building up rights to contributory benefits and therefore they are usually social security claimants (three quarters of claimants dependent on social security are women and a high proportion of these are the heads of single parent families). There the disadvantage of women's dependence on men extends to those without such men. Attempts are made to shift the burden to a 'liable relative' and particularly to obtain maintenance orders from husbands – although payment of maintenance is difficult to enforce even by law. Cohabitation with men is also regarded by the social security administration as financial dependence and an army of investigators are employed to check up on the domestic arrangements of single women claimants to ensure whether they are living with a man – an overnight stay is taken as evidence of cohabitation.

Thus, although the welfare state has had an important levelling-up effect by operating to somewhat equalise incomes and improve job opportunities, its effect in this respect is limited by the continued importance of private provision, the reflection in social provision of society's discriminatory practices and the retention of the moralistic categories of the 'deserving' and 'undeserving' and the 'genuinely' seeking work in the administration of the welfare state.

(c) *Labour demand*

The *aggregate level* of market demand for labour is determined by the aggregate level of market product. The *structure* of the demand, in terms of the tasks required of labour is determined by the technical requirements of production and by power relationships. The technical requirements of production are determined by what is produced and how it is produced. Power relationships are those between labour and capital and between the factions of labour and of capital which determines the social organisation of production. In practice the factors which determine the technical organisation of production and those which determine the social organisation interrelate and cannot easily be separated. However attention in this section will be focused on the social organisation of production and its influence on the demand for labour.

The design of the means of production and hence the level and the structure of the demand for labour is an economic and social as well as a technical phenomenon which reflects the level, structure and certainty of product demand, the ownership and control of productive resources, and the availability, quality and docility of certain classes of labour and their capabilities of, and opportunities for, organisation. The organisation of the labour process involves the application of labour to the means of production (machines and material) and, whilst the smooth running of machines as mechanical instruments can be regarded largely as a technical matter, the effective use of the labour at the disposal of the organiser of production is quite another question. Skill and effort is embodied in the labourers who decide whether, how and to what extent it is used, these attitudes being formed by education, socialisation, tradition and other social forces and implemented to a degree determined by the extent and effectiveness of organisation. Thus the relations of production are not simply technical matters but involve the exercise of power, a conclusion which applies with equal force to the structuring of production. For example, the most efficient size of production unit in terms of output per composite unit of labour and the means of production may appear to be a technical matter determined by economies of scale and benefits of vertical integration. But the massing of the means of production on a single site has other, non-technical advantages and disadvantages. On the one hand it offers the opportunity to increase the degree of control and facilitates the more effective use of machines and labour, while on the other hand it increases the organising ability and bargaining power of labour by bringing together a large number of workers on one site and increasing the possibility of disruption of production by sectional groups.

The demand for labour is also influenced by the supply side structuring to the extent that values which determine this structuring are shared by the organisers of production. Racism and sexism are reflected in the hiring policies of the firm because the hirers share the social values which classify workers on the supply side and much the same argument can be made about the ranking of workers by the educational system, professional training and craft apprenticeships. At a more practical level the representatives of various forms of exclusive clubs are to be found amongst the employment decision makers and apply the club rules in their hiring policies.

This fragmentation is not confined to labour. Wide variations in the efficiency of machines and access to finance and other basic requirements structure capital into a hierarchy based on relative market power. Such differences are reinforced and multiplied by the 'technical' advantages of economies of scale and massed resources for research and development and by trade associations, agreements and laws which concentrate market power in selected hands. Within this hierarchy of firms, subordinate relations develop. Large firms 'capture' their suppliers and can dictate the terms of trade. In the product market the 'leader' establishes the ruling price to which the 'followers' must adjust and, in terms of market shares, firms with relatively weak bargaining power fit into the interstices between their more powerful opponents. The factionalisation of capital influences the demand for labour by ranking firms according to their ability to pay and by providing the opportunity for firms to choose between centralising or decentralising production, hence allowing them to vary their demand for labour in quality and quantity.

(d) *Labour markets*

The general characteristic of labour markets is that workers are not free to move from one job to another. Whilst individuals are free to vacate an existing job, their access to others is severely curtailed. Access to vacant jobs is carefully controlled, and the higher the pay and status the more restrictive the rules of entry. Rules of exclusion operate on all groups at all levels and are mutually reinforcing in the sense that workers in each labour market group, excluded from better jobs, more carefully protect those within their control. The few jobs which are accessible to almost anyone are generally those which almost nobody would want.

Access to particular jobs, and the incomes associated with them, depends largely on social circumstances as much as ability and qualifications. The social position of married women, for instance, has made them willing to accept jobs which attract relatively low wages and offer poor working conditions. The choice of position in the labour market hierarchy is restricted by social constraints even though on purely economic criteria their productivity would open up a wider selection of occupations. In a similar way access to the small number of 'good' jobs towards the top of the labour market hierarchy is restricted by trade union and professional association rules and restrictions which are supported by custom and social acceptance.

Thus the labour market opportunities of individuals depend, on the one hand, on qualifications, aspirations and information which are determined by upbringing and by education and, on the other hand, the occupational structure which is determined by the interplay of technical and social factors and which determines the level and range of skills and of earning opportunities. Thus what constitutes the labour market varies for individuals. University graduates, for example, will have qualifications which will admit them to the highest level jobs but which will not necessarily exclude them from occupations lower in the hierarchy. Moreover they will be able to adopt a national or even international perspective on job opportunities, whereas the actual or perceived job opportunities of a worker with minimum educational attainments will be confined to a small occupational and geographical area. The localisation of job opportunities will be reinforced by the network of information and contacts by which jobs are secured and by the acquisition of specific skills, seniority rights and job experience which together determine the level of earnings and job security. Such factors serve to trap workers into declining areas and industries to a degree which is inversely related to their ability to retrain and to gain access to jobs which offer prospects comparable to those relinquished. Such potential mobility will depend on the individual's ability to signal that he can adjust to changed circumstances and these indicators – for example, educational attainment, age, sex and race – may be determined by social norms and values, unrelated to actual ability and performance.

Thus the labour force in each economy is stratified by class, race, nationality, religions, sex and many other factors. These divisions are created and reinforced by discrimination, differential access to education and training, professional associations, trade unions, employers' associations and ratified by social beliefs and conventions. The resulting inequalities are partially offset by the welfare state but in other respects the state reinforces divisions in the labour market. Supply-side structuring has its demand-side counterpart in the hiring rules adopted by firms which rest on signals transmitted by social characteristics (age, sex, race, educational qualification etc.) which are only partially objectively based but which are taken to measure the relative worth of job applicants. Thus the filtering process rations out the scarce good jobs and ensures that the workers with the least attractive features in terms of social classification are employed in the lowest paid and most insecure occupations. The important features of segmented labour markets are that relative wages are no guide to relative skills or productivity and that workers of equal skill or potential ability are employed at widely different wage levels.

The dynamics of labour markets

The fact that labour markets are divided into largely non-competing occupational groups does not mean that they are inflexible. There is no historical evidence that the supply of labour has proved to be a long-term constraint on the development of capitalism although problems of integrating newly mobilised reserves of labour may have placed a ceiling of the pace of expansion. Nor is there any lack of evidence of capital's ability to restructure the demand for labour so as to economise in its use, however its ability in this respect may be constrained by labour organisation. But the process of labour market restructuring has not been continuous and, moreover, it has periodically been reversed. The dynamics of this process is the subject matter of this section which in turn considers the supply and demand before analysing how the two sides interact in the labour market.

(a) *Supply side*

During prolonged periods of expansion of demand considerable pressure develops on the stock of labour power with a growing need to expand it in both qualitative and quantitative terms. The response to this comes in the form of an increase in the fraction of the population seeking work – recently in the form of increased employment of married women – by an increase in the hours of overtime and multiple job holding, by inter-industry, inter-regional and international shifts and by the 'upgrading' of labour by education and training. Amongst those already in the labour force, flexibility is achieved by the lower tiers serving as reserves of labour for higher tiers and this upgrading is relatively easily achieved because workers are generally underemployed and all that is normally required is a change in hiring rules rather than any radical retraining programme.

In such periods the state will come under increasing pressure to increase expenditure on education and training to facilitate the upgrading of the existing labour force and to induce entry of potential new recruits from outside. Increased employment of workers from the periphery will require increased expenditure to assist recruitment, training and possibly to subsidise transport and accommodation for new recruits. In the case of married women, who provide the most easily mobilised reserve of labour, it may also be necessary to extend child care facilities.

Periods of high employment will also generally be periods of rapid change in techniques and industry's structure and location. This will increase the already heavy pressure on government to increase the size and upgrade the labour force by more expenditure on education and training and inducements for a rapid transfer of labour from declining to expanding sectors. Health care and health and safety at work will also be given priority in periods of high and growing employment to maintain the labour force, to ensure the quick return to employment of sick workers, and to extend the working life. In this latter respect in the post-war periods, in conditions of chronic labour shortage, significant tax incentives were given to the old to encourage the postponement of retirement.

Expanding government expenditure found justification among social scientists who encouraged the government to expand further education in the 1960s in the interest of a larger and better qualified labour force. Increased government expenditure on social services, in particular earnings-related unemployment pay and redundancy pay, were also encouraged in terms of improving the working of the labour market by facilitating job search.

One effect of a high level of demand for labour was therefore to induce an increase in state expenditure to improve the labour supply in quantitative and qualitative terms. More generally, high levels of employment have increased political pressure from the trade unions and other pressure groups concerned with poverty for a general improvement in social welfare benefits. Similar tendencies are observable in the development of trade unions. High employment strengthens the bargaining power of trade unions and in particular tends to extend its coverage to incorporate hitherto unorganised workers particularly amongst the lowest paid. This has added to the pressure on government to outlaw discrimination against racial minorities, legislate in favour of equal pay for women and improved employment conditions such as paid maternity leave and the right to reinstatement to jobs after maternity leave. Thus economic, political and social pressures combined in the upgrading of the labour force in such a way as to benefit particularly those at lower levels in the hierarchy.

In periods of high and rising unemployment the upgrading process described above is reversed. Changes in hiring rules dispel the less well qualified from the upper levels of the employment hierarchy and these people in turn shunt new arrivals out of the lower levels so that there is a general downgrading of labour although unemployment – as opposed to underemployment – tends to be concentrated amongst the most disadvantaged in the labour force. Increasing unemployment has removed the pressure on the state to increase welfare state expenditure. The existence of large numbers of workers without jobs and a general downgrading of those in work means that there exists a considerable reserve of un-utilised labour power. The need to train and to facilitate the employment of peripheral groups is removed and the slowing down of the pace of technical change will reduce the needs for provision for acquiring new skills. By contrast, the imperative to acquire skills to pursue increasingly scarce jobs will enable the government to shift the burden of training to the individual and families.

As the imperative for the state to invest in human capital has reduced, the pressure opposing welfare state expenditure has increased. This has been orchestrated by 'born again' neo-classical fundamentalists who have attributed the problems of slow growth, unemployment and low profitability to growing social welfare expenditure and the associated increasing fiscal burden. It is argued that the welfare state saps the will to work by closing the gap between social provision and the industrial wage whilst high taxation has been detrimental to investment, work and acquiring skills. Such arguments have received widespread popular support as the tax burden has eroded income at lower and lower levels of income particularly since unemployment has simultaneously increased social expenditure and reduced the tax base. Resistance to the state's initiative to cut welfare state expenditure has been reduced by high unemployment and the accompanying weakening of the trade union movement. Trade unions themselves have been subject to growing criticism and held responsible for inflation by rigidifying the labour market and resisting change so as to slow economic progress.

The policy response of the Thatcher government has been twofold: a weakening of trade unions and a lowering of the floor of social welfare rights. The right to strike and to make strikes effective have been severely curtailed. The ability to enforce trade union membership has been reduced by rules which hamper the establishment and maintenance of a closed shop by very high penalties which can be imposed on unions, employers or both for the dismissal of a worker for refusing to join a trade union and by the outlawing of 'union labour only' clauses in sub-contracts. Changes in the law on the contract of employment have made it no longer 'unfair' and therefore actionable for an employer to sack strikers without notice and to dismiss strikers selectively.

The government's policies for reducing social welfare have had a general and a discriminatory effect. There have been general reductions in *per capita* expenditure on education and health and reductions in the scale of unemployment and sickness pay to make those in employment less eligible. More selective measures have also been implemented to reduce the number 'entitled' to benefit and to discriminate against the 'undeserving' poor. The earnings-related element in unemployment and sickness benefit and the dependence allowance in sickness pay have been abolished and social welfare benefits have been made liable for direct taxation for the first time. The criteria for 'genuinely seeking work' has been strengthened, women are obliged to prove that suitable child care facilities are available before they receive unemployment pay and more searching enquiries are made to ensure that long-term recipients of social security are not 'work-shy'. More generally, an increasing number of the newly unemployed are disqualified from unemployment pay by having inadequate contribution records or, by 'contributing' to their own dismissal; the administration of social security has been tightened up by a more strict interpretation of discretionary powers, more investigators have been employed to track down cohabitation and to trace fraud, and more formal rules for granting benefits have been laid down at the centre to limit the effectiveness of the local appeals procedure for claimants who have been refused benefits. These changes add up to a determined effort to reduce the income of the unemployed relative to that of the employed (unemployment pay as a percentage of average earnings is now back to that of the late 1940s), to increase work discipline by making access to unemployment pay more difficult, and to coerce the unemployed. In particular, many of the changes have been detrimental to categories of workers already disadvantaged in the labour market, especially women.

The modifications to the social welfare system which have had the effect of reinforcing the disadvantage of the disadvantaged have been accompanied by other changes in labour market policy designed to have a similar effect. Make-work schemes and youth opportunity and training schemes designed to reduce unemployment have been widely used to provide cheap substitutes for more regular forms of employment. These measures include community work by the unemployed for pay only marginally higher than unemployment pay, a substantial subsidy paid to employers who hire young workers at rates of pay below a maximum which is significantly lower than union rates, and work experience schemes by which the government pays school leavers for one year's work experience with an employer. These and other schemes serve to disguise unemployment and provide the opportunity to undercut union rates at a cost to the government not significantly higher than unemployment pay.

The government has also reduced standards for conditions of employment enforceable by law by making it easier for firms to oblige workers to 'contract out' of their legal rights to redundancy pay and protection from unfair dismissal. (This was only possible for fixed term contracts, the minimum length of which has been reduced from two to one year.) The length of continuous employment with a firm necessary to qualify for redundancy pay and protection from unfair dismissal has been increased, entitlement for maternity leave and the right to reinstatement has been reduced and for women employed in small firms they have been abolished. Finally the government threatens to end legal minimum wage laws and has abandoned the 'fair wage resolution' established in the 1880s which prohibited government contractors offering wages and conditions of work less favourable than those usual in the area.

The downgrading effect of the recession and the impact of government policy has generally been to weaken the relative position of the workers in the lower strata of the labour market. The provision of the 1980 and 1982 Employment Acts reduced the degree of immunity enjoyed by unions in the civil courts but the responsibility for taking action lies with the individual employer. Because of the possible long-term effects on industrial relations, it seems unlikely that employers faced with strong trade unions and with well-established collective bargaining arrangements will avail themselves readily of the new powers. On the other hand, in areas where trade unions are weak and collective bargaining less developed, employers will be less inhibited and consequently it is to be expected that the trade union legislation will have a disproportionate effect where wages are low and employment is less secure. Privatisation, the outlawing of union-only clauses in sub-contracts, and the worsening of the legally binding conditions of employment will also have its major effect in the sectors of the labour markets where workers are weakest, as will the abandonment of the 'fair wage' clause and future attempts to abolish legal minimum wages. In addition, the cuts in social security will tend to weaken disproportionately the positions of the relatively disadvantaged in the labour market. The reduction in family income by unemployment and cuts in social provision below what is customarily regarded as a necessary level of family expenditure may induce family members – particularly women and children – to work for almost anything they can get. If this level of earnings is threatened by high marginal tax rates, by reductions in means tested social welfare benefit or possibly by rigorously enforced exclusion rules for social security, the temptation will be for workers to seek jobs outside the formal sectors of the economy. In these cases the impoverishment of families by unemployment reinforced by cuts in social welfare will be accompanied by an attempted increase in labour market participation as the level of desperation amongst poor families increases and any consequent reduction in wages will not be recorded in official statistics because it will take place in the 'submerged' economy.

(b) *The demand for labour*

Until the late 1960s, evidence seemed to show an increasing tendency for firms to prefer long-term employment relationships. In sectors where large firms were operating capital intensive modern technology, firms offered high wages and secure employment prospects to attract and retain workers. Such firms dominated secure and stable product markets and could bear the fixed costs of determining their pay and employment practices according to their long term requirements. At the other end of the spectrum, 'competitive' employment sectors persisted in declining industries and provided certain traditional and menial occupations requiring such low levels of skill that they need never be 'internalised' in the primary sector. It was hypothesised that in the secondary sector skills were low and behavioural patterns of workers made them unsuitable for primary employment. It was generally supposed that the secondary sector would continue to be characterised by 'traditional' firms using obsolete or traditional technologies, but that technical progress, industrial development and the growing influence of trades unions and collective bargaining would further the importance and dominance of the primary employment sector.

In the 1970s, however, the employment structure was found to be developing in more divergent and thus more complex ways than had previously been recognised or expected. This divergence revealed itself in the location of industry, the nature of product markets, technological change and in the system of labour organisation. Evidence has emerged on relocation of industry from inner city to rural areas, from industrial conurbations to newly industrialising areas (for example, in the UK from London to East Anglia, and in the US from the industrial north to the 'sun belt') and from advanced industrial countries to the Third World. Within industrial countries there is growing evidence of an increasingly important role for small firms in creating jobs.

Technological developments have generally increased the complexity of changes in industrial and employment structure. In addition to increasing the potential rate of decline in employment in manufacturing, they have also provided the opportunity both for decentralisation and fragmentation of production (for example microchips allow the application of high technology to small batch, diversified production) and further concentration (for example application of robotics requires integrated high volume production).

Increasing evidence has also emerged of a continued and in some cases increased use of secondary-type employment forms such as homeworking and labour-only subcontractors – trends which contradicted the simple 'deskilling' hypothesis of progressive concentration and factorisation of manufacturing employment. The use of subcontracting was one part of a general move away from increasingly long-term and secure employment contracts. Other examples of this tendency include the growing use of part-time work, often of so few hours per week as to bring earnings below the level at which liability for the payment of social security contributions are incurred.

These tendencies which were increasingly in evidence before the onset of the current recession have been exacerbated by the increasing adversity faced by industry. The growth in the number of workers seeking employment outside the formal sectors of the economy has been paralleled by a growth in the number of the firms seeking to reduce costs by avoidance of social security and other fixed costs of employment as well as the avoidance of union rates of pay. Government policies on privatisation of national health and local authority services have contributed to this general tendency. Services provided by direct employees are substituted by those from contractors who generally employ non-union labour on a more casual basis and pay wages lower than trade union rates.

(c) *Trends in labour market organisation*

A central question is the extent to which the changes discussed above are cyclical responses to changing economic conditions which are readily reversible, or evidence of more permanent trends in labour market organisation. For example, is the growth of small-scale production shading into the black economy mainly determined by economic adversity and uncertainty faced by firms and growing poverty amongst socially disadvantaged groups, or is it evidence of an alternative form of organisation of industry to large-scale production made possible by new technology or a new strategy developed by capital to undermine the power of organised labour?

There is no simple answer to this question. Change in labour market organisation is induced by the interaction of a multiplicity of factors which can be grouped under the headings: conditions of labour supply, technology, product market conditions and power relations. Low levels of effective demand resulting in increased uncertainty amongst employers and high levels of unemployment and increased poverty exacerbated by government policy have favoured the spread of small scale production and more casual forms of employment. Technical change, the development of new products and the increased relative importance of luxury goods have in some industries lowered the minimum efficient scale of production and reduced the profits of vertical integration. These changes have facilitated a restructuring of industries towards small firms and sub-contracting and the growth of separate service sectors from those previously integrated into manufacturing – for example, design – and from new developments – the writing of consumer software. Growing unemployment, changes in government policies, technical and market conditions have all interacted with the weakening of labour organisation to change power relations and this has both facilitated and been facilitated by the access of capital to weakly organised sectors both within countries and internationally.

In important respects some of these changes are cyclical responses but others have much more long term implications because of the permanency of changes in technological and product market conditions. However, other elements of the changes outlined may be a way by which the economic and political system accommodates disruptions to established power relations. The tendency is for the costs of unemployment and structural change to be shunted down the labour market hierarchy (on both the demand and supply side) to those both least able to bear it and most powerless to resist. The unequal distribution of these costs enables the powerfully placed on both sides of industry to accommodate the changes. But the new 'equilibrium' may be unstable because the conditions for it is an expansion of the potential pool of low paid substitutes for the products and services provided by the primary core. Thus the conditions for accommodating the changing power relations is found in concentrating the costs on the disadvantaged segments of the labour market, but the size and the extent of the exploitation of the latter are a potent cause of the changed power relationships.

Moreover, many of the changes in the factors structuring the labour market are not easily reversible, particularly as they are linked to more general developments in, for example, the level and structure of product market demand and social change. The increasing labour market participation by married women has been accompanied by changes in family organisation and in the structure of demand, and it cannot be assumed that women can simply be relocated in the home without important social and economic repercussions. The increased labour market participation by married women has been accompanied by a reduction in the labour intensity of household work with the growth in the ownership of consumer durables. Whether aids to housework released women or whether women acquired this equipment to be released from housework is an important question but whichever the causal direction the increase in married women's participation in the labour market *and* in the product market had a fundamental effect on the structure of demand. Increasingly the pattern of expenditure of the family has been restructured around the needs of a working wife and mother and in the process it has become dependent for its standard of living on the labour market earnings of that working wife. Thus services, many of which were traditionally provided by women within the non-market sector, are now provided by the market but in the process both the markets for labour and products have been radically transformed.

There is more debate about the extent to which the structure of power within the family has been changed, for example how much the traditional male dominance has been eroded by the husband's sharing with his wife's financial responsibility. But there can be little doubt that labour market participation of women has reduced the resources available for traditional non-market services such as the care of the elderly and, where alternative provision is available, the care of very young children. An alternative system has evolved based on state provision but this has been financed by increased taxation, particularly at the lower levels of income.

The changes discussed above are not confined to the family. The growing participation in the non-rural labour market by workers previously engaged in subsistence farming has been accompanied by a growing mechanisation of agriculture and its increasing dependence on wage labour. This transformation of the traditional sector has been accompanied by a breakdown of traditional forms of inter-community and inter-family transfers which formed the basis of traditional forms of social welfare so that the rural sector can no longer be regarded as a sponge ready to absorb surplus industrial labour and maintain it until it is next required for industrial employment. The migration from the land precipitated long period changes which made it unable to fulfil such a role. The same story can be told about the many services for example, domestic services, launderies, shoe repairs etc. which used to provide the sponge to absorb the reserve army of industrial labour and provide for some measure of subsistence. The combination of labour mobility, technical progress, changing patterns of consumption and social reorganisation means that they have now largely disappeared. [1]

Moreover, these changes are largely irreversible. The newly urbanised workers, and particularly their children, have become habituated to urban living, have contributed to the growth and the restructuring of markets in line with their consumption needs and have become dependent on the state for social welfare and on tax-payers to finance its provision. Therefore there have been significant shifts in the source of family income from the non-market private sector to the market and the state which now provides to a greater degree the sponge to maintain the unemployed and to maintain social reproduction. Accompanying this has been a reorganisation of demand for goods and labour and the reallocation of income between private and public provision as taxation has increased and extended to encompass lower and lower income levels.

This has important implications for current policies. Firstly, a cut in state provision of a given magnitude has a much larger impact on income than it would have had, say, fifty years ago, because of the increased dependence on state provision. Moreover a cut in services without a corresponding cut in taxation has greater distributional consequences because the ones most dependent on state provision, the relatively poor, are the ones whose taxation has increased in greater proportion to their income. Secondly, the growth of state provision of education, health and social welfare has been particularly beneficial to the relatively poor because the relatively rich continue to be dependent on their own resources. The poor have traditionally depended on communal provision and a cut in its modern version – state expenditure – will concentrate the costs where they can least easily be borne. Finally, the movement of labour from the traditional to the modern industrial sectors has frequently meant long-distance migration between regions within countries and between European countries. As European unemployment grows, the reverse flows of people with changed lifestyles and expectations to societies which have at least partly adjusted to their absence has serious short- and long-term implications for those areas, not least for the demand for state provision.

5   Conclusions

The intention of this paper was to sketch an outline of the factors which are important in determining how labour markets are structured and operate.

These views are based on detailed case study work at the level of industry and the firm as well as investigation of, for example, the supply of labour and the pace of inflation at the macro level. The conclusions are tentative and some would regard them as speculative.

However that may be, further progress can only be made by more detailed investigation of the determinants of the demand for, and supply of, labour. This procedure provides the basis for both developing a general framework for understanding how labour markets operate *and* for testing that framework. It is our view that this approach is both more scientific and more fruitful than the methodology of abstract *a priori* reasoning followed by attempts to assess how far reality approximates to the theoretical abstraction.

We have also spent some considerable time developing our understanding of recent government policy in the labour market. This we felt to be important both because it illustrates some of the processes we discussed earlier in the paper and because we believe it reveals the necessity for assessing policy recommendations and responses in an integrated framework, rather than, for example, from a narrow economists' perspective of how markets are supposed to function. This is not to deny the need for theory as a basis for policy but, unless the framework of analysis is a reasonable representation of reality, the success of the policy depends on the ability to coerce the system to behave in the manner appropriate to the underlying theory.

In developing our views, we have necessarily strayed into the preserves of social scientists in other disciplines. We make no apology for this but hope that we may be forgiven for the amateurish form our trespass has taken. We believe that segmentation in the social sciences has been one of the greatest obstacles to real understanding. But our contacts in the research community suggest that there is a growing will to reduce the significance of those divisions, both in terms of subject boundaries and institutional arrangements, with a prospect of closer collaboration in the development of a general conceptual framework to which we could all subscribe and contribute.[2]

Notes

1 The disappearance of this aspect of the sponge should not be exaggerated. The current recession has seen a growth in the number of self-employed service engineers for the wide range of domestic appliances. The implication of this is that the 'shape' of the sponge is defined by current levels of the technology and patterns of consumer demand.
2 See bibliography for other publications by the authors and in addition, Elbaum and Wilkinson, 1979.

The end of convergence: corporatist and dualist tendencies in modern western societies

Introduction

The idea of 'industrial society', in its present-day acceptance, was developed in the 1950s and 1960s by both European and American social scientists within a liberal critique of contemporary Marxism. For some of the authors in question, the aim was primarily to show how Marxist analyses of modern capitalism, as well as being often empirically inadequate, were also conceptually restrictive and misleading. *All* technologically and economically advanced societies, it was argued, whether capitalist or not, displayed essentially similar structural and processual features, which were associated with the requirements and consequences of large-scale industrial production: thus, the idea of 'industrial society' must be recognised as superordinate to that of 'capitalist society', and take precedence for analytical purposes (e.g. Aron, 1962, 1968). However, for other liberal authors, to achieve such a conceptual reorientation marked no more than a first step. It was then their objective to move on to the formulation of a *theory* of industrial society, of a similar character to that of the Marxist theory of the long-term dynamics of capitalism, but which would be capable of quite transcending the latter in its scope and explanatory power.

Thus, for example, in what must be reckoned as the most ambitious and influential attempt in this direction, Clark Kerr and his fellow authors of *Industrialism and Industrial Man* (1960, 1973) see themselves as following Marx in applying deductive methods to the understanding of the emerging pattern of global social development, but at the same time they directly contest the Marxist conception of how this development proceeds (*cf.* also Kerr, 1983). The fundamental impulse in long-term social change is not, in their view, the contradictions that recurrently build up between the expanding forces of production and the property institutions of a particular epoch but, rather, the ever-present and universal exigencies of technological and economic rationality. At the level of social action, the key processes through which decisive historical change is actually brought about are not those of class mobilisation and conflict, but those of élite leadership and mass response. And the ultimate *dénouement* which may be envisaged is not the revolutionary transition from capitalism to socialism, but the evolutionary convergence of all modern and 'modernising' societies on one particular form of industrialism: namely, 'pluralistic industrialism'. This is the general model of society most consistent with the functional imperatives that a rationally operating technology and economy impose; and it is in fact the pressure of these imperatives which must be seen as forcing the development of industrial societies on to convergent lines, whatever the distinctive features of their historical formation or of their pre-industrial cultural traditions.

It has, moreover, to be added that both in the case of Kerr and his associates and of various other liberal authors who advanced essentially similar theories of industrialism (e.g. Parsons, 1964, 1966), a concern is also to a greater or lesser degree apparent to take over from Marxism the claim to provide – through a privileged cognitive grasp on the movement of history – an objective basis for political judgements (*cf.* Goldthorpe, 1971). Thus, it is characteristic of such authors that, rather than attempting to argue in any philosophical way either for or against particular political positions, they aim to justify the liberal values that they see embodied in pluralistic industrialism on functional and evolutionary grounds derived directly from their sociology. These values, they hold, are actually revealing themselves in the course of social development as those most consistent with the 'logic' of industrialism. As experience of industrialism accumulates, it becomes evident what are the 'realistic' political possibilities; and unworkable 'utopian' conceptions – such as those which inspire socialism or communism or, for that matter, pure *laissez-faire*, individualistic capitalism – are eliminated as part of the evolutionary process. In the end, therefore, 'industrial man is seldom faced with real ideological alternatives' (Kerr *et al.*, 1960: 283): he must either accept the pluralistic industrialism that is being chosen for him by history or else face disillusionment and failure.

In view of the challenges, both intellectual and political, that are thus laid down by liberal theories of industrialism, it is in no way surprising that they should have provoked extensive controversy. Thus far, apart from attempts to display 'the ideology of the end of ideology' implicit in such theories, critics have chiefly raised empirically-based objections to the claim that a convergent pattern of development is now established among the societies of the industrial world. And of course to the extent that such objections can be sustained, doubt must then also fall on the existence, or at least on the cogency, of the functional logic which is supposed to generate convergence. In the present paper, this same line of criticism will be further pursued. It will in fact be contended that over recent decades – and even if attention is confined to the industrial societies of the West or only to those of western Europe – clearly *divergent* tendencies in social development may be observed in a number of significant respects. However, what will also be attempted is to provide some account of why this should be so and, in this way, to go beyond merely empirical objections to the convergence thesis – which might by now perhaps appear *vieux jeu* – to a more fundamental argument: that is, that contrary to what would be supposed by liberal theorists, the idea of capitalist society is not outmoded or rendered problematic by that of industrial society; and further, that an analysis of the course of change in modern western societies in terms of the functional imperatives of industrialism is no substitute for one in terms of the political economy of capitalism – even though this may need to depart radically from conventional Marxist lines.

In what follows, attention will centre on claims made by exponents of the convergence thesis in three substantive areas: social stratification, the representation of interests, and industrial relations and organisation. When these claims are examined, one point should become apparent: namely, that the convergence thesis was very much a product of its time – that is, of the 'long boom' of the post-war period. What the theorists of industrialism implicitly assumed, so far as the western world was concerned, was that with the development of improved techniques of economic management, following the 'Keynesian revolution', and with the growing readiness of governments to apply such techniques, the problems of regulating capitalist, or 'mixed', economies were essentially solved; and that for the conceivable future, therefore, economic stability and dynamism would be reconciled and guaranteed. And in turn, then, it was also supposed that, within such an economic future, a virtually permanent status would attach to the post-war 'settlements' which had been arrived at in western nations between capital and employers on the one hand and labour and its organisations on the other. For what these settlements typically involved, although in varying degree from one society to another, were assurances to labour that governments had assumed responsibility for the basic economic and social security of all citizens, and for the steady improvement of their material standards of living through sustained economic growth.

In other words, there was no place in the scenarios of convergent development that were elaborated in the 1950s and 1960s for the severely troubled phase in the economic history of the western world which actually began in the early 1970s. And what then will subsequently be maintained is that it is through the responses that have emerged in different societies to the ending of the long boom – specifically, responses in what may be termed 'corporatist' and 'dualist' directions – that divergent tendencies in social development have been made most apparent. However, the argument to be presented is not that it was simply as the result of an unforeseen, and perhaps unforeseeable, decline in the performance of western economies that the convergence thesis was undermined. Rather, it will be held that the problems of inflation and of 'stagflation' with which these economies are now beset are ones that have to a significant extent been produced endogenously within the societies of the western world, and through processes *which were already in train during the post-war period* but which exponents of the convergence thesis were conceptually ill-equipped to observe.

Changes in social stratification and their consequences

In elaborations both of the idea of industrial society and of the thesis of the convergent development of western nations towards the goal of pluralist industrialism, the treatment of changes in the degree and form of social stratification and of their consequencs holds a quite central place. Three major arguments regarding stratification may be identified in the work of the leading theorists of industrialism, which, in their essentials, can be stated as follows.[1]

(i) In the course of industrial development, social inequalities of both condition and opportunity show a general, long-run tendency to decline. Industrial development based on technological advance requires an increasingly differentiated labour force, and one with progressively higher standards of education and training. Thus, the proportion of the economically active population enjoying a relatively high level of occupational status and income steadily grows. Moreover, this expansion of higher-grade employment, together with the increased provision of education, greatly enlarges individuals' chances of social mobility; and the 'openness' of industrial society is further enhanced in that economic and technical rationality impose criteria of social selection which emphasise 'achieved' rather than 'ascribed' characteristics. Finally, equality is also promoted as in all industrial societies the state intervenes in market processes in order to establish certain minimum standards of welfare as the social rights of all citizens, complementary to their civil and political rights.

(ii) In industrial societies stratification takes on an increasingly unstructured and fluid form. It becomes difficult to identify either classes or status groups in the sense of relatively stable collectivities of individuals and families displaying characteristic lifestyles and associational patterns. In particular, the former distinctiveness of the industrial working class fades away. An advanced industrial society has to be seen as essentially a 'middle-class' or, rather, as a 'middle-mass' society. The decomposition of classes and status groups results in large part from tendencies towards greater social equality and mobility, but is furthered too by the increasing cultural homogeneity which also follows from industrialism. All forms of subcultural particularism – those based on region, ethnicity etc., as well as those based on class – are broken down, on the one hand, by the need for greater geographical as well as social mobility within the labour force and, on the other, by the growing influence of mass consumption and mass communications.

(iii) In industrial nations, social stratification becomes steadily less divisive and, thus, of declining importance as a basis of socio-political mobilisation.

It is in the context of early industrialism, and especially in the 'heroic' phase of capital accumulation, that class conflict reaches its peak. Subsequently, the effects of industrialism in reducing social inequalities and in blurring the lines of class division – and also, of course, in raising living standards generally – progressively undermine the potential for such conflict. The widening of opportunities for social mobility encourages the individualistic pursuit of interests, and this can, moreover, be effectively supplemented by collective action that is organised not on a class but, rather, on a *group* basis. Thus, action directed towards furthering the interests of those employed in a particular plant, occupation, or industry usually appears as far more relevant than attempts to uphold some wider but increasingly diffuse interest, such as that of the working class as a whole.

It will be apparent enough how the foregoing arguments stand in quite systematic counterpoint to those which – at least up to the 1960s – could be regarded as characteristic of Marxist analyses; and their critical force and success in this respect must be reckoned as considerable. However, what may also be suggested is that in being formulated in this polemical context, these arguments came to share in some of the same general weaknesses of those against which they were directed: most notably, an exaggeration of the extent, continuity and consistency of the particular trends of change they sought to emphasise and, at the same time, a one-sidedness in the view taken of their implications. These weaknesses are moreover particularly evident in judgements made on the future of the working class and of class conflict.

Thus, in the light of recent research and analysis, major qualifications could be made in the following respects.

(i) Liberal theorists often took as evidence of declining social inequality what was in fact evidence simply of a general increase in living standards and welfare. Research focused specifically on the extent of class *differentials* in life-chances – for example, in health and education – has frequently found that these have altered remarkably little over the post-war decades, and that disparities existing between the industrial working class and the rest of society have been especially resistent to change (*cf.* Wedderburn, ed., 1974; Rainwater, ed., 1974). Similarly, in the case of social mobility, liberal theorists quite failed to recognise that while the 'upgrading' of occupational structures produced by industrial development does indeed widen opportunities for social ascent, it has at the same time the effect of reducing the likelihood of downward movement. And the major finding of analyses that have been made of trends in national mobility rates considered *net* of all structural effects – which provides the best indicator of changes in the degree of openness – is that such rates display very considerable stability over time (Erikson *et al.*, 1983).

(ii) This combination of structural change with constancy in relative mobility chances, rather than threatening the decomposition of the working classes of western nations, must tend in fact to increase their internal homogeneity, at least so far as the social origins and work-life experience of their members is concerned. For declining downward mobility into working-class positions – together with a decline in the influx of labour from greatly contracted agricultural sectors – means that in recent decades western working classes have, for the first time, become predominantly self-recruiting. Although in most instances reduced somewhat in size, they do now mostly comprise a majority of members who may be reckoned as, at least, 'second generation'. And while it is true that opportunities for upward mobility out of the working class have expanded, the growing importance of education as a channel of such mobility has meant that those who break away increasingly do so at a relatively early age. Thus, the bulk of working-class membership, as it exists at any one moment, is likely to be made up of those who have – as Sorokin (1927) once put it – both a 'hereditary' and a 'life-time' affiliation (*cf.* Goldthorpe, 1980, 1983).

(iii) In emphasising certain egalitarian tendencies which are indeed associated with western industrialism, liberal theorists neglected the well-attested possibility that where social inequality is reduced in one particular respect, this may, rather than lowering the potential for social conflict, actually increase it, through bringing other forms of inequality into contention. Thus, a consequence of the decay of status group structures of pre-industrial origin may be that class inequalities, for which the status hierarchy previously provided a 'traditionalistic' legitimation, become more often regarded as arbitrary and contingent rather than as part of 'the order of things', and that in turn normative restraints on what are seen as 'appropriate' rewards, entitlements and opportunities are weakened. Moreover, this process can only be encouraged as the ethos of consumerism and continuing material advancement secures wider acceptance, and as the limitations on wants and lifestyles imposed by traditional communities and sub-cultures, especially those of the working class, are undermined. Likewise, the process through which in the western world civil, political and social rights of citizenship have been extended to all members of national communities – while certainly egalitarian – has at the same time to be recognised as one which has its own dynamic and no very evident resting point (*cf.* Lockwood, 1974; Esping-Andersen & Korpi, 1985). Thus, in the post-war period a notable movement has been for citizenship rights to be further developed into the industrial sphere: that is, in the form of employees' 'rights in jobs' – pertaining to such matters as redundancy, dismissal, promotion etc. – and rights to participate in decision-making procedures affecting their working environment, conditions of service and employment prospects. From one point of view, these developments can be seen as entirely continuous with earlier ones in what Marshall (1950) referred to as the 'war' between citizenship and class – in setting limits, one could say, to the extent to which labour can be treated merely as a commodity. But from another point of view, this extension of citizenship rights into the actual organisation of production raises new, and manifestly very divisive, issues concerning managerial prerogatives and the bases of authority and responsibility within the enterprise (Goldthorpe, 1978 and forthcoming).

To identify these aspects of change in the pattern of social stratification that are neglected or misconstrued in liberal theories of industrialism has significance not only by way of criticism of various specific claims that follow from these theories. It is also highly relevant to understanding why their proponents failed to envisage the possibility that, far from western societies becoming increasingly better adapted to the functional requirements of industrialism, developments were taking place within them that could seriously threaten the continuation of their economic success.

In order to amplify this point, it is important to begin by noting that the liberalism which stands behind the idea of industrial society could be fairly described as a political, far more than an economic liberalism. This is most clearly indicated by the fact that while its adherents attached the highest importance to the freedom of individuals who recognise common interests to organise and to pursue these interests through all lawful means, they were remarkably unconcerned about the likely consequences of such activity for the free operation of market forces. In other words, there was little awareness of the contradictions that might arise within the pluralistic industrialism of the west between a form of polity characterised by the vigorous rivalries of organised interests and a form of economy which, though perhaps labelled 'mixed', remained essentially capitalist in its mode of operation; or, perhaps, as one commentator has suggested, the new liberals possessed 'an excessive faith in capitalism and in its ability to fly however much its wings are clipped' (Scitovsky, 1980). However, it is precisely contradictions of the kind in question which, of late, have become accepted by economists and other social scientists – of varying theoretical and ideological persuasions – as a factor of steadily increasing importance underlying the severity and persistence of the economic problems that western nations now confront (Jay, 1976; Brittan, 1977, 1983; Scitovsky, 1978, 1980; Thurow, 1980; Schmitter, 1981; Olson, 1982: ch. 7 esp., 1983; Mueller, ed. 1983). Their analyses have in common the recognition of two crucial facts: first, that interest groups, as they operate in the economic sphere, aim primarily at strengthening their members' market positions through action that is in some sense taken *against* market forces – for example, via organisation, regulation, legislation etc.; and secondly, that such interest groups are concerned very largely with distributional issues of a 'zero-sum' kind, in which their members' interests can only be protected or advanced to the extent that those of other groups are threatened or damaged. Thus, as the number of interest groups and the amount of interest-group activity increase, it must be expected, on the one hand, that the market mechanisms on which the efficient functioning of a capitalist economy depends will work less freely; and, on the other, that distributional conflict within society will be heightened, which will in turn add to the difficulties of carrying through remedial economic policies.

Further, though, what has also to be recognised as highly relevant in this connection – but what the theorists of industrialism succeeded in concealing from themselves – is the interplay occurring between the 'organisational revolution' of the post-war period and the evolution of class structure and class relations within western societies. Although it could certainly be said that in this period interests of all kinds increasingly sought and achieved organised expression, there can be little doubt that the major development was in the organisation of *labour* (*cf.* Korpi, 1983: ch. 3 esp.). And while the theorists in question were well aware of, and indeed concerned to stress, this development, their appreciation of its significance was far from adequate. Their expectation clearly was that as labour unions 'matured' – that is, abandoned the ideological commitments to class struggle characteristic of their early years – and concentrated their efforts on pragmatic collective bargaining and pressure-group activities, they would come to form a quite integral part of pluralistic industrialism (Lester, 1958; Kerr *et al.*, 1960; Clegg, 1960; Ross & Hartman, 1960). However, the possibility that was here overlooked was that unions could, even while perhaps modifying their previous ideological positions, still effectively represent class as well as sectional interests and, moreover, that they might do so in a way that was capable of bringing about a significant shift in the balance of power in class relations. In particular, liberal theorists of industrialism failed to appreciate the importance of two developments that became increasingly apparent, even if with some significant cross-national variation, within trade unionism over the post-war period: first, the emergence of a new 'maximising' militancy in collective bargaining, encouraged, one would suggest, by the weakening of traditional legitimations of class inequalities and traditional limitations on wants and life-styles, as well as by the rising confidence of trade-unionists in the bases of their organised power (Barkin, ed., 1975; Crouch & Pizzorno, eds., 1978; Sachs, 1979); and secondly, a growing concern shown by unions, especially through their central federations, with the direction of macro-economic policy, which they increasingly recognised as capable of exerting a crucial influence on the bargaining strength of labour as a whole (Barbash, 1972).

In sum, then, the argument is that the functional viability of pluralistic industrialism was greatly over-estimated through a neglect of the generally damaging effects of interest-group activity on the operation of market mechanisms, and further of the particular problems created by the relatively rapid increase, in most western societies, in the organised power of labour and in both the range and intensity of labour's demands. The most obvious outcome of these developments, apparent in fact already by the 1960s, was that western economies became inherently inflationary. As organisation increased the capacity of different groups to protect their incomes against unfavourable market forces, a strong downward rigidity of incomes and prices was created; and in turn, then, the response to upward shifts in relative prices that might for any reason occur was not offsetting relative price decreases and consequent changes in income distributions, but rather an upward movement in the general price level.[2] In addition, though, the increased power of labour was also crucial in undermining the effectiveness of the techniques of economic management, in particular of demand management, on which liberal expectations of stable yet steadily expanding economies were in large part founded. On the one hand, it became apparent that where attempts were made to control inflation through policies that reduced aggregate demand, then, in the face of labour's growing ability to maintain wage levels, a larger proportion of the effect of such policies would come in the form of a reduction not in the rate of price increases but rather in real output or, in other words, in the form of rising unemployment. And, on the other hand, it was no less apparent that where, perhaps as the result of union pressure, attempts were made at reducing unemployment by policies aimed at expanding demand, then, again as a result of labour's increased bargaining strength, these policies were increasingly likely to have their intended effects dissipated in a further upturn in inflation.

In the course of the post-war years the indications thus steadily mounted that to view the major features of western societies as developing on lines that would make these societies progressively more adapted to the functional requirements of modern economies was, to say the least, scarcely realistic; and indeed, as already remarked, by the early 1970s rather widespread attention was being given to the social-structural – and associated political – factors in the unprecedented emergence of persisting high rates of inflation and of unemployment as complementary rather than alternative expressions of economic disorder. However, what for present purposes is of major relevance is to recognise that, confronted by rising difficulties in controlling their economies, western societies have not, so to speak, remained passive. The period of the long boom was itself not free of economic problems yet was in most cases sustained up to the 1970s, and it is further notable that in the subsequent stagflationary period the performance of western economies has tended to become more disparate: modes of 'adaptation' have clearly varied (Scharpf, 1981). In what follows, the main concern will be to examine the nature of different responses to the central problems of capitalist economies that have formed in the west, and more specifically to see how and why these responses have involved significant – yet contrasting – divergencies from the model of pluralistic industrialism which, in the grand vision of liberal theorists, the west offered to the world as the ultimate evolutionary goal.

Corporatism

If it is the case that the problems currently faced by western economies do have a major endogenous source in heightened and more equally balanced distributional dissent, at the level of both interest groups and classes, then one possible direction of response, so far as governments are concerned, would seem fairly apparent. That is, to try to bring some greater degree of order, and hence of predictability, not only into their own relations with particular organised interests, but further into the relations prevailing *among* these interests, where their aims and their strategies for pursuing these aims are, in some way or other, interdependent. It is, one may suggest, as a response of essentially this kind that one can best interpret developments in the form of interest representation which have become evident in a number of western societies over recent decades, and which have been widely seen as indicating a return to, or renewal of, *corporatist* principles. What has been found significant in these developments is that they entail a blurring of the line of division, crucial to liberal political theory, between the state and civil society. Organisations representing private interests are accorded a role in the formation of public policy in areas that are of central concern to them, but are then required to assume a responsibility for the effective implementation of policies with which they have become associated and, in particular, for the appropriate conduct of their own memberships – being perhaps in this respect aided by the state as, for example, through various kinds of delegated powers, special privileges, subsidies etc. However, what needs to be added here is that it is not such a *Verstaatlichung* of private interests which in itself is all that novel. Rather, it is the increasing extent to which not simply bilateral, but tri- and multilateral arrangements have been attempted, in order to afford government the possibility not only of accommodating and regulating specific interests but, more importantly, of promoting the *concertation* of different interests which could otherwise be expected to compete or conflict in ways detrimental to the achievement of major governmental objectives (*cf.* Czada & Lehmbruch, 1981; Lehmbruch, 1983, 1985).

Perhaps because the 'rediscovery of corporatism' was largely an achievement of political scientists, corporatist tendencies have often been treated as a response to governmental problems of effectiveness and consent of a quite general kind. Following the organisational revolution, it has been argued, the unregulated representation of interests becomes increasingly a recipe for disorder and unrest: claims are made on government of such a volume and range and are backed with such a capacity for collective action that channels of decision-making fail through 'overload' and societies are brought close to a condition of 'ungovernability'. However, on sober examination, such contentions must seem somewhat exaggerated – and often out of a rather transparent ideological distaste for 'over-participation'. In so far as western governments have had to face recurrent crises of effectiveness and, perhaps, of consent in the recent past, these have in fact by far most frequently arisen in connection with *the management of the economy*, and in consequence of the actions of organisations representing major economic interests: that is, business and employer organisations and trade unions. On account of the control that these organisations can exercise over the key resources of capital and labour, they must be placed in a quite different category from virtually all others in their ability to exert pressure on governments or simply to frustrate their initiatives. And in turn, it may be held, it is in the case of these organisations that corporatist developments, in the sense of governmentally guided attempts at the concertation of interests, have been most distinctive and have carried the furthest-reaching implications.

More specifically, what may be suggested is that these developments represent in effect attempts by governments, in dealing with the rising problems of macro-economic policy previously noted, to find institutional and ultimately political substitutes for the declining efficiency of market mechanisms. The most common, (though by no means the only), objective has been to establish arrangements, formal or informal, for consultation and negotiation between government, employers' associations and union federations, in the context of which the latter may be induced to accept – and to commit their members to accepting – some form of restraint in their use of their collective bargaining strength. Such restraint has been seen as necessary, given the growing rigidity of modern economies, to allow governments to introduce expansionist policies aimed at sustaining employment without producing disastrously high rates of inflation; or, conversely, to allow them to introduce restrictionist policies aimed at curbing inflation without producing disastrously high rates of unemployment.

Two features of the logic of these corporatist arrangements would seem to be of key importance. First, the central – that is, the national – organisations of employers and unions are required to take on a representative function that must seek to transcend sectionalism. They must act in a way that will balance the differing interests that exist within their memberships, and concentrate their efforts on goals from which all can benefit. Such 'encompassing organisations', as Olson (1982) has termed them, should thus serve to absorb within themselves some of the distributional dissent arising from more narrowly constituted interest groups. Secondly, in the case of the unions at least, a basic change of *modus operandi* is implied. Unions are required to cede or under-utilise their economic power – that is, the power they can express in collective bargaining in labour markets – in exchange for the opportunity for their leaders to exercise political power or, at all events, political influence. Several commentators have indeed maintained that it is this exchange that is fundamental to the developments in relations between governments and unions which have been labelled 'corporatist', and would themselves wish rather to speak – as they would see it, less tendentiously – of the emergence of a form of 'political' or 'societal' bargaining, in which unions engage primarily with government rather than employers and which modifies, but can at the same time powerfully complement, conventional collective bargaining as a mode of action of labour movements (Korpi & Shalev, 1980; Korpi, 1983; *cf.* Pizzorno, 1978 b, 1981).

This view has obviously something in common with that taken here – that significant corporatist tendencies should be regarded as primarily a response to problems of economic management. However, what can scarcely be neglected, and is in fact for present purposes of central relevance, is the way in which these tendencies, even if restricted largely to the economic sphere, do still entail departures from the model of pluralistic industrialism that are of a quite major kind.

To begin with, there can be little doubt that, whether understood as 'corporatism' or 'political bargaining', the pattern of interaction between government and major economic interests which would seem prevalent in several western societies, such as those of Austria, Sweden, and Norway – and which has at certain periods been attempted in a number of others, such as the Netherlands, West Germany and Finland – is one that scarcely conforms with the model of interest representation envisaged by liberal theorists as that most appropriate to and characteristic of modern industrialism. In the view of these theorists, the complexity of the structure of an advanced industrial society must lead to the recognition by groups differently located within this structure of a great diversity of interests – economic and other – which then become represented through an equally great diversity of organisations. These bodies will compete with each other for influence over government within a kind of political market; and while this will, like other markets, be subject to governmental supervision and even, in particular cases, to regulative intervention, it is not seen as part of government's role to 'organise' the market itself. However, in those societies where corporatist tendencies have developed, an attempt to comprehend the relations prevailing between governments, employers and trade unions in terms of such a conception of 'pressure-group politics' would be obviously inadequate. For apart from it being unrealistic to suppose that the central organisations of employers and unions can be treated as interest groups like any others, it is precisely the purpose of corporatist arrangements to involve such organisations in the political process in a way that goes clearly beyond the exercise of external pressure: that is, in an acceptance of shared responsibility both for the formation of policy and for its implementation. And what then rather naturally follows from such arrangements is that governments are led to give increased attention to questions of how their 'partners' in policy-making manage their own internal affairs: in particular, to questions of how *they* form *their* policies and, more fundamentally, of how they come to *define* the interests that they exist to serve. In pluralist theory, group interests are seen as emerging directly from the positions that groups hold within the social structure, and the function of their organisations is then that of representation of a similarly direct, unmediated kind. But in corporatist practice, interests are clearly not treated simply as sociological 'givens', and the function of representative organisations is not merely to express, but actually to formulate interests, in response to pressure from both their memberships *and* from their bargaining partners, and also in the light of their leaders' own conceptions of appropriate strategies. Thus inter- and intra-organisational relations alike become of major political consequence, and fall within the legitimate sphere of governmental concern.[3]

Furthermore, interest representation in the form of corporatism, as here understood, clearly diverges from the pluralism envisaged by liberal theorists in that, far from reflecting and in turn reinforcing a process of class decomposition, it tends rather to endow class – as opposed to group – interests with a new significance. If the national representative bodies of employers and unions are to act as 'encompassing organisations', aiming to modify sectionalist demands from among their members and at the same time to win the support of the latter for a strategy of political bargaining, then it becomes necessary for their leaderships to take up a position on the obvious questions of exactly what interests will be served by this strategy and how. One possibility may be to claim that in this way distributional conflicts that are 'negative-sum' in their outcomes can be reduced, to the advantage of all parties involved. But distributive conflicts are more characteristically of a 'zero-sum' kind, and, in so far as this is so, the organisations representing 'the two sides of industry' can scarcely do other than define the interests that they seek to advance in essentially class terms.

This requirement arises most sharply in the case of the unions since, as earlier suggested, it is the nature of union activity that is most affected by participation in corporatist arrangements. The acceptance by a national union movement of restraint of any kind on processes of conventional collective bargaining must mean that certain groups of workers – that is, those with the strongest labour market positions – will yield more in the way of immediately available gains than will others. But the benefits that can be obtained as the *quid pro quo* for such restraint – through, say, employment, fiscal or social policy – will not only be somewhat deferred but will also tend to be of a rather generalised kind: for example, benefits that will accrue, if not to all citizens, then to all employees, all industrial workers, all persons with incomes below a certain level etc. Thus, union leaders engaging in political bargaining and wishing to retain the backing of their memberships are typically led to emphasise their concern with the interests of a broadly-defined working class, and usually on a relatively long-term view, as against interests of a more sectional and shorter-term kind. It can hardly be thought accidental that the national union movements which have the most consistent records of involvement in political bargaining – those of Austria, Sweden and Norway – are also ones which, as well as being highly centralised, have attached a greater importance than most others to combating sectionalism and to maintaining a sense of class solidarity and a class outlook on economic and political issues among their rank and file (Korpi, 1978; Hanisch, 1981;

Marin, 1983). It is also worthy of note that in each of these countries, in which trade unionism and socialism have strong historical connections, union movements have passed through periods of ideological questioning – in particular of *marxisant* conceptions of class struggle – but that this has *not* prevented them from remaining movements of a distinctively class-oriented kind. What is thus demonstrated is the invalidity of the assumption, which theorists of industrialism seem regularly to have made, that such ideological reassessment must imply that unions have become ready to accept the limitation of their functions simply to conventional collective bargaining and pressure-group activity, as the model of pluralistic industrialism would require.

Following from this, one may then point to yet another way in which the emergence of corporatist tendencies in certain western societies has led to a rather decisive contradiction of liberal expectations. Along with the decomposition of classes and the 'maturing' of unions, the theorists of industrialism looked forward to what might be termed the progressive depoliticisation of industrial relations. This would be achieved by the development of industrial relations institutions, principally ones of collective bargaining and dispute settlement, which would in effect create the basis of a system of industrial democracy complementary to, but separate from, that of political democracy. In this way, issues of both industrial and political conflict could be contained within, so to speak, their proper spheres, and 'spill-over' effects avoided. In particular, it was believed that if industrial conflict could be institutionally insulated from political influences of the kind that stemmed from class-oriented labour movements, its volume would be substantially reduced. Indeed, some liberal theorists were prepared to anticipate, as the appropriate institutions came into being, a virtual 'withering away' of the strike (Ross & Hartman, 1960).

However, it is evident that corporatist arrangements providing for political bargaining between governments, employers' organisations and unions, represent a kind of institutional development that goes in more or less direct opposition to those envisaged and endorsed in liberal scenarios. Since such bargaining essentially involves unions in exchanging some form of restraint on their labour-market power for a voice in governmental decision-making, it clearly implies a strategy on both sides in which advantage is seen precisely in treating certain major industrial and political issues *together*, so that they can in effect provide a basis for 'general understandings' or 'package deals'. And so far as unions are concerned, the possibility must of course be presupposed that political action can be a viable, and indeed a preferred, alternative to industrial action in the pursuit of their objectives. It may, moreover, be noted that, in this form at least, the politicisation of industrial relations cannot be linked with a high level of conflict. On the contrary, worker involvement in strike activity in Austria, Sweden and Norway, and also in the Netherlands and West Germany, has fallen to particularly low levels. And while it need not be claimed that political bargaining is the only source of this relative industrial peace, their association can scarcely be thought surprising. For where union movements are following a strategy that requires them to hold their labour market power in check, they may be thought unlikely to initiate or to encourage a form of action which crucially depends upon such power. [4]

In sum, corporatist tendencies, as here understood, represent a response to growing problems of the management of modern capitalist economies which involves the deflection or redirection of the increased power of organised labour away from the labour market into the political arena (Korpi & Shalev, 1980; Korpi, 1983; ch. 8; Shalev, 1983). In this interpretation, it may be added, the fact that the countries in which such tendencies have been most sustained are ones in which social-democratic parties have played a dominant role in government is readily intelligible: union movements will be more prepared to enter into political bargaining, and will have greater confidence of eventual gains from it, where they possess close ideological as well as organisational ties with the ruling party. But one has also to recognise, in addition to these instances of relatively stable corporatist arrangements existing under social-democratic hegemony, those further cases – as, for example, the Netherlands and West Germany – in which unions have judged it to their advantage to participate in such arrangements, at certain times and to a certain extent, in clearly less favourable political circumstances; and, at the same time, cases – such as that of Britain – in which, even under Left governments, the effective involvement of unions in political bargaining has proved difficult to establish (Tarling & Wilkinson, 1977). However, what for the present is of chief concern is not the specific pre-conditions for the emergence of corporatist tendencies, but rather the way in which, where they have in fact emerged, such tendencies mark significant departures from the liberal model of pluralistic industrialism – departures which, far from representing damaging deviations from the functional requirements of the logic of industrialism, must rather be seen as resulting from attempts to counter the economically 'dysfunctional' effects of the reality of pluralism when in conjunction with capitalism. [5]

Dualism

If the foregoing analysis is accepted, then corporatist tendencies may be thought of as a response to the current problems of western economies of an 'inclusionary' kind: the increased power of major economic interest groups – and of organised labour in particular – is offset by institutional developments designed to involve these interests in both the formation and the implementation of economic policy. As was earlier suggested, what is here implied is the granting of institutional recognition to actual power shifts as a means of compensating for their damaging effects on the functioning of market mechanisms. However, to view corporatist tendencies in this way is at the same time to become aware of the possibility of a response on quite contrasting, 'exclusionary' lines: that is, one which would entail off-setting the increased power of organised interests by the creation or expansion of collectivities of economic actors, within the sphere of production, who *lack* effective organisation and indeed the basic resources and perhaps motivations from which such organisation might be developed. Tendencies indicative of a response of this kind may be described as ones in the direction of *dualism*. This label would seem appropriate in that these tendencies do not necessarily imply any direct and comprehensive attack on organised interests, but only the enlargement of certain areas of the economy within which market forces and associated relations of authority and control are able to operate more freely than in others, and in fact in such a way as to compensate for the rigidities that prevail elsewhere. [6]

According to liberal theories of industrial society, such dualism should have little place within the modern world. Economic dualism of any kind is seen as characteristic only of the earlier stages of economic development; as the logic of industrialism imposes itself, economies are progressively unified and the social processes that underlie the functioning of markets and of production units become increasingly homogeneous (*cf*. Kerr *et al.*, 1960: ch. 10). However, in opposition to these claims two empirically-grounded arguments may be advanced: first, that during the post-war years of unprecedented growth, dualist features persisted in many western economies – and contributed to their growth – to a far greater extent than liberal theorists were able to recognise; and secondly, that in the succeeding period of declining economic performance, a strengthening of dualist tendencies can be quite widely observed.

One major source of dualism, as here understood, in the economies of western capitalist societies is that of migrant labour – recruited predominantly from the less developed regions of the western world or from former colonies. Several authors – and most convincingly, perhaps, Kindleberger (1967) – have sought to show the importance of such labour in sustaining economic growth in western European nations through, at least, to the late 1960s. Not only did migrant workers help to prevent manpower shortages which could have checked growth but, further, they represented a type of labour distinctive alike in its elasticity of supply, its responsiveness to economic incentives and its tractability in the hands of management (Piore, 1979). In the growth model proposed by Kindleberger, the availability of labour with such characteristics encourages investment, permits high profits and then in turn encourages reinvestment in a virtuous circle. Moreover, where employers can draw on migrant labour more or less at will, the bargaining position of indigenous labour is inevitably weakened, whatever its level of organisation. It is notable, for example, that where liberal theorists saw in the moderation of the wage claims of West German unions in the 1950s and 1960s a prime illustration of growing 'maturity', Kindleberger would point rather to the brute facts of labour supply (1967: 34).

By the end of the 1960s, the impetus to growth given by migrant labour was clearly reduced. With the settlement of some proportion of migrants and the consequent growth of communities of migrant families, it became apparent that increasing social costs would have to be set against the economic advantages of this form of labour supply. For this reason, therefore, and also in response to rising prejudice and hostility against migrants, governments generally moved towards more restrictive immigration policies (UN, 1979; Rist, 1979). This tendency was then strengthened with the growing economic uncertainty of the early 1970s, and those economies which had drawn most heavily on migrant workers, such as the West German, French, Austrian and Swiss, were able to extract one further advantage from them – that is, by 'exporting' some substantial part of their increasing unemployment, in pursuit of what have been called 'beggar-my-neighbour' labour-market policies (Pichelmann & Wagner, 1983). However, what must here be emphasised is that despite stricter controls on migrant workers, aimed chiefly at preventing settlement, and despite the extent of return migration, still at the present time persons of foreign birth represent from 5 to 15 per cent of the total population in most of the major countries of western Europe and generally constitute a somewhat higher proportion of the active labour force. Moreover, these foreign workers continue to be to a large extent distinctive in the market and work relationships in which they are involved, and in ways which maintain their functional importance for western economies in the straitened circumstances of the present as in the previous years of expansion.

This is most obviously the case with that part of the migrant work force which is in effect 'unfree' labour – that is, which consists of workers recruited for specific employers and jobs and for strictly limited periods. Labour of this kind, which can be hired, utilised and then discharged, as employers require, can clearly play an important part in counteracting the rigidities of indigenous labour markets. So too can the further number of foreign workers found in all host societies who are illegal or otherwise 'undocumented' migrants, and who are thus in a particularly poor bargaining position *vis-à-vis* employers and indeed highly vulnerable to exploitation. Furthermore, though, the remainder of the migrant work force, comprising its more permanent or settled members who are not tied to particular employments, is still typically differentiated as labour from the bulk of that drawn from native populations: *de jure* in lacking certain of the civil, political, social and industrial rights of full citizenship, and *de facto* in lacking organisational protection. It is estimated that only around a quarter of all migrant workers in western Europe are members of trade unions, which is a particularly low proportion in view of their occupational and industrial distribution; and moreover, unions have for the most part taken an uncertain and ambivalent attitude towards migrants and have shown relatively little concern with their specific problems (Castles & Kosack, 1973; Rist, 1979). At the same time, efforts by migrant workers to form their own organisations have not been highly effective in the face of difficulties stemming from their lack of rights, their cultural diversity and their high mobility.[7]

In the context of present-day capitalist societies, one could then conclude, migrant workers serve in part as a kind of 'industrial reserve army', whose members may be mobilised and discharged in response to major economic fluctuations, but more importantly as an important component of a 'secondary' labour force in the sense of a pool of labour, permanently available in these societies, which is highly exposed to market forces and to managerial authority alike.[8] In this latter respect, the presence of migrant labour may be seen as, so to speak, the counterpart of the success of workers within the mainstream or 'primary' labour force in gaining rights and organisational strength as a defence against economic uncertainty in general and, more specifically, against the logic of capitalism that would have labour treated as the variable factor of production. Thus Piore has remarked (1979: 42) that 'at root, the migrants provide a way in which workers in the native labour force are able to escape the role to which the [capitalist] system assigns them'. But, conversely, it could as well be said that it is in so far as these latter workers *have made their escape* that the system needs to recruit labour from other sources of a kind which can help restore its flexibility.[9]

While turning to labour drawn from outside the national community is one resort open to employers confronted with persisting qualitative as much as quantitative problems of labour supply, another and somewhat more radical response can also be identified which is similarly productive of dualism. This involves – as well as perhaps the tapping of new sources of labour – the creation or encouragement by employers of forms of production and of associated work-roles and employment relations which in themselves serve to ease or to avoid labour problems.

In liberal theories of industrialism it was envisaged that, in order to meet requirements of reliability and predictability, production would increasingly be carried out according to one standard pattern: namely, that of the large-scale, bureaucratically-organised enterprise, run by a professional management team and regulating its work-force through a complex 'web of rules' that are in substantial part negotiated 'constitutionally' with union representatives (Harbison & Myers, 1959; Kerr *et al.*, 1960; Kerr, 1983). A long-term historical shift in the direction of this pattern may perhaps be recognised, even if with a wide and persisting degree of cross-national variation. But what is now also becoming clear is not only that the dominance of the 'modern' enterprise is in many industrial societies still far from complete, but further that, in the context of present economic difficulties, there is a rather widespread tendency for other forms of production to increase rather than to diminish in importance. And what the latter tend to have in common is that they entail employment relationships which, rather than being closely rule-governed, are in large part either conditioned directly by market forces or subject to employers' *fiat*.

Thus, for example, there would now appear to be an increase in many western economies in the extent to which large-scale enterprises hive off some part of their production under subcontract to smaller concerns. As several authors have documented, this practice has assumed major proportions in France and in Italy, two countries in which traditions of small-scale enterprise have persisted particularly strongly, and in which therefore ample opportunities for such subcontracting are available (Paci, 1979; Berger, 1981; Berger & Piore, 1980; Brusco & Sabel, 1981; Brusco, 1982). Through subcontracting, employers are of course able to give themselves some protection against fluctuations in demand, but it is further attractive as a means whereby employers can avoid the labour-market rigidities and limitations on the utilisation of labour that are associated with the activities of powerful unions. Small firms can typically offer non-unionised work-forces, flexible wages and also exemption from – or disregard of – many restrictive features of health and safety regulations and other labour legislation. It is notable that a sharp upturn in the amount of subcontracting occurred in France after the strike wave of May–June 1968 and in Italy after that of the 'hot autumn' of 1969, in both of which instances the outbreak of worker militancy led to a strengthening of the unions' presence in large enterprises and to new legislation which extended workers' rights and threatened increased restraints on employers' customary powers in regard to discharges and deployment.[10]

Moreover, what is perhaps of yet wider significance is the growth of various kinds of employment which serve to enlarge another major component of the secondary labour force, namely, that of casual or marginal workers. For example, a further feature of the present-day Italian economy is the amount of 'outwork' undertaken by individuals or family groups in their own homes and also the extent of 'labour only' subcontracting, especially in the construction trades and services (Paci, 1973, 1979; Berger & Piore, 1980; Villa, 1981); and such employment – whether licit, 'black' or some shade of grey – would appear to be spreading extensively in many other western societies (De Grazia, 1980). Again, there is evidence of a general increase in temporary work, and in some countries, notably France, this is now extensively organised by special agencies which in effect deal in labour (Berger & Piore, 1980; Michon, 1981). Finally, there has in most western economies been a marked growth in part-time working, especially by married women. The increase in the participation rates of married women which has typically occurred in these economies over recent decades is substantially, and in some cases entirely, the result of an increase in part-time employment. And while not all those in such employment could be properly regarded as marginal workers – for example, many women in professional occupations in the public sector – it is none the less evident that in this way the secondary labour force has often been considerably expanded.

Like the subcontracting of production, 'non-standard' employment arrangements of the kind in question have the advantage for employers of reducing risk in the face of uncertain demand, and provide work-forces which are rendered flexible by the very terms on which they are engaged. With out-work and labour-only subcontracting, the regulation of labour is of course largely left to the direct effects of economic incentives and constraints; while both temporary and part-time workers are typically excluded from at least the full range of protection and benefit afforded under legislation on redundancy, dismissal, sick and maternity leave, equal pay, etc. as well as having only very low rates of union membership. It is furthermore important to recognise how opportunities for non-standard employment serve to mobilise a previously latent supply of labour from among groups who, for various reasons, would not otherwise regard themselves as being on offer – most obviously, perhaps, married women with young children but, in addition, juveniles, semi-retired persons, peasant-workers, and various others seeking 'second' jobs. For, what members of these groups have in common is that their commitment to the work they have taken on tends to be strictly limited and, in turn, their expectations of what they will be able to derive from it: typically, they have other sources of identity and satisfaction, and also perhaps of economic support. On account therefore of their location within the wider social structure, as well as of the form of their employment, such workers are unlikely to constitute a labour force in which any very strong interest in developing greater organisational power and in curtailing managerial prerogatives either exists or can easily be developed.

From the foregoing it should be fairly apparent how dualist tendencies in modern western societies – no less than the corporatist tendencies previously considered – entail major departures from the model of pluralistic indus-trialism which, for liberal theorists, is the focus of convergent development. Thus, the massive influx and the substantial settlement of migrant workers was not only something which itself had no place in the scenarios constructed by these theorists, but further, the consequences that have directly followed are not readily reconciled with the conceptions of the emerging social order that they offered. Most obviously, those very attributes which make migrants an attractive source of labour supply for capitalist economies – their imper-manence or, if settled, their restricted rights and lack of adequate organis-ational representation – are at the same time ones which serve largely to exclude them from the pluralist polity. In contrast with other groups definable within the social division of labour, they are seriously impeded in seeking to strengthen their economic position through collective action. Furthermore, though, migrant workers and their families represent an element in the popu-lations of western industrial societies which must stand as a rather striking exception to liberal theses of increasing equality, cultural homogeneity and social integration. In view of the concentration of migrants in the least desirable types of work, of their degree of material deprivation, and of their low levels of social amenity and opportunity, they might seem well described as forming an 'under-class' – a class, that is, inferior to the lowest strata of their host society. However, as commentators such as Moore (1977) and Giner and Salcedo (1978) have pointed out, the main qualification to such a view must be that it tends to underestimate the extent to which migrants live apart from their host society altogether – differentiated from other groups and strata not only by the nature of the economic relations and circumstances in which they are involved but further by their language, their ethnicity, and the total meaning of their presence in the society.[11]

Those members of indigenous populations who are drawn on, together with migrant workers, in the development of secondary labour forces clearly do not share in the same situation of general 'apartness'. What, rather, is distinctive in their case – but also creates difficulties for the model of pluralistic industrialism – is their lack of integration specifically into the world of industrial work or, that is, their very role as casual or marginal labour. For the implication of this is not that they are of limited economic import-ance but, on the contrary, that they are of functional value to the economic system because of the fact that they *are* highly *disponible* or, in other words, because they stand largely outside, and in fact may not seek strenuously to become involved in, the 'web of rules' which, for liberal theorists, represents the characteristically modern way of regulating employment relationships. While, then, these workers are not, like migrants, effectively denied partici-pation in the political life of their society, they are comparable with – and indeed often substitutable for – the latter (Piore, 1979; ch. 4) in that they represent labour which is largely excluded from the systems of *industrial* citizenship built up within western nations in the course of the present century. Liberal theorists emphasised the steady upgrading of employment and the institutionalisation of labour relations which they saw as following from the logic of industrialism. However, it is now evident that what they failed to anticipate was the way in which the logic of capitalism has required, as the counterpart to the evolving mainstream or primary labour force, the creation of a further body of labour that is still capable of being treated essentially as a commodity.

Alternatives for the future

In the foregoing it has been argued that far from western capitalist societies following convergent paths of development, focused on the model of pluralistic industrialism, the recent experience of western European nations would suggest that the applicability of this model is in fact tending more to diminish than to widen. Moreover, it has been contended that this is so because, rather than pluralist forms of society and polity being progressively favoured as those functionally most consistent with an exigent logic of industrialism, it has become apparent that some serious incompatibility arises between pluralism and the requirements of *capitalist* industrial economies. The increased power of organised interests – and of organised labour in particular – which pluralism facilitates and encourages within capitalist society, results in the operation of market mechanisms being impeded or restricted to a degree which undermines the effiency of the economy and frustrates standard techniques of macro-economic management. Growing awareness of this incompatibility has therefore led to movements away from the pluralist model which are of clearly divergent kinds: that is, ones going either in the direction of corporatism and aiming, so to speak, at the institutional transcendance of pluralism, or in the direction of dualism and aiming at the effective limitation of the provisions of pluralism in regard to a certain range of economic actors and collectivities.

In this concluding section, the aim is to extend the critique of liberal theories of industrialism so far presented in one other, highly consequential, way: that is, by showing that the contrasting responses to the difficulties of modern western economies that are represented by corporatism and dualism can, and often do, embody 'real ideological alternatives' of the kind which, according to liberal theorists, the coming of advanced industrialism would progressively eliminate. It is by no means supposed that either corporatist or dualist tendencies may be understood simply as reflections of dominant ideological currents in the societies in which they occur. Indeed, it is clear enough from the historical record that developments in both directions have often come about as the result of what were, for the actors concerned, essentially pragmatic measures devised in the face of immediate and pressing problems, and further that such measures have been greatly influenced by the specific, historically-formed circumstances of different national societies and the possibilities for 'solutions' that these appeared to afford (*cf.* Berger & Piore, 1980; Marin, 1983). Moreover, it is also evident that corporatist and dualist tendencies can to some significant degree *co-exist* within the same society – as might of course be expected if both are responses to the same underlying problems. None the less, what may still be maintained is that these tendencies do carry with them ideological implications in, so to speak, an objective sense; and, further, that to the extent that these implications are made manifest, they will appear as ones which stand in strong opposition to each other. Rather more sharply, the argument may be put as follows: if one envisages an industrial society in which corporatist arrangements and practices of the kind that emerged in the 1960s and 1970s were sustained and developed over several more decades, then this would have to be seen as a very different kind of society, ideologically as well as institutionally – and indeed in its entire structure of social power and advantage – from one in which dualist features had become likewise established.

It is, first of all, worth noting that in the emergence of corporatist and dualist tendencies, a marked contrast arises over which actors take the crucial role. In the case of corporatism, this is clearly assumed by the unions and their members. Although actual proposals for corporatist arrangements are likely to come from government, this has typically been as a response to the demonstrated strength of the unions in labour markets; and whether or not unions are willing and able to participate effectively must, thus far at least, be reckoned as the major issue on which the success or failure of such arrangements has turned. Instances can be readily cited in which unions have been unable to agree even the initial terms for a 'partnership' with government (e.g. Delors, 1978); or in which corporatist arrangements have collapsed either as a result of the withdrawal of union leaders or of their inability to 'deliver' their rank and file (e.g. Akkermans & Grootings, 1978; Müller-Jentsch & Sperling, 1978). However, where unions do become firmly engaged in political bargaining with government, employers, even if disapproving, may still find it hard to avoid being drawn into participation themselves, since this is a preferable option to simply standing aside. In the case of dualism, on the other hand, it is employers and their managements who are of central importance. It is they who take the lead in tapping new sources of labour supply and in developing new methods of organising production and new forms of employment. Governments may act supportively as, for example, in facilitating migration or in modifying labour or social security legislation; but, in contrast with corporatist endeavours, the dualist response is essentially a decentralised one. In this case, it is the unions who are placed in the position of being able only to react to initiatives taken by others. Their attitudes to most manifestations of dualism have been hostile, but such hostility has not in fact been widely translated into effective counter-measures.

It can furthermore be claimed that although a corporatist basis for economic policy-making and management may be compatible with, and might even seem to be favoured by, some degree of economic dualism, the continued development of both corporatist and dualist tendencies within the same society must give rise to increasing tension between them. This is so because the general orientations in economic – and also in social – policy with which these tendencies have evident affinities are of clearly divergent kinds which, ultimately, presuppose quite different balance-of-power situations.

Thus, corporatism may be said to imply not only a highly interventionist approach by government, but further one that has a quite distinctive slant. To begin with, unions engaging in political bargaining in the context of stagflation may be expected to take as their first objective that of 'equality of sacrifice' – or, in other words, that of ensuring that governments do not deflect on to labour an excessive part of the costs involved in the adaptation of national economies to less favourable conditions. And indeed it can be shown that, over the period since the ending of the long boom, a rather strong association exists between the prevalence of corporatist arrangements and levels of employment (Schmidt, 1982 a, 1982 b; Cameron, 1985). It is only in the three countries earlier referred to as those where corporatism has become most securely established – Austria, Sweden, and Norway – that the goal of full employment has been kept at least within sight. Governments acting in partnership with unions have been clearly more likely than others to make positive efforts to maintain employment levels – whether through conventional demand-management undertaken in conjunction with incomes policy, through 'active' labour market and job creation policies, or through various policies aimed at sheltering the domestic labour force against external threats – including that of migrants. Moreover, the other major element in the *quid pro quo* that is typically sought by unions in return for labour-market restraint is a commitment by government to at least maintaining, and as far as possible expanding, social welfare provisions which have some redistributive effect. And again there are indications that this strategy has had a measure of success (Schmidt, 1982 b; van Arnhem & Schotsman, 1982; Cameron 1985). However, a continuing participation in political bargaining and exchange, with outcomes of the kind in question, is not something that unions can simply opt for. On the contrary – as earlier arguments have implied – such participation is only likely to be achieved, even if desired, in so far as national union movements possess two key attributes: first, considerable power within labour markets and, second, a high degree of cohesion and discipline based ultimately on class solidarity. For without the former, unions have nothing to bargain with at the political level, and there is little reason why governments should seek to enter into – inevitably difficult – negotiations with them; while without the second, unions will be unable to overcome the ever-present threat of sectionalism and to secure their members' acceptance of the political bargains to which they have committed them.

Dualism cannot, in the same way as corporatism, be directly linked with specific objectives in economic and social policies: as already suggested, the present extent of dualistic tendencies within modern economies has to be understood largely in terms of distinctive features of their historical development. None the less, what can be claimed is that the strengthening of such tendencies – the widening of those sectors of production in which market forces and managerial authority are relatively unimpeded – accords extremely well with the policy orientations of what has of late become known as the 'new *laissez-faire*'. And what is distinctive about the latter as an approach to political economy is that, in direct contrast with that characteristic of corporatism, it involves an explicit retraction by government of responsibility for maintaining any particular level or pattern of economic activity, and an insistence that the performance of the economy is primarily dependent on those who play the key roles within markets and production units. The task of government is essentially that of providing an institutional context within which market incentives and disciplines can operate effectively and investors,

entrepreneurs and employers – the actual creators of wealth – can enjoy a
wide freedom of action (Keohane, 1978; Goldthorpe, forthcoming). Thus
it is notable that the Thatcher regime in the UK, which may be taken as the
leading exemplar of the new *laissez-faire* to date, is clearly bent on enlarging
the size of the 'exposed' work-force within the economy, whether directly
by such measures as removing 'fair wages' clauses from public contracts or
the abolition of Wages Councils, or indirectly by paring back social welfare
benefits and thus reducing the 'reserve price' of labour. At the same time
a remarkable emphasis has been given to the part to be played by small
businesses in restoring efficiency and prosperity to the British economy, not
least through the contribution which it is believed they can make to the overcoming of labour problems (Scase & Goffee, 1980; Elliott & McCrone, 1982).
It is moreover equally relevant to observe that the idea of political bargaining
with unions was rejected from the first, as endowing them with a quite
unwarranted power and influence outside their legitimate sphere of action;
and that various legislative measures have been taken, or are planned, the chief
significance of which lies in the limits they seek to impose precisely on the
unions' potential to serve as a vehicle for class-oriented – rather than simply
sectional – action, which might be of political effect. The most obvious
example here is the outlawing of 'sympathetic' and 'political' strikes, but
much of the government's expressed concern with creating greater democracy
within unions would seem in fact to be directed more towards undermining
what Pizzorno (1978 b) has referred to as their 'capacity for strategy'.

Finally, if one looks to the future, there are good grounds for expecting
that the ideological divergence implicit in corporatist and dualist tendencies
will emerge still more sharply from the different issues that they will respectively place on the political agenda, and from the different socio-political
cleavages and conflicts to which these issues will give rise. As several commentators have noted, while corporatist arrangements often face the threat of
a collapse of labour support, they have also to be seen as subject to repeated
renegotiation on account of the enlargement of the demands that unions
believe that they can – and in their members' interests must – make in return
for their participation (Martin, 1979; Lange, 1979; Schmitter, 1983;
Goldthorpe, forthcoming). And already observable developments leave little
doubt that among such new demands will be ones that imply an increasing
entrenchment on basic institutional and structural features of capitalist
society: for example, demands for greater public control over the extent and
pattern of investment – witness the recent struggle over wage-earner funds
in Sweden – or for the reorientation of various aspects of social policy on
to more decisively egalitarian lines (*cf.* Esping-Anderson & Korpi, 1985). It
may be unduly optimistic to suppose, as some authors have done (e.g.
Stephens, 1979), that political bargaining via corporatist institutions – and
under social-democratic hegemony – amounts in effect to a non-revolutionary
mode of transition from capitalism to socialism. But, on the other hand,

it would seem quite inadequate to regard corporatist tendencies in modern societies, in the manner of more orthodox Marxist writers, as reflecting no more than the latest or 'highest' form of the social control of labour under capitalism and as quite lacking in radical potential (e.g. Panitch, 1977 b, 1981; Jessop, 1978). What corporatist institutions can be said to provide is a distinctive context within which the class conflicts of a capitalist society may be carried on. The eventual outcome of such conflicts will depend on the relative success of contending organisational leaderships in mobilising and sustaining support within their constituencies; but under corporatism as here understood, labour attains a position in which it can at least make the attempt to convert its market strength into political measures designed to advance working-class interests in a wide ranging and more permanent manner than could be achieved through action in the industrial sphere alone. [12]

In contrast, to the extent that dualist tendencies prevail, it must be questionable if such measures will be on the political agenda at all. From the standpoint of the unions, the first concern must be that of how best they can secure their labour-market power against the threats that dualism can pose. And what would in this respect seem crucial is which of two very different strategies national union movements aim to pursue: that is, whether they strive to uphold a class orientation, which must entail as far as possible opposing dualism – for example, by seeking legislation which can check employers' attempts to generate it and by regarding secondary workers, even if not union members, as still forming part of the unions' constituency; or whether, on the other hand, they in effect accept dualism and fall back on the defence of the specific sectional interests of their enrolled members, in the hope that these interests may then be as much protected as undermined by dualism through the 'shock-absorber' function that the secondary work-force performs (*cf.* Sengenberger, 1981).

While both these strategies have their own logic, there can be no doubt that it is the first which is by far the more difficult to implement. Thus, for example, in the course of the 1970s the Italian unions sought to use a significant increase in their labour-market strength and in their organisational unity as a basis for a new departure into political bargaining, in which their objectives were explicitly conceived in terms of broad class interests and solidarity. Their 'core' membership, comprising mainly industrial workers in the North, were to exercise restraint in pay negotiations in return for reforms in social policy and government efforts to expand and redirect investment so as to improve labour-market prospects for workers in the Mezzogiorno and also for women and young people (Regini, 1982). In the event, however, this initiative proved disappointing to the unions in that government largely failed to deliver (Lange *et al.*, 1982; Regini, 1985); and in more recent attempts to secure a 'political exchange' – in which their own position has been weaker than before – it is notable that the unions have clearly reduced their ambitions and concentrated far more on safeguarding the employment of their core members themselves (Regini, 1984). Furthermore, what must in turn become open to question, if the ideological basis of the period of *solidarietà nazionale* is now eroding, is whether political bargaining on *any* terms will prove to be sustainable in the face of the inevitable sectionalist pressure for a return to unrestrained labour-market action, which the prevalence of dualism can only accentuate.[13] As is well brought out by several commentators on the present-day West German situation, the possibility of dispersing the costs of economic adjustment within a pool of secondary labour, rather than 'internalising' them, is a powerfully attractive one to union movements, even where they possess some tradition of more solidaristic strategies (Sengenberger, 1981, 1983; Brandt, 1983; Streeck, 1983, 1985). What may be envisaged in the West German case, and perhaps elsewhere, it has been suggested, is the progressive 'Japanisation' of the economy, in the sense of the development of extensive dualism alongside the growing involvement of members of the primary work-force in various forms of 'micro-corporatism' at the level of plants and enterprises. To the extent that national union movements do thus accommodate to dualism, there is only one long-term result that may be expected: that is – in direct contrast to the prospect of creative, if stressful, conflict afforded by political bargaining – the fundamental division and effective depoliticisation of the working class, with the concomitant disappearance of any organised challenge to the capitalist order in the name of economic democracy and social equality.

In sum, what may be maintained is that over recent decades western capitalist societies have moved in divergent directions in their responses to economic problems and further that, in consequence, they now face different sets of political choices in which 'real ideological alternatives' are in fact inherent. Which alternatives will be pursued, to what extent, and with what degree of success are questions that cannot be answered in advance and will be determined only by the future course of political action in particular nations. But what may at least be said is that there is no longer any reason for supposing, in the manner of the liberal theorists of industrialism, that either the course or the results of such action will be so constrained by the functional requirements of modern economies that 'the road ahead', whatever actors' goals may be, must lead to the one ultimate destination of pluralistic industrialism. On the contrary, it is the difficulties that have been encountered in reconciling the expression of pluralism within a capitalist society with the efficient working of the capitalist economy that have chiefly energised the corporatist and dualist departures from pluralism that are now evident. To future observers of the western capitalist world, it may well appear that the failure of a nation to achieve decisive modifications of the pluralist model – in one direction or another – is the typical concomitant of persisting economic decline.

Notes

1 The following draws on the works by Aron, Kerr *et al.* and Parsons already cited; *cf.* also the more specific discussions of industrialism and stratification found in Lipset, 1969 and Treiman, 1970.

2 It is of particular importance to the argument being advanced here that the tendencies described were ones which progressively emerged over the post-war years – thus clearly prefiguring the 'stagflation' widely experienced in the 1970s, and in turn constituting strong evidence against the claim (*cf.* OECD, 1977) that the declining performance of western economies could be largely understood in terms of an unfortunate coincidence of 'external shocks' plus policy errors. As Cagan has noted for the US (1979: ch. 1; *cf.* Sachs, 1980) – and the same observation could be made more generally – what was distinctive about the inflations of the post-war years was not the rate of price increases, but rather the fact that in intervening recessionary periods prices hardly declined at all – or even continued to rise. *Cf.* also Olson (1982: 219–20).

3 This argument obviously owes much to the critiques of the liberal pluralist model of interest representation which has been presented by authors such as Schmitter, 1974, 1981, 1983, Berger, 1981 and Lehmbruch, 1983, at the same time as they have drawn attention to the development of new corporatist tendencies in the general sense here intended. However, it could be said that one source of the confusion attending current debates on corporatism has been a tendency of some critics of the pluralist model to exaggerate the extent to which its exponents would see government as no more than an 'inert' recipient of group pressures (*cf.* Martin, 1983). The issues are clarified in so far as critical emphasis is placed on the inadequacies of the pluralist model in recognising (i) the role that governments may play in the concertation of interests; (ii) the role that organisations may play in the formulation of interests and in their 'intermediation' (Schmitter, 1974) as distinct from *either* simply representing interests *or* controlling or disciplining their members; and (iii) the qualitative difference that exists between classic pressure-group politics – even where this involves some degree of 'symbiosis' between a private interest and an agency of government – and a situation in which government engages in concerted political bargaining with two or more competing or conflicting organisations, each of which has a 'capacity for strategy' (Pizzorno, 1978 b) and can engage in interest intermediation.

4 It is important to note that although liberal writers – such as Ross and Hartman – themselves argued that increased possibilities for political action on the part of unions was a factor in reducing the recourse to strikes, the political action they had in mind was clearly that of unions acting as pressure groups – seeking improved labour legislation, social welfare provision etc. – while continuing to engage in free collective bargaining. What, however, may now be said – in the light of the industrial relations record of the 1960s and 1970s – is that the development of institutional arrangements facilitating this latter pattern of union behaviour, rather than the trade-off of labour-market for political-bargaining strength, need in no way be conducive to the 'withering away' of the strike. This point is one quite overlooked in Batstone's recent (1984) attempt to rehabilitate Ross and Hartman.

5 It is in this connection of interest to note Lehmbruch's, 1983 critique of the thesis advanced by Almond and Powell, 1966 that a linear relationship exists between the degree of 'sub-system autonomy' within a total political system and that system's problem-solving capacities. Rather, Lehmbruch suggests, the relationship may be a U-shaped one. Although the low level of sub-system autonomy

found within Eastern European socialist societies can be regarded as having
negative consequences, so too may the high level found in, say, the USA – while
some western European polities have been increasing their capacities by moving
towards an intermediate position of 'limited' sub-system autonomy. As
Lehmbruch observes, there are very obvious affinities between the conception
of a polity with high sub-system autonomy and the pluralist model of interest
representation (*cf.* also Almond, 1970).

6   Dualism, no less than corporatism, is a concept which in the recent past has
aroused a great deal of fervent, but often not very illuminating, debate – for
valuable critical reviews see Cain, 1976 and Hodson and Kaufman, 1982. It must
therefore be stressed that the way in which the concept is used here does *not*
imply any commitment to the idea of dual – or segmented – labour markets which
are identifiable either by the existence of strong barriers to mobility between them
or (necessarily) by differing returns to labour of similar quality and productive
potential. What rather is crucial is, in a phrase, the degree to which labour is
commodified: or, that is, the degree to which workers' wages, conditions, work-
tasks, job-security etc. are exposed to the effects of market forces and to the
exercise of employers' – or their managements' – prerogatives, rather than being
protected by legislation, by work-rules embodied in collective agreements (or
custom and practice), or simply by a capacity for organised action. Although
it is in principle, possible for this degree of exposure or protection to vary continuously, the central argument of the paper leads to the expectation that at least
a marked 'bimodality' will tend empirically to be found. There is an obvious
affinity between the dualism here suggested and that implicit in Hicks's, 1974
distinction between the 'fix-price' and 'flex-price' sectors of modern economies
(*cf.* also Olson, 1983).

7   It is of interest to note that in the rather exceptional British case, in which, up
to the passing of the Immigration Act of 1971, Commonwealth migrants could
generally lay claim to citizenship and Irish migrants hold a special status, it was
never government policy – as it often was in other western European countries
– to give positive encouragement to the inflow of migrant workers for specifically
economic reasons. For an insightful comparison of the British and French cases,
see Freeman, 1979.

8   For arguments on the extent to which migrant workers may or may not be usefully
rgarded as constituting an 'industrial reserve army', *cf.* Rosenberg, 1977 and
Lever-Tracy, 1983. The crucial issue is of course how far migrants may be seen
as potentially substitutable for, rather than as essentialy complementary to, native
labour.

9   This is not to deny that employers may – even in the absence of unions – accord
to at least some part of their labour force conditions of employment similar to
those that unions would seek to obtain. One motivation for this may be to forestall
unionisation; but, in addition, employers may well feel that they can thus derive
real advantages by winning the goodwill and co-operativeness of certain key
groups of workers. (*Cf.* Thurow, 1980: ch. 3.) It may be added that in their earlier
writings Kerr, Dunlop, and other American authors who subsequently became
leading exponents of the theory of pluralistic industrialism emphasised the
advantages to employers of developing 'internal' labour markets, which operated
almost independently of 'external' ones; and in this way they can in fact be
regarded as among the pioneers of an interest in economic dualism (*cf.* Cain,
1976). Yet, strangely, this idea is, as already noted, almost entirely excluded from
their later work.

10 A tendency on the part of employers to 'decentralise' production in ways often
involving increased subcontracting is, however, evident in many other western

industrial societies (*cf.* Wilkinson, ed., 1981).

11 It should not, for example, be supposed that migrant workers eligible for citizenship of their host nations will generally wish to take this up – as is shown by recent experience in West Germany. It should also be added here that to the extent that migrant workers *have* engaged in collective political activity, this has – not surprisingly – been largely expressed outside the accepted channels of parliamentary democracy. An important question for the future is that of the political orientations and modes of action of the second generation (*cf.* Miller, 1981).

12 It is, it may be noted, the Thatcher regime in Britain which has most decisively undermined orthodox Marxist interpretations of corporatism of the kind referred to in the text. Thatcher and her ideological mentors saw far more clearly than Marxists were apparently able to do the radical potential of new corporatist tendencies based on union involvement in political bargaining and have unremittingly opposed them. Arguments presently being advanced by some British Marxists to the effect that sooner or later a 'monetarist corporatism' must emerge are, to say the least, implausible.

13 A more positive view than that implied here is presented by Regini, 1984, who emphasises that so far at least 'il dualismo non ha trionfato' and sees the possibility in the Italian case of some long-term coexistence of dualism with union involvement in political bargaining, albeit on relatively restricted terms.

7 *C. C. Harris, R. M. Lee, L. D. Morris*

Redundancy in steel: labour-market behaviour, local social networks and domestic organisation

Introduction

In December 1979 the British Steel Corporation announced its intention to reduce the number of its employees from 150,000 to below 100,000 nationwide. At the BSC works at Port Talbot, near Swansea, this involved the loss of 5,800 jobs out of the 1979 total of 12,500. At that time unemployment in Britain stood at 7 per cent. It was expected that the redundancies in steel would at least double if not treble the unemployment rate in the areas dependent on the steel industry, creating a sharp differential between such areas and the rest of the country.

In the event the expected unemployment differential never emerged: as Dr Fevre's study of the Port Talbot labour market has shown (Fevre, 1983), the redundancies in steel were merely the particular local manifestation of the nationwide recession. Fevre goes on to show that employment opportunities declined during the 1970s rather less in Port Talbot than in the county of West Glamorgan as a whole. When the redundancies in steel took place, only briefly did they result in Port Talbot's cumulative job loss exceeding that of the county as a whole, where job losses produced by the deepening recession soon equalled those produced by the redundancies in steel. Hence Port Talbot never became the unemployment blackspot predicted early in 1980.[1]

The absence of any marked unemployment differential between Port Talbot and West Glamorgan, and West Glamorgan and traditional areas of Welsh migration, resulted in the lack of any significant migration response to the redundancies.[2] This posed problems for the research reported here which had been designed to compare the domestic and local social circumstances of migrating and non-migrating steelworkers made redundant from the Port Talbot plant. 'Local labour-market behaviour' was therefore substituted for 'migration response' as the focus of the study some fifteen months after its commencement.[3] Though the study had defined the local labour market of

'West Industrial South Wales' (Harris, 1982 a), and some theoretical attention had been given to the notion of a labour market at the outset of the
project (Harris, 1981), the 'local labour market' had been used in the original
study not as an object of enquiry but as a way of defining a locality which
constituted the context of migration 'decisions'.

Once the focus of the study was redefined it became vital that information
about the demand side of the labour market be obtained, but West Industrial
South Wales constituted far too large an area for the research team to undertake a detailed study. It was necessary that methods of job search and job
acquisition be studied through the surveys, but while job-acquisition data
can and have been obtained, it is very difficult to obtain job-search data
through the survey method unless something approximating to a consciously, formally *Zweck rational* orientation is adopted by respondents – a
condition rarely fulfilled empirically.[4] While the relation between migration
and non-migration and different types of network and domestic organisation
had been specified at the outset, the relation between domestic organisation,
network type and labour-market behaviour was unclear, largely because
categories for the classification of labour-market behaviour were unclear.

There was therefore a tendency to focus on the *outcomes* of labour-market
behaviour and to substitute for 'migrant/non-migrant' 'employed/
unemployed'.We were encouraged in this naivety by our reading of existing
redundancy studies (see, for example, Mackay & Reid, 1971), which have
tended to be concerned with who gets into which jobs how quickly, and in
which job-search behaviour is related to successful or unsuccessful employment outcomes. However, the data emerging from Morris's field study
showed clearly that many redundants had embarked on highly chequered
post-redundancy careers produced in part by changed employment practices,
and the survey data reflected the assortative character of the redundancy
process whereby the population of redundants came to be composed of
particular types of worker.[5]

As a result, the redundancy study has come to focus on the labour-market
histories of the redundants as the critical variable and is seeking to relate
this data, together with data on job acquisition, to data on domestic
organisation and local social networks.[6]

The approach adopted

(i) *Labour markets and households*

A local labour market is properly so-called because it performs the *function*
of a market in economic theory: it brings together buyers and sellers of a
commodity within a given area. However, it is not a market in the classical
economic sense for a number of reasons:

(a) It does not involve the exchange of a homogeneous commodity. The commodity is *not* homogeneous because labour power is differentiated by skill and experience. At the same time, prospective employers of workers, bearing in mind the necessity of converting labour power into *actual labour*, pay considerable attention to the *characteristics of the labourer* as well as to the quality of his/her *labour power*, and these factors further differentiate labour power and render it even less homogeneous.

(b) The knowledge involved on the part of both buyers and sellers is extremely imperfect and not dependent on the spatial location of the knower; indeed, a market may be conceived of as a plurality of ego-centred geographically based social areas within each of which ego is willing/able to undertake transactions.

A local labour market (LLM) is constituted by a population of a given area within which labour power is in fact bought and sold. Its reference is therefore to a concrete entity. It is a descriptive, not a theoretical concept. It does not refer, however, to a *specific* place or set of institutions by means of which labour is exchanged. If, therefore, it is the case that a given local area is an area within which labour power is bought and sold, then it is necessary to enquire as to exactly what institutional and other social mechanisms produce this 'market effect'.

Our conception of a local labour market does not therefore involve the assumption that any area and population so designated fulfils the conditions for the existence of a market as specified in economic theory. We assume, rather, that it contains practices and relationships which combine to produce the effects of a market understood as a social institution, i.e. the bringing together of the buyers and sellers of a commodity. We welcome the plea – for such we take it to be – made by the Cambridge Labour Studies Group (Craig *et al.*, this volume) that economics should return to the study of economic institutions and their operation thus making possible, once again, the sort of communication between economists and their colleagues in history, sociology and anthropology which has, in other times and places, been taken for granted.

The population of a LLM may be conceived of as differentiated, not only in terms of *whether* its members are *buyers or sellers* of labour power, but also in terms of the *type of labour power* which is bought and sold and the *characteristics of labourers* (sellers), and in terms of the *geographical location* of buyers and sellers. It is also differentiated in terms of the relation of market members to the *means of labour marketing*.

These means are of two kinds: formal and informal. The *formal* means are state-owned employment/labour exchanges (job centres), private employment agencies and public advertisement. The *informal* means are person-to-person contacts, or chains and networks thereof, which may be facilitated by institutions entirely unconnected with the buying and selling of labour power at the formal level: religious and political associations, pubs, clubs, and of course networks of kin relationships. It follows that not only is the relationship of the household to the productive process mediated by the labour market: the household's relationship to the market is mediated by its relation to the *means of labour marketing*.

To claim that households are differentiated by their position in the labour market is to claim, sociologically, much more than that they are differentiated by the types of labour power that they have to offer and the relative levels of supply and demand for that type of labour power in that area. It is to claim that they differ in their location within a local social structure, different positions within which vitally affect both the chances of their members obtaining any employment and of their obtaining particular types of employment. 'Types of employment' refers here not only to the nature of the labour they require and the differential rewards for work which they offer (wages, pensions, fringe benefits, hours of work and working conditions) but also to the degree of permanence of that employment and hence to the frequency with which the wage-earners come on to the labour market.

High levels of unemployment resulting from economic transitions transform households' relationships to production. They should be seen as doing so, however, not by affecting the number of households separated from that process by unemployment, but by affecting the *number* of households whose wage-earners *come onto the market*, the *frequency* with which wage-earners come on to the market, the importance of informal means of job acquisition relative to formal means, and hence the relative importance of the location of the household in local social structure as a determinant of its level of consumption and degree of economic security.

(ii) *Labour markets and redundancy*

Wood and Cohen (1977-8: 19–27) have argued in a sharply critical review of the literature on redundancy that there has been a general failure to examine what they describe as the 'social production of redundancy', and a specific failure to understand the relationship between redundancy and labour-market situations. Certainly as far as those workers made redundant from BSC Port Talbot are concerned, one cannot fully understand their labour-market situation without reference to the way in which they arrived in the market.

Where a decision to implement redundancy has been made, two broad problems arise for management. These are, put crudely: what is to go? and who is to go? In the case of a large-scale integrated production process, for example, the labour input associated with administration or some special kinds of maintenance may remain relatively fixed despite variations in the level of production capacity. As was the case at BSC, jobs in these sectors, while not entirely protected, may be cut back rather less in proportionate terms than production jobs. At the same time, other kinds of ancillary or support services may have a sufficiently fragmentary and self-contained character readily to permit their excision and resupply by contractors (see Rubery and Wilkinson, 1981). The way in which decisions are made in the redundancy process may therefore subsequently affect the *operation* of the labour market by changing its opportunity structure – for example, by increasing the number of short-term jobs available to those in the labour market. Furthermore, redundancy poses problems of control insofar as it introduces a process of invidious selection which leaves some individuals attached to the reduced stock of jobs while others are dismissed – a situation potentially difficult for management if individual resentment becomes mobilised into collective resistance.

One of the features of the Port Talbot redundancies was the use of 'cooling-out' mechanisms which facilitated the transition into the new and unsought status. Mechanisms of this kind include, according to Goffman (1952: 451–63): (a) the entrusting of disclosure concerning the new situation to some other thought capable of controlling resentment; (b) the provision of an alternative and/or compensatory status; (c) the maintenance of a fiction that the transition from a pre-existing role has been made willingly; and (d) the exchange of the current status for compensation.

All of these mechanisms can be seen to have operated in one way or another during the redundancies at BSC Port Talbot: the use of counsellors; the devolution of responsibility for the selection of individual redundants onto the trade unions who were in a position to formalise selection around rules such as 'last in – first out'; the offer of large-scale redundancy payments with additional premiums to be paid under certain conditions; the encouragement of early retirement, especially by those in relatively ill health; 'voluntary redundancy' (which might perhaps be more properly termed 'self-selected redundancy'); the offer of enhanced post-redundancy benefits from European Coal and Steel Community (ECSC) funds; the provision of advice on entrepreneurmanship and retraining.

A number of consequences of direct importance to the labour-market situation of the redundant follow from the deployment of cooling-out processes. Redundancy is likely to become an assortative process – that is, it encourages as a by-product of the selection process a *statistical* tendency for some groups or categories of worker to have a greater likelihood of selection or self-selection for redundancy. This is particularly true of older workers, the sick or otherwise impaired and those (like short-service workers) who have relatively little power. It is not difficult to see from this that the assortative character of redundancy will tend to produce a population of redundants biased towards those whose labour-market chances are relatively poor.

(iii) *Redundancy, labour markets and the informal economy*

One of the most notable effects of the assortative character of the redundancy process is that a significant proportion of redundants classify themselves as 'sick' or 'retired'. Hence they not only leave the books of their erstwhile employer, they also disappear from the unemployment register. For the remainder, the consequences of redundancy are not employment or unemployment, nor a transition from unemployment to different types of employment mediated by different types of job search, but a *post-redundancy career*[7] involving the movement of redundants through a sequence of post-redundancy statuses. We have provisionally termed careers consisting of a sequence of different status types 'chequered' (Harris, 1982 b). There will be variation *both* in the incidence of 'chequeredness' between different populations of redundants and between different categories of redundant. Variations in chequeredness between populations of redundants will not however simply be a *composition* effect resultant on different types and degrees of assortativeness in the redundancy process. It will also be a resultant of the types of employment available in the market in the post-redundancy period.

When the volume of redundancies is large relative to the market, the propensity of the demand for labour to engender chequered careers may be affected by the redundancies themselves as a result of the assortative character of the process of job excision. Hence the character of post-redundancy careers is a result of a complex interrelation between assortativeness in the redundancy process and the type of demand for labour in the market.

Redundancy does not necessarily involve simply the *loss* of jobs, however. It may involve the replacement of jobs of one type by jobs of another type. Redundancy from a work establishment which continues to exist after redundancy is not necessarily the result of reduced production or increased productivity or both. It can also be the result of an attempt by management not to *slim* the labour force, but to acquire greater *control over employment levels*, and this is particularly likely where the product market is extremely uncertain. If management succeeds in increasing its power to vary the size of its workforce, and does so, this will increase the 'chequeredness' propensity of the demand for labour.

Marginal jobs – those that come in and out of existence – may for a variety of reasons involve irregular employment outside the formal economy in one sense of that term. The workers in such jobs will have 'chequered' labour-market histories, i.e. mixed sequences and at least periods of employment and unemployment. Given that workers are living by means of a sequence of fixed-term jobs (whether regular or irregular), then their behaviour is best thought of in terms of an income-maintenance strategy rather than an employment strategy. Crucial to the maintenance of a given income level may well be the opportunity for ancillary employment. Hence there is likely to be an association between 'chequered' post-redundancy histories and informal economic activity.

There will nonetheless be considerable variation between redundants with regard to the chequeredness of their histories, and this will vary not only according to the supply of and demand for their particular skills but also according to their access to the means of labour marketing. Highly developed local social networks are likely to be a precondition both of obtaining a sequence of short fixed-term jobs and of obtaining opportunities for informal economic activity. However, whether or not the network of a given redundant will have this effect will depend on what it connects with, and this in turn will be related to previous labour-market history.

The relation between households and the market

Since the results of the field study of domestic organisation are reported elsewhere in this volume, this part of the research will be dealt with only briefly here and from the standpoint of the effect of domestic organisation on labour-market behaviour.

While redundancy has clearly affected domestic organisation, there is to say the least a marked continuity between patterns of domestic life before and after redundancy and a complete absence of anything amounting to a reversal of domestic roles (Morris, 1983 b). The differences that do exist between households and the variations produced by redundancy are not related in any direct way to labour-market behaviour, but are related *indirectly* through the network of social relationships within which households are embedded, precisely because these relationships connect or fail to connect redundants with work opportunities. The creation of redundancies on a large scale not only affects the character of networks but it also transforms the structure of job opportunities with which networks connect redundants and their households.

An integral part of the redundancy agreement (the 'slimline' plan) was the excision of certain functions and their supply by the use of contractors rather than by permanently employed 'direct labour'.[8] In this agreement the Corporation undertook to use its good offices to encourage contractors to employ ex-steelworkers. That contractors should have been willing to do this is not surprising since, under ECSC provisions, redundants were eligible to have their pay in employment after redundancy made up to 90 per cent of their BSC earnings for a limited period. As Fèvre has pointed out in a preliminary paper, this meant that the way was open for small, new (non-unionised) contracting firms to come in and take advantage of the rightward shift in the supply curve of redundant steel-worker labour which the 'subsidy' involved. Since most of the employment offered by contractors was of fixed term, the excision of departments by BSC and their replacement by contractors simultaneously created a population of redundants, increased the chequeredness propensity of labour demand, *and* increased the demand for redundant steelworkers to perform fixed-term jobs, thus increasing further their propensity to have 'chequered' post-redundancy careers. However at the same time it created a new breed of contractors who paid non-union rates, were not bound by national agreements and employed 'irregular', 'lump' labour (Fevre, Nov. 1983; Morris 1983 a).

The necessity to recruit ex-steelworkers, non-unionisation, and the – if not peripherally legal – at least peripherally institutional character of the employment offered by contractors, all combined to make the contractors depend heavily on informal means of labour recruitment. They wanted to recruit ex-steelworkers, eligible for make-up pay, who were not 'trouble-makers', who were 'reliable' and whose work skills (derived from the BSC experience) fitted the type of contract on which they were to be employed.

From the standpoint of the supply side, this meant that access to the work opportunities provided by contractors which replaced those lost through redundancy would depend on the access of redundants to the informal means of labour marketing. That is, redundants have differential chances of re-employment by contractors depending on the character of their networks.

In her field study Morris distinguishes three different types of social network: 'collective', 'dispersed' and 'individualistic' (Morris, 1983 c, d). Her data suggest that redundants with collective social-activity patterns are most likely to obtain work through informal means and have the best opportunity of obtaining jobs with contractors. This is not simply due to network interconnectedness, which would appear to maximise communication flow, but is rather a resultant of the moral character of the sets of 'collective' redundants. Job acquisition depends on the character of moral ties between employer and employed worker, and employed worker/collective network member and other *un*employed members of the network.

In contrast, redundants with *individualistic* social-activity patterns are least likely to be recruited to fixed-term employment, least likely to have chequered careers and more likely to experience long periods of unemployment and may be seen therefore to be in a relatively unfavourable labour-market situation.

However, it seems that 'individualistic' men have a better chance of obtaining a secure job – eventually – while the 'favourable' labour market position of the 'collectives' (predominantly skilled men with stable (non-chequered) work histories prior to redundancy) has resulted in their being shifted 'down market' into the 'secondary sector'.

In contrast to both social-activity categories are the 'dispersed' whose members have characteristically chequered pre-BSC labour-market histories and fewer skills. This category has the highest incidence of long-term unemployment.

There is some evidence to suggest that present social-activity type is powerfully influenced by previous labour-market history. Hence the character of redundants' social networks (for which the social-activity type is a surrogate) would appear to be both an historical outcome and a contemporary determinant of labour-market position. The manifold of relations in which the household is embedded not only determines the effect of post-redundancy labour-market career on the household. It is itself a determinant of the character of that career.

Labour-market careers and outcomes

That previous labour-market experience is a determinant of the type of post-redundancy career is also suggested by the survey data. Those who have chequered post-redundancy careers may be continuing a pattern established before they worked for BSC, since they are somewhat more likely to have had at least one spell of unemployment lasting a month or more before their entry into the steelworks and they are more likely to have had prior experience of self-employment. Individuals whose employment history since redundancy has been chequered are also rather more likely than those in the sample as a whole to have moved house since redundancy. In other words, as one might expect, there is a relationship between residential dislocation and employment dislocation. However, it should be emphasised that, as already noted, the incidence of moving in the Port Talbot redundancy survey is quite low and it would be a mistake to equate chequered post-redundancy careers solely with mobility.

Age is obviously a major factor associated with movement out of the labour market altogether, and it is also strikingly clear that the overwhelming majority of those who have experienced only unemployment since redundancy are aged over 50, and particularly so where they had had long periods of service at BSC. Presumably those in this position are relatively unattractive to employers and, given the length of time they have been in employment, they may be unfavourably situated in relation to the means of labour marketing. There would not, however, appear to be any clear-cut relationship between age and other kinds of post-redundancy experience.

If one distinguishes broadly between the *employed*, the *unemployed* and the *chequered* in terms of post-redundancy career, then former BSC employees who had been in *professional and managerial* positions are about evenly split between the three categories. For those formerly in *manual grades* there is little difference by skill in terms of their employment experience after redundancy. Around one-fifth of manual workers found uninterrupted employment post-redundancy, a half can be regarded as having chequered post-redundancy careers, while something in the region of 30 per cent experienced prolonged unemployment. Around one-fifth of those who had some kind of *chequered* post-redundancy career were working in the construction industry.

It is clear that the expansion of Ford's operation in South Wales in the early 1980s 'mopped up' a number of the redundant workers from BSC, with perhaps as many as a quarter of those who returned to secure employment now being involved in vehicle manufacture. For those who found employment after redundancy there has been a relatively substantial shift into service industries, though the proportions now in service occupations do not vary greatly by the character of the post-redundancy career.

As well as a shift into service industry there has tended also to be a downward movement in terms of occupational level if one compares the BSC job against the job held now. It seems that this downward movement is also a general one throughout the sample. Those with unbroken patterns of employment post-redundancy are slightly more likely to have moved up since leaving BSC than those with chequered post-redundancy careers, but they are also a little more likely to have moved down.

So variation by post-redundancy employment experience can be seen in the methods of job acquisition used for the job held now. Those who had found 'regular' employment post-redundancy were more likely to have come by their jobs through formal means, i.e. through a newspaper advertisement, the Job Centre, an agency and so on. Those whose post-redundancy careers showed evidence of 'chequeredness' also displayed a more evenly spread distribution of methods of job acquisition with similar proportions making use of formal, informal and other methods of job acquisition. It is interesting to note in the light of an earlier discussion, however, that two-thirds of those who had obtained work through 'bestowal' – that is, where they had been offered work directly by an employer – had had alternate periods of work and unemployment since redundancy.

An extensive analysis of job acquisition has been undertaken on the first and second interviewing waves (Lee 1983 a; 1983 b) with particular reference to Granovetter's suggestions (Granovetter, 1973, 1974) that job-acquisition information emanating from an informal contact is likely to be of higher quality where the contact is seen relatively infrequently. The argument here is that an individual who is not seen often is likely to move in different social circles from ego and therefore to have access to information not readily to hand. In the light of Granovetter's hypothesis and our own earlier discussion, it is interesting to note that the preliminary results of the analysis of the labour-market histories of our respondents suggests that those who moved into relatively 'permanent' employment about which they had heard from an informal source were *less* likely to have seen their contact on a very frequent basis. This pattern was quite clearly reversed for those who had had *chequered* post-redundancy careers. They were extremely likely to have obtained job information from someone seen very frequently.

Clearly, then, the *existence and nature of informal ties* is of crucial importance to the fate of redundant workers who enter and remain in the labour market. However this importance is in part the result of the change of employment practice by the redundants' previous employer, BSC, which has increased the employment of contractors, and the relatively low level of demand for labour in the market.

The most striking finding of the study is however the simple distribution of redundants over different types of post-redundancy career. No less than one-third (33.9 per cent) had *withdrawn* from the labour market either immediately or following a period of unemployment (see Walker, Noble and Westergaard, this volume).

If only those still in the market are considered, by far the largest group are formed by those having chequered post-redundancy careers (42 per cent). This group comprises those displaying an admixture of employment and unemployment and all those cases where employment and unemployment were combined with another status or statuses.

In contrast, 27 per cent had been continuously unemployed since redundancy or had had their unemployment broken only by retraining, and 23 per cent had been continuously employed either since redundancy or after a period of unemployment immediately after redundancy or had continuous employment broken only by a spell of retraining. The remainder (5 per cent) had spent some part of their time after redundancy as self-employed. These figures, together with the category definitions, make clear the variegated character of post-redundancy labour-market experience which is a product of changed employment practices, the uncertainty or fixed-term character of much available employment and the existence of alternative statuses such as 'retraining'.

Conclusions

As far as understanding *redundancy* is concerned the work reported here demonstrates the necessity of:

  understanding the social character of the redundancy process itself;
  paying attention to the changed operation of the organisation generating the redundancies and not assuming that they result simply from changes in product demand;
  collecting redundants' post-redundancy labour-market histories and not merely data on the work status occupied at the point of survey; and
  moving away from rational models of job search and seeing the behaviour of redundants as sequences of situated actions based on partial knowledge of unstable market conditions.
  It is also necessary to develop methodological strategies for examining *relations* between buyers and sellers in the market, as opposed to studying each side separately and then trying to relate the two sets of results.

Because of the particular character of the redundancies studied, it is dangerous to generalise from the Port Talbot data to the operation of *labour markets in general* under present economic conditions. The data from the study, together with what is generally known both about current dominant political attitudes to employment policies of public bodies and current employment practices in the private sector, suggest that a more widespread use of contractors is not confined to South Wales (see Craig *et al.* in this volume). This suggests that one of the effects of the recession on labour markets has been to increase the proportion of all employments formed by employment of a temporary or fixed-term character, thus increasing the proportions of the workforce coming onto the market in any given time period and the proportion of the workforce having 'chequered' labour-market experiences.

We suggest that individuals' experience of the market and their position in it are *always* potentially important determinants of their 'social position'. Hence the same systematic attention should be accorded to market experience and position as is customarily accorded to positions in the productive process and experiences of work, quite apart from the importance which market experience and position acquires in periods of recession.

Notes

1 Rates as high as 22 per cent were envisaged in some quarters.
2 On the basis of data from the first wave of interviewing we estimate that the proportion moving outside South Wales was below 4 per cent. According to data from the 1981 census, Afan – the borough within which Port Talbot is situated – had the lowest mobility rate per thousand total population in England and Wales, Devis, 1983.
3 Recognition of the absence of movers was delayed because of the time taken to complete the first wave of interviewing. This delay was due to the last-minute refusal of BSC to supply a sampling frame. The frame was eventually constructed through the good offices of MSC Wales.
4 For a discussion of some of the methodological difficulties associated with the study of job search as opposed to job acquisition see Reid, 1972.
5 It is clear from the survey that those made redundant from BSC Port Talbot were overwhelmingly male, Welsh-born, and in the older age groups. Just over a quarter had had a non-manual occupation, but only a relatively small proportion, around 8 per cent, were unskilled. Some 45 per cent were classified as skilled, although this includes production workers conventionally regarded as skilled within the steel industry, as well as craftsmen. Around two-fifths of the sample had received a redundancy payment of £5,000 or more – see Lee, 1983 c.
6 This has posed major problems in terms of the survey analysis since the critical variable is the labour-market history (LMH) which was the last piece of data to become available. The problems of computer analysis of *status strings* are formidable and in order to relate the LMH to data collected on earlier waves we have had to learn how to data-link the members of three non-identical sets. While these difficulties with the survey work have not delayed Dr Morris's field study, which is now completed, it has meant that while her work has benefited the survey (particularly the construction of the Wave 3 schedule) her work has not benefited from the survey analysis in the way that was originally intended.
7 The term 'career' is used here simply to denote a sequence of labour-market statuses and is not used prescriptively to imply an outward and upward movement through the life course. Sociologically one can consider a career either in

terms of its phases and investigate how the sequence of phases which constitute it are configured, or in terms of *contingency* – the choices, constraints and meanings which surround the transition from one status to another. Which view is adopted has, of course, implications for data analysis.

Section three

Labour markets, ethnicity and community

In this section, we look at the ways in which the economy affects, and is affected by, the salience of ethnic identity to both minority and non-minority ethnic groups. These papers show that the importance attached to ethnicity by both members and non-members depends, to a considerable extent, on economic and residential circumstances. The significance of ethnicity is also double-edged. Prejudice against members of an ethnic group can disadvantage them economically through discrimination. Yet ethnicity can be a resource used by entrepreneurs and workers to further their economic goals.

This section provides further support for the claim that the labour market is inherently imperfect, showing how ethnic stereotypes, rather than objective qualifications, determine who is employed. Richard Jenkins argues that ethnic minorities are inevitably discriminated against when so much depends on 'word-of-mouth' recruitment in firms in which the majority of employees are white, where vacancies are first advertised internally and where line managers, often the most influential in recruitment, are mainly concerned to stabilise labour relations by choosing workers who will not upset the local working culture. The occupational disadvantages of minority groups and their high rates of unemployment are thus neither the result of their lack of objective qualifications nor of crude racial bias. They result from the fact that established social relations and the categories of exclusion that defend them are basic elements in organising economic activity.

One implication of this position is that the more homogeneous a community is in terms of overlap between work and residence, then the more difficult will it be for outsiders to be accepted. Ethnicity as an overriding category in determining social interaction is thus often most pronounced when people of similar culture, religion or race live together, depend on the same economic activities and are surrounded by people of diverse cultural origins. Sandra Wallman shows, conversely, how ethnicity has relatively little significance in determining social interaction in an occupationally heterogeneous area of inner London in which most people work outside the locality. There, people draw upon neighbours as resources irrespective of ethnic origin. She suggests, however, that in areas in which there has traditionally been a close fit between work and residence, then the community is more likely to be a closed one and considerations such as kinship and ethnic origin will determine interaction.

Ethnicity is, then, not a fixed category with an unchanging significance for social interaction. Robin Ward develops this argument in terms of the economic opportunities open to ethnic minorities in different British cities. He seeks to explain why similar ethnic groups have dissimilar jobs in different parts of the country. No satisfactory explanation is to be found in the skills of the migrants or their rural–urban origins. Instead, it is clear that cities differ in the economic opportunities they offer, some providing unskilled and semi-skilled manual work, others opportunities for service employment and business. There is little, then, to suggest that ethnic groups have a 'natural' propensity for a particular kind of economic activity. However, Ward shows that ethnic ties can be useful in a certain type of economic activity – that of the small business which makes use of ethnic and kinship allegiances to lessen the uncertainties of establishing a market and securing a reliable workforce.

This is the main theme of Roger Waldinger's analysis of immigrant enterprise in New York. He concentrates on the positive contribution that ethnic ties make to developing economic activity, though reminding us of the exploitation that can accompany the use of kin and fellow-ethnics in business. He analyses the difficulties faced by small enterprises in a competitive market situation where they face the dilemma of having to cut labour costs while still needing to retain a relatively skilled and committed workforce. Ethnicity, particularly in New York where it is associated with the induction of immigrants into American society and economy, provides one solution to that dilemma. Ethnic entrepreneurs provide work for fellow ethnics and mediate between them and the wider society. The workers trust their employers and have the opportunity to learn skills that will eventually allow them to start their own businesses. This 'successful' case of ethnic enterprise depends, as Waldinger indicates, on a dynamic and competitive economy which both provides opportunities for entrepreneurs and, in a culturally diverse population, makes ethnic ties and ethnic clients the surest basis for economic activity, especially when establishing a business. His argument has wider implications than the field of ethnic business. In essence, he shows the value of binding social ties and common cultures to a common type of economic enterprise – one dependent on the quality and commitment of its workforce in face of economic fluctuation and competition.

Black workers in the labour market: the price of recession

It is perhaps ironic, although certainly not accidental, that the current high level of sociological interest in labour-market issues has only developed at a time when the market for labour is in a state of crisis, if not quite imminent collapse. This volume is representative of that interest, and many of the contributors provide convincing evidence of the depth and severity of the recession. In this chapter I shall, therefore, be content to take the existence of a crisis in the labour market, manifest in particular by high levels of unemployment nationally, the collapse of the 'traditional' manufacturing sector and disproportionately high levels of youth employment, for granted. Instead, I shall explore the impact of that crisis upon one group, namely black workers. I shall also take for granted the undisputed facts of ethnic disadvantage in the labour market; black workers have been disproportionately hard hit by unemployment, and black youth in particular is increasingly being pushed to the margins of paid employment (Smith, 1981; Troyna and Smith, 1983). In order to place the discussion in its appropriate context, it is necessary to discuss the organisational framework of the labour market outcomes of black workers, in particular, selection criteria and the recruitment process.

The study which is briefly documented here was carried out between 1980 and 1983 whilst the author was employed at the SSRC (now ESRC) Research Unit on Ethnic Relations at the University of Aston in Birmingham.[1] The major focus of the research project was upon discrimination against black workers in recruitment to manual and routine non-manual jobs. From the beginning, it was conceived as both a study of racist discrimination, on the one hand, and the processes of the labour market, on the other. As a consequence, it is hoped that the results will speak to two distinct academic interest groups, i.e. sociologists of race relations and students of the labour market.

The core method used in this project was a long, semi-structured ethnographic interview with managers who were responsible for recruiting manual and routine non-manual labour. A total of forty organisations agreed to co-operate with the research: fifteen manufacturing companies, fourteen public sector organisations and eleven retailing firms. In as much as the management structure of all of these organisations was sufficiently specialised to support a personnel function, they may all be thought of as being in the 'medium-to-large' size bracket. They were all situated in the West Midlands Metropolitan County area.

Although documentary material relating to the organisations was collected, the main source of data was the interview. All told, 172 managers were interviewed: sixty-nine personnel specialists and 103 line managers. Case-studies were made of two of the organisations, one in manufacturing (twenty-seven interviews: 10 personnel specialists and seventeen line managers) and one in the public sector (thirty-eight interviews: four personnel specialists and thirty-four line managers). Trade unionists in these two organisations were also interviewed, as were some local full-time officials.

Selection criteria: the importance of being acceptable

The analysis of selection criteria starts off from the proposal that selection criteria tend to be of two sorts: functionally specific criteria of *suitability*, which relate to competence or *ability* to do the job in question, and functionally non-specific criteria of acceptability, which relate to wider organisational matters such as 'stability', 'reliability', and 'predictability', in short, the degree to which the worker is habituated to employment or other-wise organisationally acceptable. Claus Offe has drawn a similar distinction between 'functional' and 'extra-functional' characteristics (1976: 47–99), and David Gordon's concepts of 'quantitative efficiency' and 'qualitative efficiency' also appear to have much in common with what I am saying here (1976: 22–6). Both sorts of criteria come into play in recruitment; in this research, however, I decided to concentrate on acceptability, since there are no indications that black workers are primarily disadvantaged in the market because of their inability to pass over the relatively low thresholds of suitability attached to most manual or routine non-manual jobs (Daniel, 1968; Dex, 1982; Smith, *op. cit.*). [2]

The major criteria of acceptability were divided up into three categories, *primary, secondary* and *tertiary* criteria, according to the frequency with which they were mentioned by the managers interviewed. Primary criteria were 'appearance', 'manner and attitude' and 'maturity'; secondary criteria were the interviewer's 'gut feeling', the applicant's labour market history (i.e. periods of unemployment and number of jobs), speech style, 'relevant experience', age and marital status (for male workers), literacy, and 'personality and the ability to fit in'; the tertiary criteria were English language competence and references from past employers. Two important further dimensions of acceptability which shortage of space prevents me from discussing here, are *non-verbal communication* in the selection interview and *gender*.

Presented in this fashion, these criteria are somewhat enigmatic. Elsewhere the meanings of these criteria for recruiters have been explored using extensive ethnographic quotations (Jenkins, 1982). It is clear from the data that there are differences in the criteria which are used in the recruitment of manual and non-manual workers, and in the manufacturing, retailing and public sectors. There are also differences in the pattern of criteria used by personnel and line managers which I shall not, however, discuss here, for reasons of space.

Looking at the recruitment of manual workers, managers are most concerned about 'appearance', followed by 'maturity', 'manner and attitude', labour market history and 'age and marital status'. Less important are 'relevant experience', 'gut feeling', references and speech style. Looking at those managers recruiting non-manual workers, however, the pattern is as follows: of most apparent importance are 'appearance', 'manner and attitude', and 'gut feeling', followed by speech style, labour market history, 'maturity', 'personality and the ability to fit in' and 'relevant experience'. Of lesser importance are literacy, references and the candidate's competence in spoken English. Thus while *'appearance'* and *'manner and attitude'* are very important for all workers, 'maturity', labour market history and age and marital status (for males) are more important for manual workers, 'gut feeling' on the manager's part playing a greater role for their non-manual counterparts.

If, however, we look at the differences between the public, manufacturing and retailing sectors then a different pattern emerges. In manufacturing the three most important criteria are 'maturity', labour market history and 'gut feeling'. These are followed by 'manner and attitude', age and marital status, literacy, 'appearance', English language competence, 'relevant experience', 'personality and the ability to fit in', and references.

By contrast, in the public sector organisations, 'appearance', 'manner and attitude' and 'maturity' were the criteria most often mentioned by managers. Mentioned less frequently were 'gut feeling', 'personality and the ability to fit in', speech style, 'relevant experience', labour market history, and competence in the English language.

Finally, coming to the retailing sector, there are five criteria which appear to be of major importance: 'appearance', 'manner and attitude', speech style, literacy and 'gut feeling'. Lower down the order of priorities are competence in English, 'maturity', relevant experience, and references.

Thus it is clear that there is a pattern of differences in the attributes relating to acceptability which are sought by recruiters in the organisations in the three industrial sectors in question. The sources of these differences are probably the differences between the three with respect to formal organisational 'structure' and the social organisation of the labour process.

One thing which all of these organisations and employment sectors do have in common, however, is the close relationship between selection criteria of acceptability and managerial control of the workplace. In attempting to recruit acceptable workers employers are trying to avoid managerial problems in the future, and to maintain their control of the workplace and the daily routines of organisational life. There are at least three important aspects to this. First, there is the quest for the habituated 'responsible' worker, someone who will be able to manage him- or herself in the particular work context (or, at worst, will not create any major problems). Most of the criteria which are used to judge these attribute are, to say the very least, 'unscientific', depending as much on the recruiter's hunch as anything else. Secondly, there is the desire to prevent problems arising with the existing workforce as a result of hiring new workers who may be unacceptable to them. Thirdly, there is the basic aim of recruiting a workforce who can understand and obey spoken and written orders. There are, therefore, three sides to acceptability: the recruitment of manageable workers, the avoidance of industrial relations problems, and the maintenance of communication at the workplace. All are essentially about the control of the workforce and the labour process.

The differing versions of the notion of acceptability can also have their consequences – typically detrimental – for black job seekers. The first point to bear in mind here is the routine ethnocentricity of many of these ideas of acceptability. 'Appearance', 'manner and attitude', 'speech style', and the manager's 'gut feeling', for example, are all criteria which depend to a greater or lesser degree upon shared cultural competences. This is all the more so considering the importance of non-verbal communication in the assessment of these attributes by the manager. Thus a white recruiter may choose to interpret an avoidance of direct eye contact by an applicant as indicating anything from a lack of self-confidence to 'shiftines'. However, for many job-seekers whose cultural background lies in the Indian sub-continent, the refusal of eye contact may be a respectful attempt to avoid impoliteness. For many of the managers I interviewed, such behaviour in an interview would be an indicator of unacceptability. [3]

Another example of the potential power of ethocentricity is the criterion of 'age and marital status'. Basically this refers to the notion that, if there is an 'ideal' employee, *he* is a 'married-man-with-two-kids-and-a-mortgage', an idea which has been reported elsewhere (Blackburn and Mann, 1979: 105; Nichols and Beynon, 1977: 97, 199). This rests upon two assumptions: one, that this is the 'normal', 'respectable' household type, and two, that a worker in this position is so burdened down by responsibilities that he *has* to come to work whether he wants to or not. Quite apart from the explicit sexism of this criterion (both in its content and its likely consequences), this is an extremely culturally specific model of the 'normal' family. Cultural differences with respect to the norms of kinship, marriage and residence being what they are, there is no doubt that the household arrangements of proportionately more black than white workers will fall beyond this pale of normality.

A second problem with criteria of acceptability concerns the new recruit's need to 'fit in' with the existing workforce. That this can be a source of discrimination was shown by the Commission for Racial Equality's formal investigation into BL's Castle Bromwich plant (1981). Thirdly, the fact that so many criteria of acceptability operate tacitly and implicitly not only makes research difficult for the social scientist, it also renders the selection process mysterious and opaque. This makes the investigation of complaints of discrimination more difficult than it might otherwise be, and helps to create the organisational space wherein racism can flourish.

Coming to criteria such as competence in spoken English or literacy, here there are also difficulties for black job-seekers. In the case of literacy, the major problem is the employer who sets unrealistically high literacy requirements for unskilled jobs. Looking at competence in English, however, the situation is more complex, in as much as it appears not to be formally tested for in the same way as literacy, assessment depending largely upon the subjective judgements of recruiters. Once again, this allows ethnocentricity and racism a route into the selection process. Finally, in that black workers appear to be more likely to suffer from involuntary redundancy, dismissal and unemployment (Dex, *op. cit.*: 18–25, 40–9; Smith, *op. cit.*: 67–93), they are less likely to have acceptable labour market histories in the eyes of many recruiters, thus setting up a vicious circle of disadvantage.

These are some of the implications which the notion of 'acceptability' may have for black job-seekers. It remains, however, to briefly explore one other area, the relationship between *stereotypes of acceptability* and the *ethnic stereotypes* of black workers held by managers. Many of these ethnic stereotypes (such as 'West Indians are lazy, happy-go-lucky or slow', or 'Asians are clannish and don't mix') fly in the face of the ideas bound up in the notion of acceptability.[4] To make matters worse, many of these interviewees see the employment of black workers as creating managerial problems which would not arise with an all-white workforce. This too is a further dimension of the unacceptability of black workers for white managers.

In this section I have outlined some of the meanings of worker acceptability in the eyes of the managers interviewed in this research project. Following from this, the consequences for black workers of the importance of acceptability were outlined. In the next section, I shall discuss the recruitment processes which provide the organisational settings for selection decision-making.

Recruitment processes: formality, informality and 'word of mouth'

The recruitment process can be divided up into three elements: *recruitment channels*, organisational *recruitment procedures*, and the selection *interview*. Looking at channels of recruitment there are differences between industrial sectors, on the one hand, and occupational categories (i.e. manual, skilled manual and routine non-manual) on the other.

In manufacturing, employers typically look within their own organisation first before going elsewhere. The medium most commonly employed is the internal advertisement, although non-competitive promotion and the straightforward redisposition of labour are also important. A small number of firms routinely approach the public Employment Services first, while one manufacturing organisation did not advertise at all (internally or externally), relying wholly on unsolicited applications and 'word of mouth'. If internal search fails to produce an acceptable candidate, the most popular recruitment channels are 'word of mouth', the Employment Services and newspaper advertisements, in that order.

By contrast, in the public sector, although internal recruitment wherever possible is similarly important, there is a greater subsequent use of newspaper advertisements. In some organisations, the formal policy is that canvassing disqualifies the applicant. Despite this, 'word of mouth' is the next most popular recruitment channel, followed closely by the Employment Services. Equally noteworthy is the very low first preference usage of the Employment Services, and the complete non-usage of private agencies.

Coming to the retailing organisations, the most characteristic feature is a much less definite pattern of preferred recruitment channels. There is a striking diversity in the alternatives which are used by these recruiters, particularly for non-skilled manual jobs (mainly shop assistants). However, 'word of mouth' is the channel which finds some use by most employers. In addition, all of the following have some significance: consulting files of previous applicants, unsolicited applications and casual callers, and public noticeboards. Many organisations use the Employment Services once their original recruitment channel has failed them.

Looked at with reference to occupational categories and the kinds of jobs which are being filled, there are further differences in the recruitment channels employed. Private employment agencies, for example, are exclusively used to recruit non-manual workers; unsolicited applications and casual callers are primarily a source of recruits to manual jobs. 'Word of mouth' is very important for all categories of vacancy, while internal search is the preferred channel of recruitment for everything except shop assistants. The Employment Services are more or less equally significant for all jobs in the categories under consideration, although there is some variation between sectors.

It is important to note that two of these recruitment channels, internal search and 'word of mouth', overlap to a considerable degree. This is because employers may use their workforce as a means of contacting potential applicants, and, even where this is not the case, existing employees will communicate information about vacancies to their families and friends. The widespread use of 'word of mouth' contacts in recruitment may be thought of as extending the scope of the internal labour market outside the formal boundaries of the organisation.

This brings us to organisational recruitment procedures, the procedures for processing applications and taking applicants through the stages of recruitment. There are, once again, important differences between industries. In manufacturing, the personnel function typically screens applicants before passing them on for a decision to line management. In the public sector there are two characteristic procedures: in the first, line management is responsible for the entire process; in the second, there are selection panels but line management makes the final decision. In retailing, however, one recruitment procedure characterises this area of employment: personnel specialists are responsible for all aspects of recruitment.

Looked at with respect to occupational categories, there are also some contrasting patterns. The only situation, outside retailing, in which personnel handles every aspect of recruitment involves non-skilled manual vacancies. Within the public sector, however, the influence of personnel specialists is greater in the recruitment of non-manual employees. Similarly, in manufacturing, panel interviewing becomes more important as the vacancy rises up the manual/non-manual hierarchy.

There are two conclusions to be drawn: (a) the internal market, and its extension via 'word of mouth', is the most important arena of search for employers, and (b) generally speaking, allowing for the small size of the retailing sector (relative to manufacturing or the public sector), personnel managers have only slight decision-making powers in recruitment.[5]

For reasons of space I shall not discuss the selection interview here, except to characterise it as typically a highly informal affair, both in its conduct and in the specification of job requirements. Looking at interviewing in internal recruitment and promotion, it is clear that it is likely to be even more informal than external recruitment interviewing, largely because so much is already known about the candidates.

One major aspect of this research into recruitment processes was the examination of 'word of mouth' recruitment. When asked for their reasons for using this channel, the recruiters interviewed gave the following most frequently: the reputation of the recommender serves to predict the reliability of the new recruit; the presence of the recommender in the workplace may guarantee the new recruit's 'good' behaviour; it is part of the 'family firm' ethos; 'word of mouth' is good for industrial relations; it is cheap and easy, particularly with so many job-seekers in the market; and finally, it is a good source of extra general information about the applicant. Thus, 'word of mouth' is at least three things at once: an industrial relations strategy, an efficient recruitment channel, and a criterion of acceptability in its own right. These results compare well with earlier research in the United States (Rees, 1966).

It is possible to discern in these patterns of recruitment procedures certain consequences for the black job-seeker. Given its importance as a channel of recruitment, 'word of mouth' is an ideal place to start the discussion. In the first place, particularly in organisations with small numbers of black employers or most of their black employees in low-status jobs, 'word of mouth' may result in the reproduction of the hierarchical *status quo* within the organisation. White workers will tend to have better access to job information – both in quantitative and qualitative terms – than their black peers. At the extreme, an all-white workplace with a heavy reliance on informal social networks as a source of recruits will be almost certain to remain an all-white workplace. Secondly, as 'word of mouth' is an informal process, unrecorded and largely unaccountable for, the enabling conditions for the operation of racist discrimination are created. Finally, the issue of acceptability is also of some significance. If it is important for the recommender or mediator to be acceptable, then, bearing in mind the previous section's argument about the comparative acceptability of black workers, black workers may not be influential as pivots in the chain of recommendation, certainly for jobs other than those which are seen to be appropriate for them. Once again there is the reproduction of the current labour-market disadvantage of black workers.

The general emphasis on internal search as a first channel of recruitment also has its disadvantages for black job-seekers. Internal search tends to close off the initial availability of job information to those in the organisation, or in 'the know'. If black workers were evenly distributed throughout occupations or organisations then this would not be a problem for them. As it is, however, they are *not* evenly distributed and it *is* a problem. It is a problem, what is more, which is compounded by the greater informality which characterises much internal recruitment, since informality, as I have already argued, is an enabling condition of racism.

The relative lack of influence of the personnel function may also put black workers at something of a disadvantage. As the professional people involved in recruitment they are, to some degree, the 'natural' custodians of meritocratic recruitment, fair treatment and equal opportunities. Nor is this a caricature of the personnel role: many of the personnel specialists I interviewed took this view of the personnel profession. However, the weak place of the personnel function within the political hierarchies of most organisations ensures that they rarely have the opportunity to actually practise their professional responsibilities.

Recruitment channels acquire a further significance if they are examined in the context of the job-search patterns of black workers. Looking at adult workers first, it appears from the most recent pieces of research (Courtenay, n.d.: 15–22; Smith, *op. cit.*: 98–103), that there are only minor differences in job-search patterns between white and West Indian workers. There may be a tendency for white workers to use newspaper advertisements more often as a source of information, but informal kinship and friendship networks seem to be important for both. The main differences are between white and West Indian workers, on the one hand, and Asian workers, on the other, regardless of gender. The latter appear to rely more on 'word of mouth' or direct approaches to employers; they are less likely to use the state Employment Services. According to the evidence from this study, direct approaches from job-seekers are primarily a source of applicants to manual jobs. The heavy reliance of all groups of workers upon 'word of mouth', and other informal job-acquisition strategies, limits the job-seeker to the fund of contacts which are available to his/her immediate social group by virtue of their work histories and present employment status. Because of the place of black workers in the labour market and their stereotyping by white managers, these resources may well restrict the scope of 'word of mouth' contacts to providing 'more of the same', at best. Asian workers, therefore, as a result of their concentration upon 'word of mouth' contacts and direct approaches to employers, may be limiting the effective scope of their job-search to manual jobs at the bottom end of the labour market.

The pattern for young workers, however, is different. One of the earliest pieces of research (Beetham, 1967) concluded that black school-leavers were more likely to use the Employment Services (the Youth Employment Service, at that time) to find work. The situation has not changed much, if more recent studies are anything to go by (Anwar, 1982: 19; Commission for Racial Equality, 1978: 8–9; Dex, *op. cit.*; Lee and Wrench, 1983: 60–1). Black school-leavers and young workers still rely heavily on the Careers Service and the Job Centres for vacancy information and job placement.

As a corollary, there are differences in the pattern of use of 'word of mouth': for apprenticeships for example, white school-leavers use kinship and friendship networks to a greater extent than their black peers and do so more successfully. More generally it appears that Asians use social networks more than whites, who, in turn, use them more than West Indian youth. There are also some gender differences, white girls being more likely to use newspaper advertisements than their West Indian peers. Finally, Asian youth are much more likely to use a direct approach to employers than either whites or West Indians.[6]

The importance of the Employment Services for young blacks has implications for their likelihood of finding employment, and for the type of job they may be offered. As we have seen, this research indicates that internal search and 'word of mouth' are the most important recruitment channels for employers. When jobs do come on to the open market, internal candidates will have been taken up wherever possible and they are likely to be relatively low-status, 'port of entry' jobs, at best. These will typically be the jobs which go to the Job Centres. To illustrate the nature of the problem, only seven of the organisations examined (17 per cent of the total) normally notified the Employment Services of all of their routine non-manual vacancies. Evidence from other studies suggests that the Employment Services are seen by many employers as a last-resort source of 'low grade' labour (Carter, 1966: 147; Keil, 1976: 17–19). Despite high levels of unemployment, many of the managers in this study made disparaging remarks about the Employment Services during the interview. It seems safe to assume, therefore, that the reliance by young black workers on the Employment Services may serve to further handicap them in the labour market.

However, this discussion of job-search strategies and recruitment channels is *not* another exercise in 'blaming the victim'. Job-search behaviour cannot be understood in isolation; it is heavily dependent upon the recruitment channels used by employers. Job seekers can only take advantage of the recruitment channels which are effectively open to them; many jobs are found, not deliberately sought out. Thus the differing opportunity structures for black and white workers have an important effect. All workers, for example, may use 'word of mouth'; that is not to say, however, that this strategy gives all workers access to similar jobs. It clearly does not. Secondly, black job seekers, inasmuch as they face substantial discrimination, are engaged in a more difficult endeavour than their white peers. High levels of discrimination in recruitment have been convincingly demonstrated by well-documented situation testing in 1966 and 1973–4 (Daniel, *op. cit.*: 76–9; Smith, 1977: 105–26). More recently, similar research has argued that the level of discrimination may actually have increased (Hubbuck and Carter, 1980).

Neither is there any suggestion from existing research that the dis-advantaged position of black job-seekers is a reflection of differing persistence in the job-search. In fact, in response to discrimination, black workers are *more* persistent in applying for jobs, making many more applications per job obtained than white workers (Commission for Racial Equality, *op. cit.*: 8–9; Smith, 1974: 33). Remaining with the response to racism, Shirley Dex has recently argued that the concentration upon Job Centres by West Indian youth, and their turning away from kinship and friendship networks as a source of labour market information, is a rational attempt to avoid jobs such as those held by their parents (Dex, *op. cit.*: 20). In no sense, therefore, should my appraisal of the relative utility of particular job-search strategies for black workers be interpreted as blaming them for their own labour market dis-advantage. Their behaviour may – as with all social actors in all contexts – contribute to the production and reproduction of their situation. However, due to a history of discrimination and domination, black workers have less power to make their actions count in producing labour-market outcomes than do white workers or managers. In this sense, therefore, it is perhaps most appropriate to view their job-search behaviour as a rational response to a situation over which they have little control.

Changes in the labour market: the implications for black workers[7]

Perhaps one of the most interesting results of this research is the importance which is currently attached to internal search, the internal labour market (ILM), as an arena of recruitment. Over two-thirds of the manufacturing and public sector organisations tried to recruit through the ILM first for manual, skilled manual and routine non-manual vacancies. For the other organisations in these sectors, the ILM was typically used simultaneously with external search; even in these cases it has an important role.

Of greater interest, perhaps, is the evidence that there has been an increase in the use of internal search recently. This trend is already discernible if one compares studies carried out early in the 1970s (Courtenay and Hedges, 1977; Dunnell and Head, 1973). Of the organisations in this study, 73 per cent of the manufacturing firms, 43 per cent of the public sector organisations and 18 per cent of the retailing companies reported that the present recession had led to some increase in their use of internal search, including 'word of mouth' recruitment. Although it is not easy to disentangle from other ILM procedures such as the use of internal vacancy notices, 'word of mouth' recruitment appears to be more significant than previously. An important implication of this trend is that the state Employment Services may be notified of fewer vacancies. Furthermore, if the arguments earlier in this chapter are correct, there will also be a tendency for those vacancies which are notified to be increasingly 'lower-level' jobs.

Why this increased reliance on internal search and recruitment? In the first place, it reflects the problem posed for organisations by redundancy. An organisation which finds itself having to shed labour will seek to fill whatever 'normal' vacancies may arise – and they do arise from time to time – from among its outgoing workers. Such a strategy avoids the need to pay those workers redundancy payments, and in as much it allows part of the burden of redundancy to be offset, helps to smooth over the potentially disturbed waters of industrial relations. In some cases, in fact, this recruitment strategy is as much the result of trade union pressure as anything else. The use of internal search may vary, from simply pinning notices on internal notice-boards to the regular preparation of a central consolidated vacancy sheet by the headquarters of a manufacturing group or a public authority. This approach can also be seen as extending the boundaries of the ILM outside the immediate limits of the workplace or the enterprise.

However, simply reducing the *number* of workers employed is frequently only of secondary importance to the *restructuring* of the labour process; in the words of one interviewee, 'It's a question of moving people from non-essential to essential jobs'. As a result of pressures of this kind, mobility agreements are increasingly becoming a part of the industrial relations accommodation which is being reached in many workplaces between profit-ability and some sort of fragile job security. Within this kind of context the traditional rules governing redundancy may become an embarrassment for both management and unions. When the shared goal is the retention of the most 'flexible', 'reliable' or potentially retrainable sections of the workforce, ideas such as 'last in – first out' are, by tacit agreement, laid to one side; the redundancy exercise becomes more selective than it might otherwise have been.

Another reason for turning to the internal market is because it is both cheaper and easier. A newspaper advertisement or a card in the local Job Centre might result in a deluge of applicants. 'Word of mouth' is important in this respect, vacancy information passing out of the gates only via the network of existing employees. Some of the organisations in the study consciously encourage this process, in order to limit the number of applications they receive. .

Cheapness, convenience and the problems of redundancy and restructuring are not the only, or even the main, reasons for the increased concentration upon the internal recruitment arena, however. The evidence from this study is clear: employers are using recruitment strategies of this kind for two other reasons.

In the first place, they are hoping to retain or recruit a more acceptable 'class' of worker. Keenly aware that they are, for the first time in a long time, in a buyer's market for labour, they are intent on capitalising upon that enviable position. This also affects their industrial relations stance; many employers are relishing a rediscovered militancy. Returning to the point about the selectivity of redundancy, a production manager at a metalwork plant admitted, for example, that, 'There were a few dead legs but we got rid of them, with redundancies and early retirements . . . and giving them the sack'.

The process is not always this overt; in some places union militancy has survived the recession and can still make its presence felt. The recruiters who were interviewed, however, agreed that internal candidates are much easier to evaluate with respect to their acceptability, in that they are a known quantity. In this process it is not difficult to select out the 'unreliable' worker or the 'troublemaker'. People with these kinds of reputation do poorly in internal procedures; their redundancy money may be considered a small enough price for getting rid of them. Finally, it should not be forgotten that 'word of mouth' is also centrally concerned with the recruitment or promotion of habituated, acceptable workers.

However, it is not *just* a question of worker acceptability. There is a second discernible managerial goal here: internal, or informal external, recruitment may be a more or less conscious control strategy, at both the individual and the organisational levels. As the quest is for habituated, 'reliable' workers, this is an obvious statement; however, it is also true in other respects. For example workers, particularly young workers, recruited through informal social networks, can to some extent be controlled indirectly through the mediator or wider peer-group pressure. Furthermore, if 'word of mouth' is an aspect of the 'family firm', then, paternalism being a particular approach to industrial relations, it is seen to be part of a wider control strategy, the workforce being allowed to participate in recruitment in return for co-operation and 'reliability'.

Returning to the ILM, increased managerial control is also to be seen here. As the procedure is typically more informal than external recruitment, outcomes can be more easily secured. Competitive procedures may, for example, be ignored and the acceptable person simply given the vacant job. A greater degree of control is also being exercised over manpower planning. In most organisations the managerial level at which authorisation to fill a vacancy must be sought has risen; what is more, vacancies are more likely to be approved if they are to be filled internally. This ensures that if the organisation does have to go outside for recruits, it will only be at the lowest level.

These then are some of the changes in labour market processes which have resulted from financial constraints within work organisations, on the one hand, and high levels of unemployment, on the other. Before concluding this chapter I shall briefly discuss the consequences of these labour-market changes for black workers.

Some of these consequences are, perhaps, obvious, given the discussion in earlier sections. Firstly, the shift to the internal market and 'word of mouth' means that established workers, in the sense of those who are in work at all, and *particularly* those who are in stable, 'established' jobs,[8] and the members of their social networks, are likely to have better access to job information. 'Established workers', in the sense that I am using the expression here, are disproportionate*¡ ʔ* more likely to be white than black; black workers are, perhaps, increasingly only going to hear about 'black jobs' or 'shit work'. It is ironic that those black youngsters who, as Shirley Dex suggests, are deliberately moving away from their parents' information networks in order to prevent this from happening, and using the public Employment Services, are, if the arguments of this paper are correct, possibly *increasing* their chances of being offered jobs at the bottom of the market. That is, of course, if they are lucky enough to be offered any jobs at all.

Apart from the fact that 'word of mouth' serves to reproduce the occupational *status quo*, there are other problems with this kind of recruitment. Not the least of these is its informality, which may allow scope for discrimination to operate. Similarly, as argued earlier, given that recruiters can be selective about whose recommendation to accept, there is always the possibility that black workers will not be able to introduce applicants as successfully as their white colleagues. For similar reasons, the apparent rise in the levels of acceptability which employers are looking for is a further cause for concern. Given that we live in a society which has yet to accord legitimacy to the presence of large numbers of black people, there is good reason to suspect, and the data from this study bears this out, that they are regarded as undesirable aliens by many white employers and workers. In the tight labour market of earlier and economically better days, black labour was necessary, if not desirable or acceptable. Now it is no longer even necessary. There is some evidence from this study which shows that, in some organisations, trade unionists are more concerned to protect the jobs of their white, rather than their black, comrades.

It is not, however, simply a matter of discrimination in recruitment; as I have already argued, selection for redundancy or other forms of severance may be equally discriminatory. Returning briefly to the research findings, 'the need to maintain a racial balance' is a problem with which many managers see themselves confronted in the multi-ethnic workplace. What 'balance' actually means, however, is a majority of white workers. It is clear from the interview material that 'balance' may also mean keeping black workers in their place, that is, in unskilled or otherwise undesirable jobs. There is additional indirect evidence that some managers have used a redundancy situation to remedy the matter and restore a 'balance'. A central strand in this concern with 'balance' is the reassertion of managerial control, which is seen to be undermined by the presence of too many black workers, who 'form cliques' and 'stick to themselves'. In this light, it is interesting that the trade unions are often as keen as management on the notion of 'balance'.

Finally, a further consequence of the recession has been to diminish managerial interest in the introduction of equal opportunity policies within organisations. There are a number of reasons for this: in a buyer's market, there is no longer the pressure on organisations to present themselves as 'good employers'; policy formulation and organisational change can be expensive; with the change of government in 1979, the state policy climate in the race relations area has changed; given the present levels of unemployment there may be active hostility from unions and white workers to the notion; and, finally, many employers, in their new-found militancy, are inclined to resist any interference in their affairs, which is what they may perceive the race relations legislation to be. All of these factors come together to create a climate which is hostile to the active pursuit of equal opportunities.

In this chapter, I have very briefly explored some of the changes which are taking place in the social processes of the labour market. Many of these changes have definitely detrimental consequences for black workers. Caught between their disadvantaged position in the information networks of the labour market, the subtle, or not so subtle, racist discrimination of employers in selecting for redundancy or employment, increased attempts by management to reassert control at the workplace, and a changing climate with respect to equal opportunity initiatives, it is little wonder that black workers have been so disproportionately affected by the current recession. It remains to be seen whether their position will achieve some sort of precarious stability, or deteriorate even further.

Notes

1 This research has been written up as a final report for the Unit, 'Racism and recruitment: managers, organisations and equal opportunity in the labour market', which is planned for publication by Cambridge University Press in 1985–6. The Unit has now changed its name to the Centre for Research in Ethnic Relations, and moved to the University of Warwick.

2 For a further discussion of the argument that black workers are not discriminated against because they are unsuitable, see Jenkins and Troyna (1983).

3 For a specific example of just such a case, see 'Seeing error of their ways', *The Guardian*, 7 January 1983.

4 It should, perhaps, be pointed out here that there is little evidence of consensus among these managers as a group with respect to the ethnic stereotypes they hold, although there are well-defined clusters of shared stereotypes.

5 The relatively weak position of personnel management within organisation is discussed by Watson, 1977.

6 The sources of the assertions in this paragraph are Commission for Racial Equality (1978: 8–9), Dex (1978–9: 364; 1982: 42–3) and Lee and Wrench (1983: *passim*).

7 Much of the argument in this section derives from an earlier paper jointly written with Alan Bryman, Janet Ford, Teresa Keil and Alan Beardsworth of Loughborough University (Jenkins *et al.*, 1983). I am grateful to them for their considerable contribution to that argument and their permission to use the material here.

8 To avoid misunderstanding, I am not here proposing a 'dual labour market' model.

9 *Sandra Wallman*

Structures of informality: variation in local style and the scope for unofficial economic organisation in London[1]

The study reported here deals with combinations of people and place in London. It was provoked by the observation that superficially similar areas of the inner city vary enormously in respect of their styles of livelihood, and a parallel conviction that these differences account for local variations in the success of economic policy and development or redevelopment plans. The project is interdisciplinary: we are using a combination of historical and contemporary data to map the political and economic characteristics of two inner London areas,[2] and to analyse patterns of livelihood common among residents in each.[3] The central questions are: how do the economic structures of the two areas compare? and: what styles or principles of organisation do residents in each setting use to manage the options offered by that setting?

This paper focuses on interrelations of structure and organisation in each of the two areas – *structure* being the framework of social or economic or conceptual options, and *organisation* the pattern of choices made from amongst those options (as Firth, 1964; see also Sahlins, 1974). In this perspective the notion of distinct formal and informal, official and unofficial, economic *sectors* has no analytic value: informal/unofficial systems of organisation fit into the interstices of formal/official structures – whether of factories, local markets or the urban economy as a whole. Thus the structure of the 'host' economy must be taken into account if options for informal or non-official organisation within it are to be effectively manipulated or properly understood.

This particular study deals specifically with the ethnic option – i.e. with the scope for and constraints on ethnicity as a principle of (informal/unofficial) economic organisation and group identity in two inner London areas. In the context of this discussion however, the origins and cultures of the two populations are less significant than the possible effect of local industrial structure on local styles of economic organisation – whether in the matter of employment as such, or in the way community resources are managed. If it is true that one kind of local labour market offers more – or at least different – informal economic options than another, it follows that ethnicity has quite a different organising potential in either case (Wallman, 1979 a).

Research in the first area – a part of Battersea in South West London – led us to formulate the propositions set out below. But in the course of looking for a second area in which they could be tested by comparison to Battersea, we met with difficulties caused by the fact that they fit too neatly in some areas and too crudely in others. These difficulties are spelled out here because the selection procedure itself led to a refinement of the original hypothesis and begins to illuminate the way informal/unofficial economic organisation works.

The substance of the comparison need not – indeed cannot – be given at this stage; the background to it serves only to indicate how the present problem was formulated. Only the initial focus of comparison is discussed. It is described by reference to structural heterogeneity/homogeneity and to the numerical and statistical indices used to select a homogeneous area to be compared to the heterogeneous case already studied. The reasoning behind this procedure has been entirely deductive. The Battersea case is characterised by heterogeneous industrial structure *and* by a relatively open and flexible organisational style; its heterogeneous structure is reflected or refracted throughout the local system. The comparative study was set up to see if the opposite (i.e. homogeneous) industrial structure colours the local system as it does in Battersea, but with opposite (i.e. homogeneous) effect on styles of informal/unofficial organisation in general, and on ethnic organisation in particular.

We may now set out our four-part working hypothesis, describe the initial failure to select an appropriate second area in which it could be tested, and propose a refinement to it which resolves the selection dilemma.

The original propositions are:

(i) The significance of ethnicity and so the expression of 'racist' sentiment varies from one inner city area to another because different local resource systems, different systems of organisation and identity give it different scope.

(ii) The character of a local resource system is governed in some part by the local industrial structure: as the heterogeneity of Battersea's industrial structure is echoed at all levels in the social system, so homogeneity will resonate throughout the opposite case.

(iii) The homogeneous/heterogeneous dimension also affects boundary principles and processes. In a heterogeneous area (like Battersea) localist principles are stronger: insider status can be achieved by residence and recognition. In the opposite (homogeneous) case ethnic principles will tend to prevail: insider status will be ascribed by birth, perhaps by in-marriage, perhaps through offspring. Boundaries of the first (heterogeneous) type are by this token more adaptable, more flexible than in the second (homogeneous) case.

(iv) As the resilience of any system varies with the flexibility of its boundaries (Wallman, 1978), so areas of the first (Battersea) type are relatively more resilient in the face of economic change or population movement; they are economically adaptable because a heterogeneous and open local structure offers more scope for informal/unofficial economic organisation. There is a correspondence between economic and identity resource systems in this respect; diverse options in one domain imply flexibility also in the other.

Economic, demographic and political profiles of Battersea as a whole can be described as heterogeneous and open (Wallman and Associates 1982). As a local labour market it includes (and in the nineteenth century included) a wide range of industries and occupational niches and there is no dominant employer or set of employers. Its population is and has been ethnically mixed, and although dominantly working class it includes a long-standing sprinkling of middle-class residents. Working-class Battersea is not physically cut off from riverside areas and the park to the north of it and the neighbouring middle-class districts to the south. Nor is the housing stock distinct. While a large part of the centre of modern Battersea has always been a working-class residential area, it has no unbroken expanses of similar dwellings. Our first ethnographic survey area is typical: a compact neighbourhood of no more than 500 households, the housing stock includes small cottages, imposing four-storey residences and flat-fronted modern apartment blocks; these are both publicly and privately owned and all types of tenancy are represented.

Of all the indications of heterogeneity, the most interesting is the extent to which newcomers and outsiders can be integrated as 'members' of one kind or another. This pattern is not confined to narrowly economic aspects of livelihood, nor is it new. Historical evidence shows it to be a striking characteristic of local political traditions and of expressed political ideology: in contrast to the exclusive ethnic/nationalist political style of east London for example, working-class ideology in Battersea has been consistently internationalist and its elected politicians strikingly cosmopolitan (Kosmin, 1979). Similarly, but from a different perspective, ethnographic enquiry shows in-migrants assimilating to the area with an enthusiasm which indicates that the practical or affective value of localness or localist identity regularly outweighs the resource potential of their ethnic or regional origins. Localist identity is, like any other, a two-way process: evidence for it here is the fact that newcomers both define themselves and are recognised by their neighbours as 'local' after relatively short periods of residence, and that these definitions govern the management of other resources.[4]

Localism is in this sense a principle of resource management, not a geographic focus. Battersea's localist orientation does not mean that its residents ever confined all their livelihood to a narrow local area. The point is nicely illustrated by the relation between jobs and information about jobs. The neighbourhood studied conforms to the pattern for Battersea as a whole in that most employed residents have jobs outside Battersea itself and many travel to work long distances beyond the South London area. But the ethnographic survey reveals a localist bias that the formal labour market statistics ignore: the majority of respondents with jobs heard about them from *local* information sources – whether or not the jobs were in Battersea and irrespective of the respondents' ethnic and regional origins.

The same data imply the connection between forms of structure and styles of organisation that we are concerned to demonstrate. Heterogeneous structure and localist organisation are both expressions of Battersea's boundary system. Once defined as 'local', newcomers begin to be integrated into local information networks which give them access to a range of other resources. On one side of the process they *choose* to enter the local system because it is useful to them; on the other, they *can* enter because the local system allows them in. Its overall boundary is permeable because the boundaries of its component sub-systems are not superimposed: the information network and the area of employment are not co-extensive; residents do not live and marry and work and play in a ghetto-like local area or identify with a set of others defined by a fixed set of 'tribal' characteristics – which would account, incidentally, for the minimal interest in ethnic origin characteristic of the area. The data for Battersea imply that if the local system were less heterogeneous its boundary would be less negotiable and membership to it less readily achieved. By this logic a more homogeneous structure will necessarily entail a more explicit investment in ethnic resources for economy and identity alike. The two types of boundary system are idealised in the contrast between the heterogeneous and homogeneous styles represented in figure 9.1.

Battersea's heterogeneous industrial structure sets or reflects the style of resource management throughout the local system. Either way, industrial structure is the prime *objective* measure of its heterogeneity. By this token a suitable area for comparison with Battersea will be indicated by homogeneous industrial structure. Thus: just as employment in Battersea is spread across a wide range of industries, and travel to work outside the Borough is and always has been a normal feature of local livelihood, so the contrasting case will be an employment centre – i.e. an area to which workers come rather than one from which they disperse – with a traditional leading industry or industries.

The east end of London qualifies on both counts. It has since the nineteenth century been the centre of London's dockland, clothing and furniture industries, and these have in combination dominated the industrial structure of the area and made it an important focus of employment opportunity.[5] We were not therefore surprised by the contrast between Battersea and the old dockland areas of Bermondsey and Poplar in respect of proportions of men working outside the home borough, and of the population balance after the labour force has travelled to work (table 9.1). But we had not anticipated that travel to work traditions could be so markedly independent of local geography: each of the three boroughs abuts onto the Thames and has a water boundary which constrains daytime journeys to work. The fact that this physical similarity so little affects the size and shape of the local labour market enhances the probability that industrial structure has some prior significance.

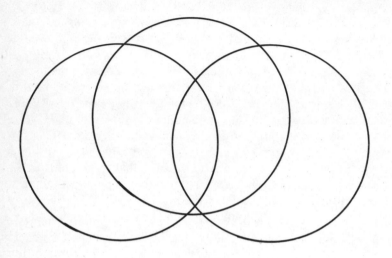

(i) Heterogeneous Boundary Type

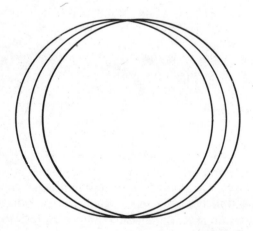

(ii) Homogeneous Boundary Type

Figure 9.1

Table 9.1 Travel to work patterns: men only (boundaries before 1965)

Area of residence and enumeration	% working outside it	Labour force balance
Battersea M.B. (pop. 75,000)		
1921	58	—
1951	61	—
1961	65	—
Poplar M.B.		
1921	33	+
1951	43	+
1961	49	+
Bermondsey M.B.		
1921	33	+
1951	39	+
1961	44	+

Source: OPCS

Its influence persists even in the face of change. The dockland, clothing and furniture industries have lately declined so much in importance that they no longer dominate the economy of London's east end, but travel to work patterns continue as before. We cannot show them by carrying forward the comparisons shown in table 9.1 because its constituent units disappeared as administrative areas when London's local government was reorganised in 1965. But even the new larger London boroughs, each made up of more or less arbitrary amalgamations of some number of old metropolitan boroughs, show similar differences. In 1971 the metropolitan boroughs of Battersea, Bermondsey and Poplar were absorbed into the London boroughs of Wandsworth, Southwark and Tower Hamlets respectively. Although each unit 'area of residence' is now much larger, a higher percentage of Wandsworth men travels out to work every day than from the other two areas, and Tower Hamlets, with more than half its employed residents working in the home borough, was still an employment centre in 1971 (table 9.2). Tower Hamlets in fact represents an unusually neat overlap of administrative and economic realities: it is precisely contiguous with the three old Metropolitan Boroughs of Poplar, Stepney and Bethnal Green which together made up the traditional east end industrial centre.

Great cities like London are never ideal settings for local labour markets studies (Norris, 1980), but the OPCS figures indicate that some parts of it may be more amenable to labour market analysis than others. These are the districts whose workforce tends consistently to confine itself to a bounded local area and which function also as employment centres, attracting people to work in them who do not live there. These districts, moreover, meet our criteria for homogeneity very closely: their economy is focused around a dominant industry or industries, and their residents' travel to work patterns imply an overlapping of occupational and residential networks and close ties between the workplace and the neighbourhood.

Table 9.2 Travel to work patterns: men only (boundaries after 1965)*

Area of residence and enumeration 1971	% working outside it 1971	Labour force balance 1971
L.B. Wandsworth (incl. Battersea) (pop. 250,000)	65	—
L.B. Southwark (incl. Bermondsey)	56	+
L.B. Tower Hamlets (incl. Poplar)	46	+

Source: OPCS

* Data for 1981 unavailable until September 1983.

Seeking a small area in which to test the proposition that the homogeneity of an industrial structure is reflected throughout the local system (as heterogeneity is in Battersea), we began by compiling a list of named east end residential neighbourhoods that looked as though they might be appropriate to the comparative ethnographic survey. We then sketched a simple socio-economic profile of each, using a combination of statistical sources, the electoral register and walkabout. The field was eventually narrowed to two, and it was in the process of eliminating the other seven that the practical and analytic disadvantages of too much homogeneity at the neighbourhood level showed up.

It is not possible to use industrial structure as a direct index of homogeneity at this level: industrial structure influences the homogeneity of a neighbourhood, but it is not the appropriate measure of it. A neighbourhood is a residential microcosm of a wide administrative area, and industrial structure is an important economic characteristic of that administrative area. So different in kind are they that a neighbourhood need not even be within the boundaries of the administrative area from which it takes its employment tradition, it is only necessary that it should be involved in the industries which structured that tradition. Hoxton, which is one of the examples given in tables 9.3 and 9.4, is a case in point. It is now in the huge London borough of Hackney which was established with the reorganisation of local government in 1965 but its style of livelihood developed over the many generations that it was integrated into the old metropolitan borough of Shoreditch. Until the administrative change, Shoreditch was a small borough bordering on two of the east end industrial boroughs (Stepney and Bethnal Green), the City (that great centre of white-collar employment) and three other boroughs. It housed branches of the east end industries although it was, as a borough peripheral to the employment centre. Hoxton, however, lay in the south-east of Shoreditch, bordering on Bethnal Green and Stepney and belonging to the same local system. The fact that it is no longer officially enumerated as a part of the industrial east end (now almost exactly represented, as we have said, by the London Borough of Tower Hamlets) does not preclude its continuing to have the formal economic characteristics of an east end neighbourhood: in 1982 the majority of businesses around Hoxton Square trade in or make furniture or clothing.

Table 9.3   Values relative to all London wards

Area	1971 Ward and borough	NCEO	Foreign-born	Public housing	Travel to work on foot
Isle of Dogs	Poplar Milwall: T. Hamlets	4	3	9	6
Riverside	Riverside: Southwark	4	5	8	8
Hoxton	Moorfields: Hackney	5	4	7	9
Medway Road	Holy Trinity: T. Hamlets	6	6	7	7
Louvaine Road (pop. 1,200)	St John's: Wandsworth (pop. 12,000)	7	6	5	6

(Morrey GLC, 1976)

Without detailed ethnographic evidence, the only data systematically collected at neighbourhood level are the Census Small Area Statistics, still available only for 1971. The Greater London Council's collation of these provides a useful starting point (Morrey, 1976). The same characteristics are abstracted for each Small Area (which comprises two to three hundred people) cumulated to borough ward level and tabled to make a standard nine point range for London.[6] This means that each area is comparable to any other in terms of the various features measured. For our present purposes, we have only taken account of four of the Small Area characteristics which together can be interpreted to say something about local boundary systems: these are shown in the 'scores' for residents of foreign or New Commonwealth (i.e. non-white) origin; for residents living in local authority (i.e. public) housing; and for residents walking to work (table 9.3). Converting the normal curve scores into more or less than average values (so that zero represents the value for 40 per cent to 60 per cent and ± 4 the value for 4 per cent of London wards) produces a more explicit measure of relative degrees of homogeneity (table 9.4).

Figures are given for only five borough/wards. The St John's Wandsworth figures pertain to the Battersea survey area which is a template for the least homogeneous (because heterogeneous) case. The other four are tabulated so that those nearer to Battersea are more like it (i.e. less homogeneous) than those further from it. The correlations are statistically crude but ethno-graphically suggestive: more homogeneity implies a pattern such that low levels of black or foreign in-migration, go with one style of tenure and formally controlled access to housing, and with an overlapping of residential and employment networks. Where the pattern is broken the anomaly is readily explained: the Isle of Dogs score for residents walking to work is out of line because of the unique combination of its peninsular shape, transport patterns and traditional dependence on the now dead docklands. By 1971 there were few local jobs left and most residential parts of it were cut off from the mainland by deserted warehouse space and too far away even from mainland Tower Hamlets for a two-way journey on foot each day.

Table 9.4 Degrees of homogeneity

	NCEO	Foreign-born	Public housing	Walking to work
Isle of Dogs	− 1	− 2	+ 4	+ 1
Riverside	− 1	0	+ 3	+ 3
Hoxton	0	− 1	+ 2	+ 4
Medway Road	+ 1	+ 1	+ 2	+ 2
Louvaine Road	+ 2	+ 1	0	+ 1

The more homogeneous areas have: fewer foreign and Commonwealth born residents (less mix); more public housing (controlled access and one style of tenure); more travelling to work on foot (work/residence overlap) than is average for London (represented by a zero score).

But while these special features of the Isle of Dogs confirm its homogeneity, they also signal that an area may be homogeneous to a degree that eliminates exactly the options we intend to test. The Isle of Dogs fits the homogeneous model (figure 9.1(ii) quite perfectly, but there is *visible* evidence that its perfection disqualifies it as a candidate for comparison. Its operative 'neighbourhood' boundary is actually a concrete buffer strip that makes a neat geographic division between insiders and outsiders, but is too inflexible to respond to the processes of change and exchange which affect insider/outsider definitions.

Social boundaries regularly occur at points of physical difference, but they are not *social* boundaries unless the meaning of the physical difference is relational, negotiable, variable. And if the boundary marking the edge of the Isle of Dogs is not social in this sense, then there is no point in trying to explain it by principles of organisation and identity characteristic of a particular social structure or style of livelihood.

Similar (and, of course, always only for the purposes of a synthetic selection procedure) very high scores for homogeneity of people and housing indicate and are reflected by the lack of certain organisational options. Because there is virtually only one landlord (the local government authority) and only one style of tenure, there is no room to manoeuvre the way housing resources are managed; and because there are so few foreign or Commonwealth born residents, so few ethnics, the ethnic option – i.e. the use of ethnicity as a prime principle of identity or (unofficial) economic organisation – is not there to be exercised.

The analytic constraint of too much homogeneity applies also in the case of Bermondsey's Riverside area but shows itself differently on the ground – perhaps only because the ground itself is different. There is no part of Bermondsey which is physically as distinct as the Isle of Dogs, but the riverside area was, like the Isle of Dogs, built up around the London docks and now shows signs of the dockland industry's decline. Some of the effects of its structure and traditions however persist. While some people have moved out and others in, no Battersea-like mix has occurred in the process. Newcomers appear instead to have settled in homogeneous population blocks such that ethnic boundaries often coincide with geographic lines – one side of a road, one housing block, one unit being almost entirely white, the other no less dominantly black.

This observation is made only on the basis of extensive walkabout in the area, but is sociologically persuasive: local dependence on a single industry may mean that, when the single industry dies, the families of people defined by it move out, in effect, blocks at a time, leaving space for replacement blocks of newcomers who take it up because their residential options and/or preferences are different.

Where, as in this case, the oldtimers are largely white and the newcomers largely black, difference by colour also coincides with difference by length of residence in the area. And because colour is more visible than the significance of time involvement, the pattern strikes the eye as a version of racial or even racist segregation. Our point is that this example of the ethnic organisation of housing should be examined as evidence of structural homogeneity, which in turn is explained by the fact that the boundaries of the various local systems coincide so exactly that the overall local system is hard to penetrate and hard to change (as figure 9.2(ii)).

The combination could account for there being so few foreign or Commonwealth born residents in the Isle of Dogs and Riverside, but also implies that there would be little scope for the reorganisation of economic or identity resources whatever the rate of influx: newcomers to any area can only take up the options it offers and so cannot avoid sustaining the local style. By this logic, where mixed population and homogeneous local structure *do* occur together, neither ethnic nor homogeneous principles need be altered by the encounter. On the contrary: each will tend to reinforce the other.

Unlike the Isle of Dogs and Riverside, Hoxton and the Medway Road area combine the two features in a way that allows the logic to be tested on the ground. They contain average or better than average proportions of foreign and Commonwealth born residents and yet show signs of homogeneous local structure in the Small Area Statistics compilations. Two inferences can readily be drawn. One is that either area is appropriate to the comparison we propose to make because each offers scope enough for variation in ethnic preference or organisational principle to be expressed. The other is that, although all four areas listed above the line in tables 9.3 and 9.4 are 'homogeneous' by contrast to Battersea, the upper and the lower pair differ from each other not just in *degree* of homogeneity, but in *kind* of homogeneity. Both inferences are sustained by the fact that the Isle of Dogs and Riverside are traditional dockland areas, while Hoxton and Medway Road are furniture and rag trade areas. Although the three industries are similar to the extent that they dominate or have dominated the local employment scene and foster or have fostered geographically narrow labour markets, the scope for control over entry into dock work is, in London at least,[7] very different from the structure of access to the other two trades. The difference shows in the number of 'gates' of entry into each. In the docks there is one: dockworkers are (were) by tradition members of one extended family, passing the occupation from father to son in a way that leaves (left) no need for or room for new recruits of any origin. In the rag and furniture trades by contrast there are many 'gates' into workshops and sweatshops, into the manufacture or distribution of specialist garments or pieces of furniture, into separate levels of the industrial hierarchy etc. Because control over a particular 'gate' implies control over access to the economic niche that it leads to, these many-gated industries may be said to account for the multi-ethnic style of London's east end. They offer economic options amenable to takeover by entrepreneurs with limited initial capital, a ready pool of dependent cheap labour, and some willingness to defer economic and status returns on their investment – all of which requirements are met by particular forms of ethnic organisation.[8] The point is double-edged: the industrial structure offers a limited range of options and only a limited range of people can deploy the resources necessary to taking up those options. In effect it is a combination of structural options and organisational styles which makes particular ethnic groups fit the local system so neatly.

The methodological conclusion is obvious: it is as impossible to compare items that contrast too much as it is to compare items that match too closely. In this case it makes no sense to test whether two London areas differ in the extent to which they use ethnicity as a principle of organisation and identity if one of those areas has no resident ethnic mix and no incoming population; and/or if the local structure contains so little room for manoeuvre that there is no scope for the expression of either ethnic or non-ethnic preference.

But if *structure* as a framework of options is distinguished from *organis-*

ation as the choices made from amongst those options, the difference between homogeneous areas that can and cannot be compared to Battersea can be taken into analytic account. Where both structure *and* organisation are homogeneous – as in the two dockland areas – there is too much difference, not enough similarity to allow any sensible comparison of styles of resource management to be made. But where a homogeneous structure contains scope for heterogeneous organisation – as in the Hoxton and Medway Road areas – the comparison is both feasible and useful. It is because these areas are similar to Battersea at the level of options for organisation that they are appropriate grounds for testing the effect of structural difference on the way those options are exercised.

It is too early for analytic conclusions, but we may venture two tentative predictions of variation on the inner London theme – the first concerns identity options and is in line with our original proposition; the second relates to economic change and rests on the revised, three-part typology.

One: there are two styles of resource management. One is *localist* and reflects a heterogeneous industrial structure, the other is *ethnic* and occurs with homogeneous industrial structure. It is as though heterogeneity opens the system and fosters a commitment to place while homogeneity closes the system and fosters a commitment to (ethnic) origin. By this token, if two areas with mixed population, one heterogeneous, one homogeneous, are compared, it is likely that ethnic difference will count less in the first area than in the second.

Two: alongside these two resource management styles, we have identified three types of local areas in terms of differences in the structure of their economic options. These terms provide a logic for their different reactions to recession and redundancy in the various local industries. Heterogeneous (Battersea type) areas will show least change – at least in the early stages. When any of the small local industries closes, some among the working population will move to others, the majority will travel further to work without moving house or altering their pattern of livelihood to any observable extent. Very homogeneous (dockland type) areas are very inflexible by contrast: the decline or death of the dominant one-gated industry will (without radical intervention) mean a parallel decline of the local area. And the inter-mediate type area, defined by homogeneous structure but heterogeneous organisation, will conform to the demographic pattern called 'ethnic succes-sion'. The traditional ethnic labour force will move out to the suburbs *en bloc*, leaving inner city niches for another ethnic group to take up. The newcomers may be recent immigrants and they may or may not have prior connections in the area and experience of the industries concerned. It is only necessary that they be adept in the use of ethnic principles of organisation and resource management, and that they will constitute a labour force cheaper than the one they are replacing.

Whatever the 'ethnic outcome' in these inner London areas, the general inference is plain. Local industrial structure makes so much difference to organisational options that it can be expected to govern the scope and style of informal/unofficial economic activity in labour markets of every sort.

Notes

1   This paper was asembled with the active assistance of Ian Buchanan and Yvonne Dhooge. It reports a phase of the Resource Options Research Programme, funded by the (British) Social Science Research Council at the London School of Economics.

2   Principal written sources are OPCS Censuses of Population 1911–71, Booth, 1889–91, and Llewellyn Smith's *New Survey of London Life and Labour*, 1935. More qualitative data sources of the economic and social history of inter-war Britain have also been used.

3   These data were enriched by a strategy of employing local residents as interviewers in both ethnographic surveys. The procedure and its contribution to the understanding of local networks and boundary processes are described in Wallman *et al.*, 1980.

4   Both localism and the systematic connection between economic and other resources are explored in Wallman, 1984.

5   In the case of London, areas contrasted by industrial structure can also be contrasted by *type* of industry. In a detailed mapping of the industries of London in 1861 and 1951, Battersea is shown as service industry oriented – if only because 'being an area of small total employment it appear(s) to contain concentrations of service workers . . . by default' – and east end areas are shown as dominated by manufacturing industry (Hall, 1964: 33–5). A particular industrial structure does not, of course, imply a single co-variant industrial type: small manufacturing industry is no less characteristic of Battersea than is its 'concentration of service workers'. But it could be interesting to consider whether industrial type of itself affects unofficial economic options at the local level. Needless to say, we have not done that here.

6   The standard nine-point scale is the numerical representation of a normal curve. It is important that a score of 5 represents the middle value pertaining in 20 per cent of cases; 0 and 9 the extremes including only the top and bottom 4 per cent.

7   Other forms of restrictive recruitment are reported for dockland areas elsewhere
    (see e.g., the ethnogaphic descriptions of Newfoundland and Israeli docklands
    included in Wallman (ed.), 1979 b).
8   It is important that only hierarchical forms of ethnic organisation are appropriate.
    Non-hierarchical ethnics – notably West Indians – do not take up these options.
    The implications of this difference are not considered here.

Minority settlement and the local economy

One of the consequences of the recession in Britain in the early 1980s has been to focus the attention of policy makers and academics on the extent to which ethnic minority business development can help to regenerate the economy, especially in inner urban areas marked by long term industrial and residential decline. The similarities between economic policy in Britain and the United States suggest that this structural pressure to maximise the contribution of minorities to economic activity may be more widely felt. Within the EEC countries in continental Europe, too, where the Gastarbeiter system has been used to recruit workers during the period of post-war economic expansion, structural unemployment seems likely to create pressure for ethnic minorities to become more involved in entrepreneurial activities, especially where repatriation is not seen as a feasible solution. These developments give an added sense of urgency to the need to develop useful paradigms for understanding the role of ethnic business in western capitalist economies. Indeed, a flurry of research activity in this area in America and in Britain has contributed substantially to this end (Cummings, 1980; Kim, 1981; Aldrich, Cater, Jones and McEvoy, 1981; Waldinger, 1983; Ward and Jenkins, 1984).

The conceptual frameworks employed in earlier studies of ethnic minorities in business drew extensively on the 'middleman minorities' model (Blalock, 1967; Bonacich, 1973); more recently the notion of the 'ethnic niche' or 'ethnic enclave' (Wilson and Portes, 1980) has been influential. There has been no real attempt, however, to establish in what circumstances such approaches can be used to explain the pattern of involvement of ethnic minorities in the economy in contrast to previous explanations which have stressed the role of immigrants as a 'replacement labour' force (Peach, 1968). Indeed, some studies of immigration to Britain (and to western Europe as a whole) in the post-war period assume that all migrants have been employees (Grammenos, 1982). It is difficult to reconcile this with accounts which stress the preoccupation of particular immigrant communities with entrepreneurial activities (Tambs-Lyche, 1980).

At an aggregate level statistics indicating the involvement of ethnic minorities in business in Britain are not revealing. The latest available national data showing the numbers and proportions of self-employed and employers (as opposed to those in the labour market) come from the National Dwelling and Housing Survey (NDHS), carried out in 1977–8.[1] Figures are given in table 10.1.

Table 10.1 Heads of households: self-employed in specified socio-economic groups by ethnic group for national sample (percentages)

| | Employers | | Self- | Own | Sum of | |
	large firms (SEG1)	small firms (SEG2)	employed prof'nals (SEG3)	account workers (SEG12)	SEGs 1, 2, 3 and 12	(no.)
White	0.3	3.8	1.0	4.9	10.0	1,101,181
West Indian	—	1.0	—	2.6	3.6	4,880
Indian	—	4.6	1.6	5.5	11.6	12,956
Pakistani/ Bangladeshi	—	2.4	0.4	5.1	7.9	4,372
Other non-white	0.8	5.7	0.5	6.0	13.0	23,036
Total	0.3	3.8	1.0	4.8	10.0	1,146,424

Source: National Dwelling and Housing Survey, special tabulation.
Note: Percentages read *across* the line and represent self-employed in designated SEGs as a proportion of all economically active household heads.

Table 10.1 shows that while West Indians are significantly underrepresented among the self-employed, there is no major difference in this respect between Indian and Pakistani and white household heads. Furthermore, breaking down these figures into different types of self-employment does nothing to alter this conclusion. Aggregate statistics simply conceal the very substantial internal differences in the employment position of ethnic minorities in British cities (Ward, 1984, ch. 7).

This chapter consists of a first step towards assessing the participation of ethnic minorities in business by classifying the settlement pattern and involvement in the local economy of members of ethnic minorities in urban areas in Britain. In so doing, it attempts to demonstrate the relevance of the main types of explanation of this phenomenon noted above. It posits five broad types of involvement in the local economy:

(i) Some areas have been largely unaffected by immigration from the New Commonwealth in the post-war period. It is hypothesised that this will occur in two quite different contexts. First, where there has been a sharp contraction in the rate of economic activity over the last forty years, it is unlikely that there has been any real opportunity for an immigrant group to obtain employment. At the other extreme, where economic opportunities and the local lifestyle have been sufficiently attractive, it is equally unlikely that members of racial minorities would have found easy access to employment or business opportunities in the area. Where either of these sets of circumstances obtain, we should expect to find a *non-settlement* area.

(ii) Secondly, in some districts a substantial number of local jobs have been abandoned by the traditional workforce, through migration either to other areas or to other places of work in the locality where terms and conditions have been more attractive. Thus, there has been a need for a *replacement labour* force to take over the jobs which have been abandoned. This thesis, set out by Peach (1968), has been widely adopted in other accounts of race and employment in Britain (see, for example, Rose *et al.*, 1969, ch. 7). The main areas of employment at issue have included foundries, cotton and wool textiles, public transport, utilities and domestic work in hospitals.

(iii) In some situations where ethnic minorities have arrived to take over such jobs they have thereby created a market which can most easily be supplied by other members of the same minority. In particular, small businesses may thrive to the extent that such consumer demand constitutes a 'protected' market. Thus the more culturally alien the minority, the more the opportunities for self-employment within the community. That is, a pattern emerges of the *ethnic niche* or *enclave* which covers both a majority of wage workers and a minority of small businesses within the ethnic community.

(iv) In other contexts, however, there may be opportunities for ethnic minorities to develop businesses which rely on the established majority for custom. The *middleman minority* model expounded by Bonacich was an attempt to conceptualise the circumstances in which this was likely to occur. Whether or not the explanation she puts forward as to which minorities are likely to exemplify this pattern is validated in the British case, the self-evident presence of some minorities, most notably the Chinese, in areas of business where they are largely dependent on the majority community for patronage confirms that this is a further pattern of involvement in the local economy.

(v) Lastly, while none of the above types will be found in a pure form, there are likely to be situations where more than one pattern is to be found. For while they are analytically separate, there is no reason to regard them as *alternative* forms of settlement. Thus, the final type could be described as a *general* settlement pattern.

Finally, it should be stressed that while each of these types is seen as distinctive, all derive from the particular structure of opportunities in the local economy, rather than the characteristics of the minority group members. Those migrating to a specific area may have distinctive characteristics (types of qualifications, for example, or business experience) but it is argued that this will only constitute an advantage where it relates to openings in the local economy.

In testing the utility of this classification scheme against data on the settlement of minorities in urban areas in Britain, it is desirable to select a minority group who are (i) culturally distinct (much of the theorising in the area of ethnic business carries this assumption), (ii) sufficiently numerous to allow the pattern of settlement in a wide range of areas to be examined and (iii) sufficiently involved in business as well as the labour market to distinguish between the various alternatives set out. For these reasons, in this analysis we use data referring to Indian and Pakistani settlement in Britain, rather than that of West Indians or the Chinese, for both of which groups one or more of these conditions would not obtain.

Patterns of immigrant involvement in the local economy

(i) *Non-settlement*

There are two types of economic conjunctures in which it was hypothesised that little or no Asian settlement would take place in an urban area. These consist of (i) a sufficiently sharp contraction in the local economy to discourage any immigration from outside and (ii) economic or lifestyle opportunities sufficiently attractive to allow effective resistance towards any Asians trying to move in. For a crude measure of this we turn to a classification of British towns and cities in the period immediately preceding large scale immigration from India and Pakistan. Moser and Scott (1961) provide an analysis of 157 urban areas by economic and other variables based on the 1951 census which is most convenient for this purpose. Of these almost one-third (49) are within the London commuting area, and since London constitutes something of a special case in looking at immigration to Britain, they are ignored for the purposes of this paper, though the same broad trends apply in London too.

It was assumed that those areas experiencing the greatest decline in the economy could be identified by the proportion of men in semi-skilled and unskilled manual work. Of the twenty-six areas with the highest proportions only two had more than half of one per cent of their population of Indian or Pakistani ethnic origin in 1977–8, according to the NDHS, compared to a figure of 1.8 per cent for England as a whole. They consist almost entirely of long-established industrial areas dominated by heavy engineering, mining and docking. Many of them had as little as one in a thousand of their population of Indian or Pakistani origin – examples include Liverpool, Hull, Barnsley and Wigan. Some of these areas had received larger numbers of immigrants from Africa and Asia in earlier years (including Liverpool and ports in the north-east of England) but more recently there have been virtually no arrivals from South Asia.

Areas with the most attractive economic and lifestyle opportunities were identified by taking those places with the highest proportion of male jobs in professional and managerial positions. The top eighteen such areas had equally minute proportions of Indians and Pakistanis. Thus about 40 per cent (42 out of 108) of urban areas in Britain outside the London commuting region, those with the least and those with the most attractive opportunities, have been virtually unaffected by South Asian immigration. So while the conventional wisdom is that Asians have settled in those areas with the worst jobs, this analysis suggests that there are a substantial number of areas where there were no jobs, as well as where higher status jobs were available but monopolised by others. This fits in with Peach's conclusion that 'the main coloured groups form the highest proportion of the population mainly in the regions of moderate industrial attraction' (1968: 67).

(ii) *Replacement labour*

The classic explanation of the settlement pattern of New Commonwealth immigrants in Britain is, as noted above, that they came as a replacement labour force to take such jobs as were no longer attractive to local labour (Peach, 1968). Whether this refers to areas where workers turned to other jobs that were available locally and preferable or to areas which were losing their labour force as workers sought better jobs elsewhere, the central notion is that black people were *replacing* the local working population.

Where immigrants from the Caribbean have played this role, they have typically been drawn into the workforce in small units in sectors such as transport and public utilities. Where whole sections of an industry needed a replacement workforce, this is more likely to have come from Asia. In an attempt to define areas where replacement labour has been dominant in the settlement pattern of Asians, to the exclusion of ethnic business development, we looked for areas where there was (i) substantial Asian settlement (over 3 per cent of the population), (ii) a heavy concentration of Asians in manual employment in local firms (over 75 per cent manual employees), (iii) little small business (less than 3 per cent of Asians in businesses with no employees except members of their immediate family, i.e. SEG 12).

Data were available from the NDHS on the characteristics of Asian household heads in fifteen towns and cities in England outside London with over one per cent of their population of Asian origin (as well as two others, Liverpool and Salford, which were non-settlement areas). Figures from the NDHS used in categorising Asian settlement patterns are contained in the appendix (table 10.2).

Five of these fitted the replacement labour form as defined above: Birmingham, Coventry, Wolverhampton, Sandwell and Walsall. All are in the West Midlands and in all of them metal manufacture and metal working are dominant in the economy. In each case at least twenty-five times as many household heads were manual employees as were running their own small businesses. Given this degree of dominance of manual labour in the employment profile of Asian workers, it is surely justifiable to refer to these areas as characterised by replacement labour, as far as Asian workers are concerned. Even if all the Asian houehold heads enumerated in the NDHS as working on their own account were in trade and commerce, there is no hint of middleman activities being any more than a minute adaptation among Asian settlers. Indeed, there is little sign of substantial numbers making a living by servicing members of their own ethnic groups, let alone acting as middlemen in businesses dependent on the host society for custom, which is presumably implicit in the middleman model. In fact, the replacement labour pattern found in the West Midlands well exemplifies Bonacich's recognition that 'many groups of sojourning migrant labourers do not enter small business' (1973: 588).

(iii) *Ethnic niche*

A recent study of Asian retailing in Britain has stressed the extent to which Indian and Pakistani shopkeepers are making a living by serving the 'protected' ethnic market (Aldrich, Cater, Jones and McEvoy, 1981; Cater, 1984). While this is not the only pattern observed (for cases where Asian retailers have mostly served the white market, see Aldrich, 1980 and Mullins, 1979), its existence suggests explanations of Asian retailing in terms of the dynamics of ethnic consumer demand at different stages of the process of residential succession. We noted that the presence of a concentrated body of Asian settlers in particular residential areas along with fellow countrymen making a living by selling or providing other services within the community has been described in terms of the 'ethnic niche' or 'ethnic enclave' (see also Auster and Aldrich, 1984). This represents the next of our types of settlement. Its main feature is a body of migrant workers engaged in manual work, as in the previous type, but in association with a substantial number of community members running businesses heavily dependent on fellow ethnics for custom.

To qualify as examples of the 'ethnic niche' settlement pattern, we postulated that over 3 per cent of the population should be of Asian origin, as before, that over 70 per cent should be engaged in manual work as employees and that more than 5 per cent should be running small businesses on their own account which depended heavily on community support. Three of the fifteen urban areas for which data was available fulfilled the first three conditions (see Appendix). From the NDHS data it is not possible to deduce the extent to which businesses serve the protected ethnic market, the final condition, but from other sources it is clear that most Asian retailers in Bradford, a centre of the manufacture of wool textiles in Yorkshire, rely greatly on support from within the community (Aldrich, Cater, Jones and McEvoy, 1981; Aldrich, Jones and McEvoy, 1984). The other two examples, Bolton and Rochdale, are cotton textile towns in Lancashire, which seem to display the same pattern (Anwar, 1979; Hahlo, 1980).

In all three areas there are still ten to fifteen times as many manual workers as small businessmen. But trade and commerce, a key feature of middleman minority settlement, at least seem to provide a larger minority with a means of livelihood. However, this does not qualify as a middleman pattern of development, since the trade is largely within the ethnic community, and by implication would not exist if the majority of community members had not come to take jobs in local firms, i.e. it is a secondary adaptation. Perhaps the most interesting question that arises from a comparison between the replacement labour and ethnic niche adaptations is whether there are more small businesses in the latter because of some characteristic posessed by those who decide to go into business or whether it reflects the lack of jobs in the local labour market which are more attractive than petty retailing. The studies of Asian shopkeepers in Bradford contain little evidence that those going into retailing are particularly qualified to do so by virtue of their background, when compared to those who take jobs in industry. For example, only one-fifth had fathers who were self-employed (Aldrich, Cater, Jones and McEvoy, 1981: 177). On the other hand it may be no accident that in the West Midlands, where Asian retailing has been less widespread, half of the manual jobs taken by Asians in industry have been at the skilled level and are likely to carry higher wage rates than jobs in the mills, the majority of which are semi-skilled.

The suggestion for further research that emerges is that where the ethnic niche model best describes Asian involvement in the economy, rather than replacement labour, this says more about the lack of good opportunities for manual work in the ethnic niche areas than about the lack of qualifications for starting businesses among Asians in areas where replacement labour predominates. In both types of area, settlement has been largely by villagers, mostly peasant farmers, who have formed encapsulated 'ethnic villages' in new and strange urban surroundings.

(iv) *Middleman minority*

The main elements in the middleman minority model are concisely set out by Bonacich:

A key variable is the orientation of immigrants towards their place of residence, with sojourning at first, and later a 'stranger' orientation affecting the solidarity and economic activity of the ethnic group. These in turn arouse the hostility of the host society, which perpetuates a reluctance to assimilate completely, or 'stranger' status (1973: 583).

Central to this model is the notion that it is those who immigrate as 'sojourners', i.e. who have a clear intention of returning home, and thus see themselves as temporary migrants, who are predisposed both to become successful in business and in so doing to maintain their temporary status until they become *de facto* permanent settlers, while retaining a 'stranger' role comparable to that of recent migrants. Sojourners show a high degree of internal solidarity. This gives rise to business success, since along with the motivation to accumulate capital found among temporary migrants, it allows the efficient distribution of resources (capital, jobs etc.) and the regulation of internal competition. It also leads to hostility against those who both live off and remain separate from the host society; and so to a reluctance to assimilate which perpetuates their stranger orientation in the society.

Bonacich recognises that middleman roles extend beyond trade and commerce and include other ways of making a living, such as the independent professions, the practice of various skills and acting as agents, contractors or brokers in different sectors of the economy. But within the world of business where middleman minorities are mostly found they are concentrated in those activities which do not require large amounts of capital to be tied up. Thus she describes them as in 'portable' occupations which can easily be practised in new surroundings – a clear advantage for those who see themselves as temporary migrants.

The fifteen areas of Asian immigration outside London were further inspected with a view to identifying places where the middleman minority form was more dominant. Unfortunately, the four categories described in table 10.1 which together make up the business population could not all be deduced from the available tabulations.[2] However, as a rough and ready way of categorising areas displaying the middleman minority model, it was determined that at least 15 per cent of the heads of household should be working on their own account and that a minority of Asians should be employed as manual workers. Two areas satisfied these conditions, Manchester and Newcastle (see Appendix).

To find Manchester emerging as a middleman minority area was no surprise, since the Asian business community based on the clothing trade but extending into various other sectors has been well researched (Nowikowski, 1984; Nowikowski and Ward, 1979; Werbner, 1984). For Manchester additional tables are available from the NDHS showing that a third of Indian heads of household and almost half (46 per cent) of the Pakistanis were engaged in some kind of business, with or without employees.

Little is known about the Asian community in Newcastle, an area of lesser Indian and Pakistani immigration, though Davies (1972) has shown that landlording was a favoured occupation among Pakistanis and that the Asian proletariat, whose housing careers in Britain have attracted considerable political as well as academic attention (Rex and Moore, 1967), were largely absent from the city. The NDHS figures show that 31 per cent of Asian household heads in Newcastle were working on their own account, to which would have to be added an unknown proportion running businesses with employees outside the family.

What has been said so far supports the middleman minority model as portrayed by Bonacich. But there are other features of Asian settlement to consider. For the explanation of this pattern that she gives to be substantiated, it would be necessary to show not only that trade and commerce was a major area of immigrant activity, but that those engaging in such activities saw themselves as sojourners and displayed the 'ethnic village' characteristics listed above. In fact, such evidence as is available points to the reverse.

First, the most distinctive sojourning group among Asians in Britain are the families of Indian and Pakistani ethnic origin who came to Britain following pressure to leave their adopted home in Uganda and Kenya. They could be said to be sojourning, certainly in relation to two homelands (India/Pakistan and Uganda/Kenya), possibly a third, i.e. Canada, where increasing numbers of community members have found a home. Further, many of them have come from a background of trading in East Africa and frequently they have transferred this to Britain. But neither Manchester nor Newcastle has been a centre of settlement for East African Asians, regardless of whatever business opportunities may be present here, and most Asian business is in the hands of Indians and Pakistanis who came direct from the subcontinent.

Secondly, while details of the personal characteristics and orientation to migration of Asians in Newcastle are not known, it is clear that members of the Asian business community in Manchester are much more anglicised than the ethnic villagers found in areas of replacement labour and ethnic niche. For example, they are much more residentially dispersed (Fenton, 1977; Ward and Nowikowski, 1981; Werbner, 1979) and more likely to have married outside the community and to be English-speaking (Nowikowski, 1980). They also show signs of the dilution of their cultural background, while retaining in most cases a strong sense of ethnicity (Nowikowski, *op. cit.*).

Thus while they may be well established in business, it is difficult to attribute this to the sojourning outlook of immigrants who see their stay as temporary and seek to separate themselves from the host society wherever possible, arousing its hostility in so doing. Indeed, as Werbner (1984) shows, a familiarity with the English way of life, including a knowledge of English, is likely to be a considerable asset in carrying on business in the rag trade, and to be reinforced by the social situations thrown up in the course of trading. That is, empirically the middleman minority pattern of economic activity is well supported but much remains to be done to establish its theoretical basis.

(v) *General migration*

The final item in this typology of Asian settlement patterns is frankly something of a catch-all. However, it is worth noting that only five of the fifteen areas we have been considering remain to be 'caught', so that while it may cover diverse situations, at least they constitute a minority. Labelling it 'general migration' is intended to distinguish it from the other types which all emphasise specific, collective adaptations, whether by manual workers or petty entrepreneurs. It is not suggested that in this final type migrants have come on a wholly different basis; rather, that they have been attracted by a *diversity* of economic opportunities. By implication it might be argued that these areas are characterised by a lack of opportunities for migrant workers to take over whole sections of manual employment in the locality or to become extensively involved in sectors of trade and commerce. The best examples of this among the remaining areas are probably Leeds and Nottingham, two regional centres where the basic industries have not drawn in large quantities of immigrant labour, but where various kinds of opportunities have arisen for Asians to make a living. In Nottingham, for example, Asians are more diverse in terms of the skill level required for their job and their employment status than in any of the other areas considered (see Appendix).

A third district, Dudley, is broadly comparable to the replacement labour areas which it adjoins but contains rather more Asian small businessmen; it has a smaller Asian population a bit more scattered over the economy; this probably reflects the fact that it houses many of those working in better class jobs in surrounding areas. It should probably be treated as a replacement labour area.

The fourth area considered under this heading, Reading, could arguably have been excluded on the grounds that it is only forty miles from London and includes among its residents London commuters as well as those working in the locality. More of its Asian population are managers in small firms, or employed as professionals or clerical workers – a pattern found to a much greater extent in London, though even in Reading over three-fifths of the Asian household heads are engaged in manual work.

Leicester, the final area caught under this heading, is certainly the least easy to classify. It could be argued that it represents all of the types of adaptation considered except, by definition, non-settlement, since it had an estimated Indian and Pakistani population (mostly Indian) in 1978 of 45,000 (16.5 per cent of the population). Thus, (i) it includes a replacement labour force attracted particularly by jobs in the knitwear and hosiery industry; (ii) there is an important business community (including a large element from East Africa) which is small in relation to the number of Asian employees in Leicester but large in comparison to the Asian business community in many other areas in Britain – some businesses depend on the protected market for custom, as in the ethnic niche areas, while others have developed a role as middlemen in the wider community (Clark and Rughani, 1983); (iii) there are also quite large numbers of Indians scattered over the economy employed as managers or professionals or in a white collar capacity, including some who have come to the city as individual households – a characteristic of general migration areas. Thus, examples of each type of adaptation could be found in Leicester, as in London, but in aggregate Asian settlement could not be categorised in terms of any of the three previous types. It may well contain the clearest example of the middleman minority adaptation as set out by Bonacich, but this is a minority element within the overall settlement pattern. It seems likely that it has grown as Indians have moved out of the manual employment which first drew them to the city, either because of the extra attractions of business openings or as a consequence of large scale contraction in local industry.

Discussion

We set out to assess the involvement of ethnic minorities in business by classifying urban areas in Britain according to the economic role played by Asian settlers. There were three distinctive patterns together with a residual category where a more diverse mode of settlement was evident, as well as other types of area where Asian immigration has not taken place. It is hardly a surprise that the places associated in each category turned out to have very similar local economies. *Non-settlement* districts (Liverpool, Salford) were traditional heavy engineering areas in an advanced state of economic decline. *Replacement labour* districts (Birmingham, Coventry, Wolverhampton, Sandwell, Walsall and to a lesser extent, Dudley) were all centres of engineering in the West Midlands and noted for the expansion of their economies over the post-war period. The three places displaying the *ethnic niche* pattern (Bradford, Bolton and Rochdale) were all textile centres in Lancashire and Yorkshire. Two districts (Manchester and Newcastle) showed a *middleman minority* model; both were regional commercial centres. This left what was described as a *general migration* pattern in Nottingham, Leeds, Reading and Leicester, to which London would have been added, given the opportunity to describe its complex immigration pattern. These are all urban industrial centres, though they have less in common than the places grouped in other categories.

The elements which singly or in combination made up the various types of Asian settlement were (i) replacing the white labour force in an area of manual work in the local economy, (ii) running a business relying for custom on members of an Asian replacement labour force, (iii) running a business oriented towards the wider, 'open' market and (iv) taking advantage of job openings on a more individual basis wherever they arose. In practice these elements will be found to different extents and in different combinations and sequences.

Replacement labour and the immigration of individual families such as is likely to be found in the general migration pattern are typical initial modes of settlement, though the speed with which Chinese from Hong Kong took over large sections of the fish and chip business in post-war Britain (a better case of middleman minority adaptation than any of those considered in this chapter (Watson, 1977)) suggests that the middleman form may emerge early on in favourable circumstances. A natural progression from the replacement labour form is to the ethnic niche, though this assumes that making a living servicing community members is more attractive than manual employment. We have suggested that in the foundry industry this was probably untrue, but that in textiles the rewards of manual employment in the mills were insufficient to deter Asians from going into trade and commerce within the protected market. How far the rapid contraction of the foundry industry in recent years has pushed Asians in the West Midlands into shopkeeping and other areas of business is not known. It is to be expected that in general structural changes in the local economy will lead to a reorientation of Asian economic activity.

What are the implications of this analysis for academic enquiry into minority business development – an area which needs much more systematic examination if the questions raised at the beginning of this chapter are to be properly addressed?

Where Asians have gone into business, it can be argued that particular industries have been selected because they both have low barriers to entry and also offer a chance for immigrants from Asia to be competitive through efficient use of the resources of labour, capital and expertise available through the community network (where the ethnic niche pattern is followed the ethnic market is also a significant factor). Thus one area in which research might usefully develop is to consider the circumstances in which businesses are started and the *strategy* behind decisions taken at the start, as well as at subsequent phases of development, together with the barriers faced at each point. This would clarify the circumstances in which the ethnic niche pattern emerges or alternatively that of the middleman minority.

A second research priority concerns *business succession*. Presumably the considerations which are most salient change over the course of a business career. At the start, however, such research as has been carried out on Asian businessmen in Britain suggests that it is the availability of a business that is the chief consideration. It is unfortunate that so little work has been done so far outside retailing, but within this sector it is those types of business which come on the market because they are least attractive to white business people in which Asian retailers are overrepresented. They include those shops which are unattractive to whites because of their location in areas undergoing residential succession from white to Asian or West Indian. Indeed, it is a feature of the 'ethnic niche' explanation of Asian retailing patterns that residential succession is closely associated with business succession (Ward and Jenkins, 1984). It may be therefore that more of the conceptual apparatus used in analysing residential succession could be usefully applied in examining business succession, such as 'push' and 'pull' models of succession.

The second type of retail outlet typically taken over by Asians in Britain is the business which has little appeal because of the long and unsocial hours involved. Newsagents, tobacconists' shops and chemists are good examples, where late working is normal, as well as the corner shop which, if Asian owned, is likely to be open on Sunday morning as well as Monday to Saturday. Running a chemist's shop also gives a chance to use a professional training in pharmacy.

Finally, following the logic of the above discussion, we can conclude that research could usefully address itself to the notion of the *business career*. We have already suggested that a middleman role may emerge in the course of settlement in contexts where replacement labour or the ethnic niche or individual migration is dominant. The same applies to the careers of individual businesspeople as well as communities. The first venture into self-employment is quite likely to depend for success on the protected market, but relying on community members for custom on a permanent basis may be a recipe for remaining small. A second path is to graduate to selling (or making) the same product or providing the same service on the open market after an initial period of dependence on community support. Among the Afro-Caribbean community in Britain, for example, hairdressing is probably the best example of this process. A third possibility is to use the capital acquired in the first, intra-community phase of the business to branch out into a separate area which requires a higher initial capital investment but offers a higher rate of return. Others again will go straight into business on the open market, with varying degrees of success, usually offering goods or services with an ethnic aspect (e.g. restaurants). All these types of business career carry the prospect of success or failure or just an ability to hang on. A systematic classification of the business careers of a sample of migrants from different origins (e.g. Asians vs. West Indians), with different characteristics (e.g. urban vs. rural background) and approaches to migration (e.g. permanent vs. temporary settlement) would be of great value, not only in facilitating a clearer understanding of the processes underlying business success but in providing some guidance as to what steps can be taken in a period of economic crisis to assist in planning business success in the future.

While the burden of this paper has been to demonstrate that the structuring of the local economy in different kinds of urban areas has been substantially responsible for the broad pattern of Asian settlement, this does not mean that the characteristics and orientation of other immigrant groups are not powerful determinants of their situation. The concentration of the Chinese in middleman roles in Britain (Watson, 1977) as well as in the United States (Light, 1972) fits in well with the interpretation put forward by Bonacich – their involvement in the restaurant and fish and chips business seems to be largely independent of inter-urban differences in Britain, since the consumer market on which they depend is not differentiated in this way. By contrast, immigrants from the Caribbean are much more evenly distributed over different localities in Britain – and, contrary to their position in the United States (Foner, 1979), substantially underrepresented in business almost everywhere (see Appendix).

Thus small business can be seen as an important, though usually subsidiary, element in the economic adaptation of Asian minorities in Britain. Reliance on the ethnic community and a middleman role are alternate strategies for business development. Some indication has been given of the uneven progress of those strategies in particular local economies. But much remains to be done by way of explaining the circumstances in which each pattern will flourish, anticipating likely trends and identifying implications for policy.

Notes

1 Most of the data from the NDHS referred to in this paper comes from special tabulations acquired by the ESRC Research Unit on Ethnic Relations.
2 In this paper 'small businesses' and people working 'on their own account' are defined by the number of 'own account workers', i.e. Socio-Economic Group (SEG) 12. This category includes all those working for themselves without using a professional skill, and with no employees outside the immediate family. SEGs 1 and 2 include both employers (i.e. those referred to in the first two columns in table 10.1) and managers employed in large and small firms. Finally, SEG 3 consists of those using a professional skill while working for themselves. Figures on the whole business population for Asians in selected areas, as in table 10.1, are contained in Ward and Reeves, 1980.

Appendix table 10.2 Data on Asians and West Indians in selected areas (percentages)

	Asians in population	Socio-economic groups of Asian household heads						no.	West Indians in population	West Indian h'hold heads in SEG 12
		1–2	3–4	5–6	9–11	12	Others			
Non-settlement										
Liverpool	0.1	(3)	(2)	(—)	(2)	(1)	(—)	8	0.3	(5.0)
Salford	0.5	(2)	(5)	(4)	(9)	(—)	(—)	20	0.1	(—)
Replacement labour										
Birmingham	6.4	8.8	3.7	7.4	75.5	2.3	2.3	216	4.8	2.1
Coventry	6.2	4.3	2.9	4.8	79.5	2.9	5.7	210	1.1	—
Wolverhampton	8.8	3.0	1.9	3.3	84.8	2.2	4.8	269	5.0	1.3
Sandwell	5.7	3.6	2.6	3.6	83.9	1.0	5.2	192	3.0	1.7
Walsall	4.2	5.2	0.6	4.5	83.9	—	5.8	155	1.0	(2.5)
(Dudley)	1.6	3.4	6.8	5.1	76.3	5.1	3.4	59	0.7	—
Ethnic niche										
Bradford	7.8	5.0	1.5	3.8	80.1	5.4	4.2	261	0.6	(3.0)
Bolton	4.7	3.9	3.9	4.5	74.7	7.8	5.2	154	0.2	(9.1)
Rochdale	3.1	5.6	5.6	0.9	74.8	7.5	5.6	107	0.2	(—)
Middleman minority										
Manchester	3.1	17.0	10.6	12.8	38.3	14.9	6.4	94	2.5	3.0
Newcastle	1.3	26.2	2.4	16.7	21.4	31.0	2.4	42	—	(—)
General migration										
Leeds	2.5	9.1	3.0	7.6	68.2	9.1	3.0	66	1.0	—
Nottingham	2.4	10.0	2.9	11.4	54.3	10.0	11.4	70	3.4	0.7
Reading	2.2	16.9	7.0	8.5	64.8	—	2.8	71	3.6	5.4
Leicester	16.5	8.8	2.0	9.4	66.7	7.0	6.1	543	2.1	—
London	4.1	12.6	9.8	22.2	42.3	6.5	6.6	4,077	4.1	2.8

Source: NDHS, special tabulations
Notes: SEG 1–2 managers; 3–4 professionals; 5–6 other non-manual; 9–11 manual; 12 own account workers
Others: Personal service, foremen, farm, armed forces, inadequately described. Actual numbers given for Liverpool and Salford because of small cell sizes

Immigrant enterprise and the structure of the labour market

This paper has two concerns: to examine labour market processes in the ethnic sub-economies emerging among the new immigrant population in New York City; and to explore the implications of these findings for segmented labour market theory. The paper develops two principal arguments: first, that the ethnic sub-economy differs from other secondary industrial sectors in the mechanisms by which labour market information is transmitted and workers are attached to firms; second, that these distinctive processes are associated with greater opportunities for skill acquisition and upward mobility.

Introduction

In the stylised model of urban labour markets offered by segmented labour market (SLM) theory, the secondary sector is the province of firms whose lack of market power and reliance on labour-intensive technologies keep wage levels depressed. Since the persistence of competition places a limit on firm size (and thereby on the articulation of structured job ladders) and also reduces the profit levels needed to pay for investment in specific skills, there are few opportunities for mobility within the firm. Skill acquisition through lateral mobility is equally impeded since most firms utilise simple processes with few intermediate positions that would provide learning opportunities. Because the wage levels are low and conditions are poor, the workforce in the secondary sector is marked by high levels of dissatisfaction and is weakly tied to any particular employer. Lacking incentives of either a monetary or non-monetary nature that would heighten commitment to work, secondary firms fall back on atavistic methods of direct control that engender antagonism and heighten turnover. The cumulative effects of instability produce an erratic career in which the succession of jobs and work relationships take on a disorganised and meaningless character. Thus, as Piore argued in his study of Puerto Rican migrants to Boston:

not all . . . [secondary] jobs possess all of the characteristics, and the reason for grouping them together is less that they are all alike in some obvious sense than that workers
and employers seem to perceive them as being alike . . . A special effort was made
to identify the common feature of the jobs; this appeared to be the opportunity for
upward mobility; all of the jobs were essentially dead-end. Not only did they offer
little chance of advancement within the enterprise, but they offered little in the
way of information, training, or institutional connections which would facilitate
advancement elsewhere in the labor market. (Piore, 1975: 11)

This conceptualisation emerged in the late 1960s as an attempt to explain
the employment problems of the then predominately black labour force concentrated in low-wage labour markets of the US inner cities. Since that time,
new immigrants from Latin America, the Caribbean and Asia have entered
the urban economy, in some instances replacing, in other instances displacing,
their black predecessors. While the empirical descriptions of low-wage labour
markets have been altered to take this development into account, the basic
conceptual framework of the segmented labour market has remained
unchanged. In fact the transformation of the low-wage labour force seems
to confirm the root SLM hypotheses. As Piore argued in *Birds of Passage*
(1979) immigrants offered a labour force ideally suited to the requirements
of secondary employers. Since the demand for labour in the secondary sector
is essentially undifferentiated, instability in a migrant workforce engaged in
back and forth moves to their home societies is fully compatible with manning
requirements. For workers, the decisive fact is that labour in the industrial
society is viewed as temporary and understood as an activity that is instrumentally linked to social conditions in the home society. Thus, immigrant
workers are indifferent to the issue of upward mobility and have the additional
advantage (from the employer's point of view) of evaluating wages and
working conditions in light of the much lower conditions that prevail in the
countries of origin.

However, the secondary sector appears to be only one mode of immigrant
labour market incorporation in the US; increasingly, immigrants enter the
labour market through the portals of immigrant-owned firms. Miami, with
its Cuban-dominated sector of more than 150 manufacturing firms, 230
restaurants, thirty furniture factories, a shoe factory employing 3,000 people
and thirty transplanted cigar factories is generally seen as the exemplar of
the contemporary ethnic economy in the US (Time, 1978; Wilson and Portes,
1980; Wilson and Martin, 1982). New York City, where the research on which
this paper is based has been conducted, is no less a stronghold of immigrant
business activity. For example, in the clothing trade, Chinese-owned factories
provide employment to over 20,000 Chinese immigrants – more than one-
sixth of the labour force in the city's largest manufacturing industry
(Waldinger, 1983). In restaurants, a conservative estimate pegs the level of
immigrant ownership at 60 per cent (Bailey, 1983). Meanwhile, Korean
immigrants have virtually taken over the city's stock of neighbourhood
groceries – much to the consternation of the supermarket chains who find that

the small immigrant concerns have cut heavily into their trade (Kim, 1981). Among tobacconists, stationers, jewellery manufacturers, construction contractors, furmakers, and taxi-owners, the infusion of new entrepreneurial blood is equally pervasive (Gallo, 1983; Korazim & Freedman, 1983).

This paper argues that labour market processes within this evolving ethnic sub-economy operate differently than they do in other secondary industry sectors. While the SLM literature suggests that labour market experiences have a random and anomic character, the evidence on immigrant-owned firms suggests that these concerns are organised around close-knit, well-established networks of kin, fellow townsmen and common nationals. The mobilisation of these networks apparently alters the interaction between labour and management, strengthening attachment to the firm. The relationship between employment in the immigrant firm and opportunities for subsequent mobility also takes on a different form than the SLM model suggests. Immigrants employed in ethnic firms appear to have substantial opportunities for skill acquisition; this in turn, combined with certain characteristics of the environment, increases the likelihood that they may successfully strike out on their own.

While this argument has been stimulated by direct empirical research, the essay itself is a work of synthesis. It draws on a variety of studies of small business activities among new immigrants in New York City. Some of these, including my own, originated as labour market studies focusing on the interactions between a diverse immigrant population and other labour force groups within a specific industrial context. Interest in immigrant enterprise emerged only in the course of research when it appeared that the role of immigrants within the various industries was mediated by their absorption into immigrant firms. Other studies referred to in this essay belong to the literature on immigrant adjustment; here the focus is on a single ethnic group whose entrepreneurial activity comprises one aspect of the broader process of ethnic adaptation. As distinct contributions, both the ethnic group and labour market studies highlight the myriad of ways by which immigrants gain access to a particular business niche. Taken together, however, the findings resonate with one another, uncovering a set of regular labour market practices that reappear across industry and ethnic group boundaries.

Immigration trends and adjustment patterns

New York is America's quintessential immigrant city and it has resumed its role as a Mecca for the country's newcomers ever since the revision of US immigration laws in 1965. Approximately 800–850,000 legal immigrants arrived in New York City between 1970 and 1980, almost 18 per cent of the total immigrant population moving to the United States during that period. To these legal arrivals can be added an indeterminate, though certainly sizeable number of illegal immigrants. Despite economic crisis and population decline, immigration mounted during the second half of the last decade when both the level of legal immigration and the numbers of foreign visitors – an indirect indicator of illegal immigration – moved upward (US INS, 1970–79; Tobier, 1982).

The New York-bound migration stream constitutes a group quite distinct from the rest of the nation's. Despite the city's large population of European descent, migration from Europe has dropped off more sharply than in the country at large. Similarly, Mexico and Cuba, which are important source countries nationally, contribute relatively little to the New York migration flow. Instead, New York's immigrants are dominated by newcomers who move from other western hemisphere countries and from China, with other important Asian-sending countries furnishing a relatively small migration flow.

In comparison to the rest of the nation, New York's immigrants are more likely to be of working-class and lower middle-class backgrounds. In part this is an artifact of the population's national composition, since Asians, the most educated group among the new arrivals, generally settle elsewhere. However, even in comparison to migrants of similar national backgrounds, New York's newcomers remain less likely to have been previously employed in professional and technical jobs. The percentage of such immigrants with higher-level training has declined among all immigrant groups, including Hispanics and Asians (Tobier, 1982).

Though immigrants experience downward mobility after entering the United States they subsequently move along an upward slope, gaining increments in pay as they acquire greater experience, firm-specific training, and greater labour market information. Research indicates that the earnings of immigrants reach parity with the earnings of comparable nationals (those born in the United States) after a ten to twenty year period; thereafter newcomers surpass nationals in earning ability (Chiswick, 1979; Waldinger, 1982). Comparable, locality-specific studies have not yet been conducted and thus it is difficult to assess the progress of those immigrants who have settled in the New York area. However, the available indicators suggest that local patterns of adaptation resemble the national norm. While *per capita* income tends to be lower among immigrants than among nationals, rates of unemployment, poverty and labour force participation among immigrants are on a par with that of the total population. Moreover, relative to the 'native' minority population of blacks and Puerto Ricans, the new immigrants do substantially better on all major indicators despite comparable 'human capital' characteristics. (Bailey and Waldinger, 1983; US Census of Population, 1980.)

The structure of the ethnic economy

The ethnic economy is structured around a series of economic processes that both create a protected niche for small immigrant firms and maximise the importance of immigrants' informal resources. The starting-point for many immigrant small businesses is the ethnic community itself. As Kinzer and Sagarin first noted, 'an ethnic group may not only have its own language, but its habits and customs that are better understood by business establishments operated by members of their own group' (Kinzer and Sagarin, 1953: 144). Among new arrivals there is often an intense demand for ethnic products of various types, whether cultural or culinary, whose provision involves a direct connection to the homeland and a knowledge of tastes and buying preferences unlikely to be shared by larger, native competitors. Immigrant businesses may also benefit from an ability to obtain the trust and confidence of the larger immigrant community. This is especially true for those businesses specialising in the process of adjustment. Since newcomers are often disconnected from the institutionalised mechanisms of service delivery, these immigrant businesses perform a myriad of functions far above the simple provision of accountancy, legal aid, or travel information and reservations. The search for security also leads immigrants to patronise their co-ethnics over outsiders. In the Colombian and Dominican neighbourhoods of Queens, for example, immigrant contractors renovate buildings and homes for other immigrants who opt for the reliability and reputation of a contractor over the lowest offer made through an ethnically open, competitive bid (Gallo, 1983). A preference for a segregated life-style also opens a niche for immigrant businesses: Israeli immigrants in Brooklyn, for instance, operate a thriving quasi-legal cab service taxiing religious Jews who prefer to utilise the services of other Jewish concerns (Korazin and Freedman, 1983).

Influences emanating from the open market provide a further spur to ethnic enterprise. In manufacturing, New York City specialises in products for which the final demand is highly unstable – with the result that the small, flexibly managed firm represents the optimal form of organisation. Immigrant clothing firms successfully compete in the production of short-lived style items and overruns on standardised goods because large firms lack the organisational capacity needed to respond to unpredictable tastes and short-term buying trends (Waldinger, 1984). In food retailing, the complexity of the New York market, with its heterogeneous ethnic mix, makes it a quagmire for national chains with cumbersome and rigid central administrations. Consequently, smaller, locally-based chains, where the span of control is short enough first to process information about highly differentiated market segments and then to service those various needs, are the dominant presence in the local market. However, these chains lack the economies of scale needed to achieve significant market power, with the result that food retailing can be easily penetrated by new immigrant-owned firms. Similar processes are at work in the food service (Bailey, 1983) and taxi (Korazin & Freedman, 1983) industries, creating more favourable terrain for small firms.

Stability and training

One strand of the original SLM literature emerged out of an institutional study of the internal labour markets of large firms. Doeringer and Piore's study (1971) showed how the internal labour market served to recruit and stabilise a trained workforce and minimise the risks associated with companies' investments in training. By restricting entry to the lowest point of the job hierarchy and providing orderly lines of progression up the job ladder, firms maximised workers' interests in maintaining tenure on the job. With the reduction of instability, employers increased the likelihood of obtaining a return to their initial investment in training.

In industries characterised by small firms the problems of obtaining and stabilising a training labour force are considerably more severe. If technological conditions are similar and skills are general, or if the labour contract is of an uncertain and limited duration, firms will be reluctant to train workers. One alternative is to lower skill levels so that the costs of training can be drastically reduced. In fact, the SLM literature suggests that this is the remedy that small firms generally pursue; as Piore argues, jobs in the secondary sector 'are essentially unskilled, either requiring no skill at all, or utilising basic human skills and capacities shared by virtually all adult workers' (Piore, 1980: 18). However, in many secondary industries, deskilling is not a viable option. For example, the industries that comprise New York's manufacturing complex are associated with a high degree of uncertainty in their final products and as a result jobs cannot be reduced to a single, simple task; similar conditions exist in other industries (food service, construction) in which immigrants are concentrated. Where the technology lends itself to a more radical division of labour, de-skilling tends to lower wages and limit the opportunities for upward mobility. But this device may intensify the recruitment problems further. If wages fall below the community norm and entry-level jobs are detached from promotional opportunities the effective labour supply declines, producing the very situation that triggered the latest migration flow.

The factors affecting attachment of ethnic workers to the immigrant firms take a considerably different form because social ties are reproduced within the workplace. Where shop size is small (as in newsstands or restaurants) labour market mechanisms may be entirely superseded by family relations. In other cases, labour requirements make it necessary to reach beyond the family circle; but in these instances jobs can be manned by fellow townsmen, or at the very least, common nationals. My research on the clothing industry, for example, showed that Dominican immigrant entrepreneurs tended to organise their firms around migration chains from a common site in the Dominican Republic. In a typical case, relatives and friends comprised the entire workforce of an eighteen-person factory owned by three brothers from a small agricultural town in the northern Dominican Republic; in a firm jointly owned by two parents and two of their adult children, half of the workers came from the owners' hometown and the remaining employees came from small towns in the vicinity (Waldinger, 1984 a, 1984 b). Such pre-existing social connections provide privileged information about worker attributes, useful in predicting behaviour on the job. The same ties also furnish a source of norms and sanctions needed to promote cohesiveness and guard against turnover – especially important in industries like apparel or construction where labour shortages typically develop during periods of seasonal activity. Thus, Korean greengrocers in New York use network hiring as a device to exclude potential competitors, who might enter into employment to learn the trade and then quickly strike out on their own (Kim, 1981). Similarly, in construction, ethnic connections substitute for unions by organising craftsmen into informal networks that promote rapid information flows and reinforce the stability of the labour supply and thereby maintain skill levels (Gallo, 1983). Workers with weak or malintegrated networks may in turn find themselves excluded from immigrant firms that hire through social connections; interviews with Chinese workers employed in the New York clothing industry underlined the employment difficulties that new and untrained workers encounter in the absence of connections to owners or employed friends willing to lend assistance in job training.

Network recruitment further strengthens firm-level attachment by redefining the employment exchange in terms of personal relationships and loyalties. 'It's been a tradition to hire the relatives of our workers', explained one Dominican clothing factory owner who announced all his vacancies to his workers. 'We consider them our friends.' Many immigrant-owned clothing firms systematically hire the newly arrived friends and relatives of workers already employed in the plant (Waldinger, 1984 a, 1984 b). Similarly, Bailey (1983) notes that some immigrant restaurants in New York serve as waystations where recent immigrants who know friends or relatives of the owners can earn a little money and make contacts while they are looking for a job.

Personal loyalties are reinforced when employers behave in ways that are congruent with normal, non-economic roles. In the clothing industry, owners act as intermediaries, intervening to assist their employees with social and legal problems or providing short-term loans that cover the rent or pay for emergencies. As one Dominican employer commented in an interview, 'The shop is like a family – people bring me problems everyday. I help them with applications, fill out their immigration papers, call the hospital to find out about relatives, and help them with anything involving English.' The case studies of both restaurant and garment industries indicate that immigrant entrepreneurs also tend to assist workers in bringing relatives over from the home country or to sponsor prospective immigrants who need a guarantee of employment in order to obtain permanent residency (Bailey, 1983; Waldinger, 1984 a, 1984 b).

In secondary firms, low pay is a source of grievance that attenuates workers' attachment to any employer. Secondary firms are also vulnerable to any expansion in the demand for better-priced labour as well as the attractions of other forms of income generation, e.g. the illegal economy or public assistance. By contrast, network hiring tends to isolate immigrant firms from wider economic influences, with the result that the competition for labour is regulated by the norms of the ethnic community rather than the standards that apply in the broader labour market. Generally, wages are interdependent because industries recruit from the same sources of labour and through similar labour market institutions. Wage claims can further be transmitted across occupational or ethnic group boundaries if jobs or union jurisdiction overlap or provide contexts for interaction. But if the competition for labour in an industry is ethnically circumscribed, or if occupational segregation isolates an ethnic group from the broader labour market, the processes by which claims and norms cross group boundaries to gain universal coverage is blocked. Consequently, when immigrant workers find themselves concentrated in ethnic firms and isolated from the influence of contrasting wage norms, demands to keep up relative wages tend to be weak. Moreover, the norms governing employment conditions often come to reflect the informal exchanges characteristic of ethnic firms, with the result that the socially acceptable conditions of employment are redefined, as the following clipping from the local Chinese press suggests:

the garment industry (is) not only one of the two economic lifelines of Chinatown, but it also plays a role of social responsibility. In a situation of inadequate day care, women workers who were mothers could come and go with flexible schedules, convenient for taking and picking up their children from school. If social security was insufficient, the garment shop allowed some old people to cut threads, and in addition to a small wage, they would also get the union's Blue Cross benefit. The Chinatown garment shops have also provided an opportunity for new immigrants, who can learn a skill and have a temporary position before, entering American society.
(*Pei Mei Daily*, 10 Nov. 1982, author's files)

Authority and control

A second function of network hiring derives from its role in the maintenance of authority and the mediation of internal strain. In the SLM literature the small firm appears riven by antagonistic labour–management relationships. Supervision is tyrannical and capricious; there are no formal grievance procedures through which workers can seek redress for their complaints; and management and labour are caught in a vicious circle in which workers respond to the harsh exercise of discipline with further insubordination. While this picture of the small firm has been generally accepted, there is another perspective that suggests that small firm size is in fact associated with co-operative worker behaviour. Research on the 'size-effect' indicates that small firms garner favourable ratings when checked against larger plants on turnover levels, propensity to strike, job satisfaction, and a variety of other indicators (Cleland, 1955; Ingham, 1970), despite all the liabilities underlined in the SLM literature – few opportunities for promotion, lower wages and inferior fringe benefits.

If size *per se* is unlikely to yield a particular industrial relations environment the contrasting findings on the effect of size suggest that it does create the potential for two quite contrasting types. Where management and labour are ethnically distinctive, as in low-wage firms in the US inner cities, face-to-face relationships may be all the more difficult to sustain. Ethnic behavioural patterns are often so divergent that simple stylistic differences are perceived in deeply threatening ways. This is especially so when management and labour engage in frequent interactions under the conditions of duress that so often confront small firms (bottlenecks, short delivery deadlines, undermanning, etc.). Repeated conflict over production quotas, behavioural rules, absenteeism, and instability tends to take on an explicitly racial character as management, in particular, interprets workers' behaviour in racially stereotyped ways. Disparities in wages, personnel policies, and general working conditions are also likely to be all the more resented when immigrant or minority workers are employed by members of the majority group. Finally, racial or ethnic conflicts originating outside the workplace may reverberate powerfully within.

In the small ethnic firms, however, antagonism is transcended because authority is secured on the basis of personal loyalties and ethnic allegiances that antedate the work situation. Thus, the simple fact of ethnic commonality provides a repertoire of symbols and customs that can be invoked or manipulated to underline cultural interests and similarities in the fact of a potentially antagonistic relations. For example, Chinese immigrant employers in the New York clothing industry celebrate holidays and shop anniversaries by holding banquets or luncheons to which all workers are invited. On the Chinese New Year, they pass out gifts (the traditional 'red envelope' stuffed with five dollars) and hold raffles whose proceeds go to the workers. Values and symbols may be cultivated on a more routine basis to broker patron–client relationships, as Wong observed:

The (clothing factory owner) is aware that he is more than employer [to his workers] and that he is consciously cultivating *Gam Ching* [sentimental feeling] with the workers . . . He used all possible ways to instil loyalty among his workers. He has had most of them since 1969. Kinship terminology such as *Je, Mui, Dai, Sou, Suk, Sam*, and *Baah* are deliberately used. He often tells them, 'You are only of the family. You can count on me.'
(Wong, 1979: 115)

Moreover, culturally-sanctioned patterns of paternalism mediate the tension and conflict that arise from instability and from the constant pressure induced by instability, bottlenecks or short delivery deadlines. Interviews conducted with Chinese employers in the clothing industry indicate that employers quite deliberately engage in gift-giving and celebrations in order to appease hostility generated by low earnings or difficult jobs.

Conflict is also mediated by ethnic management's attempt to present an egalitarian image and thereby lay claim to identification with the workers it employs. The organisation of the ethnic firm tends to reduce functional differences on both sides of the employment exchange. Ethnic owners initially negotiate capital barriers by substituting their own labour for any deficient factor of production. Once in business, they often lack the profit margins needed to pay for exclusive involvement in administrative affairs and continue to work alongside their employees. Involvement in production activities obscures differences in status and rewards, as Herman noted in his study of Macedonian-owned restaurants in Toronto:

There is a recognized hierarchy of jobs, and job status is reflected in income . . . Despite this hierarchy interpersonal behavior among all staff including the owner is normally egalitarian . . . Since, despite their relatively higher income, most owners worked more than any staff member, they saw themselves as equal to others working in the restaurant who earned without actually working, the owners might have considered themselves 'better' and so kept a social distance.

In the garment industry, these claims to identification are buttressed by awareness of the immigrant owner's inferior position in a contractor–manufacturer relationship that mirrors the overall pattern of ethnic sub-ordination. Consequently, the appeal to identity based on functional equivalence plays an important role in mediating strain within the ethnic firm, as the following leaflet, distributed by a group of Chinese garment factory owners during the course of a labour dispute, vividly suggests:

No matter if we're bosses or workers, we are one, like fingers on a hand. We're all in the same boat together in this garment industry, fighting for a decent living. Everyone in Chinatown can see the work of the bosses. Every cent is earned from sweat and blood. There's no difference at all with the workers, except going uptown to get the garments [from the manufacturers]. When [the bosses] come back, they take off their coats and sit down and sew just as hard . . .
(Leaflet distributed by a 'Group of Justice-Loving People', author's files)

In some cases, business activity will take the form of occupational or industrial encapsulation in which an ethnic group's activity is bound up with a distinct trade. To take the New York example, the Chinese are concentrated in clothing and restaurants, Greeks in restaurants and furs, Koreans in vegetable and fish retailing, and Indians in small non-food retailing (tobacco and stationery shops and newsstands). Here, occupational distinctiveness produces ethnic solidarity by creating a niche in which cultural and economic roles are congruent. Consequently, the salience of ethnic identity reduces the appeal of groups that make class-based claims, such as unions. Thus, while the SLM literature reports that secondary employers are often unionised, research on immigrant business indicates that the employment of immigrants in a context where obligations are understood to be both informal and reciprocal discourages unionisation. Even when immigrant firms are organised, unions seem constrained in their ability to significantly alter the employment relationship. Similarly, solidaristic norms shield ethnic firms from the purview of state regulation, witness this reaction by a major New York Chinese daily to government attempts to enforce wage and hour laws:

low pay is not the result of employers' exploitation nor the workers' fault. The westerners do not understand this special situation in Chinatown and label the shops as 'sweatshops' . . . The outsiders do not know the facts and causes and know only to label the shops as 'sweatshops' based upon pure imagination. It is in contradiction to the reality.
(*United Journal*, 15 October 1982, author's files)

Opportunities and labour market behaviour

One important strand of SLM theory links the behaviour of the workforce to the opportunities that they encounter and the work environment in which they function. As Harrison and Sum write in recapitulating the SLM viewpoint:

In acclimatizing themselves to local work arrangement some workers may find it psychologically as well as technically difficult to move from one stratum of the economy to another. Embedded in the dual labor market [theory] is the hypothesis that productivity and stability increase as wages increase. Thus, at the low wages prevalent in the secondary segment, poor productivity and lack of motivation are to be expected.
(Harrison and Sum, 1979: 691)

Conditions in the immigrant sector offer workers a different mix of opportunities and these in turn elicit a distinctive set of aspirations and expectations. The expansion of the ethnic economy provides both a mechanism for the effective transmission of skills and a catalyst of the entrepreneurial drive. Skills are relatively easy to pick up in the small immigrant firm, where responsibilities are flexibly defined and, due to understanding, jobs often include several tasks. Family members, brought in with the expectation that they will help out in all aspects of the business, thereby gain the chance to acquire not simply managerial training but also those contacts to suppliers and customers needed for business success. By recruiting through the immigrant community, the immigrant owner also creates the basis for trust and the delegation of authority, generally absent from the native-owned firm where prejudice often confines immigrants to low-skill jobs. For example, few native-owned restaurants in New York hire immigrants as either managers or waiters, but immigrants are employed in both of these positions throughout the immigrant business sector (Bailey, 1983).

In similar fashion, the protected market also provides an 'export platform' from which ethnic firms can expand. Greeks started out in the restaurant trade serving co-ethnics looking for inexpensive meals in a familiar environment. This original clientele provided a base from which the first generation of restauranteurs could branch out. More importantly, the immigrant trade established a pool of skill and managerial talent that eventually enabled Greek owners to penetrate beyond the narrow confines of the ethnic market and specialise in the provision of 'American food'. Currently, Latin construction contractors servicing the ethnic community are gradually edging out into the broader market as they assemble a skilled labour force and gain in efficiency and expertise (Gallo, 1983).

No less important than skill is the motivation to go out on one's own. As the immigrant sector grows it throws up a pool of potential role models whose success reinforces the drive for independence. Interviews with Hispanic and Chinese immigrant owners in the clothing industry, for example, indicated that their perceptions of opportunities were often linked to the experiences of other immigrants within their reference group. Business activity, it appears, follows an imitative pattern; initial business success signals the existence of a supportive environment, thereby encouraging other, less adventurous entrepreneurs to follow suit. As Kim (1981) notes in the case of the Koreans:

Korean immigrants who entered the United States via Latin America were the first to enter the fruit and vegetable business in 1971 . . . News of their success quickly spread through the Korean community in the area, and new immigrants from South Korea quickly followed them into the business. This economic news also spread to Philadelphia, resulting in the emergence of Korean fruit and vegetable enterprises in that city.
(Kim, 1981: 114–15)

While the immigrant sector gains new entrants on the basis of imitation, expansion may also have a dynamic effect on the customer base. Economies of agglomeration occur when firms proliferate and attract additional customers drawn by the size and diversity of the market – as in the case of stores that draw in passerby traffic from customers patronising other nearby shops. Such agglomeration economies play a catalytic role for ethnic merchants catering to the distinctive tastes of their co-ethnics, since the size of the market provides a scope for specialists whose services would otherwise not be in sufficient demand. Thus, because consumers are drawn by the tremendous variety of services that only a centralised commercial area can provide, New York's Chinatown, located in the original area of Chinese settlement, has seen business activity burgeon even though residential patterns have become more dispersed.

Conflict and constraint

An alternative to the argument developed so far would suggest that immigrant firms are privileged only in their ability to exploit the immigrant workforce. By hiring through the ethnic networks, immigrant employers engage their workers in a sponsor/client relationship whose claims extend far beyond the cash nexus. Workers entangled in close sponsor/client relationships may find that the expectations and obligations incumbent upon them serve to inhibit rather than encourage inter-firm mobility. As Wong noted in his study of Chinese businesses in New York:

The newly arrived kinsmen are thus tied to the employers and are expected to work hard and get little pay in order to reciprocate the kindness of the sponsor. A kinsman sometimes can remain in such a client-employee status for many years and be 'milked' by the employer-patron.
(Wong, 1979: 107)

The probability of movement out of the ethnic firm depends on the broader structure of opportunities in which ethnic enterprise emerges. Where immigrants are institutionally segregated from the broader labour market and/or highly dependent on ethnic trade, immigrant employers can effectively use the threat of exclusion or ostracism to maintain control and stability. Mobility may also be hindered if ethnic elites establish formal structures that regulate intra-ethnic economic activity, such as the trade guilds and marketing organisations that were common among Chinese-Americans and Japanese-Americans in the early twentieth century (Light, 1972; Modell, 1978; Bonacich and Modell, 1980). But these structures are most likely to arise when the threat of unimpeded business growth and competition stands to overwhelm the limited market for ethnic goods.

In the current context a complex of interacting psychological and economic factors diminish the potential for a captive labour force. Since the immigrant sector is in a growth state, there is little need for intra-ethnic economic control. Efforts to regulate business activity have arisen on occasion among the Chinese and Koreans but they have foundered against the immigrant entrepreneur's incessant search for individual opportunity (Kim, 1981; Waldinger, 1983). More importantly, the widening of opportunities provides a spur to ambition, and this in turn feeds into a preference for economic independence that is bred by the regimentation of low-level factory and service jobs and the constricted opportunities for advancement within the blue-collar hierarchy. The studies of immigrant clothing and construction contractors, for example, found that the desire to be 'one's own boss' was the most frequently mentioned reason for starting up a new business enterprise (Gallo, 1983; Waldinger, 1983). Exclusion from those more desirable mobility paths for which education is required further reinforces the appeal of small ownership.

Where the immigrant firm services an open market – as is the case for

Chinese clothing manufacturers, Greek restaurants, or Korean vegetable and fruit dealers – workers who seek to go out on their own can do so with little punitive threat. Since these businesses involve market relationships to out-siders, trust between sellers and customers is of reduced importance and performance is judged according to abstract criteria. Under these conditions, as the following case suggests, the demands of patron–client relationships can be evaded upon the acquisition of business contacts and managerial skills:

M. moved to New York City from Hong Kong in 1965. In 1968 she went to work for her aunt who owned a cut-make-and-trim factory and needed M. to help out in the plant. M. became involved in all operations of the firm and worked closely with the manufacturers who sent jobs to be made up to specification. M. then went into partnership with her aunt but later broke with her aunt over a disagreement about business practices. In 1979 M. found a new partner with whom she opened a new factory employing thirty-five workers. M. is now responsible for relationships with outside suppliers and customers while her partner manages production.

Since entry into business is thus unhindered by social control mechanisms, the ethnic business sectors are rife with competition and turnover rates for new businesses are high (Kim, 1981; Waldinger, 1983).

Finally the would-be owners' thrust towards independence does not necessarily conflict with the interests of the immigrant employer. From the standpoint of the worker, the opportunity to acquire managerial skills through a stint of employment in the immigrant firm both compensates for low pay and provides the motivation to learn a variety of different jobs. For the employer who hires the co-ethnic, the short-term consideration is access to lower-priced labour. Over the long term, the immigrant owner can act on the assumption that the newcomer will stay long enough to learn the relevant business skills. Moreover, the new entrant's interest in skill acquisition will diminish the total labour bill and increase the firm's flexibility. Thus, one can trace out a sequence of developments that shape regular labour market behaviour within the ethnic sub-economy: first, the development of a distinct business niche; then a community-wide orientation towards business; finally an understanding that newcomers will seek to go out on their own. For these reasons, work in an ethnic firm takes on the character of an entrepreneurial career. As the owner of a long-standing Chinese restaurant in New York noted: 'My father brought 100 people over from China. They worked in the restaurant and then went out on their own. Most of the successful Chinese restaurants in New York have someone who was trained in the House of Chan' (Neustadt, 1980: 68).

Conclusion

The ethnic sub-economy is based in the competitive sector of the economy but in the structure of its labour market it stands apart from other secondary industrial sectors. What distinguishes the labour market in the ethnic sub-economy are both the *processes* by which workers are attached to jobs and the *outcomes* of those interactions. The root hypothesis is that informal resources substitute for the institutionalised mechanisms common to large firms in organising the labour market. These informal resources, which consist of connections to a supply of family and ethnic labour as well as a set of understandings about the appropriate behaviour and expectations within the work setting, provide a conduit for the flow of labour market information and create a normative climate conducive to stable relationships to a single firm. As these resources are mobilised, the initial effect is to provide the immigrant employer with privileged access to the immigrant labour force – a factor of considerable advantage in competition against non-immigrant firms. However, the creation of stable work relationships within a context where work roles are loosely defined has the unintended consequence of facilitating the acquisition of skills that can permit subsequent movement into entrepreneurial positions. Once in place, these informal mechanisms of skill transmission facilitate the growth and proliferation of new ethnic firms beyond the original customer base. Business success then acts as the parent of an alternative motivational structure, breeding a community-wide orientation towards small business and encouraging the acquisition of business skills within a commonly accepted framework.

This paper suggests a number of implications for further research in the field. One issue concerns the differences among minority groups in rates of self-employment and small business activity. This is an issue of particular import in the United States where immigrants are more likely to be concentrated in small business than native blacks but it is of significant interest in the UK as well, where considerable differences obtain between South Asians and West Indians. Given the importance of informal resources in mobilising the ethnic labour force, one hypothesis would link business success to the strength of informal networks among various ethnic groups.

A second issue involves the relationships between those industrial structures conducive to small immigrant business and labour market processes. In SLM theory, small firm size and competition are the defining characteristics of the secondary sector, yet these conditions also create the opportunities for small business development. Rather than aligning the secondary labour market with the competitive sector, as does SLM theory, the evidence reviewed here suggests that the opportunities for small immigrant business are linked to the differences among competitive industries. One possibility is that opportunities for entrepreneurship will be concentrated among those competitive industries linked to volatile and fluctuating product markets where flexibility and informal organisational resources play a critical role. By contrast, in competitive industries making standardised products, firm size and specialised production technologies will impose excessive entry barriers both in terms of capital and skill.

Notes

1 This summary synthesises, in somewhat stylised form, a large and growing
   literature. Key works include Doeringer and Piore, 1971; Gordon, 1972; Gordon,
   Edwards and Reich, 1982; Edwards, 1979; Piore, 1973, 1979, 1980.
2 My own research on the clothing industry is reported in Waldinger, 1983, 1984
   a, 1984 b. Other labour market studies include: Bailey, 1983; Gallo, 1983; Korazim
   and Freedman, 1983. This paper also draws on research on low-wage labour
   markets that I have conducted, along with Thomas Bailey of Columbia University,
   for the New York City Office of Economic Development.
3 Ethnic group studies include: Kim, 1981; Wong, 1979.

Section four

Labour markets and gender

Until the late 1970s, social research into labour markets and employment focused overwhelmingly on the attitudes and experiences of male workers. The assumption appeared to be that women were marginal to the central dynamics of employment relationships. However, striking changes in the gender composition of the labour force in the 1970s could only heighten a growing awareness that not only were prevailing accounts of labour markets restricted in scope, but that it was impossible to provide an adequate analysis of the structure and operation of labour markets without more systematic research into the determinants of female participation and of the ways in which employers utilised female labour.

One of the most significant contributions to our knowledge in this area has been the research programme launched by the Department of Employment. Ceridwen Robert's paper presents an overview of this and discussed the nature of women's labour market participation and employment as they emerge from the Women and Employment survey carried out in 1980. This shows that the majority of women spend the greater part of their working life in paid employment and that women are returning more rapidly to the labour market after childbirth – thus eroding the traditional bimodal pattern of labour market participation. As with men, the principal reason that they seek employment is financial and women's incomes are a vital component of household income. However, the study reveals in stark form the extent of occupational segregation, a phenomenon that is particularly marked in situations in which women are employed part-time. Women's withdrawal from the labour market for childbearing imposes marked costs in terms both of lost earnings and downward occupational mobility on return to employment. Yet, while this derives from a socially constructed sexual division of labour, the research shows that women largely accepted it, believed that their main work should concern home and children, and were happy with the existing balance between home and work.

It has been noted frequently that women's earnings in employment are lower than men's and that this remains the case even at similar levels of educational qualification. This clearly raises major problems for orthodox economic theory which assumes that income differentials reflect variations either in innate ability or in investment in human capital. The paper by Stewart *et al.* presents a sharp critique of the explanatory power of market theories of income inequality in general and in relation to the specific issue of gender differentials. Moreover, using empirical data from Scotland and the southeast, they found that among the men and women they interviewed the non-market criterion of the gender composition of occupations was a major factor in the understanding of income inequalities. The 'labour market' neither operates in practice, nor is perceived to operate, according to principles. Yet, much as Roberts had found, the objective disadvantages that women suffer in the labour market do not appear to generate any very widespread resentment. Indeed, the women, even more than the men they interviewed, accepted the validity of existing gender differentials and there was certainly no strong feeling that these should be eliminated.

The growth of female participation in the labour market not only occurred in the context of a very high level of occupational segregation, but it was associated with the expansion of a type of work that was largely distinctive to women – namely part-time work. The reasons for the marked growth in part-time work and its implications for the quality of employment have been recognised widely as major issues in the analysis of the changing structure of employment opportunities in the last decade. The study by Beechey and Perkins of employer policies in Coventry revealed the inadequacy of much earlier thinking about employer utilisation of female part-time labour. They stress the shifting nature of employer motives with changing economic conditions, the centrality of the concern to increase flexibility, the close interconnection between part-time work and occupational segregation by gender, and the importance of familial ideology in influencing the way in which employers organise the labour process. The employment of part-time workers is not merely a temporary expedient to increase labour supply in periods of labour shortage, it reflects an enhanced employer concern to 'rationalise' the work process.

The analysis of the nature and determinants of the growth of female participation in the labour market is crucial for any attempt to assess the likely impact of the recession. This forms the central focus of the paper by Sylvia Walby. Walby shows that in comparison to other EEC countries Britain has an exceptionally low ratio of female to male employment. However, this does not reflect a more progressive attitude to women's employment. Rather it is, in good part, explicable in terms of the greater prevalence of part-time work in Britain and the poor conditions of employment associated with it. It is precisely because women are a particularly exploitable part of the workforce that employers are reluctant to dispose of them. Further, in her empirical study of the process of job loss in thirty establishments in the north-west, she shows that, although some of the selection criteria at the individual level may be unfavourable to women, the sectoral concentration of women in the service sector gives them greater protection than men. The post-war shift in the gender composition of the labour force seems likely then to be an enduring feature of British economic structure.

Research on women in the labour market: the context and scope of the Women and Employment Survey[1]

Introduction

This paper reports on a programme of research on women in the labour market, funded or sponsored by the Department of Employment, which I was responsible for initiating, designing and managing over the period 1978 to 1983. After describing the background to the research programme on women, I briefly outline the main themes of the research programme as exemplified in discrete research projects before moving to a fuller discussion of the main project namely the DE/OPCS Women and Employment Survey.[2]

Research on women's employment and unemployment

Equal opportunity legislation has been a major source of impetus to research on women within the Department. Indeed, in the period before major reforms in the form of the Equal Pay Act and Sex Discrimination Act were enacted, the Department sponsored two large surveys and produced four monographs on aspects of women's employment. This made a substantial contribution to public knowledge on women and work in the 1970s (Hunt, 1968, 1975; Department of Employment, 1974, 1975). The two surveys, conducted for the Department by the Government Social Survey under Audrey Hunt, provide a benchmark against which subsequent developments and changes in women's position since the mid '60s and early '70s can be measured. In her first study, conducted in 1965, Audrey Hunt focused on the interaction of women's home and work lives to describe the extent of the barriers to women's labour force participation. Her second study, conducted in 1973, examined management's attitudes and behaviour towards women as employees and identified some discriminatory views and practices. It confirmed the view that women's opportunities at work were adversely affected by employers' stereotyped treatment of women employees.

Once the legislation was passed, interest in DE in research on women initially focused on monitoring it and evaluating its impact (Snell *et al.*, 1981). Subsequently policy and research interest became broader though legislation still provided the broad context of the research. There were several reasons for this widening of research perspective. One stemmed from women's increased labour market participation; the implications of increased proportions of women in employment, particularly the growth of part time employment amongst married women coupled with a rising rate of female unemployment needed to be studied. A second reason reflected recognition at policy level that 'the causes of continued unequality are complex and rooted deeply in tradition, custom and prejudice' (Home Office, 1974). Thirdly, there was a background of research knowledge on women, conducted and published in the '70s which had begun to go beyond descriptions of women's disadvantaged position towards explanations for this in structural terms (Barker and Allen, 1976 a and 1976 b). Common to almost all the writings on women was the recognition that women's position in employment and in the labour market more generally could not be understood or explained without reference to their domestic roles and the unpaid work women undertook at home.

Against this background various projects were mounted which together comprise a programme of research on women in the labour market. Initially, individual policy research questions were set and projects mounted. In retrospect it is clear that whilst they individually cover specific issues they were broadly directed to understanding the position of women in employment, the importance of employment to women and the extent and nature of women's unemployment. Taken together, therefore, the projects go some way to establishing and explaining the position of women in the labour market in Britain in the 1980s. Legislation, however, provided the central focus for initial projects.

With the passing of the Equal Pay Act, for example, administrators quickly realised they had to know about women's pay more broadly. It was recognised for example, that we could not properly evaluate the Equal Pay Act and understand the role of legislation in promoting equal pay for the same or broadly similar work without knowing more about how women's pay was determined and the relative advantages or disadvantages of different types of payment systems. Consequently two large and separate projects were set up. The first, undertaken by the Department of Applied Economics at Cambridge, looked at informal or non-job evaluated payment systems and the way in which women's pay was determined (Craig *et al.*, 1984). The second, which is just being completed, focused on the other end of the spectrum by looking at the composition and levels of women's pay under job evaluation schemes (White and Goberdhian, 1984).

Employment legislation also provided an important impetus to work on women. One of the early projects stemmed from interest in women's use of the maternity provisions of the Employment Protection Act (1975) and the response of employers to this right. This was the focus of the project conducted by W. W. Daniel of PSI. This project, which was basically intended to monitor legislation, also gave useful insights into women's attitudes to work and motherhood and their views on the barriers to more extensive participation by women and the role of legislation in facilitating this. It also provided information on employers' use of women in their labour force and the extent or otherwise of conscious strategies about this (Daniel, 1980, 1981).

Other topics stemmed from more intractable problems and required several projects. The issue of unemployment illustrates this particularly well, although perhaps it is also true of pay. The difficulties of interpreting official statistics on women's unemployment are well known and, as might be expected, reflect the conceptual problems of defining who is unemployed amongst women without paid work. These partly arise because for women there are also several routes into unemployment. Women may become unemployed because they lose their job, for whatever reason, or because they enter or re-enter the labour market and cannot find employment. This last group will therefore comprise both young women leaving school and women returning to work after domestic absence. Its boundaries are necessarily fuzzy in so far as the processes whereby women come to want to re-enter are highly likely to be affected by the levels of local employment and unemployment and therefore known job opportunities.

It is also probable that women may become 'discouraged' workers, and therefore not 'unemployed', more easily than men. Because women's attachment to the labour market is likely to be different in some respects from men's it is also likely that not all women who leave or lose their jobs will become unemployed. (Indeed, strictly speaking, not all men will stay in the labour market after job loss – some will retire.) It is also likely that women's reactions to being unemployed will differ from that commonly reported in male unemployment studies. Accordingly, three linked projects were designed to look at particular aspects of unemployment.

The cornerstone project of the three was the DE/OPCS Women and Employment Survey. This explores differing definitions of 'unemployed' women and compares and contrasts five groups of non-working women in terms of their work intentions, and their attitudes to not working, as well as describing their levels of financial stress and the demographic characteristics of women in the five groups. In this way it could provide a useful general overview of the extent of unemployment amongst women of working age in 1980. It also shows how women become 'unemployed', whether they are moving from a job or from being economically inactive and, if from a job, whether they left this voluntarily or not.

The two other 'unemployment' studies use different approaches. The study by Cragg and Dawson, for example, is based on intensive interviewing of a sub-sample of women identified on a very broad definition as 'unemployed' in the 1980 survey (Cragg and Dawson, 1984). Interviewed between seven and nine months after their OPCS interview, not only was the women's subsequent labour market behaviour recorded, but their responses to being without a job were explored in some depth as was the meaning they attached to their status and experiences. In this way it was possible to begin to tackle, in research terms, the issue of the process and causes of discouragement as well as to throw some light on whether 'unemployment' means different things for different women and is different again from unemployment for men. The third project, the study of unemployment following redundancy by Dr Martin using the case study method, approached the issue from the perspective of a particular group of women. By following them for a period after they lost their jobs, having initially interviewed them at the time of their redundancy, Dr Martin and his research team aimed to show whether women are less attached to paid work, either in their determination to find a new job or in terms of them being less affected in financial, social or psychological terms by losing employment than men are held to be (Martin and Wallace, 1984). Taken together, the findings of these three studies will advance our knowledge of female unemployment considerably.

In all, the DE's programme of research since 1978 included approximately eleven projects, most of which were done by external contractors, a mixture of academic and commercial researchers. In addition, other programmes of research or individual projects also included women as analysable subgroups of their samples. The several projects concerned with homeworking, for example, are clearly of interest as 'homeworking' is held to be a particular 'problem' for those groups of women who are unable for domestic or health reasons to take alternative forms of paid work (Hakim and Dennis, 1982; Leighton, 1983). In addition, studies of the unemployed or particular groups in the labour market, such as young people, include both male and female respondents (Ashton, 1982; Dex, 1982; White, 1983). The largest single project and, in a sense, the project which underpinned or gave coherence to the whole programme of research women was the national survey of women of working age which is discussed next.

Special or *ad hoc* surveys are well established as a tool in social research in general and government information seeking in particular on specific topics or groups within the population (Marsh, 1982). Several previous surveys on aspects of women's employment provided, as we have pointed out, valuable sources of data on aspects of women's employment. By 1979 however, the chief of these, Hunt's study, was fourteen years old and there had been considerable changes in both the behaviour and attitudes of women in the intervening years as well as major equal opportunity legislation. A new survey, therefore, was felt to be timely. In addition, if we were to understand unemployment properly we had to know the detail of women's moves in and out of the labour market and the proportion of their potential working life they spent out of the labour market so that the consequences of not having a paid job could be better understood. Moreover, as Hunt showed in 1965, only in a special survey can women's work histories be collected and measures of the extent of women's work experience generated. For all these reasons it was felt that a new survey was needed to establish the current position of women in employment in order to identify what the effects of the changes in the '70s had been; to show what having or not having a paid job meant for women in the 1980s, and to generate data about women's lifetime employment.

The objectives and scope of the survey

The emphasis was on employment, for we were chiefly concerned with the paid work women do rather than the unpaid work they do at home and elsewhere. That is not to say domestic work was ignored completely, for women's employment cannot be understood without reference to their roles as wives and mothers and the work this involves, but we did not aim to collect detailed information on it. The survey had a large number of detailed aims, but most can be subsumed under two broad objectives. Firstly we wanted to know what factors determine whether or not women work and so identify the importance of domestic factors or the sexual division of labour in shaping women's lifetime labour market involvement. Secondly, we wanted to discuss women as workers, collecting full information about the work they do, their pay and conditions of employment as well as the way they behave in the labour market when they leave jobs or look for work and, of course, we wanted to know the importance of work to women and their job priorities. One of the issues here was to consider how far the view that women were secondary workers concentrated in low paid, insecure and low skilled jobs was true for all women.

Underlying much research on women is the assumption that the situation of women is different from that of men. For example, paid work is held to be of central importance in men's lives, but not as important in women's lives. This reflects the widespread view in our society that women have a choice about employment, at least at certain stages of their lives, in a way that men do not as they will be primarily concerned with rearing children during part of their lives and so will either withdraw from the labour market or combine domestic responsibilities with part-time paid work. Consequently, it is also assumed by many people, and embodied in the state's social security and tax systems, that married women will be financially dependent on their husbands, who are seen as the primary breadwinners, and therefore that it is less important for women to work than for men (Land, 1976). One aim of the survey therefore was to test the validity of this.

The major innovation in the survey, was the collection of detailed work histories stretching over the whole of our female respondents working lives since leaving full time education. By finding out the proportions of women who had worked at past stages of their lives it was intended to build up a picture of women's lifetime economic activity and show how this was changing. This would also enable us to test how typical the two-phase work profile, demonstrated by cross sectional analysis (Hakim, 1979), was for all women. Data on lifetime movement in and out of employment also illustrates very clearly the impact of domestic responsibilities on women's employment. In addition, to explore domestic responsibilities in some detail and so illustrate the effects of the sexual division of labour, we intended to compare the roles adopted by wives and husbands with respect to both paid and unpaid work. Since their views about the arrangements were important too, we decided to interview a small sample of husbands and compare their views with the views of their wives.

Full details about the findings and methodology of the study are found in the two reports of the study (Martin and Roberts, 1984 a, 1984 b). Brief details of the methodology are given here. A nationally representative (GB) sample of women of working age (16–59) was drawn. Interviews were achieved with 5,588 women and a sub-sample of 799 husbands/partners and were carried out using a structured interview schedule. The interviews with women lasted approximately an hour, although this was longer for older women with extensive work histories.

Data was collected on a range of topics relevant to understanding the place of employment in women's lives. Thus basic demographic, household and fertility data was collected at different points in the interview. Employment data included details of all past jobs, current economic status, details of current job and future work intentions as well as information on attitudes to working or not working, job priorities and job search strategies and behaviour. Income information was also collected as was data on the economic status and occupation level of a women's partner and his earnings/income and attitudes to his wife working, share of child care and housework, and women working in general.

The survey generated a considerable amount of data and it is impossible to do justice to the range of findings in a brief paper (Martin and Roberts, 1984 a, 1984 b; Dex, 1984 a, 1984 b; Joshi, 1984). Rather, findings are selectively presented to show the changing patterns of women's lifetime employment, to discuss women as workers focusing on their jobs, and rewards from working and to consider the consequences for women of time out of the labour market. Underlying these issues is the relationship between womens position in the labour market and the division of labour between the sexes.

The extent of women's lifetime employment

Longitudinal data provides an essential corrective to the picture of women's employment derived from cross sectional data, for the proportion of women who are working at any one point in time is always lower than the proportion of women of working age who have worked or will work over their lifetime. Our data shows that most women will spend the major part of their working life in a job. Older women, on average, have spent about 60 per cent of their working lives in employment and younger women already show signs of surpassing this.

Women rarely stop work on marriage; for most women the first break comes with the first baby, only 4 per cent of women with children in our sample had been in the labour market continuously and some of these are likely to leave subsequently to have a further child. However, nearly a quarter of women (22 per cent) with children (and most women eventually have children) will work for over 90 per cent of their potential working life. Whilst most women leave work on having a baby almost all, over 90 per cent, will return to employment. Moreover, contrary to popular thought, this is not a new phenomenon. For example, over 90 per cent of women who had a first birth in the late 1950s and early 1960s had returned to work at some stage and among older women, the proportions were not much lower; 87 per cent of women who had a first birth in the early 1940s had subsequently returned to employment.

What is new is that women are returning to work markedly more quickly after having a baby; for example, half the women who had a first baby between 1970 and 1979 had returned to work within four years, while it was considerably longer (9.6 years) before 50 per cent of women who had a first baby between 1950 and 1954 had returned. This is true too of women returning after subsequent babies. These increasingly early returns to work are interrelated with a developing pattern of returning between births. As nearly half the women (47 per cent) whose latest birth had been between 1975 and 1979 had been employed for some time between their first and latest birth, it is clear that the two-phase or bimodal pattern of women's employment is an increasingly less accurate description of how a large group of women behave in the labour market. Broadly, women with children may be divided into two groups: mothers who work between births and return to work soon after their latest birth, and the declining majority of mothers who more closely approximate to the bimodal pattern and do not return to work at all until their last child is of school age.

Obviously, part-time working has been very important in facilitating this increase by enabling women to combine caring for young children with paid work. Indeed the traditional model of women's employment assumes a pattern of movement between full- and part-time work with young children and back to full-time work once their children have grown up. Our data however shows that movement is more complex than this. Whilst it is certainly true that women are more likely to be working full-time the longer they have been back at work, some, particularly those returning to work very early, go back to full-time jobs initially and change to part-time; others work part-time throughout their post-child work phase and others return later, but to full-time work.

Clearly very few women adopt the stereotypical male pattern of continuous lifetime employment as a full-time worker and most interruptions to employment are caused for domestic reasons. However, though women with children tend to have more breaks in their employment than childless women, childless women are also liable to spent some of their working life out of employment for domestic reasons. Thus there is considerable diversity in women's pattern of lifetime employment. What is also clear from our findings is that marital status *per se* has no effect on whether women work or not; the age of the youngest child is the single most crucial factor. Marital status, however, does have an effect on whether a women works full or part-time.

Women as workers

As part-time working is an important and recent phenomenon in Britain we looked in some detail at both the number of hours women work and the time of day at which they work. The majority (56 per cent) of working women at any one point in time are working full-time, and most of these will be doing a standard nine–five day. Few working women work less than sixteen hours or eight hours a week and so work too few hours to qualify for employment protection legislation: 12 per cent and 4 per cent respectively. There is considerable diversity in women's arrangement of part-time hours however. In all, we identified nine main patterns of full and part hours of work amongst working women. The largest single group of part-time workers (29 per cent) are morning workers, i.e. they start before 10 a.m. and finish before 2 p.m., but 12 per cent work over midday and 13 per cent do evening work. Moreover, the hours women work varies with their stage in the life cycle. It is noticeable, for example, that women with young children, i.e. under five, are particularly likely to work in the evenings.

Occupational segregation

The occupational distribution of women is well known. They work in a much more restricted number of occupations than men, with markedly fewer women in the very top jobs. Part-time workers are even more likely to be in lower level occupations than full-time workers. Women are also more likely to be in service industry jobs, particularly if they work part-time. We had a particularly strong or absolute measure of occupational segregation in our study based on women's experience of segregation at work place level: 63 per cent of working women worked only with other women doing the same kind of work as them and part-timers were much more likely to work only with other women; 70 per cent did so compared with 58 per cent of full-time workers. However, women working full-time in the service industries, particularly in higher non-manual jobs are much more likely to be working with men.

An employee-based study cannot establish the causes of this marked occupational segregation; it is also difficult to establish precisely the magnitude of its effects, though we examined the factors with which it is associated. It is striking for example, that women who work with men are more likely than women who work in 'women only' jobs to have higher levels of pay and access to good conditions of employment and opportunities for further training and promotion in their jobs. It is not therefore surprising that women working in 'women only' jobs are much more likely than women working with men to think of their jobs as 'women's work' which men would not be prepared to do, chiefly because the jobs are low paid, boring or only suitable for women. Thus many women in our survey experienced the labour market as highly segregated on the basis of sex with men doing both different jobs and more of the supervisory and managerial jobs. Their husbands' experience of occupational segregation is even more marked as most (81 per cent) work only with other men and almost none (2 per cent) had a female supervisor. Husbands were much more likely than wives to think of their work as gender specific.

Full and part-time workers

While it is clear that in broad terms, men and women's experience of the labour market is markedly different as is the experience of women in 'women only' jobs it is also important to note that there were differences between women associated in particular with their employment status as full- or part-time workers. Women working part-time are more likely to be in lower level occupations: over half of part timers are in social class 4 and 5 occupations, for example, compared with just under a quarter of women working full-time, and it is likely that these broad occupational groups mask even more pronounced differences in job levels. It is these differences in occupational level which largely account for the different hourly rates of pay of full- and part-time workers, since we found no significant difference in the hourly pay of full- and part-time workers within the same occupational group.

Overall, part-time workers are less likely to have access to or to have provision of conditions of employment like paid holidays, sick pay and an occupational pension scheme. They are also less likely to have promotion and training opportunities in their jobs and less likely either to be a member of, or have the opportunity to belong to, a union. In general, a woman's employment status as a full- or part-time worker had a stronger effect on her access to good pay and job benefits than her occupational level and whether she worked with men as well as with women. While part-time workers clearly have less good pay and job benefits than full-time workers the differences in coverage by statutory provision are much less marked. 67 per cent of full-time workers were covered by employment protection legislation compared with 60 per cent of part-time workers.

Occupational segregation and employment status are clearly interconnected and have an important effect in respect of women's pay and general employment conditions. The most 'privileged' group of women are those who work with men in full-time, higher non-manual jobs. They are likely to have better pay and conditions and job opportunities than all other women, and can be seen as forming a primary sector of the female workforce. All other groups of women in varying degrees have the characteristics and labour market position associated with secondary sector workers.

Reasons for working

Having looked briefly at the jobs women do and the material rewards they get from working it is germane to look at the reasons why women work, recognising of course that we do not ask this question of men in the same way, for we do not assume the possibility of choice. In our society women are assumed to have, and indeed may feel, an element of choice in whether they work or not at certain life stages, and this may well affect how they feel about working. Our data shows that in one sense women, like men, work in large part for the money. The majority of working women had a high financial dependence on working and gave a financial reason as their main reason for working. Non-married women, particularly lone parents working full time, were more financially dependent and more likely to say they worked 'for essentials' but even so, over a quarter (28 per cent) of women working part-time said 'working for essentials' was their main reason for working. The importance of financial motivation is also underlined by the greater emphasis placed on this by women looking for a job; more said they needed a job for essentials than amongst working women generally.

The vast majority of women were committed in varying degrees to working; indeed only 6 per cent of working women definitely wished they did not go out to work. Most women gave more than one reason for working and it is clear from their responses that they work for a variety of reasons and enjoy working. However, there are differences between women in their attitudes to work. Young childless women are less attracted to working than women who have returned to work, which suggests that the pull of anticipated domesticity and motherhood reduces young women's interest in working while the experience of being at home makes some women more interested in working. In addition, childless women over thirty are the most likely of all groups to show high intrinsic attachment to work. The complexities of women's work attachment are highlighted most clearly in the responses of the group of mothers of pre-school children who work full-time. Some, chiefly those in higher level and well-paid jobs show a high intrinsic attachment to work, while others in lower level, less well-paid jobs are clearly only working because of financial necessity.

Money, however, is not the aspect of a job most women rate as most important. Both full-time and part-time workers rated 'work you like doing' the most important aspect of a job, though 'convenient hours' were equally important for part-timers. Indeed these are an absolutely crucial requirement for part-time workers for, if the hours are not right, women wanting to combine employment and their domestic responsibilities cannot work at all. The consequence of this is that part-time workers often make certain trade-offs, attaching less importance to a 'good rate of pay' than to 'convenient hours' even when they work mainly for money. They are therefore less likely than full-time workers to stress the importance of pay and a secure job and are more likely to emphasise the importance of having friendly people to work with. But, as we know from many other studies, in general people want what they feel or know is possible. Interestingly, both full- and part-time workers placed low priority on the career aspects of a job or the opportunity to use their abilities, though these were more important to younger women.

Why women leave jobs

The notion that women leave jobs to have babies or to fit in with their husband's jobs seriously distorts a more complex reality. Women obviously leave jobs and leave the labour market for domestic reasons but they also leave jobs without leaving the labour market, either by changing directly to a new employer or being unemployed. Their reasons for leaving an employer may be domestic or job-related in that women, like men, may move voluntarily to a better job, or involuntarily if they are dismissed or made redundant.

On average our survey shows that women work for between four and five employers during their working life though the range is wide. Younger women leave jobs more frequently than older women. Indeed, the highest rate of change of employer is amongst women in their first five years of work, when it is also high for young men. Overall, more women leave an employer to change straight to another job than leave to stop work and women are more likely to leave an employer for a job related rather than a domestic reason. For example, women left jobs for domestic reasons about 40 per cent of the time and were more likely to do this earlier in their working lives. Even though women with children are more likely to leave an employer for a domestic reason childless women leave jobs for domestic reasons in about a quarter of cases. After the childbearing period, more women leave jobs for job related rather than domestic reasons.

Not working and the consequences of time out of the labour market

Almost all women will experience periods in their working lives when they are not working either because they are unemployed or, more likely, because they have withdrawn from the labour market. Thus at any one point of time 'not working' is likely to be a temporary phase in a woman's life. We found that 35 per cent of our sample were neither in a job nor full-time students. Most of these women (80 per cent) were economically inactive and were in varying degrees temporarily or permanently withdrawn from the labour market. The other 20 per cent were divided into the unemployed (14 per cent), so called because they met our survey definition of the unregistered unemployed by having no paid job and looking for one, and the remainder (6 per cent) who gave a domestic explanation as to why they did not have a job but subsequently told us they were looking for work; most of the latter women were domestic returners, i.e., they were re-entering the labour market after a period of domestic absence.

Because non-working women are so heterogeneous, summary measures of their financial position and attitudes to their situation are meaningless, though in broad terms it is possible to say that women were less likely to be financially stressed and much more likely to have positive attitudes towards not working the more economically inactive they were. Accordingly, women who were least likely to work again, those who had retired permanently or had not worked for a long time, were most likely to feel happiest about not having a job since, as might be expected, there was considerable congruence between women's employment status and their attitudes. Women in an 'unemployed' category who were more likely than other non working women to be young and single as well as looking for full- rather than part-time work were most likely to be dissatisfied with not working and eager to start work. Both groups of women who were looking for work shared similar levels of financial stress and strain at not working even though unemployed women showed a higher level of financial dependence on their own earnings than domestic returners.

Absence from employment has long-term effects too, some of which our survey was able to show. Downward occupational mobility, for example, is particularly associated with both absence from the labour market for child-bearing and a subsequent return to part-time employment. The survey shows that a substantial minority of women (37 per cent) experience downward occupational mobility on re-entering the labour market when they return to work after having a first baby. Women are much more likely to return to a lower level job if they go back part time; 45 per cent of women going back to a part-time job were downwardly occupational mobile. Moreover, the longer a woman delays her return to work the more likely she is to return to a lower level occupation. By contrast the small minority of mothers who return within six months of a first baby mostly return to the same level of occupation; 76 per cent did so, usually because they return to the same employer they had before childbirth.

But, while length of service is important, employment status has the stronger association with downward mobility. Women returning to full-time work are less likely than women returning part-time after the same length of absence to move to a lower level occupation. Even women who first return to work full-time after childbearing and subsequently change to work part-time are likely to experience downward mobility though (subsequent) return to full-time working often leads to upward occupational mobility. Women therefore can, and a small minority do (10 per cent) recover the occupational standing they had prior to childbearing and some 6 per cent move higher than this. While some theorists argue that this downward mobility is a consequence of the depreciation of women's human capital, a more straightforward explanation is that since many women combine child care and paid work by working part-time, their choice of a part-time job constrains their occupational choices and they trade off job level for a 'suitable' job.

We have shown that women's years out of the labour market for childbearing are declining. However, it still has an important effect on women's earnings. Joshi's analysis of our data shows that this absence coupled with a return to part-time rather than full-time work reflecting women's greater share of domestic work depresses women's lifetime earnings by approximately 30 per cent. Thus, she argues, the costs of family formation are borne disproportionately by women (Joshi, 1984).

Employment and the sexual division of labour

It is impossible to describe women's employment position without relating this to their position in the sexual division of labour. Women were more work orientated in 1980 than Hunt's survey showed them to be in 1965 and no doubt this change in attitudes reflected the increased work involvement women had shown over the '70s which our data suggests will continue to increase. However, the domestic division of labour has not changed markedly. Our survey shows very clearly that in 1980, women, because of their role as wives and mothers do more of the work involved in looking after a family and home both at any point in time and in total over their lifetime than their husbands, whose primary economic role is that of primary wage earner. Consequently women do not participate in the labour market on the same terms as men over their lifetime and the conditions under which they offer themselves, for example, as part-time workers may go some way to explaining the segregated and secondary nature of much of the work they do.

Our data suggests that most women accept or accommodate to the sexual division of labour we have described. Only small minorities were either very traditional or very radical in their attitudes towards women's roles or position in society. In so far as older women were more traditional, and younger and more highly qualified women more non-traditional this may be evidence of a continuing shift in women's attitudes. There is certainly general endorsement of the social values underlying the equal opportunity legislation of the 1970s, but little evidence that women see themselves becoming in the near future equal or joint wage earners on the same terms as their husbands. The current arrangement of family life simply precludes this for most married women.

To a large extent women's general attitudes about the importance of paid work for women reflects this sexual division of labour. This no doubt explains why in our survey paid work is held to be less central to women's lives than to men's, even though the benefit of working is recognised either in general terms or as the best way to be independent. While only a minority of women think women cannot combine a career and children, it is clear that these are rarely considered equally important, since a majority of women feel a home and children is a woman's real aim and main job and endorse the view that family responsibilities may conflict with having a demanding paid job. That said, however, most women agree that work is financially important for women; few think wives only work for 'pin money' or should leave the labour market when unemployment is high.

Our study has shown the choices women in the 1980s are making about combining work and home and the factors which influence these choices. Most women are happy about their balance of home and work and often part-time employment has been a crucial way in which they have achieved this. For the minority of women who choose or need to effect a different balance the position is less clear cut. Some, like lone parents, as we have shown, may be particularly disadvantaged by having to combine domestic and paid work without a partner. Other women may make a different choice, emphasising paid work and if they are highly qualified and work full-time in higher level jobs they are most likely of all women to work on comparable terms with men. What is clear is that most women, unlike most men, both have the choice and often still have to choose.

Notes

1 Ceridwen Roberts, who is a Principal Research Officer in the Department of Employment, London is writing in a personal capacity. The analysis and views expressed in this paper are not necessarily those of the Department of Employment.
2 The survey was carried out jointly by the Department of Employment and the Office of Population, Censuses and Surveys. Several publications report on the data. These are Martin and Roberts, 1984 a, 1984 b; Dex, 1984 a, 1984 b and Joshi, 1984.

13 *Veronica Beechey, Teresa Perkins*

Conceptualising part-time work[1]

From 1979–81 we undertook a research project which investigated part-time employment in selected areas of manufacturing industry and the public sector in Coventry. The aim of this paper is to discuss some of the findings of this project and to consider some of the problems involved in conceptualising part-time work. The process of doing empirical research has led us to question some of the established theoretical perspectives on women's employment and to reformulate the perspectives which originally informed the project. In this paper we discuss those theoretical perspectives and also some of the project's findings. The paper is written in three parts in order to convey some sense of the *process* by which we undertook our empirical research and developed a theoretical framework to interpret the findings. The first part of the paper discusses some of the literature on women's employment which was available in the 1970s before the project commenced. In the second part we present some of the major findings about part-time work from the project, and in the final part we return briefly to some of the broader theoretical questions discussed in Part 1. Inevitably this final section raises more questions than it answers, but we hope it will stimulate further discussion of these questions. We hope, too, that the arguments in this paper will contribute to wider discussions about women's employment, the labour process and the labour market.

1 Prevailing theoretical approaches

When the research project commenced, the literature on part-time working was very scarce. The few articles in existence had been written in the 1950s and 1960s and focused very much on questions of labour supply. Like Jean Hallaire's study for the OECD, published in 1968 (Hallaire, 1968), they were strongly influenced by 'human capital' assumptions. With the exception of Jennifer Hurstfield's study for the Low Pay Unit, *The Part Time Trap*, published in 1978 (Hurstfield, 1978) and an unpublished MA dissertation by Colleen Chesterman (Chesterman, 1978) the growing body of literature on work and the labour process was silent on the subject of part-time work, a silence which was clearly related to the more general marginalisation of women's work within both industrial sociology and Marxist theory (see Brown, 1976).

(i) *The women's two roles paradigm*

The main body of literature concerned with women's employment in Britain was the 'women's two roles' approach. This was firmly located within British empirical sociology and was, as one of us argued in 'Women and production' (Beechey, 1978) strongly influenced by a modified version of structural functionalist theory. This perspective on women's employment was widely deployed during the 1950s, 1960s and early 1970s when Britain experienced a severe labour shortage in the long post-war boom, and was reflected in official studies of women's employment carried out by the government and by international agencies like the ILO and OECD. Taken as a whole, these studies were principally concerned with factors affecting women's participation in the labour market, with the problems women faced in combining two roles, and with policy implications. They subscribed to a very optimistic view of the possibilities for progress, itself seen as a result of technological change and the extension of social democracy. They regarded the development of marriage as a partnership and women's increasing participation in the world of paid work as part and parcel of the general growth in equality and democacy in post-war Britain.

Such writers had a good deal to say about part-time work. Since one of their major concerns was with the increasing participation of women in the labour force, and in particular the role of married women as an untapped labour reserve, they heralded part-time work as an important means of enabling women to participate in the world of paid work, as the following quotation from Viola Klein makes clear:

With single women being employed today at nearly the same high rate as men, married women are the only untapped labour reserve left in our society. It would therefore seem imperative to investigate the conditions under which this reserve can be drawn upon. It is possible – and the results of this enquiry would appear to make it likely – that expansion depends largely on an increase of part-time jobs.
(Klein, 1965: 82)

People writing within this framework unquestioningly accepted the association of women with maternal and domestic responsibilities. Viola Klein goes on to quote favourably a statement by the National Manpower Council of Columbia University that:

Women constitute not only an essential, but also a distinctive part of our manpower resources . . . distinctive . . . because the structure and the substance of the lives of

most women are fundamentally determined by their function as wives, mothers and homemakers.
(Klein, 1965: 83)

Part-time work was thus seen as an ideal means of enabling women to combine their domestic responsibilities with paid work; 'For some years now and for millions of married women in Western countries, part-time work has been a factor making for equilibrium between the duties of a wife and mother and economic necessity' (Hallaire, 1968: 37). Furthermore, the construction of certain jobs as part-time was unquestioningly associated, in the theories, with the assumption that women were primarily wives, mothers and homemakers. Myrdal and Klein suggested that 'some types of work lend themselves *by their nature* to part-time employment (Myrdal and Klein, 1956: 113, my emphasis); and cite as examples domestic work, catering, social services (e.g. home helps, school meals and social welfare work) and child-minding. They argued that apart from these primarily domestic occupations and a few 'special cases', employers were largely disinclined to employ people on a part-time basis except when driven to by acute labour shortage or by a temporary need for extra shifts.

Jean Hallaire suggested that 'part-time jobs may be regarded as adapting work to the man [*sic*]' (Hallaire, 1968: 33). His analysis makes it quite clear that he saw part-time work as one solution to the problem of marginal groups wanting to work. Clearly married women were the largest marginal group, but Hallaire argued that part-time work should not be adopted for women only, but for all workers subject to 'limiting conditions'. Among the other groups for whom he considered part-time work a possibility were retired people and students. Myrdal and Klein were clearly worried lest part-time employment become associated solely with women. They argued that it might be a good temporary solution for women wanting to resume their careers later, a kind of 'refresher course' but that it was neither practicable nor desirable as a more permanent pattern of work for married women. And they argued that women needed to be regarded as full workers and not as 'helping hands' if the difficulties married women faced in attempting to reconcile a career with family life were not to be perpetuated. It was in this context that they advocated a whole range of policy changes, some of them quite radical – for example, extended maternity leave, training for the over forties, houses built for working women, better planned distribution, rationalised housework, public services, school meals, day nurseries and nursery schools and domestic help.

One of us had criticised the 'women's two roles' perspective in 'Women and production' for its overly optimitic view of 'progress', for its unquestioning acceptance of the sexual division of labour, and for its exclusive emphasis on the family and on questions of labour supply, and these criticisms seemed to be particularly relevant to our research project. Since this body of literature completely ignored the demand for labour, workplace organisation and the labour process, it seemed to be rather limited as an approach for studying part-time work. Furthermore, it seemed important to break radically with the assumptions embodied in theories of women's two roles that part-time work and married women's work were synonymous, that married women were 'naturally' suited to certain kinds of work, and that part-time work was a marginal kind of work.

Two major theoretical developments in the 1970s directed attention away from questions of labour supply towards questions relating to the demand for labour: dual labour market theory and Marxist labour process theory. Although the recession was in its early stages in the early and mid-1970s, there was an increasing awareness that everything in the economic garden was not rosy. Black struggles in the United States in the late 1960s had drawn attention to the unevenness of employment and to the incidence of unemployment among blacks, and in Britain and other west European countries there was a growing interest in the problems faced by immigrants within the labour market. Furthermore, the renewal of the feminist movement drew attention to the fact that, despite a steady increasing rate of participation in the world of paid work, women were in a position of structural inequality when compared with white male workers. It was these conditions which led many people interested in questions to do with work and in ethnic and gender inequalities to turn to dual labour market theory and to Marxist labour process theory as frameworks for analysing these inequalities.

(ii) *Dual labour market theory*

Dual labour market theory grew out of studies of local labour markets in the USA and originally emerged in the 1960s from attempts to understand the problems of poverty and what was at that time called 'underemployment'. It was widely used to analyse the position of blacks within the American occupational structure, and has more recently been used to analyse the position of women, both in the USA and the UK. Dual labour market theory has since become very popular with researchers into women's employment. There are now substantial variations on dual and segmented labour market theory as the framework has become more sophisticated.

There was not, in the 1970s, any specific discussion of part-time work by dual labour market theorists, but dual labour market theory did offer a framework for analysing gender divisions within the labour market. An early attempt to use dual labour market theory to analyse the position of women in the labour market in Britain can be found in Barron and Norris' paper, 'Sexual divisions and the dual labour market' (Barron and Norris, 1976). The basic argument of this paper is that the labour market is subdivided into primary and secondary sectors, a division which results from the strategies used by employers to tie skilled and technical workers into the firm. It is argued that employers privilege primary sector workers (by paying them

higher wages and tying them into the firm's career structure) because they
need to have a stable workforce in jobs which require extensive training and
investment and because they wish to weaken the unity of the labour force.
Secondary sector workers, by contrast, tend to move between industries and
occupations, from one unskilled or semiskilled low-paying job to another:

> If it is in the interest of the employers to maintain and expand the primary sector,
> it may also be in their interest to ensure that instability and low earnings are retained
> in the secondary sector . . . Of course, the strategy is necessarily related to the
> availability of a supply of workers willing to accept the poor pay, insecurity, low
> status and poor working conditions of secondary jobs.
> (Barron and Norris, 1976: 52)

In Britain, according to Barron and Norris, 'the secondary labour market
is pre-eminently female' (p. 48), because women have all the attributes of
secondary sector workers. Indeed, they suggest that one reason why dualism
in the British labour market has often been obscured is because the
primary–secondary sector division coincides with gender divisions.

When we formulated the research project dual labour market theory seemed
to offer some advantage over the 'women's two roles' analyses because it
shifted emphasis away from labour supply factors towards an analysis of
the demand for labour and it emphasised the fact that women were heavily
concentrated in poorly paid and insecure occupations which were generally
segregated from men's occupations. It seemed problematic as an explanatory
framework for analysing part-time work, however, because it abstracted the
question of employers' behaviour in the labour market from an analysis of
production, it ignored the role of trade unions in creating and maintaining
labour market segregation, it conflated the multifarious forms of women's
employment into a general category of secondary sector work, and it relegated
the sexual division of labour to the status of an exogenous variable. It also
seemed not to be very promising as an heuristic device for getting to grips
with the variety of forms of part-time work in Coventry. We were therefore
drawn towards Marxist labour process theory as a framework of analysis
in formulating the research project.

(iii) *Marxist labour process theory*

At the same time as the growth in dual labour market theory there was a
renewed interest in Marxist analysis of the labour process. A full version of
the *Grundrisse* (Marx, 1973) was translated into English for the first time
and published in 1973, so some of Marx's most important writings on the
labour process became more widely available, and Harry Braverman's book,
Labour and Monopoly Capital (Braverman, 1974), which was published in
the USA in 1974 was quickly welcomed as a very important attempt to apply
Marx's labour process analysis to contemporary capitalist society. Labour
process theory was less concerned with employers' strategies than dual labour

market theory, and more concerned with the ways in which the laws of capital accumulation impact upon the labour process. When analysing the labour process in capitalist societies, Marxist theory has been principally concerned with the changing forms of subordination of labour to capital, and with the effects of transformations in the labour process on the structure of the working class.

It is common knowledge that Marx had very little to say specifically about women's employment. Nevertheless Marx's analysis of the labour process was extremely influential on both theoretical and empirical writings about women's employment during the 1970s. Harry Braverman showed in his book, *Labor and Monopoly Capital*, that the classical Marxist framework could be broadened to take account of the fact, as one review put it, that 'the working class had two sexes' (Baxandall, Ewen and Gordon, 1976) and he paid considerable attention to the implications of women's increasing participation in the labour market for the changing class structure in the USA.

A number of feminists interested in women's employment suggested, however, that it was difficult to escape from Marx's naturalistic assumptions and to give adequate weight to the sexual division of labour between men and women without substantially revising the Marxist framework, and the term 'Marxist feminist' was widely used to refer to reconstructed versions of Marxist theory. There were two alternative versions of Marxist feminist theory proposed by people analysing women's employment and the labour process. In the first version the concept of patriarchy was introduced into the analysis of production.[2] This, it was suggested, would permit the Marxist framework to take account of the structures of male domination and female subordination which were otherwise missing from its analysis of production. In the second version, the Marxist analysis of production was broadened through an analysis of the family-labour process relationship.[3] Thus in the first framework of analysis the position of women in the labour force was analysed as resulting from the interrelationship between patriarchy and the 'needs' of capital, while according to the second version the position of women as a cheap, unskilled and disposable workforce was thought to result from the conjuncture of capital's 'needs' and the sexual division of labour.

(iv) *Approaching the research*

The assumptions with which we approached the research were largely derived from the Marxist framework just discussed, and particularly from the reconstructed framework which broadened the Marxist analysis to incorporate the family–labour process relationship.

These ran as follows. Part-time workers are overwhelmingly women, and are a particularly exploited sector of the workforce. Their gender is a major reason for their exploitation, since as women they perform both domestic and wage labour. It is the sexual division of labour in the family, and the familial ideology based upon this, which determines the conditions in which women sell their labour power and enter the world of paid work. We were aware, however, that this set of assumptions was very general, and that it was necessary to approach the research with more specific questions. We decided, therefore, to investigate the forms of part-time work and the situations in which part-timers worked, to analyse the demand for part-time labour in different kinds of enterprise, to examine the relationship between the expansion of part-time labour and the decline in employment opportunities for other groups of workers (e.g. full-time women and full-time men), and to investigate the extent to which the growth of part-time employment could be related to the growth of new industries or sectors. We were particularly keen to test out two alternative hypotheses about women's employment to find out whether part-timers were being substituted for full-time workers, thereby becoming a more permanent part of the labour force; or whether they were being disposed of, and thereby further marginalised.

When we started our fieldwork we had ambitious plans to study enterprises in all three sectors of Coventry industry (manufacturing, state services and private services), and to complement our study of the labour process with an analysis of the family. We wanted to do this in order to establish how the supply of part-time labour was related to other variables, for example, household structure and family income. Because the research proved to be extremely time-consuming, we had to abandon private services and also our proposed analysis of the family. We therefore concentrated on the demand for part-time labour. We decided that in any given workplace we wanted to cover all part-time workers. We did not want just to focus on production occupations, or to study large concentrations of part-timers, such as assembly workers on evening shifts. We generally found that within a single workplace part-time labour was used in a variety of ways and that the relationships between part-time work, full-time men's work and full-time women's work were quite complicated. The next part of the paper outlines our findings about the patterns of use of part-time workers in those industries/sectors we studied.

2 Patterns of use of part-time work in selected Coventry industries

(i) *Manufacturing industry*

Within the manufacturing sector four industries were studied: electrical engineering (which in Coventry is almost entirely telecommunications), baking, vehicles and mechanical engineering. Part-time workers in the machine tools and vehicles industries are a group which in 1976 formed 12 per cent and 7 per cent of the female workforce respectively.[4] By 1979 there were very few part-timers remaining in either industry, and there were no longer any on the shop floor. The handful of part-timers who were employed worked as telephonists or receptionists, or as punch card operators on evening shifts. There were also a few isolated copy-typists and clerks – isolated in the sense that they were always the only part-timer in the section. The telecommunications part-timers comprised 8.7 per cent of the total female workforce in 1976, but the numbers had been much larger five years earlier. All the part-timers were employed in a single occupation, wiring. Whereas there had been considerable employment of part-time wirers on both day and evening shifts, by 1979 part-time wiring took place only on the evening shift. There were no part-time clerical workers. Indeed telecommunications was the *only* industry in which there were a total absence of part-timers from clerical work.

By contrast, in the baking industry, in which part-time women comprised 58 per cent of the industry's female workforce and 16 per cent of the total workforce in 1976, part-timers were found in a wide variety of occupations, working enormously varied hours. There were evening workers, weekend workers, part-week workers, and part-timers employed to cover meal breaks. Part-timers were employed in the whole range of clerical and confectionery production jobs, but not in the production of bread which (with the exception of roll-packing) was done entirely by men. In some cases a part-timer was the only part-timer doing a job which was mainly done by full-timers, some jobs were done mainly by part-timers (e.g. clerical work), while others were done by full-time and part-time women working alongside each other.

The most common explanation offered for the rapid growth in the employment of women (both full-time and part-time) in the 1950s and 1960s is that it was a response to the shortage of labour which existed during this period of long boom,[5] and there was clear evidence of women being employed on a part-time basis during this period in a number of the industries studied. There were two basic patterns of use of part-time female labour during this period of expansion. First, management employed women on a part-time basis during the day if they could not attract women to work full-time in manufacturing and clerical occupations. The precise reasons why they were unable to attract full-time labour are not clear, but the argument which is couched purely in terms of labour shortage would seem to be an over-simplification. It may be that there was a labour shortage relative to wages, and that certain employers could not attract full-time labour because they paid such low wages. This was certainly true of the telecommunications firm and one of the textiles firms studied by Colleen Chesterman. Or it may be that the firms could not attract full-time labour *into particular occupations* and were forced to make certain jobs part-time in order to attract women to work in them.

The second pattern of use of part-time female labour during the period of economic expansion was the employment of part-time women on twilight shifts. These were devised as a means of extending the length of time during which production was carried out to meet short-term increases in demand for the product. Personnel managers who had been engaged in recruitment in this period said that they had had to make some concessions to accommodate women's own needs in order to encourage them into paid employment – for instance, by organising twilight shifts at hours when women could leave their children at home with their husbands. These shifts often lasted only a few months.

The period 1970–80, on which our fieldwork focused, has, in contrast, been a period of deepening recession for Coventry's manufacturing industry, and there has no longer been a labour shortage. The trend both nationally and in Coventry has been for women's part-time employment in manufacturing industry to decline, and there was substantial evidence that part-time women had disappeared from production occupations in some industries and also that part-time clerical work had declined. It is difficult, however, to generalise about the reasons for the decline in part-time employment. In some cases the fact that firms no longer had difficulty in recruiting labour is the salient factor. In other cases the decline seems to have been more closely connected with changes in the organisation of the labour process. In telecommunications, for instance, part-time work declined in manufacturing occupations because the jobs on which part-timers had been concentrated were severely cut back due to the introduction of new technology, and managements and trade unions had reached agreement that part-timers would be the first to go. Also, part-time jobs disappeared in a number of engineering workplaces because managements engaged in large-scale rationalisation of their labour forces when faced with increased competition, and introduced new grading structures which part-time work did not fit into.

Part-time work had not, however, disappeared across the board from Coventry manufacturing industry. Since the period 1970–80 has been a time of deepening recession in Coventry, with a steady increase in the level of unemployment, the continuing presence of part-time workers cannot be adequately explained in terms of arguments about a labour shortage. There were three patterns of employment of part-time women in Coventry manufacturing industry in this period. First, part-timers were used to extend the length of time during which production was carried out, for instance, on a Sunday shift. Part-timers were also employed on twilight shifts in a number of Coventry industries in order to extend the length of the working day. This was true of clerical workers in the baking industry as well as production workers, and of women working in computer rooms in some factories. Managements were more likely to use women to work on twilight shifts if there was a normal day shift operating; when double day or continental shifts were used, part-time work was generally phased out. Second, part-time workers were used to provide a flexible labour force to cover peaks and troughs in production over the working week. In the baking industry, for instance, women were employed part-time to cope with the problems of a daily production cycle and with changing demand over the working week. Finally, part-timers were used to fill in gaps and cope with overflow. Receptionists and telephonists, for instance, were frequently employed part-time in order to avoid the problems of covering meal breaks. Either a part-timer was brought in to cover meal breaks, or – more typically – two part-timers were employed, one in the morning and one in the afternoon; each also worked on alternate Saturdays.

We found, then, rather different patterns of use of part-time labour in the period of recession from those which had prevailed in the earlier period of sustained economic growth. In the period of expansion managements employed part-time women in certain manufacturing and clerical occupations during the day because there was a labour shortage relative to wages or because they could not attract full-time labour into particular occupations. They also employed part-time women in certain occupations in order to extend the length of the working-day. In the period of recession, however, part-time women were employed in certain occupations to extend the length of time during which production was carried out, to provide a flexible labour force over the working day or working week, and to fill in gaps and cope with overflow.

There was a high degree of occupational segregation of women's and men's work throughout Coventry manufacturing industry. In all industries clerical work was done by women. In some industries (for example, vehicles, mechanical engineering) the labour force in production occupations was exclusively or overwhelmingly male, while in other industries (for example, baking and telecommunications) there was a definite occupational segregation between men's jobs and women's jobs within production occupations. The use of part-time female labour was directly related to the pattern of occupational segregation throughout the industries studied. Where the full-time labour force was female, managements generally used part-time women to extend the period of time in which production was carried out, or to cover peaks and troughs of work over the working week. Where the full-time labour force was male, by contrast, managements devised other means of extending production and coping with peaks and troughs. In most cases, overtime working was used to extend the period of production and cover peaks where men were employed. In the baking industry, however, full-time male casual labour was sometimes used for these purposes. It appears then that managements use different ways of attaining flexibility when they employ women from the ways they use when they employ men, and that the continuing use of part-time female labour in manufacturing industry can be understood in terms of this difference.

This argument is well illustrated by the case of one of Coventry's largest car firms.[6] During the 1960s management needed to build up production of some components, and took on a twilight shift of male workers. This used the plant between 4.15 pm and 8.00 pm, that is, between normal shifts. However, management created a twilight shift on quite different terms from those which firms employing women had devised. It assumed that the labour force, being male, would need to earn a full 'family wage'. The men were therefore kept on to work on other machines from 8.00 pm until midnight, working alongside the male night-shift workers. The twilight shift was therefore effectively a full-time shift, and the men were paid as such with generous shiftwork bonuses.

Clearly since our fieldwork was limited and concentrated on selected industries one must be cautious about drawing general conclusions about the whole of manufacturing industry from our research. We have, however, discovered some important patterns of employment of part-time female labour which go some way towards explaining the conditions in which women have been employed on a part-time basis in Coventry's manufacturing industry.

(ii) *The public sector*

In the public sector we investigated women's part-time employment in the health service, in social services and in the education system. We found quite a complex situation, although the sheer size of part-time employment in the public sector does make it easier to say with some confidence that patterns exist. It is perhaps important to stress that the state is by far the largest employer of part-time workers. In Coventry in 1976 the education sector alone employed one quarter of all women part-timers. [7] The bulk of women's part-time work in the public sector was domestic work – cleaning, catering, home helps, etc. But there was also some part-time professional and para-professional work (teachers, nurses, paramedics, social workers) and part-time administrative and clerical work.

(a) *Health*

Between 1971 and 1977 part-time employment became an increasingly important component of health service work and an increasingly typical form of women's work within Coventry's health service. Part-timers increased as a proportion of the total female workforce from just over one third (35.4 per cent) in 1971 to just under one half (49.2 per cent) in 1977, and part-time women increased as a proportion of the total workforce from 29.5 per cent in 1971 to 41.4 per cent in 1977. [8] Our fieldwork was concentrated on part-time employment in the hospital sector, mainly in Coventry's two large general hospitals. At one of the hospitals just over half the nurses worked part-time, while the figure was slightly lower at the other. Just over half the part-time nurses worked as nursing auxiliaries (unqualified nurses), but a considerable number (44 per cent) were concentrated in the lower grades of qualified nurses. [9] Virtually all the part-time registered nurses were employed to do night duty. Part-time women were employed in a variety of paramedical occupations, but were systematically concentrated in the lowest grades. Women worked part-time in administrative and clerical occupations at both hospitals. Part-timers were concentrated in either specific tasks (e.g. medical records) or time-specific tasks (e.g. ward clerks working at weekends) or in the most routine clerical jobs like copytyping. Finally, most manual work in both hospitals was done by part-time women. Within manual occupations there was 100 per cent occupational segregation by sex, with men working as porters (a full-time occupation) and women working as cleaners and catering assistants. Both women and men worked in the hospital kitchens, but the men were employed as trained cooks while the large number of part-time women worked as kitchen and dining room assistants.

(b) *Social services*

Social services was another major employer of part-time workers in Coventry. In September 1979 nearly 63 per cent of the workforce employed by Coventry Social Services Department worked part-time.[10] There was a small number of part-time social workers, who tended to be concentrated either in caring for the elderly or in specific, non-typical areas of social work. As in nursing, there was a clear hierarchy between male and female social workers, with men being concentrated in managerial and senior positions. Part-time women were generally in the lower grades of qualified social workers. There was some part-time administrative and clerical work. Unlike the hospital sector, there was no central or typical locus of work in the social services, but a wide range of types of work and an enormous number of places of work. Part-timers were scattered throughout the many workplaces which make up the terrain of social services work. Part-time work in social services was massively concentrated in manual work, either in residential homes, or in supportive services for the elderly (particularly home helps). A large part of this work was necessary to the running of residential establishments; and a substantial amount of the caring work in homes for the elderly was done by part-time care assistants. This contrasts with the caring work in residential children's homes, which was mainly done by qualified full-timers. Supportive services for the elderly (e.g. home helps, mobile meals) were staffed almost entirely by part-time women.

(c) *Education*

Within education, like the other sectors, there were a few part-time professionals, some part-time administrative and clerical workers, and large numbers of part-time manual workers. We had difficulty getting hard data about part-time teachers in Coventry, but our interviews with teachers suggest that Coventry was similar to the national pattern. The numbers of part-time teachers appeared to be in decline, and those that remained were concentrated in specialist areas rather than in typical classroom teaching. They were all on Scale 1 posts. There were some part-time clerical assistants employed in Coventry schools (all on Clerical Scale 1) and the offices of primary schools were staffed entirely by part-time clerical workers. As in the social services these part-timers were scattered in ones and twos throughout a lot of the different workplaces. In the education sector almost all the manual workers employed by Coventry's education department worked part-time. There was a clear segregation between women's and men's manual work, with men working predominantly as caretakers, and women being concentrated in catering and cleaning. The school meals service (unlike the hospital meals service) was staffed almost entirely by women, the vast majority of whom (93 per cent in 1981) worked part-time.

(d) *Patterns of part-time employment in the public sector*
As was suggested by our analysis of Coventry manufacturing industry, it seems likely that different factors would operate to create a demand for part-time labour in a period of economic expansion from those which operate in a period of recession. Thus, until, the mid-1970s a shortage of labour undoubtedly contributed to the public sector's demand for part-time workers. In Coventry, in particular, there was a sudden and very rapid demand for labour in the mid-1960s with the more or less simultaneous opening of a large new hospital, a college of education, the university and the reorganisation of the polytechnic. But to explain the increase in part-time employment solely in terms of arguments about labour shortage is not a sufficient explanation. It does not explain *why* managements opted for part-time work as a solution to labour scarcity rather than adopting some other strategy (e.g. paying higher wages, or providing workplace creches). Since the period of expansion of part-time jobs in the public sector was also a period in which women's full-time employment in manufacturing industry was on the decline, there are *prima facie* grounds for assuming that there were women available who wanted to go on working full-time. Why, then, were so many jobs in the public sector created as part-time jobs?

One explanation is that managements employed women on a part-time basis in order to attract already trained and experienced women back into employment when their skills were in short supply. This has been true of professional occupations throughout the sectors we studied, although these have not been constructed as part-time jobs. Part-time work has tended to be the exception rather than the rule, and part-timers have been employed to do tasks which full-timers were unable to do, for example, working at nights or weekends. Part-time professionals were also employed to do specific tasks, for example, remedial care and special care for the elderly and disabled. Professionals working part-time have nearly always been employed in the lower grades.

The unqualified nursing, teaching and social work jobs have, in contrast, mainly been constructed as part-time jobs. There were several reasons for this. First, women working part-time have been used to extend the length of the working day or working week, a use which was very similar to the use managements made of part-timers in manufacturing industry. In the hospital sector and the residential sector in social services, for instance, part-timers were extensively used to enable care to be provided on a twenty-four-hour basis. In other areas of hospital care (e.g. catering, administrative work on the wards) coverage was not required for twenty-four hours, but it was required for more than a normal working day or working week, and part-timers were used to provide this additional coverage. Time factors were also important in the education sector, where much of the need was for periodic care. In the education sector some part-timers worked full-time school hours during terms, but not in the holidays. In all the sectors we studied part-timers were employed to do jobs which were only needed at a particular time or times of the day (for example, school meals workers, children's crossing wardens, hospital kitchen workers, mobile meals staff).

Although these kinds of factors associated with the need for a flexible labour force were clearly important in all the sectors we studied, it seems unlikely that these provide a sufficient explanation as to why so much of the non-professional caring work and domestic work in the welfare state is done by women working part-time. Another factor clearly has to do with the role of familial ideology. It was quite clear from our research that managements saw women, and especially wives and mothers, as ideal employees to work in certain domestic and caring occupations because these jobs are similar to women's unpaid domestic work in the home. Thus, while it is possible to specify constraints on the ways in which work can be organised and to point out the advantages of employing women on a part-time basis – showing, for instance, the importance of cleaning hospital wards before doctors' rounds, or cleaning classrooms when children are not at school, or making the fairly obvious point that the preparation and clearing up of meals generally takes place in the middle of the day, it appears that a major part of the reason why so much domestic work is part-time is because it is women's work. In employing women to do jobs which are similar to those performed, unpaid, within the home, managements make use of gender-specific skills which women have learned informally at home, yet the women's jobs are generally not classified as skilled. It would be wrong to suggest, however, as Myrdal and Klein did, that women are 'naturally' suited to such jobs, but more accurate to say that domestic work and much unqualified caring work in the public sector *has been constructed* in such a way that it replicates women's domestic role within the home. Familial ideology has an important role to play in the process of constructing jobs in this way. Like all pervasive ideologies, familial ideology is well grounded in the sexual division of labour, and makes a woman's position in the workforce *appear to be* a natural extension of her place in the family.

(e) *Part-time work and occupational segregation*
In the research project we tried to identify features of the organisation of the labour process which could account for the fact that certain jobs were part-time. But one thing which became absolutely clear is that these features only resulted in jobs being organised on a part-time basis when women were employed. Where men were employed, in contrast, managements used other mechanisms for attaining flexibility. Two examples illustrated this point. Within the hospital sector there was 100 per cent occupational segregation between portering, done exclusively by men, and other manual work, done by women. Now one could advance similar arguments as to why portering should be part-time to those we have advanced for women's manual occupations – twenty-four hours coverage is needed, there are peaks and troughs of work, etc. Yet portering was done by men working on a three-shift system, while women's manual work was all part-time. The second example is from baking. Both bread and confectionery production required a lot of flexibility of labour. There were peaks and troughs over the working week, and since bread and cakes are perishable, work had to be organised in a concentrated way when demand was high. Yet bread production, done entirely by men, was organised on a full-time basis, and flexibility was attained by extensive use of overtime and by some use of casual labour. Flexibility within the predominantly female confectionery production, however, was attained by extensive use of part-time labour, and a complex variety of patterns of work had been devised to attain this flexibility.

It appears, then, that a crucial part of the explanation as to why certain jobs are part-time is that they are typically done by women, and that the demand for part-time labour is inextricably linked to the presence of occupational segregation.

Wider theoretical considerations

These findings from our research project should be regarded as tentative since the project was limited to particular industries in a single labour market. They should perhaps be thought of as hypotheses warranting further investigation. Whether or not these arguments can ultimately be sustained in the light of more systematic social enquiry, they do raise some important and more general theoretical questions. We shall consider some of these, very briefly, in the final part of this paper.

As stated earlier, we approached the research with a set of assumptions derived broadly from the Marxist and Marxist-feminist frameworks. These asserted that women's specific position in the labour force derived from a conjunction of capital's needs for a particular kind of labour force – cheap, unskilled, and disposable – and sexual division of labour which consigned women to domestic labour within the family, and determined that, when they entered the labour market, they constituted a distinctive kind of labour force. The main advantage of the classical Marxist analysis of the labour process is that it directs attention towards an analysis of production and the demand for labour. These were questions which were absolutely central to our research project. As a result of doing the research, however, we have become aware of some fairly crucial problems with both the classical Marxist and Marxist feminist frameworks.

The first problem is that people using these frameworks have frequently adopted too formalistic an interpretation of Marxist theory, as one of us has argued elsewhere (Perkins, 1983). This has led them to assert that female labour will be used in one particular way within capitalist societies, and to overlook the historically changing ways in which women have been employed and the variety of uses to which female labour has been put. Irene Breughel has argued, for instance, that women are employed on a part-time basis because they can easily be disposed of, and that part-time female labour fulfils the role of an industrial reserve army of labour within contemporary capitalist societies (Breughel, 1979). While we did find some examples of part-time women being disposed of first, in the telecommunications company we studied, for instance, our research suggests that part-time women were employed by Coventry employers for a variety of different reasons (mostly to do with flexibility) and that these reasons for employing women on a part-time basis changed over time in accordance with the state of the economy.

Our analysis of part-time work also suggests that the question of gender must be incorporated into the framework of analysis. We found considerable evidence to suggest that gender is important in the organisation of the labour process: that it is invariably women's jobs which have been constructed as part-time jobs; that part-time working is inextricably linked to the existence of occupational segregation; that employers have gender-specific ways of attaining flexibility within their labour forces; that both employers and trade unionists make gender-specific assumptions about what kinds of work are appropriate for women and why married women do part-time work; and that many jobs in the public sector have been constructed in such a way that employers reap the benefits of skills learned by women as daughters, wives and mothers in the family without granting these formal recognition. It is difficult to know how to build an analysis of gender into an analysis of the labour process itself, but it seems increasingly clear that this needs to be done. It seems clear, too, that neither the classical Marxist framework with its sex-blind categories nor the Marxist-feminist framework which introduces gender into the analysis of production either through an analysis of the family–labour process relationship or through a rather formalistic analysis of patriarchy has proved to be entirely satisfactory.

The family clearly does have an important role to play in explaining women's part-time employment. The DE/OPCS study discussed elsewhere in this volume by Ceridwen Roberts found that women with children were more likely to work part-time than women without children, and that married women were more likely to do so than unmarried women. The survey also found that convenient hours were important to women working part-time, something we too found in interviewing women. Our research does suggest, however, that part-time working cannot be explained solely in terms of the family and female labour supply, and that an analysis of the labour process and of employers' demand for part-time labour is also a crucial part of the explanation. It suggests, too, that it is difficult to separate out questions of supply and demand. While it is clearly possible to distinguish *analytically* between the supply and demand for labour, and to argue about the pros and cons of approaching women's employment from the perspective of labour supply or demand, as soon as one begins to investigate the processes of recruitment of labour, and to try and analyse the reasons why certain jobs are part-time, it becomes increasingly evident that supply and demand are highly interdependent. Employers demand female labour, or part-time female labour, because a supply of this appears to be available, and conversely, women present themselves for particular kinds of work because they make some assessment about the likelihood of their labour being demanded.

Our research also pinpoints the importance of ideological constructions in this context, and suggests that the demand for particular kinds of labour may depend less upon some actual supply of labour (which is in any case hard to measure in the case of female labour because much of it is latent and hidden within the family) than upon managements' perceptions of what kinds of labour are available, and what work is appropriate for married women or women with dependents. Likewise it seems that the supply of part-time labour may itself be filtered through the prism of women's perceptions of the labour market, and their assessment of the likelihood of obtaining particular kinds of work. This interdependence of demand and supply factors and the ideological elements which enter into both became particularly clear in our research because we were undertaking a concrete investigation within a particular local labour market. One major advantage of analysing employment in the context of a labour market is that some of the complexities of the relationships between family and labour process, supply and demand, are revealed.

Conclusion

The paper has discussed some of the prevailing approaches to part-time employment, and also some of the findings of a research project into part-time employment in selected sectors of Coventry's manufacturing industry and the public sector. The research project turned up a number of interesting findings; that part-time work is an important means by which managements attain flexibility in the organisation of the workforce; that most women's non-professional domestic and caring work is organised on a part-time basis; and that part-time work is inextricably linked to the presence of occupational segregation. More generally, the project found that (with a few exceptions) it was only women's jobs which were constructed as part-time jobs and that gender was crucial to the ways in which managements organise their workforces.

It is difficult to know how to build an analysis of gender into a more general theoretical framework for analysing production in capitalist societies and there seem to be several choices as to how to proceed. One is to continue to use abstract categories for analysing production which are sex-blind and to assert that gender is only important at a concrete level of analysis. Another is to try and generate new categories which can take account of the complexity of gender relations within the real world at a theoretical level. The latter strategy seems to be a more promising way of both generating theoretical analyses and conducting empirical research. However, if this strategy is adopted much work remains to be done before we have a framework which can enhance our analysis not only of women's employment but of work more generally in industrial capitalist societies.

Notes

1 This paper was drafted by Veronica Beechey, and based on a research project undertaken jointly by Veronica Beechey and Teresa Perkins between 1979 and 1981. The final report, *Women's Part-time Employment in Coventry; a study of the Sexual Division of Labour*, was submitted to the EOC–SSRC Joint Panel, which funded the research, in May 1982.

2 This version is mostly commonly associated with the writings of Heidi Hartmann (Hartmann, 1976). It has always been more popular in the USA than the UK, although it can be found in Cynthia Cockburn's recent book (Cockburn, 1983).

3 Veronica Beechey argued for this broadening of the Marxist framework in two early papers (Beechey, 1977, 1978).

4 Unless specified to the contrary, the statistics in this section are calculated from the 1976 Census of Employment. These were the most recent Census of Employment statistics available at the time of our research.

5 See, for instance, Hallaire, 1968.

6 Colleen Chesterman cited this example in Chesterman, 1978.

7 Figures calculated from the Census of Employment, 1976.

8 Coventry Area Health Service Statistics.

9 *Ibid.*

10 Summary of all staff of Coventry Social Services Department in post, September 1979 (SSDS001).

Approaches to the study of gender relations in unemployment and employment

Introduction

My research over the last few years has been concerned with gender relations in unemployment and employment. This is an interest born of a concern both with the practical policy related aspects of unemployment as a social problem and with the potential light an examination of this area can throw upon theoretical issues in the explanation of gender inequality. Thus, on the one hand, I have asked questions such as: do women bear a disproportionate share of the burden of unemployment? and, is there sex discrimination in the process of job loss?, whilst on the other I have sought to develop a more adequate theoretical account of changes in gender and class relations. I have found these questions to be closely related to each other. The issue of the gender distribution of unemployment demands a consideration of the shifting boundaries between paid and unpaid work, which in turn requires an adequate theorisation of the sexual division of labour. This issue raises problems which include not only those of theory but also of method. The measurement of women's unemployment is itself a tricky problem as is the actual identification of the processes which do differentiate between men and women in times of employment loss. Thus the questions relating to gender and unemployment are a complex mixture of the theoretical and the empirical.

This paper will begin with a brief review of the problems identified with much existing literature on gender and unemployment (see Walby, 1985 a for a fuller account). It will continue with an account of the three main ways in which I have approached this area in my own research. That is, I shall discuss my work on a comparison of gender rates of unemployment in the EEC, a study of job loss practices in thirty UK establishments, and a historical study of exclusionary employment practices directed against women.

Existing research into gender and unemployment

Much research on gender and unemployment has accorded too much importance to the attractions of the family for women, and too little on exclusionary practices in the labour market directed against women. Too much emphasis is placed on consensual relations in the household and insufficient on conflictual relations in the labour market between different groups of workers. This is a problem common to both neo-classical economists such as Mincer (1962, 1966) and to some Marxists such as Beechey (1977, 1978). Both Mincer and Beechey suggest that in times of declining employment opportunities women are more likely than men to leave paid work and that they instead perform other work in the form of unpaid household tasks. Women are seen to move from paid work under market conditions to unpaid work within domestic relations. Mincer does not see married women who lose paid employment as really unemployed. Both see married women as a labour reserve who are drawn into waged labour only when the economy is in an expansionary phase and who leave in times of economic recession.

These explanations are, however, both theoretically and empirically flawed. Historical evidence of movements in women's paid employment do not substantiate these claims. Women have not left the paid work force in greater numbers than men in the economic recessions of the 1930s nor the 1970s and '80s. Theoretically the arguments are weak because of their failure to consider patriarchal forces in the labour market. Neither writer adequately specifies the mechanism through which women rather than men are induced to leave paid work. Mincer suggests this is a result of rational household decision making. Yet inequality between men and women in the family makes the use of the family as an undifferentiated unit of analysis untenable. While Beechey's more recent writings (1983) have paid more attention to the structuring of the labour market, her writings on the reserve army (1977, 1978) emphasise the explanatory significance of the needs and demands of capital. This makes the suggestion that employers would let go their women workers before men, despite the fact that they are cheaper, a contradiction within her own argument. If the demands of capital are primary then why are not the more expensive men shed before women?

Attempts to explain away this empirical discrepancy whilst retaining the basic thrust of the argument have engaged several writers. Milkman (1976), Bruegel (1979), OECD (1976) and Rubery and Tarling (1982) have argued that the effects of the sexual segregation of the work force have masked the underlying reserve army mechanism. Women, they have argued, are concentrated in the service sector of the economy, and, as this area of employment has been less affected by the twentieth-century recessions, then, so has women's employment been protected. The problems with these arguments are the taking of sexual segregation of employment as a fact rather than as a problem in need of explanation and the resulting inadequate treatment of the empirical character and theoretical basis of the processes of job loss. Underlying these problems, I would suggest, is an inadequate theorisation of gender relations which is related to a refusal to conceptualise patriarchal relations as analytically independent from capitalist relations. Yet it is only by theorising this independence and then by tracing the connections between different sets of patriarchal relations and analysing their articulation with capitalist relations that gender patterns in unemployment and employment can be grasped.

Before I could proceed further with my own analyses it was necessary to clarify the concept and method of measurement of women's unemployment. I began by rejecting the assumption made by Mincer (1962, 1966) and others that a married woman could not be unemployed because when she left paid work she would engage in unpaid housework. This assumption is sometimes buttressed by notions that married women place so many restrictions on possible employment that they are not fully available for work (Interdepartmental working party, 1972), and that the financial support of a woman by her husband materially affects her status as unemployed.

These assumptions, however, permeate the existing sources of data on women's unemployment. The official rate of unemployment based on the number of people registered as unemployed and collecting benefits is now commonly known to seriously underestimate the number of unemployed women. This is primarily because married women are not allowed to claim supplementary benefit in their own right, but rather are dependent upon their husband or male cohabitee to claim it for them; thus they are omitted from the official figures. This undercounting renders the government unemployment figures unusable for any research on gender rates of unemployment.

These assumptions about married women also permeate unemployment figures based on social surveys to varying degrees. The Census is very badly affected (leading, in 1961, to less women being counted as unemployed than in data based on registered unemployed). The most likely explanation of this is that unemployed married women were entered as 'housewife' rather than 'unemployed' by a male head of household who sought to enhance his own status as a conventionally successful breadwinner.

The more detailed questions of the General Household Survey makes its figures on women's unemployment more likely to be valid. However, its relatively small sample size precludes the possibility of some of the more interesting analyses.

The best source of data on gender rates of unemployment is that provided by the EEC Labour Force Survey. However, this is limited by being carried out only every other year and by a time series which goes back till only 1973 for the UK. Nevertheless, it is the best which exists, and was the data source for my first investigation of gender rates unemployment.

Comparative analysis of gender rates of unemployment

My first attempt to try out the theoretical arguments that I was developing was a comparative analysis of gender rates of unemployment, which utilised data from the EEC Labour Force Survey (see Walby, 1983 a, for a fuller account). I first compared the gender rates of unemployment in 1979 across the nine EEC countries (still the latest for which this data is available), and then compared the rates in the different regions of the UK. There are very great variations in the ratios of female to male unemployment between EEC member countries as table 14.1 shows. The ratio of female to male unemployment varies from the female rate being 1.3 times the male rate in the UK in 1979 to being 3.2 times the male rate in Belgium in the same year. In the period 1973 to 1979 the UK consistently has the lowest or next to lowest ratio of female to male unemployment.

Table 14.1 Unemployment rates in the EEC, 1979

	Percentage unemployed			Ratio of female to male unemployment
	Total	Male	Female	
W. Germany	3.0	2.3	4.2	1.8
France	6.9	4.6	10.2	2.2
Italy	7.9	5.3	13.3	2.5
Netherlands	6.7	4.8	11.1	2.3
Belgium	7.3	4.1	13.5	3.2
Luxembourg	2.4	1.7	4.2	2.5
United Kingdom	5.2	4.6	6.0	1.3
Ireland	9.8	8.2	13.6	1.7
Denmark	6.9	4.8	9.6	2.0
All EEC	5.8	4.2	8.3	2.0

This uses the extended concept of labour force membership and includes persons with a main occupation, unemployed persons, and non-active persons with an occasional occupation or seeking paid employment, all aged fourteen and over.

Source: Calculated from Eurostat (1981), *Labour Force Survey 1979*, Table 18

One possible explanation of this difference is that Britain has less patriarchal structures affecting women's employment than the other EEC countries; that women in the UK are allowed greater access to paid employment than in other European countries and hence suffer less unemployment. Indeed women's participation in paid work is higher in Britain than most other EEC countries.

However, I would argue on the contrary that women's higher rates of participation in paid work in the UK are due not to these relations in employment being less patriarchal, but rather because women in the UK are concentrated in worse jobs than in most other EEC countries. Despite the high participation rate of women in the UK, only a low percentage are to be found in professional, managerial and administrative jobs as compared to other EEC countries (Walby, 1983 a).

A further aspect of the disadvantaged position of women in the UK as compared to other EEC countries is that of the conditions of part-time workers in the UK. The UK has one of the highest proportions of part-time workers among women in paid work in the EEC as table 14.2 shows. These workers are largely concentrated in service sector jobs which developed in the post-war period.

Table 14.2 Part-time women as a percentage of women with an occupation in the EEC, 1979

W. Germany	27.6
France	17.0
Italy	10.6
Netherlands	31.6
Belgium	16.5
Luxembourg	18.1
United Kingdom	39.0
Ireland	13.0
Denmark	46.3
Average EEC	25.6

Source: Eurostat (1981), *Labour Force Sample Survey*, 1979, Table 20.

The conditions of employment for part-timers are on average considerably worse than those for full-timers. Rates of pay amongst part-timers are, on average, lower than those for full-timers. Job security is considerably less established among part-timers than full-timers. This is not only due to custom and practice and the activities of trade unions but also because much employment protection legislation does not apply to part-time workers. Part-time workers are overwhelmingly female. As a consequence of this differentiation of part-time and full-time work a high proportion of women in the UK suffer particularly bad employment conditions as compared with men, while part-time workers are particularly attractive to employers. Women part-time workers are thus attractive because of the poor conditions under which they can be employed in the UK.

Further advantages accrue to employers who use part-time workers who work particularly short hours. In the UK employers of such part-time workers have the possibility of nil or reduced National Insurance payments because of the threshold beneath which payments need not be made. They are also exempt from the provisions of the Industrial Relations, Redundancy Payments and Contracts of Employment Acts. The extent of differentiation of part-time and full-time workers is unique to the UK. In other EEC countries social security contributions are either made irrespective of the number of hours worked, as in Germany and the Netherlands, or else the threshold on earnings is extremely low, as in France (Manley and Sawbridge, 1980). Thus an important part of the difference in employment conditions between women in the UK and other EEC countries is due to differences in state policies.

It is often argued that the main factor affecting women's labour force participation is their responsibility for child care. Thus one possible explanation of the differential European rates of women's labour force participation is related to differences in child-care arrangements. The figures for the UK which show the highest participation rates for the ages before and after the years of child care would appear to support this. However, the UK is almost unique in the EEC with such a pattern. In most EEC countries the highest participation rates are found during a woman's twenties and early thirties which are the childbearing years. This is strong evidence that differences in child care are not the main reason for differences in European women's participation rates since it is in the years of a woman's life *after* childbearing and child care that the greatest differences in participation rates occur.

Thus I argued that the lower ratio of female to male unemployment in the UK as compared to the rest of the EEC is due to the greater severity of patriarchal relations in employment in the UK. A most important component of this is the greater proportion of women workers in the UK who labour under particularly poor conditions in part-time work, primarily in the service sector of the economy. The generally poorer conditions have also been seen in the lower proportion of women in higher level occupations in the UK as compared to the other countries of the EEC. These conditions make women workers particularly attractive to employers and contribute importantly to the lower rate of unemployment of women as compared to men in the UK as compared to the rest of the EEC.

The *reasons* for the greater patriarchal structuring of labour market conditions for women in the UK than in the rest of the EEC cannot be found by examination of the statistics of employment and unemployment; but require rather a wider ranging historical analysis of their development.

Regional differences in gender rates of unemployment 1973–9

The further comparisons of gender rates of unemployment in Britain which are possible using the EEC Labour Force Survey data are ones between different regions of the UK and between the years 1973, 1975, 1977 and 1979. Table 14.3 sets out the figures necessary for such a comparison.

No clear picture emerges from such a comparison. The changes over time for the UK as a whole are limited and do not appear to bear any relation to any other rates of unemployment or employment. Some of these variations may be seen to be the result of changes in the conduct of the survey and to sampling error, however, this can only account for some of the variation. There is also a problem in the use of regions as the units in such analyses.

The theory of women as a reserve army of labour was tested against this data. The theory predicts that when the overall level of unemployment rises that of women rises disproportionately fast. However, the EEC LFS data shows that while the change in the UK between 1973 and 1975 fits this hypothesis, that between 1977 and 1979 does not. Thus this data does not

Table 14.3 Unemployment rates and ratios of female to male unemployment by region 1973–81

	1973		1975		1977		1979		1981	
	Total unemp.	Female/male ratio	Total unemp.	Female/male ratio	Total unemp.	Female/male ratio	Total unemp.	Female/male ratio	Total unemp.	Female/male ratio
North	3.6	0.3	6.3	0.9	6.2	1.0	8.1	0.9	12.2	
Yorks & Humberside	2.2	0.7	4.5	1.5	4.2	0.9	5.6	1.5	9.8	
N. West	2.8	0.5	5.1	0.9	5.4	0.8	4.3	1.1	11.8	
E. Midlands	1.7	0.7	4.4	1.4	3.8	0.9	4.1	1.6	8.7	
W. Midlands	1.7	0.9	4.0	1.4	4.5	0.9	3.5	1.3	12.7	
E. Anglia	1.1	1.1	4.0	1.5	4.5	1.1	4.7	1.7	8.7	
S. East	1.3	1.0	3.7	1.4	3.8	1.0	4.9	1.6	7.0	
Wales	2.1	0.5	5.1	1.3	4.8	0.8	6.5	1.4	11.7	
Scotland	3.7	0.9	5.5	1.2	6.5	0.8	7.2	1.2	12.0	
N. Ireland	4.6	0.8	7.1	1.4	8.5	0.9	8.6	0.7	15.4	
UK	2.1	0.7	4.6	1.2	4.7	0.9	5.2	1.3	9.7	0.9

Sources: calculated from Eurostat (1980), *Labour Force Sample Survey 1973, 1975 and 1977*, Table VII/3; Eurostat (1981), *Labour Force Sample Survey 1979*, Table 60; OPCS (1982), *Labour Force Survey 1981*, Table 4.16

support the hypothesis although it is hardly a conclusive refutation. Similarly, regional comparisons do not provide either support or a conclusive refutation of the reserve army hypothesis.

Little obvious pattern emerges from these figures. Such a pattern would only be expected if unemployment was something which had a single cause. Rather, the level of unemployment is the outcome of complex increases and decreases in employment in different industries, occupations and areas, as a result of the intersection of capitalist and patriarchal relations. Patterns of employment and unemployment are the outcome of the accumulation over time of rounds of restructuring of gender relations in employment. Thus it is to be expected that the gender rates of unemployment by UK region appear chaotic and unrelated.

A study of job loss in thirty establishments

One of the problems of the type of study based on cross-national comparison of unemployment statistics is that it necessarily cannot provide an account of the actual mechanisms through which workers of different kinds are likely to lose their jobs to different extents. This second study was designed to look simply at this aspect of unemployment.

Methods

Thirty employment establishments in the north-west were examined in some detail for the processes of job loss which were utilised. The intention was to ascertain why particular strategies were adopted and whether these had a differential effect on men and women in employment.

The process of job loss was investigated by interviewing management and unions in these firms which were selected to have a broad range of characteristics. The north-west was a region with a higher than average rate of unemployment at the time of study and for a considerable period prior to it. Thus management and unions were typically familiar with the issues surrounding job loss. Almost all the establishments that were contacted had experienced recent contraction of some form or another, thus eliminating the need to search for such firms. The period of fieldwork was 1981–3 and all managers and trade unionists were asked questions about the preceding two years. Thus the period of job loss covered by this report extends over 1979–82, a period of high job loss both regionally and nationally.

The employment establishments were selected by quota sampling so that a wide range was represented. Certain characteristics which might be pertinent to processes of job loss were identified and the establishments were selected so that there were some with each. So it was ensured that the establishments selected were drawn from both manufacturing and services, employed manual and non-manual workers, had a large, medium and small number of employees, were mixed sex, employed largely men and employed largely women; were part of multinational corporations, locally privately owned, owned by national capital, and state owned; and were unionised and non-unionised.

Types of job loss

Compulsory redundancy is only one of several types of job loss, even if the most highly visible variety. Indeed its high visibility is one of the reasons for the undue focusing on this form of job loss by social scientists. Other major forms include voluntary redundancy, early retirement and natural wastage. Other ways of cutting back on labour include the use of temporary contracts and the cutting down on the number of hours worked by each employee. Each of the major types of job loss can itself have different varieties. Table 14.4 shows the types of job loss and their occurrence in the sample.

Gender distribution of employment loss

The effect of compulsory redundancies on the balance between male and female employment depended upon the criteria used in the selection of those made redundant and the application of those criteria in relation to divisions between departments in the establishment. It was not a form of job loss which in itself has necessarily more consequence for one sex rather than the other.

Instances of direct discrimination against women as women were very rare, being found on only one occasion. However, various forms of job loss led indirectly to women losing their jobs more than men in particular situations of labour contraction. In particular, the sacking of part-timers first and the sacking of those with shortest service as in 'last in–first out' had a greater impact on women than men. However, the use of 'age', 'efficiency' and 'task' criteria did not have a sex specific effect.

The sex segregation of employment makes the unit of selection for reduction by compulsory redundancy of overriding importance. Very often the selection of particular departments for reduction by redundancy led to the pool of potential redundants being almost entirely of one sex or the other. The decision as to the selection criteria thereafter could do little to affect the implications for each sex of the ensuing redundancy.

Voluntary redundancies are never totally voluntary but always include an inducement of some kind; these different incentives have differing gender implications. There were negative inducements which included the offer of a different job, either in the same establishment or in a different city or town, as the only way of staying with that employer, and positive inducements which usually meant a financial benefit of some kind.

Table 14.4 Distribution of types of job of job loss in the sample (a)

Natural wastage:		20
simple	16	
delays in reappointment	3	
enhanced	1	
Compulsory redundancies		13
selection criteria (sometimes more than one used):		
least essential tasks or skills	6	
last-in, first-out	5	
least efficient	4	
part-timers first	4 (b)	
near or over retirement age	3	
least personal hardship	1	
disliked by management	1	
Voluntary redundancies		10
induced by:		
financial benefit (state minimum)	5	
geographical redeployment (only alternative)	2	
financial benefit (above state minimum)	1	
internal redeployment (only alternative)	1	
change of hours (end of twilight shift)	1	
Early retirement		9
induced by:		
financial benefit (above state minimum)	4 (c)	
internal redeployment (only alternative)	4	
geographical redeployment (only alternative)	2	
hours cut	1	
bonus cut	1	
financial benefit (state minimum)	1	

(a) Some establishments used more than one type of job loss hence the numbers add up to more than thirty
(b) Not all these cases unambiguously belonged to this category
(c) In one case there was the dual inducement of both financial benefit above state minimum and the threat of internal redeployment

There were clear differences in the gender rates of job loss in cases of voluntary redundancy according to the nature of the incentives to leave. The offer of a job in a neighbouring locality as an alternative to redundancy led to a higher proportion of redundancies among women as compared to men, unless the costs of this are paid by the employer. This was largely due to the fact that women are less likely to be earning a wage which made the ensuing travel worthwhile. The differing effects of this process of job loss are thus a consequence of other aspects of the employment situation of

women. Women's lower pay is the basic cause of women being unable to
retain jobs when faced with the choices between geographical redeployment
and redundancy. Yet when the costs of moving and travel were met by the
employer women did not lose their jobs in greater numbers than men. All
these processes were affected by the sexual segregation of the work force
in the same way as the compulsory redundancies.

Where early retirements took place under the positive incentive of service-
related payments there was a tendency for more men to go than women. This
may be explained by the greater benefits men typically derive from such
schemes as compared with women, because of the greater likelihood of
their having the long unbroken service which leads to the largest payments.
As in the other forms of job loss the sex-segregated nature of employment
is often of significance in the sex composition of early retirers.

More than half of the establishments in the sample were utilising natural
wastage in order to reduce the size of their work forces. While in a third
of these this was the only method used, in the remaining two-thirds it was
used alongside more precipitate forms of job loss. Where it was possible to
distinguish the effects of natural wastage alone it was found to result in a
greater loss of women's jobs than those of men. This was to be expected
because of the higher turnover rates of the jobs typically occupied by women.
The process of natural wastage was sometimes enhanced, retarded or otherwise shaped by the management. Thus, while natural wastage in itself tended
to produce a greater loss of women's jobs than men's, there existed in actual
practice ways of shaping this process which had varying but strong sex specific
effects.

Sectoral distribution of job loss

This account has so far focused primarily upon the variations in the methods
of job loss and their impact. However, the distribution of job loss itself across
the range of employers has a significant effect on the distribution of job loss
between men and women. The establishment with the greatest contractions
in employment were largely located in the manufacturing sector and employed
a relatively high proportion of men, while those with the smaller contractions
were largely located in the service sector and employed a relatively high proportion of women. The sample of thirty establishments reflected the behaviour
of the national economy in this respect. Across the spread of the sample,
men were more likely to be in a situation of job loss than women. Thus
although in any given situation of job loss the practices often employed were
more likely to lead to the loss of a higher proportion of women's jobs, men
were more likely to be in such a situation than women. The concentration
of women in the sector of the economy least affected by the current recession thus protected women's employment as a whole. So, for instance, while
part-timers, who were almost exclusively married women, were more likely

to lose jobs than full-timers in a situation of job loss, the bulk of part-time jobs were in the service sector which was the sector undergoing least job loss.

Conclusion of job loss study

There existed simultaneously two distinct sets of processes, one of which meant that women were more likely to become unemployed than men, and one of which meant that women were less likely to become unemployed than men. The aggregate figures of men's and women's unemployment and employment must then reflect the sum of these two contrary processes. The very similar levels of men's and women's unemployment rates at this time (according to the EEC Labour Force Survey) thus reflect the outcome of two opposite tendencies, which are hidden in aggregate national or regional figures.

Some commonly used forms of job loss do mean that women are more likely to lose their jobs than men. This situation is primarily the outcome of women's position in a structured labour market and of negotiations between unions and management. Most of the forms of job loss which disadvantaged women *vis à vis* men stemmed from the prioritising the claims to employment of those who have been in specific jobs longest, a category of worker which is also the best represented in work place discussions and negotiations. Women's disadvantaged position in society is thus reflected in the work place in processes of job loss.

However, since the areas of employment in which women are concentrated are experiencing less contraction than those in which men are concentrated, the net outcome is for women's employment as a whole to be contracting less than that of men.

The analysis of the situation of job loss provides only one part of the explanation of gender patterns of unemployment, however. It does not explain why women are concentrated in areas of employment which are more buoyant than those in which men are primarily located. That is, it is necessary to explain the gender distribution of employment in order to explain the gender distribution of unemployment.

The explanation of the distribution of male and female patterns of employment requires an examination of how these have built up over time. They are the product of industrial development and social struggle over a long period. They result from the accumulation of round after round of restructuring of gender relations in employment. The contemporary location of a higher proportion of women workers in the buoyant sections of the economy and a higher proportion of men in areas of employment decline can only be explained by a historical analysis of these overlapping rounds of restructuring. This analysis is essential to a full understanding of contemporary gender patterns of unemployment, and it is to this that my third project turned.

Historical analysis of the development of patterns of gender relations in employment and unemployment

My third approach to the study of gender and unemployment was a historical analysis of gender relations in employment and unemployment (Walby, 1983 b, 1984, 1985 a). There are three processes which must be separated in order to explain uneven rates of decline of employment for men and women. Firstly, there are different rates of decline of employment in industries and occupations in which different sexes predominate. If male-typed forms of employment decline at different rates than female-typed forms then this produces different rates of employment loss for each sex and differential unemployment rates. Secondly, there is the ejection of one sex more than the other from any particular type of employment. Historically, there have been instances of well-organised men making women bear a disproportionate amount of employment loss. Thirdly, there is the possibility of uneven rates of increase in employment for women and men. All three processes were operating historically, and indeed today, and they should be seen as interrelated though distinct processes. When women's conditions of employment are depressed beneath those of men by patriarchal forces it is to be expected that employers developing new products will endeavour to devise forms of labour process and locational policies to take advantage of women's labour. The restructuring of gender relations takes place in the context of both patriarchal and capitalist struggles (and indeed ethnic struggles).

Thus for an analysis of gender rates of unemployment it is necessary to explain the uneven distribution of men and women in different industries. The sex-ratio in particular industries is remarkably stable over time, so in order to explain the current concentration of women in particular parts of the economy it is necessary to go back to examine the times when those industries developed and their sex-ratios established. Current gender patterns of employment, and hence of unemployment, can only be understood by a historical analysis of the rounds of restructuring of gender relations. I found a modification of Massey's concept of 'rounds of restructuring' (Massey, 1978) a particularly useful way to conceptualise this process (Walby, 1984).

In my historical analysis I focused on three major areas of employment: cotton textiles, engineering and clerical work. They were selected so as to meet three criteria: significance for total employment, contrasting gender compositions, contrasting forms of workplace organisation and state intervention. Thus cotton textiles, engineering and clerical work were three major areas of employment in Britain. The gender composition of the workforce in each area is different: mixed in cotton textiles, predominantly male in engineering, and predominantly female in clerical.

At crucial points of their development there were different forms of workplace organisations and state intervention: in cotton textiles there were non-craft unions together with legislative attempts to control women's labour; in engineering there were craft unions in the early days with late development of general unions, together with occasional legislative attempts to control women's labour; while in clerical work there were limited forms of workplace organisation.

The history of the gender relations in each of these areas of employment is marked by periods of rapid change, usually, but not exclusively at the points of their expansion and development, together with long periods of relative stability. It is the analysis of points of change which is of importance in the analysis of the gender relations in employment. I analysed the broad developments in gender patterns of employment followed by more detailed consideration of such changes in the gender relations of cotton textiles, engineering and clerical work as occurred in different historical periods since industrialisation. The historical work showed the importance of examining the variations in the nature of patriarchal relations in the workplace and the specific ways that they interact with capitalist relations to produce any given pattern of gender distribution of unemployment and employment.

I identified patriarchal workplace organisations, and in particular trade unions, as crucial agencies in determining gender patterns of employment. There are two main strategies here: firstly, that of excluding women from paid employment; and secondly, that of confining women to jobs which are graded lower than those of men. Since the last quarter of the nineteenth century an increasing proportion of trade unions used the grading and segregation rather than the exclusionary strategy. This shift has taken place in two ways: within unions and with the growth of unions which have only ever adopted the second strategy.

The level of unionisation and the nature of the strategy followed by such unions varied significantly across different industries and was a most important factor in the determination of the sex-ratio in that industry. The circumstances which facilitated such union developments were, of course, the key to this analysis. The decision as to which strategy was followed was determined by a variety of factors, the most important of which was the extent of continuity of the process and organisation with the related pre-factory forms of labour. Thus in engineering the gradual movement of small-craft production to the factory assisted the maintenance of strong, craft-based organisations of the workers, who adopted a policy of exclusion in order to retain the scarcity of their labour, and thus the price at which it could be sold. This general exclusionary strategy facilitated the adoption of a patriarchal strategy based upon exclusion, rather than the one based on grading, which was retained until women were admitted to the AUEW in 1943. In the case of clerical work the absence of strong organisation among the male clerks precluded their adoption of an effective exclusionary strategy against women when clerical work began to expand rapidly at the end of the nineteenth century. Although there are indications that this was tried, these attempts rapidly gave way to the strategy of confining women to work which was graded lower than that of men.

The strategy adopted against women by these unions could not be reduced to a defensive strategy against employers, but rather had an independent patriarchal dimension. For instance, the discrepancy between the use of the grading in, for instance, the organisation and grading of semi-skilled and unskilled men in engineering while simultaneously attempting to exclude women completely, demonstrates the independence of patriarchal relations from those between capital and labour. Many unions at the end of the nineteenth century excluded women from membership and tried to exclude them from areas of paid work even though they recruited semi- and unskilled men.

While trade unions were one of the most important agencies involved in patriarchal strategies in the workplace, they were not the only source of patriarchal intervention. The state has also played an important role in supporting such practices, especially before 1919. During the nineteenth century a series of pieces of legislation attempted to restrict women's access to paid work. This legislation was fought for by an alliance of patriarchal interests including male workers and bourgeois philanthropists, against the opposition of many, though not all, manufacturers. This political struggle by these patriarchal forces was not entirely successful since women's employment in the cotton textile mills, which was their primary focus, did not diminish in this century. Nevertheless, this struggle should be seen as one in which the state acted in the maintenance of patriarchal interests. Further instances of such action include the moves of the state in restoring patriarchal employment practices which were suspended for the duration of the wars. The state should not, however, be seen as the direct instrument of the patriarchal workplace organisations. Rather these actions were the outcome of struggles on the political level which have a degree of autonomy from economic interests. Patriarchal actions by the state on issues of women's unemployment and employment are less intense today than they were previously. The legislation which currently exists supports women's access to paid employment, although this is not vigorously implemented. The political struggles of women were important in changing this policy of the state. It should not be seen as the result of some inevitable drift of progress.

These varying sets of patriarchal relations interacted with capitalist relations to produce the gender patterns of unemployment found today. There was not a once and for all fixing of these relations, but rather at each new phase of capitalist development new struggles with patriarchal relations produced a set of gender relations in the new industry. These patterns in industries remained relatively fixed within specific industries until these industries were further subjected to technological change or other causes of expansion or contraction such as war or depression. Each new fixing of the sex-typing of employment was built on the foundations of previous rounds of restructuring, and was significantly affected by it. These patterns of inclusion and exclusion have given rise to the contemporary situation where women are more often to be found in industries which are contracting their labour requirement less than in those in which men are primarily located. This is the essential background to explaining the paradox as to why women, despite being more likely to lose their jobs in any particular situation of job loss than men are, nevertheless, not substantially more liable to unemployment than men.

Future research

I think a fundamental issue behind most questions concerning gender patterns in employment and unemployment is that of the sexual segregation in work. This is something which crops up repeatedly in both work by myself and others. It is a key to the relative protection of women from higher rates of unemployment in Britain in the current recession; women being concentrated in the service sector which is less depressed than manufacturing.

We know very little about the impact of the current high levels of unemployment on the sexual segregation of the workforce. It is time we did.

15 *A. Stewart, R. M. Blackburn, K. Prandy*

Gender and earnings: the failure of market explanations

The market and stratification

Markets, or, more frequently, 'the market', have had a central place in the sociology of stratification and inequality: a place which has gone substantially unchallenged until very recently.[1] For example, in Parkin (1973, 1979) and Giddens (1973) market forces are given the central role in the negotiation of inequality in western societies though each argues that there are further processes of distribution which cannot be traced to the market. Recognition of the need to supplement the processes of the market, as explanations of the structure and maintenance of inequality, with different determinants of differential returns, is argued by each to illustrate the superiority of Weber's sociology over that of Marx.

More recently, the problems of market models have received more attention, especially in discussions of the nature of female employment and in consideration of the lower levels of return to women than to men in employment.[2] On the face of it differential returns by gender suggest that establishing a market in which both types of labour occur could be difficult and one broad thrust in the face of such data is to accept, initially, that gender divisions act to modify markets or produce different markets – dual, fragmented, local or whatever.[3] The former position, that gender acts upon markets, such as is proposed by Wright (1979) among others, can be quickly shown to be incoherent.[4] The divisions by gender do not in any sense supplement the processes of the labour market, they contradict them. There cannot be two prices for the same quality and quantity of labour in a coherent market model. The latter position, that there are different markets for male and female labour, seems initially more plausible and fits with the data on employment which show that men and women are seldom employed alongside one another in jobs that are represented as the same. However, the processes by which separate markets have been established and are maintained are difficult to specify and most theories of dual or fragmented markets collapse back towards market models with women located at the lower end. Attention then shifts from the direct consideration of differential returns as the problem to the processes by which women are excluded from privileged market positions, whether by limits upon their education and training, by restrictions upon their labour market participation as a consequence of family responsibilities, or by social exclusions such as male definitions of skill.[5] The characteristic of each of these arguments is that it accepts that there is a single price for the same quality and quantity of 'labour' even if the definition of 'labour' is based upon social conventions which are problematic.

It is our view that there are indeed real problems for labour market theories of incomes, but that the type of argument outlined above cannot deal with these problems. In fact, the discrepancies between the different attempts to re-establish market explanations illustrate their incoherence. Consider, for example, how the argument that men control the definition of skill, and so impose divisions between forms of labour to the disadvantage of women, relates to arguments that women are excluded from the acquisition of appropriate education and training. For the market to operate upon both of these processes levels of education and levels of skill would have to coincide even if each was a consequence of disposable social conventions. Yet if they do coincide the male definition of skill is unnecessary to processes of discrimination since the latter could be explained by the manipulation of education alone. The male definition of skill arises to explain the *deviations* from market outcomes expected on the basis of education and as such it can have no substance *within* such market explanations. However, we believe that concern with it reflects a real issue – an issue of the adequacy of market explanations.

The thrust to re-establish the 'market' derives from a perceived need for coherence, but the coherence it seeks cannot be in terms of the elements of the failed explanations. Although we are sceptical about the solutions, we accept the need to take the problem seriously. Something of the force of pressures towards the coherence of a market model can be seen if we look at the relationships between gender, education and income, where we can also see some of the problems associated with it. Available figures for advanced industrial societies show that there are discrepancies between the earnings of men and of women matched by education, whether we consider mean hourly earnings or earnings for matched full-time employment. It is precisely this type of problem that male definitions of skill are meant to address; differentiations in rewards which, on the face of it, cannot be explained by differences in the quality and quantity of labour power. It would seem that even if women are discriminated against in the acquisition of education this is insufficient to explain their low earnings, and further factors must be adduced. We may be sceptical of a conspiracy of male employers and male employees to maintain differentials to the benefit of male employees in an otherwise market economy, but at least such an explanation recognises the problem.

Another response is to argue that the problem has no real substance. The education of men and women may look alike, but as it bears upon employment this appearance hides real differences in labour capacity as a consequence of experience and commitment.[6] This argument tries to re-establish the market by refining the categories in such a way as to neutralise the difficulties. It is not well established in practice and this article will examine its claims in some detail.

Our interest in the operation of the market extends beyond the issue of gender and labour,[7] though that issue highlights many problems. We do not believe that market models have ever been as efficacious as their proponents claim and in some of their forms they are merely attempts to justify inadequate understandings of the *status quo*. The most extensive statements of the market are those proposed by the classical economists and by Marx. In somewhat different ways they seek to establish markets upon labour power, where all exchanges tend towards equality in their labour content. All of the writers experience difficulties in producing statements of the nature of labour in terms of which all exchanges are equalised, and subsequent statements of the market have tried to solve this problem by arguing that the difficulties internal to labour theories of value can be removed by extracting labour from the internal statement and making it an input with a form, or forms, determined by social processes which are external to the market. The market is thus predicated upon social processes that it does not contain.

While accepting that the problem of 'labour' is real we believe that attempts to solve it by accepting the categories of the problem and making some of them the basis of additional, *ad hoc* factors merely reify the failures. On examination the market is not predicated upon these factors, they contradict its operation.[8] This is not surprising since the origin of the factors is the deficiency of the unified statement. For example, the neo-Ricardian argument that the solution to the transformation problem in Marx's writings is to recognise that the market operates in terms of definitions of labour produced in social conventions external to the market, displays all of the characteristics of its origin in the transformation problem. The definitions of labour are 'conventional' in form only because they cannot be given 'real' substance within the explanatory undertaking. This entails the sort of division between the economic as 'real' and the social as 'conventional' that Marx sought to attack. The use of the term 'conventional' signals the location of factors in primitive values, tastes, appetites etc. which contradict the operation of existing 'determinant' processes. The novel factors are no more than the reflections of the deficiencies of these processes.

Weber's theories, and those of neo-Weberians, are not superior to those of Marx in their greater extensiveness. That extensiveness is merely the acceptance of the perceived deficiencies of his statement as the substance of the explanatory task. The market is supplemented by 'status' processes which contradict its operation[9] and is drained of all explanatory force by assuming that it operates and so equalises inputs. 'Market capacities', it is argued, derive from diverse sources and their value is what they will exchange for in the market. Thus the fact of exchange is assumed to be sufficient to establish the operation of a market, and exchange and equality of exchange are conflated. This is precisely the form of neo-classical assumptions of the operation of the market where the market processes reveal the tastes and preferences of the parties to exchanges. Each failure to predict outcomes on the basis of past assumptions is the occasion of the operation of new preferences. If this sort of procedure could work there would never be an issue of the operation of the market, but the market would never afford insights beyond the direct apprehension of supposed exchanges.

In fact, the conventional limits upon the operation of the market can, in all specific instances, be shown to be contradictions of market principles rather than additions to these principles. Our main purpose in the paper is to illustrate this for gender as a factor which must be taken into account in addition to market principles. The efforts to re-establish market understandings are attempts (though sometimes the problem is only dimly perceived) to escape the consequences of the contradiction. Their failure indicates the need for the transformation of theories of inequality in such a way as to account for stable processes of distribution in other than market terms.

A survey approach to market issues

In order to examine the problems of market explanations in more detail we shall use information from a survey of male and female employees.[10] At the outset we should make clear some of the issues raised by the use of survey data to address social processes. We most emphatically are not arguing that values are the foundation of social experience. Social processes are complex negotiations of practical circumstances not primitive projections upon the world.[11] However, their substance is the knowledge and practices of members of the society. Though such knowledge may not encompass the totality of social arrangements it must be consistent with such arrangements if processes are stable. Where there is a contradiction in understanding and practices the instability so produced can be solved only by the creative reformulation of objects and relations. This is the true task of social science whosoever undertakes it.

The understandings of social participants are thus vital social scientific data. In the case of markets the understandings of participants are obviously crucial. In integrated statements of markets shared understandings of exchanges are necessary. In statements which attempt to found the market upon values or preferences, participants are seen as the only source of relevant information. If in either case the understandings of processes cannot be accommodated to market explanations, then market explanations must fail.

The survey was carried out over several months beginning in January 1981. It covers 381 respondents, 215 male and 166 female. They are divided between Scotland (principally the Glasgow area) and the south-east (the Cambridge area and London in the main). Scotland provides 217 respondents, the south-east 167. The respondents were chosen to cover employment in manufacturing and tertiary sectors, private industry and government service and manual and non-manual occupations. Most were interviewed at their place of work though a few were interviewed at home or at other arranged venues.

Table 15.1   Occupations in the analysis

Solicitor	Butcher in own shop
Civil engineer: design work for construction company	Toolmaker in medium-sized engineering company
Primary school teacher	Supervisor of TV assembly line workers
Bank manager, medium-sized branch	Police constable
Social worker	Supervisory cook in NHS hospital kitchen
Sales manager for medium-sized chemical company	Compositor for local newspaper
Journalist on local newspaper	
Nurse (SRN) in NHS hospital	Bus conductor (Corporation)
Production manager in large engineering works	Motor mechanic
Head of drawing office in large engineering company	Person delivering milk
Estate agent	Sewing machinist: ready-made suits
Executive officer (DHSS): administers supplementary benefits	Post Office mail sorter
Laboratory assistant: routine testing in chemical works	Turner in medium-sized engineering works
Secretary to a middle manager (shorthand typist)	Cleaner in Council offices
Wages clerk for Gas Board	Glue machine operative in cardboard box factory
Telephone operator (GPO)	Assembler of electrical components
Publican	
Sales assistant in department store	Punching press operator in large engineering works
	Council labourer
	Packer in food factory

The data for this paper are drawn from assessments, covering a variety of characteristics, of the thirty-six occupations shown in table 15.1, which were chosen to represent variations by industry, manual and non-manual tasks, public and private employment and gender composition. Obviously, if the task was to be kept to reasonable limits each respondent could not assess all thirty-six occupations so we formed twelve separate sets of six occupations. These sets were randomly assigned to respondents for the assessments, each occupation appearing in two different sets. The occupations were each assessed, therefore, by about sixty respondents on average. The groupings of occupations within sets were not random. They were chosen, as far as possible, so that each set covered a wide range on the variables in which we were interested.

We asked respondents a number of questions about characteristics of the occupations and their incumbents. Every respondent was given a set of six cards, each having one of the occupations printed upon it. For each characteristic of the occupations they were asked to place the cards in order of their possession of that characteristic. When they had completed the task for the first characteristic they were given an additional card on which was printed 'Your own job' and were asked to place it in the ordering. Each subsequent task repeated this process.

The estimates upon which this analysis is based were formed by first calculating the mean position of every occupation in all sets of occupations (which gave two means for each occupation since each occurred in two sets) and then taking an unweighted average of the two means for each ocupation. Since the occupations vary between sets, the values so produced are comparable only because assessments on all variables are made within the same set of occupations and insofar as we were able to make the sets broadly similar. Since the occupations of respondents vary and they placed their own occupations in the orderings the equivalence of means depends upon the random assignment of respondents' occupations over sets. We know that this is close to the truth. There are other more complex methods of producing compatible scores which use the overlaps between groups in multi-dimensional scaling analyses and we have used these on other occasions. However the simpler procedures provide substantially similar results and are adequate for present purposes.

There are certain advantages to the use of aggregate data. In a sense the refinement of the values on the different variables affords a more direct assessment of the structure of relationships between them. If a significant correlation, e.g. between education and income, is found in individual level perceptions the only condition under which the level of the correlation would not converge upon unity with aggregation is that the structure of the errors in the individual level correlation is not random, which means that the relation is non-linear. This may be due to an orderly basic relationship where different units of measurement could capture linearity, or it may be because of more or less specific discontinuity in the structure of the relationship. Whatever the source of deviation (from linear relationships with random errors) it must occur within the population and aggregation can provide evidence of its substance. For example, the relationship between estimates of skill with the hands and estimates of income is of the order of −0.35 in the aggregate data. Among non-manual occupations the relationship is negative, among manual occupations it is positive and because of the concentration of high incomes in the non-manual area it is negative overall. The low level of the aggregate correlation is a consequence of these different processes as they occur in the population.

However, caution is required in the interpretation of aggregate relationships. Though a substantial deviation from unity is always worth pursuing, values may approach unity in cases where there are somewhat contrary trends for sub-groups of the population. In other words whereas deviation from unity indicates a non-linear structure to relationships the approach to unity is not necessarily an indication of only random deviations from a *single* structure of relationship in the population; it may conceal significant variations.

We conducted separate analyses for male and female respondents but, although there were some marginal differences that were interesting and corresponded to differences of experience, the main structures of results were very similar and we shall present only the results obtained by combining male and female respondents.

Earnings and gender

In this section we shall look at the respondents' perceptions of the labour content of jobs, relating them on the one hand to their perceptions of earnings and on the other to perceived characteristics of incumbents. This, in a sense, looks at the two processes postulated as central to the labour market: the relationship between the form of labour and rewards to it and the relationship between this form and labour power, which is often measured by education and training. We shall examine how gender bears upon each of these processes showing that there is an assymetry which undercuts markets explanations. Gender operates in the relationship between labour and labour power only in the sense that female occupations are, in general, low on both characteristics. There are no substantial differentials that require specific gender explanations. In the relationship between labour and rewards, however, there are important differentials by gender. This means that in the perceptions of our respondents rewards from employment cannot be explained by a market model since there are differential prices for the same quality and quantity of labour.

The first set of variables we shall examine are those that can be associated with characteristics of occupations which might be thought of as bearing upon their labour content. They are: the amount of thinking each job calls for, the skill with the hands required, the amount of responsibility each involves and, perhaps a little more controversially, the amount of personal decision-making and control each job affords.[12] This last item may be more immediately perceived as a reward of the job rather than a requirement which involves paying a premium in a labour market, but each of the variables has a dual characteristic of both requirement, drawing upon more or less scarce resources, and reward to those exercising the resources.

The duality is a constant difficulty for thoroughgoing market models of personal incomes. It is never clear, for example, in human capital theory where investment (as consumption forgone) ends and consumption begins. Even the acquisition of skills in education and training might in many cases be more easily regarded as privileged consumption than as self-denial in order to accumulate capital, but the more serious difficulties are associated with the tendency of earnings of the most highly educated groups on entry to employment to rise steeply over most of their working lives and to become increasingly, favourably, distinguished from the earning of less educated groups. Why should this be so? The answer that Mincer, for example, provides is purely circumstantial and implausible. He argues that the growth of inequality with age can, within a human capital model, 'be explained by the correlation between the stock of human capital at any stage of the life cycle and the volume of subsequent investment. The correlation is understandable, if factors of ability or opportunity which affect individual investment behaviour tend to persist over lengthy periods of a person's life. For example, the absolute growth of dollar earnings with experience is greater at higher schooling levels'. (1976: 152)

The problem with this position is that the acquisition of capital must now occur in the exercise of employment tasks and these tasks are most frequently given, by the financially most advantaged, as the most rewarding characteristics of employment. Some meaning can be given to consumption forgone in education given the relatively low earnings of full-time students (though this depends upon the spurious equation of the social and intellectual experience of student status with cost), but what is forgone in the development of a successful career is much more difficult to specify, and if the determination of income depends upon the accumulation of capital after entry to the labour market human capital explanations are at best speculative, but more likely, merely rhetorical.

Given our scepticism about any of the variables as 'market' resources there seems no point in excluding the control of personal circumstances experienced by employees. In any case these are arguments that the extent of personal control is a major factor in the determination of income.[13]

We asked respondents 'How much do you think an average person in each of these jobs earns?' If they had difficulty in making an estimate we asked them to place the occupations in order of earnings. For the most part we are concerned in this paper with the mean order of earnings (usually derived from the figures for actual earnings) because of its similarity in form to the mean orders of other variables under consideration. We shall, however, use the mean estimates of income for some purposes.

Table 15.2 contains the correlations between income and the various characteristics of occupations. Apart from skill with the hands the variables are all highly intercorrelated. We have already discussed the difficulties of the relationship of skill with the hands to income and very similar problems occur in relation to other variables.

Table 15.2 Correlations of occupational characteristics

	Income	Responsibility	Skill with hands	Thinking
Responsibility	0.83			
Skill with hands	− 0.35	− 0.40		
Thinking	0.86	0.97	− 0.37	
Control	0.90	0.95	− 0.41	0.92

When multiple regressions are performed with income as the dependent variable only control occurs as an independent variable whether the analysis is performed stepwise, with forward inclusion or with backward exclusion. [14] The R^2 is 0.81. This indicates that the relationships among the job characteristics are broadly similar and that, with the exception of skill with the hands, which adds nothing significant to the explanation, they relate to income in much the same way.

There are characteristics of incumbents that could contribute to the determination of income independently of the characteristics of jobs, though this would involve, a negation of the market relationship of 'labour power' and 'labour'. We next included respondents' perceptions of two of these, age distribution and level of education and qualifications. In fact, there are two variables associated with age distribution since we asked for separate estimates of the ages of women doing the jobs and of men doing them. [15] When these three variables are added to the analyses one of the age variables, that based on the age distributions of women doing the jobs, enters the equation along with control. To a large extent the age distributions act in similar ways in that the male age variable takes over if the female age variable is removed. There are some differences between them, but they need not detain us here. It is not surprising that the mean level of education and qualifications does not enter the analysis since it correlates 0.99 with the mean amount of thinking the job requires and that latter does not appear. The very high figure for this relationship (together with the fact that the mean values are almost identical and there are no discernable differences for sub groups) shows that the underlying perceptions of these factors are very similar. It would appear that there are stable and consistent processes relating 'labour power' to 'labour'.

When the female age variable is included the R^2 rises to 0.84. Thus when we consider the combined effects of job characteristics and incumbent characteristics we find that only control and the age distribution of women doing the jobs make any significant contribution. This suggests that, with the exception of the age variable 'labour power' and 'labour' factors are consistent with each other and relate in much the same way to income.

What we now wish to consider is a potential non-market characteristic, the perceived sex composition of the various occupations. If gender is related to income determination, but only through processes assigning women to lower positions in the labour market by denying them access to the acquisition of the means to better jobs, then the gender composition of occupations should make no contribution to the determination of income once 'market' factors have been taken into account. In fact it makes a substantial contribution, as we shall see, which is strong evidence for the absence of a true market for labour in that the same quality of labour exchanges for differential prices.

As a first, visual indication of how much gender matters we present in Figure 15.1 the plot of the standardised residuals of the regression of income upon control and female age distribution with those occupations which are

Figure 15.1   Income and 'market' factors: plot of standardised residuals

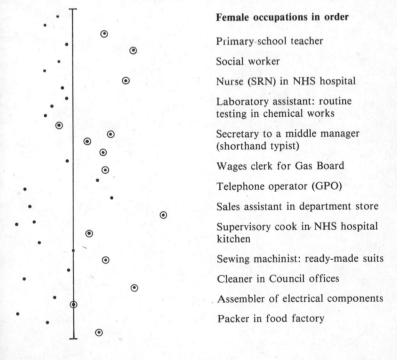

Female occupations in order

Primary-school teacher

Social worker

Nurse (SRN) in NHS hospital

Laboratory assistant: routine testing in chemical works

Secretary to a middle manager (shorthand typist)

Wages clerk for Gas Board

Telephone operator (GPO)

Sales assistant in department store

Supervisory cook in NHS hospital kitchen

Sewing machinist: ready-made suits

Cleaner in Council offices

Assembler of electrical components

Packer in food factory

judged by our respondents to be, on balance, more female than male ringed
and itemised. This shows clearly the tendency for male occupations to have
higher actual values than predicted and female occupations to have lower.

The gender composition variable was formed from answers to questions
about which sex more typically did each of the jobs or whether both did. [16]
The variable was formed by combining the percentages who fell in each of
the three categories, multiplying female percentages by 0, both by 1 and male
by 2. In fact there was a very strong tendency for agreement on whether
occupations were performed by one or other sex or by both. There are no
occasions where the population is very strongly divided in identifying jobs
by sex. The correlation of the residuals with gender composition is 0.70, which
shows clearly that it must make a significant contribution when added to
the multiple regression.

In fact, when gender composition is included with all other job
characteristics and incumbent characteristics it makes the most important
contribution after control. Including gender changes the structure of the
equations somewhat and education and qualifications now also make a significant, though small, contribution with forward inclusion. The R^2 is now 0.93.
Table 15.3 summarises the various regressions.

Table 15.3 R^2 values for multiple regressions

	Including: Job characteristics	Plus incumbent characteristics	Plus gender composition
All occupations	0.81	0.84	0.93
Female occupations	0.92	0.92	—
Male ocupations	0.95	0.95	—

Another illustration of the importance of gender can be given by separating
the occupations into those done, on balance, by men and those done by
women, in the judgement of our respondents, and conducting separate regressions with income as dependent variable for the two groups. When this is
done control occurs in both regressions; in the female occupations as the
only significant contributor and in male occupations together with education and qualifications. In neither does age distribution make a significant
contribution. The R^2s are much higher than for the combined analysis (when
gender is excluded). For female occupations it is 0.92 and for male 0.95. For
male occupations education and qualifications makes the larger contribution. If we consider only education and qualifications the R^2 remains little
changed at 0.95, if only control is considered it is 0.91. This does not represent a difference between 'labour power' and 'labour' effects upon income
since thinking correlates 0.99 with education and qualifications and maintains the level of the R^2 if the latter is omitted from the regression. What

it does mean is that control makes a slightly different contribution than other job characteristics for male occupations.

Separating the occupations allows us a further illustration of how gender affects income in ways inconsistent with the operation of a labour market. As we have seen, some commentators have attempted to argue that identical qualifications held by men and women do not really indicate the same quality of labour power. Though the educational standards match this gives a false impression of relation to the labour market because it fails to take into account other factors affecting the quality of labour. As a consequence differential rewards by gender are held to reflect real differences in market capacity.

The analysis to date suggests that this is not the case. Education and qualifications relates very well to job characteristics and they all relate to income in much the same way. If qualifications had differential meaning by gender, then we would expect that female and male occupations would have been different relationships to placement in employment. When the thinking the job requires, the responsibility necessary and the control exercised, are estimated from perceived education and qualifications, then female occupations should afford lower values than male occupations. If on the other hand the education of those in female occupations stands in much the same relation to job characteristics as the education of those in male occupations while at the same time their incomes are perceived as much lower, then we must conclude that in the perceptions of our respondents the differences in income are not a reflection of different labour power or different labour quality. The underlying processes assigning people to employment might be intelligible and orderly, but they would not be those of a market for labour.

The results of the various regressions of job characteristics on education and qualifications, for both male and female jobs, are given in figure 15.2 and the regressions of income on job characteristics are given in figure 15.3. Although the range of education and qualifications is different for male and female occupations, the relationships with job characteristics are very similar. Only control shows a notable advantage of male jobs over female jobs (because the variables are mean ranks high value represent low estimates) and even there the differences are slight. When we turn to regressions of income upon job characteristics the situation is quite different. Once again there is broad similarity in the relationships of each job characteristic to income for the male occupations, and for the female occupations considered separately, but there is now a very considerable difference by the gender of jobs. The two figures, taken together, illustrate how education and qualifications of those in female occupations relate to job characteristics in much the same way as does the education of those in male jobs, while male jobs afford higher incomes. The differences in income by gender composition in the perceptions of our respondents cannot be explained by the operation of market forces.

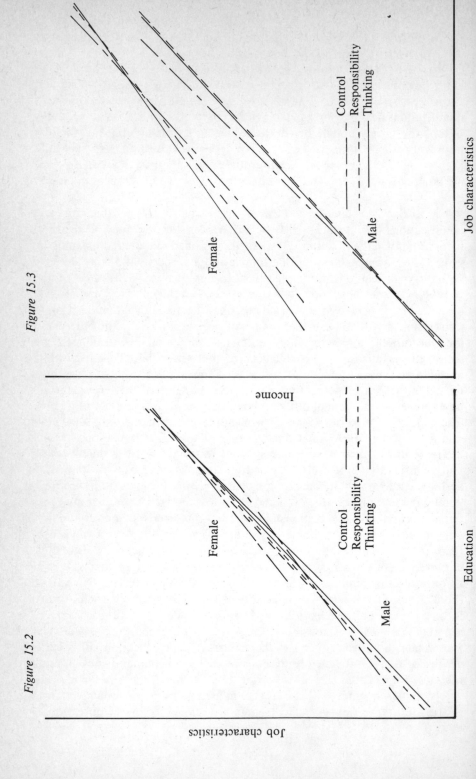

Figure 15.3

Job characteristics

— — Control
— — — Responsibility
——— Thinking

Female

Male

Income

Figure 15.2

Education

Control — · —
Responsibility — — —
Thinking ———

Female

Male

Job characteristics

Perceptions and published statistics

At the outset we argued that important social processes must consist in the knowledge and practices of members of the society. We should stress that the answers to the questions sociologists form do not stand in unproblematic relationships to such processes, nor are the 'attitudes' or 'opinions' or 'values' of respondents the source of social processes. As a consequence we must constantly relate findings derived from surveys to other information on processes. It is not always possible to do this over the whole range of issues and, in any case, the greater extensiveness of survey data can solve problems otherwise intractable, but they must, where possible, be confirmed by data produced by other means.

From various sources we have compiled estimates of income for each of the occupations at the period of the interviews. For the most part these are drawn from the Department of Employment's New Earnings Survey supplemented by other government and private sources where the former is insufficiently precise. We formed separate estimates of mean male and mean female incomes (where appropriate) and for the purposes of the present analysis we produced a single estimate for each occupation weighted by the gender composition of that occupation as perceived by our respondents. The R^2 obtained by regressing mean perceived income on the estimate of mean actual income is 0.88. Obviously, though the level of co-efficient is high, there is still scope for a fair number of cases where estimates by our respondents are out of line with the estimates from other sources. This does not necessarily mean that our respondents are always less accurate in their estimates. The figures otherwise available often cover rather different, less precise, groupings and since we asked respondents for an estimate of what a 'typical person doing the job would earn' while the other estimates are based on mean earnings, the relationship between them will depend upon the distribution of earnings among the members of an occupation. This may go some way towards explaining the consistently lower estimates of our respondents, since we know that modal earnings are typically below mean earnings. At all levels of earnings there is a difference of about £1,400 between the estimates of income from other sources and those estimated from our respondents' perceptions of typical incomes. [17]

The two occupations whose incomes show greatest underestimates by our respondents are police constable and bank manager. In both of these cases we believe our respondents, in line with the population in general, are unaware of just how high rewards to these occupations are. Three occupations show particularly high overestimates by our respondents, estate agent, production manager and head of a drawing office. The last is probably explained by the impressive nature of the title, but the other two may reflect more accurate assessments by our respondents than are available for the imprecise categories in which the other two occupations occur in available statistics.

We have also compiled estimates of the sex composition of the occupations. For this purpose we have used the Economic Activity Tables of the 1981 census. Ironically, the change in the occupational classification between 1971 and 1981, which in other contexts has caused much difficulty and confusion, has allowed us, through the double classification of 1 per cent of the 1981 census (to the 1970 and the 1980 classification of occupations) used to dispel some of the confusion, to locate more accurately the content of particular occupational titles. The R^2 is 0.94. Despite the different ways in which the estimates were formed (the mean of estimates across our respondents and the mean composition in the external estimates) the relationship should be more or less linear if the distributions of respondents' estimates are sensitive to actual gender composition. This seems to be the case. The differences between the variables are not due to systematic under- or over-estimates by the level of gender composition.

As with income the estimates of our respondents are not necessarily worse than those we have derived by other means. Published figures are often at a higher level of aggregation, from which our specific occupations are difficult to extract and we do not always have adequate, alternative sources. In general, occupations in manufacturing are perceived as more male by our respondents than they seem from the other estimates. The greatest discrepancy is between the 91 per cent of our respondents who identify punching press operators as male and the 66 per cent who are male in the other estimate. The latter may be wrong in that the categories of press operators are imprecise. However, our respondents are also less likely than would be expected on the other estimates to see glue machinists, electrical assemblers and supervisors of electrical assemblers as female. This tendency is more marked among female respondents than among male and it corresponds with their lower level of participation in manufacturing. The occupations that more of our respondents see as female than we would expect on the basis of other estimates are estate agents, laboratory assistants and police constables. The last may be due, in part, to the prominence of policewomen in television programmes such as 'Juliet Bravo'!

Overall, then, our respondents, perceptions agree with information from other sources and some of the deviations that do occur may be due to a lack of equivalence in the measures rather than deviations of means perceptions from actual distributions. Whatever deviations might remain with refined measures they are not such as to call seriously into question the processes associated with our respondents' perceptions.

The stability of gender differentials

We have established that our respondents have, on average, fairly accurate perceptions of income and gender distributions and we have shown that the relationships they see between them cannot be explained by the operation of a market model. What we now require is an examination of whether the gender-related differentials are stable or whether they are seen by our respondents as distortions of the market which should be corrected. Do they believe that the market should operate even although they see that it does not?

After asking our respondents about the earnings of the average person in each occupation we then asked the following questions:

> Could you now look at these jobs again and this time consider whether there need be such differences in earnings, or on the other hand whether they need to be greater in particular cases.
> (a) Are there any of these jobs that you think could be paid more, even though others would then have to be paid less?
> (b) Are there any that could be paid less?

If our respondents believed that the gender differential was a distortion of the market for labour which should operate, their answers to these questions would be such that when they were taken into account they greatly diminished or eliminated gender as a factor in the distribution of income. Perhaps the easiest way to understand this is in terms of the effect of these factors on the standardised residuals of the regression that included only those independent variables with 'market' implications, i.e. job characteristics and age and education of respondents. If there were a wish to reduce 'market' distortions then those perceived to be paid above 'market' income would be candidates to be paid less and those paid below would be candidates to be paid more. Since the gender divide is highly correlated with these 'market' residuals the desire to pay more or less should reduce that correlation in so far as it represents a commitment to a market.

The variables we created were the percentages of our respondents who wished to pay more to each occupation and of those who wished to pay less. In general our respondents wish to pay more to those who receive least, and less to those who receive most. Since the female occupations are on average paid less than the male occupations there is, by this token, a negative correlation between gender composition and the percentage who wish to pay an occupation more and a positive correlation between gender composition and the percentage who wish to pay less. This could, erroneously, lead to the conclusion that our respondents were more favourably disposed towards female occupations. As we shall see this is not the case. The adjustments they wish to make do not reduce the operation of gender as a factor in the determination of income. The two new variables act in similar ways and only the percentage wishing to pay more enters the equations. When it does the variable for age distribution of women in the occupations drops out, which suggests that our respondents do not approve of its effects. The R^2 rises from

0.84 to 0.91 which demonstrates that the variable is having considerable influence in tidying up deviations from the 'market' structure or, more accurately, deviations from the general processes of distribution. However, it has little effect upon the gender component of these deviations. It will be recalled that the relationship of the gender variable to the standardised residuals of the 'market' regression was 0.70. When the desire to pay more is taken into account it remains substantially unchanged at 0.69. The only female occupation that is peculiarly advantaged by the percentage wishing to pay its members more is nurse (SRN). Gender makes a somewhat larger contribution to an overall explanation of income distribution than does the desire to pay more (remember that its inclusion with 'market' factors produces an R^2 of 0.93), but they are largely complementary and when both are included with 'market' factors the R^2 is 0.98.

Differences of income by gender are clearly perceived by our respondents; they cannot be explained by the perceived location of women in a market for labour and our respondents appear prepared to tolerate them. This latter is even more true of our female respondents than of our male respondents although their perceptions are very similar. As men and women employees they are subjects of their own understandings and the fact that there is no systematic commitment to eliminating gender differentials suggests that they are embodied in stable social processes. Their perceptions are largely consistent with data from other sources and such perceptions could not be stable if they were at odds with the perceptions of other participants in the employment relationship. If, for example, employers operated according to market principles, gender differentials would soon disappear since employers of men could buy the same quality and quantity of labour power more cheaply by employing women. Equally, if the true value of labour power embodied in female occupations is lower than perceived by our respondents, but correctly perceived by employers then it is difficult to see how our respondents' perceptions could remain out of line given the real consequences of employers' correct perceptions and an official policy of equality by gender in a labour market. The perceptions depend upon a system of income distribution which cannot be explained in market terms.

Consideration of how the processes maintaining income inequalities are closely associated with the ways in which employment is related to wider aspects of social experience will have to await another occasion. However one point should be made in conclusion. Our search for the relatively stable bases of distribution will eventually converge upon the areas where the deleterious consequences of mistaken understandings are concentrated. Erroneous market explanations of income distribution may have little immediate effect upon the actual processes of distribution as experienced by our respondents, but they must have consequences. Practices and policies founded upon deficient understandings are regressive.

Notes

1 For his helpful comments and for his general contribution to the approaches that inform this work we should like to thank our colleague John Holmwood. Janet Siltanan's work on gender and employment helped to form our thinking and we should like to express our gratitude.

2 For recent discussions see Wilkinson, 1983 and the paper by the Labour Studies Group in this volume.

3 See e.g. Doeringer, 1973, Doeringer and Piore, 1971, Edwards, *et al.*, 1975, Barron and Norris, 1976.

4 For a discussion of this point see Stewart *et al.*, 1980: 265–73.

5 Purely as an illustration of how these different arguments occur to re-establish market explanations, consider these quotations from two recent sources: 'women in employment tend to have lower average hourly earnings than men in the same industry, to be graded as having less skill, and to have less authority.' Purcel, 1984: 57. There is market symmetry about these factors. 'Some of the present inequality is undoubtedly the product of mechanisms over which the movement has little control, such as an employer's manipulation of vulnerable groups of workers, or biased systems of education and training. But some of it is the result of explicitly male interests – practices excluding women from skilled work and attempts, often successful, to define the work that men do as skilled and the work that women do as unskilled.' Barrett, 1984: 93. Similar statements could be found in most writers considering these issues, including the present authors on a previous occasion.

6 See e.g. Barron and Norris, 1976.

7 For more extended discussions see Prandy *et al.*, 1982 and 1983 and Holmwood and Stewart, 1983.

8 In addition to Stewart *et al.*, 1980: 265–75 mentioned above see Holmwood and Stewart, 1983.

9 See Holmwood and Stewart, 1983.

10 The survey entitled 'The understanding and evaluation of income inequalities' was financed by the ESRC.

11 For a discussion of this point see Stewart *et al.*, 1980: 1–11.

12 The actual questions asked were:

I should now like to ask some questions about jobs – how they differ in various ways, the kinds of people that do them, and so on. Here is a list of jobs (hand to respondent) that I should like to have your views on.

(a) Let's start with skill with the hands.
   Would you please choose from the set the job that calls for the most skill with the hands. Then the next and so on until you have ordered them all. If you think any of the jobs call for about the same degree of skill put them together.

(b) Would you now put your own job in this set in terms of skill with the hands.

(a) Now I should like you to consider the amount of thinking a job calls for. As before, would you choose that which calls for most thinking, then the next most and so on until all are ordered. Remember jobs can be tied.

(b) Would you place your own job in terms of the thinking required.

(a) Can we now do the same again, considering the question of the amount of responsibility that jobs involve. Would you please order them from that which requires most to that which requires least.

(b) Would you place your own job in terms of responsibility.

(a) Another difference between jobs is the amount of control that can be exercised by the individuals doing them. In some jobs it is possible to make almost all important decisions; in other jobs it is other people who make all the important decisions. Again, would you please order the jobs from that where the individual has most control to that where he has least.

(b) Would you place your own job in terms of control.

13   For arguments from very different perspectives see Jacques, 1961 and Wright, 1979.

14   The analysis in this paper was facilitated by the SPSS programme.

15   The actual question on age distributions for women doing the jobs was worded as follows:

Now I should like us to consider the ages of people doing jobs. Some jobs are done by people of any age; some are usually done by younger people, some by older people and others by those in the middle of their working lives.

First of all, thinking only of jobs that might be done by *women*:

Will you go through the jobs one by one and say whether you think the job would be done by women of all ages or women in particular age groups [the categories were: under 25, 25–35, 35–45, over 45, not applicable]. The process was later repeated for men doing the jobs.

The process was later repeated for men doing the jobs.

The education question was:

(a) Will you now think of the qualifications and education that people doing these jobs would *normally* have, and order them from that which would have the highest level of education or qualification to the lowest level.

(b) Would you place your own job in terms of education or qualifications.

16   The question was:

Some jobs are mainly done by men, and some mainly by women.
Others are often by both men and women.

Could you look through the cards and say

Which of these jobs are done by both?
Which ones are mainly done by men?
Which ones are mainly done by women?

17   When we compare the two estimates of income with the actual incomes of our respondents in jobs similar to those in the analysis we find that in most cases the external estimates are higher than the actual incomes and our respondents' estimates lower. Our respondents' estimates are closer to the actual. We have similar findings (that respondents underestimate actual mean earnings, and that actual earnings are below published statements of earnings) from other surveys and they warrant further investigation.

Section five

The implications of unemployment

One of the most dramatic transformations of the economic structure of capitalist societies in recent years has been the emergence of levels of unemployment unprecedented since the inter-war period. This caught social scientists largely unawares. Preoccupied with the effects of apparently inexorable economic growth, researchers had come to regard unemployment as largely a matter of historical interest. With a few notable exceptions, our knowledge of the social implications of unemployment was still based primarily on research of the 1930s. Yet as it became evident that high levels of unemployment might well become an enduring feature of advanced western societies, its implications for the quality of life of individuals, households and indeed entire communities have become an increasingly central issue for research.

Research evidence for the 1930s was fragmentary and uneven in quality. Moreover, given the development of welfare state provision and the social structural and cultural shifts of the post-war era, it was far from evident that the experience of unemployment in the 1980s would be the same as in the inter-war period. Might it not be that in a context in which the financial deprivations of unemployment were less severe and in which the importance of family and leisure values were thought to have increased, unemployment would be no longer a major source of psychological distress? Indeed, might one be entering an era in which unemployment would become a socially acceptable and individually valued way of life? Clearly, if this were the case, it would have fundamental significance for the functioning of labour markets and the wider character of social organisation.

The most systematic attempt to address this problem has been the research carried out by the Social and Applied Psychology Unit at Sheffield. Peter Warr's paper provided an overview of a wide array of studies that have focused on the implications of unemployment for workers' psychological well-being. The message that emerges from this research is remarkably consistent across a range of different samples and of different measures. The experience of unemployment in the 1980s still produces a marked deterioration in psychological health. It increases anxiety and depression, and it undercuts self-esteem and self-confidence. Certainly the psychological impact of unemployment is mediated by peoples' prior commitment to work, but the evidence indicates that the great majority of the working population feels some degree of commitment to employment, a commitment that is not reducible purely to the financial rewards that employment provides.

If there can be little serious doubt in the light of this research about the psychological distress brought about by unemployment, the implications for physical health are much more controversial. As Roy Carr-Hill points out, many of the more extreme claims that have been made are based upon evidence that is methodologically unsatisfactory and open to conflicting inter-pretations. Given the poor quality of work conditions in many of the establish-ments in which people are employed, it is at least open to question whether unemployment may actually improve the physical health of certain categories of the population. This is clearly a highly controversial area of research and, in the light of the enormous methodological difficulties that it poses, it is unlikely to be resolved in any definitive way in the near future.

The general psychological implications of unemployment appear to affect most categories of the working population. However, the effects are more severe on some groups than on others. For instance, middle-aged men would appear to suffer greater distress than those who are younger or older. It would seem that the effects of unemployment depend not upon inherent features of human personality, but upon the specific social conditions under which it occurs. Yet, this said, the argument that there are 'less vulnerable' categories of the workforce must be treated with caution. As Walker shows in his study of older redundant steelworkers in Sheffield, the majority of older workers regarded being out of work as either the worst or nearly the worst thing that had happened to them. If older workers were more likely to withdraw from the labour market, this, he suggests, reflects, in part, discouragement at the virtual impossibility of finding new employment and, in part, the influence of a pervasive 'official doctrine' that priority for jobs should be given to the young.

Given the evidence of the sharp financial costs and the psychological distress caused by unemployment, a central issue is the way this affects peoples' understandings of the wider social order, their political commitments and indeed their commitment to the prevailing political institutions. These issues are taken up by Fraser and Marsh. They point out the ambiguities of existing evidence and the remarkable paucity of research in this area. One important paradox is that, while in recent years unemployment has been seen consistently as the most important issue facing the country, its impact on voting choices and political allegiances would appear to be less than decisive. The authors point to ignorance of the implications of party policies, and to the wide-spread belief that the world recession is the major determinant of unemployment, as crucial factors leading to the depoliticisation of the issue. However, they also question the view that unemployment undercuts radicalism in the wider sense of the term and point to some initial evidence that the experience of unemployment, and contact with the unemployed, may increase peoples' readiness to engage in non-violent protest.

Twelve questions about unemployment and health

The official United Kingdom unemployment rate has risen from around 3 per cent to more than 12 per cent in the past ten years. There are wide variations around that overall level, with 20 per cent to 30 per cent rates in some groups. Teenage workers, those who are older, unskilled or previously employed in declining manufacturing industries are particularly likely to be without jobs, as are members of ethnic minorities and disabled people. The number of *long-term* unemployed people has also increased substantially: over a third of the registered unemployed have been without a job for more than twelve months. Such a long period of unemployment is likely to be quite different from a short gap between jobs, which was the typical experience in some earlier decades.

The large majority of people out of work are clearly employable and clearly want to have a job (e.g. White, 1983); their unemployment cannot plausibly be attributed to personal features. That contrasts with periods of very low unemployment (in the 1960s, for example) when it was reasonable to argue that differences between employed and unemployed people were largely due to their prior characteristics rather than representing the effects of unemployment (e.g. Tiffany, Cowan and Tiffany, 1970; Goodwin, 1972).

Research in this field has expanded in recent years as unemployment has become more widespread. This chapter reviews findings about health in relation to unemployment, and is organised around twelve principal questions.

1 How does unemployment affect psychological health?

In respect of men, research has clearly demonstrated a significant deterioration in psychological health caused by unemployment. Many studies have been cross-sectional, comparing people who are at the time employed with those who are unemployed. That does of course present problems of causal interpretation, but there have now been sufficient longitudinal investigations to permit conclusions about causal priority.

Table 16.1 Research into unemployment and psychological health

	Measure	Type of study	
1.	Happiness	CS	L
2.	Present life satisfaction	CS	L
3.	Positive affect	CS	
4.	Experience of pleasure	CS	
5.	Negative affect	CS	
6.	Experience of strain	CS	
7.	Negative self-esteem	CS	L
8.	Anxiety	CS	L
9.	Depressed mood	CS	L
10.	Psychological distress	CS	L
11.	Diagnosed psychiatric illness		
	(a) neurotic disorder	CS	
	(b) psychotic disorder	CS	

CS: Cross-sectional comparisons
L: Longitudinal comparisons

Table 16.1 summarises eleven areas in which cross-sectional studies have revealed lower psychological health among unemployed samples. References to these investigations are provided in the Appendix. Consider initially the first ten features, from happiness through to general psychological distress. Different investigators have employed different measures, but these are in fact significantly intercorrelated across the ten areas. For that reason we can extrapolate from longitudinal studies using measures 1, 2, 7, 8, 9 and 10 to fill in the gaps shown for measures 3 to 6.

For example, one measure of psychological distress which has been used in longitudinal research is the General Health Questionnaire. This was devised by Goldberg (1972, 1978, 1981) as a self-administered screening test for detecting minor psychiatric disorder in the general population. It contains questions about recent experiences of strain, sleep loss through worry, lack of confidence, inability to concentrate, feelings of depression, a sense of personal worthlessness, and so on. As a measure of general psychological distress it thus covers all the features 1 to 9 in table 16.1. Longitudinal research has recorded significant increases in distress as workers lose their jobs and significant reductions after they become re-employed (e.g. Banks and Jackson, 1982; Jackson, Stafford, Banks and Warr, 1983). We may be confident that changes in employment status cause these changes in distress, and that similar causal relationships are also present for the more specific measures 1 to 9 in table 16.1.

The General Health Questionnaire (GHQ) may also be used in its role as a screening instrument, since scores are known to be strongly related to the probability of being designated a case in psychiatric examination (e.g. Henderson, Duncan-Jones, Byrne, Scott and Adcock, 1979; Banks, 1983). In practice the GHQ is an indicator of neurotic disorder (11(a) in the table), and we might therefore infer from the longitudinal changes in GHQ scores that there are also longitudinal changes in diagnosed neurotic conditions. As far as I know, this has not been demonstrated directly, although Finlay-Jones and Eckhardt (1981) included in their psychiatric examination of unemployed young Australian workers an inquiry about date of onset of each diagnosed disorder. They concluded that in 43 per cent of cases (mainly of depression), onset had followed unemployment in the absence of any other apparent provoking stressor.

What of item 11(b) in the table? It is clear from cross-sectional comparisons that psychotic illness is disproportionately more likely among unemployed people (e.g. Jaco, 1960). However, causal interpretation is particularly difficult. It is not clear which mechanisms associated with unemployment might be expected generally to provoke psychotic illness, and as far as I know there have been no longitudinal investigations of the topic. We are not at present justified in viewing unemployment as a significant causal agent in respect of psychotic disorders, although this may be shown by future research.

In passing, we should note the logical difficulties attached to any attempt to demonstrate that unemployment is 'a significant causal agent'. One is seeking to show that unemployment causes significantly more distress (or psychosis, physical ill-health, etc.) than would otherwise have been present within the group investigated. Suppose that unemployment provokes a psychotic reaction in a number of individuals: would these people in any case have developed similar reactions to environmental pressures of other kinds in the absence of unemployment? That is difficult to assess without conducting comparisons between groups to identify relative risks. Individual persons in which unemployment appears to provoke a negative outcome do not on their own demonstrate that unemployment is a significant causal agent at the level of a group.

Another approach to the first ten features of table 16.1 is to ask unemployed people whether their health has changed at all since job loss. Studies of that kind by Klausen and Iversen (1981) Fröhlich (1983), Warr and Jackson (1984) and Payne, Warr and Hartley (1984) have shown that between 20 per cent and 30 per cent of unemployed men are likely to report a deterioration in their health since job loss. In respect of psychological health, changes are typically described in terms of increased anxiety, depression, insomnia, irritability, lack of confidence, listlessness and general nervousness. Problems in concentrating and taking longer over activities are also widely reported (e.g. Fryer and Warr, 1984). In addition, deterioration is described in what might be termed 'psychophysical' conditions: dermatitis, eczema, headaches, high blood pressure and ulcers.

However, it is important to note that around 10 per cent of men in these studies are likely to report an *improvement* in their health since becoming unemployed. In some cases this is in respect of physical illnesses which had been exacerbated by working conditions (bronchitis, back problems and so on), but it is also found that a small number report improved *psychological* health since job loss, usually because they are now free from job stressors. This reported improvement is particularly likely for those who have only recently become unemployed (Warr and Jackson, 1984).

In summary, it is clear that unemployment impairs psychological health of the kinds described, at least among men, and that this impairment extends into psychophysical conditions. However, despite a substantial overall shift, not everyone is affected negatively when they become unemployed.

2 What are the processes through which unemployment impairs psychological health?

The aspect of unemployment which is likely to have greatest impact on psychological health is the reduced income which it yields. For example, studies of unemployed working-class men in Britain suggest that about two-thirds of them have a household income which is half or less of their income when employed (e.g. Warr and Jackson, 1984). It is also found repeatedly that financial anxiety is high (e.g. Daniel, 1974; Estes and Wilensky, 1978), and that worries about money strongly predict unemployed people's overall distress scores (e.g. Jackson and Warr, 1984; Payne, Warr and Hartley, 1984).

Second, without paid employment a person's behaviours and environments are likely to be relatively restricted. This is partly a question of being required less often to leave the house, and it is also a function of reduced income: you cannot afford to go out as often as you could when you had a paid job. Studies of behaviour change after job loss find, not surprisingly, that unemployed men take on significantly more childcare activities and meal preparation, but there is also significantly more inactivity, merely sitting around, sleeeping during the day, and watching television (e.g. Kilpatrick and Trew, 1982; Miles, 1983; Warr and Payne, 1983; Fagin and Little, 1984; Warr, 1984 c).

A related feature arises from the importance of goal structure and the concept of 'traction'. It is apparent that many forms of activity are made up of interrelated sets of tasks and goals. Committing yourself to a certain goal also commits you to other goals and tasks; you become drawn along by the structure of your work. Hence the term 'traction'. It is often the case that paid employment introduces more traction in this sense than is present when one is without a paid job (e.g. Feather and Bond, 1983). This process is particularly important in generating and sustaining motivated activity and creating links with the purposes of other people.

A fourth feature associated with unemployment which is likely to impair psychological health is a reduced decision latitude, a smaller scope for decision making. In one sense of course an unemployed person has a great deal of freedom, but this is in most cases limited to small repetitive decisions about daily routine. In respect of larger decisions, for example about lifestyle or major purchases, the range of realistic options available to an unemployed person is usually quite small, since material resources are severely curtailed.

Fifth, there is considerable evidence that much of the satisfaction derived from jobs comes from the development and practice of skills. Not all jobs offer opportunities of that kind, and they are of course also present outside paid employment. However, it seems likely that for most people unemployment brings a reduction in skill use and development. This comes about through diminished personal and material resources and the absence of complex behaviours required by one's employed role.

A sixth process is in terms of an increase in psychologically threatening activities. Unemployed people are committed to seeking jobs where they will probably be rejected, they have to deal with a society which often views them as second-class citizens, and they may have to struggle to raise money through official agencies or through borrowing and selling. In general they are liable to experience a large number of threatening life events. Associated with this is a seventh feature of unemployment, insecurity about the future. A high proportion of unemployed people report anxiety about not knowing what will happen to them in the future, whether they will become unemployable, lose their self-respect, or have insoluble money problems (e.g. Payne, Warr and Hartley, 1984). Current threats are thus compounded by a sense of uncertainty about the future.

An eighth feature of unemployment is in respect of interpersonal contact. Unemployed people may have more restricted social contacts of several kinds, for example because of the absence of job colleagues and because of reduced availability of money to visit clubs, pubs or other social settings. In general the *amount* of social interaction after job loss does not appear to decline (e.g. Fröhlich, 1983; Stokes, 1983; Warr and Payne, 1983; Warr, 1984 c), but there are many suggestions that its *quality* is reduced during periods out of paid work.

Finally, we must consider the changes in social position which accompany unemployment. There is no doubt that on becoming unemployed a person loses a socially accepted position and the roles, self-perceptions and self-evaluations which go with it. And the new position is widely felt to be one of lower prestige and social acceptability.

3   What factors statistically mediate the impact of unemployment?

A number of factors have been found statistically to mediate the negative effects of unemployment. Results in respect of eight features can be summarised as follows.

First, employment commitment. Most unemployed people are locked into a strong commitment to find another job (e.g. Warr, 1982). However, there are variations between people in the degree to which having a job is personally salient. It is widely found that strength of employment commitment is strongly positively associated with the degree of psychological distress during unemployment: higher employment commitment goes with higher distress (e.g. Warr, 1978; Feather and Davenport, 1981; Feather and Bond, 1983; Jackson, Stafford, Banks and Warr, 1983; Jackson and Warr, 1984).

A second mediating variable is age. At least among men, age is curvilinearly associated with the negative effects of unemployment: middle-aged unemployed men experience greater distress than those who are younger and older (e.g. Daniel, 1974; Hepworth, 1980; Jackson and Warr, 1984). In part this is associated with greater financial strain among the middle-aged group, who often have more demanding family commitments.

Length of unemployment is a third mediating variable. There are some ambiguities in the literature here (see Warr, Jackson and Banks, 1982; Brinkmann, 1983; Warr, 1984 b), but in general it seems that there is a gradual decline in psychological health during the first months of unemployment, with some stabilisation at a lowered level after about six months. However, for teenagers and men approaching retirement age there appears to be no association between duration of unemployment and psychological health (Jackson and Warr, 1984; Warr, Banks and Ullah, 1984).

Turning to a fourth and a fifth mediating variable, it is clear from several studies that both financial strain (Little, 1976; Estes and Wilensky, 1978; Brinkmann, 1983; Warr and Jackson, 1984) and a low level of activity (Feather and Bond, 1983; Hepworth, 1980; Payne, Warr and Hartley, 1984) are significantly associated with psychological ill-health during unemployment. The causal pattern here is probably a cyclical one, in that financial strain and low activity levels are likely both to be outcomes of unemployment as well as themselves influencing other outcomes.

Those two features come together when we examine social class as a sixth possible mediator. It is generally found that working-class unemployed people have substantially greater financial problems than middle-class unemployed people, and also that they have greater difficulty in filling the time. The difference in activity level is partly a function of the working class having less money to spend, but there are suggestions in the data that the difference is also a matter of greater internal control and self-directedness among the middle class (Payne, Warr and Hartley, 1984).

A seventh mediating factor is the sex of an unemployed person. The impact of this depends upon marital and parental role. For single women or other women who are in effect principal wage-earners, the pattern of unemployment effects is the same as for men. But for mothers of young children there is apparently no general association between having a job and experiencing higher psychological well-being. Neither does there appear to be an association between paid employment and psychological health for mothers in general, defined as a group irrespective of the age of their children (Warr and Parry, 1982; see also Cleary and Mechanic, 1983).

Finally, let us note the importance of personal vulnerability. It is obvious that in general terms some people have greater difficulty than others in coping with stress of all kinds. This may be because of their personality characteristics or because they have already been subject to an accumulation of problems. In either case such people are likely to exhibit lower mental health in response to the stress of unemployment than are less vulnerable people.

4   How does unemployment affect primarily physical health?

As described in relation to question 1, we know that unemployment harms psychological health and that the effects can extend into what might be termed 'psychophysical' problems: dermatitis, headaches, ulcers, etc. But what about illnesses which are primarily physical, with no psychological causes or at least with very little psychological input? Bronchitis, the cancers or pneumonia might be taken as examples of such primarily physical illnesses. If unemployment is to bring about illness of this kind, the causal mechanisms are presumably different from those yielding psychological ill-health. Most probable is an increase in poverty, leading to deficiencies in clothing, heating or nutrition or to some other harmful change in lifestyle.

We know that there are cross-sectional differences between the physical health of employed and unemployed people (e.g. Wilder, 1980; Verbrugge, 1983), such that the unemployed are overall less healthy, but it has not in general been possible to distinguish between ill-health leading to unemployment and unemployment causing ill-health.

In their cross-sectional study of men aged between forty and fifty-nine in twenty-four British towns, Cook, Cummings, Bartley and Shaper (1982) distinguished between two groups of unemployed men: those who reported that their unemployment was due to ill-health and those who indicated that being unemployed was not connected with their health. Comparisons were made between employed members of the sample and the two unemployed groups, in respect of bronchitis, obstructive lung disease, ischaemic heart disease and hypertension. The group who said they were unemployed because of their health had significantly higher rates of bronchitis, obstructive lung disease and ischaemic heart disease than the employed group, but no difference was present in respect of hypertension. The unemployed men who indicated that their being out of work was unconnected with the state of their health were not significantly different from the employed sample in respect of bronchitis, obstructive lung disease or hypertension; however they did exhibit significantly more ischaemic heart disease, a difference which persisted after controls were introduced for age, social class, town of residence and smoking behaviour.

These results are of special interest in a number of ways, but as the authors point out longitudinal research is still required.

One longitudinal investigation has been described by Kasl, Gore and Cobb (1975) and Kasl and Cobb (1980). This found no evidence of significant decrements in physical health associated with the transition from employment to unemployment. However, the durations studied were rather brief, up to fifteen weeks unemployment in the subsequent two years. A more extended inquiry was reported by Narendranathan, Nickell and Metcalf (1982). Obtaining retrospective reports from 17,707 British men for the period 1965 to 1975, they examined the relationship between periods of unemployment and of sickness which lasted at least three months. Although a clear cross-sectional relationship linked to occupational level was found (unskilled men were most likely to have periods both of sickness and of unemployment), no longitudinal association was present: there was no indication that unemployment spells raised the probability of subsequent sickness.

There is thus at present no strong evidence from these individual-level studies that unemployment leads to ill-health of a primarily physical kind. It seems likely that it could have this effect when coupled over a long period with a very low standard of living, but such a pattern has not yet been demonstrated unequivocally.

5 What is the effect of unemployment on mortality rates?

This fifth question extends the discussion into one specific and extreme index of physical ill-health: the probability of dying. Research in this area has usually been at the aggregate level, investigating features of communities or nations as a whole. Several such investigations have been of a longitudinal kind, examining the association between aggregate health indices over a number of years.

For example, Brenner (e.g. 1980 a) investigated the relationship between overall mortality rates and several economic variables, including unemployment, for the United States between 1909 and 1976. He reported that, after controlling for other variables, national mortality rates are significantly associated with earlier unemployment levels; unemployment is said to have a lagged effect (greatest at between two and five years) upon United States overall death rates. He reached a similar conclusion from his analysis of mortality data from England and Wales between 1936 and 1976 (Brenner, 1979, 1980 b), and (using a more complex model) for England and Wales and for Scotland between 1954 and 1976 (Brenner, 1983).

Brenner's concern is with rapid economic change of two kinds, growth as well as recession, both of which are said to increase stress and to inhibit the long-term decline of mortality. In respect of increases in unemployment, all members of society (not merely those who lose their jobs) are thought to be at risk. Indeed his analyses of data from both USA and England and Wales reveal the strongest relationship between aggregate unemployment and mortality for people who are out of the labour market: adults aged above seventy-five and children aged below ten. (See Brenner (1973 b) for separate examination of foetal and infant mortality rates in USA between 1915 and 1967; and Brenner (1983) for an investigation into infant mortality in England and Wales between 1925 and 1950.)

These time-series studies of overall mortality have been complemented by studies focusing specifically on ischaemic heart disease. Significant lagged relationships between unemployment levels and IHD mortality have been reported in USA between 1915 and 1967 (Brenner, 1971), in Australia between 1921 and 1975 (Bunn, 1979), and both in England and Wales and in Scotland between 1955 and 1976 (Brenner and Mooney, 1982; Brenner, 1983).

This evidence is impressive and has been taken by some people to indicate that economic recession causes death rates to rise, or more precisely retards the long-term improvement. However, there are a number of problems with the method and the findings, and we must be cautious in our interpretation (see also Eyer, 1977; Kasl, 1979 b, 1982; Spruit, 1982; Winter, 1983). Six points deserve mention.

First is the fact that many investigators present very few details of their findings, so that assessment of their conclusions is extremely difficult. For instance, it is common to cite only the 'optimum lag', that period, up to five or ten years, which yields the greatest association between the variables. The probability of obtaining a statistically significant result clearly increases with the number of tests which are made, so that merely citing the largest association does not permit assessment of its significance. Interpretation is made more difficult by the fact that the business cycle is often around five years in length, so that a lag of five years from peak unemployment often corresponds to a period of expansion; separating the effects of recession and recovery is difficult.

A second problem arises from the fact that other different results are obtained after rather minor procedural changes or with different data sets. For example, Gravelle, Hutchinson and Stern (1981) observed that significant relationships in England and Wales data disappeared when the period of analysis was extended from 1936–76 to 1922–76. Forbes and McGregor (1984) analysed Scottish male data between 1956 and 1978, finding no evidence of a lagged relationship between overall unemployment and overall mortality. (They did however record some significant lagged correlations for the 40–69 age group.) John (1983) also failed to observe the predicted relationship in an examination of West German data between 1951 and 1979; the impact of unemployment was opposite to the prediction in twenty out of thirty-four sub-group analyses. However, significant lagged associations in the predicted direction were found for infant and maternal mortality.

Third, a number of possible confounding variables have been identified.

For example, Gravelle, Hutchinson and Stern (1981) demonstrated that Brenner's (1979, 1980 b) positive findings in respect of mortality in England and Wales between 1936 and 1976 were almost entirely due to a substantial decrease in unemployment between 1940 and 1942, at the same time as major improvements occurred in diet, medical treatment and availability of health service facilities. Separate analyses of mortality data for shorter periods within the original range of years failed to reveal any significant relationships with unemployment. This was confirmed by Brenner (1983), who argued instead that a more sophisticated model (including alcohol and tobacco consumption) was applicable in post-war England and Wales, USA, Canada and Sweden; on the other hand, the earlier, simpler model was said to be appropriate for post-war France, Italy, West Germany and Spain.

Difficulties also arise from the very high intercorrelations between predictor variables. In addition to unemployment rates, a range of indices of welfare expenditure and economic growth are typically included in order to maximally predict the health outcomes. In such analyses it is not always possible to distinguish between effects from several highly correlated variables.

A fourth reservation about this type of investigation has sometimes been termed 'the ecological fallacy'. This has been described by Catalano and Dooley (1983) as 'the logical error of assuming that an association between two characteristics of a population aggregate, e.g. unemployment and mean hypertension, will generalize to those characteristics when measured across individuals' (47). This problem is of course recognised by Brenner and colleagues, who agree that 'while the macro [aggregate] study can make valid and testable inferences to phenomena at the same macro level, it can only suggest inferences and hypotheses about behaviour at lower levels' (Brenner and Mooney, 1983: 1135).

Fifth, causal interpretation is not possible. The existence of a significant association between aggregate unemployment and mortality does not permit the statement that increases in unemployment cause increases in mortality. That may in fact be the case, but from the correlational evidence alone we do not know about causal priority.

A sixth limitation of aggregate time series research is that it is inevitably based upon periods in the past. Long series of years are desirable within the analysis to enhance reliability, but in extending further back into time these series bring in conditions which are progressively less similar to those of today. Furthermore, most published analyses use series which terminate in the mid-1970s. There is a clear logical difficulty here: how can time-series investigations of the past tell us about relationships between variables in the present?

My overall conclusion about these aggregate studies and their problems is thus one of caution. The results are certainly intriguing and suggestive, but from them on their own we do not know whether or not unemployment has a causal impact upon mortality.

Longitudinal research at the individual level would be of great value, and a promising start has been made by Fox and Goldblatt (1982). They analyse mortality data for the years 1971 to 1975 according to individual characteristics recorded in the 1971 England and Wales census. Among males aged fifteen to sixty-four the standardised mortality ratio in the subsequent period was considerably greater for people unemployed and seeking work than for those in jobs at the date of the census. (However, no difference was present for women aged fifteen to fifty-nine or for men aged sixty-five to seventy-four; in all groups the subsequent SMR for people unemployed and sick was particularly high.) This prospective investigation is to continue, and analyses to control for possibly confounding variables are envisaged. For example, the difference between employed men and those unemployed and seeking work may have arisen from differences in age, social class or geographical region; these factors were shown to be associated with both mortality and unemployment.

6   How does unemployment affect use of health service facilities?

This next question has been approached by several investigators through aggregate time-series investigations of mental hospital admissions. Brenner (1973 a) examined first admissions to New York state public mental hospitals between 1914 and 1967, reporting a significant lagged relationship with changes in the manufacturing employment index. This finding has been questioned on a number of grounds, such as the omission of data from private mental hospitals and state general hospitals, variations between years and sub-samples, and possible failure in matching community areas for economic and psychiatric variables (e.g. Marshall and Funch, 1979, 1980; Ratcliff, 1980). A similar study of admissions (including re-admissions) to mental hospitals in England and Wales between 1950 and 1976 (omitting 1961–3) revealed no synchronous or lagged association with unemployment rate, although synchronous correlations for two age-groups of women were found to be statistically significant (Stokes and Cochrane, 1984).

Some American investigations have examined more short-term changes, on a month-by-month basis. In general there are hints of a relationship between unemployment rate and admissions, but results are inconsistent between studies and across patient groups (male or female, inpatient or outpatient, first admission or re-admission, public or private hospital).

Research by Catalano, Dooley and Jackson (1981) revealed significant relationships between both male and female inpatient admissions and local unemployment levels two to four months earlier. For outpatient admissions the correlation was significant only for males. In the study by Ahr, Gorodezky and Cho (1981), associations with unemployment lagged by two or three months were statistically significant for inpatient re-admissions but not for first admissions; in general the relationships with outpatient admissions were non-significant. Barling and Handal (1980) recorded from their analyses a single significant finding, which as they point out does not exceed chance probability. Similarly, of thirty-three group and sub-group lagged correlations in Frank's (1981) study, only three reached statistical significance at the 0.05 level, one of which was opposite to the direction predicted.

All these studies are subject to the reservations described earlier in respect of aggregate mortality data. They have the additional problem that the dependent variable (hospital admissions) is reactive to demand both positively and negatively. As demand increases so will admissions, but only up to hospital capacity; thereafter treatment decisions are likely to change, in order to cope with patients at an earlier stage in the health care system.

Causal interpretation of the few significant correlations is extremely difficult. Both Catalano, Dooley and Jackson (1981) and Ahr, Gorodezky and Cho (1981) consider that an 'uncovering' explanation is more likely than one in terms of unemployment 'provoking' greater ill-health (see also Catalano and Dooley, 1979). Health service facilities may become more accessible or attractive to people when they are unemployed, or high unemployment may reduce a community's ability to cope with illness at home; in both cases observed increases in hospital admissions may be due to an uncovering of previous illness more than reflecting new illnesses caused by unemployment.

Note, however, that the association has not yet been demonstrated beyond doubt. Indeed there is reason to suppose that the threat of unemployment might lead to a *reduced* call upon health service facilities. It is possible that people who remain in jobs are reluctant to present themselves for treatment, fearing that absence from work might place their employment at risk. Once again, firm evidence is lacking.

In respect of people who become unemployed, Jacobsen (1972) observed that significantly more workers sought medical advice in the month in which their factory closed and in the succeeding month in comparison with the same months in the preceding year. A six-year study of Danish bricklayers showed that 'unemployment increases the risk of hospital admission, and conversely that admission to a hospital increases the risk of unemployment' (Lajer, 1982: 9). However, the processes underlying this relationship are not clear from the data presented.

Catalano and Dooley (1977) set out to link together aggregate and individual-level information, through study of associations between local unemployment levels and self-reports of depressed mood. Significant associations were found after a two-month lag. However, a second investigation failed to replicate the result (Dooley, Catalano, Jackson and Brownell, 1981). A further study found some evidence that economic contraction led to more undesirable life events, which in turn were associated with higher risk of physical illness or injury (p<0.05); however, this was observed for only one of three social-class groups, with no relationship for a second group, and the reverse relationship for the third group (Catalano and Dooley, 1983). The picture thus remains unclear.

7   How does unemployment affect suicide rates?

Possible associations between economic conditions and suicide have been discussed for at least 150 years. Even now a firm conclusion appears impossible.

Individual cross-sectional studies indicate that people committing suicide are disproportionately likely to be unemployed (e.g. Platt, 1984), but it is apparent that over time the same personal and environmental factors may have operated to yield both unemployment and suicide (e.g. Shepherd and Barraclough, 1980). Aggregate time-series investigations in the United States regularly find a positive association across years between suicide and undesirable economic change (for example, shown in high unemployment rates), but the evidence from European studies is much more conflicting (Platt, 1984). In any case, as we have seen, data of this kind are extremely difficult to interpret.

Research has also examined parasuicide ('attempted suicide') as a function of unemployment. Cross-sectional studies again reveal a high probability of parasuicide among the unemployed, especially among those without a job for more than a year (Platt, 1983). However, interviews with people who have survived parasuicide rarely point to unemployment as a major precipitating factor. Some form of interpersonal relationship problem is most often seen as the principal proximal cause (Platt, 1984).

Of course, unemployment may increase the chance of having interpersonal difficulties, and it remains true that many researchers in these interview studies have not devoted close attention to employment factors. Nevertheless, evidence about the causal impact of unemployment in respect of both suicide and parasuicide must at present be viewed as ambiguous.

8   How do health-related behaviours change after job loss?

There have been no longitudinal studies which record everyday behaviour before and after job loss, and research into behaviour changes is limited to a small number of studies obtaining retrospective or current reports from people who are at the time unemployed (e.g. Kilpatrick and Trew, 1982; Miles, 1983; Warr, 1984 c; Warr and Payne, 1983).

In terms of health-related behaviours, there are suggestions that unemployment is accompanied by an increase in smoking, at least among working-class men (Cook, Cummins, Bartley and Shaper, 1982; Anon, 1983 b; Warr and Payne, 1983; Warr, 1984 c). However, consumption of alcohol is reported to decline with increased financial constraints after becoming unemployed (Smart, 1979; Klausen and Iversen, 1981; Warr, 1984 c; Warr and Payne, 1983). Cook *et al.* (1982) found no significant difference in the proportion of heavy drinkers (those reporting more than six drinks a day) between employed and unemployed men, after standardising for age, social class and town of residence (see also Anon, 1983 a, b). On the other hand, people who already have serious drinking problems may consume more alcohol when faced with the stress of unemployment (Sharp, 1979). Armor, Polich and Stambul (1978) describe survey results indicating that the male problem drinker is three times more likely to be unemployed than the average man, while the alcoholic seeking treatment is fifteen times more likely to be unemployed.

9 Does unemployment cause family strain?

Several authors have pointed out that a husband's unemployment can cause increased strain within the family (e.g. Moen, 1979; Schlozman and Verba, 1979; Thomas, McCabe and Berry, 1980; Leventman, 1981; Madge, 1983; Fagin and Little, 1984). Liker and Elder (1983) gave particular emphasis to the relationship problems caused by heavy income loss. However, we have no firm information about the impact of unemployment on the probability of divorce.

Child neglect and abuse may be thought to be particularly probable in families with unemployed fathers. Such an association is indeed found in cross-sectional comparisons (e.g. Gil, 1971), but causal interpretation is difficult in view of significant correlations between neglect and abuse and a wide range of indices of social deprivation in addition to unemployment. Furthermore, reports to official agencies are likely to be unreliable estimates of true prevalence (e.g. Light, 1973).

Steinberg, Catalano and Dooley (1981) adopted an aggregate time-series approach, relating overall levels of reported child neglect and abuse in two US counties to local economic conditions over a thirty-month period. No evidence was found for a lagged relationship between economic conditions and child neglect, although the authors claim support for the hypothesised link with child abuse: in both counties there was a significant negative relationship between reported abuse and size of the work-force two months previously. However, three out of six reported lagged relationships (one, two and three months in each county) were in the opposite direction, and the evidence may thus be thought to be equivocal. Further studies are required before conclusions can be drawn with any confidence.

10   What are the effects of high unemployment rates on people in jobs?

The outline findings in relation to this question are clear: the level of tension is significantly increased in economically difficult times. This has been shown in the study of plant closure reported by Cobb and Kasl (1977) and Kasl (1979 a), where a strong 'anticipation effect' was observed before closure, in terms of increased depression and feelings of insecurity. Jacobsen (1972) observed considerable excess morbidity from the month in which workers learned about the proposed closure of their factory.

Similarly raised tension levels have been shown in companies in financial difficulty but not scheduled for closure. For example, Erikssen, Rognum and Jervell (1979) reported significantly raised systolic blood pressure among male workers during a company's economic difficulties; however, no differences were observed in a small sample of women. Significantly higher psychological distress, assessed through the General Health Questionnaire, has been reported in companies with financial problems (Wall and Clegg, 1981). Increased tension of these kinds is likely to be found both among managers faced with difficult decisions and accumulating problems and also among subordinate workers subject to insecurity and potential job loss. Previous unemployment may itself exacerbate this tension in workers who have only recently found new jobs, since there is a widespread convention whereby those who commenced work most recently are in difficult times required to leave the company first (the 'last in – first out' procedure).

11   What are the differences between countries?

It is extremely probable that the experience and consequences of unemployment differ between countries, because of differences in welfare benefits, availability of free medical services, cultural norms, traditional levels of unemployment, social support networks and so on.

However, this issue has not been addressed in any systematic way, and authors tend to assume that findings from one country can be generalised to any other country. That is almost certainly false, but we do not yet know the limits of generalisation or the bases on which countries should be treated as similar or dissimilar.

12   What is happening to the place of paid employment within society?

It seems certain that in many countries in the foreseeable future there will not be enough jobs to employ everyone, at least if a job is expected to fill thirty-five or forty hours of each week. We need to examine how society is changing to cope with this development.

Ideas are starting to gain ground in terms of job sharing during a week or in alternate weeks, or having a paid job for only a limited number of months in each year. 'Early retirement' is becoming more common. Unemployed people are increasingly undertaking work for voluntary groups, attending short-term or part-time educational courses, or having access to free recreational facilities. But there are substantial practical and financial difficulties in changing the role and status of unemployed people, and the issue raises many deep-rooted emotions and values.

One possibly useful perspective is to consider the minority of people who appear to be relatively unharmed by unemployment. What is it about these people and their personal circumstances which distinguishes them from the majority who suffer during unemployment? The processes identified under Question 2 are likely to be influential here. For unemployment to be psychologically tolerable it must be accompanied by relatively high levels of some or all of these: money, variety, goals and traction, decision latitude, skill use and development, a sense of security about the future, interpersonal contact and a valued social position (Warr, 1983). Societal and individual changes may be envisaged which can reduce the harmful effects of unemployment through building upon these primary features.

Appendix

Studies examining the relationship between unemployment and psychological health (see table 16.1)

A. *Cross-sectional investigations*
  1. *Happiness:* Bradburn, 1969; Bradburn and Caplovitz, 1965; Tiggemann and Winefield, 1980.
  2. *Present life satisfaction:* Campbell, Converse and Rodgers, 1976; Cohn, 1978; Donovan and Oddy, 1982; Gaskell and Smith, 1981; Hepworth, 1980; Miles, 1983; Schlozman and Verba, 1979; Warr, 1978.
  3. *Positive affect:* Bradburn, 1969; Warr, 1978.
  4. *Experience of pleasure:* Warr and Payne, 1982.
  5. *Negative affect:* Bradburn, 1969; Warr, 1978.
  6. *Experience of strain:* Warr and Payne, 1982.
  7. *Negative self-esteem:* Feather and Bond, 1983; Lawlis, 1971; Warr and Jackson, 1983.
  8. *Anxiety:* Cobb and Kasl, 1977; Donovan and Oddy, 1982; Kasl, 1979 a; Lawlis, 1971; Warr, 1978.
  9. *Depressed mood:* Cobb and Kasl, 1977; Donovan and Oddy, 1982; Feather, 1982; Feather and Bond, 1983; Kasl, 1979 a; Radloff, 1975.
  10. *Psychological distress:* Banks and Jackson, 1982; Cochrane and Stopes-Roe, 1980; Donovan and Oddy, 1982; Estes and Wilensky, 1978; Hepworth, 1980; Miles, 1983; Pearlin and Lieberman, 1979.
  11(a) *Neurotic disorder:* Bebbington, Hurry, Tennant, Sturt and Wing, 1981; Roy, 1981.

11(b) *Psychotic disorder:* Jaco, 1960.
12.   *Suicide:* Many studies are reviewed by Platt, 1984.

B.   *Longitudinal investigations*

1.   *Happiness:* Tiggemann and Winefield, 1980.
2.   *Present life satisfaction:* Cohn, 1978; Tiggemann and Winefield, 1980.
7.   *Negative self-esteem:* Warr and Jackson, 1983.
8.   *Anxiety:* Cobb and Kasl, 1977; Kasl, 1979 a.
9.   *Depressed mood:* Cobb and Kasl, 1977; Frese, 1979; Kasl, 1979 a; Tiggemann and Winefield, 1980.
10.   *Psychological distress:* Banks and Jackson, 1982; Jackson, Stafford, Banks and Warr, 1983.

17 *Alan Walker, Iain Noble, John Westergaard*

From secure employment to labour market insecurity: the impact of redundancy on older workers in the steel industry

Introduction

Older workers (age fifty-five and over) have long been a disadvantaged minority in the labour market, experiencing relatively high levels of unemployment, long-term unemployment and difficulty in finding work even in periods of 'full employment' (Reubens, 1970). In the current recession attention has been focused on the position of younger people in the labour market, with comment, research and policy being concentrated on school leavers especially. The purpose of this paper is to help redress this imbalance. We report some findings from recent research on redundancy in the steel industry. We have interviewed more than 370 workers made redundant when a large private steel company in Sheffield closed one of its divisions in 1979. Over half of those interviewed were aged fifty-five and over and the survey provides information on the impact of redundancy on this group and their labour market experiences in a period of high and rising unemployment and declining opportunities.

In particular the results allow us to look behind the bald and simplified picture provided by unemployment and economic activity statistics and analyse the relationship between redundancy, unemployment and early retirement. This suggests that the threat or experience of unemployment, coming after an extended period of employment, has had the effect of discouraging many of older workers from seeking work. Thus a considerable boost has been given to trends already visible towards fixed age retirement and, more recently, early retirement (Walker, 1980). Since it is within this context that the results from our local survey of the recent post-redundancy experiences of older workers can best be understood it is to longer-term trends in economic activity that we turn first.

Economic activity among older workers

The proportion of elderly people (men sixty-five, women sixty) who are economically active has been falling steadily if not uniformly over the course of the last fifty years. In 1931 one half of men aged sixty-five and over were in the labour force, in 1951 the figure was 31 per cent and by 1982 it had fallen further to only 10 per cent. This decline in labour force participation by elderly men is common to all industrial societies (Townsend, 1979: 654).

The downward trend of economic activity among married women over retirement age has been less marked. Moreover, a larger proportion of women than men remain in the labour force after pension age. The earlier age of retirement for women than for men may help to explain this. But this is not the way older working women themselves see it: they give money as their main reason for continuing to work, followed by enjoyment of work (Parker, 1980: 29). The weight they attach to financial considerations is not surprising. While a much lower proportion of both men and women who work beyond pension age receive occupational pensions than those who retire at, or before, pension age, women workers over pension age are more than four times less likely to receive occupational pensions than men.

Since the mid-1970s the decline in economic activity among men aged sixty-five and over has been extended quite dramatically into the age group immediately below retirement age. From the high rates sustained through most of the post-war period (around 85 per cent), labour force participation among men aged 60–64 has dropped to figures now fluctuating around or below 70 per cent. A smaller fall has taken place since the mid-1970s among non-married women than for men; and, although economic activity has fallen in the last few years also among married women in the five-year-pre-pension age group, the longer-term trend in their case has been upwards. Between 1951 and 1977 the activity rate of married women increased by nearly threefold from a low base of 19 per cent.

These changes in labour force participation rates should be seen, in part, to reflect the use of older workers as a labour reserve (for a full discussion, see Walker, 1981, 1982). This, in turn, is one aspect of what Sinfield (1981: 139) has referred to as the 'shifting patterns of exclusion and inclusion' from the labour force as a whole. Whether or not these will prove to be temporary or permanent trends rests on factors such as the level of demand for labour, government economic and employment policies and attitudes, particularly those of employers, to the participation of older workers in the labour market.

It is clear that a large proportion of older males are now withdrawing from the labour market prematurely, that is before the customary retirement age – a larger proportion than at any other time since World War II. This growth in economic inactivity or 'non-employment' is almost wholly accounted for by the increasing trend towards early retirement among some groups in the 60–64 age range. Britain shares this changing pattern of retirement with other advanced industrial societies although there has been no formal lowering of the general retirement age (Tracy, 1979). Explanations are often expressed in individual terms that refer to changing preferences or declining abilities on the part of older workers (see, for example, Heidbreder, 1972; McGoldrick and Cooper, 1980). The research which we report here, however, supports the quite different conclusion that the employment, redundancy and unemployment experiences of older workers currently generate pressures which go a long way to explaining their differential withdrawal from the labour force.

The 'after redundancy' study

The study was based on structured interviews with some 370 former employees of a privately owned steel company in Sheffield who were made redundant in and shortly after the summer of 1979. The firm's management approached us in the summer of 1980 asking if we could find out 'what had happened' to their former employees and agreed to provide the names and addresses of those who had lost their jobs. Interviews were conducted between October 1982 and February 1983. The questions concentrated on the following key areas of inquiry: reactions to redundancy, receipt of redundancy payments, the record of economic activity over the three years following redundancy, income, attitudes towards work and the experience of unemployment as well as retirement and early retirement, socio-political views, voting patterns and trade union membership. Excluding those who had died during the three years from redundancy to survey, the final response rate was 79 per cent.

The redundancies arose when, following the take-over by a large multi-national in 1978, the reconstituted company reached the conclusion that its forging division could not survive in the face of a contracting market and enhanced capacity on the part of its main British competitors (another private firm and the BSC, both operating in Sheffield). It was decided to close the whole division, sell its order book and some ancillary activities to the rival private-sector firm, and arrange for the latter to re-employ part of the labour force being dismissed. For the rest of the labour force affected, a redundancy scheme was negotiated with the unions. In the final agreed form the scheme added to redundancy payments required by statute: a tax-free lump sum in lieu of notice and a sum equivalent to one week's pay for every year of service in the case of employees at least five years from normal retirement, one and a half week's pay for older employees. The great majority (90 per cent) of those made redundant accepted it 'voluntarily' under this scheme, although, of course, there is serious doubt whether individuals ever freely decide to take redundancy (see Herron, 1975; Wood, 1980).

Sheffield had until recently experienced little unemployment during the post-war period. Though unemployment had risen to high levels in the city in the early 1930s, this was limited to a fairly short span of years and was, at the time, a new experience for the bulk of the local labour force (Pollard, 1959: 248). Unemployment in Sheffield has been below the national average over the whole of the post-war period. This contrasts directly with other parts of South Yorkshire, such as Rotherham and Dearne, which have experienced unemployment levels up to double those in Sheffield for many years. The relative prosperity of Sheffield has been based partly on the production of special steels (carbon steel, alloy steel and stainless steel) and related manufacturing industry. The special steels industry, however, is closely related to that of vehicle manufacture which has experienced a marked decline in recent years. In addition the steel industry in Sheffield has suffered from the 'dumping' of special steel imports into this country. From the late 1970s, therefore, parts of Sheffield have begun, rapidly, to experience that deterioration of the economic fabric which has been felt elsewhere in the county of South Yorkshire for much longer (Walker, 1981 a). Indeed, at the time the redundancies under consideration took place, unemployment was rising faster in Sheffield than in other areas of South Yorkshire: by 48 per cent in the city over the period December 1978 to June 1980, compared with increases of 34 per cent for Barnsley and 25–9 per cent for Doncaster, Rotherham and Dearne. By late 1982/early 1983 unemployment in Sheffield had risen further to an average of 14 per cent (the same as the national average), 18 per cent among men and 9 per cent among women.

This is the local employment context within which the redundancies took place. We now turn to the experiences of those who were made redundant. The majority (55 per cent) were older workers of fifty-five and over when interviewed, and it is on this group that attention is focused in this chapter. An age bias of this order was expected – only one in seven were under the age of thirty – because the workforce in the steel industry is of relatively high median age (Jolly, Creigh and Mingay, 1980: 91), because older workers are more likely than younger ones to be made redundant (Mukherjee, 1973; Daniel, 1974) and because of the 'voluntary' nature of the redundancies in question. The gender distribution also followed a predictable pattern, with the overwhelming majority, 85 per cent, being male. Among the older age groups the proportion was even higher; just under 90 per cent. Thus we are not able to say much about the post-redundancy experiences of older women previously employed in this sector of industry. This is unfortunate in view of the relative neglect of women in studies of redundancy (see Daniel, 1972; Barron and Norris, 1978) but it was inevitable. However, two further characteristics make our group a particularly interesting one for study of the labour market experiences of older male workers in a period of high unemployment.

First, two-thirds of the entire group, and still more (69 per cent) among those aged fifty-five and over, were manual workers. This contrasts with other recent non-representative research on early retirement, carried out by McGoldrick and Cooper (1980), which concentrated on those in higher socio-economic groups (see also Wood, 1980). They found that the majority were satisfied with early retirement. Although doubt is cast on that finding by the results of the national survey (see Parker, 1982: 90) McGoldrick and Cooper's research was conducted after the national survey and it has encouraged a view that favourable attitudes towards early retirement are on the increase among older workers (see, for example, Social Services Committee, 1982). It is important, therefore, to compare the conclusion of that work with the results of our research based on different socio-economic groups. There has in fact been little recent study of what befalls older manual workers following redundancy.

Secondly, a large proportion of the older workers we interviewed had had a long period of service with the same company before being made redundant. Only 17 per cent had been with the company for less than ten years (only 5 per cent for less than five years), while 68 per cent had twenty years' service or more. Over two in every five of them had worked in the company for at least thirty years. The majority therefore had experienced secure employment for long periods of time. Only one in six of the older workers had ever experienced redundancy before 1979, over half of these people who had less than ten years service with the company.

The experience of long-term secure employment prior to redundancy contrasts with the findings of other research which has examined the labour market status of older workers, but which has sampled directly or indirectly among the unemployed (Hill, Harrison, Sargeant and Talbot, 1973; Daniel, 1974; Wood, 1982). Although more representative of the whole unemployed population than our study, research on the unemployed alone is insufficient to judge the specific impact of redundancy, especially on older workers – many of whom do not choose to declare themselves as unemployed, or do so only while entitled to unemployment benefit – and the experiences of economic insecurity following relatively secure employment. Thus we are able to examine a range of post-redundancy experiences related to the labour market – the main additional one to unemployment considered in this chapter is early retirement.

The impact of redundancy

By the time we interviewed them in late 1982 and early 1983 the older workers were divided almost equally between those still economically active and those now inactive – 51 per cent and 49 per cent respectively – according to the standard definition of such activity. However, in common with some previous research (Sinfield, 1968; Norris, 1978; Townsend, 1979; Walker, 1982 a), our data raise questions about the precise distinction between economic activity and inactivity and especially about assumptions which underlie this crude dichotomy.

Rather than a static indication of the potential population available or not

available for paid employment, these economic classifications are dynamic
and interrelated, expanding and contracting primarily in response to the
demand for labour. Thus it is not only unemployment that increases when
the overall demand for labour falls substantially, but also the categories of
economic inactivity – 'housewife', sick, disabled, retired and in full-time
education.

So, in our study, over three in every four of the older people were without
paid employment when we interviewed them some three years after they had
lost their full-time jobs with the company. Unemployment, by conventional
definition, was sizeable, yet only the large tip of the iceberg: about one-fifth
of those aged fifty-five and over had no job but were still looking for one.
The rest of the workers had withdrawn from the labour market. As many
as one in three of the entire group of older workers had now retired; but
the large majority of these had done so before normal pension age. Some
others (7 per cent) were in 'near retirement', having given up any search for
work though they were still registered as unemployed; while another group
(12 per cent) said that ill-health or family commitments now prevented them
from taking employment. Among these older workers 'economic inactivity'
– effective withdrawal from the labour market – thus accounted for more
of the worklessness that followed as a common long-run consequence of
redundancy than did 'unemployment' as conventionally defined.

Table 17.1 shows the distribution of employment status for different age
groups both immediately after leaving the firm in question and, approximately
three years later, at the time of interview.

The impact of redundancy on the employment status of older workers was
remarkable, with only one in six moving at once from employment with the
steel company to a further spell of employment and only one in seven to
full-time work. Although these proportions altered subsequently, particularly
among the 55–9 age group, after three years only just over one in five were
in work.

The respondents' first employment status, shown in table 17.1, was
compared with their immediate intentions following redundancy. This
revealed a considerable mismatch between what was intended and what
actually happened. The job aspirations of the 55–9 and 60–4 age groups were
particularly often frustrated. Taking the 55–9 age group first, nearly one-
fifth intended to have a holiday, one-tenth to retire and three-fifths to find
a job (most of them saying they wanted a job as soon as possible) – yet fewer
than two-fifths actually found a job then. Among those aged 60–4, 14 per
cent had intended a holiday, 29 per cent to retire and 47 per cent to find
a job (32 per cent as soon as possible) but only one in six managed to find
employment at the time. Turning to the over-65s, 5 per cent intended to take
a holiday, and 67 per cent to retire, but there were still 22 per cent who hoped
to find a job (most of them as soon as possible) as against the less than 5
per cent who actually did so.

Redundancy had the most immediate impact on the employment status of older workers compared with younger ones. Initially the flow out of the labour force and into retirement was concentrated among men within three years of pension age. Three years after redundancy the picture had changed, with the level of employment rising among those still under pension age and the level of unemployment falling. But whereas for the 55–9 age group the fall in unemployment was compensated by an increase in employment (though also in sickness and disability) for the 60–4 age group early retirement together with sickness and disability increased more substantially than employment. Among those sixty-five and over when we interviewed them, hardly any had work three years after redundancy and the great majority had retired. But common enough as that may seem at first sight, most of the retired had done so early without waiting for normal pension age to come.

Table 17.1 First and latest employment status following redundancy (per cent)

Employment status a first b latest		under 40	Age at time of interview 40–54	55–9	60–4	65+	All 55+	All ages
Employed	a	64.2	42.5	(39.5)	17.2	4.6	17.3	33.6
	b	69.1	66.2	(53.9)	24.4	1.5	23.2	40.6
Unemployed	a	30.9	50.7	(50.0)	49.4	24.6	40.8	40.6
	b	17.3	27.0	(25.6)	27.9	1.5	18.4	20.0
Retired – early	a	0.0	0.0	(0.0)	10.3	44.6	19.9	11.0
	b	0.0	0.0	(0.0)	16.1	72.3	31.1	17.1
– at pension age	a	0.0	0.0	(0.0)	1.2	6.2	2.6	1.4
	b	0.0	0.0	(0.0)	3.4	20.0	10.5	5.8
Sick or injured	a	0.0	2.7	(5.3)	9.2	7.7	7.9	4.9
	b	1.2	2.7	(12.8)	15.1	1.5	10.0	6.4
Looking after family	a	3.7	2.7	(5.3)	1.1	0.0	1.6	2.3
	b	11.1	1.4	(7.7)	1.2	0.0	2.1	4.1
Other*	a	1.2	1.4	(0.0)	9.2	12.3	8.4	5.2
	b	1.2	2.7	(0.0)	12.8	1.5	6.3	4.3
Total		100	100	100	100	100	100	100
Number		81	74	39	87	65	191	346

Notes: First = employment status after being made redundant; latest = employment status
           at time of interview
* includes those registered as unemployed but not seeking work and 'semi-retired'

Table 17.2 shows the major knock-out effect of redundancy: even by conventional definition the rate of unemployment three years after redundancy was high across all age groups in the sample and particularly so among older workers.

Table 17.2 Economic activity and unemployment (per cent)

Economic activity		Age at time of interview				All	All
	under 40	40–54	55–9	60–4	65 +	55 +	ages
A. Economically active as percentage of total	86.4	87.5	(79.5)	52.3	3.0	41.4	63.2
B. Unemployed as percentage of total	17.3	27.0	(25.6)	27.9	1.5	18.4	20.0
C. Conventional unemployment rate (B as percentage of A)	20.0	30.9	(32.2)	53.3	50.0	44.3	31.7
Total	100	100	100	100	100	100	100
Number	81	74	39	87	65	191	346

Unemployment and non-employment

The dynamic pattern of experiences implied by the two cross-sectional snap-shots shown in table 17.1 was confirmed by analysis of the respondents' records of economic activity over the three-year period following redundancy. As table 17.3 shows, those in the 60–4 age range were more likely to be unemployed (in the conventional sense) and for longer periods than other older workers since being made redundant. Secondly, in addition to their disproportionate share of long-term unemployment, people in this age group were more likely to be *non-employed*, whether looking for work or not. In turn, while those in the 55–9 age group showed no marked difference from younger people in their experience of unemployment over the three years, more of them had been unemployed and for longer. This emphasises the point made earlier, that unemployment is only one indicator of the under-utilisation of labour (Sorrentino, 1981: 168). To assess the impact of redundancy on the labour market status of older workers a more comprehensive indicator of under-utilisation is required. We have used the concept of non-employment.

What do we mean by this? We do not use the concept to mean under-utilisation of individual skills or education in jobs which are below the ability of the incumbent (Sorrentino, 1981: 167), but to refer to an under-utilisation of labour associated with lack of opportunities for paid employment or restricted access to employment (Walker, 1982 a: 86). It may be seen, therefore, as one dimension of 'subemployment' – the other dimension being low wage employment (Gordon, 1972; Vietorisz, Mier and Giblin, 1975: 3–4).

Non-employment, as we use the term, is the extent to which individuals were not in paid employment during the three years or so after redundancy – for whatever ostensible reason, whether unemployed by conventional definition, retired, sick, or tied by family commitments.

A detailed record of each change in employment status was collected from respondents and from these records we have calculated the proportion of time available actually spent in some form of employment. (Those who had passed normal pension age were excluded from this calculation.) Caution is required in using the notion of non-employment because it is simply a guide to the distribution of employment as opposed to unemployment among a given population over a given period of time. It contains no reference to the nature of the employment, as would a more elaborate subemployment index; nor to whether or not those involved would *choose* to take up employment if it were available. It is not helpful, therefore, to apply it to the population as a whole, because many will not be willing or able to enter the labour market; but it is revealing when used in application to a group which is known to be seeking employment such as recent school-leavers (Walker, 1982 a) or which, as in the present study, had until recently been in full-time secure employment.

Our results thus bring out the contrast in post-redundancy experience between older and younger workers more sharply when we look at the total record of non-employment rather than the record of unemployment alone, either at a particular point of time (table 17.1) or over the three year period (table 17.3). Nearly two in every three of the older people had paid work for less than half the period since redundancy, a rate of non-employment more than twice that for the two younger groups shown in table 17.3.

Table 17.3 Proportion of time since redundancy spent employed and unemployed (per cent)

Percentage of time spent: employed and unemployed	Age at time of interview				All 55+	All ages
	under 40	40–54	55–9	60–4*		
employed						
none	13.1	17.6	(25.6)	58.2	52.5	30.4
one but less than 25	8.3	9.5	(10.3)	10.1	10.2	9.1
25 but less than 50	3.6	4.1	(7.7)	3.8	5.1	4.3
50 but less than 75	15.5	10.8	(7.7)	5.1	5.9	10.1
75 but less than 100	22.6	18.9	(17.9)	15.2	17.8	21.0
100	36.9	33.8	(30.8)	7.6	15.3	27.2
Total	100	100	100	100	100	100
unemployed						
none	53.6	43.2	(43.6)	41.4	42.4	47.1
one but less than 25	21.4	25.7	(23.1)	17.2	19.2	22.1
25 but less than 50	8.3	5.4	(5.1)	9.2	8.0	7.6
50 but less than 75	4.8	4.1	(7.7)	4.6	5.6	5.1
75 but less than 100	7.1	9.5	(12.8)	8.0	9.6	9.1
100	4.8	12.2	(7.7)	18.4	15.2	11.6
Total	100	100	100	100	100	100
Number	84	74	39	79	118	276

Note: * excludes those over pension age

Redundancy and the process of exclusion

How do we explain these patterns of economic activity and inactivity on the part of older workers? Our data provide some indication of reactions to work, redundancy and early retirement and pave the way for more detailed enquiries into the experiences and attitudes of older workers.

We start from the assumption that if the plant had not closed those now under pension age would still be employed. This is supported by the overall length of service of the majority, their attachment to the particular employer and their answers to specific questions about redundancy and early retirement. More than three-quarters of those retired did so before pension age. But when asked whether they had thought about early retirement before the issue of redundancy came up, only just under one-quarter said yes.

There were no signs of a widespread dissatisfaction among older workers with employment or their employer prior to closure. In fact, the opposite was true. Older workers were more likely than their younger counterparts to have expressed satisfaction with the firm and its management. For example, three-quarters of the older respondents said that they would not have left the company to do the same job, but for a little more money, with another firm in Sheffield, compared with three-fifths of those under forty. Older workers were more than twice as likely as those under forty to say that they had a great deal of respect for the top management at the firm (72 per cent).

Redundancy, linked as it was to a substantial fall in demand for labour, was the immediate reason for the scattering of a previously stable and relatively secure workforce into the variety of different employment related statuses shown in table 17.1. Redundancy marked the end of secure employment and for some this proved also the end of their working lives.

The disadvantage of older workers in the labour market

The employment prospects of older workers are particularly severely affected by redundancy. In the first place, they are more prone than younger people to illness and disability, and manual more so than non-manual workers (Townsend and Davidson, 1982: 130–33). Reduction in working capacity on this score may remain invisible or small, or may receive special consideration by a sympathetic employer while the person is in a job; and this has been so for a few older workers in our study just before redundancy. But it becomes a considerable hindrance to any search for new employment.

Secondly, older workers are at a great disadvantage in the job market because of age discriminatory recruitment practices (Jolly *et al.*, 1980). Most of those in the 60–4 age group who were unemployed had more or less given up looking for work: in the words of one sixty-three-year-old man, 'Because I'm sick of trying and being told I'm too old'. Redundancy exposes the disadvantages associated with class which affect other aspects of the older worker's life when in employment, such as the poor working conditions characteristic of manual employment (Townsend, 1979: 440–42); and it opens the door to new ones related, in part at least, to age. So, for example, the majority of older workers in our study had received minimal education (primary level was the furthest two out of three had gone) and little training (one in four had not received any and a further one in two had been 'trained' only on the job). Coupled with the specific nature of their work experience this lack of formal education and training is a considerable disadvantage in the labour market. One man had joined the company as an office boy nearly fifty years before being made redundant and had worked his way up to a professional grade job, but had no qualifications. He had been seeking any form of clerical work but remained unemployed through the three years. It may well be that long-term, relatively secure employment of a manual kind is the worst possible precursor to redundancy and the changes that long-term unemployment or re-employment may demand.

Once redundancy became a real prospect and they were faced with the closure of the plant that they had worked in for a long time, the older workers, along with the younger ones, took 'voluntary' redundancy in order to qualify for the negotiated package. Undoubtedly too the lump sum involved – over £5,000 for most of the older workers – was a considerable inducement. But whatever the reasons why they lost their jobs in the first place, what explains the subsequent differences among them in patterns of economic activity and inactivity? Why did some withdraw from the labour market prematurely while others stayed on?

Employment and unemployment

As tables 17.1, 17.2 and 17.3 indicate, we found, in common with other research (Parker, 1980: 13), that the nearer to statutory pension age the more likely people were to withdraw from the labour market. Nevertheless, just over half of the 60–4 age group remained economically active, by conventional definition, for at least three years, together with the overwhelming bulk of the 55–9 age group (table 17.1). They stayed in the labour force despite the concentration of non-employment and unemployment on this group. This suggests that the individuals had little choice for financial or other reasons but to remain economically active. But was it also the case that older workers responded to unemployment differently from younger ones? Our data suggest so.

All those respondents who had experienced at least one period of unemployment since redundancy were asked about their feelings about being out of work. It is important to stress that the majority of those asked said it was either the worst or nearly the worst thing that had happened to them. But there were variations in response among the older workers. The 55–9 age group clearly felt very hard hit by the experience of unemployment: nearly three in every four of those among them who had been unemployed for part or all of the time since redundancy saw this as the worst thing that had ever happened to them, compared with half the under-thirties and three in five of the middle-aged. Yet among the 60–4 year olds in the same situation, only two in every five chose the phrase 'worst thing' to describe their experience; and the figure for those over sixty-five was 54 per cent. This difference between the 55–9 group and those still older can be seen at the other end of the scale in the proportion saying that they did not really mind being unemployed: 5 per cent for the 55–9 year olds, but 23 per cent for the 60–4 group.

So, by this indication those close to pension age found the experience of unemployment less personally distressing than those a little further from it. Since we found no significant difference in employment commitment between the two groups, the main reason for their difference in reaction to the experience of unemployment is likely to be that those nearer retirement age could reconcile themselves more easily to being without a job because a pension was within reasonable sight and they would not need to stretch their finances so far as the younger group. The latter, 55–9 when we interviewed them, were in the 52–6 age range when they became redundant. That meant, for men, a minimum of nine years and a maximum of thirteen years to go before reaching pension age: a daunting prospect, in the knowledge that after one year the redundancy payment and any other savings must be reduced to below £2,000 (£2,500 from November 1982 and £3,000 from November 1983) before entitlement to the poverty level income provided by supplementary benefit.

Of those currently unemployed at the time of the interview both the 55–9 and the 60–4 age groups were aware that their chances of finding a job were slim: four out of every five thought their prospects 'not at all good', compared with one in four of those under forty. These differences were reflected in the incidence of 'negative affect' in the few weeks prior to the interview. Negative affect is a scale devised by Bradburn (1969) which asks if informants had suffered any of five common symptoms of psychological distress during the few weeks prior to interview. Older workers (excluding those aged sixty-five and over) were the age group most prone to negative affect and within the group it was the 55–9 year olds who were slightly more likely than the 60–4 year olds to have registered negative affect (see also Warr, 1984).

Information about job-searching between the announcement of the redundancies and the time when respondents actually left the plant supports the drift of these findings. For example, while older workers as a whole were much less likely than younger ones to have looked for alternative employment before leaving the firm – 24 per cent compared with 78 per cent of the under thirties – the 55–9 age group were more than twice as likely as the 60–4 age group to have done so (48 per cent versus 21 per cent). Even when we look for this purpose only at those who told us that, on redundancy, they had intended to find a job as soon as possible, the 55-9 year olds among them were still more likely than the 60-4 group to have looked for a job already before they left (65 per cent compared with 48 per cent).

When asked if they had been worried at the prospect of not having another job to go to when they left the firm, older workers as a whole were the least worried (31 per cent of them were worried or concerned compared with 50 per cent of those under thirty and 68 per cent of those aged 40-9). But again, the 55-9s were much more likely than those aged 60-4 to be worried (62 per cent and 38 per cent). Similarly when it came to registering as unemployed, the 55-9 age group did so much sooner than those nearer pension age: 59 per cent of those among them who registered did so within one week: twice as many as among 60-4 year old registrants, and four times the rate for the over-sixty-five group. The latter groups were much more inclined to leave registration for longer than one month than the 55-9 age group. Here, as from the evidence set out earlier, the greater anxiety of the 55-9 year olds about finding work is plain. But the oldest group – those sixty-five or more – were the most likely of all to register at *some* time, even though they were relatively slow about it. This was almost certainly due to their concern to protect their state pension rights.

Although the level of employment among older people was low relative to younger groups, just over one half of the 55-9s and just under a quarter of the 60-4s were employed when we interviewed them (table 17.1). While a more detailed analysis of the data on those older workers in employment has yet to be conducted, several important findings can be reported at this stage.

There was little or no difference in the degree of commitment to employment (as measured by our scale) between employed and unemployed older workers, nor for that matter between the sick and the employed. In the 60-4 age group slightly lower levels of employment commitment were found among the early retired and those who were registered as unemployed but not seeking work. The length of time spent unemployed did not appear to affect commitment to employment (see Warr and Jackson, 1983). Differences did emerge, however, in relation to respondents' immediate intentions on becoming redundant. Our results here suggest that the degree of *urgency* with which older individuals first sought re-employment may have been an important factor in their subsequent success or failure. Take the 55-9 age group first: those in employment when interviewed were far more likely than those unemployed (79 per cent and 30 per cent) to have said that their intention had been to find a job as soon as possible. True, in the 60-4 age group, where it must be pointed out that cell sizes were larger there were no marked differences on this score: forty-five per cent of the employed and 42 per cent of the unemployed said they had been keen to find work as soon as possible. Even so, a further 25 per cent of the employed said that they had been concerned to take their time in finding a job, compared with only 5 per cent of the unemployed. None of those in employment when interviewed said their intention had been to retire, but 16 per cent of the unemployed did.

There is some indication from our data (again at this stage we can put it no stronger than this) that older people who were successful in finding subsequent employment had to accept jobs (and presumably pay) below their previous level of skill. In the 60–4 age group such downgrading was widespread with, for example, skilled workers of long standing accepting jobs as unskilled labourers. Their reasons for staying in the workforce, even at a lower level of skill – 'I just don't like being out of work', 'The last thing I wanted was to be on the dole', 'Well, you don't want to stop work when you've been active all your life' – displayed the same 'paid employment ethic' and distaste of unemployment that kept the unemployed older workers searching for jobs for so long before becoming disillusioned.

Money, of course, is an important component of the 'paid employment ethic', hence our preference for that term in contrast to the conventional 'work ethic'. Not surprisingly those in employment were considerably better-off financially than other groups. The mean total income for the respondents' income unit was £83 a week for those in the 60–4 age group who were employed, compared with £37 for the unemployed and £53 for the retired. As a result a much lower proportion of those in employment than those not employed had been forced to cut down on expenditure since leaving the steel firm. So, among those aged 60–4, 30 per cent of the employed, 36 per cent of the early retired, 83 per cent of the unemployed and 92 per cent of the sick said they had to make cuts.

Early retirement and discouragement

The major exit route from the labour force was early retirement. Just over half of those who retired prematurely did so at the time as their redundancy. The rest retired at different points over the following three years. Again the initial redundancy was the major spur to early retirement.

How did the older workers who took the early retirement option come to their decision? Two approaches may be contrasted. On the one hand there were those who, once the prospect of redundancy had been raised, were reconciled to early retirement and to some extent relieved at leaving work, although they were attached to their employer and would not in all probability have left prematurely of their own volition. In the words of one sixty-four-year-old man who took early retirement, it was 'due to the fact that I was made redundant. I'd been at [the firm] all those years and worked really hard and felt I could get through alright without working. I felt I'd done my duty'.

On the other hand, there were those who gave up work reluctantly and would have preferred to have kept on working, but for reasons of health and lack of alternative employment chose early retirement. As one put it:

'I was accepting early retirement but psychologically I was being pushed out'.

The early retirers in our study were split evenly between the first group who had no regrets about retirement, even if their decision was precipitated by redundancy, and the second who would have preferred to continue to work (this compares, incidentally, with just over one quarter of those who retired at the normal pension ages who would have preferred to keep on working).

In common with previous research on early retirement (Parker, 1980; McGoldrick and Cooper, 1980), we found that ill-health was a crucial factor in the decision. It was the most frequently mentioned reason for early retirement. In fact the dividing line between the status of sickness, unemployment and early retirement was often difficult to draw. For example, one sixty-year old man with a cataract considered himself to be early retired, another sixty-three-year-old wanted a job following a major operation on his leg and a sixty-four-year-old was registered as unemployed, despite severe illness, and looking for light work.

Our findings also confirm those of previous research (Friedman and Orbach, 1974; Parker, 1980; McGoldrick and Cooper, 1980) that another important factor in the decision whether or not to retire is finance. We have already shown that those in full-time employment were substantially better off than other groups. But the early retired, in turn, were better off than the rest. They were more than three times as likely as the unemployed to have income unit incomes over £100 per week (14 per cent and 4 per cent) and one-third as likely to have incomes of less than £50 a week (19 per cent and 41 per cent).

These income differentials were underpinned by differences in occupational class. Thus there was a clear bias in the social class distribution of retirement and early retirement, with the semi-skilled and unskilled being most likely to wait until the statutory pension ages (31 per cent and 5 per cent of the retired in each social class) and the supervisory and managerial group were the more likely to retire early (95 per cent and 69 per cent).

Age itself, in conjunction with age-barrier retirement policy, had an important bearing on early retirement (see Parker, 1980: 13). We looked at proximity to the pension ages in 1979, when the redundancies took place. The proportion of time spent retired increased dramatically the closer to pension age. Thus the mean proportion of time spent retired for those within four to six years of pension age was 19 per cent, compared with 57 per cent for those within three to four years and 84 per cent for those with one to two years to go before reaching pension age. Differences between occupational classes in the propensity to retire early increased with distance from pension age. Take those within one to two years of the pension age first, the aggregate of time since redundancy spent in retirement by non-manual workers (86 per cent of the total time) exceeded that for skilled manual workers (67 per cent) by nearly one third. For those within two to four years of pension ages the figures were 77 per cent and 59 per cent and for those four to six years away from normal pension ages 38 per cent compared with 8 per cent.

High and rising unemployment and knowledge about the poor prospects of older workers will undoubtedly have contributed to the decision to take early retirement even by those who had no regrets. But the others – the reluctant early retirers – conform directly to the description of 'discouraged workers' presented in some American work (Sorrentino, 1980: 168). They are people who would like to work but believe no work is available, lack the necessary schooling, training, skills or experience, are regarded by employers as too young or too old or who have other personal handicaps in finding a job. The small number of older (and younger) women who gave up paid employment following redundancy to become housewives may also be included in this group of discouraged workers. They have given up the idea of gaining paid employment and withdrawn, temporarily or permanently, from the labour force.

Others too, especially the long-term unemployed, while not leaving the workforce, had effectively given up searching for work. They had been discouraged by the difficulty of finding secure employment and while they had applied for jobs in the early stages of unemployment were not doing so any longer. Nearly all the unemployed people aged 60–4 mentioned the bias towards younger people in recruitment. The following comments are representative:

'They have lost interest in me because of my age.'

'You're told that they are looking for someone younger everywhere.'

'You lose interest and you can see the situation as it is – you're not going to be set on, and who's going to set me on at 63?'

Official labour market intermediaries in the Job Centres are an important source of information about employment prospects and are, therefore, crucial in transmitting discouragement. For many older people in our study the process began as soon as they registered as unemployed, because they were then much less likely than younger people to be interviewed by Job Centre staff, and if interviewed they were likely to be told their prospects of obtaining employment were nil.

'When I went to the Job Centre they said they couldn't do anything for me at my age (63).'

'I've given up the idea of finding a job – since my wife was snubbed at the Job Centre – she was looking for a job herself and asked the girl about one advertisement for a turner at Worksop. When she asked the girl said it was too far away and anyway I was too old – it was a job for a younger man. I've not bothered since then, I felt very bad after that.'

Discouragement, as already noted, operated differentially according to socio-economic grouping. Among the early retired it was the manual workers as opposed to the non-manual who were most likely to have wanted to continue working and who were therefore forced into early retirement; conversely it was the non-manual group who were more likely to have wanted to retire. But even among the non-manual group there were those who felt that they were coerced into retiring prematurely:

'I saw the writing on the wall. Despite promises people were losing their jobs or being moved to uncongenial jobs, I think on purpose to make them leave. I don't think any staff were sacked, but things were made uncomfortable and if I hadn't accepted the generous offer I might've been given the push one or two years later without the extra redundancy pay'.

All those who retired prematurely were compelled by redundancy to make a decision about their future employment status. Half of those who retired at that point or subsequently were effectively forced into early retirement by ill health or the lack of job opportunities. Only three people among the retired group had worked since redundancy and only one of those did so for more than half the time between redundancy and our interview. So for the bulk of those who delayed a decision about early retirement, unemployment or sickness amounted effectively to the same thing as early retirement: non-employment. But considerably more social stigma attaches to the status unemployed than that of early retired. In this respect older workers have at their disposal a socially acceptable alternative role to unemployment, while younger workers do not. The formal decision to retire prematurely, when it came later, was to some extent a rationalisation and an improvement in the individual's situation. (The terms that older people themselves used to rationalise early retirement are discussed below.) Between November 1981 and 1983, moreover, men aged 60–4 in receipt of supplementary benefit were made significantly better-off by declaring themselves early retired rather than unemployed and so becoming entitled to the long-term rate of benefit.

Conclusion: social exclusion and the construction of age

The discouraging effects of prolonged unemployment, experience in the labour market with employers and official intermediaries, public statements by political and economic commentators, politicians and employers about the future of employment: these are all part of a social process of exclusion, which began for the individual older workers in our study even before the redundancy itself. Attitudes towards employment, retirement and early retirement are not formed in a vacuum; and quite apart from the long-term devaluation of the industrial worth of older people (Walker, 1980), the periods leading up to and after the redundancies in question were marked by frequent public references to the need for earlier retirement and more importantly by social policies – such as the Job Release Scheme and changes in supplementary benefit regulations – aimed at encouraging it (see Walker, 1982).

Together, official labour market and social security policies and policy statements reflect an overwhelming official concern in the current period of high unemployment with the position of young people in the labour market and conversely, a lack of interest in any positive action to improve the employment prospects of older workers. Not surprisingly perhaps, when the agenda has been set so thoroughly by public statements and practical policies, the general public have reflected the same ageist bias. Thus a Marplan public opinion poll, in December 1982, found that four out of five of those questioned thought that early retirement was a desirable measure for alleviating unemployment. In our own study support for compulsory retirement at an earlier age was nearly as widespread, with one-third saying it would be very effective and two-fifths saying it would be quite effective. And, for all the regrets which many early retired people expressed about a decision at least in part forced on them, it was the group that we have already identified as the most likely to be non-employed, the 60–4 age group, which was most likely to say that early retirement would be very effective in dealing with unemployment: 46 per cent, compared with 34 per cent of the 55–9 age group and 30 per cent of those under the age of thirty.

Statements by individuals in response to other questions about early retirement also often reflected the dominant official concern. It appears that older workers themselves had internalised the ageism which underpins policy. The terms they and others used to justify or rationalise early retirement often dwelt on the position of young people in the labour market. One man who took early retirement at sixty-one because he had been made redundant echoed the view of many others when he described as an advantage of early retirement: 'The fact that there were so many young people out of work and I thought I'd done a lifetime's work and might as well leave it for the young ones'. Similar responses have been found in other research (see McGoldrick and Cooper, 1980: 860).

So, the context of public debate and policy within which the redundancies took place and our respondents were to experience subsequent difficulties in the labour market, was one indifferent or hostile to the special needs of older workers. Yet it had in effect also prepared these older workers for the non-employment and its hardships which so many of them had to face. There can be no doubt that official and public attitudes to older workers – which in turn determine their inclusion in or exclusion from the labour force – rest primarily on the demand for labour. Thus, at an earlier stage of Britain's post-war history, people of retirement age were urged officially *not* to retire and 'sink into premature old age' but to work a little longer and therefore have 'a happier and healthier old age' (Phillipson, 1983: 33). At the same time, it was hardly an accident that medical and social science research began to indicate that retirement had detrimental effects.

Today a formal lowering of the male retirement age to sixty has been rejected on grounds of cost (House of Lords Select Committee on Unemployment, 1982; House of Commons Select Committee on Social Services, 1982), but high rates of unemployment among the male 60–4 group together with official encouragement for unemployed men to leave the labour force have amounted to a tacit policy of increased early retirement for men. Of course this is considerably cheaper than awarding full pension rights to men at sixty. But while this policy may relieve the short-term burden of unemployment from some older men, our study shows that this burden is also rather easier to bear for the group nearest retirement age. It is those in their mid- and late-fifties who must pay the full cost of official indifference. Moreover, the long term consequences of this tacit policy of early retirement, such as deeper poverty in advanced old age, have so far been virtually ignored in public debate (Walker, 1982: 66–9).

The processes of exclusion from the labour market in operation currently play an important part in the social construction of the definition and redefin-ition of the labour force, the economically active and inactive, the unemployed and retired, the productive and unproductive, and therefore of working age and old age (Walker, 1980; Phillipson, 1983). These are processes whereby the state encourages and legitimates increased dependency in the form of unemployment and early retirement among elderly people, while subjecting others not only to substantially lower incomes but also to control procedures intended to ensure that they continue searching for work.

Whither (research on) unemployment?

Dedication: To my many friends who have demonstrated the errors of macho hyperactivity: and to Paul Lafargue, who rebelled against the promotion of an ideology of work by his father-in-law (Karl Marx). More concretely, to Jeanette Thorn, who, yet again, practised the opposite of what I preach in transforming my illegible script into something legible at a moment's notice: and to Barbara Dodds and Glennis Whyte for 'producing' the final polished copy.

The fundamental contradiction of capitalism (whether of the private, state or Heinz variety) still remains in the necessity for capitalism on the one hand to reduce workers to simple executors of tasks and, on the other, to the impossibility for it to continue functioning if it succeeds in so doing. Capitalism needs to achieve mutually incompatible objectives: the participation *and* the exclusion of the workers in production as of all citizens in relation to politics.

(taken from Cornelius Castoradis, 1959, *Modern Capitalism and Revolution*)

Introduction

Peter Warr has provided us with a comprehensive review of research into the relationship, on the individual level, between the status of unemployment within British capitalism today and mental or psychological health. Thus, in Sections 1, 2, 3 and 10, he presents findings on the effects of unemployment on psychological health, processes through which unemployment impairs psychological health, factors mediating the impact of unemployment and the effects of recession on people in jobs. Warr is careful in his discussion of them and I have nothing to add provided they are taken literally as demonstrating the impact *not of unemployment per se* but of unemployment within this particular British context.

Warr is also properly circumspect in the second section where he discusses 'what we need to know'. Apart from his speculations (in sections 8 and 9) on alleviating the lot of the unemployed (see below), these can be divided into ignorance on an individual level (the effects of unemployment on physical health in section 4, and detailed information about the impact of unemployment) and ignorance on a macro level (the relation between economic recession and mortality rates, the use of health service facilities and (para) suicide – in sections 5, 6 and 7).

Quantitative macro studies of the latter sort are notoriously difficult to interpret, often degenerating into a haggling match between two statisticians as to whether or not to lag and, if so, by how much.

Thus, Eyer (1977) believes that, contrary to Brenner (1979), the sources of social stress which occur *with* the boom are responsible for the business cycle peak of the death rate. The net impact of stress during booms is greater than that of health risks which increase during depressions. Moreover, Gravelle, Hutchinson and Stern (1981) who tested Brenner's model with more extensive data concluded that: 'We were unable to demonstrate a significant effect of unemployment on mortality for a longer period (1922–1976) or for the post-war period (1952–1976), [where] the estimated coefficients fail appropriate tests of structural stability' (1981: 677).

Some progress can, however, be made by examining the theoretical models underlying research on the impact of unemployment both on the macro and micro level. First, I shall make a few remarks about the effects and impact of unemployment other than upon psychological ill health. Then I summarise the arguments about the impact of unemployment upon 'crime' seen as one of the main social consequences of high unemployment (Hakim, 1982). Finally, I set the whole debate in a broader context to question the direction and motivation of all this research on unemployment.

Effects of unemployment on physical ill-health and other problem behaviour

Peter Warr reports studies of cross-sectional differences between the physical health which show that the unemployed are overall less healthy. Similar findings have been reported during the present (fourth Krondatiev long wave) recession since Daniel's (1974) study showed that: (a) younger unemployed workers were much more likely to have found jobs than the elderly; (b) workers with lower self-ratings of their own health status were less likely to have found a job.

These findings prompt discussion of the healthy worker effect, where an unhealthy worker is the first to be made redundant, or does unemployment produce ill health? Hence, the importance of studies of long-term unemployed over their career of unemployment. The few longitudinal studies that do exist are ambivalent. Warr quotes Kasl and Cobb (1980) but rightly criticises them for too short a follow-up. Of course, Fox and Goldblatt (1982) have analysed mortality data for the years 1971 to 1975 according to individual characteristics recorded on the 1971 England and Wales census. Much play is made of the difference they find for males aged fifteen to sixty-four in the standardised mortality ratio in the subsequent period between people unemployed and seeking work than for those in jobs at the date of the census. Much less is made of their finding that there was *no* difference for women aged 15–59: the explanation given is that

society would expect unemployed men of working age to seek work and this would have the effect of including among those seeking work a disproportionate number of less healthy men. Since this expectation would not apply to women, or to men of pensionable age, the category 'seeking work' at this age would describe self-selected groups which exclude people on health grounds. (1982: 26)

An equally plausible view would be that in our sexist and ageist society, the financial consequences of unemployment are more severe for men of working age than for either of the other two groups.

Yet there is a wealth of historical evidence to suggest both that many occupations are bad for your health and that idleness is good for you. In the former category, we can start with Engels (1958), cite countless studies of fishermen, miners and soldiers, and refer to dozens of sociological studies (of some ten years ago) or to any report of the Health and Safety Executive (a useful summary of recent evidence for the UK is provided by Clutterbuck, 1982). In the latter category, the fact that the British aristocracy who never lifted a finger (literally, in some cases) lived far longer than the rest of the population seems to me a knock-down argument in favour of unemployment being conducive to good health.

I *do* realise that there is a small matter of the rather widely disparate relative income levels associated with being an aristocrat and with being unemployed; but you have to search very hard through the literature to find any studies which control for income levels in assessing the relationship between unemployment and health. Thus, Watkins (1982) in an extensive review of the links between recession and health acknowledges that an 'alternative explanation' for all the studies he reviews about the links between unemployment and ill-health is that 'they are demonstrating not the effects of unemployment but the effects of multiple deprivation' (13). He says that:

We know that poverty is damaging to health and that the unemployed are poor. We know that life changes damage health until the individual readjusts and we know that losing your job is a life change and that you are not supposed to adjust to worklessness. We know that social networks are important to health and that the unemployed lose the social network of work and also that they withdraw from other social interactions because of stigma and lack of money.
(Watkins, 1982)

I would go further and argue that each of those 'associated deprivations' fundamentally reflect a loss of income and that all the other observed effects are consequential (see below). But what is interesting here is how he follows that summary. He claims that:

In order to argue that unemployment does not damage health, one would have to postulate some beneficial effects of unemployment to outweigh these damaging aspects. The postulated benefit would presumably be absence from the damaging health effects of work. Thus, if it were found that unemployment did not damage health that would be an even greater challenge to our social organisation, suggesting that work damages health even more than being poor, stigmatised or lonely. The Ecology Party could have a field day.
(Watkins, 1982)

The picture becomes clearer: so long as objective academics and/or all right-thinking supporters of a parliamentary 'democracy' (with two or two-and-a-half parties) hold ranks, then the work ethic will hold, and so we don't have to worry too much about redistributing income and wealth. In contrast I would claim that poverty and, increasingly, unequal shares, is what it is all about. The emphasis on unemployment is myopic (see below).

In another section of his review, Warr summarises research on the impact of unemployment upon other behaviours. Catherine Hakim (1982) introduces her piece by saying

There is widespread consensus that unemployment has deleterious effects both on the individual affected, and on the community as a whole . . . Yet this belief in the social damage wreaked by unemployment seems to be at variance with the fact that the very high and rising levels of unemployment currently experienced appear to have been absorbed without widespread breakdown of the social and political order . . .
(Hakim, 1982: 433)

In fact, in this latter category she skates rather rapidly over the 'patchy evidence' (her words) relating unemployment to homelessness, family stability, children's education, racial tension and public attitude.

Of course, other papers at this conference have provided detailed case histories of the activities of the unemployed, but there have been no detailed longitudinal studies which could verify any of the rather general assertions that Hakim makes. Once again, it would seem to me more parsimonious to rely on the *known* and repeatedly *proven* associations between low income and other negative life events such as homelessness, family instability and inadequate education for the children, rather than speculate about the effects of unemployment *independent of a drop in income*. Equally, it might be more profitable to castigate the contribution made by scribblers of all kinds to exacerbating racial tension and negative public attitudes by focusing upon the unemployed, rather than endlessly proposing further research as part of an academic job creation exercise.

Unemployment and crime

It has become commonplace to claim that unemployment causes crime. In the public domain, the House of Lords Select Committee, reporting in May 1982, claimed that: 'We believe unemployment to be among the causes of ill-health, mortality, crime or civil disorder'. Catherine Hakim says, 'There is extensive evidence . . . that unemployment is a factor contributing significantly to crime and delinquency' (1982: 450). Indeed, she claims that a study by myself and Stern 'confirm[s] the association between crime and unemployment, and suggest[s] that it has been increasing over time' (1979: 452–3). This is taken up below. Finally, of course, there is Brenner (1976) again, whose first foray into correlating trends in economic indicators and 'social problems' was in the field of crime.

First we have to set the debate in context. In 1970 there were 1,568,000 and in 1981, 2,794,000 recorded serious offences. It is important to emphasise that the majority of these 'serious' offences are minor. This can be best illustrated through the Metropolitan Statistics as they provide some further detail as to the *amounts stolen* or the *actual harm done*. Thus, there were 631,238 total known recorded offences in 1981 of which *c.* 95 per cent are property offences and about two-thirds of those involved property worth less than £100 (Sir James Crane, *Guardian*, 9 March 1982). The *typical* offence is therefore a *small property* offence and this must be borne in mind when discussing the impact of unemployment below. In contrast, there were 5,889 recorded offences of robbery in the open following sudden attack in 1981 (popularly known as 'mugging'), representing 0.9 per cent of all serious recorded offences in the Metropolitan Police area. Whilst not wishing to play down these offences, it is important to note that a study of a sample of 'mugging' incidents by Dr Michael Pratt – a senior civilian employee at Scotland Yard – shows that 58 per cent received no injury whatsoever and a further 37 per cent received injuries which were described as slight. Furthermore, 81 per cent of the victims were male, and only 14 per cent of the victims over sixty years old, whilst 53 per cent of victims were between seventeen and sixty.

We next ask *a priori* how one might expect unemployment to affect crime. There are a number of possible relationships and we look at three: the unemployment rate may affect (i) the actual number of offences committed; (ii) the numbers of offences recorded for a *given* number of offences, through effects on recording; and (iii) other variables, for example, the number of policemen *per capita* which may, in turn, affect the number of offences recorded. We look at the possible directions of these effects (see also Carr-Hill and Stern, 1983 b).

Let us consider first the possible effects of a higher unemployment rate on 'criminogenic' behaviour. Where there is more unemployment it is possible that communities are poorer and this may make individuals less prepared to take risks (see Carr-Hill and Stern, 1979, chapter 2A). The unemployed may perceive themselves to be subject to heavy punishment and this would also work to reduce offences. Finally, the employed may be less likely to commit offences if they fear unemployment more. There are, of course, influences which may operate the other way. Enforced idleness might lead to criminality through either more time available at low cost or because the unemployed were angered by their position. A drop in standard of living might lead the unemployed to attempt illegal ways of maintaining it and so on.

There are, therefore, a number of arguments either way and we cannot pretend that the effect of unemployment on behaviour is clear, *a priori*. It is important to note that this question of a link between unemployment and criminality is part of a wider debate within criminology as to the relationship between socio-economic status and criminality. It is instructive to note the conclusion of a contribution by Tittle *et al.* to a series of articles on this theme:

Finally, we do not know what the 'true' relationship between socio economic status and criminality is . . . [and] we do not believe he [Kleck], Braithwaite, or anybody else knows either . . . Our review of the comparable empirical literature suggests that our disciplinary faith in a negative relationship may be false and that we therefore ought to make sure our theoretical eggs are not all in one basket. (1984: 437)

Secondly, we have the possibility of effects operating through the recording of offences. Here firms may report more crime at times of high unemployment. And where offences are committed outside work they may be more visible. Thus, the effect of unemployment is probably to increase the likelihood of a given incident being recorded as an offence.

Thirdly, unemployment is likely to make it easier to recruit policemen: indeed it is striking that the police force, for the first time, reached their establishment levels (the numbers of police the authorities think are required) in the late 1970s. More policemen may imply either more recording or more deterring of crime. The effect could go either way.

Thus, taking these three *a priori* effects together we see that there is great ambiguity. We cannot pretend to know in advance of empirical investigation whether unemployment will increase or reduce recorded crime. It is not, however, helpful to say that 'the precise nature of the causal links between unemployment and crime are not of crucial concern' (Hakim, 1982: 453). Whether rising levels of (officially classified) unemployment lead directly to more (legally classified) crime or make it easier to recruit policemen or policewomen who 'find' more offences to record is of paramount importance in deciding upon policy both about crime and towards the 'necessity' for increased police surveillance of the unemployed. But the complexity of the relationships means that it will be very hard to learn from an empirical study which of the many effects are operating.

But what does one learn from the empirical studies? First, Carr-Hill and Stern (1979), in cross sectional studies for 1961, 1966 and 1977, found no significant effect of unemployment in the equation explaining recorded crime. This is in contrast to Hakim's commentary on our results (1982: 452) where she makes two claims. First she says that the authors' reject the hypothesis about unemployment contributing to crime on theoretical (subjective) grounds. We showed in our comment (Carr-Hill and Stern, 1983) how the effect of unemployment upon the (recorded) crime rate *could not* be tested in isolation from the processes determining the clear up or conviction rate and the number of policemen *per capita*. When we do that, the most probable conclusion is that unemployment affects the number of policemen *per capita* but nothing else. Second, she suggests that we were biased against official crime statistics and for data from self-report studies. Once again, in our comment we showed how our concern was with the quality (in terms of reliability and validity) of the data from whatever provenance. Whilst this led us to emphasise the importance of the social processes producing the official crime statistics, we did not rely on self-report studies in any of our interpretations.

Secondly, there is the much quoted study by Brenner (1976) which claimed to find for the UK a significant relationship showing that unemployment increased crime. However, his results cannot be taken seriously since he took no account of recording or simultaneity. Further, he used a time-series approach which must be regarded with suspicion since Stern and I found that the relationships changed quite markedly from one year to the next.

There have been several other empirical studies but there is no point in presenting their results at length here since there have been a number of useful recent surveys, for example by Tarling. He concluded (1982: 29):

Such studies are subject to a variety of difficulties not the least being that recorded crime may not be a true measure of the level of actual crime. These difficulties will be discussed later, but even leaving them aside the results of the studies do not satisfactorily resolve the question of the impact of unemployment on crime and no discernible pattern amongst the results emerges.

It is clear that the problem of disentangling the relationship between unemployment and crime is complex and simple examples of increases or decreases may be misleading. It is tempting, however, to look at simple historical cases and one or two examples may underline the difficulties involved.

Firstly, unemployment was very low during the second world war (below 1 per cent most of the time) yet recorded crime (in the form of indictable offences) rose by more than 50 per cent from around 300,000 at the beginning to approximately 470,000 at the end.

Secondly, unemployment rose sharply in the USA in 1982 but recorded crime fell by about 4 per cent. This led to articles purporting to explode the myth about the relationship between unemployment and crime (see, e.g. *The Standard*, 30 March 1983: 7). There should not have been a myth and in any case the figures for one year cannot clinch the case one way or the other.

Thirdly, Stern and I recently (1983 a) looked at the correlation between increases in unemployment, increases in the police and increases in recorded crime in England and Wales in the 1970s. Only that between increases in unemployment and increases in the police was statistically significant.

The conclusions from the *a priori* arguments, from the more systematic evidence, and from the preceding examples, must be that we just do not know whether or not unemployment causes crime. Stern and I concluded that 'This [analysis] puts increases in crime and their possible relation with increases in unemployment in a very different perspective . . . ' It is quite wrong to pretend that there is a well-attested relationship. Similarly, it is absurd to lay great emphasis on increases in total serious offences when most of that increase is due to a change in the proportion that is recorded. The issues involved are too serious to be treated in the casual way invoked in recent utterances. In particular, given that unemployment is likely to remain high for several years, it is grossly unfair on those who may be or become unemployed to associate them with an increase in criminality when the link is not established and the increase itself may be spurious.

It is more important to situate any relation between unemployment and crime within an overall context of law and order. Thus, research on how the unemployed are treated when they come in contact with the police, or are brought before the courts, or try and get parole would be useful. Similarly, the extent to which the promulgation of a probably mythical link between unemployment and crime has faciliated the extension of police powers during a period of rising unemployment would bear examination.

Research on unemployment

Whatever we may individually mean by 'unemployment' nearly all the research is obliged to take on board the official category on the basis of which unemployment statistics are collected and published. The definition adopted in the Census since 1951 encompasses those people out of work through the Census week who were seeking work or who had found a job which would start after the Census. The Department of Employment, who produce the monthly *Employment Gazette*, has, however, recently adopted a rather more 'fluid' approach to the definitional problem, especially in respect of school leavers.

However, whichever definition is used, it is obvious – or should be – that unemployment is not the same as not working or not wanting to work; conversely, employment is not the same as working or wanting to work. On one level, of course, this is 'just an ideological quibble' and determining the specificity of, for example, the category of 'not wanting to work but employed' is just an academic exercise. But, if we want to know *how* unemployment might relate to other statuses, then we have to know what the various characteristics of the sub-groups which go to make up the concept are and how those might motivate or predispose people.

Another obvious point is that the two categories of employed and unemployed are by no means exhaustive. In 1980 the majority (55.2 per cent) of the population of the UK were neither employed nor unemployed (these and other figures in this paragraph are from *Social Trends*). Whilst most of these are either children of school age (the under fifteens constitute 23 per cent of the population), or over retirement age (males 65 + and females 60 + contitute 17.5 per cent of the population), there is also a large category of housepersons and others (the remaining 14.7 per cent of the population). Are all these groups permanently depressed? lazy? suicide-prone? Obviously not – but they are also not in paid employment.

Apart from these definitional points, the research on the effects and impact of unemployment is myopic. What about the effects of the kind of jobs that present-day long-term unemployed are most likely to get if some government were returned to power on some kind of Keynesian platform to create jobs (whether in the state sector or by state fiscal intervention)? Consider the worries over the ignoring of safety regulations in the variety of temporary work schemes. What would they be producing and, as a corollary, asked to consume? As Andy Brown (1983) says:

Both Western and Economic systems function so as to absorb people's lives in struggles which have no meaning. The one system eggs on to work in order to consume, without ever establishing the meaning of work or the products we consume, while the other functions so as to break people's spirits [very unsociological that] and to teach them the value of obedience and conformity even at the cost of economic efficiency.

This kind of argument prompts discussion of a trend which is forgotten among the rising clamour over unemployment and . . . that is, the refusal to work. Some have argued that absenteeism and sabotage will disappear in the face of rising unemployment (Reeve, 1976). But, amidst growing unemployment there are contrary trends; first, workplace crimes or diddles including absenteeism remain popular (see Mars, 1983). Second, Britain has exceptionally low productivity in many industries. Compare the growth of OECD industrial production to the 'growth' in UK output over the last ten years (Department of Employment, 1984: 58). Third, the DHSS recently gave in to the rising levels of sickness claims by allowing employees to declare themselves sick for up to a week.

The research on the nature and impact of unemployment is very extensive. It *looks* thorough; in fact, the theoretical underpinnings of most of the research are flabby. Thus, Jahoda (1982) develops the following argument: that involvement in a paid job provides not only an income but also access to five socially important categories of experience (physical activity, social contact, collective purpose, a time structure and social status); she claims that these are crucial to the maintenance of psychological integrity. Peter Warr and Stephen Watkins have been making a similar point. But the social importance of physical activity, social contact, collective purpose, a time structure and social status are, in large part, *defined in terms of employment status*. I am sure that Charlie Brown would understand the problem.

What Jahoda, Warr, Watkins (and many others) seem to be trying to do is to promulgate a form of 'good' unemployment as against 'bad' unemployment. For example, the implications of Jahoda's argument are that new forms of activity and social organisation which improve unemployed people's access to the (five) categories of experience could have beneficial effects. Warr's ten characteristics of acceptable unemployment are: money, striving variety, goals/traction, decision latitudes, skill use and development, lack of psychological threat, security, interpersonal contact, valued social position. Watkins (1982) admits that 'it is probable that poverty contributes to the health damage of unemployment'. But 'probable' is only his third category of likelihood and he obviously thinks that the matter is not resolved because he concludes that 'more research is needed'. In contrast, he argues that the health damage of unemployment is clearly related to the importance of social support, the strength of the work ethic, self esteem and time structuring and he proposes a series of measures for 'sustaining the unemployed'.

Clearly, if Jahoda (1982), Warr and Watkins are right in claiming that the non-monetary characteristics of a job are more important (for health, for psychological well-being) than the *derived income* then this would have important implications for the organisation and viability of 'alternatives to employment'. First and foremost, there is nothing like full employment; and if you can't be employed then you should make unemployment as much like employment as possible through improving 'unemployed people's access to the categories of experience'.

One particular set of arguments revolves around the supposed trend towards the self-servicing economy. In this view, there will be an absolute increase in the total amount of unpaid work as households 'invest' in domestic capital goods and shift their labour resources into the increasingly productive 'informal' sphere. Gershuny (1983), comparing data over thirty years, comments that since the early 1960s all social classes have shown a similar fall in domestic work time. But this latter fall is due to an enormously increased *productivity* of domestic work – in other words, the total value (whether evaluated privately or social) of domestic work has almost certainly increased.

Instead, Gershuny and Pahl (1980) predicted not only that there might be a shift from the formal to domestic economy, as a reaction to high unemployment, new technology and government policies, but they also forecasted a great increase in informal work since the relative autonomy, personal fulfilment, self-direction and self-pacing which characterised it would, of itself, encourage its growth despite the lower financial rewards involved. Similarly, Clemitson and Rodgers (1981), Clark (1982) and Dauncey (1983) have written of the potential benefits to be derived from a positive approach to unemployment, e.g. lifelong education, occupational pluralism, community projects, 'sabbatical' schemes, developing hobbies, etc.

In contrast, Turner, Bostyn and Wight (1983) conclude after a case study of the work ethic in a situation of declining employment that

The values relating to work and consumerism are very persistent, even when a large proportion of the population lack prestige exactly because of this ideology. Very few of the unemployed come to terms with their situation by altering that attitude towards work, and most attempt to maintain their previous levels of consumption. (1983: 8)

Yet the case histories they quote do not really confirm this. Thus R.T. wants a job 'so long as it would be for what he considers a decent wage'; 'when M.S. discusses work, it is usually in terms of the money it brings'; J.O. 'does not want regular formal employment so much that he would accept a low paid job' and he would not take a very monotonous job (unless well paid); T.M. 'would take nearly any job – as long as it gave her at least £20 above the amount she [now] gets and as long as she found it enjoyable' (all taken from the Appendix to Turner, Bostyn and Wight, 1983: 9–16).

Whilst it seems to me quite possible that people will switch their energy and imagination to domestic work and the informal economy, this does not necessarily imply that people need to be involved in apparently productive activity all day. Indeed, there is little evidence that people will 'expand the work to fill the time available' (Parkinson, 1958: 4) if there is no increase in the actual output for them. Surely, Sahlins (1974) was right: many, perhaps most, people will gladly opt for a four-hour working day if they can live comfortably thereby.

Concluding remarks

In this brief tour of the research on the supposed links between unemployment and health, between unemployment and crime and on unemployment and work, I have been arguing that it is a distortion for research to concentrate on a narrow examination of how the unemployed fare or what they do independently of their change in income. We should, of course, be concerned with and do appropriate research on the basic issues of poverty and of unequal shares which, with the present *contingent* economic, political and social arrangements, are linked to being in or out of paid work. Thus, employment status is one, temporarily very visible, way of sorting people into rich and poor, high and low status, in our stratification system. The dominant characteristic for the disabled, those excluded from paid jobs, the low-paid, the sick – and the unemployed – is their poverty. Instead, the present direction of research on the impact of unemployment wrongly emphasises the work rather than the wage, and thus draw attention away from the fundamental problem of the distribution of income and wealth in our society.

Thus, whilst I agree with Hakim (1982) when she says:

As long as paid work is a financial, social psychological and moral imperative (for all men and for the great majority of non-married women), unemployment must

necessarily be an unwelcome, damaging and degrading experience carrying negative and deleterious consequences for those who are caught in it.
(Hakim, 1982: 461)

I cannot agree with her policy recommendations:

to make it a more positive experience, by removing the social stigma attached, by breaking down the rigid distinctions between paid employment and other productive or useful activities, by removing the stigma and suspicion attached to benefits provided for those not in paid employment, by removing perhaps the distinction between unemployment benefits and other social security benefits for those unable to work, or even moving towards a single maintenance scheme for people both in and out of employment.
(Hakim, 1982: 462)

She goes on to claim that:

such change might make it socially acceptable to share out more equitably available opportunities for paid employment and opportunities for other types of productive activity, be they voluntary work, child care, community work, education or training.
(Hakim, 1982: 461)

They will not: the attached tract (Appendix) shows the logical conclusion from Hakim's (and Jahoda's and Watkins's and Warr's) kind of argument. If we want to reach a situation where it is thought of as equally valuable to be in paid employment as being involved in voluntary work, etc., then the income we receive must be more or less independent of the work we do.

Appendix

When I read this tract a couple of months ago I gave a belly-laugh at its outrageous cynicism. Sadly, having read the papers for this workshop, I find it to be a rather accurate if somewhat wry commentary on the state of thinking about unemployment.

Millions of people, in present economic conditions, have difficulty in attaining the self-respect that comes from a long spell of that right and duty fundamental to all who have nothing but their chains, namely Wage Labour.

Whole generations now lack the incentive to wake up, one of the most salutary traditions of our way of survival. They miss the Monday Morning feelings so crucial to reproducing the good humour and regularity of the Honest Worker, who sweats productively, obediently, ever tightening his belt. Instead they fall into confusion, anguish, and deviance. Abstention from work seduces them into crime. Long term laziness only encourages disorder and sedition. Moreover, millions of scroungers now have to contend with the overwhelming guilt of receiving an income without being able to contribute to the community. Sociologists and psychologists agree. Work is the perfect optimal remedy for drug abuse, hooliganism, pederasty, bestiality . . .

In the sixties boom everyone (even women, blacks, and vegans) was encouraged to donate their surplus effort to the cause of Economic Growth. Some incorrigibles however, so far abandoned this wholesome ethic that they degenerated into refusing the enriching discipline of work by striking, go-slows, absenteeism, and sabotage.

Indifferent to the joys of travail, they made unrealistic wage demands. This threat to Civilization forced employers to remodel work. Through Austerity measures such as redundancy, speed-ups, incomes policy, inflation and other necessary remedies they have restored the Dignity of Labour.

For workers the current mass unemployment opens unexpected prospects for toiling harder, more exuberantly, teaching them to repress excessive expectations. They should grasp the chance of labouring not only for personal fulfilment or family obligation but for the Company, Investment, and Nation.

The Demand for the Right to Work fits excellently into the context of World Recession and will hopefully stimulate competition between those in jobs and those without. Workers should recognise the sanctity of this demand and cease all activity which threatens the rules of employment. This will maximise Job Satisfaction. Work must be valued once again – it's not enough just to do it for the money. And why be content with only 8 hours a day?

It is fitting to congratulate the entire Labour Movement for its efforts in organising on our behalf. The last Labour Government especially showed how union/government cooperation can make work bracing enough to be worth doing. The TUC must be encouraged to continue marching, regimenting, and representing the victims of blind market forces. How else are they to learn to go on their knees to beg?

The Left are also to be commended for refraining from complicating matters with excessively critical theory or over-imaginative activities. They help stabilize a dangerous situation by their diverting show of opposition. They popularize the litany that identifies class with work. Socialists all over the world are committed to elaborating the rewards of restraint. Through job-sharing, co-ops, and other ingenuities they aspire to reform the system so that none are excluded. For a lucky few they offer interesting jobs, participation, training, high morale. Accountable police will be given new powers to assist those genuinely seeking work.

A NEW HOPE

For all those temporarily denied a career but not oblivious to the gratifications of Exchange, We propose Local Authority grants for the following occupations:
1. Eradicating graffiti from walls, municipal buildings, churches, and toilets.
2. Voluntary work as soldiers or policemen in seaside resorts.
3. Mime classes to teach individuals to mimic work while at home.
4. Extension of Time and Motion principles to all sexual acts.
5. Moral re-education for absentee workers.
6. Haircut and alternative comedy competitions.
7. Poverty sharing, voting practice, and cycling lessons.
8. Aversion therapy for illegal or autonomous activity.

Remember: Sacrifice is not enough – we must immolate ourselves!
(from *Solidarity*, I, 3)

Political responses to unemployment

For a variety of reasons, including the predictions of virtually all British economists, a very reasonable expectation is that either moderately high (say between 5 and 10 per cent) or high (say above 10 per cent) rates of unemployment will persist throughout the 1980s. By 1990, moderately high or high unemployment will have prevailed for at least fifteen years. According to opinion polls, unemployment has been seen by the general public as the single most urgent problem facing this country since the summer of 1980; since then the proportion mentioning unemployment first in Gallup polls has always been above 80 per cent.

It would, in these circumstances, be surprising if detectable political reactions to unemployment did not emerge in some form or other, as indeed they appear in 1984 to be doing within, for example, the National Union of Mineworkers and the City Council of Liverpool. Yet very little, if any, systematic evidence is available on political responses to unemployment in the United Kingdom. Reviews of recent empirical evidence either make little or no reference to political reaction to unemployment (Showler and Sinfield, 1981; Sinfield, 1981) or else comment on their failure to find systematic evidence on the issue (Fraser, 1980). In part this strange silence may stem from problems in perceiving and specifying precisely what forms these might take.

Political response can be studied at national, community and individual levels, at least. Our current interests lie with individuals and communities; a consideration of the policies of governments, national political parties, trade unions and the like, with some regret has to be left to others. That division of labour reflects our own skills and capacities; it does not imply any judgement by us as to the most likely sources of overt political reactions. In the first section of this chapter, we shall review the literature relevant to three focuses for the study of political responses to unemployment. In the second section we shall briefly present some findings from an exploratory survey we conducted in Cambridge four days before the general election of June 1983, in which the views about unemployment of individuals of one community are related to their voting intentions.

Three focuses of enquiry

Of the various ways in which political responses to unemployment might be approached, three focuses are of particular interest to us.

1 *Unemployed individuals*

Such discussion of political reactions to unemployment as does occur appears to focus mainly on the unemployed themselves and to be dominated by two contradictory representations or orthodoxies.

The 'older orthodoxy' represents the hopes and fears which are derived from the notion that the unemployed are particularly likely to be politicised and radicalised by their experiences. Even though they may not be expected to destroy the integument of capitalism at one fell swoop, the unemployed, according to this view, are at least expected to become politically aware and involved, to march and protest, to vote for their interests, and perhaps occasionally to create mob mayhem. The persistence of this older outlook is revealed amongst a wide spectrum of politicians, as well as among the public at large, by homilies and warnings about the long-term danger to the social fabric of our land. Such homilies and warnings were particularly prevalent immediately following the urban riots of 1981, for which unemployment was the single most popular explanation offered by the general public, by most professional politicians who made their views known, and by a sample of the young unemployed (Kettle and Hodges, 1982; MORI, 1981).

At times other than during the aftermath of riots, however, a 'newer orthodoxy' has become commonplace in recent years. The unemployed, the argument runs, far from becoming politicised, become politically inactive and even withdrawn. After all, it has been persuasively argued that the internationally widespread, sustained unemployment of the 1930s, far from producing political revolutions, produced no single sustained political party or sustained large-scale protest movement from amongst the unemployed in any of the major industrialised countries (Garraty, 1978). And many people believe that the unemployed today have acquiesced in their own fates. Thus, the view that the unemployed become inert and apathetic is held to apply as readily to their political stances as to their mental states.

What does social science research have to say about these two contradictory views? In this country, surprisingly little, as has been noted above. But occasionally social scientists elsewhere, and particularly in the United States, have looked at one aspect or another of the political views and actions of unemployed people. Not surprisingly, the limited and scattered literature which we have been able to locate suggests that neither of the common orthodoxies is an adequate account of the political responses of the unemployed in recent years. The empirical evidence, which typically is derived from comparisons between samples of the currently employed and unemployed, suggest:

(i) unemployed samples do tend to express more critical and/or radical political attitudes than do employed samples: in USA, Schlozman and Verba (1979); Street and Leggett (1961); Useem and Useem (1979); in Cuba, Zeitlin (1966); in UK, Breakwell, *et al.* (1984).

(ii) when they vote, the unemployed tend to vote for parties inclined more towards higher public expenditure and economic expansion. They are more likely than the employed to vote Democratic in the USA (Kinder and Kiewiet, 1979; Schlozman and Verba, 1979) or Labour in this country (Economist Intelligence Unit, 1982). In the USA, unemployed Republicans are, possibly, more likely to switch parties than are employed Republicans (McIver, 1982; Schlozman and Verba, 1979) though voting Republican and voting for the incumbent were confounded.

(iii) the unemployed are less likely than the employed to register as voters and to turn out to vote: in USA, Rosenstone (1982); Schlozman and Verba (1979); in UK, Todd and Butcher (1982); Economist Intelligence Unit (1982).

(iv) the unemployed are less likely than the employed (in the USA) to be active participants in unions or other politically relevant organisations, to participate in political activities like letter-writing or money-giving, or to express an interest in politics (Schlozman and Verba, 1979); they are probably less likely to participate in traditional political activities or protest activities (Jackson, 1973).

(v) amongst the unemployed, those who are politically active or radical tend to be members of unions (Leggett, 1964; Aiken and Ferman, 1966 – in USA) or other workers' organisations (Klandermans, 1980 – in Netherlands; Gordon and Scott, 1972 – in USA).

Thus the evidence does not provide unequivocal support for either of the two 'orthodoxies'. Although points (iii) and (iv) appear to show that the unemployed tend not to be active participants in overt political action, point (ii) suggests that the unemployed are not completely passive, and points (v) and (i) seem to imply that increased organisation of the unemployed might tap critical political attitudes which are relatively common amongst the unemployed. A tentative generalisation might be that, in the absence of organisational support, the more commitment to action that a political response requires from an individual, the lower the proportion of those making it who will be unemployed. Such a claim might have some descriptive value, but should not be taken to imply psychological rather than structural determinants. And its tentativeness must be stressed, given the nature and quality of much of the evidence from which it is derived.

Little evidence comes from very recent years which have seen high unemployment levels in many countries. Most of the evidence comes from the United States and, for several reasons, may not be directly applicable to European societies. Only the most conventional of political activities have been examined. Problems of adequate sampling of 'the employed' and 'the unemployed', together with difficulties in distinguishing between differences associated with pre-unemployment characteristics of the unemployed samples, and differences relating to the experience of unemployment itself, characterise many of the studies. The practice of contrasting samples of the currently employed with samples of the currently unemployed as if current, and often temporary, employment status should explain all, is particularly problematic (see Daniel, 1981) and is elaborated elsewhere (Fraser and Marsh, 1984).

Despite these shortcomings, it is interesting to note that the findings of the three British studies included in the above review are compatible with the American evidence regarding points (i), (ii) and (iii). It should be noted, however, that Breakwell's evidence comes entirely from a smallish sample of young people, that the OPCS evidence is derived from a limited number of London boroughs, and that in all three studies the evidence relevant to political reactions was subsidiary to other aims and hence was of limited scope and depth. Only two other British studies are known to us. Robins and Wormalds (1979) reported that unemployed teachers became more politically active, though not more radical in their views, the longer they were unemployed. The sample size was not actually stated, but appears to have been very small. A MORI survey (1981) of young unemployed included some questions about attitudes towards unemployment as well as political attitudes. The data, and possible samples, are not of very high quality and there is no employment sample to act as a benchmark for comparing the views of the young unemployed.

Thus, the systematic British evidence is very limited indeed. As an absolute minimum, some descriptive investigations are called for on the political responses to unemployment of the unemployed in this country.

2 Employed individuals

There are at least two sets of reasons for justifying the study of the impact of unemployment on the political attitudes and behaviours of the employed population: (a) to help make better sense of the impact of unemployment on the political responses of the unemployed, including making better sense of the type of evidence cited above; (b) for its own sake.
(a) The studies above imply that, at least in a rough and ready way, the impact of the experience of unemployment is captured by the difference between the responses of samples of the unemployed and samples of the employed. One difficulty which has already been pointed to concerning that view is that in many studies it is not possible to separate the effects of unemployment itself from pre-existing differences between the employed and unemployed.

A second major difficulty relates to the absence of adequate information about changes, in response to changing levels and prospects of unemployment that may already have occurred amongst the employed. If, for example, rising unemployment had already increased the prevalence of politically radical attitudes amongst the employed, then the observed mean differences between employed and unemployed samples could underestimate the radicalisation that had occurred amongst the unemployed. On the other hand, if increasing unemployment had strengthened conservative attitudes amongst the employed, then the unemployed/employed difference would overestimate the radicalising effects of unemployment on the unemployed. A third difficulty with looking for the effects of unemployment among the unemployed arises from the impossibility of distinguishing them sharply from the employed; many of those currently employed will have had recent experience of unemployment, and some of those currently unemployed will have reasonable expectations of shortly re-entering employment.

The implication of these arguments is that a major investigation of political responses to unemployment should include not only a comparison of unemployed and employed but should also be conducted longitudinally, for example, as a panel study.

(b) The employed, however, are worthy of study in their own right. For they, rather than the unemployed, may prove to be the focus of major political reactions to unemployment. In the case for example, of Germany in the inter-war years, numerous studies of voting patterns (e.g. Lipset, 1960; McKibbin, 1969; Childers, 1976; Bessel, 1982) demonstrate the naivety of examining only the voting behaviour of the unemployed in an attempt to understand the role of unemployment in Hitler's rise to power. And some studies of much more recent American voting behaviour (e.g. Brody and Sniderman, 1977; Kinder and Kiewiet, 1981) claim that variations in voters' perceptions of the nation's economic and political condition are better predictors of voting behaviour than are differences in first-hand experiences of economic problems and difficulties.

Thus study of attitudes amongst the employed towards the unemployed, levels of unemployment, fear of unemployment, and government's responsibility for unemployment levels should be part of the study of political responses to unemployment. To the best of our knowledge, such information is almost non-existent.

The studies reviewed on pp. 353–4 are of little help. Typically they made no attempt to assess relations between variations in attitudes towards (or even past experience of) unemployment on the part of the employed and variations in their political views and actions. The most ambitious and informative of recent studies (Schlozman and Verba, 1979) raised such issues, but decided 'not to attempt to determine the degree to which attitudes towards unemployment colour partisan identifications' (305).

The only British evidence which, as yet, we have managed to locate consists of snippets from opinion polls. From two Gallup polls (November 1980 and January 1982) it appears that the public is very ready to blame both the unemployed for lack of effort and the government for doing too little about unemployment. In both surveys, two-thirds of the employed expressed confidence about security of their own and their families' jobs.

Again, however, the conclusion must be that detailed, systematic descriptive studies of political responses to unemployment amongst the employed themselves need to be undertaken to help elaborate the very inadequate and sketchy information currently available on their views.

The unemployed and the employed together constitute the economically active population. Over one-third of the adult population is 'inactive', including housewives, students, the disabled, the sick, the retired. Even less information exists regarding their responses to unemployment as an issue.

3   Local political structures and organisations

There is a danger that surveys of samples of employed and unemployed individuals may inadvertently lead to an unduly individualistic account of political reactions, or lack of reactions, to unemployment. In our view, Schlozman and Verba (1979), for example, did not succeed in avoiding that danger. Their model of political mobilisation appears to imply that individual unemployment and deprivation will eventually lead to individual political response without any form of social or organisational mediation being necessary. Although one hypothesised mediating factor is increased class consciousness, no social mechanism is postulated for bringing that increase about. The implicit model is one whereby large numbers of unemployed individuals separately experience the same sequence of psychological changes and, as a result, independently hit on the same sets of overt political reactions. If they were ever to engage in collective protest or action they would, presumably, create the meeting or march by chance.

One safeguard against falling prey to such views is to study the part played by formal political structures, parties and organisations in conditioning or creating reactions to unemployment, and our interests and competences lead us to do so at a local, rather than national level. Again, there are two sets of reasons for such a focus.

First, the study of local political tradition, culture and organisation should throw light on variations in political reactions amongst employed and unemployed individuals. As we suggested above by the studies in point 1(v), awareness of, membership of and access to relevant parties, unions and organisations should be a major factor in encouraging, or inhibiting, the political responses of individuals. Knowledge of such links to political organisations directly or indirectly concerned with unemployment may help us understand variations within as well as differences between samples of employed and unemployed individuals. We know of no evidence of this kind from studies conducted in this country.

Secondly, the study of local political organisations and responses to unemployment is of considerable interest in its own right. It may well be that the origins of political reactions lie in such organisations and that very large samples of individuals would have to be drawn before enough activists were identified by survey methods to justify any claim to having detected a political response at all. Local political organisation as a context for the development – or inhibition – of individual political views, involvement and action is, to the best of our knowledge, a relatively unresearched area as far as the issue of unemployment itself is concerned. But there are related literatures which can be of some help. The 1960s marked the high point of 'political culture' as a concept and framework for research and analysis. The foundations of this approach to the study of political interest and action of groups and individuals having been laid down by a number of American political scientists (e.g., Almond and Verba, 1963; Pye and Verba, 1965), the ideas entered British political analysis via American contributors such as Nordlinger (1967) and British sociologists, or sociologically orientated political scientists such as Mackenzie and Silver (1968).

More recently there have been attempts to identify and analyse local political and historical traditions without explicit reference to political culture as such. These studies serve to show that individual political beliefs and action occur and develop in the context of collectively shared experience. Examples of local militant traditions examined in this way include Branson's (1981) study of Poplarism in the 1970s and McIntyre's (1981) study of 'little Moscows' between the wars. Local political life in parts of London during the 1960s, and subsequently, has also received some attention, in the contexts of both general discussions of community politics and activism (e.g. Hain, 1976) and consideration of specific areas and issues, for example Lambeth and the housing/squatting issue (Cockburn, 1977). The overlapping of trade union organisation and political experience in areas of traditional industries and distinct occupational communities has been noted by numerous authors, e.g. Hill's (1976) study of London dockers. Finally, recent studies of collective responses to threats of specific mass redundancies – e.g. Herron (1975), Rainie and Stirling (1981) and Coates (1981) on resistance to closures in shipbuilding and ship-repairing on the Clyde and the Tyne; and Baker (1981) on resistance to the BSC closures at Corby – provide some insight into the strengths and weaknesses of industrial and local political cultures in promoting or inhibiting such resistance industrially and politically.

Although each of these lines of work, and indeed others not mentioned, may throw some light on our current concerns, none of them has directly examined the extent to which local political organisation has been penetrated and affected by the growth of unemployment. Equally, the impact of organised labour, and its expressed views on unemployment, upon communal political consciousness at a local level merits study.

4 *Comment*

In this review of three focuses of enquiry, the primary emphasis has been on descriptive empirical research rather than on the elaboration of theoretically derived questions. That has been deliberate. It is not that we are unaware of or uninterested in theoretical issues. As has been implied in passing, we see many important theoretical questions which could and, eventually, should be related to the phenomena which interest us. These include, from social psychology, questions of attitude-behaviour relations and the importance for action of different patterns of causal attributions, and, from sociology, issues concerning relations between work situation, class consciousness and ideology, as well as questions relating to local political organisation and culture. Above all, we expect that in the future we shall examine critically and constructively existing theoretical analyses of political mobilisation. In the light of our own, cross-disciplinary interests and backgrounds, we hope that one of our eventual theoretical contributions will be a systematic examination of interactions between structural analyses of political culture and organisation, on the one hand, and social psychological experiences and changes of individuals on the other. But sound empirical evidence from the United Kingdom which could help guide and constrain such theoretical endeavours is so close to being totally non-existent that we feel the first priority must be description rather than theory building.

Unemployment as an issue and voting intentions

This second part is offered as a modest contribution to the description of the impact of unemployment on one aspect, voting intentions, of the political responses of the non-unemployed, i.e. the employed and those deemed economically inactive, whose reactions, as pointed out on p. 356, have been relatively unstudied. It reports some findings from a survey conducted in Cambridge four days before the general election of June 1983, supplemented where possible by data drawn from national surveys. A number of the issues raised have been discussed in national terms by Richardson and Moon (1984). Technical details of fieldwork and sampling are given in Marsh (1984); only a summary is presented here.

Staff and students of the Social and Political Sciences Committee of the University of Cambridge designed and carried out a survey of electors in the Cambridge constituency for the *Cambridge Evening News*. A two-stage systematic random sample of the whole electorate was drawn. Interviews were obtained with 455 electors, representing 59 per cent of the potential respondents whom we have no reason to believe could not be interviewed, a response rate which, though not as high as was hoped for, represents something of an achievement for an untrained fieldforce working on a particularly fine summer Sunday. The sample was well spread across all the wards of the constituency; employed persons appear to have been somewhat overrepresented, and retired and unemployed persons somewhat under-represented but weighting the sample to correct for those biases had a neg-ligible effect on aggregate voting intentions. Only 2 per cent of the sample described themselves as currently unemployed rather than the 4 per cent which might have been expected from the census data (see Marsh, 1984), and thus we could not examine correlates of current unemployed status. All respondents were asked voting intention and biographical questions. A random sub-sample were also asked a number of questions about experience and attitudes towards unemployment. Most of what follows depends upon this sub-sample of 125 respondents.

The interviewers were university and sixth-form college students, carefully briefed but otherwise untrained. Because of that, the interview schedule avoided open-ended questions, problematic codings and complex filters, which meant that some questions were simplified into closed options more quickly than we would have desired. The questionnaire proved relatively problem free in actual administration.

Some findings relating past first-hand experience of unemployment and current contact with the unemployed to reported political responses other than voting intentions are presented elsewhere (Fraser and Marsh, 1984). What follows is an account of our data on the impact of unemployment as an issue on individuals' reported voting intentions.

Unemployment as an election issue

The most straightforward way of ascertaining the importance of unemploy-ment in an election is to see if people nominate it as an important election issue. 71 per cent of our sample thought it was the most important issue facing Britain today, a very similar result to the findings of the national polls. This is much higher than in 1979, when the proportion was only 32 per cent (BBC/Gallup, 1979). Moreover, the proportion climbed steadily throughout the campaign, from 50 per cent at the end of April to 71 per cent in the week before the election (*Sunday Times*/Mori I–IV, 1983).

However, it is easy to overinterpret the significance of unemployment as a major election issue for the individuals who voice this reply. In the Cambridge survey, unlike most others, respondents were also asked if the issue they had named as the most important for the country would be the most important in influencing how they would vote, and 44 per cent said it would not. For many voters the first question was a test of their knowledge of 'the' election issues, rather than a personal value statement. For only 40 per cent of the Cambridge electors was unemployment both the most important issue facing the country and the issue that would have most influence on their vote.

Nevertheless, 59 per cent in our version of this question claimed that it was the top or second top issue in influencing how they would vote. But before this reported belief in the importance of a single issue can be translated into a vote for a party promising to do something about unemployment, at least two conditions would seem to have to be satisfied: people must be convinced that parties and policies can have an impact upon unemployment; then they must value one party as having a 'better' policy for dealing with the issue than other parties.

Ability of parties to influence unemployment

The first stage in the process of turning unemployment into an election issue involves people believing that the future course of unemployment is altered by an election. One common way of approaching this is to obtain from respondents their perception of what would happen to unemployment if each party got in.

This question was put to electors by Gallup before the 1979 election, and showed clearly the ignorance that existed at the time about the likely consequences for unemployment of the Conservative's deflationary economic policy; 59 per cent believed that unemployment would stay the same or go down if they won in 1979. Moreover, Mrs Thatcher managed to sustain and increase this tide of economic optimism throughout her period of office. Monitoring of repeated MORI findings on 'Perceptions of the future of the economy' reveals a striking pattern which may well help to explain why there has not been the popular outcry that many predicted would ensue from high levels of unemployment. From the general election of 1979 to that of 1983, as the number of officially unemployed steadily increased, so did the percentage expressing confidence in the future of the economy. Those expecting it to get worse steadily declined in number, while those expecting it to improve steadily increased, until by May 1983, the latter were more numerous than the former.

Table 19.1, from our Cambridge survey, suggests some change from the Gallup results of 1979, but perhaps not as much as might have been expected. It is interesting to note that, although the Labour Party was selected by a majority as the party most likely to reduce unemployment, a sizeable proportion also thought that it would increase unemployment, larger than the proportion was thought an Alliance win would increase unemployment. A breakdown of table 19.2 by party support (not shown here) reveals unsurprisingly that Labour supporters are the most convinced that their party could deal with unemployment, and that Alliance supporters were most pessimistic about the effect of a Conservative victory, but much less optimistic than Labour supporters about the Labour Party's ability to solve the problem.

These findings from the Cambridge survey may seem at first sight to be contradicted by other national findings. The *Sunday Times* panel, for example, was asked whether it agreed or disagreed with the statement:

'Whatever government is in power, unemployment will remain over two million throughout the 1980s', and an unwavering majority of over 80 per cent endorsed this at all stages of the election campaign. It may be, however, that this question elicited a strong acquiescence bias. Furthermore, since the majority of Cambridge respondents who thought unemployment would come down felt it would so 'a little', the two sets of figures are not necessarily contradictory.

Table 19.1 Perception of future unemployment

Question: If there is a . . . government after this election, then over the next five years do you think unemployment levels will:

If	Conservative	Labour	Alliance government
Go up a lot/little	48	29	21
Stay about the same	30	20	38
Come down a little/lot	22	51	41
	(N = 118)	(N = 116)	(N = 111)

We split our sample into two groups: those who appear to think parties could alter the course of unemployment, because they did not answer each question about the effect of a victory for each party identically, and those who saw no difference. We found 80 per cent giving different responses, and, among those with experience of unemployment the proportions were even higher.

To argue that people clearly perceive differences amongst the parties in their policies on unemployment is not the same as arguing that they think such policies are the major causes of unemployment. After piloting some of the commoner reasons given for the current high levels of unemployment, we offered our respondents a choice of eleven, and asked them to say whether they thought they were very important, quite important or not important as reasons. The responses are shown in table 19.2, and presented in rank order of popularity of the explanation.

Only two of the profferred explanations were not supported by a majority – 'level of unemployment benefit' and 'married women wanting jobs'. The very large number of endorsements for each explanation suggests that in future we shall have to find ways of exploring other people's beliefs more subtly, without inducing acquiescence bias.

It is striking that the most popular explanation was that it is the world recession that causes unemployment. The policies of the Conservative government were seen as very or quite important by 80 per cent of our sample, but only come third in the list, after world recession and lack of investment. The rank order of explanations shown in table 19.2 held good for those who had contact with the unemployed as well as those with none. The only variable which produced significant differences was car ownership, a proxy measure of wealth. The better off you were the more likely you were to blame the trade unions and the less likely the government.

Table 19.2   Popular explanations of unemployment

Question: Could you tell me whether, in your view, each of the following is *very important, quite important*, or *not important* as a cause of current unemployment.

| | Importance: | | |
	Very	Quite	Not
World recession	57	37	6
Lack of investment/modernisation	41	50	9
Policies of present Conservative government	42	38	20
Inflation	28	52	20
Quality of managers in British industry	31	47	22
New technology	36	38	26
High wage rates	25	44	31
The trade unions	17	47	36
Immigration to Britain	20	32	48
Married women wanting jobs	14	33	52
The level of unemployment benefit	15	32	53

(Average: N = 105)

We performed a factor analysis of responses to these eleven items, and found that the second factor to emerge was a simple distinction between those who blamed world recession and those who blamed the government; perhaps in a future survey we should force a choice between these two. The first dimension selected respondents who tended to blame women working, high dole levels, immigration, high wages and trade unions.

In conclusion, then, these results suggest that the general public did perceive major differences between the parties on this issue; the first condition for turning unemployment into an election issue seems to have been met. While 80 per cent laid some blame for past unemployment at the government's door, we noted, however, that two other explanations of unemployment were more frequently endorsed, and that the government's policies was only one of half-a-dozen explanations endorsed with very high frequency.

Party with the best policy on unemployment

Cognitions alone are insufficient, however. We want to know how people value various consequences and policies if we are to understand their impact on voting. The Labour Party was still perceived as the party with the best policies on unemployment; of those who thought it the most important issue, 41 per cent thought Labour, 36 per cent thought the Conservatives and 23 per cent thought the Alliance 'would be best at handling it'. Results from a national poll lead one to wonder what this question means to respondents;

when asked 'which political party do you think has the best policies on unemployment?', 32 per cent said Labour, 28 per cent said Conservative and 16 per cent said Alliance (Mori/Yorkshire TV, 1983). However, when the same respondents were asked 'Which party's policies do you think would be most likely to bring about *a long term* reduction in the level of unemployment?' (our emphasis) 34 per cent said Conservative, 28 per cent said Labour, and 16 per cent said Alliance. It seems as though one should be very careful to link expectations of the future to rather precise time limits.

Moreover, the BBC/Gallup surveys document that the Labour Party had lost ground since 1979 as the party best equipped to deal with unemployment, and the *Sunday Times* panel surveys show that it lost further ground during the election; the steepness of the decline was so sharp that it suggests that the party lost the intellectual battle in the eyes of the public. There was therefore considerable doubt in the mind of the public about the likely success, especially in the long term, of Labour's unemployment policy.

At the end of the day, of course, it is interesting to see if these cognitive and attitudinal items actually correlated with voting intention. There was a clear differentiation by party in naming unemployment as an important influence upon how they would vote, with two-thirds of Labour supporters naming it, 54 per cent of Alliance supporters and 37 per cent of Conservative supporters. This, however, does not mean that it was people worried about unemployment who voted Labour; it is equally plausible that it was Labour supporters who were worried about unemployment.

Conclusions

Cambridge voters, like the country at large, saw unemployment as the most important issue facing Britain today, but as attitude-behaviour models which stress the need for comparability of generality or specificity of attitude and action (e.g. Ajzen and Fishbein, 1980) might predict, by no means all who held that general view were likely to act on it when it came to casting their specific vote. Many voters did see differences amongst the parties regarding their policies on unemployment, but there was only a small difference between Labour and Conservative, favouring the former, with regard to which party was seen as having the best policies on unemployment, and in a national poll that difference was reversed when respondents were asked about policies for a long-term reduction in unemployment.

Those findings give us some clues as to why the existence of mass unemployment did not sink the government at the last election. Other clues are given by the evidence pointing to the government's success in at least partially decoupling the link between perception of the problem of unemployment and perception of governmental responsibility for it (Richardson and Moon, 1984), and by the government's apparent ability, in the fact of ever-worsening unemployment to convince increasing numbers of voters that the economy would improve.

The first part of this chapter implied that the likely, non-governmental sources of political response to unemployment are as yet by no means clear. The second part suggests that, so far, one effective political response has been that of the Conservative government in communicating the view of unemployment and economic change that it wishes to see prevail.

Section six

Household roles in the changing economy

The papers in this part jointly start from the perspective that, rather than juxtaposing men (*qua* economic actors) to women (*qua* domestic managers), the domestic *and* the employment involvement of both men and women should be seen as equally problematic. Thus questions are raised about the implications of economic arrangements and changes for gender roles within the household, about the results of unemployment for both the men and women themselves *and* for their spouses, and the ways in which activities and roles within the household may or may not be changing in response to the current economic situation, together with the possible effects of this within the household itself and more widely.

From this, one of the main themes to emerge is the economic significance of the household itself. Household work, well described as 'self-provisioning' in Pahl and Wallace's paper, not only takes up much time (especially but not exclusively women's) but also, it seems, forms one essential part of non-market economic activity. Further, social relations and expected roles within the household apparently often crucially affect both careers in the formal job market outside the household (most obviously for women, as discussed in the paper by Barrère-Maurisson *et al.*) and thus, perhaps, ultimately the well-being of the household and its members as a whole.

The research reported here questions some previous assumptions about the social implications of current economic patterns. One prediction of the response to recent high levels of unemployment was that as the formal economy (of paid jobs) shrank, so informal opportunities would expand: in the 'black' economy, through unpaid work and exchanges in the local community, or within the household. This expectation, partly stimulated by some of Pahl's earlier work, was sometimes expressed in the optimistic form that, despite unemployment, people could just keep up their standard of living by transferring from formal to 'informal' economic spheres. Several papers here throw doubt on that expectation (also the paper by Turner *et al.* in section seven). It is clear both from the paper by Pahl and Wallace (helpfully honest about the ways in which their actual findings failed to confirm earlier expectations) and, from McKee and Bell's report, that it may well be precisely those households who have the *time* to engage in unpaid work (being unemployed) that lack the financial resources to carry it through (no money to buy paint for home decorating is one vivid example). In terms of perceived value too, any increase in time spent on domestic work (by the unemployed women studied by Martin for instance) is not regarded as sufficient compensation for the social as well as economic rewards of employment – domestic work, it appears, cannot in practice fill the gap of the job that had been lost. There are also some indications (noted especially by Pahl and Wallace) of an increasing polarisation between earning and non-earning households, the former, perhaps paradoxically, more likely to be able to engage in informal and self-provisioning activities, a polarisation sometimes leading, for the less fortunate, to a sense of despair. How far this polarisation in access to economic resources and activities is confined just to certain areas or dates, and how far it is a generally emerging pattern remains one of the tasks for further research.

The second expectation questioned by some of the research here is of a likely shift in domestic and employment roles, as they are renegotiated to meet current economic changes, particularly widespread unemployment. As men become redundant, for example, will women become the breadwinners and/or men take over domestic tasks once assumed to be the preserve of women? The papers here suggest that the gender division of labour within and outside the household is a complex matter not to be easily summarised, but certainly do not support this perhaps facile expectation in any simple manner. The social concepts of male versus female spheres within the household are certainly not a given of nature, but nevertheless appear deep-seated in our society and to be held by women as well as men. (Interestingly, it appears in examples cited in the papers by both Morris and McKee and Bell that it is women no less than men who sometimes see a threat in any move to change the traditional division of labour within the household.) There is also the significant finding, noted in the same two papers, that it is often in precisely those families where the men are, or have become, unemployed that women are least likely to have a paid job: something perhaps due not only to the perceived constraints of social security arrangements and to the lack of opportunities in specific localities but also to certain abiding concepts about the social division of labour. Certainly there have been changes over the years in male and female expectations – not least in female aspirations *outside* the household, well brought out in Martin's study – but it seems that the framework of male and female spheres within the household goes deep, to be negotiated in part, perhaps, in relation to particular tasks and situations, but not readily relinquished *in toto*.

Indeed, the other theme that emerges from the papers here is the significance of people's values, diverse and varied as these are. There are of course very real constraints on people's choices (some of them, as several contributors note, with 'tragic' implications), but at the same time not everything is determined by economic motivation in the narrow sense. Up to a point people *choose* to engage in the kind of self-provisioning described in Pahl and Wallace, *prefer* to maintain male and female spheres in the household (mentioned in almost all the papers). Social arrangements within the household are, it is clear, directly affected by current economic changes; but at the same time the values associated with the family and the socially constructed division of labour related to it do not just follow the economic, but have their own effect on the organisation of economic life.

Forms of work and privatisation on the Isle of Sheppey

Speculation about the future of industrial society was encouraged by the observation, widely noticed in the 1960s, that the motor of industrial development could be maintained with fewer workers. This has led to a focus on the shift in the *nature* of employment: jobs in the manufacturing sector may decline, but many considered that the service sector would then expand to take up the slack. For a time this indeed seemed likely. The expansion of education, health and welfare in the 1960s encouraged commentators to extrapolate such an expansion of employment to other new spheres: whole new sectors of service employment were envisaged. This shift from manufacturing to the service sector was compared with the shift from the primary, mainly agricultural, sector into the secondary or manufacturing sector at an earlier period. The transition might be painful – particularly for individuals – as it seemed unlikely that displaced male factory workers could be readily retrained as office workers or computer programmers.

Two main themes stimulated our work; namely, the decline of manufacturing employment and an understanding of the complexities of forms of service provision, particularly as this relates to activities of household members within their local areas. Evidently, the growth of domestic technology is a new and significant trend which deserves careful analysis, both for its implications for class and gender relations and for its impact on forms of employment. The imputed growth of unpaid work of household members in the home can be seen to be related both to affluence and to the recession and the growth of a pauperised unemployed element. Any notion of 'the' household acting in a universal and distinctive way is surely hard to sustain, but without detailed analyses of specific household work practices, the argument could not be developed. This encouraged us to develop a deeper understanding of all forms of work in context, by focusing on the specific work practices of a sample of households in a given labour market.[1] Once the unexceptional point is made that not all economic activity is counted or analysed by economists, there is little more analytical value in the term 'informal economy'. We do, nevertheless, distinguish three kinds of work which we relate to three distinctive spheres.

In the *first* sphere, the social relations of work are determined by the way the formal demand for labour is constructed or determined: wage labour may be recorded or unrecorded, protected or unprotected and the social relations of wage labour may be more or less modified or moderated by the actions of the state.[2] Where wages and salaries are exchanged for labour, we argue that the nature of work is intrinsically the same whether or not that work is formally recorded in the national accounts. Within this sphere there may be petty commodity production with its distinctive social relations of work and which again has its undeclared, darker side or shadow. How far this 'shadow' wage labour and a *fortiori* petty commodity production is accurately recorded in national accounts is to a degree arbitrary, depending on the state policies at the time.

In the *second* sphere of domestic work, we refer to all the production and consumption of goods and services undertaken by members of the household within the household for themselves, irrespective of the pattern of motivations determining these activities and the pattern of constraints under which they may or may not be done. Here the emphasis is on who does the work and where it is done. This is essentially the sphere of self-provisioning.

The *third* sphere refers to all those activities carried out by members of other households, whether or not they are related to them. By and large this work does not depend on payment, or, if it does, the payment is not based on strictly market principles. More likely, goods and services are exchanged according to norms of reciprocity, which may, in particular localities, be extremely forceful and binding. However, again we are concerned with all this activity, irrespective of the pattern of motivation or the pattern of constraints under which the work may or may not be done. Here the work is defined by the distinctive social relationships and local context in which it is embedded.[3]

These three spheres are not necessarily mutually exclusive, nor should they be considered to relate to distinct physical contexts. Evidently petty commodity production very often takes place in the household and reciprocal exchanges can take place at the formal workplace. However, the analytical distinctions between these three spheres are important as means of understanding more clearly all forms of work taking place in distinct territories. The intention is to understand how these three spheres of work interrelate and how the whole assemblage of work in distinctive milieux relate to the restructuring of capital and the current economic recession.

We began by expecting to be able to document the *shifts* between these distinctive spheres of work as households developed more ways of getting by under difficult circumstances.[4] As will be explained below, this expectation was not validated.

It is important to avoid too mechanistic an approach. People's work

practices differ substantially – even under broadly the same material conditions. Evidently, what people do is as much dependent on their cultural
values as on the exigencies of the local labour market, the current practices
of the political system or the opportunities presented by technological
innovation. Happily, people do not respond uniformly and puppet-like to
oscillations in the cycles of capital accumulation or to Kondratieff cycles of
product innovation and development. Nor, indeed, are patterns of behaviour
entirely voluntaristic and independent of material conditions. This dialectical
interaction is the essence of the process that structures social formations.
A realistic research strategy demands some simplification and our present
position is to disaggregate household work practices into *specific tasks done
by members of specific households in specific contexts.* In this way we ground
our theoretical argument in detailed empirical observation and analysis. The
work practices of households are perhaps too frequently disaggregated into
the economic activity of individuals, as if the social relations of the household
and the context in which households live were of little importance.

The context for household work practices

A concern with the work undertaken by households without putting those
households in context may well produce generalisations which mask crucial
variations. As we remarked above, one of the inevitable weaknesses of the
aggregated data is that households are plucked out of context, or the context
has to be aggregated up to a level at which important local differences cease
to have significance.

Whilst each household is in some way unique in the way it allocates its
time and resources to get work done, distinctive patterns emerge dominated,
of course, by the need to get money from land (rent), capital (interest), labour
(wages) or the state (benefits and allowances). Hence the markets for land,
labour and capital and the nature, range and style of state intervention and
provision crucially determine the potential for household work strategies.
Furthermore, these factors change in emphasis and importance over time:
the changing market for land and the changing availability of skilled labour
may be crucially important in, as it were, 'allowing' a given style of household work strategy to emerge. Once a given pattern has emerged with its distinctive practices, this in turn helps to reflect back upon and partially creates
the material conditions for a later period. However, it should be emphasised
that the centrality of the household work strategy is not intended to imply
that the actions of households are the central determinants of economic and
social life. It is simply that we see the actual *practices* of households as being
a useful tracer of the effects of the restructuring of capital in specific milieux.
The same process of investment can have different consequences in different
milieux and this is both revealed in and caused by household work strategies.

In order to put our detailed knowledge of household behaviour into its material context, we did parallel studies of the local context, the Isle of Sheppey in Kent, a detailed account of which would be complex and lengthy.[5] The island presents a distinctive pattern of opportunities and constraints and it is to this that households must accommodate more or less passively.

Different layers of investment on the Isle of Sheppey took place at different historical periods and in different sectors of the local economy. The interaction of these flows of capital into land, housing and industry created a distinctive local political economy based on distinct social milieux in different parts of the island. The involvement of the state in directing capital and providing intrastructure is also important.[6]

In terms of present-day employment, it is clear that a heavy dependence on manufacturing and a poorly developed service and small business sector makes the island dependent on the fluctuating market for its manufactured products. In 1983, the level of unemployment was hovering around 20 per cent. A survey of its main employers in 1981 had demonstrated that its vulnerability was likely to continue: if economic conditions improved, employers were likely to put in more capital equipment in the hope of maintaining jobless growth in productivity, and if the economic climate did not improve, many saw the likelihood of closure or of moving their plants overseas. By and large, wage rates were very modest: skilled manual workers earning around £120 per week and semi-skilled workers around £85 a week at the time of the survey in 1981. Twenty per cent of the jobs in the largest twenty-five employers of labour were done by women. Increasingly, employers in manufacturing industries prefer to employ female factory workers: they receive lower rates of pay, being classified as semi-skilled workers, no matter how objectively skilled the work they do may be, and women are also more likely to be employed on a part-time basis with the greater insecurity that this implies. In so far as one can generalise about typical households of ordinary working people, it does seem that not only does the local labour market depend increasingly on female labour in the factories, but households are increasingly dependent on the extra income provided by a further earner.

We may summarise the position for the workers of the Isle of Sheppey as being extremely precarious. Low wages and the need for multiple earners for households to get by puts an added squeeze on those without employment. Most people in the island find employment through friends and relatives. Evidently that is easier if members of the household are already in employment, since they are much more likely to find or to hear of employment for their partners or older children than those who are unemployed. Employment tends to generate further employment; unemployment tends to generate further unemployment. Wives of the unemployed tend to find it not worth their while to carry on working when their earnings are offset against the unemployment and/or supplementary benefits to their husbands.

The particular characteristics of the local employment situation make it extremely difficult for youngsters to find work. With no office development and an underdeveloped service sector, job opportunities are limited and most employers prefer to employ a married woman part-time than what may unfairly seem to be an untried and risky youngster. Hence, few youngsters are likely to be able to afford to establish their own household for many years after leaving school. Many are, therefore, forced to stay at home and play some part in the work strategy of their parents' household.

The local labour market, therefore, encourages multiple-earner households by the level of wages, the opportunities for employment for married women and the lack of long-term job prospects for youngsters. In certain male occupations, such as stevedores, which are highly paid but which make less demands in terms of time and physical effort, more time and energy are available for other activities. This provides a distinctive type of household headed by a manual worker with time, resources and very often craft skills: it is perhaps unsurprising that when these households have multiple earners they are particularly well-placed to engage in a wide range of domestic activities.

There are other aspects of the local context which should also be emphasised. House prices on the island are substantially less than on the mainland.[7] The differential in house prices is greater than the differential in wages. Furthermore, there is an existing stock of dwellings available for owner-occupation due to the construction of housing for dockyard workers already described. A programme of private refurbishing, making use of what grants were available, enabled people to get better accommodation for a given expenditure than was possible at that level of income in other contexts. In this sense, dwellings in less adequate condition can be seen as a resource to be exploited by households to improve both their existing conditions and their capacity for capital accumulation.

There has also been a tradition on the island since the early years of the century for people to acquire land and to build their own dwellings, either with their own labour, with the help of colleagues, or by commissioning a local builder to do it for them (Pahl and Wallace, 1982). Sometimes ownership was ambiguous: determined or devious people could get access to land in a way not normally possible in many localities. Public services and facilities were often rudimentary: sewerage and street lighting were slow in coming and the roads are still not all made up. It is evident that this is very fertile ground for the development of a flourishing petty bourgeois ideology of domesticity and an inward-looking privatisation.

The island has a singularly high level of home ownership. Also, the local authority is supporting a policy of sale of its own stock of dwellings to individual households. It is perhaps therefore not surprising that as seven out of ten households on the island own their own homes, there will inevitably be substantial home refurbishing and maintenance. The material and ideological encouragement for such activity is substantial: Sheppey is a frontier of privatisation.

There is also very strong material encouragement for the private acquisition of the means of transport. The island is not well served by public transport. Most of the services are centred in Sheerness at the north-west tip of the island. However, the hospital is at Minster in the centre of the island and, in the summer, the beaches at Leysdown at the east end of the island are the focus for discos and various forms of live entertainment. Elderly people tend to retire to Minster or to the east end of the island and this creates a further demand for transport. There is only one combined road and rail bridge connecting the island with the mainland and this inflexibility, coupled with a poor rail and bus service, makes car ownership highly desirable, if not essential. Travel to mainland towns for entertainment and shopping is possible but inconvenient by public transport and attendance for specialist medical treatment at the larger and better equipped hospitals is almost impossible by public transport from the more scattered settlements away from the main train stations at Queenborough and Sheerness. The lack of state or public provision forces people to private provision.

Overall, the class composition of the island is much the same as that for the country as a whole, but that is more an artefact of the Registrar-General's system of classifying occupations. There are very few top managers or professionals on the island, but there are enough relatively senior people in business and industry for the higher class categories to be proportionately similar to the national average.[8]

Forms of work on Sheppey

In the spring and summer of 1981, a one in nine sample survey of the island produced information on 730 households. This sought to document all the forms of work undertaken by all household members. We did not ask, as those doing similar work frequently do, simply 'who does the housework?', or whatever. Rather, this and all other spheres of activity were disaggregated into specific tasks, and questions were asked about these, even though they might later be presented in an aggregated form. The survey covered a range of essential household tasks including home maintenance and improvements, cleaning, cooking, washing, childcare, care maintenance and gardening. It also covered less essential 'self provisioning' tasks such as beer-making, bread-making, knitting and clothes-making.

In this chapter we have been obliged to limit the presentation of our data in order to keep it to a manageable length.[9] Households do carry out a remarkable amount of work for themselves in spheres where one might reasonably expect the task to be provided by a formal contractor. Four out of five of all 730 households do their own painting and a quarter do plastering or fix the brakes on the car themselves. Perhaps more astonishingly, fifty-six households put in a reinforced steel joist (RSJ) themselves – more than those who got the job done by a contractor (thirty-one) or informally through neighbours or kin (twelve). [10]

These would be among the most likely activities that could be paid for informally, whether or not in cash, to people outside the household, but not in their formal capacities. If there *was* evidence of a shift to informal provision in the black economy, we would expect it to be reflected here. In the event, we could not show that this was happening. Moreover, this local labour market had been chosen precisely because it contained features such as high unemployment and casual seasonal employment which would encourage an informal sector to flourish.

Turning now to informal work outside the household, respondents were asked an open question about all the other unpaid, informal work they might do for friends and neighbours. [11] This covered a very wide range of activities from voluntary work to babysitting, and we were reassured to discover that there was no important task which members of one household might do for another which we had not asked about more precisely on the interview schedule. A quarter of our sample claimed to do at least one other informal task outside the household. [12]

Further questions were asked, designed to elicit information about other informal work that was paid. In response to the question, 'Do you do any own account work for extra money?', 4 per cent of the sample replied in the affirmative; a further 1 per cent of our respondents acknowledged that they did other work for an employer or firm for which they got paid (presumably in cash or some other informal way). Analytically this is what we term 'shadow wage labour': that is to say, payments may or may not be declared to the Inland Revenue. Our respondents were alternately male and female, and when we analysed the twenty-seven respondents who acknowledged that they got extra money informally, some striking contrasts emerged. Of the eleven men, only one was unemployed – he appears to be the single 'honest scrounger' on the island! Furthermore, of the ten male full-time workers, half were in high income households. [13] By contrast, of the sixteen women, half were full-time housewives and ten were in low-income households. Clearly, the relationship between economic circumstances and paid informal work seems to be sharply differentiated by gender.

Returning to the one in four of the sample who engaged in unpaid informal work outside the household, it is interesting that broadly the same proportion of each social class reported doing some form of informal work. As we shall document below, greater class differences emerge when focusing on informal work done by members inside the household. Thus, whilst engaging in informal work is fairly randomly spread across our sample, there appears to be a division based on gender in the *kinds* of work that is done. Women are more likely to do routine domestic work (shopping, housework and washing, for example), presumably largely for elderly dependants, to undertake personal services for people and pets in other households and also to participate in more structured voluntary work. Men, on the other hand, are more likely to do improvement and maintenance work for others (such as gardening, decorating, repairs and carpentry). Unpaid, informal work outside the household is therefore highly gender-specific.

It is frequently asserted that the unemployed are more likely to be doing unpaid informal work than those in full-time employment. However, we did not find this to be so. Indeed, if the sexual division of labour in informal work is taken into account, it is clear that *men* who are in employment are *more* likely to be doing work than any other male category and unemployed *men* do least; 31 per cent compared to 19 per cent respectively.[14] This pattern is reversed for women, reflecting again the division of labour in unpaid informal work by gender. Men need tools and materials for their work – women more often simply need energy and some capacity to care for others.

This relationship between male economic activity and involvement in informal work does not accord with conventional wisdom. It is possible that as unemployment increases, the possibilities for informal work decline. It is perhaps when the unemployed with skills are surrounded by people in full-time employment that most opportunities exist for getting extra money for doing odd-jobs for others, sometimes on a reciprocal basis.[15] More research on the interaction between different kinds of work on a longitudinal basis is needed.

Our sample survey of households provided an unequivocal answer to the question of who does what work outside the formal economy: *members of households do it for themselves.* It is this work that we term *self-provisioning.* Reciprocal exchanges between households seem very poorly developed, according to our data. Similarly, attempts to elicit information about second 'informal' jobs, work for cash and all other possible ways of exploring participation in the so-called 'black' economy produced remarkably few cases.[16] Some households engage in informal work outside the household on a reciprocal basis for others; a very few engage in such work for cash. But these are a very small minority. Most informal, unpaid work is being done by household members for themselves and other members of the household. It is to a detailed analysis of this type of *self-provisioning* that we now turn.

Overall, the domestic is the most important sphere: of all tasks, if they are done at all, 84 per cent are done by household members in the household, and this applies particularly in households where both a male and female partner are present, as opposed to those households with only one parent or elderly people living on their own.

Household income is highly significant in relation to the amount of work that is done: by and large, the more income, the more tasks are done *within* the household. However, these results relate to the whole sample of 730 households and so one reason for, say, less routine housework amongst those on low incomes may almost certainly be explained by the fact that elderly single people may be unable to do certain tasks for themselves. Hence the results show the effects of age as much as of income.

It is clear, therefore, that analysis of the forty-one tasks at the aggregated level can only be taken so far. Households which do their own home maintenance, for example, may be newly-married couples getting their house in order, whereas those growing their own vegetables may be middle-aged working-class men who may or may not be living in dwellings that they own. For this reason, we shifted our analysis from the total number of tasks to measure *the spread of activities* of the *same* household across a broad spectrum of tasks. Why do some households do a wider range of tasks in and around the house than others? The issue we are exploring relates to the *range* of tasks, not the number of tasks in one area. Thus, we are not concerned here with whether a household is able to do its own plastering *and* painting *and* glazing, but whether it has the capacity to do *one* of these activities *as well as* vegetable-growing *and* car maintenance task, and so on. We devised a six-point scale based on distinct spheres of household or domestic tasks which could be done by household members, but which could equally well be bought in the market. People can buy vegetables, cakes and jerseys; they don't have to dig, bake and knit. These six clusters of tasks produced a *Self-Provisioning Scale* (SPS).[17] If it were the case that the domestic sphere could compensate for the decline of formal employment then we would expect low-income households with unemployed members to be doing the most self-provisioning work. On the other hand, these households would also be least likely to own such things as a car and a house and therefore less likely to maintain them themselves.

The 730 households of the complete sample were distributed on the self-provisioning scale as shown in table 20.1.

Table 20.1 Household type by self-provisioning scale

Household type	\multicolumn{6}{c}{Self-provisioning scale}	N =
	1	2	3	4	5	6	
	%	%	%	%	%	%	N
Couple households	—	3.0	13.3	28.3	39.7	15.6	526
Other male-headed	—	12.5	37.5	30.0	17.5	2.5	40
Other female-headed	—	31.1	31.1	28.0	9.1	0.6	164
ALL	—	9.9	18.6	28.4	31.6	11.5	730

Similar scales were constructed to measure the extent to which households used formal sources of labour or informal, communal sources of labour. The results from an analysis of these scales found that the extent of formal service provisioning closely reflected self-provisioning, whilst informal service provisioning did not. Hence, those households who were high self-provisioners also used the most formal services and the least informal services.[18]

Households with a male and female partner scored most highly at points 5 and 6 of the scale. Indeed, dichotomising the self-provisioning scale into 'low' (2–4) and 'high' (5–6), demonstrates that one-half of couple households (55.3 per cent) scored high on the scale. This is a better basis for our assertion that substantial domestic work by households does take place, since it avoids the problems posed by certain tasks being appropriate only at certain stages of the life-cycle: particularistic circumstances are ironed out by using the scale.[19] From now on we shall refer simply to 'low' and 'high' self-provisioners.

The first issue to be explored, following our earlier discussion, is how far involvement in the formal economy affects the household's capacity to score highly on the SPS.

More self-provisioning is done in households where the chief male is employed (60 per cent were high) than where he is unemployed (44 per cent were high). Furthermore, we found that the extent of self-provisioning depended not only upon the employment status of the male head of household, but also upon that of the wife. Hence, in households where the woman was also employed full-time, self-provisioning was higher, and where other members of the household were also employed self-provisioning was higher still.

This is a significant finding: *employment and self-provisioning go together, rather than one being a substitute for another.* One might have expected that those earning more or in a higher social class would be more likely to pay others and to do less self-provisioning themselves. If anything the reverse was the case: households were categorised on the basis of the Registrar-General's Socio-Economic Groups into three classes.[20] Amongst middle-class households 64 per cent were high self-provisioners, but amongst the lower middle and working class the percentage was 59 and 50 per cent. This must, of course, be partly a function of the higher incidence of car and home ownership in higher class categories, but it still does not follow that these households should necessarily do so much for themselves. This seems to be an indication that people actually *choose* to do this domestic work.

Since we are concerned with a *range* of self-provisioning activities, it is perhaps not surprising that the more adults there are in the household, the higher the score. In a phrase, households do more and a wider range of activities in and around the house if they have access to land, labour and capital. Growing their own vegetables requires access to a garden or allotment, and coping with activities as diverse as knitting, jam-making, repairing the car and painting the house requires a gender-divided pool of hands to do the work. Finally, unless households have the capital equipment of a car and, of course, the house itself, they are unable to score on all the points of the scale. Nevertheless, it does not follow that people's behaviour is mechanistically determined by the ownership of property and consumer durables. It is simply not the case that households with a given mix of the factors of production will *necessarily* do such work in their dwellings. More affluent households could pay for the task to be done in a garage or by a building contractor or painter and decorator. Many items of self-provisioning can be obtained more cheaply by buying them in the shops – jams or jerseys, for example.

Single variable analysis, as we have seen, can be confusing: for example, differences in class may be masked by multiple earners in lower-status households reducing the class gap in household incomes.[21] Yet, whatever the precise statistical measures to account for the differences, the differences themselves are overwhelmingly apparent. There appears to be a *process of polarisation* which produces at one pole busy households with many workers, some of which are in employment, and where a wide range of domestic tasks get done; they own their own homes and cars and have the money to maintain and service them. At the other pole are the households with only one or no earner,which do not own a house or a car or, if they do, do not have the resources for the materials to maintain them adequately.

Domestication and privatisation

In the previous sections we have discussed three kinds of informal work: the production of goods and services for consumption within the household; doing work for cash for others on one's own account or for an employer; and unpaid informal or communal work outside the household for non-household members. We have demonstrated that, in global terms, the first of these is by far the most important.

We have demonstrated with our empirical data that certain types of households are consistently high self-provisioners, whereas others consistently low: households with more income, either because of the size of individual incomes, the number of individual earners or a combination of the two, are likely to be high self-provisioners. The more adults in a relatively affluent household, the more work will be done. Households of higher status not only do more work for themselves, they are also more likely to get others to do work for them. Such households produce more and consume more, formally and informally. Hence, employment status is the key to participation in *all* forms of work, not simply that in the formal economy. Put negatively, unemployed men are more likely to be in households doing little self-provisioning and doing little or no informal work outside the household themselves. Hence, we argue that on a number of frequently overlapping dimensions, there is a process of *polarisation* between the busy, highly work-motivated households, generally well-off with multiple earners and potential household workers, and others who are at the opposite end of the scale.

This process of polarisation, we suggested, is partially supported and encouraged by the distinctive mix of opportunities and constraints provided by the local labour market. It is here that the possibilities for given household work strategies are embedded. Polarisation in the sphere of production is achieved through the distinctive earning capacities of household members; polarisation in the sphere of consumption is achieved through multiple adults in the household. In a different context, no doubt, households would adopt different strategies to get by. In Sheppey, the relatively low wages, coupled with relatively easy access to home ownership, have produced both polarisation and high levels of self-provisioning.

Self-provisioning is the production of goods and services outside the market by household members for their own use and enjoyment. *Domestication* is the product of a value system which puts home-centred activities as the central focus of a distinctive lifestyle. Household members may *choose* to, say, maintain their own car, even though they could afford to have it serviced in a garage, or they may be *obliged* to do such work for themselves because they cannot afford the market price. The same process may, therefore, be produced as much by choice – domestication – as by constraint, and households in different objective situations may end up equally domesticated. *Privatisation*, on the other hand, relates to the market provision of goods and services which had previously been provided publicly. Here again there is an element of both constraint and choice. A household may choose to provide its own means of transport by buying a car, even though public transport may be perfectly adequate or, on the other hand, a household may be obliged to run a car simply in order to get to employment and basic services. Such a constraint operates over much of the Isle of Sheppey, where public transport is poor and the population not living in Sheerness is relatively scattered. Evidently, increasing privatisation can encourage increased self-provisioning, and people's values can influence the degree to which they decide to buy private transport, health, housing, education and so forth. We return to this theme below. Self-provisioning is a product of both the cultural values of domestication and structural privatisation. Some welcome the self-provisioning imposed by privatisation; others are more obliged to respond to the forces that act upon them.

Self-provisioning is, therefore, partly created by a home-centred value-orientation. Households may choose to pay others to do work such as painting, decorating and gardening or they may choose or be obliged to do it themselves. The level at which they are satisfied again varies according to the value orientations of the household. However the work is done, and to whatever standard, the domestication value which unites many households in self-provisioning sees the house and home as a central defining and determining feature of a lifestyle and as a symbolic and material expression of success in life. Very often, households make very precise calculations about the balance of work between that which is paid for and that which they do themselves. Given the goal of achieving a predetermined standard of domestic comfort and style, households work out the best means of achieving it. Hence it is very hard to say in a given case whether a household is working for itself, either according to one kind of rationality by which it is calculated that it is 'cheaper' (in a limited economic sense), or according to another kind of rationality, which supports the activity in terms of other satisfactions – overall higher standards achieved, more work done, or the self-fulfilment from seeing a job well done. This produces a mixture of rationalities (for which we see little point in providing labels) which is inevitably complex and in some cases would be impossible to disaggregate. People know that they have mixed motives and, if they are encouraged to concede a reduction of salience to one form of rationality, they will simply 'top up' with another in an unconcernedly pragmatic way. Exploration of this matter is best done by extremely detailed, in-depth study of specific cases.

The self-provisioning households of Sheppey make sure that their homes are well decorated and often extend or modify them in various ways to make them more comfortable. They grow their own vegetables and 73 per cent of our sample had a deep-freeze, compared with the national figure of 47 per cent as a whole. [22] Women in employment augmented the resources of the household, but then very often used these same resources to do more of other forms of work in the household. Here again we meet problems. Households may choose to own their own dwelling and a private car and then find that they are obliged to maintain them, becoming, as it were, reluctantly self-provisioning. Whilst the mixture of rationalities suggested above enables some households to aim higher by extending the potential for household work, there may also be a ratchet effect on other households, who feel obliged to keep up to the standards of their local *milieu*, even though their household resources barely allow them to do so. What is 'choice' and what is 'constraint' under these circumstances is as hard to disentangle as is the mixture of rationalities. Indeed, the modes of rationalisation and the awareness of the contextual constraints in which such justifications are grounded are clearly interrelated. Households in the same material circumstances may choose to use these resources in fundamentally different ways, whereas those in different material circumstances, but with similar goals and values, may work to achieve similar outcomes and styles of life. Whilst we do not have space to discuss the issue in detail, we must emphasise that the current trend to the privatisation of housing and other services and facilities is a powerful support to the growth of self-provisioning which we have described. But both self-provisioning and privatisation can be highly divisive, especially within the working class. Lower-income households, who cannot get the resources to provide services and facilities for themselves, will become increasingly isolated, politically impotent and socially invisible. Forced to rent because they cannot afford to buy and maintain their homes, forced to use a declining public transport because they cannot afford to own, tax and maintain a private car and increasingly unable to retrieve their position through their own efforts, such households are likely to make the process of polarisation more acute in the years ahead, as the labour market continues to contract and privatisation continues as the policy of the government.

In this respect our account of informal work in this chapter is dramatically different from that in other contexts, particularly in the Third World. There is nothing in our findings to suggest that the work outside employment on the Isle of Sheppey generates much growth or provides communal support and benefits. All the work is private, inward-looking and concerned with domestic comfort. However, it is not enough to echo Galbraith by emphasising private affluence and public squalor. What we are describing is a polarisation between a precarious household work strategy, entirely dependent on the wages of multiple earners in a declining labour market, and those households cut off from even that modest security. Indeed, it is arguable that those doing well now would suffer the more if their income was drastically reduced through redundancy. Our interviews have documented the despair of those living in their own homes, with their own tools, with time on their hands and with urgent decorating jobs staring them in the face, but without the money to buy the paint.

Faced with their powerlessness in the face of economic realities, households are clearly in a more secure position when owning their dwelling outright, keeping it in good repair and also owning a car and other domestic consumer goods. Those who desire such a modest degree of security and are unable to achieve it seem even more excluded. It is difficult to say how much this desire for a modest self-sufficiency is at all widely shared, although we did find some evidence amongst certain households we interviewed. There may be more security to be found in the sphere of consumption than in the sphere of production. An inward-looking concern with private comforts might be one way of coping with the consequences of global processes of capital accumulation. Another way might be to drink oneself silly: a pattern more common in vodka drinking lands. This point is not entirely frivolous. Alcohol is one escape from circumstances over which one has no control; enormous quantities of beer are drunk on the Isle of Sheppey: there are over one hundred licensed premises on the island. Evidently there are *alternative* ways of coping with conditions in a context. It would be wrong to postulate a value consensus on the island. Indeed, we were struck as much by the *diversity* of values as by the polarisation in practices of self-provisioning on which we have focused here.[23]

Work in a wider context

At the level of larger-scale analysis, we suggest that the Isle of Sheppey is not an atypical, unusual spatial context in the declining periphery of one of the core capitalist countries. Rather, it is typical of those parts of the country experiencing de-industrialisation and the restructuring of capital. Over half the main employment on the island is controlled by foreign capital – German, French, Canadian, Japanese, American and so on. Substantial profits leave the island and substantial investment comes in. A new factory recently opened by Klippons – a German-based electrical components manufacturing company – produced twelve new jobs for an investment of £1.4 million.[24] By and large, however, most companies are contracting and our survey of employers suggests that this will continue.

There is very little that ordinary people can do about their position in the local labour market. Militant trade union activity is likely to be counter-productive. Investment decisions are taken off the island, more likely in another country. Multinational companies are, if anything, more paternalistic than smaller, local companies and are likely to take greater care of fewer people. A sound, pragmatic strategy for such people, concerned to get by as comfortably as possible, is to put their resources of time, energy and skill into making their domestic world more secure. At least in that sphere they have some control.

Our initial hypothesis that extra-household informal work would play an important part in household work strategies has been shown to be mistaken. Very little extra work is done for others, even though there might be a logic in the reciprocal exchange of specialist skills or in certain economies of scale. The only co-operative venture which we could document in detail was connected with growing vegetables. The Sheppey Horticultural Society buy fertiliser, garden tools and equipment and so forth in bulk and sells at favourable rates to members.

What reciprocal work there was between neighbours and the generations was related to the domestic cycle. Parents helped children substantially when setting up home and children visited elderly parents to do their shopping or decorating when they were retired. Even baby-sitting was more likely to be done by members of the same family at different stages of the domestic cycle rather than by neighbours at the same stage. From the experience of five years' fieldwork on the island, we would judge that if working-class married women in employment required help and support looking after their young children, this would typically be provided by a 'nan'. Three out of four working-class (Class 3) households had another relative living on the island and even 60 per cent of middle-class (Class 1) households did so. The emphasis by Gershuny and others on separate economic spheres distracts attention from the continuing importance of family and kinship networks. When times are hard, people may feel the obligations of kin become stronger, but this is a question which we explore elsewhere.[25]

Much work is certainly being done by some households for themselves, but this is for many precariously dependent on multiple earners. Household work strategies take place in specific contexts and reflect distinctive value systems. The material conditions provide the structural frame, but how and what people consume is fundamentally determined by their values.

Our analysis suggests a tragic precariousness at the centre of people's lives. The households which we are able to describe cannot achieve any real independence from market services in their nest-centred lifestyle. A few fortunate ones, perhaps, do achieve a remarkably close approximation to self-sufficiency and resent having to own a car or to have a telephone. But these are exceptional. About the rest, with all their ideological eggs in the domestic basket and *more* heavily dependent than they are perhaps aware on the fragile basis for gaining income in a declining labour market, we are inclined to be pessimistic. We feel that we are describing a *dependent* domesticity: the more capital goods and equipment they own, the more they are dependent on market services to maintain them. The security associated with home ownership and a high commitment to work for self-provisioning can be shattered overnight with an unexpected redundancy. The overwhelming dependence of all forms of informal work, including self-provisioning, on the money from formal employment is the basic fact underlining our polarisation thesis.

Notes

1 For a more detailed account of results arising from the project see Pahl and Gershuny, 1979; Pahl, 1980; Pahl and Dennett, 1981; Wallace, Pahl and Dennett, 1981; Buck, 1981; Pahl and Wallace, 1982; Pahl, 1984, 1985; Wallace, 1984.
2 We recognise that 'formal employment' covers a great variety of occupations at different levels of the social structure. For the purposes of this schema however these have all been classified together.
3 Informal relationships and patterns of reciprocity in the local neighbourhood have been documented in more detail elsewhere Wallace, 1984.
4 Shifts in the different forms of service provisions are more fully explored by Gershuny, 1979 which was the basis for our initial hypothesis.
5 Studies were made of local employment Pahl and Dennett, 1981, public and private housing Wallace and Pahl, 1981 and the Sheerness naval dockyard in the nineteenth century Buck, 1981. These unpublished studies have been submitted to the SSRC/ESRC as part of the final report of the respective projects.
6 These historical layers of investment are documented more fully in Pahl, 1985 and Pahl and Wallace, 1982.
7 An analysis of similar houses in Sheppey and in the nearest towns on the mainland advertised in the same paper on the same day revealed that in July 1981 ordinary terraced houses or bungalows were 20 to 40 per cent cheaper in Sheppey and the cost of a small plot of land was less than half the price.
8 The extent to which Sheppey reflects national trends is described in Pahl, 1984 b, chapter 4, which discusses national data relating to forms of work outside employment.
9 A fuller documentation of the survey results can be found in Pahl and Wallace, 1985.
10 Putting in an RSJ is important on Sheppey where many small terraced houses can be improved by making the two downstairs rooms into one by knocking down the intervening wall and building on a kitchen at the rear.

11 Much of the work outside employment which we discuss in this chapter is referred
    to as 'informal'. This carries no analytical weight.
12 Since the 730 households included many elderly and single person households,
    we focused much of the analysis of the tasks on those households based on couples
    – a man and a woman, generally married partners, but not necessarily so.
13 Households were divided into three income groups:
    Low income   – less than £70 per week.
    Medium income – £70–149 per week.
    High income   – more than £150 per week.
14 See tables 20.2 and 20.3 below.

Table 20.2   Economic activity of respondent by whether he/she engages in unpaid
              informal work outside the household*

Economic activity of respondent	Yes %	No %	Total N
Full-time work	28	72	287
Part-time work	22	78	81
Unemployed	26	74	42
Retired	22	78	148
Full-time housework	22	78	168
Other, did not answer	—	—	3
% =	25	75	730
ALL N =	179	548	—

* The question on the interview schedule was: 'Are there any jobs that you do *outside*
your home, for other people?'

Table 20.3   Economic activity of respondent by whether he/she engages in
              unpaid informal work outside the household, by sex of respondent*

Economic activity of respondent	Men			Women		
	Yes %	No %	Total N	Yes %	No %	Total N
Full-time work	31	69	206	21	79	81
Part-time work	40	60	5	21	79	76
Unemployed	19	81	26	38	63	16
Retired	21	79	63	22	78	85
Full-time housework	0	100	1	23	77	168
Other, did not answer	—	—	2	—	—	1
% =	28	72	—	23	77	—
ALL N =	84	218	303	96	330	427

* The question on the interview schedule was: 'Are there any jobs that you do *outside*
your home, for other people?'

15 Anecdotes about this kind of activity provide the main support for popular
    speculation for the so-called informal economy.
16 In order to be sure that this was not simply the understandable caution of
    respondents who might be reluctant to reveal all their activities to an anonymous

interviewer on the doorstep, we carefully selected thirty households for more detailed interviews in-depth. In some cases these households were interviewed more than once by each of us in turn. Furthermore, we have knowledge of families on the island stretching over a period of five years, and we are confident that our assessment is correct.

17 The self-provisioning scale (SPS) was devised to measure the production of goods and services by households themselves, which could also be purchased formally. Therefore, we selected tasks from our questionnaire which were sometimes purchased formally and sometimes done within the household, and individual households were ranked according to the number of such tasks which they performed. The SPS therefore gives a measure of the tasks performed by a given household. It was decided that it would be more accurate if SPS measured the *range* of tasks done by a household rather than the gross number of such tasks, since the tasks covered such distinct areas of activity. Thus, we wanted to discover not just whether a household did a great many housing repairs, but whether it repaired the car, grew vegetables and provided personal goods such as clothes as well. Hence the tasks were divided into six clusters and the household could score one SPS point if it did just one task within each cluster, up to a maximum of six points for all the clusters. Tasks of a fairly routine nature were only included in the SPS if they were performed with some frequency, but the major tasks were included if they had been performed at any time at all. The clusters of tasks for the self-provisioning scale are as follows:

SPS 1 Vegetable growing at any time
SPS 2 Either painting or plastering or mending a broken window in the last year
SPS 3 Either checking the oil level or tuning the engine or doing work on the brakes of a car at any time
SPS 4 Either putting in an RSJ or double glazing or central heating or building a bathroom or an extension or converting an attic at any time
SPS 5 Either making jam or beer or wine either fortnightly or regularly
SPS 6 Making clothes or knitting at any time

18 These complementary scales are explained and discussed more fully in chapter 9 of Pahl, 1984.

19 For present purposes we are excluding non-couple households from the analysis, simply because single parent households and single retired person households have special and distinctive problems and we have problems enough in accounting for variations between couple households.

20 These social classes have been reduced from the seventeen socio-economic groups as follows:

Class 1 = SEGs 1, 2, 3, 4, 13 (i.e. professional and managerial)
Class 2 = SEGS 5, 6, 8, 12, 14, 16 (i.e. junior and intermediate non-manual, foremen, own-account workers, farmers and armed forces)
Class 3 = SEGS 7, 9, 10, 11, 15 (i.e. all manual workers, personal service workers)

The fourth class, which we do not use in our present analysis, comprises those in SEG 17 (unclassifiable) and those who have never had paid employment.

21 In an attempt to get a more precise measure of what seemed to be the three main variables affecting households' position on the self-provisioning scale, multiple regression analysis was used for couple households. The variables taken were the social class of male chief earner (defined as in note 20), the number of adults in the household and, thirdly, an income variable dividing households into those with incomes under £100 a week and those with £100 or more. These three in-

dependent variables were described as Class M, Adults and Povline respectively and the dependent variable in the equation was the Self-Provisioning Scale described in note 17. The three coefficients were highly significant, the coefficients for Class M and Adults being almost precisely the same as the Povline coefficient being slightly more significant. The full equation is as follows (NB: Self-Provisioning Scale = SPS):

$$\text{SPS} = 18.8 - \underset{(-.07)}{0.108} \text{ (Class M)} + \underset{(.08)}{0.100} \text{ (Adults)} + \underset{(.03)}{0.13} \text{ (Povline)}$$

22 *Social Trends*, 1983.
23 We have also documented other styles of getting by than those which are the focus of discussion here. These will be discussed in forthcoming publications.
24 *Sheerness Times-Guardian*, 11 March 1983.
25 See Wallace, 1984, *op. cit.*

Marital and family relations in times of male unemployment

The general objective of our study is to draw conclusions about the impact of unemployment on family and marital relations. It aims to extend our understanding of the relationships between husbands and wives and between parents and children when men are out of work. It relies on couples' perceptions of their relationships and by talking in depth and at length to husbands and wives attempts to convey the different meanings men and women attach to the experience of unemployment and to their marriages and family lives. The conventional way of studying unemployed men tends to focus chiefly on an 'economic model of man', or man as an 'ex-worker'. Considerations of the man's other relationships within the family and community are taken either as secondary or dependent variables. (One exception to this is the classical study by Komarovsky, *The Unemployed Man and His Family*, carried out in the 1930s.) Our own study also incorporates a review of the man's work status but gives equivalent weighting to his family membership, especially his relationship with his wife and children. It is especially focused on families with young children and we will provide details of the sample selection criteria later.

Widespread unemployment provides a tragic circumstance in which to explore the structure of contemporary family life. With the removal of large numbers of men and women from the labour force, the home or 'domestic workplace' becomes accentuated as a location for much social life and inter-action. Attention is accordingly drawn from the public sphere to the private and from the corporate to the conjugal.

In particular, male unemployment creates a 'laboratory situation' (Komarovsky, 1940: 2) in which it is possible to examine facets of the male provider role more closely. Recent family research has stressed that many modern fathers experience a conflict between the worlds of work and the family, with breadwinning and childcare and domestic responsibilities being in direct competition (Moss and Fonda, 1980). Men's 'greedy' occupations are often blamed for low paternal engagement in housework and childrearing and for preventing egalitarianism or role interchangeability within the home (Hughes *et al.*, 1980). It is noted that men work the longest hours of their working lives when their children are small and, conversely that married women with pre-school age children are those least likely to work outside the home. In contrast, there is another trend which shows that increasing numbers of fathers of young children are becoming unemployed as the recession deepens. As well as actual numbers in this category rising quantitative data suggests that the spells of unemployment for male family heads are lengthening. Rimmer and Popay (1982: 32) in a review of the 1980 General Household Survey, comment:

If married men only are considered, the rate of unemployment for married men with dependent children (5 per cent) is higher than for men without children (4 per cent), and for men with four or more dependent children it is nearly two and a half times as great (12 per cent) as for married men with no children.

What then are the implications for families when men's attachment to the labour market is broken? Does the loss of the economic provider role result in changes in the domestic division of labour? Are men freed to become more participative fathers and more active home makers? How are the lives of women and children affected by male unemployment? What is the relationship between economic provision and power and authority within households? Does increased male unemployment herald a breakdown in patriarchal structures and enhance wives' spheres of authority?

The study takes these questions as central and this paper will summarise how we went about posing the questions and the sorts of answers that emerged.

The approach to families and the research locale

Turning firstly to the study design and methods, it was felt that such precise questioning about family patterns and behaviours could best be achieved through detailed case study work using in-depth interviews with a small number of families. Our emphasis was on getting 'close to' the dynamics of domestic and family life and we believed that this could only be successfully achieved by skilled focused interviews and observations. The strengths of this method would depend largely on the degree of rapport and trust established between families and the investigator. It would also depend on the development of a sensitive, responsive research instrument which encouraged families to share intimate reflections and experiences.

For these reasons, we decided to use one main fieldworker; to restrict the sample size to forty-five couples; and to employ a largely unstructured, conversational interview style.[1] Furthermore, since the main focus of the research is on unemployment as an 'occasion' in which to identify a diversity of familial behaviour and values, we should seek a fairly heterogeneous group of families. We decided that men and their families should be eligible to take part in the study if they met the following general criteria:

(a) registered as unemployed at the first point of contact;
(b) having at least one dependent child of ten years or less;
(c) living in 'complete' families – that is families consisting of father, mother and children living together. Legal marriage[2] or biological parenthood were not selection criteria and cohabitees and stepfathers were included;
(d) living within the study town and its immediate villages. Residents from a neighbouring town using the Unemployment Benefit Office were excluded.

Wives' employment status, duration of unemployment, religion, family size and occupational status were not held constant. Our intent was to capture the range of problems faced by unemployed families; to detail the processes by which they cope and to describe the variations in life experiences.

We also felt quite strongly at the outset that the families should be drawn from a single locale. The value and efficiency of using a single location was emphasised in a recent text on 'the cycle of deprivation' (Coffield, Robinson and Sarsby, 1980), where the authors note how their fieldwork was enhanced and enriched by first gaining a comprehensive review of services available in the town where their sample lived. This enabled them to appreciate fully the situation in which deprivation occurred. We felt similarly that a study of 'unemployed families' would benefit from our familiarity with a specific community and its network of local agencies and while our aim was not to do a 'community study' our primary task was to build up a detailed profile of the area.

As well as insisting on a single location, we felt that the area selected should meet a number of other criteria: it should have a readily identifiable local labour market;[3] its experience of unemployment should be fairly serious and recent so as to allow comparison with others where massive unemployment has been a persistent and endemic problem (North Tyneside CDP, 1978; Sinfield, 1981); its pattern of employment and unemployment and its regional position should not deviate markedly from neighbouring areas and for pragmatic reasons of cost and fieldwork practice it should be reasonably accessible to us as researchers. The availability of local statistics, expressions of interest and cooperation and some ready-made ties between the researchers and the community were also important influences in the selection procedure.[4]

Finally, after lengthy investigations, we were impressed by the suitability of the town of Kidderminster, a small industrial town in the West Midlands. It was characterised in the past by a traditional stable employment pattern and enjoyed relatively high levels of employment and prosperity. Like so many other manufacturing towns in the West Midlands it appears to be experiencing what is being called 'de-industrialisation'. For example, unemployment in Kidderminster rose from 5.2 per cent in April 1979 to 11.7 per cent in 1981.

Kidderminster's communication position as a satellite of the Midlands conurbation and of Birmingham also made it an ideal choice, for in this way it resembles many other towns that could be selected. Kidderminster in our view met all the criteria we had set and was useful both for its uniqueness and typicality.

Details of the place of the study and comments about its changing face arose again and again in respondents' accounts and we felt this alone later justified our ethnography. Themes of the town's decline were reiterated. Images of empty factories, poor amenities, burgeoning consumerism in the growth of new supermarkets and new dual carriageways being built to lead out and away from the town, hit our consciousness with force when we survey our respondents' experiences. Some extracts impress this upon us:

'Kiddy's a ghost town ain't it? At one time everyone of my mates was at work. I bet you I can't even name one that's at work now.'

'They're closin' down factories every day.'

'Kiddy's gone to the dogs.'

We decided to use the method of direct recruitment outside the Unemployment Benefit Office. We do not have space here to discuss in detail the merits and disadvantages of 'street sampling' nor indeed its relationship to the wider population of the unemployed/employed.[5] However, it is noteworthy that for our purposes it was:
(a) quick and efficient, access could be instantaneous;
(b) respondents gave their own direct permission to be researched;
(c) respondents met in person or saw the investigator and could ask questions;
(d) no intermediary or facilitator was involved and the research relationship involved genuine confidentiality between researcher and researched.

The interviews

Initially, it had been hoped to interview wives and husbands separately and then together, however this aim had to be modified in the light of the sampling delays and fieldwork practice where the presence of the other spouse was difficult to manipulate. Instead, we quite quickly decided to allow the couple themselves to structure the composition of the visit and to interview whoever was available when we called, returning if necessary at a later date to interview the 'absent' spouse. In the main, interviews proved to be joint including the accounts of both husbands and wives. In two cases husbands only were contacted (one opted for a telephone interview because his wife refused to cooperate), for the remainder, contact was made with both partners at some point. We are now convinced that this kind of 'joint' interviewing and non-directive approach may be productive. The quality of data has been of central concern and it has become apparent that much can be learnt about the nature of the marital relationship through observation of husband/wife interaction. We have taken seriously, and made explicit issues such as who talks most, who interjects, contradicts or interrupts; who claims 'ownership' of the interview; the differential quality of talk whether 'confiding' or 'factual'; the degree of conjugal openness or consensus; and empathy. We also noted practical matters such as who offered or made tea, interaction with children and who was at home when we called. We made it clear that both partners were to be interviewed, but if only one was at home when we visited we conducted the interview there and then and returned later to see the other partner. We also found it surprising how many opportunities arose for brief conversation with one partner where 'secrets' could be disclosed. By leaving the interview structure open, husbands and wives can come and go. They can carry on their daily routines, fetching children from school, going off with a friend who has called, making the lunch, keeping fixed appointments. This can provide further insights and make the interview less obtrusive.

Evaluating the interviews

We would like now to briefly review some of the issues intrinsic to this methodological approach, especially in relation to the content of the fieldwork interviews. We list these items almost without comment to encourage discussion.

(a) The value of separate/joint interviews needs to be assessed especially in the context of achieving a 'naturalistic' approach.

(b) If joint interviews are elected as the preferred mode, consideration needs to be given to affording spouses an *equal* hearing and receiving confidential information. In this study men's employment and unemployment histories tended to dominate women's experiences. The topics of sexual relations and marital violence were sometimes suppressed in the presence of the spouse.

(c) Unstructured non-directive interviewing may move the focus of the research away from the initial research brief. Marital and family relations, for example, may become a minor issue if the respondent has another burning issue to get off his/her 'chest'. We tried to allow respondents to attach their own 'weighting' to different aspects of being unemployed. This for us was an essential part of building the rapport with couples which allowed for a later expansion of marital and familial intimacies.

(d) Witnessing severe hardship, and deprivation, we often felt uneasy in our role as interviewers in the face of widespread poverty and unhappiness.

(e) The degree of involvement in respondents' lives is not easily prescribed for interviewers who take an unstructured approach. This may involve both direct and indirect pleas from respondents for help, advice, aid and guidance.

(f) Combining the collection of quantitative and qualitative data: here we devised a brief structured questionnaire as an aid to recording 'fact sheet data' on age, marital status, place of origin, etc. However, we have since discovered other types of information which may have benefited from more systematic collection and recording, especially to do with income and expenditure.

(g) Collecting employment and unemployment histories: This proved very complex and in a number of cases we have respondents who have experienced repeated spells of unemployment through their adult lives. There are others for whom unemployment has been more usual than employment.

(h) The impact of the fieldwork on the interviewer is seldom considered. However, where research is concerned with hardship, deprivation and extreme distress this may need to be considered at the outset. Management of marital hostilities, physical danger or abuse need explicit airing.

(i) With regard to the receiving and reporting sensitive or 'illegal' information, the ethical position of researchers party to sensitive information continues to pose problems in the field of unemployment research. More rehearsal of these issues might be warranted.

Wives' experiences of unemployment

One of the earliest findings to emerge from the research is the need for the experiences of the 'wives' of unemployed men to be taken seriously.[6] In this last part of this paper we give our reasons for this and point briefly to some of the fundamental ways in which women can be affected in the circumstances of male unemployment. We observed firstly during the course of the interviews that wives were often deeply and peculiarly affected by their husband's unemployment. When talking they sometimes became emotional and showed signs of strain. Often they mentioned that the interview itself had been therapeutic and/or revealing, as one wife remarked: 'Now I know how Norman feels about being unemployed, 'cause we've never talked about it'. In other words, wives pushed themselves forward and commanded our attention and concern.

There are, too, a number of academic justifications warranting a separate analysis for wives of unemployed men. On the one hand, commentators on the family have suggested that recognition should be paid to 'the impact of unemployment on the *family*, rather than on the unemployed as individuals', concluding that 'three times as many people, as registrants may be affected by unemployment' (Rimmer and Popay, 1982: 31). On the other hand, paradoxically, it has been increasingly pointed out that 'members of families do not necessarily share the same standard of living' or indeed quality of life experience (for example, Land, 1983). Here it is argued that the household as a unit of analysis obscures degrees of disadvantage, suffering and inequality. Some of the data that has now been gathered on the distribution of resources within families indicates that *mothers* may fare less well than other members of the family in relation to food, clothing, space and money (Land, 1983).

Whether we underscore the model which sees the unemployed as comprising family units, or the model which sees the family units as comprised of individuals, we conclude equally that a wife's perspective on unemployment must be developed.

Women's jobs

The first striking observation that can be made is that male unemployment has profound implications for *female employment*. (See the useful international comparisons in Barrère's paper in this section.) Women's propensity to take up paid employment outside the home, to continue in jobs, and to search for work may all be affected by their husband's employment status. One might expect wives to enter the labour market in greater numbers in response to men's unemployment, to replace lost earnings. Findings from large-scale surveys of the unemployed as a whole show this supposition to be false. 'Overall about 50–60 per cent of all wives are in work, but only 30–35 per cent of the wives of unemployed men and only 10–15 per cent of the wives of men unemployed over a year are in work' (Hakim, 1982: 441). In the present study, working wives were a minority. Only two wives could be said to have entered permanent (but part-time) employment as a direct consequence of their husband's job loss. Three other wives maintained their jobs despite their husbands' unemployment and were characterised by either having well-paid or longer established jobs. The remaining wives either engaged in temporary, casual or informal work, withdrew from work, postponed or rejected totally the return to work.

The fragmentation of wives' orientation to and participation in waged work was bound up not just with the structural opportunities for women's work or with the period in the lifecycle and availability of childcare facilities but also importantly with the operation of the social security system and with social values about 'proper' marital and parental roles. Husbands were described as primary claimants, thus depriving women of their own unemployment status. Some wives did not realise they 'could' sign on, or more usually could not see the point of signing on. Often, wives engaged in an accounting procedure estimating how much they could realistically earn in the labour market and how much would subsequently be deducted from husband's benefits, finding, when expenses for travel, childcare and incidentals were included a *reduction* in the family's overall standard of living. Few women opted for, or remained in paid work in the face of these costs. The data from the present study suggest a willingness in many wives to work to better the family's overall income, thwarted by financial disincentives.

Underpinning many of the barriers to women's economic autonomy or independence then is the concept of the 'family wage' and the persistence of the family model of male breadwinner/economic provider and economically dependent female. At the level of social values and beliefs a number of husbands and wives themselves subscribed to this organisation of family life, seeing it as the right, natural and proper order. Issues of masculinity, authority, identity, marital stability and pride were reported to depend on the man's retention of his right to provide for his wife and children. Wives and husbands frequently become emotional at the prospect of wives becoming chief breadwinner, stereotypes of the 'kept man' who was ineffectual and weak were raised; men supplementary to powerful women (the example of Denis Thatcher was given) were referred to derisively; jokes were made ridiculing such men as failures and so on. These deep-seated and often passionate views about breadwinning could not easily or obviously be related to social class alone and did not necessarily correspond to other views and beliefs about gender roles. They were often espoused by men who were highly participant in housework and childcare as well as by those with more traditional views on male domesticity. Even in the two cases where fathers accepted their wives taking chief economic provider roles, there was much evidence of prejudice and ridicule against these men.

There were, then, few families in our study for whom role-reversal was an appropriate and easy solution. Many men could accept wives working in a supplementary way or even temporarily, but full-time working wives were seldom seen as providing a permanent option. Setting values aside, many husbands and wives also realistically pointed out huge discrepancies in the earning potential of men and women, recognising that few women's wages would adequately 'keep' a family. These preliminary findings therefore confirm that unemployment of husbands does little to create new opportunities for women workers but instead can be restrictive and perpetuate male/female inequalities in the labour market. At the level of ideology male unemployment within families seems to have minimal impact on the tenacity and rigidity of beliefs about male economic provision and female dependence. These beliefs persist and may be reinforced in the circumstances of unemployment even though men may penetrate the facets of female culture such as child-rearing and domestic work. We would suggest that men's control of the 'right to provide' is far from disintegrating despite the recession.

Certainly (before concluding this discussion of female employment) there were additional factors discouraging women in this study from taking up paid work – factors distinctive from husbands' employment status. Some wives simply did not *want* to work, finding full-time motherhood preferable and believing that young children need close and continual contact with mothers. Other women worried about husbands' abilities as childminders and a few felt husbands needed looking after. As one wife put it: 'I've often said I ain't got two kids, I've got three, cause I count Tommy as a kid as well'.

Money

In the same way that unemployment of husbands accentuated and sustained male provider roles, it would seem that male unemployment may carry a heavy *managerial* role for wives. This seemed especially true in families where the 'whole wage system' (see Jan Pahl's important work, 1980 and 1983) was operative. 'Making ends meet' was cited as the worst aspect of unemployment for a large percentage of the sample and many families were living in real financial hardship. Money (and the lack of it) was cited as the source of marital rows in many instances, as divisive between husbands and wives, between parents and children and between families and their wider kin. Rows broke out over how the money was spent, on whom and what, where money came from for example if loaned by relatives, over who had a 'right' to the money, whose needs were greatest in the family, men against women, young children against older children, stepchildren against biological offspring and so on. Indeed, management of the money did not bring control for many wives, with husbands insisting on their own personal spending money with no equivalent allocation of personal money to wives. Some wives felt they had to 'check' their husbands' spending.

Even where there was no overt conflict over 'ownership' of the money or its distribution many wives found the sheer enormity of meeting everyday costs on social security benefits alone, distressing. Debts were common in the sample, especially rent arrears, and although families had negotiated many financial solutions such as extensive use of meters, bills had to be juggled, diets maintained with ingenuity, fuel usage cut back, and shopping conducted with skill and care. The data suggest that it was often wives who had to live on their wits, variously hunting down bargains, devising new 'economic' meals, locating borrowing sources, placating hungry children, refusing children spending money or treats, patching and mending clothes, going without food or taking less nutritional meals themselves and sometimes dealing with the creditors. There is, too, some evidence of wives protecting husbands from the financial reality or concealing their own worries about money. Indeed, a few wives (and husbands themselves backed them up) described their husbands as 'not the worrying kind' or were told explicitly by their husbands to 'stop worrying'. The inability to confide in husbands about money troubles was a recurrent theme. At the extreme, the responsibility for financial management and coping with money matters were portrayed by women as damaging their health. Our implication is not that all unemployed men are financially irresponsible or indeed cushioned from hardship, but we merely wish to stress how in certain households patterns of *unequal* responsibility and suffering may evolve.

Friendships and social life

As well as the differential gender effects connected with financial affairs in the circumstances of male unemployment, we also found that male unemployment could deeply affect wives' social networks and friendships. Isolation and a reduction in social contact have been frequently reported to affect the unemployed. What is less well-known is the exact way in wives' social ties and interaction patterns could be devastated. Wives could be restricted in their contact with female friends. This seemed to cut both ways: friends could stay away, not wanting to intrude on marital privacy, *or* wives were discouraged by husbands from pursuing an independent social life.

Even when female friends continued to call, despite the unemployed husband's presence, the quality of interaction could be affected and some women reported that conversations were inhibited. Husbands served as 'gooseberries' on these occasions. Some husbands themselves confessed that they found· it difficult to accept their wives' separate day-time social life and put themselves in direct competition with her friends and interests. Wives were torn between keeping husband's company and sustaining former bonds and routines. Martin's paper in this section clearly demonstrates the isolation of unemployed women albeit at a later stage of the life cycle than most of the families we studied.

Childcare and domestic routines

Finally, we conclude by suggesting that husbands' unemployment may affect wives' domestic and maternal routines. Here we do not consider the central issue of 'who does what within the home' but focus rather on the general tenor of everyday domestic and parental life. Two key observations can be made.

Firstly, male unemployment and its consequent financial stringency may be associated not just with an extra pair of hands to share domestic responsibilities but also with an *enlargement* or magnification of the domestic role. Secondly, the presence of the unemployed father in the home may not simply be a support for mothers in the care of their young children but may also create a threat to women's child-rearing practices with open conflict breaking out over standards of child discipline and control.

Much of the evidence we have gathered suggests that living on a small income commands much sophisticated time and effort; as one wife quoted above said, 'you've got to work at being unemployed if you want to survive'. For example, shopping was reported by many to be a very elaborate routine involving visits to numerous stores and to an array of markets, rummage sales, charity events, buying one item here, one item there, finding the lowest prices. Such canny shopping is time-consuming and involves effort when it is considered that many of the shoppers travelled by foot and often for long distances between market sources. The significance of shopping therefore increases in the domestic timetable by its very fragmentation. Similarly, the nature of the planning and cooking of meals may be altered by a small budget.

A number of families described a meticulous routine of writing weekly menus so as to ensure food was on the table every day. Casual selection of meals or indeed purchases were reported to be rare. Furthermore, cleaning and housework routines could take longer or be increased through the husband's presence at home. It is difficult to generalise on these matters. However, wives gave examples of the rearrangement of meal times to suit husbands, of bedrooms that could not be cleaned due to sleeping husbands, of husbands generating extra mess in the home – in short, the stereotype of husbands 'getting under wives' feet'. Even when husbands themselves were active in the home, say through home-decorating, this could frustrate the wife's goals. Many women complained about men leaving messy or unfinished jobs, and indeed this was cited as the source of marital friction in a number of homes.

We are not trying to suggest that the full domestic burden or indeed the enlarged domestic role affected only wives, what we do wish to stress is that the home may not function as a harmonious domestic unit with all parties acting in each others interests or bearing equal domestic responsibility. Again, it may often be women 'who carry the can' although this will vary in degree and form from case to case.

Sometimes he gets me [mad] when he's sat in and I'm doing it [the housework] and you've got to keep asking him to move. I mean he just can't sit in the kitchen while I do in here and then come in here while I'm doing the kitchen . . . The other week he was behind me all morning and it got so . . . in the end I told him I'd give him two quid and I said 'now clear off to the pub'. I said, 'I've had enough, just get out of my way so I can get it done'. Course you just can't get nothing done. And then like when it's time for the kids to come, you ain't done this and you ain't done that.

The potential for conflict over child-rearing was also alluded to by a proportion of mothers. Unemployed fathers could observe wives closely and spouses were variously described as 'too soft' or 'too hard', or 'giving in too often'. Indulgences and spoiling cropped up as regular themes with mother and father even taking sides over and favouring, different children. Again, it is difficult to generalise and several wives appreciated having husbands to share in childcare, and were able to use husbands as unpaid childminders, freeing themselves from the constraints of motherhood from time to time. There were others though for whom the husband served as critic and a judge of maternal practice. Children were also described as having divided loyalties and of sometimes transferring allegiances 'He's all for him now' and some mothers felt as if their authority had been eroded.

Conclusion

The last section of this paper has indicated, albeit in a preliminary fashion, the quality of the data that we have. Our study is, at one level, small scale and modest. We would though point out that this kind of intensive (we would prefer the word 'involved') non-bureaucratic research has many strengths – particularly with regard to data quality. We do know just how good our data are – in two obvious senses. Our data are very rich and we controlled their collection directly. This has naturally been as always at the expense of the number of families in the study – yet we do know a great deal about these families and the context in which they live and are sure of what we know.

Notes

1   The development of the research instrument was aided by some detailed pilot work. We were fortunate at the outset in being able to draw a sub-sample of unemployed families, who fitted our criteria, from a complementary study of young parents being conducted in Birmingham ('Fathers, childbirth and work' – funded by EOC). Fourteen couples were interviewed at this pilot stage, nine of whom were interviewed twice and in-depth by ourselves. Detailed case-notes were also kept at this time, where interviewing problems and observations were recorded. This pilot work was essential in the developing of the final interviewing check-list and in guiding the interviewers over issues such as joint or separate interviews, duration of interview, time of day to visit and interviewing style. We held regular research meetings to reflect on these matters, and one of the investigators, Lorna McKee, undertook an analysis of all the unemployed parents (44) and their characteristics for the complementary study 'Fathers, childbirth and work', Bell, McKee and Priestley, 1983.

2   The term 'wife'/'husband' is used to refer to a stable relationship, but does not necessarily refer to legal marriage only.

3   For example, Birmingham was considered and rejected because of the complexity of its labour market.

4   Contacts were made before the research submission with the manager of the Job Centre; with two local industrial chaplains who organise a weekly group for the unemployed; with trade union officials; with trades council members; with health authority officials and members and with representatives of local political parties. All offered cooperation and support at this early stage.

5   The eventual sample of forty-five had the following characteristics:
    Briefly, they are *young* families and a high proportion have pre-school-age children. Thirteen (29 per cent) fathers and sixteen (35 per cent) mothers are under twenty-five years of age; thirty-four (75 per cent) fathers and thirty-seven (82 per cent) mothers are under thirty-five years of age. Some seventeen (38 per cent) families have a baby of one year or under and thirty-eight (69 per cent) families have at least one pre-school-age child. The majority are at an early stage in the family lifecycle and in their marriage. Most of the fathers, thirty-eight (84 per cent), had been formerly employed in manual occupations and nineteen (42 per cent) held unskilled jobs ranging from construction work and labouring through to general agricultural work. Five had previously held managerial positions and nineteen skilled were working at stage one, two full-time and three part-time, and there was a preponderance of men with four or more children (nine). In terms of duration of unemployment, nineteen (42 per cent) fathers in this study had been out of work for less than twelve months and twenty-six (58 per cent) had been unemployed continuously for more than twelve months. As for place of origin, the families

are predominantly local people and white, twenty-six (58 per cent) husbands and twenty-seven (60 per cent) wives were born in the town itself and a further ten husbands and twelve wives were born within the West Midlands area. Only four husbands and three wives were born outside the United Kingdom.

6 This part of the paper refers to preliminary analysis of stage one interviews only. For a further analysis see 'His Unemployment: her problem – the domestic and marital consequences of male unemployment'. In *The Experience of Unemployment* ed. S. Allen, K. Purcell, A. Waton, L. S. Wood. Macmillan, 1985.

Renegotiation of the domestic division of labour in the context of male redundancy[1]

Introduction

One aspect of post-war change in the UK economy which is increasingly attracting the attention of social scientists is the contraction of employment opportunities in the traditionally masculine occupations associated with heavy industry, coinciding with the expansion of the service sector and consumer-based light industries employing a large proportion of women.

It seems reasonable to assume, as a number of writers do (Urry, 1981; Massey, 1982; Morgan, 1983), that such changes 'will significantly alter the nature and composition of the local working class, and can lead to important conflicts of interest between men and women' (Bowlby *et al.*, 1983).

South Wales provides us with a prime example of an area which has recently seen increased participation by women in the waged labour force, alongside the shedding of a predominantly male work force by heavy industry.[2]

In this paper I seek to demonstrate, with reference to a sample of forty redundant male steelworkers, all married, that redundancy, in the context of a wider economic recession, is unlikely to produce a reversal of pre-existing patterns of sex-role behaviour. I go on to argue, with specific reference to male *unemployment*, that there are powerful social forces at work which militate against, though without necessarily prohibiting, a renegotiation of the domestic division of labour.

Although I found some evidence of a blurring of boundaries between the sexes in the division of domestic tasks, I consider it in no way sufficiently extensive as to constitute a strong challenge to the established division of labour within the household.[3]

Whether the changes which *have* occurred represent a minor adaptation permitting the maintenance of pre-existing sex roles, or are rather the first step in a long process of renegotiation in the domestic division of labour, prompted by a restructuring of the economy, is still open to speculation and debate.

Female economic activity

Before reporting in detail on the selection of my sample, and the characteristics of domestic organisation in the context of male redundancy, it may be useful to have some background information concerning the recent trends in participation in the waged labour force by married women. In contrast to a falling economic activity rate among single women,[4] the trend throughout the 1970s for married women was towards rising participation in the waged labour force, producing an increase which stabilised between 1978 and 1980.[5] For the 16–59 age group the rate of economic activity rose from 52 per cent to 62 per cent – a rise substantially accounted for by an increase in part-time working.[6]

The greatest differences between rates of female employment are found when age of the youngest child is taken into account. Women are increasingly likely to work as the youngest child gets older, though where there is more than one child in the household the increase is concentrated in part-time employment.[7]

The implications for a renegotiation of the domestic division of labour are obvious. A woman with a very young child is likely to be inhibited from taking on paid employment, be it full-time or part-time, unless there is readily available childcare. Although one might expect male unemployment to facilitate an arrangement whereby a husband cares for children while his wife is gainfully employed, the GHS for 1980 reports rather the opposite tendency.[8] Amongst couples of working age (i.e. husband aged 16–64, wife aged 16–59) 57 per cent were both employed in 1980. However, only 35 per cent of wives of unemployed men worked outside the home, in contrast to 62 per cent of wives of men in employment. A number of informants explained their reluctance to consider a change in traditional roles by the conviction that a woman would be unable to earn as much as a man could claim in benefit.

Methodology

It is in the context of these general, complex trends in the employment pattern of married women that I wish to present my data. My sample of forty redundant male steelworkers, resident in and around Port Talbot, was selected from a larger random sample of 750, made redundant from BSC's Port Talbot plant in the summer of 1980.[9] Given my particular interest in the potential for flexibility in domestic organisation as a result of redundancy for a male main earner, I decided to contact only households of married men likely to expect to continue to be economically active (i.e. aged 20–55).[10] This meant that the households concerned would also be likely to be involved in some stage of child-rearing. Indeed, the vast majority of my sample have pre-school children (nineteen cases) or school-age children (fourteen cases). The critical test of whether or not there is any fundamental renegotiation of the domestic division of labour in the context of male redundancy will be in households containing young children, and in this respect my sample is ideal. This does not of course mean that we learn nothing from those homes without children, but simply that in such cases the test is less rigorous.

In another respect the sample is less than ideal. Most of my interviewing was carried out in the summer of 1982, just two years after the redundancies were announced – sufficient time for changes in domestic organisation to have manifested themselves. However, various factors dependent on the availability of funds from the European Coal and Steel Community[11] whose influence was felt quite some time after the redundancies, have had the effect of softening the blow for many households, and postponing the full financial and psychological impact of the redundancies. Such circumstances may well have assisted what can be seen as a post-redundancy struggle to maintain the old order of gender relations, thus making it difficult to say with any certainty to what extent there will be significant changes now that these special factors are no longer operative.

I would also stress that I am concerned with responses to male *redundancy*, which may or may not be followed by male unemployment. This paper examines the sexual division of labour inside and outside the home in response to male job loss. It is important that the sample should not be *confined to* the male unemployed – although the resultant variety in the sample means, of course, that my conclusions must be based on rather small numbers.

Central issues

This paper, then, attempts to trace the complex interrelations between the labour-market experience of men and women, and the organisation of domestic labour in the wake of male redundancy. The central questions, crudely put, must be the following: how is work outside the household distributed amongst its members, how is work within the household distributed amongst its members, and what is the relationship between these two divisions of labour? One must then ask whether or not any non-residents contribute to domestic labour, and what effect their contribution has on the division of labour negotiated within a given household. To address the issues in this way is to distinguish two different aspects of the household's organis- ation. The distribution of paid work *outside* the household, between its members, will be termed 'the domestic division of labour'. The distribution of domestic tasks *within* household, between its members, will be termed 'the division of domestic labour'. This being said, in examining my data I shall deal firstly with the domestic division of labour (external), i.e. the distribution, between household members, of responsibility for the task of providing an income sufficient to meet the collective needs of the household.

The notion of collective needs requires some explication. First, it does not presume that all members have equal access to this income, though the manner in which it is controlled and allocated within a household is too complex to deal with here and will be the subject of another paper. Second, the term does not in any way preclude or ignore the posibility that non-members of a household may contribute to that household's income. Third, needs are not regarded as fixed; indeed, the renegotiation of levels of need is an important element in the response to redundancy. [12]

In the context of redundancy for a male earner we are especially concerned with whether or not there is a change in the domestic division of labour (external) as a result of redundancy, and to what extent this has been dependent on a renegotiation of the division of domestic labour (internal). I shall also focus attention on the more specific question of male unemployment, examining its effects on both types of labour.

The domestic division of labour

Out of a total sample of forty households there were only two households in which the woman had become the main earner, and remained so throughout the post-redundancy period, up until the time of interviewing. In one case all the children had grown up and moved away, and the woman (aged fifty-three) holds a well-paid and responsible position – a job she held at the time of the redundancies. In the other case the couple have no children and the woman (aged twenty-seven) works as an insurance bank clerk, again having held the job for some time prior to her husband's redundancy. In four other homes the women were gainfuly employed during fairly long spells of unemployment for their husbands – i.e. a period of one month or more without paid work.

Comparing the pre-redundancy employment status of women with their employment status at the time of interview (eighteen months to two years after redundancy) we find:

Pre-redundancy		Post-redundancy
23	Not in paid work	24
—	Self-employed with husband	1
12	Employed full-time	7
5	Employed part-time	8

The most marked change is, in fact, a fall in the number of women gainfully employed on a full-time basis. Although the number of women workers employed on a part-time basis has risen since the redundancies, compared with their pre-redundancy counterparts these women are employed on average for fewer hours. [13]

Clearly, any likelihood of a woman taking on the role of main wage earner has been reduced by the impact of the recession on the availability of employment for women. Nevertheless, fifteen women did have some form of paid employment at the time of interviewing, and we must now ask to what extent, if at all, this relates to the employment status of their husbands. The easiest and clearest approach to this question is to look at changes in the employment status of women, comparing pre-redundancy to post-redundancy employment status, and asking why the changes occurred. Let us first examine the cases in which a woman's gainful employment ended at some point after her husband's redundancy. Ten changes were due to redundancy for the woman, coinciding in four cases with the husband's redundancy, two changes were a result of the woman leaving employment because of pregnancy, and two changes were due to the women leaving employment because it was no longer financially worthwhile (one for tax reasons, one because her husband was claiming supplementary benefit).

A number of women commented that financially it would not be worth their while to work, since their earnings would be deducted from their husband's claim for supplementary benefit. This number is likely to increase as more households move from dependence on unemployment benefit to supplementary benefit. [14] Other women felt they should nevertheless keep their jobs, on the assumption that their husbands would eventually find work, and that they themselves were by no means sure of finding another job should they leave their present one.

Cases of a woman *taking on* paid work after her husband's redundancy accounted for thirteen changes in employment status, but in only two cases was the man unemployed at the time, and in each case the wife's job was part-time and temporary. The nature of a woman's decision to take on paid employment is in part reflected by the informal and fortuitous way in which the women found their jobs: nine by chance through information conveyed by friends, two entered joint ventures with their husbands, one returned to a previous job, one applied in response to a newspaper advertisement.

In summary, then, only four changes in employment status for women were directly related to changes in the employment status of their husbands: the two who gave up work for financial reasons, and the two who took on temporary jobs just before Christmas because their husbands were unemployed.

The division of domestic labour

We may now turn to the rather more complex issue of the division of domestic labour (internal). As the figures presented at the beginning of the paper were intended to show, a crucial question influencing a woman's ability to take on paid employment is whether or not she is responsible for the care of young children.

We must therefore ask who provided childcare when necessary in households in which the mother was gainfully employed, and compare the pre-redundancy and post-redundancy periods. Prior to the redundancies, of the twelve women gainfully employed on a full-time basis, seven had no children, and two had only adult children. The other three women had school-age children, in one case old enough to be independent, though under the supervision of a friend in school holidays. One woman's nine-year-old child was cared for by an older sister for a brief period after school, and one woman was able to determine her own hours of work, calling on her mother or sister, both of whom lived opposite, should assistance be required.[15] In other words, none of the women relied upon their husbands for childcare.

The number of women gainfully employed full-time had fallen from twelve to seven by the time of my interviews. Two of the husbands had experienced significant periods of unemployment,[16] but arrangements for childcare did not change fundamentally. One man would occasionally cook for himself and his school-age children whilst awaiting his wife's return from work, but this was by no means a regular or even predictable occurrence.

If we look at part-time workers then the pattern is similar. Prior to the redundancies, of the five part-time women workers, two would depend on their own mothers for childcare, one of whom was relieved by the husband on his return from work, two had children old enough to be independent, and one woman worked an hour a day as a school dinner-lady, her two children having dinner at school.

As I have already noted, part-time women workers increased from five to eight after the redundancies. Two of these cases were mentioned above and experienced no change in their arrangements. Of the remaining six, one took her pre-school child with her, collecting payments from house to house; one worked school hours only; one woman worked an hour a day (again as a dinner-lady in her children's school); one woman exchanged childcare services with a female friend living nearby (despite her own husband's unemployment); one depended on her mother-in-law; and one paid a baby sitter, her husband having left her.

In three cases of women taking on short-term temporary work, one called on her own mother and mother-in-law for childcare, whilst two relied on their unemployed husbands, one of whom simply took the child to his own mother.

As we can see, both before and after the redundancies the participation of men in childcare in order to free their wives to take up paid employment was minimal.

If we look more broadly at the division of domestic labour (internal), which of course includes childcare, then the question to be posed is double-edged: (1) We are interested in how domestic work within the home is distributed, given the fact that the woman, who traditionally performs the vast majority of domestic tasks, may have taken on additional work outside the home.

A number of authors[17] have convincingly argued that the minimum cost of waged labour is lowered as a result of the existence of domestic labour, an arrangement which necessarily operates to the advantage of capital. This does not in any way explain the process by which women have become primarily responsible for the domestic sphere,[18] though it does draw attention to their role in reproducing and maintaining the labour force.

(2) The question of who performs domestic labour when the main male earner becomes unemployed is of particular interest in this context. It seems clear (see Gardiner, 1975; Molyneux, 1979), that the only way in which a previous standard of living can be maintained with falling income is by an intensification of domestic labour. Where the division of domestic labour is along traditional lines male job loss may mean an increase in activity and responsibility for the woman, just at a time when the man has been deprived of his major focus of activity. Hence, where redundancy has resulted in long-term male unemployment, then we must ask whether the availability of free time for the man leads to his assuming domestic tasks within the home from which he has traditionally been freed by virtue of his labour outside the home. This question is of interest *whether or not* the woman is gainfully employed.

Role reversal?

Bearing in mind the paucity of examples of female main earners in my sample, I shall approach the first part of this question by the use of a brief case study in which I examine the implications of the notion of a 'role-swap', a term usually applied in situations in which the woman rather than the man has become the main wage earner in a household. The case I have chosen is the one which of all the sample demonstrates the *greatest* degree of flexibility on the part of the man:

Mr and Mrs D. have three children, aged six, eight and ten, and live on a large council estate close to Mrs D's mother. Mr D's parents live on the same estate but rather farther away. After his redundancy Mr D. experienced ten months of unbroken unemployment. His wife had taken on an evening job as a factory cleaner about a year prior to her husband's redundancy. Despite the fact that her husband's benefit was reduced because of her working Mrs D. decided to keep her job, on the assumption that he would eventually find work (as he did). Later, the couple jointly decided that Mrs D. should take on an additional part-time job as a home help. Mr D. had originally suggested that his wife seek full-time work, thinking she might have a better chance than he had of finding job. Mrs D. was not enthusiastic: 'Well, I wasn't very keen on the idea of him doing the housework because he wouldn't do it properly anyway, and I'd still have the lot to do after work.' During the period in which Mrs D. held two jobs and Mr D. remained unemployed, Mrs D. worked mornings until about 2 pm, and evenings from

5 pm until 8 pm. The children had their midday meal at school and Mrs D. would prepare their tea before leaving for work at 4.45 pm, leaving the dishes for her husband. She would then return from work to cook an evening meal for herself and Mr D.

Although in theory Mr D. took on the task of keeping the house clean, Mrs D. was far from satisfied with the arrangement:

He doesn't like housework anyway. I suppose he thinks it's not manly. He'd dust and tidy downstairs but he won't do upstairs because no-one sees it, and he won't clean the front windows in case the neighbours see him. I don't mind housework myself as long as I've got the time to do it, but I get irritable at the weekend when there's a backlog of things to do and he won't help. He just tells me to leave it. He doesn't understand that it's got to be done sometime. A full-time job would have been just impossible, but I think we'd have driven each other mad if one of us hadn't been out of the house for a bit in the day.

The couple shopped together while Mr D. was out of work, a change from the previous pattern, because Mr D. was available to drive his wife to the cheaper shops: I'd try to get him to come round the shelves with me and I was glad of the chance to show him the prices. I try to tell him now they've gone up but it doesn't sink in.' Nevertheless, Mrs D. had total responsibility for budgeting and for planning and catering for the household's weekly needs.

In principle Mr D. is against the idea that a woman might permanently become the main wage earner, while her husband runs the home:

A 'housewife' means just that. She's supposed to stay at home . . . While I was out of work I felt I wasn't playing a part in things, ashamed that I wasn't keeping my family. I suppose tension would have been worse if the wife hadn't been working, but I'd spend sleepless nights. I'd get up and come downstairs sometimes, at three in the morning, worrying that I'm the man and it's my job to see that everything's right between these four walls. If it's not then it's my fault.

The point to note about this particular case study, then, is that although the couple perceived the situation as a 'role swap' (albeit one expected to be temporary), in effect the woman continued to run the house, with minimal assistance from her husband. From his point of view, however, he had made a significant shift in the extent to which he participated in domestic labour within the home, in response to his wife's employment. He was also going against a well-established cultural tradition in the area. His comments may be taken as fairly typical, and were echoed by other men in similar situations.

Mr D., however, was more flexible than most. One woman, who had held a full-time job predating her husband's redundancy by about a year, spoke of his six months out of work and the viability of swapping roles:

It wouldn't work. He wouldn't stand it and there'd be more quarrels than its worth. I'd rather do the work myself . . . His mother used to throw it up at his family that she worked you see, and he'd never let it happen here. Anyway, I couldn't stand the strain. He'd be out with the horses most days (his friend runs a stable) and I'd get home at tea time to find nothing done. He wouldn't do a thing. 'What do you think I am,' he'd say, 'some old housewife?' It killed him some days seeing me getting up for work though. I'd like to have dropped the job just to show him, but we just couldn't do without the money.

Another woman in a similar situation expressed her feelings rather differently: 'If there was any way that I thought giving up my own job would help him get one I'd do it like a shot. It's hard on any man to be out of work.' There is clearly a strong feeling on the part of both men and women that it is the man's place to be the main wage-earner, and that any other arrangement will necessarily be in some sense stressful for one or both partners.

Spheres of responsibility

I wish now to consider more specifically the organisation of labour within the home. As always, when dealing with case material, and especially from such a varied sample as this, one is faced with the question of the representativeness of the emotions, attitudes and ideologies embodied in particular case studies. As a means of having some measure of this with regard to the division of domestic labour (internal) (hereafter DDL internal), I examined my data on the division of domestic labour in all the households at the time of interviewing, regardless of employment status for either husband or wife.

It is clear from the data collected that there are culturally established spheres of responsibility which guide the division of labour within each home, though some men will offer assistance in the 'woman's sphere' more readily than others. All of the literature attempting to deal with the division of domestic labour runs up against the same methodological problems. Normative statements from respondents do not necessarily offer a clear guide to their behaviour. Indeed, the men who most readily identified areas of domestic labour to which they would not contribute were in fact those who in general proved to be most flexible. Those men whose behaviour was most rigid in refusing to contribute to domestic labour often denied that there was any particular task in which they would not participate.

My solution to the problem has been to identify a core domain of female domestic activity and ask to what extent there has been any blurring of the boundaries in terms of actual behaviour. Assistance by men in the 'woman's sphere' was usually in the nature of 'occasional help'. By this I mean reasonably frequent assistance which, though not in any way regularised, is neither so rare as to be insignificant. The areas in which this kind of help is most commonly proffered are preparation of food, transport for shopping, help with the dishes, minding and playing with children (for short periods). In contrast to these areas of activity we find that the woman is responsible for washing and ironing clothes, bathing children, cleaning the house and planning the weekly shopping. There were twenty men who identified areas of domestic labour in which they refused to participate. Between them, these twenty men made thirty objections to activities related to the washing and ironing of clothes, and ten objections to tasks which were specifically seen as highly visible.

I shall refer to the pattern of domestic labour (internal) implied by the above as 'traditional', and go on to identify variations on this arrangement. The incidence of different patterns in my sample is as follows.

(a) *Traditional* (as described above) – sixteen households.

(b) *Traditional rigid* – fourteen households in which there is no evidence of a flexible attitude towards DDL (internal) on the part of the man, nor any actual blurring of boundaries between male and female spheres.

(c) *Traditional-flexible* – six households in which men have shown a significant degree of adaptability at some point since their redundancy, but in which domestic organisation is nevertheless based on the traditional pattern.

(d) *Renegotiated* – four households in which the man assumes responsibility for a substantial number of tasks traditionally regarded as 'female', although one can still identify a remnant of the traditional division of labour.

We might compare these findings with Oakley's remark that: 'In only a small number of marriages is the husband notably domesticated, and even where this happens a fundamental separation remains' (Oakley, 1974: 164).

If we examine the six households in which the division of domestic labour (internal) is traditional but flexible then we find no clear association between flexibility and the employment status of either spouse. In the six households in question only one woman was gainfully employed for a period which overlapped with a time of unemployment for her husband. In the remaining five households none of the women were gainfully employed, two of the men had experienced significant periods of unemployment since redundancy, one had been in almost constant employment though by virtue of a series of short-term jobs, and two men had experienced no unemployment.

Looking at the four households with a 'renegotiated' pattern of DDL (internal) we find that three of the women work full-time, whilst one is in ill health. Three of the men concerned are unemployed and one in full-time employment. This might suggest that full-time female employment, especially in combination with male unemployment, is an important contributory factor in bringing about a renegotiation of the DDL (internal). However, in the remaining six households where the woman is gainfully employed on a full-time basis the situation is somewhat different. Five of the homes are classified as having a traditional-rigid DDL (internal), and one a traditional DDL (internal), despite the fact that five of the men had experienced significant periods of unemployment. This suggests that some other factor must be present in addition to employment status to constitute a sufficient condition of renegotiation. It also suggests that, for at least some men, a response to unemployment, especially if the wife is working, may be to emphasise their traditional role. Let us look, now, at the second part of the question I posed earlier – the effects of unemployment on the DDL (internal).

The effects of male unemployment

In my sample of forty, eleven men experienced no unemployment after redundancy, and three were out of work for periods of less than a month only. Of the remaining twenty-six: six were unemployed for periods of 1–3 months, eight were unemployed for periods of 3–6 months, six were unemployed for periods of 6–12 months, and six were unemployed for period of 12 months or more. (These figures refer to their longest period out of work, and it may be that some of them experienced more than one period of unemployment.)

The responses of these men to the experience of unemployment were varied, but certain tendencies should be remarked upon.

It is clear that a number of men have reacted to unemployment by slightly increasing their contribution to domestic labour but without significantly departing from the traditionally established pattern described earlier. In other words, there may be an increase in general tidying about the house, help with the dishes, and possibly with food preparation. This seems to have occurred mainly where the woman is gainfully employed, but in no way represents a major assumption of domestic responsibility (internal) on the part of the man, and is in almost all cases viewed as a temporary arrangement. Mr and Mrs D. provide a good example. On the other hand, in certain cases where the wife lost her own job at the same time as her husband's redundancy, there has been a contraction in the man's contribution to domestic labour (internal) because the wife was then considered to be fully available to carry out such labour herself. As Oakley has noted, 'Legal definitions current in our culture tie the status of ''wife'' to the role of unpaid domestic worker' (Oakley, 1975: 135).

However, one may see an increase in male participation in domestic labour (internal), but again within the traditional framework outlined, in cases where the woman is not gainfully employed, and usually as a response to boredom on the part of the man. This pattern is likely to be short-lived for two reasons: on the one hand the woman usually finds interference disruptive of her own routine, and judges the standard of work performed by her husband to be low. On the other hand, often in the face of irritation on the part of their wives, men soon tire of domestic work, and anyway seem reluctant to make a commitment to regularly performing particular tasks.

Of the twenty-six households in which men have experienced significant periods of unemployment,[19] ten fall into one or other of the above patterns. Before considering the third pattern an illustrative case study may be helpful.

Mr and Mrs J. (aged respectively twenty-seven and twenty-five) have an eighteen-month-old child, and live in Maesteg, some three miles from Mr J.'s parents and five miles from Mrs J.'s. Since his redundancy Mr J. has experienced three months' unemployment, followed by one year's retraining, and a further year of unbroken unemployment. Mrs J. took a shop assistant's job towards the end of her husband's retraining course, lasting a month into this second period of unemployment. She left the job because her earnings were deducted from her husband's benefit claim. During the three months she spent in paid employment, Mrs J. continued to have full responsibility for running the home, while her mother-in-law looked after the child. During Mr J.'s time of unemployment and while Mrs J. was employed, he was to have responsibility for the child, but in fact went with her up to his parents' home.

Although Mr J. has difficulty filling the day, he participates very little in the domestic labour of the household. Rather, he gets out of bed as late as possible, reads, gardens, watches TV and spends occasional afternoons watching his father's video. He did some work on the house during his earlier spell of unemployment:

Then you start slowing down. I'm often not up till eleven because there's nothing to do. At night you can sit up late watching TV and reading. You lose your energy, can't be bothered with anything. The wife thinks I could do more. At first I did but you lose interest in everything. I'd rather go out and dig the garden – anything to get out of the house. She's always on the go and gets on at me to help, but if I try I do it wrong, or she does it again anyway, and gets annoyed at my interfering.

Mrs J. gives much the same account:

I like to do the housework myself really, because I need something to do, and don't want to be bored. If he does something I just do it again, but I still get cross to see him sitting about doing nothing and getting in the way . . . It disturbs my whole routine, and my friends don't like to pop in any more with him here . . .

Mrs J.'s comments reflect a feeling I detected in a number of other women, that is, that the home is their personal environment and the running of it something which they simultaneously resent and value. It is their domain, and the location of their identity. The very presence of their husband at home during the day is seen as disruptive.

The third and final pattern of response to unemployment on the part of men takes the form of an extreme reaction against any surrender of the traditional division of labour, which will be maintained by his creating some surrogate form of work. Sixteen of the twenty-six men who experienced significant periods of unemployment may be characterised in this way. Many took on the task of completing major structural alterations to the house – a popular use of redundancy payments (encouraged by the DHSS ruling about eligibility for supplementary benefit) and/or performing similar tasks for kin and friends. This response shades into a pattern of performing tasks for particular individual clients, for which some form of payment – not necessarily in cash – will be made (see Lee *et al.*, 1983). Alternatively, a man may accept paid employment which is not declared to the DHSS. In most cases such bouts of employment are short-term and unpredictable. In a few rare instances they will be full-time and long-term. Slightly more common is a pattern of fairly regular, though nevertheless insecure and unpredictable odd jobbing which may be for an employer, or an individual client.

It is interesting to note that of the sixteen men who had had such additional sources of income at some point since their redundancy, only three had done so whilst holding a relatively secure job. Mr and Mrs T. provide a good illustration of this kind of response to male unemployment.

A case of surrogate occupation

Aged respectively twenty-nine and twenty-seven, *Mr and Mrs T.* have two children, aged four and eight, and live on a large council estate in the same street as Mr T.'s parents. Mrs T.'s parents live a ten-minute drive away. Apart from one spell of employment lasting two months Mr T. has been unemployed ever since his redundancy. Initially he spent a good deal of time completing alterations to the home. Now he spends as much of his day as possible out of the house – gardening, or welding in a small garden shed, doing odd jobs for kin, neighbours and other contacts, and occasionally taking on a job jointly with a friend who lives nearby and dates back to school days.

Mr T. has a wide range of contacts within the locality, and a particular crowd of friends whom he sees regularly at a sports club. The only contribution he makes to the day-to-day running of the home is to occasionally prepare food, and to provide transport when his wife goes shopping, although he maintains that if his wife could find a well-paid full-time job he would gladly take over the running of the home. Mrs T., on the other hand, maintains that she could never consider a full-time job: 'He's hopeless. Not domesticated at all. With some it would be all right, but not Jim. He just couldn't manage. My work takes longer now he's home because somehow if he's there he's always in the way and never helps.'

Mrs T. has recently taken on a part-time job in her father's shop. During these afternoons working she relies on a friend to collect their youngest child from nursery class, along with her own son, and to mind him until tea-time. In return Mrs T. takes her friend's child for the full day each Thursday while his mother works for the day in her grandfather's shop.

What is remarkable about this case is that despite the recent change in the woman's employment status, and the long period of unemployment experienced by Mr T., the division of labour within the home has not been in any way affected, and Mr T. continues to organise his life as far as possible as if he were still in a full-time job.

Factors external to the household

Perhaps I can end this paper by making some tentative remarks about the possible influence of factors external to the household upon the domestic division of labour.

In an earlier paper (Lee *et al.*, 1983), I documented the mutual aid networks between men which support informal economic activity, and which clearly play a vital role in determining responses to unemployment. The suggestion was that where one finds an extensive local network of acquaintances between whom there is a high degree of mutual trust and regular contact there will be an informal exchange of information and services, producing opportunities for economic activity, whether formal or informal. A typical focus for the development of such a network would be a local sports or social club.

Elizabeth Bott's work (see Bott, 1957) has suggested that there is an association between the nature of a married couple's social networks and their degree of marital role segregation. Role segregation, she maintains, will be most marked where the couple are most deeply embedded in close-knit social networks. Harris (1969) has developed this idea and drawn attention to the vital importance of whether or not spouses after marriage retain membership of a single-sex primary group outside the family. Although there are aspects of Bott's work which are both confused and confusing,[20] her central insight has been extremely valuable in orienting more recent writing on similar issues (see Fallding, 1961; Turner, 1967; Edgell, 1967). In my own research, and on the very specific issue of the division of domestic labour there are a number of questions which arise in connection with Bott's hypothesis and its later development by Harris.

The most obvious concerns the readiness or reluctance of a married man to assume tasks within the home which are culturally defined as 'women's work', and the extent to which his attitude may be reinforced by membership of a predominantly male social network. Quite apart from the pressure towards role conformity which is likely to result from membership of a cohesive, all-male group, it seems also to be the case that membership of such a group can supply an unemployed man with ways of coping which do not require the renegotiation of the domestic division of labour – informal economic activity as a surrogate for paid employment and a source of personal income which would not otherwise be available, given the minimal provision made by supplementary benefit payments.

My data suggest not simply that men with highly developed local social networks are most likely to be presented with opportunities for informal economic activity, but that they are also most likely to maintain a rigid approach to the traditional division of domestic labour within their own homes.

The attitudes of women may, of course, be similarly influenced by the nature of their local social networks, but here the issues are not so clear-cut. On the one hand, a highly developed network of female friends and/or kin could provide domestic assistance, usually childcare, which would free a woman to take on paid work outside the home, whilst on the other hand, membership of such a network may be the source of social pressure reinforcing her traditional role, and emphasising her obligations within the home as a wife and mother.

Conclusions

The questions raised above will be more fully investigated at some future date, and I would like to conclude by referring back to the question originally posed: What is the potential for flexibility in the domestic division of labour (internal and external) in the context of redundancy for a male main earner?

In its broadest sense renegotiation is dependent not on male unemployment but on the availability of employment opportunities for women, which have fallen considerably in Wales as a result of the recession, albeit to a lesser extent than employment opportunities for men. In my sample the number of women working full-time has shrunk in comparison with the situation prior to the BSC redundancies, and though the number employed part-time has increased the average number of hours worked has fallen.

Where paid employment is available to women then there are three options concerning the division of domestic labour:
(a) The woman does two jobs – one in the home and one outside the home.
(b) The man assumes an increased share of domestic labour (internal).
(c) The woman remains responsible for domestic labour (internal) but looks beyond household members for assistance.
Of course some combination of these options will be likely to be adopted in any given case, and I have suggested that the sorts of arrangements arrived at will, in different ways, be influenced by the nature of the local social networks of each member of the couple.

Male unemployment raises further questions related to the potential for flexibility in the division of domestic labour (internal) whether or not the wife is employed. What I have reported here are a number of variations occurring on the basis of a massively taken-for-granted division of labour. Although there is some evidence of a blurring of the boundaries which segregate male and female labour (both inside and outside the home), there is no evidence of a fundamental shift away from the traditional pattern.

What I suggest is that we are witnessing a renegotiation of certain details of everyday life within the household which is so far distinct from any serious renegotiation of the underlying principles. My respondents appear to be dealing with a period of personal confusion in a context of dramatic social change by endeavouring to maintain some continuity with their past life, and this is, of course, an understandable initial reaction. Whether it will persist, or whether the slight indications of flexibility we have seen represent the first step in some more far-reaching reorganisation of domestic labour, it is impossible at this stage to say. One can only remark here that there are powerful social forces at work which will tend to preserve the *status quo*.

Notes

1   Based on research financed by the Social Science Research Council (SSRC) and

first presented at the 1983 British Sociological Association's conference 'Beyond the Fringe'.

2 Between 1971 and 1978 the male waged labour force for Wales as a whole fell by 2.4 per cent and the female waged labour force rose by 20.4 per cent. Between 1978 and 1981 the male waged labour force fell by 11.9 per cent and the female waged labour force by 7 per cent. In 1979 the rate of economically active women (41.2 per cent) was nevertheless low compared with the male rate of 75.8 per cent. We should also note, however, that in the league of female employment by region for the UK, Wales in 1979 was lowest with 41.2 per cent female participation as compared with the highest-ranking region, Scotland, with 48.8 per cent, and a UK average of 46.6 per cent (Labour Force Survey 1979, Table 4.5, Office of Population Censuses and Surveys).

3 Ann Oakley (1974: 136) has suggested that social science has played a part in popularising an egalitarian image of modern marriage which may be based on false premises.

4 From seventy-two to sixty-one between 1973 and 1980 – see General Household Survey, OPCS, 1980, Table 5.2.

5 See GHS 1980, *op. cit.*, Table 5.1.

6 Full-time employment rose from 25 per cent to 26 per cent for married women, 1973–80, whilst part-time employment rose from 28 per cent to 33 per cent (Table 5.2, GHS 1980, *op. cit.*).

7 GHS 1980, *op. cit.*, shows percentages respectively of 30, 62 and 71 as the age of the youngest child increases from 0–4 to 5–9 to over ten years, as the table below shows:

Age of youngest child	Mother's employment status		
	% Full-time	% Part-time	% Total
0–4	6	23	30
5–9	14	48	62
10+	28	43	71
TOTAL	16	37	54

8 GHS 1980, *op. cit.*, Table 5.10.

9 Each couple was interviewed jointly, and later as individuals in the absence of the other spouse. In contrast to Oakley, 1974 (*op. cit.*: 137), I was afraid not only of overestimating the male input to domestic labour but also of collecting distorted data which reflected certain resentments about the content of gender roles.

10 Men over fifty-five were likely to have responded to redundancy by opting for early retirement.

11 *E.g.* retraining, previous salary, preferential earnings-related benefit, the redundancy payment itself, make-up pay for those in jobs paying less than their BSC wage, etc.

12 There is, of course, an extent to which need is socially defined – see P. Townsend, 1979.

13 Pre-redundancy, four worked fifteen hours a week.
Post-redundancy, three worked five hours a week, one worked twelve hours a week, and three worked fifteen+ hours a week.

14 The length of time prior to the transition to supplementary benefit was lengthened for many by periods of retraining, on make-up pay, or by spells of short-term employment. Earnings Related Benefit had not yet been abolished.

15 Similar patterns of female-centred networks of mutual aid have been observed in various Third World cities – see L. D. Morris (July 1981).

16   I use this term throughout to refer to uninterrupted periods of unemployment
     lasting one month or more. In the two cases in question the men had been out of
     work for periods of four and six months respectively.
17   For a review of the literature concerned, see Paul Smith, 'Domestic Labour and
     Marx's theory of value' in Kuhn and Wolpe (eds.), 1978 and Rushton, 1979:
     32–48).
18   T. Gardiner has addressed this question in her article 'Women's domestic labour',
     New Left Review, 89, 1975: 47–57 (see 52–7).
19   See 16.
20   For comment see C. C. Harris, 1969: 162–175.

Women and unemployment: activities and social contact

This paper examines the question of 'what do working women do when they become unemployed'? And how far does unemployment lead to social isolation? The evidence is drawn from a study entitled *Female Unemployment – Redundancy Studies*, which comprised five case studies of redundancies. Women workers were interviewed approximately six weeks before leaving their pre-redundancy jobs and four to seven months after leaving those jobs. Of the 196 women interviewed twice, 164 experienced unemployment, of whom twenty-five were working when interviewed; the average length of time unemployed was 19.6 weeks. As the rate of re-employment was low we were interviewing women in the (relatively) early stages of long-term unemployment – a view confirmed by a follow up postal questionnaire three months later. The case studies were carried out in the Midlands (2), north-west (2) and south-east (1). The women had been primarily in the second stage of a bi-modal working career, employed in manual and clerical jobs in large scale manufacturing industry: they had been primarily employed full-time. Full details of the project, including a discussion of the jobs obtained by the minority of women who secured re-employment, will be published in a full report *Working Women in Recession: Work, Redundancy and Unemployment*, to be published by the OUP in 1984: this paper is concerned with only a small part of the study.

The extent to which unemployment causes financial hardship depends upon the financial resources available to the household unit, and is thus dependent on the financial contributions of all household members. However, for all women unemployment involved at the minimum a major change in their daily pattern of life – a change which they had not anticipated, and had not prepared for: 70 per cent of the women interviewed before the redundancy had anticipated working without a break until retirement, and 65 per cent had worked for their pre-redundancy employer for at least ten years. The women also experienced a major change in social environment: all the women had been working in plants of one hundred or more workers, but 66 per cent lived in households of three or fewer, resulting in an inevitable constriction on social horizons.

The extent and consequences of this change are discussed in detail in this paper. We outline what the women did when they became unemployed. We also discuss their evaluation of their activities during unemployment with their work activities (*not* their comparison of the state of being unemployed with the state of being at work). We conclude by discussing whether unemployment led to social isolation.

Activities

Before the redundancies the women expected that they would undertake a new non-domestic activity if they became unemployed – voluntary work – or extend a creative pastime – knitting, sewing or other craft work. Few women envisaged extending their domestic work significantly – only 15 per cent mentioned housework and none mentioned gardening. The actual activities which replaced going out to work are summarised in table 23.1.

Table 23.1 Activities replacing work for unemployed women

Women mentioning specified activity

	%
Housework	68
Visiting/entertaining/going out with friends/relations	44
Gardening	35
Knitting/sewing/crafts	35
Home decoration	28
Shopping	16
Reading	15
Walking/walking dog	15
Sport/gym	11
Baking/jam-making/freezing	10
Assisting relatives	6
Looking after relatives' children	6
Voluntary work	6
Hobbies n.e.c.	5
Looking after own children	5
Looking for work	5
Other	15

In general the range of activities mentioned demonstrated that most women filled most of the hours left free by not going out to work by expanding their existing role of housewife, rather than branching out into new activities. Some of the 'visiting and entertaining' was among family (35 per cent) and seemed to be considered as part of general family duties.

The focus upon domestic tasks was characteristic of the most frequently mentioned activities in all case studies and, less predictably, independently of marital status. Single, or married women without children, were no less likely than married women with children to mention housework as a substitute for paid employment. As they were mostly young women living with their mothers, their friends were usually at work during the day, and often their parents also: they tended therefore to assume more responsibility for running the house than they had done previously. No fewer than 79 per cent of single and childless women mentioned housework as one of the major activities that replaced going out to work: 58 per cent mentioned knitting and sewing; 47 per cent mentioned gardening; 42 per cent mentioned visiting, entertaining and going out and 32 per cent mentioned home decorating.

Social activities as a pastime varied greatly between firms, possibly reflecting local cultural patterns, the women from the two northern towns mentioning visiting, entertaining and going out with friends or relatives significantly more often than the women from the two Midlands towns. Variations in patterns of social contact are significant in assessing the impact of unemployment among women, as those women whose domestic lives are highly privatised are likely to be dependent upon going out to work for social contact. This aspect of unemployment is discussed later. Knitting and sewing were mentioned most often by garment workers, many of whom used their skills in making garments for friends and relations and occasionally for private sale.

Significantly, two of the most commonly mentioned activities did not provide a regular occupation. Home decorating was initiated as a practical use for redundancy money, mostly involving repainting and wallpapering, often after tradesmen had completed building repairs or renovations. Once completed it would not need to be done again for some time. Gardening, one of the more popular activities, is to some extent seasonal and mainly a summertime activity. A number of women mentioned in passing that, although unemployment might be bearable in the summer, they were dreading the winter when their activities would be further restricted.

The next most frequently mentioned group of activities were mostly directed towards recreation, but were mentioned by far fewer women: shopping (16 per cent); reading and visiting the library (15 per cent); walking and taking the dog for a walk (15 per cent); sport and gymnastics (11 per cent); baking, jam and wine-making and freezing (10 per cent).

The final group of activities were again task-oriented: helping or looking after sick or elderly relatives was mentioned by 8 per cent, whilst looking after nieces, nephews or grandchildren, looking for work, charity work and hobbies were each mentioned by 5 or 6 per cent of women. Only 4 per cent of women mentioned looking after their own baby or young children as a major activity. The remaining thirteen activities, mostly recreational, were each mentioned by only one or two women.

To a large extent the unemployed women simply spent more time when unemployed doing the things they had previously done during their non-work hours. However, we also asked the women which of their present activities they had started since becoming unemployed. A minority, 35 per cent had started no new activities, although 29 per cent had initiated more than one, including 7 per cent more than two. The activities most commonly mentioned as being new were: social (16 per cent); home decorating (13 per cent); gardening (9 per cent); knitting and sewing (9 per cent); walking/walking the dog (8 per cent) and reading (7 per cent). Amongst the two most commonly mentioned were the short-term activity, home decorating, and the seasonal activity, gardening. There were few indications of new activities replacing paid employment as a permanent means of spending time, much less of establishing a new identity.

The number of new activities did not increase with time out of work; on the contrary, there was an inverse relationship, the average length of time out of work being longer for women who reported having no or only one new activity than for women who reported two or more. The availability of redundancy money may have heightened people's opportunities for a short period after the redundancy: home decorating, gardening, knitting and sewing are all activities which require at least a small outlay of money.

Having documented how the women spent the time which they had available during unemployment, we were also interested to find out how the women rated their activities subjectively: in simple terms, to discover whether they found their domestic activities as satisfying a way of filling time as they had their paid employment, or whether they missed the activities involved in paid employment. The time available during the interview did not permit a detailed analysis of the rewards of the various specific activities with which the women filled the day: they were simply asked to rank each of the three activities on which they spent the most time according to whether they found the activity more or less interesting or about the same as the paid work they had been doing. Obviously, because of the multi-dimensional nature of the rewards of activities, not all ways of filling in time are directly comparable: household activities involve autonomy and a degree of freedom in time and space, in addition to the intrinsic interest (or otherwise) of the tasks themselves; market employment provides opportunities for companionship, especially in the jobs in which the women were engaged. Moreover, different values were attributed to the activities: in domestic life, the knowledge that the activity is performed for the benefit of family, and in market employment the feeling of performing a socially and economically useful and recognised service, possibly make domestic and paid occupations difficult to compare. However, the feelings of subjective satisfaction gained from different activities, no matter how unlike, were in many instances comparable. The majority of women were able to make a comparison, although this varied according to which activity was being compared with market work, the routine task activity of housework being the most easily comparable, recreational activities the least.

Housework was the activity on which women spent the most time. It was also likely to be considered less interesting than their previous paid employment: as table 23.2 shows, 52 per cent of women who included housework as one of their three major activities said that it was less interesting than their previous paid work, 18 per cent that it was about the same, and 10 per cent that it was more interesting. One woman summed up her post-redundancy activities as 'just basic housework you know. Just completely bored. Nothing else. I'm not clever at anything else'. On the other hand, knitting and sewing, productive activities which produced articles for gifts or even sale, were more likely to be ranked the same as or more interesting than paid employment (the high proportion in the 'not comparable' category being due to the high proportion of knitters for whom knitting was a subsidiary activity, done while visiting, watching television or resting). Social activities were regarded as only slightly more interesting than paid employment; we have already suggested that some 'social' activities were considered as duty rather than recreation. Gardening ranked about equal with paid employment, and home decorating slightly below, the high rate of non-comparability in the latter case being due to the temporary and non-routine nature of home decorating as a task. 'Other' activities were mostly recreational and were likely, but only by a small margin, to be more interesting than the job, with a large proportion not comparable.

Table 23.2 Rating of most time-consuming activities.

ivity	More interesting than paid work %	Less interesting than paid work %	About the same %	Not comparable %	Missing %	N
usework	10	52	18	18	1	109
ial	30	28	15	26		53
rdening	24	24	24	27		45
itting and sewing	30	12.5	27.5	30		40
me decorating	24	36	12	27		33
ier	29	23	16	33		146

(N = number of respondents mentioning each activity as one of the three on which they spent the most time)

When comparing the satisfactions afforded by domestic activities with those afforded by paid activities preference depends upon the intrinsic qualities of each and the environment within which they are carried out. However, differences in environment made little difference to the comparisons made by the women interviewed, if the woman's occupational status and husband's income can be used as proxies for environmental differences. Preference for home activities was not linked to occupational status or husband's income, although the numbers involved are too small to be conclusive. High status and high household income are likely to be associated with good conditions at work and at home: the privileged were comparing two privileged environments, the deprived two deprived environments.

In discussing 'recreational' activities there was a predictable change: activities involving expenditure declined, whilst activities involving little expenditure increased, although the changes were not dramatic – the most common response being 'about the same'.

Table 23.3 Changes in social activities whilst unemployed

	More %	Less %	About same %	Never done %
Going with friends to pub	9	19	37	35
Going with friends for meal	6	30	31	34
Visiting relatives	51	4	41	3
Having relatives to visit	34	5	56	4
Friends dropping in	45	7	39	9
Having friends round for meal/drink	11	9	47	33

Ten other recreational activities were also listed, involving only the respondent or her immediate family. Of these, gardening, sewing and other personal hobbies, and reading were likely to be done more by a majority of women, watching television was likely to be done more by a large minority. Other recreations listed: sport, going to sports events, going to the theatre or to bingo were most likely not to have been done at all before or after the redundancy. There was no difference in regional patterns worth noting.

Table 23.4 Changes in other recreational activities: individual activities

	More %	Less %	About same %	Never done %
Taking family on outing	18	9	43	30
Gardening, sewing, hobbies	67	2	25	6
Sports	18	4	22	56
Reading, bought	54	8	29	9
Reading, borrowed	41	2	21	35
Smoking	19	8	16	57
Watching television	37	9	51	3
Going to sports events	4	8	20	72
Going to cinema/theatre	4	12	15	61
Bingo	4	2.5	15	79
Having a bet	2	6	32	61

In comparing being unemployed with going out to work the women saw some advantages, the most frequently mentioned being the absence of pressure

(54 per cent mentioned this) and greater freedom, especially at the weekend (34 per cent mentioned this). In addition, only 30 per cent said that they felt that they had time on their hands either every day, or nearly every day. However, the majority of women believed that, in general, you get bored if you didn't have a job (70 per cent) – the proportion agreeing with the statement not varying with age, marital status or occupational status.

Social contact

Most of the unemployed women were married, but only 30 per cent had children under fifteen and only 52 per cent had children living at home. Since most of the husbands were working and most of the children were at school, in practice a large number of the unemployed women were at home alone during the day, and an even larger proportion at home alone during school hours. The change in the pattern of social contact following redundancy was therefore considerable. Moreover, some of the women commented that the pressure of work and domestic responsibilities had left them little time to form social networks outside work and family. Forty-one per cent said that they did not know many people in their own neighbourhood. Although it is commonly supposed that mobility is one of the causes of social isolation, there was no relation in our sample between being born in the district and knowing many local people.

We had expected that the women would spend more time with their family and non-work friends on ceasing work and that this would to some extent replace the loss of social contact from work. The women were asked if they saw more of their neighbours, friends, husband, children and other family on ceasing work. Only 12 per cent said they did not see more of any of the groups mentioned. A minority of women said that they saw more of neighbours and non-work friends after ceasing work, the proportion (32 per cent) who saw more of their neighbours being smaller than the proportion who said they knew many local people. It is possible that a large proportion of the people whom the women knew locally were at work during the day.

Unemployment did not necessarily mean that all women saw more of their immediate families: only 40 per cent saw more of their husbands or boyfriends and 37 per cent more of their children. The twenty-one women who had non-working husbands and the cleaners who had previously worked the 'unsocial' hours of evening or early morning when the family were at home saw more of their immediate family on becoming unemployed. But most husbands were at work during the day and children working or at school. In this respect unemployed married women probably find their circumstances significantly different from those of unemployed married men, many of whom are likely to have their wives at home to provide company.

Since household chores could now be done during the day instead of when the family were at home, family contact may have improved in quality if not in quantity. However, patterns of family interaction are probably slow to change, and only a few women mentioned increased family contact as one of the advantages of being out of work. Members of the immediate family were simply usually not present to provide an alternative to the social contact of the workplace during the day.

On the other hand a majority of women (54 per cent) tended to see more of their wider family. Although 16 per cent of women had no husband or boyfriend and 29 per cent had no children, only 7 per cent had no other family; neighbourhood networks may atrophy from neglect when women go to work, but family ties can provide a permanent – if sometimes only latent – link that can be strengthened when circumstances require. Many women had retired parents, or mothers, sisters and other adult female relations who did not go to work, either because they had young children at home or because they belonged to an older generation when women were likely to stay at home. These women were available to provide company during the day.

Table 23.5　Contact with other family since leaving work.

	Total %
More	54
The same	38
Less	1
No other family	7

Only 20 per cent of women said that most of their personal friends came from work. However, the advantage of social contact in the workplace is that it is easily accessible, whilst a private friendship network is normally limited by constraints of time and distance and often unable to provide day to day company. Nearly all the women had found their work groups congenial, 86 per cent of the unemployed women saying in the interview before the redundancies that the atmosphere in their work group was normally good or very good, and only three women referring to work group relationships as poor. Nearly all of the women had some personal friends among their work mates – 83 per cent had at least one and 74 per cent had more than one. Moreover, work provided social contact which, although not described as personal friendship, was nevertheless considered valuable in itself.

The likelihood that most friends came from work increased slightly the lower the occupational status, except for a relatively small group in occupational status 5, who were mostly part-time cleaners and had few workmates, with whom they spent relatively little time. The inverse relationship between job status and work friendships may have reflected the varying opportunities within each status to cultivate friends: the higher the status the more likely that the woman worked for much of the time on her own in a competitive situation and under pressure, under conditions that did not encourage the cultivation of many personal friendships.

Stage in the life-cycle, and possibly also regional cultural patterns probably influenced the degree to which women relied upon the workplace for companionship, and therefore the effect of unemployment on social contact, depending upon whether they are young and single or middle-aged and married: social life for the former often revolves around courting and going out with friends at night, for the latter the extent to which most non-work social contact revolves around family, meeting with other women during the day, or going out and visiting with husband and other couples during evenings and weekends probably varies considerably from one group to another.

Table 23.6   Social contact on leaving work by marital status

Marital status	Social contact				
	More %	Less %	The same %	Other comment %	N
Single	29	43	29	0	14
Widowed/sep./divorce	29	40	40	0	20
Married	24	63	11.5	1.5	130
Total	24	58.5	16.5	1	164

Changes in the amount of social contact after the redundancy show variations by marital status and stage of life cycle. Single and younger women were thus likely to say that they had the same amount of social contact after the redundancy as they did before, although a substantial minority (43 per cent) had less, as indicated in table 23.6. Some lived with retired parents or a non-working mother and therefore were not alone during the day, and for most the focus of their social life was going out with friends or boyfriend at night, activities which appeared to increase, not diminish, on redundancy. As mentioned before, married women were likely to be alone in the house during the day: the large majority of married women and women over thirty-five therefore said that they had less social contact on becoming unemployed. Married women were also the most likely to say they felt more isolated: 55 per cent of married women said they felt more isolated as compared with only 27 per cent of single women.

Differences in age were slightly more significant statistically than differences in marital status, with older women more likely to say they had less social contact on leaving work, as shown in table 23.7.

The women were invited to comment generally on the changes they perceived in their social life and contacts since ceasing work: 34 per cent could not think of any major changes, 13 per cent mentioned more than one. A minority of comments, 19 per cent, centred on the enrichment of general

Table 23.7 Social contact on leaving work, by age

Age	Social contact				
	More %	Less %	The same %	Other comment %	N
18–24	40	20	20	20	5
25–34	17	55	28		29
35–44	20	61	17	2	59
45–54	29	59	12		51
55–59	25	65	10		20
Total	24	58.5	16.5	1	164

social life, and a further 9 per cent on the enrichment of family life: among this group the main points commented upon were that it was possible to see more of friends in the day-time, to stay out late at night without having to get up early, to get out and about in general and to meet local people in the streets and shops.

You are just freer, you have more freedom. You have no social life when you are working – it's so limited, so you are freer to choose when you're not working. It could be a dinner dance during the week you can go to now because you don't have to worry about being tired the next day. (Valve assembler)

Being at home and around the shops you bump into local people much more and more of different members of the family – you can be more useful to your relatives at home. (Engineering asseembler)

I'm closer to my family but I spend more time on my own during the day than I've ever done. That's a mixed blessing, sometimes I'm glad of it, sometimes not. (Machinist)

A further 10 per cent of comments related to a change in social life without any implication of impoverishment or deterioration: mixing with a different group of people, spending more time with elderly neighbours, mixing less with men, no longer going to the pub with workmates. The majority of comments (61 per cent) related to a deterioration in social life, some demonstrating extreme loneliness and feelings of losing touch with society.

I feel as though I'm drifting – it's only when I'm working with people that I feel I have a purpose to life or a pattern to life. I can't come to terms with the life I lead, doing housework over and over, sometimes you think of things – you haven't got anyone to talk them over with. (Machinist)

You can become in a little world of your own, nobody to say hello to. You get very lonely. I've been out for a walk around just to see another person. (Engineering assembler)

Others related to a deterioration in the quality of social life, or to a social world that had begun to shrink:

Generally less mentally stimulating people to meet. (Clerk)

I see less of everyone except my husband. We've always got on well but since we are both not working I feel we *might* get on each other's nerves. (Machinist)

The home is always here – you know everything everyone is going to say. (Cleaner)

I think you get out of touch – like in the morning I used to sit with the men for my lunch and it's surprising the worldly conversation, and things you learn. You would hear other opinions when at home you have only yourself to think about and no on really to talk to all day. (Valve assembler)

The common use of the word 'social' to mean contact with other people in a recreational context only rather than all contexts including work and family resulted in some difficulty of communication over questions which were designed to discover the extent and quality of changes in the women's contacts with other people in general. When asked directly about whether they felt from their own experience that unemployment led to loneliness and increased isolation, the majority of answers were affirmative: 67 per cent of women agreed that 'you often get lonely when you haven't a job', and 52 per cent said that they felt more isolated on leaving work. Fewer women felt that the quality of their social life had deteriorated: only 32 per cent said their social contact was less satisfactory, and 35 per cent that their circle of acquaintance was more restricted. That the social contact previously provided by their work environment was important to the women even if it was not a major source of personal friendships is apparent from the responses from factory E. Only 10 per cent of the women from that factory said that most of their friends came from work, and only 54 per cent said they had any personal friends at work, but 82 per cent agreed that 'you often get lonely if you haven't got a job'. Nearly all the women missed the company they had enjoyed at work: when asked what they missed most about their jobs 80 per cent of all the unemployed women mentioned missing the company of their workmates.

Although areas could not be rated as close-knit or otherwise on the basis of questions, there was a difference in the proportions of women in each factory who felt socially deprived by unemployment. This indicated a regional pattern, the women from the two West Midland towns and the south-east being more likely to feel socially deprived than women from the two northern towns. Table 23.8 shows the proportional variations from the average for each factory in answers to the questions on whether they had less social contact, whether it was more restricted and less satisfactory, and whether they in general felt more isolated on leaving work.

There were no significant differences in feelings of social deprivation between different occupational statuses, although women from lower statuses had been more likely to draw most of their friends from work; women from statuses 1 and 2 were just as likely to say that unemployment led to loneliness, that their social life and contacts were less satisfactory and they felt more

Table 23.8 Social deprivation on leaving work, by factory

Factory	Less contact in general %	More restricted %	Less satisfactory %	Feel more isolated %	Total %
C2	+ 3	+ 9.5	+ 19.5	+ 15	+ 47
C1	+ 14	+ 8	+ 1	+ 9	+ 32
A	+ 8	+ 11	+ 5.5	+ 1	+ 25.5
E	+ 1	− 4	− 5	− 2	− 10
D	− 10	+ 2	− 8	− 9	− 25
B2	− 1	− 15	− 25	− 2	− 43
B1	− 12	− 24	− 10	− 14.5	− 46
Base (%)	58.5	36	32	52	

isolated. The numbers are too small to be significant, but the twelve unemployed women from status 1 were more likely than average to say they felt more isolated (75 per cent), that their social life and contacts were less satisfactory (50 per cent) and that their circle of acquaintance more restricted (42 per cent). This may indicate that the value of association with others in the work environment is independent of the number of personal friendships made.

Table 23.9 Unemployment leading to loneliness, by marital status

	Marital status			
	Single %	Separated/widowed/divorced %	Married/cohabiting %	Total %
Agree	46	65	69	67
Disagree	46	35	28	30
No opinion	8	—	2	2.5
N =	13	20	130	163

Married women were significantly more likely to say they had less social contact on leaving work than single women. It is therefore not surprising that they were more likely to feel that unemployment led to loneliness. 69 per cent of married women agreed that unemployment led to loneliness, compared with 46 per cent of single women.

There is a risk of injuring people's pride in asking questions about the extent to which they suffer any form of deprivation: people often blame themselves for their misfortunes. In asking the women about their subjective feelings of deprivation as a result of unemployment we ran the risk not only of offending them but of their answers being biased by pride or a feeling that it showed weakness to complain. People are likely to be particularly sensitive about questions to do with their own success or failure in maintaining an adequate level of social contact. We tried to deal with this problem by asking the women to compare their post-redundancy with their pre-redundancy life where possible, rather than make any absolute assessment of their present life, and also asking some questions impersonally: whether they agreed or disagreed with statements that are 'sometimes said' about unemployed people in general rather than themselves personally. A higher proportion of women (67 per cent) said that they agreed with the statement that 'you often get lonely when you haven't a job' than said they themselves were 'more isolated' (52 per cent) or 'had less social contact' (58.5 per cent). This leaves us with no way of knowing whether some women answered the impersonally phrased questions according to how they considered the majority would feel, whilst excepting themselves, or whether more women were likely to reveal their true feelings when questions were phrased obliquely rather than directly. We can say that a minimum of 52 per cent of women felt 'more isolated' and a smaller proportion, 32 per cent, felt that their social life and contacts were 'less satisfactory' since leaving work.

The answers to these questions do not reveal how serious a deprivation the women felt this to be. There is, however, a strong association between decline in social contact and the incidence of self-reported periods of depression following the redundancy (PR = 0.023), and an even stronger association between depression and feeling that social life and contacts were less satisfactory (PR = 0.000); 72 per cent of depressed women said they had less social contact compared with 48 per cent of women who were not depressed.

Conclusion

This paper has outlined the consequences of unemployment for the activities and social contacts of formerly working women. Such changes are not the most dramatic consequences of unemployment: economic hardship, ill-health, 'loss of identity' are more dramatic – and likely to be less common. However, changes in activities and contact happen to everyone. For the majority of women unemployment resulted in a constriction of social horizons, and to some extent social isolation. The activities which replaced going out to work were in themselves, on the whole, less highly regarded than going out to work; the most frequently mentioned activity was housework, which was also the most time-consuming, and regarded as less interesting. Similarly, unemployment did not lead to an extended social life, although the changes in the level of social contact generally varied substantially between regions: there was some support for the *gemeinschaft* allegedly characteristic of Lancashire (in contrast to the Birmingham conurbation).

For the majority of women unemployment did not lead to inactivity. But it did lead to time being spent on less interesting activities and to reduced social contact. Womens' activities whilst unemployed were heavily domestically centred, and did not usually involve social contact. Significantly, reduced social contact was especially common amongst married women, 55 per cent of married women saying that they felt more isolated now that they no longer worked. The reduced social contact led to the obvious danger of social isolation, and in extreme cases signs of depression. Equally, it reduced involvement in the informal networks which are helpful in providing access to employment opportunities – especially part-time employment opportunities which do not justify the expense of formal advertisement. Overcoming social isolation, especially in major conurbations, involves the expenditure of money (on fares, shopping, pubs, cafés), at a time when the redundant women had fewer financial resources than previously, and activities involving expenditure were being reduced.

The effect of unemployment was thus to reinforce the domestic preoccupations of the previously employed women. Such preoccupations did not provide the basis for any but the most attenuated 'role' since the majority of women no longer had dependent children – the role available was that of housekeeper rather than mother. When full-time working women become unemployed they do not move from one role to another, they simply lose one – like men.

24 *Marie-Agnès Barrère-Maurisson, Françoise Battagliola,*
Anne-Marie Daune-Richard

The course of women's careers
and family life

Translated by A. Gordon Kinder

Introduction

The increase in female activity observable since 1960, which has maintained
its progress until quite recently, in spite of the economic crisis and latent
underemployment,[1] leads us to make an enquiry into the underlying determinants of the phenomenon, which is often said to be irreversible.[2]

This study of women's progress at work and its connections with family
life has the aim of shedding light on certain aspects of the logistics of how
women enter employment. Taking account of the connection between progress at work and family life in this way does not provide a subject for study
predetermined as such, rather, it results from approaches made in research,
and arises from an attempt to build up a theory.

These approaches represent more than a mere juxtaposition of the two
spheres of activity. They break with traditional methods of approach in terms
of choice and plurality.[3] These last-named, in fact, suppose that women,
and in particular married women, are 'kicked about' between the two
extremes of paid work on one side, and the home and motherhood on the
other, in such a way that they are forced to choose one by abandoning the
other, or to hold both at the same time. This concept implies that two
autonomous spheres exist: paid work on one hand, housework on the other.
Because of this, women's professional activity is analysed with reference to
family life, notably to family responsibilities, which is not the case with men.[4]
Conversely, studies are made, for example, of the impact of women's professional life on their conjugal life.[5]

Our approach breaks with this type of analysis, to the extent that it tries
from the outset to grasp the phenomena of professional life and family life
in so far as they are connected with each other, because they arise out of
a single principle of logic. This is the principle of the division of labour which
assigns to men as well as to women their place in the family and in industry.
It has taken specific forms in our societies: men have been primarily assigned

to the working world and charged with maintaining the social status of the family group; women have received primarily, but not exclusively, the charge of the family. Indeed, the fact that women have had devolved on them responsibility for doing the work of the household has not excluded them from paid employment, but the technical and social division of work is based very closely on the social differentiation of the sexes, which tends to place men and women into different social groups.

This is why the place of women in the working world cannot be analysed as a mere reflection of their place in the family. Conversely, by making observations at the level of connections between work and home, the effects of the coming and going between the two spheres may be grasped. In analysing simultaneously social relationships as they operate in the family and in the workplace, for example, we need to identify the progress of women, whose motivation is not to be found solely in the desire to master one field or the other, but rather in movement between one and the other, and the direction and content of this.

Our approach also marks a break in relation to work which analyses the situation of women as particularising a general model which is male, or as arising out of determinants which are intrinsically female, i.e., linked to women themselves as a biological sexual category. These analyses tend, in our estimation, to abstract women from the social relationships in which they are bound up, and thus to isolate them as a subject of study. We feel that it is important to place women in the social relationships that are their determinants, so that we may understand how the differentiations between men and women are produced, and of what they consist.

It is in order to study exactly how these differentiations are constituted through the professional life of women that we have been led to plot the course of their progress at work (= professional trajectory). Setting in motion such a diachronic approach permits us to follow the professional evolution of women from their education and training to their first employment, to pick up interruptions in and resumptions of activity, as well as professional mobility, i.e., changes of employment and the operation of qualification or disqualification. By putting together such professional trajectories, it is possible to understand how they are built up, step by step, and how each step continues the one before it, and foreshadows the one that follows it. Taken as a whole, the professional trajectory assumes a direction, and each occurrence, to be understood and interpreted, must be situated within the whole of the course pursued.

The professional trajectories of the women have been constructed from an analysis of interviews which asked questions with the object of finding out biographical information.[6] In this way we were able to retrace the chronology of events. Thus may be picked out the relations between women's place in production and in reproduction at different stages of their lives. The interest in this biographical approach is that it allows at one and the same time various methods of reading the results of the interviews:[7] a thematic reading, that is to say, synchronic (on themes relative to the life-cycle, as, for example, the apportioning of roles within the family); a symbolic reading; and, above all, for our objectives, a reading of events (or a diachronic reading), throwing light on comparative chronologies of men and women, as family life unfolds. An attempt may be made in this way to display tangibly the emergence and development of the processes: viz., the professional trajectories of women as they overlap with family life.

The samples[8] to which this article will refer, obtained from different pieces of research, are of limited size. In this respect they do not aspire to be 'representative'. The ambition of this article is first and foremost to have a qualitative nature. The specific function of the approach here operated is to assess the value of the processes through which professional life and family life are connected: the time, the places, the methods by which they are linked together, to make up the determinants of the professional trajectories studied.[9] What these samples have in common is that they gather together interviews with women who belong to relatively homogeneous social categories, factory and office workers for the most part,[10] which make up the majority of active women workers. Some of the women have been continuously active, others discontinuously, having left professional life and gone back to it. They are all mothers of families, and are relatively young (mostly between twenty-five and thirty-five).

Comparison of the results of the various pieces of research presented here with those of other approaches, both qualitative and quantitative, has, moreover, allowed us to give a wider context to the problem studied.

In order to throw light on the processes which allow us to understand how the professional trajectories of women are made up in their connections with family life, we shall follow a chronological order. Thus, after showing the role of the family as it affects women's entry into the machinery of production, we shall attempt to illuminate the connections between the content of activity, the kind of employment, and family life. Finally, we shall try to see how the upward progress of women is organised in their place of work in relation to their place in the family.

Method of women's entry into employment and family of origin

Drawing up professional itineraries, anchored in individual biographies, has allowed us to show how much the role of women in the family intervenes from the earliest age to structure their entry into production, and to mould their relationship with their professional work. In this respect, the professional and social destiny of women appears to be already strongly indicated by their place in their family of origin.

So we shall study in this first part interactions between professional tra-

jectories and family life successively through the education and training of
girls, the form of socialisation they encounter in their families, and the role
this plays as a means of access to employment.

Differential schooling and training according to sex and sibling group

The women interviewed came generally from lower-class families. The father
was a factory worker or a tradesman, more seldom an office worker or
middle-class. The mother had no job, or had occupied, more or less discontinuously, a job as a cleaner or factory worker; several of them were cleaning-
women in farmers' or tradesmen's houses.

Taken as a whole, differences which could be important are noted in the
level of training attained, and the kinds of jobs occupied, by the girls and
the boys who are siblings. In fact, the analysis of the interviews shows that
from the youngest age the families develop educative attitudes about schooling
and training, which affect children differently according to sex. Indeed, some
women[11] had their primary schooling interrupted because they had to help
(or replace) their mothers with the younger children. This situation is always
linked with the financial problems of these working-class families, which are
greatly increased when one of the two parents disappears (by death or
divorce), but it affects girls differently from boys.

When the time arrives for a course of professional training to be followed,
the boys are most often directed towards an apprenticeship (with the Certificat
d'Aptitude Professionnelle in view), and the girls see their professional future
laid out within the fairly well defined limits of their roles in the family, and
particularly their place in the sibling group. So it is that frequently one of
the girls takes a first job straight after the end of compulsory schooling
'because' the brother is taking a training course. According to the composition
of the sibling group, there is a division of roles amongst sisters: one takes
on the task of 'bringing some money in' whilst the other 'looks after the
house'.

In this way, girls often have to give up the idea of obtaining any training,
or put off the idea of going out to a job,[12] or perhaps both together, in order
to help or replace the mother in her household chores. In this respect, the
number of brothers and/or sisters, as well as the place amongst the siblings,
appears to play a determinant role for the daughters of those working-class
families whose financial difficulties limit their capacity to take on the cost
of training for each of the children. In this situation, the eldest daughters
of large families have a tendency to have thrust on them numerous handicaps
before they even begin to go out to work.

But the influence of the family of origin on professional training interferes
also with the 'choice' of the content of the training. The latter is dictated
by various considerations. First of all, it can be established that the means
of advancement chosen have the common denominator of being at the same

time very 'feminised' and considered as potentially 'useful' to a married woman and mother. So there are such things as sewing ('it will always come in useful'), or office work where the hours and the possibility of taking days off or working part-time allow women to 'reconcile' their professional activity and their family responsibilities. [13]

Material considerations also affect the choice of what training girls may take. These bring into play the place and role assigned to girls in the family. Indeed, some girls were not able to put into operation their plans for professional training because they would have had to leave home to go and live in another town. In every case this consideration met with parental refusal, and this happened regardless of the family's financial means. Women who mentioned this kind of difficulty came from relatively favoured families [14] (compared with others in the sample we are dealing with), and they were composed of comparatively few children: most often one boy and one girl, or an only child. The father had experienced a definite process of upward mobility. In fact, it is always an opposition of 'principle' and not one motivated by financial considerations that is mentioned. [15]

In all, this kind of difficulty results in a short training-period, or one interrupted prematurely by lack of interest, an entry on to the labour market very underqualified compared with the level of education, and an unstable professional trajectory. Thus, a woman with a technical baccalaureate (A level in technical subjects), then one year of Institut Universitaire Technique, began her professional life working on a department-store check-out and is now an unskilled worker.

Relationship between professional future and family future according to sex and class

By offering different opportunities for access to training, families impart a relationship with the professional future which is not the same for children of both sexes. From the earliest age, girls find themselves subjected to the inculcation of their role as future mothers and wives in the family, and this is done not only through the control of their 'morality' (supervision of the use of their time and occupations outside school or work, the impossibility of 'going out alone', and *a fortiori* of living alone, [16] but also through a definite assignment of household chores. [17] Indeed, even if the degree of their participation in the chores implied by the latter varies according to the profile of the family (composition of the sibling group, and rank occupied within it, mother having an outside job or not, one-parent families, and/or in financial difficulties), it is nevertheless true that it is *always* the daughters who help or replace the mother when the need is felt. Their help is called for much more often than their brothers', whether it be at the level of daily domestic chores, or of much more onerous responsibilities (such as looking after younger children, or sometimes even the management of the entire household). Their assignment to the time-space of the home is clearly – and in detail – laid down from infancy.

The transmission of a domestic complexion to daughters concerns not only 'know-how', but also the relationship of service in the family which links the women as a group to the men as a group.[18] The former, *by reason of this fact alone*, find they are relatively interchangeable when it comes to household chores. Trained from their earliest days to help, and, when needed, to replace their mother, girls are thus prepared for a future which revolves *par excellence* round the management of family life and the allocation of household chores. Their encounter with professional work is made through the 'filter' of their role in the family: choice of training 'adapted' to this end, being put to paid work which answers the need for an additional wage rather than the need to acquire a trade. The transmission of a relationship may appear to differ somewhat according to the social level and position of the mother. To begin with, professional entry of girls into unqualified jobs allows them to wait for marriage, and sets their feet more or less on a course which will be available only to intermittent workers: or, on the other hand, what is transmitted may value continuity of professional activity as such (interrupted possibly by marriage) – professional activity providing financial independence through social contacts and a wage – a continuity their mothers were not able to achieve, given their precarious situation.

The conditions in which boys are led to find a professional direction take account of their future responsibilities, so that the income and social status of the family may be assured. Aiming at the acquisition of a professional position, and, by the same token, a social one, they have a relationship with household chores that has little compulsion, and they enjoy a measure of independence outside the family circle. For the girls the opposite is the case; moulded to their domestic role, tied down to the time-space of the family, their relationship with professional work – and with the future – is very much defined by the family circle. They are directed towards professional activity in accordance with criteria almost exclusively to do with the family. The question for them is to acquire a skill (e.g., sewing) which they can use for various members of their future family, or to take a job which will provide a 'useful' source of income for the family, but in any case the motive is not to reach a position in society by that occupation.[19] Boys are directed towards permanent jobs which allow them to envisage a certain development in their career, whilst girls are led to take jobs which present an 'immediate' usefulness in accordance with these criteria, even though their initial qualifications differ according to the milieu in which they originate.

Network of access to employment and family of origin

From the research done in Marseilles,[20] it appears that the family of origin has a decisive role to play in the manner of access to employment. Indeed, two-thirds of the women interviewed made direct use of family contacts to obtain a job,[21] either someone known to the family, or people of the same neighbourhood – who, depending on how well the family is integrated into the district, are often the same people. Other research (Fournier, 1982; Gaudrey-Turpin, 1982; Gokalp, 1981) confirms these characteristics, which would appear to be particularly marked amongst women from working-class backgrounds, and/or who have a low level of training. Unfortunately, we have not found statistics which compare the courses of men's careers with women's in this respect. The work of Gokalp (1981) which presents the results of an enquiry by INED amongst young people under twenty-five does not distinguish between boys and girls (pp. 72–3). The secondary use made of this study by Fournier (1982) considers girls only, but the groupings she uses preclude comparison on this point with the table cited.

In any case, and beyond the quantitative picture of the phenomenon, the latter does not have the same significance in the two cases. Firstly, because it does not concern the same people. When boys find a job 'by family inter-mediaries', it is most often the father who is concerned.[22] When we come to girls, the research in Marseilles we are considering here shows that this is rather an exception. In the majority of cases, it is women who come into the picture when a job is sought: most often the mother, but almost as often an aunt, sometimes a female neighbour. In one case the woman in question was a grandmother.

These results are in fact no more than illustrations of the context in which the differential courses of the careers of men and women originate and find a direction. For boys it consists of an initiation by the father into the world of men by obtaining a male occupation;[23] for girls it is the female network that comes into play to gain access into a female job. The former will form a masculine view of professional employment and of their role in the family; the latter will see in an 'exemplary' manner how women enter jointly both family and productive structures.

In fact, assigning women to the time-space of family life, and the differentiation between boys and girls which operates from the very beginning, involve 'naturally' a greater dependence of girls on the family, including this dimension of 'network of employment'. Like girls, boys, especially when they have few qualifications and come from working-class families, are very dependent on the family for access to employment,[24] but the dependence of girls, even though it appears to be statistically greater,[25] is above all of a different nature: it is not only that the means (in terms of acquaintance, kinship, etc.) are less available to women than to men for help in finding a job, but rather that priority is given to their assignment to the family circle, which limits the range of possibilities for them.

Education and professional training moulded by the housework which they must (or will have to) take on, assignment to the time-space of family life, and subordination of professional work to the latter: such is the direction imposed by families of origin on the entry of women into a career. In fact, these ideas are part and parcel of the transmission to girls of domestic habits: 'know-how', but also a code of conduct and integration of a pattern attaching to their future role as wives and mothers. For women, the significance and the place of professional occupation are defined within these limits; in this direction their relationship with activity and with their employment is built up – as much at the level of what they actually do as of patterns provided – as a corollary to their place and role in the family.

Professional activity, employment, and domestic group

After showing how the different methods whereby women obtain jobs are tied up with their family of origin, we shall now attempt to bring out by what means their professional activity (i.e., activity as opposed to inactivity) and their employment (i.e., type of job possessed) are modelled by the life of the family group to which they belong.

First of all, we shall consider the problems tied up with the activity and the employment of women, in order to grasp how the different components of family life help to determine the content of that activity, and how much they determine their progress in a job. Then we shall attempt to see how much the choice of employment is influenced by the problems women feel are tied up with the relationship between professional work and housework, and what role the domestic group plays in this.

Professional activity, employment, and family life

The analysis of the situation of women in the face of activity and employment, as it is at different moments of professional life, from the moment of taking the first job, and then over the whole of the professional career, will allow us to understand how the family components and the individual components (such as professional training) are linked together; and to understand, on the other hand, how these links mould the exact manner of entry into employment. We shall consider in turn the problem of the first job in its relationship with the training acquired, then the cycle of activity, before identifying the main tendencies concerning the course of women's careers.

Training, first job, and family life
The role of initial training is a determinant of the entry of women into a profession, and has a direct influence from the moment of taking the first job.

In the enquiry carried out in the Paris region concerning women with qualifications (e.g., trained office workers, technicians, management), it is averred that only one woman in three had a first job on a level with the training acquired, in which case entry was relatively late. Another third of the women had a first job which did not correspond to the training acquired: here it is a question of women who failed the course of training they were taking, or of women whose level of training is distinctly higher than that needed for the first job. This includes women with the type of university education which does not automatically confer a well-paid job, or those whose education was interrupted, notably because of taking a job earlier than expected for financial reasons. The final third of the women had no training at the time of taking the first job. What has been noted earlier about the schooling of girls in the family of origin allows us to understand what really are the conditions in which entry into employment is accomplished (in working-class families, quite often without any preliminary training).

Entry on to the labour market is in fact very premature for many of these women. In the sample of wives of unemployed men – as with female factory workers and office workers interviewed in Marseilles – one woman out of two began work at eighteen; some of them had even held a full-time job from the age of fourteen.[26]

This is the reason why most women enter professional life at a disadvantage, earlier than they ought to, and in conditions that compare very badly with their qualifications. Moreover, the conditions which apply on entry into professional life contribute to moulding the course of the professional career,[27] and seem once more to be determinants of the level and quality of jobs gained on re-entry after a break in employment.

Professional activity of women, professional work, and domestic work in the family

If we consider the development of the professional activity of women during their lifetime, that is, their cycle of activity, three groups of women may be distinguished. The first is of women who have never worked (they are said to be 'totally inactive'), of whom there are very few at present, 3 per cent according to the survey of the Centre d'Etudes d'Emploi in 1974 (Chaudron, 1984). The second consists of women who have had continuous activity, and are said to be 'totally active' (for the moment this group represents about one-third of the women). By far the largest group is the remainder, which we have called 'intermittently active'. The latter have experienced one or more interruptions and re-entry into activity during their professional life. Although the general movement in the activity of women tends towards a certain homogeneity which has almost reached stability,[28] the phenomena of intermittent work are still very important for certain categories of women.

The simultaneous analysis of the development of the cycle of women's work activity, and of the cycle of their family life, permits us to see clearly the imprint of family life (*equally* family events and the professional life of the male partner) as it affects the professional activity of the women. This is what we have attempted to bring to light as it concerns women who, after a break of several years, are re-entering professional life.[29] We have here a fairly homogeneous population as far as the content of activity and family structure go, although there are divisions between qualified women married to middle or upper-class husbands, and unqualified women married to qualified factory-workers.

If we compare the development of their professional activity from their first entry on to the labour market with that of their male partner (likewise from his entry on to the labour market), and put this alongside the development of family life, a number of noteworthy facts appear.

In the first place, we note that men exercise a 'trade' for the whole of their professional lives, an occupation which they take up early and which they pursue steadfastly in spite of some interruptions in activity. These interruptions, when they take place, are due to military service early on, then, later on, events linked with the very exercise of their professional activity: industrial accidents, unemployment, etc. From the fact that changes in direction are rare, the trade exercised allows them to 'make a career of it' to a certain extent. Women, on the other hand, experience frequent breaks in activity, of varying duration. Sometimes their marriage causes a break, because it often involves a removal. Mostly they interrupt their activity for reasons directly concerned with the family: removals to follow a husband where his career takes him, and especially having and bringing up children. Returns to activity are equally motivated by family reasons (generally financial problems) which require the woman to replace her husband, e.g., taking a job when he is prevented from working. These returns to activity, like leaving it, are not always the result of personal choice on the woman's part. In contrast with their husbands, because of frequent interruptions, they do not exercise a 'trade' which would require them to follow a career, but have 'jobs' of a temporary nature, of differing sorts and durations according to the periods of activity.

Thus a real division of labour is set up in these families, which at the same time allocates role and tasks.[30] This allocation of roles fixes the men in production, and the women first and foremost in the home, with a possible second role as worker. It constrains women to work for family reasons only, such that this work sometimes takes the form of an occasional substitution for the head of the family, and sometimes becomes a more or less permanent contribution towards maintaining the level of family income. But in any case, the woman's employment must be compatible with her primary role in the home.

Thus, all the time, as family life develops, the balance of tasks between housework and paid employment is maintained. When the husband is the only worker, the wife takes charge of domestic work; when she replaces her partner in taking paid work, she still continues to ensure that the necessary domestic work is done. *It is for this reason that professional work of women seems to have a specific role in the family*: if we consider the whole of the development of family life, it does indeed ensure a role of *regulation within the family.* [31] This method of regulation permits the balance between the total of paid work and the necessary domestic work to be maintained all the time. The fixed point of this balance is domestic work. The wife keeps on adapting herself, passing, according to how family life develops, from the role of mother to that of mother and worker, as family necessity dictates.

Career courses and family life

The development of the professional career, already very strongly imprinted from the moment of beginning the first job, suffers, as we have just seen, the repercussions of family life, such that the intermittent character of professional activity linked with family life, expressed for many women by a continual see-saw motion between activity and inactivity, weighs heavily on the quality of their re-entry into employment. Each break in activity, indeed, is a factor of disqualification, such that they are led to take up progressively jobs which are of a lower level and of greater instability. In the case of women without training, each break in activity accentuates the precariousness of their situation. In every respect, the intermittent nature of their activity, linked with family life, determines the weak degree of re-entry into the machinery of production.

However, two sets of figures seem to emerge with regard to the degree of sufficiency which exists between the level of training and qualifications for the first job. Indeed, for the women who have been able to reach this degree of sufficiency (generally, qualified women, as we have seen), re-entries are concerned with taking jobs which operate as help in emergencies: women are led to play the role of occasional substitutes for the head of the family. So the courses of their careers are marked by a process of disqualification. On the other hand, women who had no training, or who had a first job different from the training they had acquired, when they re-enter take up jobs 'to bring some money in'. These amount to brief, temporary jobs to make a contribution to household income, since all re-entries are motivated by the overriding financial needs of the family. We do not observe any process of disqualification in the case of these women, for the simple reason that they are not qualified in the first place! But their entry into employment corresponds simply to bringing funds into family life, whenever there is a need, with a return to the home as soon as possible.

This is why, when a situation arises such as a long period of unemployment of the partner, we see unqualified women returning temporarily to the labour market, but returning home not long afterwards; whilst qualified women, having had an unqualified job for some time, change it for a qualified job and envisage a permanent re-entry. The husband's unemployment has merely brought this forward.

It seems quite clear that the level of initial training, strongly determined by the family of origin, contributes to the nature of women's activity, or to its rhythm (continuous or intermittent activity). A low level of training favours discontinuity for family reasons. This has important consequences for the quality of the later course of the career, and contributes to the division of women between stable and unstable, qualified and unqualified employment, with increasing mobility, or, on the contrary, progressive disqualification.

Thus, there would seem to be two kinds of professional career for women, corresponding to two kinds of progression between a certain sort of training and certain types of employment (or even networks of jobs);[32] on the one hand stable careers with continuous activity and mobility to jobs of equal or higher standard; on the other fragile or unstable careers, which feature re-entries with frequent breaks in activity, temporary jobs, and mobility to jobs of lower standard.

Connection between professional activity and domestic work, and the family network

We shall examine here the effect of the connection between professional work and domestic work on the choice of employment, and the role played by the family network in this respect.

Connection between professional activity and domestic work, and criteria of employment

Whether women are trying to re-enter, or are seeking their first job, the criteria of a 'good job' illustrate above all the subjection of their professional activity to the exigencies of household work. The practical considerations which guide a woman seeking a job, more especially when she is also a mother, are to earn a wage that will better the family income, whilst having working hours that will allow her to carry out the housework.

Beyond the fact that it is devolved by society on women, domestic work is characterised by being at the disposition of the family. Moreover, it is – it has to be – 'invisible' work, hidden, carried on in the main away from the presence of other members of the family, particularly the men. The 'choice' of a job is very strongly influenced by her having to seek one which offers the best conditions for her to carry out this domestic work: the overriding criterion is that she should be out of the house for the shortest possible time. Thus, the distance from the workplace, the possibilities offered by the firm as to the working conditions (notably the hours to be worked), are the points primarily considered, long before the requirements of the job or the level of wage offered. The directions imposed by the family of origin on the course of women's careers are thereby reinforced. When they have succeeded in finding a firm that offers good conditions according to these criteria, the women interviewed describe their activity as a possibility of improving the family income that does not interfere (or interferes very little) with doing the housework at home.[33] The acceptance by women of the working conditions and remuneration which are offered to them when they do their professional work in their own homes must be examined in the light of these data.[34]

If the chance of acquiring a qualification or making a career are often seen to be compromised at the outset by the conditions of education offered to girls in their family of origin, these are diminished still further by the burdens of motherhood. Thus, we found a factory worker, who, after becoming a forewoman, interrupted her professional activity to bring up her children. When she wished to go back to work, she looked principally for something 'near home', and did not even think of mentioning the qualifications she had previously. She has now been an unskilled worker for seven years.

The matter of hours to be worked plays a great part in the relationship of women with work, because it has a big influence on the way in which housework can be done, and on the availability of the wife/mother to her family. In any case, strategically, women aim for as big a concentration as possible of the hours of professional activity in the day or in the week. In this respect, continuous days, staggered hours, forty hours worked in four and a half or even four days,[35] shift work, are working formulas prized by the mothers of young families interviewed in the Marseilles enquiry. Such timetables offer a substantial lack of overlap with the working hours of other members of the family, which allows them to carry out an important proportion of their housework in the space of time left free, and to be relatively available to their husband and/or children when the latter are at home. The management of their timetable by women appears therefore to be based on criteria of the alternation of working and not being at work.[36]

Besides, taking an overall view, we notice a distinct preference for hours (or shifts) which begin in the early morning,[37] which permit women to have some time alone in the house and still to be available to the children when they come home from school, by robbing some of the hours of sleep. Let us emphasise that this primacy of housework often involves additional burdens for women in their daily rhythm of sleeping and waking, and also on the development of their professional work. Thus, in a firm whose work was concentrated into four days, working on a continuous-day basis, a factory worker reduced the forty-five minute break halfway through the ten-hour stint to fifteen minutes to allow her child half an hour longer in bed in the morning.

Such hours out of phase with the rest of the family, so sought-after by women, are part of the logic of the invisibility of housework, but they have as a corollary the greater rigidity of conjugal roles. The division of chores between husband and wife tends to be reduced to a minimum, since everything is done when he arrives. Even when a wife is on the afternoon shift permanently or alternately,[38] she has prepared the meal in the morning, so that her husband has only to 'warm it up'. When she is on the morning shift, she has most often got the children's clothes ready and laid the table for breakfast. The only exceptions in this direction concern couples working in the same firm on opposite shifts, so they can relieve each other in the care of the children; this is met with more often in certain office-worker milieux [39] than in working-class milieux. [40] We must note, however, that quite a lot of women who are employed on regular day-work, both office and factory workers, rise early and do between half an hour and one hour of housework before waking the rest of the family, preserving thus – at least in part – the invisible character of domestic work. [41]

Role of kinship network in the relationship between professional activity and domestic work

The criteria which guide women in their choice of a job thus depend to a great extent on the material circumstances in which they are able to carry out concurrently professional activity and housework. Now, at least in the socio-professional categories we are considering here, [42] these circumstances seem to be very strongly tied up with the make-up and proximity of family connections. Indeed, it seems that the division of household chores – and thus the degree of constraint they impose on the women's professional activity – is far from being restricted to the couple themselves, but cuts right across the whole of the family network. However, the role played by the latter in the execution of the household tasks of the conjugal family functions in accordance with precise rules.

In the first place, it is the wife's family that is basically concerned. Appeal is made to the husband's family only if the wife's is absent (parents dead, geographically distant, or the wife brought up in an institution). In other (rare) cases of recourse to the husband's family, a tension between the wife and her own family may be noted. [43] Secondly, it is almost exclusively the female members amongst the wife's relatives who come into the picture: essentially the mother, to a lesser extent the sisters, sometimes an aunt. This observation confirms the hypotheses which arose from the previous work, [44] which show the collective character of women's allocation to domestic work, and their relative interchangeability in this respect within a given family.

Particularly in the Marseilles sample (factory workers and unqualified office workers) we note a relative rigidity in the conjugal roles, and at the same time what may be called a mother/daughter axis as far as sharing of household chores goes. [45] This concerns largely the care of children, either full-time, or as a 'stop gap' before or after school hours, or on Wednesday [a half-holiday in France], or during the shorter holidays. We can see what importance such help holds for women who have staggered hours or shift work. Thus it is not unusual, when the woman goes off to work very early in the morning, for her mother to come and get the children up, make their breakfast, and send or take them to school. [46] But this help does not stop at looking after children, it affects meals as well: often the mother brings a cooked dish to her daughter for the evening meal, or invites her to the mid-day meal when she is on the morning shift. And finally, it is she who sees to the mending and darning for the family. To a lesser extent, grandmothers knit and sew for their grandchildren. The other members of the family (sisters, aunts) give help on a more occasional basis, rarely more than just looking after children.

Everything is done as though the domestic help offered by the family – principally by the mother – constitutes for women in the socio-professional categories we are looking at here an element which permits professional continuity after the children are born. [47] The amount of this help, together with its flexibility, allows a certain material relief – not to say moral support (knowing that children do not have to be left alone). But another dimension of this kind of organisation appears to be possibly even more of a determinant: the circulation of domestic work within the confines of the female members of the family, passing on the collective allocation of the women of one single family, allows it not to be sub-contracted outside the family-group, thus sparing the women the feeling of having abandoned their domestic role.

The preferential recourse to the mother can then be understood better, as can regrets expressed when she is not available or far away . . . and the stratagems developed by the women interviewed to get nearer their family of origin, especially by those who are factory workers. In the Marseilles sample, nineteen out of thirty-four women who had mothers living, live in the same block, or in the same neighbourhood as her, even in some cases living with her. [48] Amongst the rest, several expressed the hope of getting nearer to their mothers, either by moving, or by getting her to move nearer to them.

Thus, for women whose level of training is low or nil, the conditions for exercising their professional activity seem to be strongly structured by the nearness of the family network. By tending to reduce the distance between their homes and their parents' on one hand, and between home and workplace on the other, they maintain and develop their place within the family network which facilitates their access to work and their chance of remaining in it after children are born. In fact, we note a greater professional instability and more significant risks of disqualification amongst women who are – or who have been – cut off from their family network. [49]

As far as the course of women's careers goes, these efforts to reduce the physical distance between the conjugal family, the extended family and the workplace, tend to facilitate women's professional activity [50] and its continuity. [51] But, at the same time, the great importance given to the idea of a 'good job' has a negative influence on mobility. When the organisation that allows women to reconcile professional activity and domestic responsibilities appears to be satisfactory, the inclination to change jobs is almost nil, and arises only under the effects of external events (closure or removal of the company, family happenings). Indeed, every change in working hours, of the means of transport, of the time taken to travel between home and work, risks jeopardising the balance between professional activity and domestic work. This lack of professional mobility reinforces the conditions obtaining at the initial entry of women onto the labour market (low level of training, direction towards female sectors in maintaining them in career patterns which have no future). Additionally, the attitudes of reserve they develop with reference to professional training proceed from their initial level of training, but also from the material complications that this training would bring into the adjustments between professional activity and domestic work (at the same time, as we shall see in the next paragraph, as possibilities of promotion and training offered to women in the companies). In this direction, the fact that women are in a 'good' family network – particularly when they are poorly qualified – works in favour of a stable career profile, but also one where promotion is often blocked.

In fact, the role that parentage plays in the course of women's careers does not function in one direction only, and ought to be analysed in its complexity. The support it offers, looked at as a network of access to employment and system of circulation of household work, represents an important element in the facilitation of female professional activity, particularly at low levels of pay and qualifications. At the same time, the initial conditions of education, training, and entry into employment offered to girls by their families of origin, as well as the efforts to maintain the family network, developed by the women themselves, constitute cumulative factors in blocking careers. The high degree of importance given to family structures, and to mother–daughter relationships, may be analysed in terms of social mobility: even though we should not ignore the support mothers bring to the professional activity of their daughters. Although they themselves may most often be inactive, they demonstrate a positive attitude to the professional activity of their daughters, convinced that these days the wife's wage is indispensable in order to guarantee the level of resources of a household, as well as the mental equilibrium of a married woman (and her financial independence, if this was felt to be necessary). At the lower levels of qualification possibilities of promotion exist because of this support. It is by counting on the household help (and the material aid) of their mothers that some women have managed to involve themselves in a process of training and of professional mobility, with the aim of obtaining better qualifications.

The courses of women's careers are, then, deeply affected by doing the work in their own homes, which falls primarily on them. Since it is up to them to regulate the balance between sources of income and domestic work within the conjugal family, their conditions of access to work and the course of their careers are largely dependent on maintaining this balance. The hazards which affect the husbands' professional careers (geographical mobility, type of working hours) induce, as far as wives and mothers of families are concerned, unstable and interrupted professional trajectories, which according to their initial level of training, may also be disqualifying. In this context, we note that the fact that women are in a family network often coincides with better enablement/training/job, and exercises a stabilising influence on their careers by intervening at two levels: as a network of access to employment, and as a support in carrying out the household chores. In any case, the criteria of a 'good job' for women are first and foremost determined by the conditions available to enable the household tasks to be accomplished, and these are even lower than the level of initial training – and the wages. In the groups included in this survey, we distinguish two types of outline for women's professional trajectories: either the activity is discontinuous and the breaks in it are progressively discounted by disqualifications; or it is more stable, but, in certain kinds of employment, progress appears to be blocked.

Sexual differentiations of types of employment, and positions in the family differentiated by sex

The characteristics of women's employment are more often related to the peculiarities which arise from their position in the family structure. Indeed, we have seen so far to what extent the courses of women's careers bear the mark equally of their place in their family of origin, as of that in the family to which they presently belong. Turning now to differentiations according to sex, job, career, we may ask ourselves whether these do not more than translate the 'inequalities' produced elsewhere within the processes of reproduction (the family, the school, etc.), or whether on the contrary, the differentiations between men's and women's trajectories do not respond to specific modalities of resources, of labour management, which engender a sexual division which superimposes itself on the social division of labour, in conformity with the machinery of production.

Thus, making employment precarious (work on an interim basis, fixed-term contracts, part-time work, etc.) which affects female labour particularly, appears to be actually indispensable to companies in the framework of transformations of the wage-relationship.

On another level, the disqualification of women does not always correspond to an absence of qualifications, but to the fact that the qualifications looked for by the management are not rewarded when they are feminine characteristics. This is the case, for example, with manual dexterity and nervous resilience. [53]

Or again, because women are 'precious' and 'irreplaceable' in the jobs they occupy, openings towards other work are excluded for women who do certain jobs. [54]

Sexual division of labour in industrial production

The conspectus of research done in recent years on the place of women in the machinery of production is that technical and social division of labour is strictly superimposed on sexual division (Molinie & Volkoff, 1980).

In this setting the different destiny of men and women in the production system appears to be one of the forms taken by the relationship between the social groups constituted by men on one hand and women on the other. These social relationships between the sexes go right through the whole of our social structure, in the production system as well as in the family. Women's (and men's) professional trajectories are the result of their enmeshing.

The analysis of this enmeshing has been our concern during two of the studies quoted: one carried out in Marseilles amongst female factory and office workers, and the other in Lyons amongst male and female office workers.

The sexual division of labour which manifests itself through the differentiation of jobs and careers rests on the respective positions occupied by men and women in the framework of the family, but it cannot be reduced merely to that. We shall see how it is established and reproduced by specific procedures: a policy of personnel management, a whole series of informal rules, tactics of officials; all of them are to be found in the social relationships of men and women in the productive machinery.

As far as female factory workers go, it must first of all be emphasised that the majority are unskilled or manual workers (79 per cent), whilst this is the case with fewer than half of male factory workers (40 per cent). Female workers are primarily submitted to the constraints of work done at often very fast rates, to its fragmentation, and to hierarchical relationships which take on a disciplinary aspect more often than they do with men. Moreover, the employment structures are such that there is no way of promotion open to women. The training available in companies is aimed primarily at men. Thus, in one case we see a training course for technicians, which, because it requires a Certificat d'Aptitude Professionnelle in mechanics, is in practice accessible to men only, whereas elsewhere courses for sewing and dressmaking are offered to unskilled women who work in a cooked-meat company.[55]

In the tertiary sector, where, after all, the recent strong increase is due essentially to female labour,[56] a comparable sexual division of labour is observable.[57] In the Social Security service, women represent 73 per cent of the personnel, but more than three-quarters are in subordinate jobs, as against half of the men. As service becomes longer, the gap between men and women employees increases still further.

Men and women enter this service very young, and with comparable entrance qualifications (generally a Brevet d'Etudes du Premier Cycle or a CAP in office work), and at first they occupy the same jobs 'at the bottom of the ladder'. Recruitment, not very selective, goes in harness with an intensive system of promotion, which aims (at least until very recently) at permitting every employee to mount all the rungs of that ladder progressively. But the rule of 'equality of opportunity' is applied in a very selective manner, depending on whether men or women are concerned.

After about ten years of service, men and women occupy very different positions: some of the men have become office managers or specialist officers by way of a competitive examination which gives access to a training-course, most often one that depends on internal promotion on recommendation by heads of section. Men who have not been promoted occupy 'marginal' jobs for the most part, on mobile teams, at the counter, on telephone claims, maintaining equipment. These jobs have a greater element of independence than other non-promoted jobs, and are less subject to pressure from the hierarchy, the need to produce results is not so pressing, and the pay is often rather better.

On the contrary, amongst the women, few manage to gain promotion, the majority occupy 'basic' positions which are most subject to technical division of labour, and to the criteria of producing results; they are in sedentary and repetitive jobs, such as entering clients' details into the computer.

The differentiation, then, between male and female clerks, concerns not only access to staff posts, but also the kind of jobs held. This second discrimination, which does not involve any difference of classification, is much less visible than the first. Nevertheless, it is a clear sign of the gulf between the sexes within the confines of the institution. As in the factory, where there are workshops for men and others for women, there are in the Social Security offices sections which are rather more male, and others which are more female. Men and women are subject to different working conditions. This split reproduces the socially dominant position of men (mobility, independence, capability of making decisions, exercise of responsibilities) and the sexually dominated one of women (sedentary occupation, subjection to the need to produce results, to the decisions and the rules of the hierarchy).

The processes that lead men and women from a common departure point to different jobs are hidden, which benefits the dominating ideology of the institution, according to which the position of women is related to the nature attached to their sex ('it's women's work') or to the way they are seen primarily as belonging to the family sphere, which alone explains their lack of professional competitiveness ('they come to earn a wage that will augment the family income', 'they only think of their family').

This ideology of the respective places of men and women is expressed equally by a whole array of social measures which aim to allow women to reconcile professional activity and domestic work: maternity leave (on half pay, or without pay), days off to look after sick children, possibilities of working part-time. Such possibilities are offered to women only, either in the Social Security offices or in private enterprises where the women clerks' partners work. The result is a stagnation of the careers of those women who take advantage of them.

This discrimination between the sexes is not so much deliberately thought out, as the result of a body of day-to-day practices which give expression in the working world to the respective social positions of men and women. As we have seen, these positions are inculcated in the family of origin, and are made more positive at the time of marriage; workplaces in their turn reinforce them, especially by their procedural rules.

Practices and strategies of men and women: reciprocal influences between the division of labour in the workplace and in the family

The practices and strategies of managers are deployed in accordance with the following two definitions:

(a) by the sexual division of labour within the company: differential posibilities, according to sex, of access to certain jobs, to the routes to promotion, to 'authorised' interruptions in employment;

(b) by the sexual division of labour within the family: after their marriage, the essential household work falls on the women.

As far as unskilled workers are concerned, after taking due account of the structures of the firms where men (or women) work, one of the ways of improving qualifications and wages consists in changing companies or following an additional period of training. This is what working men do (or did, before the rigidity of the labour market caused by the crisis), then accepting longer working hours or travelling time. For women, such a strategy of sideways mobility, and/or seeking qualifications, comes up against the constraints of daily life. For married women and mothers of families, continuing in work implies indeed the existence of an organisation which will allow them to take on both professional activity and domestic work. Such an organisation rests in large part, as we have seen,[58] on the circulation of household work between mothers and daughters, and the restriction of the geographical space between conjugal family, extended family and workplace.

Clerks of the Social Security have a possibility of being promoted in the same workplace, or, at the very most, promotion implies a change of centre in the same town. But, for women, undertaking a promotional strategy, or trying to obtain a coveted position, requires a greater mobilisation of energy than for men of a similar standing. They must bring their aptitudes to the notice of the hierarchy (essentially male) and enter into competition with the whole group of men that surrounds them. Indeed, the routes towards promotion are drawn according to sex. The majority of men 'rise' by way of internal promotion. This route appears to be closed to women. Those women who are armed with sufficient scholastic luggage aim at preparing for a management course by taking a competitive examination;[59] a much more difficult route which requires considerable preliminary personal work. What is more, preparing for this examination, then gaining access to a management course demands a new daily organisation (longer working hours, more travelling . . .). She requires the participation of other members of the family, and therefore their support in her professional plans. If the mother is not available to relieve her daughter in carrying out her housework,[60] the relationship between man and wife within the couple is put in question by the wife's professional strategy. We have never met with such a case in our enquiries.

Clerks are in the great majority continuously active.[61] If almost all of them extend their maternity leave to the three months on half-pay allowed by the Social Security, few have recourse to a longer parental leave. Having at most two children, they are thus absent from work on average twice six months during their active life. In addition, a few ask to work part-time.[62] Moreover, the women who take a long maternity leave, or work part-time, have a substantial length of service (between six and thirteen years). It is after making efforts to gain promotion, or experiencing progressive disqualification in their job, that they decide to interrupt their activity briefly or to reduce their working hours when a new birth occurs.

Thus, the arguments so often put forward to 'explain' sex discrimination in employment and careers (absenteeism or breaks in professional activity) are found to be questionable. If it is certain that such breaks, when they occur, are rewarded by a disqualification,[63] the sexual division of labour sanctions for all women – continuously or discontinuously active – first and foremost their social position within the sphere of reproduction.

But, in return, the sexual division of work within the limits of the workplace acts on the family function in the direction of making more rigid the positions traditionally devolved on men and on women.

Thus, strategies of sideways mobility by working men, or their obtaining promotion often imply a change of company, which will increase the distance they have to travel and their working hours. This means that women assume the responsibility of doing practically all the housework.

In the same way, promotion of male office workers or their access to more gratifying posts is translated on the level of the family to an increasing delegation of the housework to their wives. The husbands' participation tends to be reduced to looking after the children in the morning, whilst the wives, on the other hand, begin their work as early as possible, so that some time is freed in the evening to devote to their children and to housework. The husbands' working hours stretch further into the evening, and when they return home 'everything is done'. Thus the professional plans of the husband tend to structure the daily organisation of the whole family group. On the contrary, the woman's time is subjected to the demands of the other members of the family for her to be permanently available, which is characteristic of domestic relationships;[64] professional strategies of the wives may in no way upset their fulfilment of household tasks. As one of them says, 'you must have a mother if you wish to prepare for the competitive examination to get into the management school . . . ' – her husband has just obtained a management post by internal promotion!

Moreover, the progressive specialisation and disqualification that women suffer often engender a degree of disillusionment vis-à-vis what they expected from their job, particularly office workers: job satisfaction, getting to know people, service to the public. Also, many clerks, like female factory workers, have an ambivalent relationship with their work.[65] The lack of interest in the job is a bitter criticism, but, all the same, the women have a strong attachment to their jobs. For them, indeed, a job is never an attainment reached; it always needs to be justified, even defended. For women, the most 'natural' outcome of a job which ties them down and pays little is . . . when it comes to an end! But, all the same, they are attached to this opening (of their homes) to the world outside, to the relationships established there, to all the social life which is woven within the framework of their job.[66] 'Working' is to experience independence, self-determination with reference to the family, which penetrates into private life, and cannot leave totally unaltered the relationship of dominance within the conjugal pair.[67] As Borzeix and Maruani (1982; 1984) demonstrate in the case of female strikers employed by CIP, disputes at the factory make something move at home. Reconsideration of the manoeuvres of exploitation and domination suffered by women at business and in the home cannot fail to disturb both of these 'spheres'.

Sexual division of labour in business on one hand and in the family on the other proceed from the same reasoning: to assign women to the domestic sphere, whilst at the same time using them as a continuing source of semi-skilled workers (i.e., mobilised and used as though they were semi-skilled).

Whilst women's professional positions are related, in the classic manner, to their place in family structures, men's are conceived of as independent of all family integration.[68] Nevertheless, the logic of the working world, just like men's professional strategies, rests on the expectation that elsewhere someone will take responsibility for all the work connected with reproduction. The requirements of working hours, of mobility, of 'nervous investment', of 'aggressiveness', imply a 'free' worker, free of all domestic encumbrances, totally available to industry, whose invisible, reverse side is the permanent availability of women, active or not, to industry.[69] In the same way, within the bounds of industry, devolving on women the subordinate tasks that have no future provides a springboard for men's professional advancement. In this sense, 'woman is (certainly) man's future'.

Conclusion

The construction of women's professional trajectories requires us to take account of the interrelationship between professional life and family life as they develop in parallel. Indeed, the events which punctuate family life (marriages, births . . .), as well as the professional destiny of the other members of the family group, condition very strongly the continuity or discontinuity of women's professional activity, and the forms that the course of their professional career takes. This obvious interreaction between the two spheres in which women's practices and strategies are deployed does not for all that mean that their professional positions are merely a reflection of their position in the family. In order to get behind simply recording social and professional inequalities between men and women, it seems necessary to submit an examination of the problem of social relationships between the sexes to analyses which view family responsibilities in terms of handicaps (or obstacles) to professional life. As we have attempted to show, sexual division operates simultaneously in production and within family structures. Its effect on women's place in social relationships of sex (and of class) is therefore increased in both spheres.

From the family of origin onwards, the processes of socialisation, conditions of access to training and the content of that training, sort girls and boys out in accordance with their (future) position in the relationships of sex and class, and sketches out for them different futures within both family and production. Training for 'feminine' occupations, and the segmentation of the labour market according to sex, contribute to setting girls in specific channels in employment, which they enter mainly by means of the network of their female kinship. This orientation towards 'feminine occupations' foreshadows the future position of the women in their families. From the moment of marriage, and, *a fortiori* after the birth of a child, assignment of women as a priority to the household is typified by the interruption of their professional activity, or by setting in motion a daily routine which dovetails professional activity and housework. [70] The fact that women have recourse to the help of relatives (most often mothers) or to other arrangements which give a greater or lesser place to sub-contracted services, does not alter the fact that the responsibility for housework that falls on them moulds in part the course of their careers: the demands of working hours, the need to reduce the distance between home and workplace to a minimum, etc., and contributes to reducing their professional mobility. The sexual division of labour in the family context also contributes to fashion the supply of women's work, but for all that, their position and the course of their careers do not proceed in a linear manner from their priority assignment to the domestic sphere. Equally, the productive system, in its functioning, rests to some extent on the sexual division of labour, by mobilising and making use of manpower which is differentiated according to sex. The processes at work in the employing enterprises write into their systems the social position of men and women differently from its application in the family. Treating men and women differently, providing each with different opportunities for qualification and career, the processes of manpower management reinforce in their turn the division of labour in the domestic sphere: the men carry out their professional strategies by delegating housework to the women of the family group; the women adjust, as well as they can, to the demands of their employment to ensure that the household chores are carried out.

Thus, in their concrete evolution, the courses of women's careers (and men's) result from the articulations between production and home, and from the alternation between these two spheres of activity.

This kind of approach to the course of careers, plotted in response to questions which arose concerning the course of women's careers, leads us in its turn to question men's social position.

The assignation of men as a priority to production leads to their being given situations which correspond exclusively to their places in the social relations of class. This is acting as though their position in the social relationships of the sexes, their belonging to a family (whether the family of origin or the present one), had no effect on their social and professional future. Nevertheless, the socialisation of boys – like that of girls – at home and at school – is achieved in a manner differentiated according to sex and class. Men – like women, but in a different way – are liable to social mobility by marriage, and not just by entering a profession. Just like women's, the courses of men's careers are not to be understood only by reference to their position in the family structure: disengaged from the responsibility for housework, settled mainly as the principal 'providers' of financial resources, and for that reason also providers of the social status of the family, they are only 'free' to pursue their professional plans to the extent that their wives are assigned primarily to the tasks associated with reproduction.

This analysis thus throws into relief the dominant way in which the courses of men's careers are analysed, particularly in studies of social mobility. [71] It encourages us to equip ourselves with the conceptual and methodological tools which will allow us to grasp jointly the social position of men and women in the working world and in the family structures, each as groups sexually divided. In the end it succeeds in breaking down the barriers between various disciplines: sociology, economics, demography, as well as those between various fields within the same discipline which are usually kept separate: sociology of work, sociology of the family.

From this point of view, social and professional trajectories are not seen only as class trajectories, but also as trajectories with a social content. In the social class, men and women have different social, professional, and even matrimonial and family destinies.

Finally, this approach in terms of reinforcement of the logical connections between the productive system and family structures provides not only a better understanding of the processes at work in each of the two spheres, but also a dynamic method of grasping the relationships: relationships between the offer of and the demand for work in so far as they are linked to family structures. The offer of work and the professional training of individuals – men and women in a different manner – are seen to be closely tied to the types of family in which these individuals originate and those of which they are now members. [72] On the other hand, the companies' demand for workers, their way of managing labour, and their strategies in the matter of employment, are based to a great extent on the differentiated types of family structure and the positions occupied within them by individuals according to their sex.

Notes

1 P. Laulhe, 1981.
2 M. Huet, 1982.
3 This is one of the ways the studies of budgets and time, for example, look at the problem. The notion of choice is often also one of the elements of a political speech about the family and women's work.
4 *Cf. Données sociales*, Chaudron, 1984.
5 *Cf.* A. Michel, 1974.
6 Thus it is not a question of 'life-stories', properly so-called (*cf.* D. Bertaux, 1980), nor even of 'social biographies', nor 'personal accounts recorded in a homogeneous milieu' (*cf.* A. Borzeix and M. Maruani, 1982).
7 Y. Chevalier, 1979. For use made of biographies as they concern career-courses and family life, see M. A. Barrère-Maurisson, 1984.
8 The samples are the result of four separate studies:
   (a) The first considers women returning to work because of their partners' unemployment (sample starting with 2,000 men unemployed for more than six months in the Paris area); interviews with their wives are discussed and analysed. It concerns qualified women (office workers or technicians), married to men in middle or higher management, and unqualified women (unskilled workers or unqualified office workers) married to qualified factory-workers (*cf.* M. A. Barrère-Maurisson, 1982 a).
   (b) The second also considers women seeking to return to work after a fairly long interruption (between two and ten years) in their activity owing to having children. Twenty women found jobs; all had few qualifications (factory workers, shop assistants, office workers, cleaning women before leaving their jobs), whose husbands are factory workers, clerks, or more seldom middle management. These couples live in a new town (L'Isle d'Abeau) near Lyons. *Cf.* F. Battagliola *et al.*, 1982.
   (c) The third study concerns twenty couples where at least one of the pair works in the Social Security offices in Lyons: sixteen female and ten male clerks were interviewed. Their male partners were either factory workers or management; the female partners were either 'inactive' or middle management. The interviews with the clerks and their partners were complemented by interviews with their personnel managers and union representatives. Further, observations were made at their workplace (A. Pitrou *et al.*, 1983).
   (d) The fourth concerns a sample of thirty-eight active women (factory and office workers) chosen from the lower levels of wage and qualifications (one to one-and-a-half times the guaranteed minimum wage), of whom the majority were married. Besides this, the mothers of ten of them were able to be interviewed, thus permitting an analysis of the female line. This enquiry took place in Marseilles in 1981, and was funded jointly by CNAP and the [French] Ministry of Labour (*cf.* A. M. Daune-Richard, 1983).
9 Samples consisting of 113 women.
10 These categories comprise 62 per cent of the active female population, 80 per cent including women in middle management, of whom several were contained in the Paris sample, notably higher-grade technicians.
11 Even young women; one of them was twenty-eight.

12   This is particularly true of the families of farmers and shopkeepers, where the daughters share the work of both the home and the family business.
13   Moreover, a parallel could be drawn with girls from more favoured milieux, who, for the same reasons, are directed towards teaching qualifications.
14   The better-off edges of the shopkeeper class, but also some from middle and higher management.
15   An illustration of this may be found in the case of a woman whose parents owned a flat in the town concerned, but they did not wish her to live there 'alone'.
16   Very few women interviewed during the course of these enquiries left their family of origin before their marriage, even though many of them had been earning wages for several years beforehand (sometimes as many as seven or eight years).
17   F. Battagliola, 1982.
18   D. Chabaud *et al.*, 1981.
19   Note that in this respect there are several exceptions, which concern either only daughters, or daughters who had one much older brother, the professional positions of the fathers being different, but all characterised by a process of upward mobility.
20   The result of interviewing thirty-eight female factory and office workers. The selection of those who were clerks in the Social Security offices was too specific to enable these hypotheses to be verified.
21   In the majority of cases this was the family of origin; only in a few cases was it the husband's family.
22   *Cf.* N. Gaudrey-Turpin, 1982.
23   In this sense, the influence of the crisis on young men finding jobs is felt partly because their fathers are unemployed, and thus cut off from professional relationships. *Cf.* F. Stoeckel, 1982, who notes that in such cases the boys often have recourse to what may be called the 'substitute' network of their mothers.
24   F. Stoeckel, 1982, shows the importance of family connections in obtaining jobs by working-class boys.
25   See n. 19.
26   Most of them were between thirty and thirty-five at the time of the enquiry.
27   This is demonstrated likewise by the study carried out by the Centre d'Etudes de l'Emploi (see A. Labourie-Racapé *et al.*, 1977).
28   In fact it is moving from the bimodal curve of the 1968 census towards a U-curve with a longer stay in activity and late entries (see M. Huet, 1982).
29   M. A Barrère-Maurisson, 1982 a; and F. Battagliola *et al.*, 1980.
30   See M. A. Barrère-Maurisson, 1982 a.
31   As n. 30.
32   See M. A. Barrère-Maurisson, 1982 b.
33   For an illustration of this kind of statement, see A. M. Daune-Richard, 1982.
34   *Cf.* M. Haicault, 1980.
35   The research on which this article is based dates from before the law restricting work to thirty-nine hours a week.
36   A point developed by D. Linhart and R. Tourreau, 1981.
37   Except when the problem of waking the children and taking them to school has not found a satisfactory solution. This question of shifts and preferential morning working hours was at the roots of unrest, more or less evident, in several Marseilles firms, aimed at keeping to a system of staggered hours or to bring about a move to alternating working hours, because the system of fixed shifts caused injustices and created tensions between the morning shift and the afternoon shift.
38   Usually 1.00 pm to 9.00 pm; sometimes 12.00 noon to 8.00 pm.
39   Which may be noted in the research carried out at IEST under the leadership

of Agnès Pitrou amongst families of employees (male and female) of the [French] Post Office and Telephones.

40 We have not met any in our enquiries, but Françoise Pernot-Escourrou points out several cases in her thesis (1980). Likewise, several couples where both the man and the wife are ward orderlies or nurses adopt this way of working in the sample of families working in the health service studied (together with the Social Security clerks we are considering here) by the Franco-Swedish ATP (1983).

41 The publications reporting the budget-time research indicate both the times of rising and the total time spent on housework during the day; but they take no account of the timetable of how this is carried out, so that we are not able to make general deductions from them on a wider scale. *Cf.* for example, B. Riandey, 1976.

42 But let us not forget that these make up the majority of the active female population.

43 Preference for the mother's help in the home has already been emphasised by A. Pitrou's work (1977).

44 *Cf.* D. Chabaud *et al.*, 1981.

45 *Cf.* A. M. Daune-Richard, 1984.

46 *Cf.* A. M. Daune-Richard, 1982.

47 F. Pernot-Escourrou, 1980: 293–4 had already made a similar observation amongst female factory-workers, but she interpreted it as a palliative against the absence of crèches in a semi-rural area (which is not at all the case in the Marseilles sample, for example; it is known that the crèches in the northern districts of Marseilles have many unoccupied places).

48 Information going in this general direction may be found in L. Roussel and O. Bourguignon, 1974: 32. We see that the headings, 'lives with parents', 'in the same parish', and 'less than 20 km away' account for 57 per cent of all married daughters, but only 51 per cent when they are inactive, and 59 per cent when they are active. Moreover, 74 per cent of married daughters who are factory workers are in this situation, against 56 per cent who are office workers (however, the heading 'unskilled office worker' includes people with very widely differing qualifications and salaries; it would be better if these could be distinguished for comparisons to be made).

Another confirmation of these observations about mothers and daughters living near each other in the working-class sections of society may be found in the outstanding study of connections of kinship in the urban milieu by M. Young and P. Wilmott, 1957.

49 The same observations may be found in F. Pernot-Escourrou's thesis (1980).

50 An earlier study had already drawn attention to a 'very close connection between women's activity and their originally belonging to the region'; *cf.* F. Lantier, 1971: 257.

51 We note in the Marseilles sample that the women who complain of tiredness and/or health problems (particularly nervous) are the same ones who are cut off from their family network.

52 *Cf.* M. Huet, 1982.

53 *Cf.* D. Kergoat, 1978.

54 *Cf.* A. Labourie-Racapé, 1981.

55 The study carried out amongst Marseilles women factory workers entirely confirms the analysis of A. F. Molinie and S. Volkoff, 1980, as well as the work of D. Kergoat, 1978; 1982, and that carried out by the *ad hoc* group, 'Articulation du système productif et des structures familiales: méthodologie des approches comparatives hommes-femmes' Xe Congrès Internationale de Sociologie, Mex-

ico, 1982; papers to be published in *Le sexe du travail*, in Editions PUG.

56   Between 1968 and 1975, 83 per cent of the net creation of new paid jobs was
      in tertiary activities. This development leans heavily on the call upon female
      labour, which has provided in all 60 per cent of the increase in paid employment
      in the tertiary sector (P. Bouillaguet-Bernard and J. F. Germe, 1981.

57   *Cf.* F. Battagliola, 1984.

58   *Cf.* pp. 422 ff.

59   This competitive examination may be prepared for by taking courses during work-
      ing hours, on proposals made by office managers.

60   Married female office workers are more often distant from their family of origin
      than are female factory workers (*cf.* L. Roussel and O. Bourguignon, 1979).

61   Which confirms the study by A. Labourie-Racapé *et al.*, 1977.

62   12 per cent of the women working at the CPAM [Social Security Office] in Lyons
      having at least one child under three years old at home, against 6.2 per cent of
      all the personnel of the Social Security in the whole of France (statistics from
      UCANSS). In March 1981, 15.5 per cent of the active female population are
      working part-time (enquiry on employment, INSEE).

63   *Cf.* p. 438.

64   D. Chabaud *et al.*, 1981.

65   A. Borzeix and M. Maruani, 1982; 1984.

66   Thus we can understand the reasons why women place so much importance on
      the atmosphere prevailing in the workplace, sometimes going as far as to make
      it a criterion for changing jobs.

67   *Cf.* A. Michel, 1974.

68   Whilst numerous statistics about active married women take note of their
      matrimonial status, the number of their children and details about their husbands,
      such data is rarely met with when the active male population is considered.

69   The fact that a different value is placed on diplomas on the labour market depend-
      ing on sex and matrimonial status confirms this analysis; F. de Singly, 1982.

70   Which tends to become most often the case.

71   *Cf.* M. Chaudron, 1984; F. Battagliola, 1984; and D. Bertaux and I. Bertaux-
      Wiame, 1981.

72   *Cf.* M. A. Barrère-Maurisson, 1982 a; and A. M. Daune-Richard, 1984.

Section seven

The meaning of work: value and identity

This final part once again draws our attention to the *moral* dimension of the conduct and construction of economic activity. It is clear from the research reported here that not everything is subject to the profit motive of the market place or to the principles of 'rationality', for other values play an equally – if not more – significant part in people's lives. Among these are people's views of what it is that is important about *themselves*, and the relative value they attach to one or another aspect of social and economic action. Economic activity – even, indeed, 'work' itself – is not just a matter of the objective character of jobs, pay, market forces, physical conditions or even security (though all these may be important) but also involves people's *perception* of these. Furthermore, an equally influential factor is the *value* placed on various activities by society (or, more immediately, by particular sections of society or by significant others), including the socially constructed (and doubtless changing) definitions of 'work' and 'not work', and the 'identity' which people hold in relation to these values.

Issues of these kinds come out in all the papers in this part. Is work in the sense of formal employment becoming less important to our sense of identity, perhaps to be partly replaced by other characterisations such as gender, ethnic affiliation, religion, leisure (Brown)? Or does this vary with the type of occupation (see Brown's discussion) or in different areas of the country (compare the various accounts in Brown, Turner *et al.* and Breakwell)? And does shifting our focus from the ideal of 'rationality' (well challenged in Breakwell) or the model of 'the market' (as Davis suggests) give us greater insight into people's actual choices? The answers to such questions are not fully agreed, and perhaps all need further empirical research as well as theoretical elucidation, but they are pertinent ones for trying to grasp the actual nature of people's attempts to tackle the issues taken up in the research reported in this part.

'Identity' is one of the central concepts here. The term is focused on in differing, if complementary, senses in the first three papers: *occupational* identity (as a miner, say, or a boilermaker), the sense of being employed (a 'worker') as against being unemployed (often very dependent on what other people think, or are believed to think, about you), or the *processes* by which people (in this case young people) form their views of themselves, as in Breakwell's research. Other senses too emerged in discussion, both in the papers themselves and orally: certainly the concept of 'identity' is no simple one. What seemed to be common to all, though, were the implicit *moral* connotations of people's views of themselves and their activities, both the 'value' association frequently found in the term 'work' (and hence in people's involvement or otherwise with something which could be called 'work') and the important, if often unstated, assessment of the *value* of certain activities and characteristics.

The same theme of the significance of the moral is also prominent in the final paper: Davis's discussion of rules. As he points out, people's choices are affected by their values, and these are not all to be defined in terms of the profit motive. Indeed, it may be that the 'blue economy' (Davis' neat term for the formal economy represented in government blue books of statistics etc.) may not necessarily be dominant in economic life; and, furthermore, that the model of 'the market', far from being the dominant and, as it were, 'normal', mode of economic activity in industrial society (with other forms to be taken as marginal or unusual) is itself problematic both in its functioning and extent. Is the concept of a non-local macro-market, then, perhaps not a guiding principle of our economic life after all, but only a model, 'a moral and economic goal of a particular segment of the population' (Davis)?

Whatever the answer to that challenge, the recurrent theme of this part is clear: that people are moved not just by the profit motive or by their part in the labour market or even by the very real constraints in their situation, but also, and very importantly, by the essentially moral dimensions relating both to appropriate economic action and their views of their own roles within this.

Attitudes to work, occupational identity and industrial change[1]

Introduction

With the number registered as unemployed firmly stuck at well over three million, and the number of those who would like to have paid work but who can't get it probably well over four million, it is not surprising that there has also been a marked increase in writing and research on work and worklessness. What is noticeable about the recent and current growth of interest in this area, however, is that it extends beyond concern with the incidence of unemployment and the plight of the unemployed, to raise the more basic question of the future of paid work in our society (and other industrial societies). Such a question directs attention not only to the economic and fiscal problems to which long-term or permanent high levels of unemployment might give rise, but also the nature of the paid work which most people have had to do since the 'industrial revolution', to the structure of jobs, and to the personal and social meaning and significance of employment in our sort of society.

Such issues are too extensive to be discussed within one paper. I want to focus on the question of the significance of their occupations for those who are employed, or would like to be, and to consider the implications for this question of the research we have carried out in Durham since 1978.[2] As Fox (1980) and Jahoda (1982), among others, have emphasised, paid work has meaning for those who do it in several major ways in addition to providing an income. It is important therefore to consider in what ways changes in the structure and distribution of employment are likely to affect those in or seeking work, and how far employment in the future will continue to provide such significance.

Attitudes to work

An initial assessment of the significance of paid work for those who do it, and of how far this may have changed during the last two decades, can be gained from our review of published studies carried out for the Department of Employment at the beginning of 1982 (see Brown *et al.*, 1983). This project considered research since the early 1960s which had produced findings about the orientations to work and levels of job satisfaction of manual and/or routine clerical workers, in order to try to establish whether or not there was evidence of changes over time. It also included more detailed consideration of various projects, by ourselves and others, which had been carried out on Tyneside since 1969. Conclusions from surveys of attitudes are clearly subject to all sorts of reservations, but they can both negatively and to some extent positively provide a starting point for my discussion.

The most important characteristic of a job in general was the level of earnings. This was as true in the later as in the earlier studies; some small categories of workers appeared to place less emphasis on pay, but they tended to be rather heterogeneous and atypical. The larger and more representative samples of manual and routine clerical workers emphasised pay, if anything more strongly in the 1970s than in the 1960s, and also security, which tended to be considered the second most important consideration when looking for a job. Thus 'orientations to employment' were predominantly 'economistic' or 'calculative'. This did not exclude other factors being considered important; for example, skilled and some semi-skilled men in the chemical industry, in engineering and in shipbuilding gave high priority to interesting work; and some women to 'convenient' hours, working arrangements and/or location. Indeed, when sources of satisfaction and dissatisfaction with a particular job are being considered it was these other factors which were cited rather than levels of pay or security, though when the question was put directly, most claimed to be satisfied with their pay. The nature of the work itself and of social relations at work appeared fairly frequently as sources of satisfaction, whilst – depending on the situation – working conditions could be a reason for either liking or disliking a job.

We did not find grounds for arguing that there has been any general trend in orientations to work, or in the sorts of factors which make for satisfaction or dissatisfaction in a job; neither did we find any convincing evidence of an overall decline in work obligations or, for that matter, the opposite. There were some signs of a greater stress on the importance of pay and security (not altogether unexpected given the prevailing rates of inflation and rising levels of unemployment), but they are not altogether unambiguous. Nor was there any clear evidence of consistent changes over time, in either direction, in general levels of job satisfaction. The systematic differences between types of respondents which could be discerned seemed to us to be related much more closely to position in the life cycle (age and sex) and to type and level of skill. These conclusions were broadly reinforced by the additional review we made of relevant research carried out on Tyneside since 1969. In this case the data included one set of repeat interviews with the same respondents in

1979 and 1980: dissatisfaction had increased over the period between the two interviews, especially – and understandably – dissatisfaction with perceived job security.

Surveys using questionnaires or interviews are far from the most satisfactory ways of finding out about the meaning of work for those who do it, although equally clearly in many situations there is no realistic alternative to their use. I would like, however, to pursue my argument by looking more closely at the evidence about the significance of work which comes primarily from studies of particular occupations, and then suggesting what overall changes may be occurring in the subjective experience of work on the basis of an examination of the changing industrial and occupational structure of our society.

Occupational identity

One of the key notions which has informed the study of the meaning and significance of work for many years is that of occupational identity. By this I understand a reference to the ways in which a person's identity, his or her sense of who they are, derives from their occupation, their place in the division of labour, the more or less distinctive paid employment they undertake to earn a living. The important point about this notion for my present purposes is that jobs differ in the extent to which they offer the possibility of a strong sense of occupational identity, and they differ too in the sort of occupational identity they offer. Thus if the occupational structure is changing that may well mean that certain sources of distinct occupational identities are being lost with consequences for the more general significance of work in our society. Such changes are likely to be of greater importance than the more superficial and uncertain changes in attitudes to employment.

More than thirty years ago Hughes wrote, 'Thus a man's work is one of the things by which he is judged and certainly one of the more significant things by which he judges himself . . . Many people in our society work in named occupations. The names are a combination of price tag and calling card . . . ' and, after discussing some examples, 'These remarks should be sufficient to call it to your attention that a man's work is one of the most important parts of his social identity, of his self' (Hughes, 1958: 42–3).

More recently Berger made a similar point:

To put it simply, for most of history men have *been* what they *did*. This did not have to mean that they particularly *liked* what they did – the problem of 'job satisfaction' is as modern as that of 'meaning of work'. To say 'I am a peasant' was, very probably, a far cry from pride, enthusiasm, or even contentment. Nevertheless it provided a self-identification for the individual that was stable, consistent, and so recognised by others and by himself. To put it simply again, work provided the individual with a firm profile. (Berger, 1975: 166)

If their occupations have such an implication for individuals this could be a far more powerful source of commitment to work and attachment to the job than pay or any of the other sources of satisfaction I mentioned earlier. To be fair, it should be pointed out that Berger clearly has doubts about whether any contemporary occupation can provide such a source of identity. The quotation continues:

This [a firm profile] is no longer the case with most work in industrial society. To say 'I am a railroad fireman' may be a source of pride but the pride is as precarious as the occupational title. To say 'I am an electroencephalograph technician' means nothing to most people to whom it is said. To say 'I am an addressograph operator' means nothing for a different reason, not because people do not understand what kind of work it entails, but because it is next to impossible to derive any sort of self-identification from such an occupation, not even the self-identification with an oppressed proletariat that sustained many workers in earlier phases of industrialism. (Berger, 1975: 166)

I think Berger has exaggerated the extent to which – at least until recently – an industrial society like our own failed to provide manual workers with occupations capable of providing and sustaining a strong sense of occupational identity. It is probably no accident that the attention of sociologists and others has been attracted by occupations with just such distinctive identities.

Coal mining, for example, has clearly been such an industry and set of occupations. Writers like Dennis, Henriques and Slaughter (1956: 73), and Allen (1981: 71) have referred to the fact that 'pride in work is a very important part of the miners' life', to the 'identification of a man with his work', and to the miners' 'skills acquired through years of commitment, learning, effort and exposure to injury and disease'; whilst their accounts and others by men who have themselves worked in the industry indicate clearly the significance of that experience for the miner's life and view of himself and his world (see Chaplin, 1978: 59–61 esp.; Beavis, 1980).

Certain manufacturing industries were the source of a similarly strong sense of occupational identity. Eldridge, for example, has written about skilled workers in shipbuilding:

It may be inferred that membership of such an occupational group was of central importance in the life experience of the group member. Not only did his craft training implant in him a sense of his exclusive competence in relation to a particular range of techniques, which members of the trade could undertake, but his work expectations were geared to that particular craft. To this extent he was a captive by his occupation and, upon the fortunes of his occupation in the labour market, hinged his own personal and familial security. (Eldridge, 1968: 93)

Such a judgement and its implications for occupational identity would be supported by our own past work in shipbuilding (Brown and Brannen, 1970; Brown *et al.*, 1972).

Many of these same occupations could be found in heavy engineering, and with the same strong occupational identity. In his study of engineering workers made redundant by Vickers on Tyneside Frank Pyke wrote:

For some of these men the closure had been devastating. Losing your status as a Vickers Engineer is not like losing a position of box-packer or button-pusher. One redundancy is not the same as any other – even if they're equally paid. It is a question of pride, self-identity, and sense of direction. Vickers Scotswood was not 'just a job', it was a *good* job, and people who worked there were people of worth; and they knew it. They had put a lot of themselves into the trade and committed themselves to it. (Pyke, 1982: 49)

The steel industry and printing, are just two other manufacturing industries whose main occupations also give rise to a strong sense of occupational identity. In the service sector, among manual workers, such occupations appear to be found less frequently, but they are, or were, not unknown. Railwaymen, dockers and lorry drivers, for example, have all been described as having a strong sense of identity with their occupations.[3]

Four comments, I think, should be made about these examples of occupational identities before I pursue my main argument further. Firstly, it is significant that none of them is an occupation or group of occupations in which women are employed, at least in more than very small numbers. This is not to suggest that there are no occupations in which women have customarily worked which provide a strong sense of occupational identity (nursing would be a good example), but it is an appropriate reflection of the fact that this would be the exception rather than the rule for women manual workers (textiles might provide such exceptions); and it indicates something of the occupational segregation in our society. It also accounts for my neglect of women's work in much of what follows.

Secondly, the length of time workers spend in a particular occupation and/or industry is likely to be both a consequence of and a reinforcement for a strong sense of occupational identity. The experience of Williamson's grandfather, who spent his whole working life as a miner, would not be exceptional in the coal industry (Williamson, 1982). More than seven out of every ten skilled men we interviewed in shipbuilding in 1969 had spent all or virtually all their working lives in that industry. Frank Pyke reports how skilled engineering workers saw working in Vickers as 'a job for life'; and working on the railways was often described in the same terms.

Thirdly, there is clearly a close connection between occupations and/or industries which are noted for the sense of occupational identity of their workers, and those which have given rise to occupational communities. Many such 'communities' are clearly rooted in a particular locality or region, though as Salaman (1974), for example, has argued the term can legitimately be used in the case of occupations which are not so confined and where the orientation of members is 'cosmopolitan'. Nevertheless it should be noted that the employment (and unemployment) experience of workers in Newcastle upon Tyne, discussed in this paper, must be considered in the context of the specific industrial structure and history of that city and its region, where the former domination by certain large and locally-based employers had crumbled in recent years; and that spatial or geographical changes in the division of labour can have major consequences for occupational identity. The wider debates about the correlates of occupational community are also of importance for the discussion of the implications of a decline in occupational identity (see especially Bulmer, 1975).

Fourthly, the absence of accounts of a strong sense of occupational identity in many industries other than those mentioned is not just because they have been neglected by social research – though some of them may have been. As Berger's remarks indicated, work in many industries and occupations does not provide those who do it with 'a firm profile'. One important part of the message of the *Affluent Worker* studies, for example, was that the worker of the future no longer sought or had such an attachment to occupation or industry (see Goldthorpe *et al.*, 1968). A similarly clear statement came in Blauner's discussion of operators in the chemical industry in the USA. Under the heading 'the automated operator's identity crisis' he wrote: 'Because of the public's lack of familiarity with automated technology, it is probably difficult for the chemical operator to gain the respect of others through identifying with his work – in contrast to the printer or the railroad engineer' (Blauner, 1964: 159). The chemical industry has been a growth sector of the British as well as the American economy, and studies of British workers in chemicals, or similar industries like oil refining, would suggest a very similar picture (see Nichols and Beynon, 1977; Gallie, 1978). Significantly after further discussion, Blauner continued: 'With occupational identity so problematic, production workers in the continuous process industries are drawn toward the company, and this institution tends to become the focus of worker loyalty, in contrast to the situation in craft industries' (Blauner, 1964: 162). I shall return to this point but first must consider 'industrial change'.

Industrial change

With few exceptions the industries and occupations which provided their workers with a strong sense of identity are industries and occupations in decline, in some cases dramatic and apparently irreversible decline. In many cases this decline has been going on for a relatively long time, for decades rather than for years. Though the most easily available figures refer to industries (and thus to all occupations in them) the general trend is clear. The number of men working in coal mining, for example, has fallen from more than 700,000 in the late 1950s to something over 200,000 today; in shipbuilding and marine engineering from nearly a quarter of a million in the late 1940s to less than 140,000; in metal manufacture (dominated by the iron and steel industry) from over half a million at the end of the fifties and throughout the sixties to less than 300,000; more than half a million men were employed on the railways in the late 1940s whilst the total now is less than 200,000 (Department of Employment, 1971: 1983 b).

In some of these and in some other cases the decline in employment has been particularly rapid during the last few years, part of the collapse of British manufacturing industry which has seen employment fall from over seven million in 1978 to less than five and a half million at the beginning of 1983 (Manpower Services Commission, 1983). The jobs 'lost' in this period include 90,000 in metal manufacture, 220,000 in mechanical engineering, 110,000 in electrical engineering, and 35,000 in shipbuilding and marine engineering (Department of Employment, 1983 a: table 1.2); many of these jobs, though of course by no means all, were the sorts of skilled manual work which provided a strong sense of occupational identity, and the current expectation appears to be that for whatever reasons – technical changes, greater productivity, automation, loss of markets to overseas competition, 'deindustrialisation' – few of them will return even if and when the current recession ends.

In specific localities the impact of these changes has been particularly great. To give only two illustrations: employment in mining in County Durham has fallen from 110,000 at the end of the 1940s to around 20,000 today (and many of those under threat); a major and dramatic transformation of what 'work' means for many living in that county. On Tyneside the heavy engineering plants of Vickers in Scotswood and Elswick employed 18,500 at the outbreak of the second world war, and more at the end of it; they still employed 7,000 in the early 1960s; they are now both closed, and sold or dismantled. What this means for the experience of work in such localities has been well caught by Austrin and Beynon (1980: 16–17):

In the pre-war economy of the North East, the labour force was separated into a number of clearly defined occupations. Men who worked in the shipyards, or in the pits, tended to see themselves as employed as boilermakers or miners for their lifetime. Today though, the labour force of the region is increasingly a 'mass' labour force not divided by occupations but graded bureaucratically within each of the corporations as they hire and fire. This is only a tendency, of course, but it is one which works itself out in many aspects of life in the region. Work (for manual and white collar employees) is increasingly of a routine repetitive kind, tied to the clock and to the pursuit of numbers.

Organisational commitment

It might fairly be asked whether there have not been compensating developments of new industries and occupations providing those working in them with some sense of identity. To some extent there are, of course, but such examples seem rare and perhaps rather marginal to the general direction of changes in our industrial and occupational structure. Clearly to be a computer programmer or a systems analyst is to have an occupation which scarcely existed twenty or thirty years ago but would now have meaning and significance for most of us, and provide the basis for an occupational identity for those who perform it (see for example, Hebden, 1975). Much manual work in manufacturing, however, and manual or routine white-collar jobs in the service sector, lack such an identity, and unlike computer programming, perhaps, are unlikely to acquire it with time. In so far as skill and distinctive competence are a necessary condition for occupational identity, the reasons for this may lie in the processes of restructuring manual and non-manual work so as to remove such elements which are generally discussed under the heading of the 'deskilling debate' (see for example, Wood, 1982). Rather than enter that particular minefield now, however, I would like to turn to a rather different, and perhaps more important, possibility.[4]

In the past, and more recently, some workers have acquired a sense of identity from their work not so much from the particular job they did – miner, shipwright, engine driver, or whatever – as from long service and close attachment to a particular employer. Their identity was organisational rather than occupational or industrial. The two are not incompatible, of course, as reference to Vickers' engineering workers will have indicated, but in any specific case one might predominate over the other, and they could be alternatives to each other.

In the past, identification with a particular employer was commonly the product of the paternalistic employment practices of that firm, practices which succeeded, at least for a long time, in creating a quasi-family out of their workforce. Ironically, two of the best cases come from studies of redundancy, the experience which more clearly than anything else demonstrates the inherent limitations of paternalism. Martin and Fryer's study of the workforce of a floor-covering factory in north-west Lancashire found that 'Belief in the value of loyalty as a means of acquiring respect was part of a sub-cultural value system whose other elements included an emphasis on the virtues of obedience and respect, upon the acceptance on managerial authority, and upon the value of security . . . ' and 'loyalty, obedience, and acceptance of managerial authority were highly regarded values' though 'this was not associated with a general *identification* with management and acceptance of a unitary conception of the firm'. Significantly 'the redundancy destroyed an occupational identity and status constructed over a work life spanning, in some cases, thirty years; a new identity . . . had to be constructed' (Martin and Fryer, 1973: 75–8, 135).

The Benwell CDP study of the closure of Adamsez, a small sanitary-ware manufacturer in west Newcastle, revealed a similar picture. Though some of the jobs were quite highly skilled, pay was poor and conditions of work for many had been bad. Yet the investigators reported, apparently rather to their surprise, that 'most people we talked to claimed to have enjoyed working at Adamsez. This loyalty is reflected in the fact that most people had stayed there for years, often decades, as well as in the considerable regret at the demise of the firm'. (Benwell CDP, 1980: 46). For such workers it is plausible to suggest that their occupational identity may not come so much from the precise job they did, which might change over the years, nor from the industry they worked in, but from being a valued and long-serving employee of a particular firm.

The paternalist strategy is not easily available to the large impersonal modern corporation. A possible substitute is the creation of 'employment dependence' (Mann, 1973: 40–53 esp.); this is secured through the creation of an 'internal labour market' which offers dependable long service employees the prospects of promotion within the firm to higher-paid and higher-status, and possibly somewhat more skilled and responsible, jobs. Such a strategy may be successful from the employer's point of view in securing worker attachment without creating any affective involvement and without having much effect on employees' sense of identity. Indeed Mann suggested that the workers he questioned, whose commitment to their employment with Birds' foods led many of them to move house from Birmingham to Banbury when the firm relocated, had a predominantly calculative attitude in which high wages and security were the most important considerations, though the opportunities offered by the internal labour market did render these economic ties more diffuse. In some circumstances however – the clearest case would appear to be in Japan – promotion of an internal labour market and the encouragement of loyalty to the firm certainly does have more far-reaching consequences for identity (see Dore, 1973).

Despite the Japanese example, there must be doubts as to whether occupational identity based on association with a particular employer could, in the case of manual or routine clerical workers, ever have the same significance as the traditional sort of identity based on a distinctive occupation. A necessary precondition for such occupational identity must presumably be the experience of stable employment in one organisation. Both general studies of the labour market, and our own research in Newcastle upon Tyne, however, suggest that such a precondition may well be the exception, especially for manual workers.

Labour market experience

Contemporary conceptualisations of the labour market tend to be organised around some notion of labour market segmentation into primary and secondary sectors. Jobs in the primary sector are seen as characterised by relatively high pay, good working conditions, job security and possibilities of training and advancement, and jobs in the secondary sector by the opposite of these conditions. A further development of these ideas stresses the difference between the 'independent' primary sector and the 'subordinate' primary sector, a distinction which to some extent parallels the difference between jobs which offer social identity based on an occupation, and jobs which offer the possibility of a social identity derived from employment in a particular organisation. 'Independent' primary workers have general skills acquired through some widely recognised training or education and they are consequently able to move between different employers. 'Subordinate' primary workers are on the whole less skilled and their skills have been acquired on the job and within the enterprise and do not provide much basis for job mobility (see Gordon, Edwards and Reich, 1982). A conceptualisation of the labour market of this sort, especially if allied to a prediction that jobs in the primary sector are increasingly 'subordinate' rather than 'independent', would appear to indicate some potential for employer- or organisation-based occupational identity.

Our findings for a study of the labour market in Newcastle upon Tyne cast some light on whether or how far such developments are taking place, at least in Britain, rather than in the United States which has been the major source of writing in this area. In this particular study we investigated samples of the economically active in three small areas of the city, two inner city areas and one a working-class suburban housing estate.[5] They cannot be regarded as representative of the resident and/or working population of the city as a whole. Nevertheless our evidence suggested that, especially for men, the labour market was city-wide rather than more local, and that there were many similarities between inner city and outer areas, so our findings are of some wider relevance.

Our conclusions are that in general our respondents' experiences in the labour market, which we recorded in detail for the ten years from 1969 to 1979, formed a continuum rather than displaying sharp breaks between different 'types' of worker or labour market sector. Looking at the records for the previous ten years of the men we interviewed, about half or more of the sample had experienced unemployment, including in many cases long-term unemployment, skilled manual work, work in more than one industry and/or in more than one occupational category, and employment in 'heavy' manufacturing industry, in the public sector and/or in the 'light' service industries (categories which overlap on Tyneside (see table 25.1).

Table 25.1 Occupational and industrial experience of male workers in Newcastle upon Tyne 1969–79

Percentage who had experienced:	(N = 434)
Unemployment	47
Unemployment for longer than six months	20
Employment in:	
Skilled manual work (Socio-economic group 8 or 9)	63
Two or more industries (Standard Industrial Classification)	54
Two or more occupations (OPCS Occupation Orders)	49
'Heavy' manufacturing industry (SIC 2, 4–12, 16)	53
The public sector	52
'Light' service industry (SIC 23–7)	45

In a detailed examination of the evidence for a secondary sector in the labour market, my colleague Jim Cousins defined 'secondary' workers in terms of the characteristics of their current job, deriving a list of relevant attributes from the literature on labour market segmentation (i.e. non-skilled work, no training on the job, short length of service, no change in grade or status and no promotion prospects within the job, and so on). In fact, the group which scored heavily on such items showed up as little different from respondents as a whole in terms of the nature and variety of their experience of work and unemployment. He concluded 'This does throw doubt on any clear dividing line, or even difference, between the "secondary worker" group so constructed and respondents as a whole . . . There is a broad base of experience of unemployment, instability and poor prospects' (Cousins *et al.*, 1982: 93–4).

On the other hand, certain minority groupings could be observed who did have different patterns of employment experience. This was most clearly revealed in a cluster analysis we carried out of some forty-one attributes of respondents' labour market experience (Brown, 1983; Cousins *et al.*, 1983: 105–15). Of the eight clusters so distinguished the majority were characterised by considerable instability of employment; five of them, covering 62 per cent of all respondents, included no one who had spent an average of five years or more in each job during the previous decade, though a quarter of all respondents had had such job stability. This job instability was associated with considerable instability as between industries and occupations, and in most cases high incidence of unemployment and redundancy. In contrast, three of the clusters displayed the sort of stability of employment experience which would be expected of those in the primary sector. One of these stable clusters consisted largely of non-skilled workers (11 per cent of all respondents), without educational or occupational qualifications, who probably represented that grouping largely neglected by segmented labour market theories, workers who have stable work histories but based on non-skilled, low-paid jobs with few prospects or special advantages. Many but by no means all of them were employed in the public sector.

Of the remaining two clusters one consisted entirely of some seventy-eight skilled manual workers (18 per cent of the sample), half of whom were apprentice trained, who had very little experience of unemployment (only 13 per cent ever) or redundancy (only 10 per cent in the last ten years), and who had virtually all worked in one occupation in one industry for the previous ten years. Nearly two-thirds of them were working in 'heavy' manufacturing. They seem likely to be representative of the 'independent' primary worker described in the literature – and to have the basis for the development of a strong sense of occupational identity.

The third very stable cluster (in occupational and industrial terms) was a smaller grouping of thirty-nine men (9 per cent of the total sample) who mostly had educational qualifications and had spent all the previous ten years (and in many cases their whole working life) in non-manual work, mostly (more than 80 per cent) in the service sector. Such a grouping were clearly 'primary sector' workers, and in the light of their educational qualifications and their exclusively non-manual occupations some may have been 'independent' though others were likely to be 'subordinate' primary workers.

Thus although it was difficult to identify a 'secondary' labour market, at least for men, which was markedly different from the labour market in general, and although stability of employment was not in itself a sign of being in the primary sector, there were two groupings of respondents whose work histories and current employment appeared to be very much those of primary sector workers with a stability of occupation and industry which could provide some basis for a sense of occupational identity. Significantly, however, those most likely to develop an organisation based occupational identity were all non-manual workers.

Some further light can be thrown on these two groupings, and possible differences between them, by considering the data we have on apprenticeship, and on internal labour market changes. Apprenticeship is clearly valuable as a basis for primary sector employment. The work histories of the 112 men who had served their time were less varied than those of other workers, even than those other workers who had had experience of skilled manual work; nearly three-quarters of the apprenticed men were still in skilled manual work at the time of the survey, or had moved into white collar jobs. On the other hand, only thirty-six of these 112 men had work histories which took them into the cluster of stable skilled manual workers just described.

Promotion within an organisation suggests the existence of an internal labour market and of the possibility of identifying with the organisation as a 'subordinate' primary worker. Maggie Curran has examined the characteristics of the 30 per cent of our respondents who had experienced a change of grade or status within the same 'job' (period of employment with one employer) (Curran, 1983). They were found especially frequently in white-collar work, among employees with five or more years of continuous employment with one employer, and in the service sector rather than in manufacturing industry. Internal labour market changes in grade were inversely related to change of job in the external labour market and were not especially common for those who served an apprenticeship. They were less frequent than average for skilled manual workers, for workers in 'metal and electrical materials processing or repairing' occupations, and for those working in the 'heavy' manufacturing and in the construction industries. Thus there does appear to be some separation of workers whose experience of promotion makes them possible candidates for 'subordinate' primary status, and those manual workers whose skill and pattern of secure employment suggests location in the 'independent' primary sector. The great majority of manual workers, of course, are in neither category.

One final point: the cluster of presumed 'independent' primary workers were employed predominantly in a group of industries we labelled 'heavy' manufacturing; basically engineering and shipbuilding but including mining. It was the workers in these industries who were among the most pessimistic about their job security and future job prospects, and not without reason. Despite this negative evaluation of the future prospects of Tyneside's traditional industrial base, however, when asked to suggest 'a good job for a boy leaving school around here', an apprenticeship, typically in engineering or related industries, remained the predominant choice; and skilled work in engineering the best available job for themselves. Although metal manufacturing and processing industries are declining, in the opinion of our respondents there has been nothing which satisfactorily fills the gap which this leaves. White-collar work, which can apparently provide the basis for stable employment and possibly for occupational identities based on employing organisation is not, or not yet, seen as a realistic and/or desirable alternative.

Conclusions and implications

The results of our review of studies of attitudes to employment concluded that there was little evidence of significant changes over the last couple of decades in orientations to work or in job satisfaction, though there were some differences related to age and sex, and, more important for present purposes, to level of skill. Following that rather negative point, I suggested that longer term changes in the significance and meaning of work in our society for manual and routine white-collar workers might be more adequately grasped by considering the question of occupational identity and the extent to which their occupation contributes to most people's sense of themselves. In the past a range of occupations have provided the basis for strong occupational identities, but many of them are in industries which are in decline; and there are grounds for doubt as to whether most new or growing occupations will provide the same basis for occupational identity.

An alternative source of strong occupational identities could be the employing organisation, and in some cases it clearly has been. In the present day world this would appear to be most likely to happen in firms which develop an internal labour market offering their employees the possibility of increasing security of employment and chances of promotion in return for loyal and dependable service. In our study of the Newcastle labour market there was evidence of such employment situations, but they were associated more with white-collar than manual work. This is probably the case nationally where the banks and certain retail chains, for example, have more or less successfully pursued such employment strategies for their predominantly non-manual labour forces and fostered a sense of identification with the organisation. Those *manual* workers who had stable employment records were either skilled men in the sorts of traditional and declining occupations and industries which have been the source of strong occupational identity in the past; or non-skilled men in low-status jobs. The prospects for manual workers of finding jobs with which they can identify and which will contribute to their sense of self seems to be increasingly remote.

Even if this is happening, does it matter? People work for predominantly instrumental reasons; their relationship to the job and the employing organisation is calculative and probably always has been; and the things which matter to them are largely or entirely in their lives outside work. Indeed is this just as well given the inability of our society to provide full employment?

I think there are probably more, and more far-reaching, implications than this sort of dismissive judgement would suggest. One example will have to suffice. The sorts of industrial and occupational milieux which have fostered a strong sense of occupational identity, in some but by no means all cases, have also fostered strong trade unions – miners, boilermakers, engineers, printers, railwaymen, transport workers – and as a direct reflection of identification with the occupation. These unions have been central to the growth and activities of the labour movement and the Labour Party. Their involvement in trade union and political activities, however, always had an element of ambivalence: on the one hand the solidarity which goes with strong occupational identity has been an enormous source of strength; on the other hand they have often been seen as furthering occupational and sectional interests and privileges at the expense of the interests of the labour movement and/or working class as a whole. Indeed such ambivalence is structurally induced in so far as their ability to contribute to the trade union and labour movement depends on the preservation of a strong occupational/industrial base, one which is privileged compared to the situation of many manual workers. If this base is crumbling, then clearly there will be important changes in the labour movement, possibly ones which will weaken it.

In contrast, one consequence of the decline of traditional industries seems to be an increasingly wide-spread common and shared experience of work in (and unemployment from) jobs which are no longer distinctive, but for that reason no longer divisive. In some respects this represents an increasing proletarianisation of the (manual) labour force, which may have consequences for class consciousness and class action. Alternatively, the decline of work as a source of social identity of any sort may lead to increasing salience being given to other social or personal characteristics, such as gender, ethnic origin, property ownership or leisure activities, a development which could have very different consequences. Certainly the question of occupational identity should be seen as an important element in the study of the whole future of work in our society.

Notes

1   Earlier versions of this paper were presented to the Department of Sociology Discussion Week, University of Leeds and to a seminar at the Centre for Urban

and Regional Development Studies, University of Newcastle upon Tyne, as well as to the ESRC Labour Markets Workshop, and I am grateful to participants on all three occasions for their comments. I am also grateful to my colleague Robin Williams for some helpful advice about and references to the general literature on 'identity'.

2   This research has been carried out in close co-operation with two colleagues, Jim Cousins and Maggie Curran, who indeed deserve the major share of the credit for the production of the findings to which I refer below. Full reports of the projects have been published elsewhere (see Cousins *et al.*, 1982; Brown *et al.*, 1983; Curran, 1982 a and b, 1983). Many of the ideas in this paper arise from discussions with my colleagues; they are not, however, responsible for the ways in which I present them here.

3   For steel, see Scott *et al.*, 1956 and McGeown, 1969; printing, see Cannon, 1967 and Cockburn, 1983; railwaymen, see Salaman, 1974; dockers, see University of Liverpool, 1956 and Hill, 1976; and lorry drivers, see Hollowell, 1968. It will be apparent that the situations mentioned include both those where the identification is primarily with an occupation, often, but not always (e.g. lorry drivers), one entered through apprenticeship, and those where it is with an industry which comprises a number of more or less distinctive occupations.

4   The definition of 'skill' is highly contentious partly, but not only, because a claim for a distinctive competence may be used as a basis for a strategy of social closure and exclusion in furthering occupational interests (see Parkin, 1979). 'Skill', in the sense of the ability to perform certain manual or mental tasks, is also often confused with 'autonomy' on the job. Clearly the whole question of which occupational characteristics contribute to, or even are preconditions for, the development of a strong sense of occupational identity needs much more careful consideration than it receives here; see, for example, the discussions by Becker and Strauss, 1956; Becker, 1960; Becker and Cooper, 1970 and Hebden, 1975.

5   The project, entitled 'Employment in the inner city – attitudes, aspirations and opportunities', was supported by the Department of the Environment as part of their Inner Cities Research Programme. Further analysis of the data was made possible by a grant from the Social Science Research Council. In no way should the views expressed in this paper be taken to be those of the Department or of the Council.

The work ethic in a Scottish town with declining employment

Introduction

'It's built into ye, work.'

There has been much speculation as to how people will adapt to Western society's entry into the 'post-industrial age'. While some deny that current levels of unemployment signal a radically new technological era, others suggest that this 'second industrial revolution' could provide a great liberation for the working masses and break down the alienating dichotomy of work and leisure. Our research is intended to provide empirical data on how one small community in central Scotland, known here as Cauldmoss, is coping with the 30 per cent male unemployment rate caused by the collapse of the major heavy industries in the region.

Since Cauldmoss lies in the centre of a region that for centuries was predominantly Calvinist, it might be expected that traces of the Protestant work ethic (Weber, 1930) would be found here if anywhere. In this paper we provide a description of how people perceive 'work', what they seek from it, what moral values surround it, and how folk cope, economically and psychologically, when they are deprived of the central norm in this culture. These themes will be illustrated by five case studies describing how particular individuals react to their lack of employment.

A small-scale locality study of this kind allows detailed investigation of the moral dimensions of work and unemployment, which are so often ignored or taken for granted by social scientists. The use of participant observer methods (in this case over a period of eighteen months) encourages informants to be frank about their values relating to working, claiming benefits, 'fiddling' and so on. This has enabled us to form clear ideas of people's attitudes in areas often too elusive for more formal research. The advantages of this approach are discussed at greater length in the paper in this collection by McKee and Bell.

Cauldmoss lies approximately seven miles from the main industrial conurbation of central Scotland: Boness, Grangemouth and Falkirk. Three-quarters of the population live in council houses and the rest in modest privately-owned houses or on small farms. There is no marked social structure since the inhabitants have no general way of classifying themselves, except by differentiating between locals and incomers. The vast majority of people are manual workers, and very few use class terms to distinguish villagers.

Until the 1840s Cauldmoss was a dispersed agricultural community. As coal began to be exploited on a large scale the population rose from about 1,000 to 7,000 by the 1890s. At this time Cauldmoss served as the focus of several small mining communities, but from the beginning of this century pits were being exhausted or abandoned and miners sought work elsewhere. By about 1930 the population stabilised at around 3,000, but after 1950 it fell further to the present level of 1,800. The village has become part of what the historian Harvie describes as:

an unlovely 'third Scotland' sprawled from South Ayrshire to Fife . . . old industrial settlements that ought to have been evacuated and demolished . . . but were preserved by buses, council housing and lack of long-term planning . . . Somewhat isolated, ignored, lacking city facilities or country traditions – even lacking the attentions of sociologists . . .
(Harvie, 1981: 66)

After the second world war, industries in the nearby conurbation and numerous small businesses within the village – mainly haulage, breakers' yards and a brickworks – provided most of the workforce with employment until the late 1970s. Today unemployment has risen in Scotland as a whole to a rate of 16.2 per cent, in the Falkirk district to 19.6 per cent, and in Cauldmoss, according to our 10 per cent sample of houses, to at least 30 per cent.

The inhabitants have definite perceptions of the village, the most forceful images portraying Cauldmoss as an ex-mining village, as an especially unattractive place, as particularly lawless and as a small highly interrelated community rife with gossip. Kinship plays a very important role and some estimate 60 per cent of the inhabitants to be related: 'If ye speak ill o' yun, ye speak ill o' all', they say. The help that relations give to each other extends to every economic sphere, and, perhaps most crucially, they often provide the personal contacts through which jobs are found.

In short, the village under study conforms largely to the kind described by Turner in his typology of Scottish culture areas as 'East Lowlands Mining Town': 'Mostly council houses built 1920–1960 . . . mostly Protestant; low level of church-going; hereditary miners' culture . . .; high unemployment; low mobility . . .; high vandalism' (Turner, 1980 a: 11).

The meaning of 'work'

The word 'work', while highly morally loaded, is obviously polysemic.

Wallman (1979) suggests that we should identify the different dimensions that work has, and then study how they are interrelated.

In a questionnaire we conducted, a variety of activities were listed (loosely based on Gershuny and Pahl's 1980 classification of the 'formal', 'hidden' and 'domestic' economies), and respondents were asked to classify them as work or 'something else'. Our analysis of indigenous definitions of the terms 'work' and 'job' revealed that these describe an activity which is done in return for money (the most common definition), or which involves effort of some kind, or which is unenjoyable, or which is something that *has* to be done. Often all four criteria were given. The results suggest that there are two semantic possibilities for the word 'work': 'work' and 'real work', the former being inclusive of the latter. A nice illustration of this came when a man was asked if, when he dug the garden, he saw that as work. 'No', he said firmly, 'with the garden you're working for yourself'.

Since the most central feature of the concept of work in Cauldmoss is employment for money, it is no surprise that this is the first thing people state they seek from work. But even in industrial society economic objectives are not in an autonomous sphere, for 'economic purposes are hemmed in by the social prescription of means and ends' (Wallman, 1979: 4). Money is sought for social consumption: in Cauldmoss principally drinking in the pubs, going to bingo and other forms of gambling, buying clothes, furniture and household gadgets. Several of the unemployed that Marsden (1975) interviewed in the early seventies were very conscious of the social pressure to live at an accepted level of consumption, but one might assume that this would now be felt less acutely since far more are out of work. In Cauldmoss, however, where over 30 per cent of men are out of work, it appears that the pressures to spend, coming from friends and acquaintances, the media and expectations from a more affluent past, are just as strong today amongst both workers and unemployed as they were a decade ago.

Frequently people comment that it is pointless to take a low-paid job because they would be working for little more than they would receive from the DHSS, and the net financial advantages of a job are often calculated, taking everything into account, including the lost benefits and the cost of bus fares. Parker (1982) takes £10 net gain per week as the absolute minimum to offset the disutilities of employment; many people in Cauldmoss have suggested £20 to be their minimum (see case studies 1, 3 and 4).

It is striking how few people talk of getting any satisfaction from the actual activity of working, or from the product of their work (as is the case with M.S., case study 2). This is almost never a primary objective and people talk of switching jobs 'to follow the cash'. This order of priorities may be a legacy of the people's mining background, where for generations work was largely unskilled hard graft for which comparatively high wages were expected. Contrasting attitudes have been found by Turner in a Scottish fishing community (1980 b). However, there did exist a strong sense of occupational identity among Cauldmoss miners, which today tends to be found only among skilled men in the community, both in those with jobs and those without (see Richard Brown's paper, this volume).

Apart from money, there are two other things that people say they value in work. One is the changed environment which the work place gives, enabling a person to 'get oot the hoose' and relate to another social group, and the other is the structure that employment gives to a person's life. In general, and especially amongst the older workers, folk appear to want to be part of a work force, rather than to be self-employed. (The case of B.I. in particular reveals the importance of these aspects of work; see case study 5.) This suggests that there is a desire for the discipline and time structure involved in working, an hypothesis supported by the general wish for a forty-hour working week. It seems that the substance of work is less significant than its form, and the most important thing for men is that they go out to work in the morning with their 'piece', come back dirty, wash, have tea and then maybe go out to the pub.

Amongst the older generation the importance of a full working week is very clear. They condemn young people because 'they'll neither work nor want'. One or two in the village say they would work for low pay rather than 'sign on' because they prefer 'to be able to hold their heads up in the street'. Though such evidently moral attitudes about work are not heard from the younger generation, they do persist in a less clearly articulated form. When an unemployed teenager was asked what he thought of the hypothetical prospect of the majority of people living on a decent wage on the dole, because technology had replaced them, he replied 'It'd no'be their fault'. Though many people are accused of it, very few in Cauldmoss actually *say* they do not want to work (even amongst the young offenders), and those that do are ostracised for this very reason.

The work ethic

What is at the root of this shame about unemployment? The set of norms which put pressure on a man to achieve an approved level of consumption for his family (which largely explains J.O.'s motivation to work, see case study 3) constitutes a moral dimension of work in itself, but the monetary implications are more complicated than this. Whenever motivation for work is discussed, the financial arguments are inevitably deemed paramount, as if this were the supremely valid rationale for one's actions, but in practice people do not always act in ways that accord with this rationale. Twice men have belittled our enquiries as to why they work, stating adamantly that it was simply to earn money: as soon as they found they were gaining no more than the dole they would stop. But their wives then told us that their husbands could *never* stop working, whatever they were paid.

So far, no one has told us that they consider work to be the best way of glorifying God. But it is clear that many folk believe that to work well in regular employment is a vital part of leading a decent life, and work is defined as the same arduous, methodical activity that it was for the Puritans whom Weber (1930) describes. The relationship between this belief and *religious* goals seems no longer to be as evident to individuals as it may have been in the past. For many individuals in Cauldmoss their sense of duty seems to be directed towards themselves and their families rather than towards God.

Although it is tempting to draw on Weber's historical explanation, perhaps we should not go further than the accounts given by our informants. It may be the case that an individual is simply afraid of being perceived, or of perceiving himself, as lazy. One man who claims to be earning no more than he could get on social security, when asked why he works said aggressively ''Cos I'm no' lazy yet . . . I'm no' fuckin' lazy!' Some people are certainly ashamed of being unable to support themselves and their dependents by *their own efforts*. This might be best understood in terms of the principle of reciprocity. Individuals want to feel they have *given* something in return for their reward; as one man said: 'Ye're better *earning* your money.' This would explain why the take-up rate for contributory benefits is significantly higher than that for non-contributory benefits. How much is the urge to work simply a wish to conform to the 'normal' pattern of life, to attain full adult status (especially among males)? If this is the case, then we would expect to see a decline in the desire for work; as increasing numbers fail to comply with the norm, then the norm itself may change.

Case studies

The following case studies provide some insight into the way the unemployed in Cauldmoss cope with their situation.

1   R.T.

R.T. is the youngest of five children in a Cauldmoss lorry driver's family. He is seventeen, still lives with his parents on the council estate, and has never worked since leaving school at sixteen, nor has he been on any Youth Opportunities scheme. His attitude to these, which pay £25 a week, is simple: 'I wouldnie git oot a' bed fa £25!' His sister says that all her brothers have very little wish to work because they have seen how their father spent fifty years working for a profitable firm with only meagre wage rises and nothing to show for it at the end. They all feel they can do better for themselves without formal employment: by 'wheeling and dealing' and gambling. Nevertheless, R.T. definitely wants a job so long as it would be for what he considers a decent wage – probably about £50 'clear' (after tax). However, he is realistic about the very slight chance he has of getting work, and apart from the occasional attempt, like approaching council workmen renovating houses in Cauldmoss, he makes little effort to find employment. He is quite clear that the reason he wants work is the money.

Until he is eighteen, R.T. will receive £15.80 supplementary benefit a week, but he is regularly fed by his mother and can persuade his parents to provide him with all the new clothes he needs. Thus his benefit is almost all 'spending money', and many considered him to be spoilt.

One of R.T.'s main pastimes is gambling on the horses, with help from a well-informed elder brother. His other main interest is football, and he plays for an amateur team about eight miles away, considering himself above the Cauldmoss team. He trains hard for this, and explains his uninterest in the local 'magic mushrooms' and other drugs by saying they distract him from the sport. He has followed his family's interest in the Orange Order and has been on an anti-IRA march in London, but his other activities have caused him to be banned from the local Freemasons.

Easily bored, R.T. is often involved in petty crime. His friends say that R.T. would never have got involved in such trouble if he had been employed, which seems very likely, but he got very little sympathy from many in Cauldmoss. It might be that, in the long term, the most important consequence for R.T. of his criminal activities is his loss of respectability in the community, which might put him more firmly outside the social circles through which informal work is found.

2   M.S.

M.S. is eighteen, single, and lives with her parents on a small farm just outside Cauldmoss. She is currently without a job, although she has had a great deal of work experience for her age. While she was still at school she had a part-time job serving in a shop in the village, and she continued to work there after leaving school at sixteen, although she also claimed social security benefits. This went on until someone who disliked her reported her to the DHSS. She stopped working there and had to repay all the money she had claimed fraudulently. After that, she got a place on a year-long Youth Opportunities Programme, where she did odd jobs at the Community Centre in Cauldmoss – cleaning, typing and general clerical work. She then worked for several months as a machinist in a factory producing jeans in Falkirk, followed by a short period in a cannery until she was laid off quite recently.

Her main interest in life is cars, and she says that it is to finance this hobby that she wants money. In her desire for money, M.S. seems to be representative of the youth of Cauldmoss, although the wish to use it to buy a car is usually evinced by boys rather than girls. In general, young people want cash to buy clothes, records, cigarettes and drink.

When she was made redundant from the cannery she told us: 'It's the *money* you miss' and the degree of satisfaction gained from the work itself is much less important to her. Although she left school with several qualifications it seems that the type of jobs she prefers are not those likely to be the first step in a 'career', but more temporary and relatively highly-paid work, which demands less commitment.

While working at the jeans factory and the cannery, M.S. was able to save enough money to sell her old car and buy a newer one (with some financial help from her father). Now that she is unemployed, she spends much of her time cleaning and tinkering with the car, and her chief fear is that there will come a time when she will find it impossible to run the car on her dole money, and the extra she makes by baby-sitting and giving lifts. It is this fear that will prompt her to look for another job.

3   J.O.

J.O. (thirty-five) was born in Cauldmoss, the son of a miner. He did well at school but did not get on with his teacher, and consequently chose not to continue to the high school. He could have been apprenticed for £2.29 a week and learnt a trade, but he wanted to bring home good money (partly because his father had just switched jobs, from being well-paid as a miner to low-paid as a council worker), so he worked as a bricklayer earning £13 a week. At eighteen he was employed by a major concrete firm in the local town, and he worked there for sixteen years. He was promoted and found the work satisfying because 'I could see a job from start to finish', unlike those working under him who were just shifting cement. However, demand fell, and in the last few years the concrete firm reduced its work force from five hundred to forty; in 1981 J.O. was made redundant.

J.O. lives in a council house with his wife and young son. He receives benefit of £23 a week for himself and the child, because his wife is earning £23 a week in a part-time job in the local shop. His wife can earn up to £16, above which the extra income is deducted from his benefit, and because she is employed they cannot get a rent rebate. J.O. finds this ridiculous since they would qualify for one if he had a low-paid job.

J.O. initially tends to present himself as one of the unfortunate victims of the present government's economic policies. He expresses strong, if rather incoherent, socialist sentiments, and refers to how poor one is when living on 'the bru' (welfare payments). On television people talk about the new age of leisure, he says, '. . . but we've no *money* for our leisure time'. 'There'll be an awful lot o' men sore-hearted because they've nothing for their wains [children] at Christmas', he added, and this is exacerbated by the fact that the children have got used to expecting good presents. He is emphatic about his wish to find work, and relates this to the social stigma of unemployment. He was asked if they would get more income in benefits if his wife was not working:

I dinnie ken if we'd be better off or no' . . . but she's like me, she'd rather be workin' than claiming on the bru . . . Ye're looked on like a scrounger . . . Ye'll always get scroungers on the bru . . . but the majority of working men *want* to work . . . to be able to hold their heads up in the street.

He now regrets the decision he made in the past for ready money which has left him with no real qualifications at thirty-five.

In fact, J.O.'s life-style is not consistent with the meagre dole money he receives, and it becomes apparent, from the whisky he offers visitors in the middle of the afternoon, his smart car and his regular evenings in the bowling club, that he has some other source of income. 'The government is losing an awful lot from insurance and income tax 'cos of people workin' on the side . . . ' he told me, 'I've tried it myself – if that's not official' (laugh). In practice his side-work can occupy most of the week, doing a job for his sister-in-law, labouring for a local builder or doing a few weeks with a drilling firm. J.O. thinks he is typical of many unemployed men in Cauldmoss: 'An awful lot of men are workin' on the side . . . men who'd like to be workin'' (in a formal job).

However, J.O. does not want regular formal employment so much that he would accept a low-paid job. He scorns the vacancies advertised in the local Job Centre, 'Nobody's going to take £50 a week nowadays!' Last year his dole was withheld for a while because he refused a job at Cauldmoss post office with a take-home pay of £58 a week. Furthermore, he would not take a very monotonous job (unless well-paid): 'I'm lookin' for a job, but I wouldnie like to think it's wheelin' a wheel-barra' around . . . that's every bit as degrading as being on the bru'.

From this, and from the examples of others, it appears that demanding what used to be the rate for the job in affluent times goes deeper than simply trying to maintain standards of remuneration. It seems that experienced, and particularly skilled workers, feel their personal worth would be diminished if they accepted significantly less than they used to be paid: they would be selling themselves cheap.

4 *T.M.*

T.M., who was born in Cauldmoss, is in her mid-thirties, and is divorced from her husband, who lives in a nearby village with their two children, aged seventeen and thirteen. She lives on the council estate with a divorced man, K.G., whom she met while she was living with her husband. The couple are three doors away from T.M.'s parents, both of whom are in ill-health, and with whom T.M. is in frequent contact, as she is with her sister and her brothers, all of whom live either in or near Cauldmoss.

She has been claiming supplementary benefit for two years, since she left her husband and stopped working. K.G., who was made redundant from his job as an engineer almost a year ago, receives about £40 per week invalidity benefit, eczema on his hands preventing him from handling machinery. T.M. believes that it is the present government's policy to allow individuals to claim invalidity benefit for as long as possible, and so avoid including them in the official unemployment figures.

Out of her £25 benefit each week, T.M. buys the groceries with which she feeds herself, K.G., one of her brothers fairly regularly, and her children when they visit her at the weekends. She also buys two bags of coal at £4 each every week, and pays other household bills. K.G. contributes a small amount to the housekeeping and her brother occasionally gives her cash. She worries that the DHSS will discover K.G. is living with her and cut off her benefit, and she will not accept more help with the household expenses from him because she wants to retain some independence. She says she finds it hard to manage, the amount of her benefit being '. . . very inadequate'. She often has to borrow a couple of pounds from her mother, and was recently granted £75 by the DHSS to buy new furniture. In order to ease the financial burden, K.G. 'fixed' the electricity meter, an act that T.M. worried about to the extent that when the inspector came to read the meter, she hid in bed. They have also stolen peat to supplement the coal they burn.

T.M. says she '. . . would take nearly *any* job', as long as it gave her at least £20 above the amount she gets in total from the DHSS (including rent), and as long as she found it enjoyable. Ideally, she would like to do community work with young people, but she has worked in shops and enjoyed that.

She visits the Job Centre regularly, and looks in the local paper at job advertisements, and she has even tried inquiring in shops if there are any vacancies. This, she says, was a good way of finding work in the past, but now they all deal only through the Job Centre. The fact that she knows so few people who are in employment means that she does not hear about any jobs that do fall vacant, she says.

A typical day for T.M. is to spend the morning out walking if the weather is good, or else doing housework, and the afternoon crocheting ('. . . but I canna' always afford wool') reading ('. . . *stupid* books!') or visiting her 'mam'. In the summer, she and K.G. often spend whole days out fishing. After she has made the evening meal she watches television, although she says that there are only a few programmes she enjoys. Three nights each week she and K.G. help to run a youth club in Boness, for which they are paid only their expenses. In this, the couple are fairly unusual; there are very few unemployed folk in Cauldmoss involved in similar activities. Most weekends she is occupied with her children.

Discussing her reaction to unemployment, T.M. says that she went through a stage where she felt that she would take any job at all; she thought:

I'll need to get out o' here – this is shuttin' in on me . . . I hate Cauldmoss . . . ye actually begin to hate living . . . but that [stage] passes like everything else. Ye just begin to accept it . . . [ye] just need to make the best o' the day as it comes, and try and fill it in as best ye can.

She frequently contrasts her present lifestyle with the way she lived when she was with her husband, when they both earned quite good wages. The family always had a good holiday every year, and the money she earned was spent on 'luxuries' such as a music centre and a ceramic hob. Now, any new clothes she gets are given to her by her mother, and she says if she won the football pools, her first priority would be 'A new pair o' jeans!' Extra money would mean that when cooking dinner she would not have to bother about always using the leftovers from the day before which '. . . depresses ye a wee bit. It *does*, although ye dinna' ken it'.

Her attitude towards unemployment has changed:

I used to think it'd be *great* not to work . . . when I was working . . . I'd think 'imagine having a day off' – it was a treat. Now, I've got every day, and every week, and every month . . . and maybe every year . . . to do *nothing*. There never used to be enough hours in the day for me when I was working . . . now, I know what like an hour is . . . it just drags round.

Her attitude towards people who are unemployed has altered, too: 'I would be rushing to my work and rushing home . . . and I'd see people who didna' work, and I thought 'gee, they're lucky'; and they never seemed to be without. But ye dinna' realise they were struggling to keep an appearance up.'

5   B.I.

Born in a nearby town, B.I., who is now in his mid-fifties, moved to Cauldmoss when he married a woman from the village. They live on the council scheme, near their only child who married recently. He worked for long periods both for British Aluminium and British Steel, reaching the position of quality controller before he was made redundant a year ago. He managed to find a temporary job almost straight away, but this lasted only a few weeks.

His wife, who was trained as a nurse, was not working when B.I. lost his job, although she has managed to find work over the past year – first, as a stand-in assistant at an old people's home, and then, more recently, a permanent job in an office in a nearby town.

B.I.'s redundancy pay, together with his wife's earnings, have meant that the couple have not suffered too much financial hardship as yet, and it seems that the family have made a conscious effort to maintain an appearance of financial well-being; they ran two cars when their daughter (who was also unemployed) lived at home, and they always had a stock of food and alcohol. Only rarely do Mr and Mrs I. mention not having much money; even then, it might mean renting only one video film rather than two. However, B.I. complained that, as a recipient of unemployment rather than supplementary benefit, he is not entitled to have all his rent paid or to free prescriptions and dental treatment. When asked directly how he manages on his benefit he answered, 'With difficulty!'.

B.I. says he would love a job, but thinks that he will never get one because he is too old. He feels extremely 'bitter' that, although he possesses excellent references from all his previous employers, he cannot get a job because he lacks the formal qualifications to enter on application forms. He reminisces about the past when it was possible to walk into a foundry or mill and be given a job on the spot – now, you need to fill in forms and have formal interviews, and unemployment has become 'a social disease'.

The psychological impact of being made redundant after many years in the same job seems to have been softened for B.I. by the fact that he found another job soon afterwards, albeit a temporary one. Even when this came to an end, although he worried about the future and his employment prospects, he managed to remain fairly cheerful, filling his day with chores in the house and attempts to find work.

He also passed the time by making wooden toys (which provided a little extra income). He is very skilled at this work, but any suggestion that he set up a full-time business making and selling toys was always rebuffed. Although he would not say why he did not like this idea, it seems that he did not regard this as a legitimate way of making a living, possibly because it would entail his taking full responsibility for organising his working day.

While he was working, B.I. did not go out in the evenings very often, apart from occasionally attending meetings of the Masonic Lodge, and carrying out church business in his capacity as an elder, which included going to some of the social functions organised by the church. When he became unemployed he continued to join in with these activities. During the past few months, however, he has gone out even less than usual, a trend which has culminated recently in his ceasing to attend church services. He has also given up making toys. He continues to rise early each morning and busy himself with chores but his search for work has become much less intensive. His personality seems to have changed; his wife and daughter frequently complain about him being 'crabbit' (bad tempered) and say 'He's going mad just sitting in the house', usually in front of the TV. Mrs I. often warns him that he will give himself a second heart attack. He has become taciturn, and sometimes he will not even return a greeting. He seems to be cutting himself off from social contact, turning his own words, 'People make you feel like a leper', into a self-fulfilling prophecy.

Strategies for coping

The initial reaction of older men who become unemployed seems to be to try to maintain the old familiar routine of their lives and to find another job. Work is found through the state Job Centre or through newspaper advertisements, but far more often through personal contacts. 'It's no *what* ye ken, it's *who* ye ken', is the frequent summary of the situation. If after a few months no job has come up, the attitude of even the most positive person seems to change, and the initial sense of freedom changes to boredom and depression; a finding common to most studies on unemployment from Jahoda, Lazarsfeld and Zeisel's classic study *Marienthal* in 1933 to Seabrook's writings in 1982.

Most of the young say they want work, but this is expressed more as a wish for money than employment, and several teenagers think it beneath them to work on state Youth Opportunities Programme schemes for £25 a week (illustrated by case study 1). For many of the young unemployed, several of whom have never had regular work since leaving school, phases of unsuccessful job hunting alternate with periods of apathy and delinquency.

Breakwell (this volume) points to the lack of creative activity among the young unemployed she studied, but, unlike her sample, we found that jobless teenagers in Cauldmoss do *not* tend to be socially isolated, thanks to the strength of cross-kin and cross-peer group ties in the community.

While some of the unemployed try to fill their day with 'leisure' activities, others (such as J.O., case study 3) are lucky enough to realise a strategy that both occupies their time, provides some money and helps satisfy their work ethic. Working 'on the side' when registered as unemployed is morally condoned to a greater degree than most other illegal economic activity, and our impression is that most people out of work will take any 'side jobs' available, although opportunities are usually limited, perhaps to a few days each fortnight, and one needs the right contacts. Parker (1982) has demonstrated the enormous financial incentives to work on the side, due to the cut in benefits and high taxation which legitimate work involves. Several people condemn the few who are signing on who have a virtually full-time job, but the more typical reaction to irregular work on the side is: 'That's a fly job – I'd say guid luck ta her'. Nevertheless, people are very discreet about their 'sidework' for there is a great fear of 'grassers', whose phone calls or letters can lead to 'snoopers' from the social security being sent round in cars to watch an individual's movements. The motive of informers is usually assumed to be jealousy, and as might be expected in a tight-knit community, the incidence of grassing and snooping is much exaggerated in people's talk.

The kind of informal jobs done range from undeclared work by self-employed tradesmen to unskilled labouring for unscrupulous employers and the small-scale mowing of gardens, walking dogs, and so on.

Amongst the younger generation there are several who argue that the only way to cope on social security is to develop a new strategy of 'making do' or 'cheating'. Older folk condemn most thefts and 'fiddles', and despair that for many young ones 'If it's no' too hot, it's no' too heavy', but amongst younger people 'fiddling' to save money is more common: 'Money's money after all. Ye got to save it where ye can.' Examples include fraudulent benefit claims to the DHSS and fixing the electricity meter.

Many of the unemployed state that they are forced to borrow money (usually from relatives) to make ends meet. Fewer people resort to theft in order to supplement their dole cheques, and those that do steal are often succumbing to temptation, rather than committing a premeditated crime.

Although there are fundamental differences in the crimes Henry studied in *The Hidden Economy* and those committed by the unemployed of Cauldmoss, there are some similarities. Stolen goods are not always sold at their potential price, for pricing is influenced by the relationship between trading partners. Henry notes two motives that certainly exist in Cauldmoss: the element of competition between criminals and the aspect of playing to beat the system, 'to gain control over personal action' (Henry, 1978: 95), both of which help to relieve the normal monotony of life on the dole.

Another means by which several of the unemployed cope financially is collecting fuel locally, normally for their own consumption but occasionally to sell. Peat is taken from drying stacks made by a commercial peat company, coal is dug out of the hillside where small seams are exposed, and trees are cut for fire wood. In general, collecting fuel for one's own use is not regarded as wrong, even when it is recognised as illegal.

Paths not taken

This adaptation, finding one's own fuel, is the kind of shift from the formal to the domestic economy which Gershuny and Pahl predicted would happen in a general way as a reaction to high unemployment, new technology and government policies of tax and control (Gershuny and Pahl, 1980: 7). They also forecast that there would be a great increase in informal work, since the relative autonomy and personal fulfilment which they argue are found within it, would encourage its growth despite the lower financial gain. Other sociologists and radical pcliticians have written optimistically of the potential benefits that could come from a positive approach to unemployment, mentioning lifelong education, occupational pluralism, community projects, 'sabbatical' schemes, developing hobbies, etc. (Clemitson and Rodgers, 1981; Clarke, 1982; Dauncey, 1983, amongst others).

Unfortunately for all those sympathetic to such views, our evidence suggests that few of these possibilities hold any attraction for the population of Cauldmoss. Apart from the case of gathering fuel, household activities seem not to have changed in the last five years or so: people do not make more of their own clothes, grow more of their own vegetables or rely less on convenience foods. Although one might expect that the legal restrictions on working when unemployed would encourage the barter of skills and goods, in fact it is the illegal sphere of the informal economy that seems to be developing in Cauldmoss, either providing cash or saving folk from paying it. As we have shown, the principal things most people seek from their work are consumer power (which the informal economy in general only partially provides) and a structure to their life (which it hardly provides at all) rather than the satisfaction of a productive job or community involvement, which Pahl talks of as its greatest rewards.

Cauldmoss folk are strikingly conservative about some of their values, many of which originate from an era when there was work for everyone and social status and self-identity were largely related to conspicuous evidence of consumer power. As Klein has shown, in a small close-knit community: '. . . none can escape the sanctions of gossip and public opinion. In these conditions, people tend to reach consensus on norms and exert a consistent informal pressure on each other to conform. This is the way a tradition is perpetuated . . .' (Klein, 1965: 128). The values relating to work and consumerism are very persistent, even when a larger proportion of the population lack prestige exactly because of this ideology. Very few of the unemployed come to terms with their situation by altering their attitude towards work and they are unwilling even to discuss changes in the workplace to better distribute available employment. This suggests they want to avoid a tacit acknowledgement that they may never be employed again, as if to do so would imply they are no longer seeking work and thus are no longer 'deserving' unemployed. Most attempt to maintain their previous level of consumption (at least outwardly) while some even feel that this objective validates their breach of other social norms, such as not stealing.

Young people in and out of work

Social psychology is the study of the person in social context. It examines how macro-socio-economic processes influence the attitudes, beliefs and behaviour of individuals directly and indirectly through changes in their interpersonal networks. This concern with individuals and their intimates distinguishes the approach of social psychology to the study of the labour market from those of the other social sciences. This distinction only holds at the crudest level, however, since most analyses of the labour market make assumptions about psychological functioning. For instance, many economists assume a rational model of man and consequently hold a whole array of preconceptions about how people process information and come to decisions. What other disciplines take as given in the analysis of the labour market, psychologists normally regard as the target for analysis. Instead of taking rationality for granted, psychologists have sought to find out whether it reigns supreme in decision making. In fact, there are numerous proofs that it does not (Brandstatter *et al.*, 1982). This tendency to make problematic what is often held as axiomatic has led social psychologists to concentrate upon what people think and feel about their economic activities and upon how people actually conduct themselves in work settings.

There has been great emphasis upon the experience of work. Cook *et al.* (1981) report 249 scales designed to measure aspects of the experience of work: job satisfaction, involvement and motivation; alienation and commitment; occupational mental health and ill-health; work values, beliefs and needs; the perception of work colleagues and leadership styles; and effects of work role, job context and organisational climate. This plethora reflects the centrality which work is assumed to possess in most people's lives and the assumption has been empirically supported time and again (Jahoda, 1982) in studies of the psychological impact of paid employment, unemployment and redundancy (Warr, 1983). It is worth adding that most of these investigations have been concerned only with work done under contractual arrangements for material rewards. It is doubtless true that there are other forms of work: any intended action directed at achieving a goal is work. Work of this kind would include housework, voluntary work, do-it-yourself jobs, hidden economy work, some forms of self-employment, and work in contemporary non-industrialised societies. There is no question that these other forms of work are sometimes important shapers of self-concept and self-esteem, social standing and interpersonal networks. They have the potential to serve the same psychological functions as paid employment even when they fail to fulfil its material contribution. However, they have been studied only rarely by psychologists and then often only to examine how they act as substitutes to 'real' work, i.e. paid employment. For instance, it has been shown that women who lose a paid job but who have housework and child care to do fare better than women similarly redundant who have no home and family to run (Warr *et al.*, 1982).

So, no matter how one chooses to define work, it seems to be vital to a person's identity, their sense of self and its evaluation. If one's working life is fraught with difficulties it can be predicted that identity will be threatened. This may entail a changed self-concept containing new self-descriptions. For instance, losing one's job, at the simplest level, may mean it is no longer legitimate to call oneself an engineer, another label may be needed. Alternatively, it may entail changes not in self-description but self-evaluation. For instance, being shown to be incompetent may not mean losing the label engineer but may mean fundamental re-assessments of one's worth as an engineer. Of course, sometimes both sorts of change will occur simultaneously in response to new information about one's working life.

The research reported below was designed to explore how people cope with threats to their identity posed by their position in the labour market. Three sorts of position were studied: unemployment; temporary employment on job creation schemes; and employment in sexually atypical jobs.

The people studied were between sixteen and nineteen years old. Adolescents were chosen for a series of reasons. Firstly, there is a dearth of evidence about the experiences of young people in the labour market, particularly young women. Secondly, adolescence is a time conventionally assumed to be associated with great crises and renovations of identity. The transition from school to work has been considered both the culmination of preparation for adulthood and simultaneously just the start of the long road to independence and responsibility. It is deemed a time of self-appraisal and reconstruction of the self-concept. But these psychological cameos of the move into the labour market were generated during times of full youth employment when there was little challenge to the sex-typing of occupational roles. The picture has shifted now that jobs are scarce and equal opportunity legislation calls into doubt the sexual division of labour. The salient issue becomes: how is adolescent identity reframed amid economic doubt and sex role confusion. Finally, adolescents were chosen because the research formed part of a wide initiative by the then Social Science Research Council for psychological studies of adolescence.

The research concentrated upon the consequences of threats to identity in four domains:

1. the impact upon self-image and psychological health;
2. the effects upon attitudes towards their own position, towards others in that position, and towards those thought to have put them there;
3. the development of attributions: how they explained why they were in that position;
4. the patterns of behaviour: the action strategies used to cope.

In presenting the data, an attempt will be made to organise them around these central domains. The data from young people who were unemployed and those on Youth Opportunities Programme schemes are presented first; those from young women in sexually atypical jobs (that is, jobs conventionally done by men and stereotypically associated with men) second.

Effects of unemployment and temporary employment

The young people in the unemployed sample were interviewed, using structured schedules, during the 1980–1 in the Midlands. They were drawn randomly from the Careers Service Lists of unemployed 16–19 year olds. They resided in an area traditionally associated with full employment both for adults and young people. Few of their parents had ever experienced unemployment. This is, of course, important since these young people had not been brought up to expect unemployment and its impact was probably all the worse for that. Even at the time of the interviews the area had a low rate of unemployment (8.9 per cent overall). Two groups of young people were studied: a cross-sectional sample of seventy-two, one-third of whom had been unemployed for under three weeks, one-third for 3–9 weeks, and the remainder for 9–25 weeks; and a longitudinal sample of forty first interviewed within three weeks of becoming unemployed and followed through the next three to four months during which time some found employment, others got a place on a YOP scheme, and the rest remained unemployed. Both unemployed samples were stratified by sex. The sample in temporary employment were on a government YOP scheme called a WIC (Work Introductory Course) in the same area. There were twenty-one young people on the course which comprised three days a week work experience upon employers' premises and two days in college learning various life, social and technical skills. The young people on this scheme were similar in all socio-economic and educational respects to those in the unemployed sample and comparison across samples seems valid.

In order to understand the adjustments open to the young people it was also necessary to understand something of how they were treated by those with some authority over them. There was consequently a second focus for the research: the careers officers, the YOP tutors, the workplace supervisors, training officers and employers involved. The attitudes of these people who were significant in the 'working' life of the young people were targets for exploration and are reported when relevant. It was assumed that these authority figures would play an important role in moulding the work identity of these young people. The purpose of the study was to show how this might occur. It was assumed that the rhetoric they use would be important and this was tested. Interviews with these authority figures were conducted and, where possible, they were observed in interaction with the young people. In the case of the YOP study, participant observation was used in the college-based portion of the course over a twelve week period.

(i) Effects on psychological health and self-esteem

Comparisons across the two unemployed samples and the YOP sample allow certain assertions to be made and questions to be answered. The first set of questions concern psychological well-being, self-esteem and life satisfaction. Warr (1983) has reported that for adults unemployment is associated with declining well-being (higher levels of anxiety and depression), self-esteem (greater self-doubt and criticism), and life satisfaction (satisfaction with one's social life, past education, familial relations, etc.). The current findings support this. The young people who were unemployed were characterised by lower levels of psychological well-being, self-esteem, and life satisfaction than either those on YOP or those in 'real' work (where 'real' is equated with any paid employment not part of a YOP scheme). Interestingly, YOP and 'real' work did not have significantly different effects upon these psychological factors. The young people vehemently criticised the YOP scheme but it had very similar psychological benefits to 'real' work. This may, of course, say more about the character of 'real' work available to the unqualified young person than it does about YOP schemes.

Stafford *et al.* (1980) have suggested that work involvement – the individual's personal commitment to and desire for work – mediates the psychological impact of unemployment. The idea has the stamp of common sense: those wanting work most suffer most when they do not have it. Nevertheless, the present data do not support this notion. There was no positive significant correlation between work involvement and psychological distress when unemployed. It seems that all of the young people studied had extremely high work involvement. Variations in response to unemployment are not always associated with levels of desire for work. Having said that, it was noticeable that in the longitudinal sample those who suffered greatest initial distress were more likely to gain a 'real' job. Adjusting well to unemployment was associated with a lower likelihood of getting a job.

A subset of the question about the psychological impact of unemployment must concern the effects of duration. Until recently, it had been assumed that there is a three-stage response to unemployment: initially shock, active job search and optimism about regaining employment; followed by growing pessimism after successive fruitless attempts to find work leading to anxiety and depression; and, finally, fatalism, inertia and acceptance of 'joblessness as a way of life'. This process was thought to take nine months. In fact, there is little evidence to support this picture. Most recent studies have found no direct relation between duration of unemployment and psychological state. Examination of the data from the cross-sectional sample of unemployed would also lead to the rejection of the three stage model. However, it was found that those unemployed for about six weeks suffered significantly more than either those unemployed for shorter or longer periods. This group had lower self-esteem, life satisfaction and well-being.

The explanation for this may lie in the specific situation these young people found themselves in. Due to rules about access to YOP scheme places which dictated, at the time of the study, that young people had to be unemployed for six weeks before they became eligible for a place, these young people shared a common anxiety: the problem of gaining a place that they would want. They shared a common anxiety and showed a common pattern of response. It seems from this and other data on variations in response to unemployment that specific situational variables may be formative (Breakwell *et al.*, 1984). A situational analysis would result in a more finely grained model of the psychological impact of unemployment and would explain why there are vast differences in response between different ages, classes, ethnic groups, etc. It may also explain why there were no sex differences in psychological responses in these samples when other investigators have found big differences: these young men and women shared a similar phenomenological situation.

(ii)   Attitudes to the employed and unemployed

A second set of questions which can be asked concern the stereotypes which these young people hold of the employed and the unemployed as categories of people. This can be considered to be important since the stereotype that these young people hold of the unemployed may be acting as a template for self-image. Therefore, the unemployed and YOP samples were asked to describe, on a series of twenty-three semantic differentials, what they personally thought were the characteristics of the employed and the unemployed as groups. The unemployed samples were also required to say how they thought other people would describe these two categories. This second measure was used as an index of how critical these young people felt the rest of their society was of the category to which they belonged.

The results have been presented elsewhere (Breakwell *et al.*, 1984) and they portray a clear picture. The unemployed young people, regardless of length of unemployment, believed the employed to be superior to the unemployed on every dimension of comparison. Perhaps more importantly, they believed that other people would be even more critical than they of the unemployed and more complimentary about the employed. To some extent these young people were right, when a sample of school children (15–18 year olds, numbering 290) were given the same task of describing the two categories they were more critical of the unemployed and more positive about the employed than the unemployed sample had been. However, the school pupils were not quite as polarised in their views as the unemployed sample expected. It seems that the unemployed young people had unnecessarily pessimistic beliefs about how others see them. This is especially noticeable when data from the YOP sample are considered since these young people did not differentiate between the two categories anywhere near as much as expected – though they still regarded the employed as better on every dimension. Nevertheless, what counts in the development of self-image is how one thinks others feel and think about one and one's group memberships. Clearly, the attributions that the young unemployed made about the attitudes of others in this case left them feeling that they were regarded as inferior due to their employment status.

This pattern of attitudes held by the unemployed and perceived by them to be characteristic of others may explain why unemployment has such drastic effects upon self-esteem and psychological health for large numbers of people. It is not simply being unemployed which is damaging due to the removal of the manifest and latent benefits of work but the social stigma attached to unemployment which causes harm. Many social psychologists have talked about unemployment being damaging simply because it means one loses the benefits of work. That is probably true but it has to be supplemented by an examination of the nature of unemployment too. Unemployment is not merely the deprivation of work, it carries with it societally-created prescriptions about identity, role and value. Just as work establishes an identity; unemployment erects an identity.

This has practical implications: it may not be possible to alter levels of unemployment but it may be possible to change the social role allotted to the unemployed. Changing what Moscovici (1976) would call the social representation of unemployment would entail considerable changes in the value attached to work. It would certainly entail changing stereotypes held by those dealing with the unemployed. For instance, a study conducted as part of the present research programme showed that employment assistants in the Careers Service held unrealistically negative attitudes towards the young unemployed with whom they were daily dealing. Since these employment assistants currently receive no formal training, it might not be inappropriate to start with them when attempting to introduce changes in social representations of the unemployed. Changes in their attitudes would have an immediate impact upon the young people reliant upon them for access to jobs.

(iii) Attributing blame

In explaining the effects of unemployment on identity, questions about how blame is allotted, both for unemployment in general and for one's own unemployment in particular, are interesting. Firstly, if a person feels responsible for their own position the effects on identity will be different from those where other people or the socio-economic system are held responsible. Secondly, these explanations of their predicament are likely to shape how they seek actively to cope with their unemployment. For instance, if I consider my unemployment to be due to my own inadequacies it may be in my power to change things, assuming those inadequacies are remediable, and to regain a job. On the other hand, if I believe my unemployment to be due to a world economic recession, since it is beyond my power to control, I may cease all struggle to gain employment.

When asked to explain their own unemployment and unemployment in general the young people in the unemployed samples were able to do so. With virtually a single voice, they said unemployment in general was due to failures of the system (the government policy or worldwide economic trends) but their own unemployment was due to their personal inadequacies (lack of qualifications, experience, age, etc.). These responses can be compared with those of the young people doing a YOP course. These, when asked about the reasons for their own past unemployment, did not accept personal responsibility. They were much more likely to articulate the idea that they were mere victims of the system's failure to produce the appropriate jobs. In saying this, they were, in fact, echoing the rhetoric used by the tutors on their YOP scheme who explicitly taught that unemployment (including their own) was structurally determined. The rhetoric surrounding the young people involved in the YOP scheme was designed to enable them to reconstrue their past employment and unemployment history. This may be one reason why those involved with the YOP scheme fared so much better psychologically than those who were unemployed. The psychological benefits of YOP schemes may largely accrue from the fact that they can provide new understandings of failure and success besides providing new social networks, a time structure for the day, and occasionally the promise of future employment. This may explain why some YOP schemes failed to provide psychological advantages and others succeeded. If some provided the rhetorical milieu which enabled the reconceptualisation of past experiences in the labour market and others did not, one would predict differential efficacy. The rhetorical framework can remould self-concept and self-esteem.

The longevity of this phoenix-like rhetorical reforging is, however, questionable. Follow-up studies of young women who had been on another YOP scheme and who had returned to the dole queue after it finished, showed that the improvement evident in measures of psychological functioning while they were participating in the scheme was annihilated within six weeks of leaving the scheme (Breakwell, in press). It seems that the 'truths' learned during the scheme faced severe attacks when the young person was left alone again to deal with unemployment. To be maintained, the changes in attitude, attribution and self-concept developed during the YOP experience, seem to need careful servicing. Where this back-up provision was not available the changes evaporated. The young people were left with a strong sense of loss: in retrospect the scheme was deemed to constitute a marvellous and valuable experience even though they had been highly critical of it whilst on it.

Perhaps the loss of the 'truths' absorbed on the YOP schemes is not as sad as it at first appears. There is, in fact, a certain ambivalence in their operation. Structural explanations of unemployment may assuage guilt, turn aside self-blame, and consequently protect the self-concept. This can be viewed as positive. However, they also carry the connotation that the individual is powerless to change his or her position. Not only can this sense of powerlessness be damaging to the self-concept, it may also prevent the individual from actively seeking to overcome remediable problems. The reasoning would be: I'm powerless to do anything, so why bother. In reality, the rhetoric which would lead to the optimal survival strategy would need to promote the idea that there is an interaction between individual and societal responsibility and that, therefore, the actions of the individual can have an impact within certain limitations. None of the young people interviewed propounded this interactive model.

(iv) Action strategies

All the talk above of identity, attributions and attitudes has omitted action. There has been a considerable amount of work recently on what people do while they are unemployed (e.g. Bunker and Dewberry, 1983). Much of this work emphasises that unemployed people withdraw into their homes, shun social contacts and become increasingly isolated, inactive and bored. There has however been some suggestion that this pattern may not hold true for young people. Coffield (1982) argued that young people do not withdraw into depression and apathy when faced with unemployment but instead respond creatively, finding substitutes to provide what work would otherwise offer. Sometimes this means starting a rock group, a street theatre, or simply a youth club. In fact, the evidence for this is slender. In the unemployed samples studied here no 'creative adaptations' were reported – at least, not ones which would be creative by the norms of standard society. These young people stayed in bed, watched the TV for long stretches, and stressed their utter boredom. They had not found a substitute source for the latent concomitants of work and were socially isolated and economically constrained.

Perhaps this is because these young people did not come from a region of traditional high unemployment where an unemployed subculture can cushion the effects of unemployment. These young people had no norms of coping by regrouping within the community.

Their isolation and apparent failure to identify with others in their community may explain something of their political response to their situation. Questions about the political attitudes of the unemployed are interesting because there is little data available and because one might expect them to be interested in changing a system which offers them little reward. In fact, the young people in the unemployed samples were unanimous in their disinterest in politics. They belonged to no political parties, had no faith in politicians as a route to bring about change in their position, and regarded economics as largely outside of the control of politics. However, virtually all claimed to be ready to bring about political or economic change, given the opportunity, by other means. Most saw the prospect of bloody strife on the streets as realistic.

This pattern is important: the young unemployed person is socially isolated and sees no future in attempts to work with other people in the community to bring about change through democratic means. It may be, of course, that the lack of trust expressed about standard political parties does not extend to other pressure groups or social movements. Yet these young people reported no membership of such groups. If these young people are anything to go by, one would not expect the unemployed youth to be a political force.

(v)   Some conclusions about identity and unemployment

There is a clear syndrome of attitudes, attributions and actions which differentiate the unemployed from those in 'real' work and those on YOP schemes. All three components of this syndrome reflect an identity structure typifying the unemployed; this identity is characterised by self-deprecation, self-blame and perceived powerlessness. The findings reported above examine the social influence processes which engender this identity. The important thing to recognise may be that this identity *is* a product of social influence processes (rhetoric, the impact of significant others, social representations, etc.). This means that it is not the inevitable consequence of being out of work in any absolute sense. It is the product of being out of work in a specific social context where specific influences are operative. It means that people learn what their identity should be as an unemployed person. It equally means that this identity can be changed.

Effects of sexually atypical employment

The second part of the research project was designed to examine the ways in which young women cope with the problems associated with doing sexually atypical jobs. These young women were doing jobs conventionally done by men and stereotypically associated solely with men. They were engineering technician trainees (only 2 per cent of all technicians in Britain were women at the time of the study and the job can therefore be considered sexually atypical).

The thirty-five young women in the sample comprised over a third of all female trainees at an equivalent stage of training in the South and Midlands areas. They were scattered across twenty-four different firms and were interviewed twice with a six month interval. Their supervisors and the firm's training officers were also interviewed.

The central purpose of the study was to examine what self-images these young women evolved, how far this was dictated by the demands of their work colleagues and whether the occupational identity of girls with difficulties were in any way different from those who coped well. Before summarising the findings in these areas it is sensible to consider the basic demographic characteristics of these young women.

(i) Background characteristics

The majority of the girls came from families in which at least one member had a job in engineering and their families were supportive of their decision to become an engineer. Boyfriends tended initially to be critical of the decision but those who continued to be so were abandoned once the girl started training. Being a member of an engineering family tended to facilitate entry into the job but it did not ensure success. Those who came from non-engineering families and whose passage into the industry tended to be more difficult were less likely to get into difficulties during their training. Perhaps this was because these were a more highly selected group: the ones with lower determination having been weeded out.

The majority of the girls were academically well-qualified with five or more 'O' levels. They were all 17–18 years old.

(ii) Occupational self-image

These young women had a very clear notion of their own self-concept which they could describe with alacrity. They engaged in overt and spontaneous social comparisons to assess their own worth and social standing, just as Festinger's (1954) theory would predict. When asked to compare themselves with what they considered to be the average female technician they claimed to be equal to her or better. Even when they compared themselves with what they considered to be the 'ideal' technician they felt that they compared favourably, being superior in dedication and responsibility. Comparing themselves with the average male trainee they claimed their own superiority in everything except leadership skills and technical abilities. In everything they said it was clear that these young women had a very positive occupational identity.

It is interesting that their supervisors echoed this evaluation: the girls were rated higher than their male counterparts on the qualities of neatness, reliability, punctuality, and, most importantly in the eyes of the supervisors, commitment. The supervisors considered the girls less able technically and less capable of leadership, just as the girls had commented in their self-ratings.

This unanimity of trainees and their supervisors about their occupational self-image is not surprising. It seems likely that the girls were simply absorbing their self-image from the feedback given by the supervisors.

In fact it seems that acceptance of the role constructed by the supervisors was a precondition of avoiding problems in the workplace. It was noticeable that those girls who failed to internalise the consensus self-concept were the ones who had difficulties. The girls with difficulties had two sets of characteristics. Firstly, they asserted that they did not wish to differentiate themselves from other women; claiming that there is no difference between those who become engineers and all other women. They, therefore, were not buying into the imagery which claimed distinctiveness and positivity for women who braved criticism by breaking sex-role expectations. They were rebels from the party line. Secondly, in keeping with the first, they sought to maintain their femininity in the workplace: this they expressed by being deferential to others, occupying when the opportunity arose caring roles in relations to others, avoiding assertiveness and refraining from competition.

The majority of the young women who coped well with the workplace emphasised that those with problems were simply not using the right strategy. Nor was it enough to simply be the opposite of feminine; the goal, they said, was not to copy the men. These young women recognised that copying might be perceived as outright competition and thus as threatening. Instead, they had to excel in a role which was uniquely female but also uniquely that of an engineering technician. The ideal female technician is a very different animal, in the eyes of her supervisors and male colleagues, from the ideal male technician. The girls knew that they had to model themselves on her, not on him. The ideal female technician is not too assertive or aggressive; not too dependent or shy; not too sexy; but is punctual, reliable, and conscientious.

Some of the young women considered themselves career engineers, being determined to return to engineering after they had reared their children. These were self-consciously analysing what was required of them in terms of self-presentation from their supervisors and were feeding it back to them in the identity they created for themselves at work. They fulfilled their role obligations as specified by the supervisors and were rewarded as a consequence. These young women carefully distinguished themselves from the sort of woman who could not be a technician. In fact, they positively revelled in their distinctiveness. Nevertheless, they were careful not to reveal their pride in their distinctiveness or uniqueness to their workmates because women who were thought to do the job simply to be different were anathema to the training officers and supervisors.

It seems that reliance upon the traditional female self-image is likely to lead to problems in this sort of sexually atypical job but seeking to adopt the traditional male self-image is equally counter-productive. Happiness in the job and, indeed, success in the short term is dependent upon conforming to the images which others create for the female technician. In reality these young women are abandoning simple notions of gender or occupational identity and moving towards an integrative framework.

The development of this identity is 'more than just a process of internalisation of the parameters established by supervisors. It goes beyond conformity to the norms of the workplace. The majority of the girls were actively aware that they were part of a process which is restructuring sex roles. They knew that they had to play the game to the rules made by others most of the time if they were to gain success. They also knew that they had a certain latitude of freedom to introduce innovations since the rules had yet to gain the immobility which comes with age and venerability over generations. They were breaking out of one set of expectations about women's abilities and nature, not simply succumbing to another set. They were essentially contributors in the process which was generating the revised version of expectations in the engineering industry. There is consequently a sense in which these young women were agents purposively building their own identities. They customised their own individual occupational identity but also as a result simultaneously laid down a template for any women who follow in their footsteps.

Conclusions about the impact of a threatening position in the labour market

A person's identity is fundamentally influenced by his or her position in the labour market: attitudes, attributions and actions which constitute identity can be predicted from that position. It also seems fair to say that accepted social psychological theories of social influence processes can be used to explain how identity is derived. This does not exclude the possibility of individual agency in the growth of identity at work or out of work but it does suggest that it will be circumscribed. People are not free to evolve any identity they choose in the labour market; their choices are constrained. Moreover, it has to be accepted that this occupational input will reverberate throughout the self-concept and affect other aspects of self-definition and value.

Rules not laws: outline of an ethnographic approach to economics

In the last ten years or so, sociologists have begun to rely much less than before on a class model in their analyses of industrial society. No doubt there are many reasons; among them are trends and shifts in society itself – a general trend towards the right, perhaps; but certainly, also, other shifts of a possibly more permanent kind: a rising social importance of ethnicity and race relations, for example, which does not fit easily with traditional class models. The women's movement, equally awkward in that sense, has had consequences for the style and focus of sociological work: as a social fact it commands attention; as a social influence on sociologists, it also has its consequences.

One of the major characteristics of class analyses is that they take the market as a given: classes are produced by markets, and so if there are classes, there must be markets. It was not necessary to examine them, for they produced class-based society, and that was what they were supposed to do. If at times it seemed there were discrepancies, they could often be accommodated in the analysis of relative deprivation, or working-class conservatives were shown to be products of class-dominance, and at a pinch the notion of false consciousness – not that anyone wrote much about it – could be invoked to explain why things were not as they should be. But the decline of class analysis has given greater space to the ethnographic strand always present in the British sociological tradition but sometimes obscured or ignored: the tendency for sociologists to listen to what people say seems, to an outside observer, to be increasing. In particular, sociologists have heard people speak of their economic activities, and as a result have begun to think about how economies work. For example, one of the assumptions of class analysis is that workers sell disembodied labour power, but any open-eared sociologist must now be aware that the vast majority of domestic work is done by people whose labour power is not detached from themselves. It is, rather, provided by a long-term contract which involves whole persons, and the majority of the population is brought up to believe that that is the best kind of contract to make and hence, presumably, the best kind of work they can aspire to. [1] But in this case, what price the market? Some of the most searching investigations into labour markets are stimulated by the evident failure of markets to do what markets should do, which is to create a price at which supply and demand can be matched, the market cleared. What is revealed is a range of economic activities which are not grounded in formal, legal, regulated markets at all, but rather in relations of kinship, friendship, neighbourliness; in partiality, sympathy and altruism which – from an economist's point of view – constitute imperfections: they are those other unequal things which prevent the striking of a bargain at the efficiency wage. It is not only failure which reveals imperfection: as Professor Waldinger shows, the immense success of the New York rag trade in meeting up-to-the-week demand for fashion clothes depends on a depressed labour force which has low wages, works in foul and dangerous conditions and is tied to the market by kinship, ethnicity, bewilderment and inability to communicate. The point is that like their failures, the success of markets is also not always based on an impersonal detached labour power, but on men and women whose personal characteristics are essential to the bargain: it is based on imperfection.

Craig and her colleagues at the Cambridge Labour Studies Group, say in their paper here that 'imperfection' is the category for reality which does not fit the Marshallian model of competition. It is thus similar to false consciousness: even if destruction of falseness is not quite the attractive goal for sociologists that elimination of imperfection is for economists, they are both model-sustaining categories. They both permit their users to slip from objective scientific analysis into moral judgement, and back again. For some sociologists, abandoning class analysis has opened a rich vein of human experience, understanding, intention. And, at any rate for Craig and her colleagues, abandoning the model of a perfectly competitive market allows researchers access to 'the real world'.

The point must be that sociologists who explore economic action in an ethnographic way should be led to question the model of the market, which was previously taken for granted. If they have found a princedom by kissing the toad of falseness, they should now embrace imperfection. But in fact they have at best been tentatively rebellious. In Pahl's stimulating and sensitive accounts of Sheppey the market is somehow superimposed on an inferior 'informal' economy, and fluctuations in self-provisioning are dependent on market force. Gershuny and his colleagues set about 'rebuilding the foundations of economics', but their new socio-economic accounting system, for all its subtle re-jigging, seems to operate with the established categories of the system of analysis they seek to revise.

In these circumstances it may be helpful to suggest some questions, and to draw attention to work done on economies in which the market is not a salient integrating creation. These economies are exotic; but they reveal something of the range of human creativity, may suggest ways of taking varieties of intention and meaning into observers' accounts of economic activity. It would be wrong to suggest that anthropologists have answers ready for potting-on into ethnographies of large-scale societies. On the other hand, they have discussed the working of economies in an ethnographic way, and have had to find solutions to the problems which arise whenever students of society take experience rather than a model as the touchstone of reality. It may be that these discussions suggest ways of coping with problems, even if they provide no solutions. And it should be said, too, that the discussion in anthropology is not finished: most of the points made in what follows are controversial.

The topics may be grouped under four headings or slogans, as follows:
– self interest and profit-motivation are distinct;
– economic notions are human creations;
– the categories of economic action are moral categories;
– the blue economy may not be dominant.

Self interest and profit are distinct

This is an important point because of economists' hegemonic claims: they say their discipline is the study of all choice: 'Economics is the science which studies human behaviour as a relationship between ends and scarce means which have alternative uses' (Robbins, 1932 [96]). The choices are therefore rational, or can be analysed as if they were (and if they really are not, that is because they are affected by imperfection). Moreover rationality is specifically market-rationality, involving the notion of profit. The point is elaborated by, among others, von Mises (1949), an unacknowledged precursor of Homans. People who wish to question the importance of market in economic analysis might start by questioning the pervasiveness of the profit motive.

In general terms, people do wish to be good examples of their kind; and they usually have a range of opportunities for excellence: mother, husband, teacher, shopkeeper, friend. Some statuses, in some cultures, are more exclusive: samurai and (Christian) saint are examples; but it is commoner for people to judge themselves and others on a variety of standards, each a more or less coherent sub-set of local notions of 'good'. It is clear that this is an important source of that ambiguity and indeterminancy which people in many societies find essential. Actions are in a person's self-interst when they are directed to excellence in this sense. But it is clear that the economic aspects of these statuses are not all dominated by profit motive. 'Shopkeeper' and 'mother', in all societies which have both, require different kinds of economic action, and people expect them to make their decisions on different principles. It is quite easy to discover this, by asking people what they think of shopkeepers who do not make profits at all, or who make 'excessive' profits; or by asking people what they think of mothers who make profits out of their children. At this point theoreticians dominated by a market model say: in the very long term mothers get a material return in the form of comfort and support in their old age; and mothers do make an immaterial profit because they gain esteem and self-esteem. The first of these points is of course an empirical matter, and it should be possible to know, in any particular society, what sort of risks mothers accept on long-term investments. In some milieux, you might guess, mothers would get a better return for their outlay by taking out an insurance policy. It is empirical, too, in the sense that you can ask mothers if that is why they try to be good mothers; and you can ask their neighbours if it is an acceptable motive for undertaking motherhood. So far as the 'immaterial profits' argument is concerned, it is better to leave it. For, while no one would deny that mothers get pleasure from being good mothers, and from being recognised as such, it is clear that shopkeepers also get pleasure from being good shopkeepers; and really successful shopkeepers get public honours in recognition of their success. So shopkeepers also get immaterial rewards; and it follows that any argument, to the effect that the immaterial rewards of motherhood make motherhood a profit-motivated activity, must be cast in terms of amounts of immaterial reward – it is simply not the case that only mothers get immaterial rewards: it is a question of how much immaterial reward a mother gets, how much a shopkeeper. So it would be necessary to identify an abstract mother-power, detachable from the person, and then to show that the quantities of immateriality which reward it, are greater than the sum of material and immaterial rewards received by shopkeepers. Nobody has tried to do that, although, in analogous cases, they have assumed that the sums would come out so. In some societies public honours are awarded to especially prolific mothers; and in these cases it may be that the rewards of success (taking native definitions of success into account) do constitute a profit. But at any rate in western capitalist societies it seems probable that shopkeepers stand a better chance of public immaterial reward than mothers do. Of course, public honours are easy to talk about, because they are quantifiable: a defiant immaterial rewardist has to retreat to the trench called 'unquantifiable immaterial rewards', and in the last ditch may nurse the axiom that unquantifiable material rewards always vary sufficiently to show a profit on the account. That is a shoddy argument on which to base hegemonic claims for the universality of a style of analysis.

The principle that people can pursue self-interest by other means than making profits is stated quite clearly in Mauss (1954), demonstrated in the work of Malinowski (1922, 166–91) and others. Profit is a relation between receipts and outlay in which the former exceed the latter. Reciprocity is a relation in which a donor's receipts, in his estimation, are of equal value to his outlay. Potlatch is a relation in which income is less than outgoings: that condition can hold for only one of two parties to an exchange, and so it is agonistic. And so on. The range of kinds of exchange principle is explored in Meeker (1972), and a preliminary attempt to elaborate that further is in Davis (1975). The points, for present purposes, are that the logically possible relations between income and outlay all occur in known economies; that people can pursue their self-interest in a variety of ways, one of which is profit; and that economies can be integrated by economic institutions other than the market.

Economic notions are human creations

This is really an injunction to carry out zero-ethnography: to regard every-thing economic as problematic. While the reader will not need to be reminded of this, it might still be useful to some other sociologists, who have not yet escaped from the idea that some economic behaviour is governed by natural laws.

Some anthropologists argue that society could not exist without exchange: it is a part of the definition of society, indeed of humanity, and so bridges the gap between nature and culture. Exchange, in this case usually taken to be the exchange of women, or conceptually detachable aspects of women, would therefore be given. That is largely a definitional problem, containing essential circularities, and is of rather acutely specialised interest (Lévi-Strauss, 1949; for a modern feminist discussion see Rubin, 1975). That argument apart, anthropologists have been able to break down apparently integrated notions into component parts, to show that they are absent, or combined or distributed in different ways in different societies. The most stimulating example of this activity is Codere's discussion of money (1968). It has long been customary to point out that the functions of money (storing wealth; means of exchange and so on) are separable, and may be present or absent, vested in different objects in the same society. Codere's contribution is to emphasise that modern money is itself a composite: raw, naked money, so to speak, is a symbol of value. Its effectiveness in modern societies derives from its association with other symbolic systems: with number systems – themselves ethnographically problematic (Crump, 1978); with weights and measures; with writing. True, only one monetary system is known which exists independent of number, and in all others values are not merely greater or lesser, but are summable and subtractable. Nevertheless, the essential point is made: money is complex not only in its functions but in its structure, and it is composed differently in different societies. It follows that fundamental institutions of the market – such as money – are human creations, and hence purposive. Of course, an opponent might argue that what is variable is human capacity to make real some eternal and independent notion of money: some peoples have only imperfect money (or markets, or economies). That is not an argument calculated to persuade sociologists and others who are interested in how real economies, how real money are made. The point is, that once you escape from the hegemonic claim that economic activity is necessarily either rational or imperfect, you are able to appreciate the immense variety of ways (some of them indeed profitable) in which people have pursued their self-interest. In fact it is usually the case, and may even necessarily be the case, that they have more than one path open to them: certainly, anthropologists know of societies which are partly commercial (Bohannan and Dalton, 1965: 1–34), in which some activities are governed by market rules, others by rules of other kinds. Malinowski, (1922: 166–91), lists no less than seven main types of economic principle current in the Trobriands of the 1910s. Admittedly, his way of classifying principles seems odd nowadays. Nevertheless the general point remains, that Trobriand economy was integrated by a variety of motives. In such societies social convention, moral approval and disapproval, and sometimes legal sanctions partly regulate people's self-interested choices among alternative forms of economic action: they suggest when profit is a worthy motive, when reciprocity. They suggest when parts of selves can be detached and sold, and when whole persons have to be transacted.

The categories of economic action are moral categories

An ethnographer of economic activity should therefore recognise that the performance of any given economy is a result of human ingenuity operating within a framework of categories which in some cases are created by and in the interests of powerful people, but which in all cases are also moral categories.

Most work on exotic taxonomies has been concerned with flora and fauna: the items are relatively simple, and the activities of European biologists provide a touchstone for comparison which stimulates inquiry. The research suggests that such taxonomies are relative to the interests and pre-occupations of the people who make them, and of local validity (Ellen and Reason, 1979). To understand why the cassowary is not a bird (Bulmer, 1967), in other words, requires careful understanding of the ecology, economy and symbolic order of Karam society. The only sustained attempt to show that all taxonomies divide 'reality' into the same categories has concerned colour (Berlin and Kay, 1969) and has run into acute problems (Bousfield, 1979). It is characteristic of taxonomies of all kinds that they produce anomalies, things which do not fit into the categories. The classic study of anomalies is Douglas's analysis of the prohibitions of Leviticus (1966): anomalous things and anomalous behaviour are 'abominations' in the eyes of God. Ellen's introductory essay to the most recent general survey (1979) identifies seven main categories of variation in classificatory systems.

Taxonomies of action are fraught with greater difficulties: flora are relatively stable phenomena and human actions are fleeting and changeable from performance to performance. Moreover, such classificatory systems usually involve a series of taxonomies: in economic activity, for example, at least three taxonomies are involved: one which sorts goods into kinds; one which sorts people into kinds, and a third which sorts relations between income and outgoings into kinds. The institutions of an economy in effect are a matching of categories from different taxonomies: goods of kind x should pass between people of kind y in mode z

Taxonomies of anything are local, non-exhaustive, and relative. It is extra-ordinarily rare for diacritics in one order to match perfectly with those in another. The mismatching, and the ambiguities and indeterminacy which result, give opportunities for innovative re-interpretation by individual and groups and corporations, and give rise to moral and sometimes legal arguments.

These remarks seem to apply as much to Britain as to exotic economies. Items appear in the newspapers which are clearly derived from arguments about the proper classification of economic activity. The moral and legal notion that bearing a child normally confers rights to raise it is brought into question by the offer of 'surrogate mothers'. Disputes about insider trading, about the taxation of building societies on the same basis as banks, about the lack of human dignity in televised acquisitive games, are all disputes about the logic and morality of classification schemes, and arise out of indeter-minacies produced by lack of correspondence between different taxonomies. During the years of purchase tax parliament was frequently treated to displays of wit and indignation as members contested the classification produced by customs and excise men, to determine the rate of tax; and the index to *Hansard* for those years usually has an entry 'Purchase tax – anomalies'.

The phenomena associated with classification are observable not only in minutiae, but also in broad terms. The category names 'black', 'informal', 'irregular' are cases in point: in their different ways they each have a moral connotation; the category referred to is ill-defined and the adjacent categories are usually unnamed. If you will allow a christening: all economic activities which are recorded (because they are declared for tax purposes or because they are activities by government) appear in the National Income blue books, and they might be called the blue economy. The black economy includes all those activities which are either criminal or would be taxed if they were dis-closed. Informal economy seems to include also those activities which are neither black nor blue. And so on.

These are local native categories rather than sociological ones. Like all native categories they have consequences, and can therefore be studied. But they do not aid analysis because they are essentially purposive. Indeed, you could argue that economic analysis is deficient because economists derive most of their empirical data from the blue economy and extrapolate from that to the other categories. If the notions of blue and informal are confusing in the UK context, they are even more so when applied to the economies of

Third World cities, as they are – cleverly, influentially, misguidedly by Hart (1973). Ethnographic sociologists are not so limited in their data, but their ideas may be rather too dependent on the models created to account for blue phenomena.

You may define economics as the study of substantive activities – production, distribution, consumption; or as the study of choice. In either case, the range of evidence to be accounted for is in fact much greater than is provided by the blue economy. If you accept that people may be self-interested and still not profit-motivated, you may also accept the suggestion that anthropologists find useful, that people act from a variety of motives, make choices bearing in mind a variety of indicated goods and relationships and acceptable outcomes. There is no doubt that people expect and admire different actions by shopkeepers and lovers; that part of economic activity is governed by market principles – is integrated by the profit motive; and that other parts are governed by principles appropriate to friends, parents, neighbours and so on: are integrated by the reciprocity motive, by the altruistic motive. That is true to people's understanding of their own actions; it is true to what others round about them say: they acknowledge moral categories of action, and pursue self-interest within them, exploiting the indeterminacy of the categories, and the ambiguities of criteria.

The blue economy may not be dominant

This really involves two questions: what are the relations between the moral composite categories? And what is the outcome of different combinations of composite categories? Do economies perform differently because they have different conceptual structures? Neither question really has an answer.

The terms used often imply what is sometimes made explicit, that markets are more powerful than other kinds of economic nexus; or that the informal sector exists to serve the formal sector, and so on. That is a model which obviously bears some relation to local British understanding, and is supported by the evidence from the blue books, that the blue economy is very large; and by native understandings that 'everything is being commercialised'. Well, yes. But part of the success of markets which allegedly take over ritual feasts such as Christmas is due precisely to the importance that people place on the non-market exchanges they make with goods bought in the market. You might want to argue at least for an interdependence of the gift-goods and gift-givers and reciprocity nexus with the seller-buyer and profit-motivation and gift-goods nexus; the successes of markets do not always derive from ideal market conditions.

Social scientists are particularly impressed with measures: size, volumes of goods and services transacted are likely to influence their judgement as they assess the relation of one nexus to another. Measures of the volume of non-blue activity are notoriously hard to make, although Pahl and others have tried; and Pahl, gallantly apposite, has plausibly shown variation in volumes of informality and blackness. Ruggles and Ruggles (1970; see also Kendrick, 1967) have assessed the value of unpaid labour in the US, and reckon that if it were paid for, it would increase the United States' GNP by a half (for 1965). That includes items which are neither black or blue, such as the domestic and matrimonial services of women ($144 billion *pa* at 1965 prices, allowing for the fall in prices of these services if every American man were to divorce his wife and employ a housekeeper). These figures are notional, as is the estimate that gifts in the UK had a market value of not less than 10–12 per cent of GNP in 1969 (Davis, 1972). In spite of that, they may give pause: it is not quite so certain that marketers transact such huge, overwhelming quantities of goods and services that they dominate every other category.

The question whether economies perform differently according to their conceptual structures is crucial: if there were clear differences in categories but no differences in outcomes, it might be sensible to use blue data and blue ideas. Ethnographers would lose the pleasure of listening to what people say, but they would save a lot of time. Davis (1972) tried to argue that that part of the UK market which supplies goods which are then further transacted as gifts is protected from fluctuations which affect sales of other goods: but it is not an elaborate argument. The only anthropologist who has been reasonably successful in this area of argument is M. D. Sahlins (1972) whose discussion of 'the diplomacy of primitive trade' suggests that 'price' formation in reciprocal exchange systems is essentially different from that in commercial ones. The initial (and unsolved) problem is that conventional measures of performance are statistical, and that statistics are generally available only from blue books. That is a handicap for anthropologists who study exotic economies; but it may not be so for ethnographers of British society. At least they can use the data, even if they are persuaded to treat blue categories and assumptions with caution. It therefore seems probable that advances in understanding the consequences of economic activity will come from the new sociology, rather than from anthropologists working in unregistered economies.

Anthropologists have no answers or reach-me-down solutions to the problems of explanation which sociologists confront. But it may be that their experience of exotic economies is suggestive. In particular: ethnographers who make a distinction between self interest and profit hear what people say about their motives for production and their purposes in exchanges. They may then be encouraged to examine native economic notions and the ways in which these are associated with what are essentially moral categories of appropriate economic action.

Ethnographers of British economic activity usually work with relatively small segments of the population. It is easy for them to imagine that beyond the limits of their segment – as it were, superimposed on it – there is a macro-

economy, higher, impersonal, governed by natural laws, and more determining than the day-to-day expedients which their subjects create in order
to scrape by. That is perhaps open to question: it is possible that all real
markets are in some sense local ones, and that the only non-local market
is a model of perfection, a moral and economic goal of a particular segment
of the population. Now that they have so successfully thrown away so much
of the bathwater, the ethnographers should carefully examine what is left,
to see whether there was ever a baby there at all.

Note

1   Finley, 1973: 65, argues that slavery originates in the combination of two factors:
(i) a demand for labour greater than a domestic unit can supply and (ii) a social
and conceptual unwillingness or inability to separate labour power from person.
Some people argue that family relationships, also characterised by (ii), are the
conceptual model for the involuntary status of slave.

Directions for the future

I was asked by the Social Affairs Committee of the Economic and Social Research Council to provide an overview of current research requirements with regard to the social implications of current patterns of economic change. The present paper represents a first step in this process. It examines in a broad way the range of further questions raised by recent research into changes in the labour market and into the consequences of unemployment. The suggestions here derive partly from a reading of the existing state of research and partly from consultation with more than 200 academic and government researchers – sociologists, psychologists, social anthropologists and economists.

The structuring of employment opportunities

There is widespread agreement that further progress in our understanding of the structure and operation of labour markets requires a simultaneous examination of both the way in which employment opportunities are structured on the demand side and of the factors that affect labour supply. (This point is also well developed in the paper by Craig *et al.* in this volume.) Past research has tended to focus upon one or the other, thereby undercutting the ability to make any serious assessment of the relative weight of demand and supply determinants of labour market structure.

There have been three particularly influential strands of theory focusing on the way that employers structure work opportunities – theories of the labour process, of labour market segmentation and of the spatial division of labour. Labour process theory has generated a considerable range of case studies (for instance, Zimbalist, 1979; Wood, 1982; Crompton and Jones, 1984). While breaking down the simplicities of earlier versions of the thesis, such research has led to a largely indeterminate view of the direction of change – emphasising the diversity of managerial strategies and the importance of forms of worker resistance. The most influential theoretical statements with regard to segmented labour market theory have come from the United States (Edwards, 1979; Berger and Piore, 1980; Gordon *et al.*, 1982). However, there have been significant attempts by British researchers to explore its empirical basis. In particular, Craig *et al.* (1982) and Hakim (1979) have used it to interpret their findings about womens' employment opportunities, while Ashton *et al.* (1982) have argued for its value in understanding the youth labour market. Theories of changes in the spatial division of labour have emerged primarily from the work of industrial geographers (Massey and Meagan, 1982; Massey, forthcoming), but are becoming influential in sociological research (see, for instance, Austrin and Beynon, 1980; Murgatroyd and Urry, this volume).

In each of these areas we lack the type of systematic comparative work required to provide meaningful answers to the questions raised; research has tended to be based on the possibly idiosyncratic case study. Further, there has been little attempt to explore the interrelationships between the propositions of the different theories, i.e. between developments in the labour process, forms of segmentation, and changing company locational policies. Perhaps most crucially, we know little about the way they are affected by recession.

If we are to cast light on the major existing theoretical arguments we require further research into (a) employer labour recruitment strategies, and (b) employer work organisation strategies.

Recruitment strategies

Broadly, we need to know the prevalence of different types of recruitment strategy, the conditions affecting their utilisation, and their consequences for inequalities of opportunity in the labour market. More specifically:

(a) What characteristics are employers looking for when they recruit?

(b) How do they operationalise these criteria in terms of screening devices?

(c) Have there been major shifts in the type of labour seen as desirable – i.e. from young adults to married women?

(d) Do employers have explicit preferences about internal versus external labour market recruitment?

(e) What influence do differences in technical conditions have over recruitment strategies?

(f) At local labour market level, how important is the industrial relations record of the area in locational decisions?

(g) Does the level of unemployment in the local labour market affect either the criteria or mechanisms of recruitment?

Employer work organisation strategies

The thesis is frequently advanced that the structure of work opportunities in the labour market is being altered by a change in employer work organisation strategies. These are seen as deriving from a concern either to reduce wage rigidities or to use capital equipment more intensively. They are held to have major consequences for the level of job security and the type of labour used. Key questions include:

(a) Has there been a substantial increase in the hiving off of work from the permanent work force to subcontractors and in the use of temporary labour? If so, what factors influence such decisions and do employer preferences vary in any systematic way between types of labour market?

(b) Does the slackness or tightness of the local labour market influence employer decisions about whether or not to intensify the work process through changes in job structure and the tightening of control mechanisms?

(c) What factors influence employer work hour strategies – for instance to utilise part-time workers or to introduce rotating shift work? And how do these affect the pattern of labour recruitment?

It is clear that in any future research programme we would need a clear understanding of the specific structure of work opportunities and of the ways in which these are changing, in order to understand the pattern of constraints affecting the labour market behaviour of individuals and households and their responses to loss of employment. Although outside the remit of the Social Affairs Committee, there is clearly an urgent need too for further research into the role of state agencies in moulding the labour market and into the decision-making processes that underlie the selection of priorities and forms of intervention.

Worker involvement in the labour market

Very roughly, research here can be grouped into five themes. (1) Workers' orientation to work; (2) their understanding of the operation of the economy; (3) their attitudes to job mobility; (4) their attitudes to technical and organisational change; (5) their commitment to collective organisation of their interests. The amount of past research in these areas is highly uneven – some (e.g. orientation to work) have been central research themes, others (e.g. understanding of the operation of the labour market) remain virtually untouched. In all cases, our knowledge of the implications of varying levels of unemployment in the local labour market for worker attitudes and behaviour must be judged to be negligible.

Orientations to work

This has been a major research area in the last two decades, focusing both on the nature of workers' aspirations and expectations of work and on the influence of such attitudes for job choice. In the 1960s, Goldthorpe *et al.*

(1968) had suggested that a substantial degree of choice was being exercised by workers in certain sectors of the labour market, that the consequent process of self-selection had major implications for experience of, and attitudes towards, employment, and that there was a long-term trend towards more instrumental attitudes to work. Much of the literature of the 1970s represented an exploration of and debate with these ideas. The outstanding contribution was Blackburn and Mann's 1979 study of unqualified male manual workers in the Peterborough labour market which emphasised both the instability of measures of work orientations and the structural constraints upon effective worker choice. A more recent development in the field has been the development of cross-cultural studies of work orientations (Yankelovich *et al.*, 1983).

Although providing one of the most stimulating debates in recent industrial sociology, the work orientations literature also reveals some of the most basic deficiencies in part (and current) social research. Despite Brown *et al.*'s attempt (1983) to create some element of order among the diversity of studies, the *latent* message of their work must clearly be the chaotic and non-cumulative way in which studies have been carried out and the difficulty, despite a wealth of research, of making any well-grounded judgements either about variations in orientations between different categories of the labour force or about changes in orientations over time.

The single most pressing research need in this area is to obtain some consensus over, and consistency in the use of, measuring instruments and to ensure careful replications over time. This would enable us to address the following issues:

(a) Is there any evidence of a decline in the work ethic – in the sense of a belief in the *moral* value of work? Is there any evidence of a decline in commitment to employment? Is there any evidence of a decrease in commitment to work *per se*? These, of course, are three distinct issues and require different types of evidence.

(b) Is a change occurring in people's orientation to employment – that is to say, in the relative importance that they attach to different aspects of a paid job? For instance, is there any evidence that aspirations are rising with regard to intrinsic job interest, even if pay remains the most fundamental criterion influencing job choice?

(c) Do pay expectations vary in a systematic way in different local labour conditions? Are they influenced by sub-cultural variations in lifestyles (possibly differing by region)? If they are, are differences in sub-cultures being eroded and does this influence labour market behaviour?

(d) Is there any evidence of growing incongruence between people's expectations of employment and the types of employed work that are available? In particular, does higher unemployment accentuate the misfit between expectations and opportunities?

(e) What are the implications of social relations in the household for orientations to paid work? What are the implications of changes in family values

and of the mode of organisation of unpaid work for attitudes to employment and for the prevalence of the dual earner pattern?
(f) What are the effects of changes in employment opportunities for attitudes to unpaid work? Do higher levels of unemployment lead to a reassertion of traditional views about the domestic division of labour or to its renegotiation?

Perception of the economy

The extensive literature on orientations to work has failed notably to place the issue of the individual's job preferences within the wider context of his or her economic understanding. The most relevant research in this area has been by psychologists (Behrend, 1964, 1966, 1977; Furnham 1982 a, b, c; Lewis 1982 a, b). The questions that need to be addressed here remain then very elementary:
(a) Do people have 'economic models' in any meaningful sense of the term?
(b) If they do, how consistent are they?
(c) Do such models influence behaviour – whether in terms of labour market participation, job choice, attitudes to consumption?
(d) What are the processes of socialisation into specific modes of economic thinking and how would one explain variations between modes?

Attitudes to job mobility

This is a crucial issue for labour market theory and we know precious little about it. Evidence from the Labour Force Survey and from the General Household Survey suggests that there has been a significant decline in mobility between jobs which set in *prior* to the oil crisis of 1973–4. Inter-regional mobility, which has probably been rather low in Britain for most of the current century, also showed a decline in the 1970s.

Why should job mobility have declined? Can it be attributed to changes in employment legislation, to changes in the housing market, to shifts in the age structure of the work force, to the increased importance of local non-work involvements (influenced by an increase in leisure time), to the increase in two-earner families or to the effect of higher unemployment on attitudes to job mobility?

Attitudes to technical change

There was a substantial literature focusing upon reactions to technical change in the 1950s and 1960s – much of it concerned with the implications of the development of continuous-process production techniques (see Gallie, 1978, ch. 1). More recently, however, we have seen the extension of the potential impact of automation to hitherto relatively protected categories of the workforce – in particular, women and non-manual workers. At the same time we have entered a markedly different period in that rapid technical change is occurring at a time of much higher levels of unemployment. While there have been a number of case study projects, there has been little attempt to get a wider view of the way in which current technical change is being perceived and assessed.

(a) Do people have 'generalised' images of the effects of technical change on the quality of work life, or are their views about technical change workplace specific?

(b) What are the relative distributions of 'optimistic' and 'pessimistic' views about the implications of technical change? Do people view it primarily as undercutting skill levels and generating unemployment, or do they view it as improving work conditions and as a potential source of new jobs?

(c) How do people's direct experiences of technical change in the workplace affect such more generalised images?

(d) What are people's views about the most appropriate ways of making decisions about technical changes that affect working conditions? Do they see these as a legitimate sphere of managerial authority or do they believe that such changes should be the subject of negotiation?

(e) What are people's views about the ways such decisions are taken in practice in their own workplaces?

(f) Are women workers more likely to be receptive to technical change than male workers?

(g) Are non-manual workers more likely to be receptive to technical change than manual workers?

(h) What are the implications of substantial experience of unemployment or of high levels of unemployment in the local labour market for attitudes to technical change?

Attitudes to collective organisation

One of the deeper mysteries of the culture and behaviour of the British working population is its attitude to the collective organisation of its interests in trade unions. While surveys consistently reveal a rather critical attitude towards the power of trade unions, Britain has one of the highest levels of union density among capitalist societies. Given the speculation rife on these issues outside the academic scene and the central importance of an understanding of the dynamics of collective organisation for adequate theories of wage determination and class formation, we need to know:

(a) how the paradox of high effective membership but unfavourable evaluation of unions (on the indicators used) is to be resolved;

(b) the implications of high levels of unemployment for attitudes to trade union objectives and trade union membership.

The labour market and gender

One of the most striking changes in the composition of the labour force in the 1970s was the rise in activity rates among women (42.8 per cent of those of working age in 1971 as against 62.3 per cent in 1979). This was accompanied by heightened research interest in: (1) the determinants and life cycle pattern of female labour force participation; (2) the extent and pattern of development of occupational segregation by gender; and (3) the characteristics and employment conditions of the types of work into which women were being recruited.

Female participation in the labour force

The major recent study of the factors underlying the labour market participation of women is the Women and Employment study carried out by the Department of Employment (see C. Roberts, this volume). This has underlined the crucial importance of child rearing (as distinct from marital status) in accounting both for the likelihood of being in paid work and for the type of paid work taken. It underlines the financial dependence of families on womens' employment and provides our first systematic evidence on womens' orientations to work. However:

(a) The data were collected in 1980. They will therefore tell us very little about the impact of higher unemployment rates upon women's attitude to participation. All that we can say is that given current evidence about queuing principles this effect could well be substantial.

(b) Given that the studies have focused exclusively on women we still have very little firm knowledge about the degree of similarity or difference between women's and men's orientations to employment. A particularly important question, that we cannot even begin to answer, is whether there has been any convergence in expectations about employment among men and women over time.

Occupational segregation

Although British research on this issue lacked the resources and sophistication provided by the major longitudinal studies in the United States, it has been shown nonetheless that occupational segregation in Britain is very sharp indeed and that its overall extent (although not its internal composition) has remained remarkably stable over the century (Barron & Norris, 1976; Hakim, 1981). Moreover the available trend measures based on aggregate labour force statistics probably underestimate heavily the extent of segregation at workplace level (Hunt, 1975; Martin and Roberts, 1984).

However, if we now have substantially improved descriptive evidence about the extent and stability of occupational segregation by gender our understanding of its determinants must be judged to be fairly minimal. The major competing theses – those stressing the implications of employer job construction and recruitment policies versus those emphasising self-selection on the part of workers themselves – have not been systematically tested. Moreover it is clear from the trend evidence in the 1970s – when a period of rapid desegregation (1973–7) was followed by a sudden reversal of trend – that adequate explanation is likely to be very complex and will need to move beyond simpler earlier assumptions to take account of the impact of legislative changes, of the level of unemployment, and of shifts in the occupational and industrial structure.

The employment experience of women workers

Although there have recently been a number of somewhat impressionistic studies of women in employment, our knowledge is clearly much weaker than it is of male employment. Given that women now constitute some 39 per cent of the overall work force, this seriously undercuts our ability to understand both changing patterns in the utilisation of labour and workforce attitudes to collective organisation. In particular:

(a) The marked rise in part-time work in Britain in the 1970s has been widely recognised as of major importance, but detailed research remains thin. Elias and Maine's (1982) analysis of the National Training Survey indicated that part-time work was associated with particularly disadvantageous work conditions in terms of pay, skill and unionisation. Beechey and Perkins (1982, and this volume) examined the nature of employer demand for part-time work, rejected the cruder reserve army of labour theory and emphasised the importance of employers' search for greater flexibility. Robinson and Wallace (1984 a, b) came to similar conclusions. Their study of fourteen companies also revealed the central importance of grading and payment systems – usually negotiated with the trade unions – in accounting for the low pay of part-time workers. However:

(i) We know very little about the experience of part-time work: the kind of work involved, work conditions, the flexibility of hours, and the way in which work is controlled.

(ii) There is evidence (Elias and Maine) that a significant proportion of women re-entering the workforce after having children tend to enter part-time jobs that represent objective de-skilling. But is this perceived as such and does it generate lower work satisfaction and lower motivation?

(b) Our case study knowledge of women's work is largely focused on manufacturing work, whereas the major expansion of women's work has been in the service industries.

(c) Studies tend to focus exclusively on either men's or women's reactions to the work situation. We have little evidence that directly compares the experience of and attitudes to work of men and women. Are there major differences by gender in attitudes to authority, flexibility and collective organisation? One fragmentary piece of evidence suggests that there may be important differences: GHS data show a consistent pattern in which women express greater satisfaction with their pay than men despite substantially lower earnings.

(d) Women are generally located in occupations with limited prospects for upward career mobility (compare Stewart *et al.*, 1980, with Crompton *et al.*, 1982, on differences between male and female clerical workers). Is there any evidence of growing career frustration among younger, more qualified women on re-entry to the workforce after childbirth?

(e) We know very little about the implications of women's employment for the non-work aspects of their lives. Does it influence status in the community (or the woman's perception of her status)? What are the implications for social relations in the household?

In general, the most central message that emerges from a consideration of recent research on women's participation on the labour market is that most of the crucial questions simply cannot be answered by research that focuses uniquely on women. We need a major shift from what has been the prevailing pattern of research towards studies that permit precise comparison by gender.

Ethnicity and the labour market

Although this has been the subject of lively theoretical debate in the last decade, there have been very few published empirical studies. The Handsworth study (Rex and Tomlinson, 1979; Ratcliffe, 1981) provides one substantial study of the ethnic minorities that embraces labour market issues, but there is little available that allows comparison between different labour market settings. Research still in progress will help fill some gaps. The Research Unit on Ethnic Relations is in the process of completing projects investigating the nature of discriminatory biases in employer recruitment policies, the labour market experience of Indians in the foundry industry and the changing character of state policy towards ethnic employment. There are studies in progress on small ethnic businesses and the employment conditions they provide (Hoel, 1982) and Sandra Wallman's study of Battersea and Bow (this volume) will indicate how the importance of ethnicity for labour market experience may vary between local settings. Finally, a major national study of the ethnic minorities, providing information on some aspects of employment disadvantage, will be published in 1984 (Brown, C.).

The future 'employment programme' of the Ethnic Relations Unit (RUER) is likely to focus, in particular, on the content of Equal Opportunities policies in different regions, on the implications of the Youth Training Scheme for the ethnic minorities and on ethnic business development.

However in addition to this we need research on:

(a) the implications of different types of labour market settings for employment aspirations;

(b) the implications of generally higher levels of unemployment on aspirations for upward occupational mobility. Are these being increasingly frustrated, for instance among UK-born ethnic minority members? If so, how do they respond in terms of employment decisions and training? Are members of ethnic minorities particularly likely to look to self-employment as a means of circumventing blocked career chances?

(c) the implications of recession on the attitudes of white workers to the ethnic minorities. Is increased competition in the labour market leading to a growth of resentment/scapegoating? How do black workers perceive the evolution of attitudes towards them among white workers?

(d) the implications of higher unemployment for black communities. Does it lead to increased cohesiveness? Does ethnic identity provide a buffer to unemployment and give access to a better economic support network? Or does economic recession lead to the frustration of the earlier expectations of migrants and result in increased re-emigration?

(e) the implications of unemployment for female blacks of West Indian descent. Given the higher frequency of one-parent families and the relatively higher labour market participation of this group, it would seem to constitute a particularly vulnerable sector of the ethnic minority population.

(f) Brown's forthcoming study will show a significant difference between the disadvantages experienced by blacks in the public and private sectors. How is this to be explained? Why should disadvantage be greater in the private sector? To what extent can this be attributed to specific organisational policies?

(g) how are the ethnic minorities being affected by shifts in the industrial infrastructure – the decline of traditional heavy industries and the growth of new computer-based industries? Are they managing to get jobs in the expanding sectors of the economy such as electronics and computing?

(h) evidence from studies of the clothing industry suggests that recession is encouraging the growth of small ethnic businesses in the inner cities that provide particularly poor employment conditions. Can a similar pattern be detected in other industrial sectors?

(i) the impact of labour market conditions on relations between ethnic minority workers and the trade unions. In the light of their higher membership rates than whites, will there be growing resentment of lack of influence in the decision-making echelons of the unions? How are trade union policies with regard to ethnic discrimination perceived and evaluated?

In general, given that there are substantial grounds for thinking that the labour market position of the ethnic minorities is exceptionally vulnerable to current changes in the economic structure, and given historical experience of the strains that recession can place on social relations between ethnic groups, this must be regarded as an area that requires a major expansion of existing research effort.

The informal economy

An important focus of research in recent years has been the 'informal economy'. Heavily influenced in this country by a series of articles by Gershuny and Pahl, (Gershuny and Pahl, 1979–80, 1980; Pahl, 1980) a number of researchers have sought to measure the prevalence of informal work, to assess whether or not it increases with unemployment, and to examine its implications for social stratification. The most important research project on this theme was Pahl and Wallace's study of the Isle of Sheppey (this volume). This raised major doubts about earlier views of the extent, significance and direction of change of the 'informal economy'. Although self-provisioning was extensive, paid informal work and reciprocal work between households were rare. Informal work tended to increase the advantages of those already employed, rather than to offer an alternative source of work and of income for the unemployed. These conclusions are remarkably similar to the findings of the major French study of the informal economy (Stankiewicz, 1982).

By far the most controversial area of research among people that I have consulted concerns the informal economy. There are those who think that the SSRC was mistaken in the first place to make this a central area for financial support; there are those who consider that, given the theories developed in the later 1970s, it was worth initiating research, but that the results of this research have effectively destroyed the theories that stimulated it. And finally there are those who argue that this remains one of the single most important areas in which there should be further funding. There is a difference by discipline: on the whole sociologists are unfavourable to further research on the informal economy, while anthropologists are much more in favour. This may of course reflect the relative efficacy of their distinctive methodologies at uncovering the activities in question (contrast for instance the patterns found by Pahl and Turner *et al.*, this volume).

There are a number of possible directions in which work in this area could develop:

(a) Existing studies that have revealed rather unimpressive levels of informal work have focused on areas of rising unemployment (Sheppey, South Wales). It might be that, in contradiction to earlier expectations, the informal economy flourishes best in areas of relative prosperity where it can feed upon a growing industrial base and where households have the disposable income to buy the services it can provide.

(b) Alternatively, it has been suggested that the most probable location of the growth of widespread informal work is in areas of 'catastrophic' economic collapse, where the possibility of re-insertion into 'normal' economic activity must appear particularly remote.

(c) Following a similar logic, research in this area might focus on the long-term unemployed.

(d) Possibly the assumption that there would be any shift towards informal work by mature workers who had been disciplined over the years into the norms of formal employment was rather naive. Rather if any significant change in types of work activity is occurring one would expect to find it among younger adults, in particular unemployed youth, who are less likely to be constrained to respectability by family commitments, and have been exposed for a shorter period of time to dominant norms about work.

(e) There has been no major attempt to investigate the level of informal work in a predominantly rural setting in Britain.

(f) Finally, it might be argued that even if it is implausible that research will uncover widespread informal work in any particular structural location, nonetheless it is important to investigate more thoroughly the implications it has for the minority who are involved. This might influence policy decisions about the types of work in which people might legitimately engage when unemployed. Is there any evidence that involvement in informal work reduces the psychological costs of loss of employment? Is there any evidence that involvement in informal work provides a good springboard for the development of new businesses?

The social implications of unemployment

In a sense it is artificial to start with a separate category of themes termed the 'social implications of unemployment'. As we have seen, many of the questions that need to be answered about the development of employer strategies, worker involvement in the labour market, the influence of gender differences on labour market behaviour, and the conditions of growth of informal work revolve around the way in which higher unemployment may be modifying traditional patterns of economic activity. However, we are concerned here with the direct effects of loss of employment on the individual and household rather than with the wider implications of higher unemployment for the functioning of the labour market.

Three major longitudinal studies have provided us with a picture of the type of people that become unemployed, the effect of unemployment on income levels and the determinants of the duration of unemployment (the DHSS Cohort Study, the MSC Cohort Study and the DE study of the long-term unemployed). The DHSS Cohort Study (Wood, 1982; Moylan and Davies, 1980, 1981; Moylan, Miller and Davies, 1982) and the MSC Cohort Study (Daniel, 1981, 1983) – based upon samples of the unemployed flow – emphasise the recurrent nature of unemployment and the particular vulnerability of those in low skilled and low paid work. The study of the long-term unemployed (White, 1983) – based upon a sample of the unemployed stock – revealed the importance of structural rather than individual determinants of long term unemployment and the relative insignificance of the benefits system as a factor influencing the intensity of efforts to find new work. A new large scale survey has been launched by OPCS and DHSS to examine the living standards of the unemployed, and the Department of Employment has set up a major study into long-term unemployment among young adults.

Given the DHSS's interest in replacement ratios we know a fair amount about the implications of unemployment for household income, and after the current OPCS survey, we will have substantial knowledge about its implications, at least in the shorter term, for material living standards. I shall focus then on its implications for attitudes to work, physical health and psychological well-being, social relations in the household, integration into the community, and citizenship.

Attitudes to work

Research on mature adults in the workforce suggests that there is little reason to think that the experience of unemployment has major implications for employment commitment *per se*, although the indicators used have been relatively crude and it remains possible that unemployment affects the quality of such commitment. However there are a number of areas in which our knowledge remains altogether rudimentary.

(a) While there has been much research on the short-term effects of youth unemployment, we know little about its longer-term effects on people's attitudes to careers, training, work commitment and mobility. The hypothesis, of course, is that it is the experience of unemployment at the formative stage of people's first encounter with the labour market that is likely to be decisive for their later attitudes. The timing of the National Children's Bureau 1958 Cohort study makes it difficult to use for this purpose. A serious investigation of the thesis would require a new large-scale longitudinal study that would extend over a substantial period of time.

(b) We know little about the implications of unemployment for men's attitudes to women's employment. In particular, will it lead to a reassertion of traditional role definitions and to the growth of pressure on women to 'return to the home'?

(c) Perhaps not unrelated to the previous point, there is the widely-remarked-upon puzzle of why a much lower proportion of wives of unemployed men have jobs than of wives of employed men. The frequent assumption that this is an effect of the benefit system has to meet the objections that (a) it would be somewhat dubious economic rationality for wives to abandon secure employment for short-term benefit gains if there was any expectation that the husband would find employment again in the near future, and (b) it is clear that *new* unemployed male registrants are far less likely to have working wives than average. As this problem clearly has major implications for household poverty as well as for the operation of the labour market it deserves careful research.

Physical health and psychological well-being

As this is an area in which there are almost as many 'reviews of literature' as empirical studies, I shall be brief. The literature on the implications of unemployment for physical health is inconclusive. There are significant statistical associations bctwccn physical ill-hcalth, mortality and uncmployment. The data here is not dependent merely on the co-variation of aggregate figures *à la* Brenner – see for instance the OPCS Longitudinal Study (Fox and Goldblatt, 1982) and the British Regional Heart Study (Cook *et al.*, 1982) – and the association is evident even among those who do not regard themselves as ill. What remains mysterious is the direction of causality. The evidence on psychological well-being on the other hand is remarkably consistent (Warr, this volume). Although the severity of effects varies depending on the specific category of the population, there is overwhelming evidence that loss of employment increases levels of anxiety and depression. Indeed, to my mind, work in this area could be seen as one of the major recent achievements of British social science and a good deal of this can be attributed to the research conducted by the Social and Applied Psychology Unit at Sheffield.

Physical health
(a) An immediate problem for any research design here is that of obtaining adequate indicators. A careful scrutiny of some studies (e.g. Jackson and Warr, 1983) suggests that self-reporting indicators are rather volatile in the face of differences in question format. The usefulness of available health records can be vitiated by problems of differential use of health facilities. What is needed is professional medical assessment of samples specially selected from the population for the study in question. The logistical problems of this are substantial and such a study could not be contained in any simple way within a wider-ranging sociological project on 'economic life'.
(b) As a second best we can continue to accumulate data on a self-reporting basis. Any such design would have to be longitudinal. One suggestion is to carry out a comparative study of samples of workers made redundant from comparable factories in different regional areas. This looks good at first sight but the practical difficulties are formidable. As the model Cobb/Kasl study indicated (Cobb and Kasl, 1977), effects are often anticipatory and first wave interviews would need to be prior to closure. Matching of factories – if taken seriously (and there would be little point in doing the study if it wasn't) – would be exceptionally difficult. This, when combined with recent experience

of access problems, makes the chances of a successful realisation of the research design very slim indeed. Redundancy is not synonymous with unemployment and the generalisability of findings would be restricted. All in all, a comparative longitudinal community-based study would probably provide better quality data.

(c) Apart from self-report indicators, a study might examine what could plausibly be viewed as major intervening variables affecting the relationship between unemployment and health – diet, housing and heating are obvious candidates.

Psychological well-being

(a) The oft-repeated critique that causality is still to be established in this area is in one sense out of date. More recent SAPU work has convincingly established an adequate chronological sequence. The most important area for future work is the precise nature of the causal determinants.

(b) How important is economic deprivation? While this is touched upon in SAPU studies, the economic indicators are crude. However, the current OPCS Living Standards survey will provide a more comprehensive data set for investigating this.

(c) Other postulated causal determinants – loss of time structure, lack of sense of collective purpose, loss of status, stigma, etc. remain largely unexplored. Miles (1983) has indicated the type of work needed, Trew and Kilpatrick's data (1983) establish that there is no easy way out of a more carefully designed research programme.

(d) While there is a consistent pattern of findings about psychological consequences, there must still be doubt about quite how serious they are. Psychological ill-health seems to evaporate remarkably rapidly on re-employment. Yet the yo-yo scenario seems a little implausible. One wonders whether a more probing inquiry might not reveal that psychological distress leaves its mark on attitudes, even after re-employment, albeit in a transformed way.

(e) SAPU preference for strategic, non-random 'sampling' has obvious advantages in terms of cost and rapidity. To my mind, however, it may pose greater problems in unravelling the relative weights of causal determinants than SAPU recognises (at least in its published work). Replication using representative random samples is still needed.

Social relations in the household

This is a poverty area in terms of serious research. Preliminary results of intensive studies recently carried out (compare Bell and McKee with Morris) suggest sharply contrasting findings and we have little idea whether this is explicable in terms of financial circumstances, life-cycle position, regional cultures or merely interviewer effect. We need:

(a) carefully designed comparative studies that enable us to take account of factors such as financial circumstances, household structure, and the character of pre-existing social networks;

(b) Studies that focus not only on the quality of marital relations and the division of domestic labour but on the issue of the implications of unemployment for the socialisation of children. This must be regarded as one of the single most substantial gaps in our present knowledge. How does unemployment affect:

(i) the character of relations between parents and children?

(ii) parental attitudes towards children's education and career strategies?

(iii) children's own attitudes towards education and employment?

(iv) the typical quality and range of experience that children have of their environment and its implications for their cognitive and emotional development?

(v) the significance of variations in type of household structure for the implications of parental unemployment for children's experiences and attitudes.

If we are concerned with the longer-term effects of unemployment for the labour market and family patterns, then, however difficult it may be, we need a substantial expansion of research in this area.

Community

One of the strongest messages that emerged from the literature on unemployment in the 1930s is that unemployment was a source of social isolation – leading the household to withdraw within itself and to cut its traditional patterns of interaction with the community. In some ways, one might expect that even if the same effects were apparent today their psychological implications would be less severe, for one of the dominant trends in post-war family life has been held to be its voluntary 'privatisation'. However, some evidence suggests that the difference from the pattern of the 1930s may be greater than this and that unemployment in the 1980s may be conducive to an increase in local social interaction (Martin and Wallace, 1983; Martin and Wallace, this volume; Warr and Payne, 1983). However, existing data are fragmentary and we need careful comparative studies to answer the following questions:

(a) How important are prior regional differences in the character of local networks for the experience of social isolation?

(b) Are there important gender differences in the implications of unemployment for social isolation?

(c) What are the implications of the type of household structure for vulnerability to social isolation?

(d) Do communities vary significantly in the efforts of organised groups to stimulate activity among the unemployed and, if so, do such efforts make much difference?

More generally, what are the wider implications of unemployment for the pattern of community life? If the thesis is correct that unemployment leads households to withdraw from active participation in the community, then presumably high levels of unemployment could lead, by a chain effect, to an undercutting of activities and facilities that would affect the wider quality of life in the community. A frequent comment is that we lack a contemporary equivalent to the Marienthal study.

Citizenship

Any thorough consideration of the implications of unemployment for the quality of life would need to investigate the extent to which it encouraged, undercut or altered the character of people's participation in the decision-making arenas that determine their life chances. At the local level this overlaps heavily with the themes considered under 'community' – for it raises the issue of people's involvement in local associations that can operate as pressure groups and their degree of integration into local networks that could facilitate mobilisation around local issues.

For the national arena, there has been only fragmentary research into the implications of unemployment for political attitudes and behaviours.

(a) At the most elementary level, we lack an equivalent of Schlozman and Verba's study (1979) of the implications of unemployment for political attitudes in the USA.

(b) We lack studies into the effects of *local* differences both in cultural traditions and in modes of political, trade union and associational life, on the interpretation given to unemployment.

(c) We need rather better conceived studies than those that have been carried out elsewhere to unravel the ambivalence in attitudes that emerges at the level of opinion polls. Why should unemployment have been consistently regarded as *the* major issue facing the country since 1979, and yet apparently have played a far from decisive role in determining voting preferences?

(d) While the available evidence on the implications of unemployment for political attitudes is ambivalent, there is substantial evidence that it is linked to low registration and low voting turnout. Why should this be? Does it reflect political apathy, one aspect of wider demoralisation and withdrawal, the mobility of the unemployed, or prior social characteristics?

(e) What is the importance of the immigrant density of the population in a local labour market for the interpretation that is given to unemployment and the political response to it?

(f) Given past research on political partisanship, it seems unlikely that even quite marked upheavals would lead to dramatic changes in the structure of political attitudes for the bulk of the adult population – although they might well lead to subtler shifts of emphasis. What past research would seem to indicate, however, is the crucial importance of the social climate prevailing for those who are *entering* the political arena for the first time and whose political beliefs are still relatively malleable. The most strategic research focus would be on those aged 16–25 and possibly on the implications of unemployment for the earlier and more basic processes of political socialisation.

(g) The most significant set of issues that need to be addressed in the political domain relate less to the implications of unemployment for partisan preference than to its implications for underlying commitment to democratic procedures. Perception of and attachment to the institutional framework of politics has been, in general, a rather neglected area and research into the effects of unemployment would need to ensure an adequate basis for comparison.

Some of these issues are now being addressed in a pilot study, others will doubtless be illuminated by the analysis of material collected in the Nuffield and LSE 1983 election studies. However there are no studies currently under way that are likely to have both the extensiveness and the depth needed to provide answers in what is clearly a very difficult area of research.

Finally, a general point on studies of the implications of the experience of unemployment: a fair amount of the rather small body of past and current research on these problems has been vitiated by poor research design. Further research must adhere to at least two very elementary methodological principles:

(a) It is quite futile trying to make inferences about the effect of unemployment unless there is an adequate control group.

(b) Current employment status may be a very poor indicator of lifetime experience of unemployment. The reconstruction of adequate work histories is then a *sine qua non* of effective research. Samples selected on the basis of current status may be quite misleading. Since the great majority of existing studies into the social consequences of unemployment fail to satisfy these two criteria, we must judge our present level of knowledge on any of the major thematic areas that we have been considering to be fairly minimal.

Labour market experience, unemployment and social stratification

Despite the profusion of primarily theoretical studies on the British class structure in the 1970s, our understanding of the dynamics of patterns of social and cultural differentiation and of the perception, evaluation and response to social inequality has made little progress. There was little in the literature that provided any purchase either on the long-term acquiescence of the disadvantaged to the prevailing structure of privilege and opportunity, let alone on the apparent collapse of commitment of the skilled working class to the Labour Party that occurred in the 1970s. However the issues raised earlier about the evolution of work opportunities, labour market involvement and unemployment may have a direct bearing on these issues and certainly deserve investigation.

(a) Has the decade witnessed a diversification of contractual statuses within the working class that has undercut traditional class identities and solidarities and weakened attachment to traditional institutions of the labour movement?
(b) Have there been significant changes in conceptions of desired 'styles of life' and in their salience to social identity that cut across patterns of collective identification and that help to account for the wide variations in social attitudes among those sharing a similar work situation?
(c) Has there been an increased polarisation within the working class due to:
  (i) an improvement in the living standards of the regularly employed at a time of declining living standards among those with substantial experience of unemployment,
  (ii) a growing differentiation between families with no earners and families with two earners.
  (iii) a high level of spatial segregation between employed and unemployed at both regional and local community levels with implications for the quality of the local environment and the pattern of social interaction.

Conclusion

This report by no means seeks to provide an exhaustive list of major issues that require research in these areas. However, it is clear that our knowledge remains very fragmentary and that certain major areas of enquiry have been as yet barely touched. Given the centrality of the issues in question for the development of our principal theoretical interpretations of social structure and their evident relevance for the quality of life of the people directly concerned, there are strong grounds for a major new research initiative to examine in a more systematic way the social implications of current patterns of economic change.

Bibliography

Abercrombie, N. and Urry, J. (1983) *Capital, Labour and the Middle Class*. George Allen and Unwin

Abrams, M. and Rose, R. (1960) *Must Labour Lose?* Penguin Books

Ahr, P. R., Gordezky, M. J. and Cho, D. W. (1981) 'Measuring the relationship of public psychiatric admissions to rising unemployment'. *Hospital and Community Psychiatry*. 32, 398–401

Aiken, M. and Ferman, L. A. (1966) 'The social and political reactions of older negroes to unemployment'. *Phylon*. 57, 333–46

Ajzen, I. and Fishbein, M. (1980) *Understanding attitudes and predicting social behaviour*. Prentice Hall

Akkermans, T. and Grootings, P. (1978) 'From corporatism to polarisation: elements of the development of Dutch industrial relations'. In Crouch and Pizzorno (eds.)

Aldrich, H. (1980) 'Asian shopkeepers as a middleman minority: a study of small businesses in Wandsworth'. In Evans, A. and Eversley, D. (eds.), *The Inner City: Employment and Industry*. Heinemann, 389–407

Aldrich, H., Cater, J., Joncs, T. and McEvoy, D. (1981) 'Business development and self-segregation: Asian enterprise in three British cities'. In Peach, C., Robinson, V. and Smith, S. (eds.) *Ethnic Segregation in Cities*. Croom Helm, 170–90

Aldrich, H., Jones, T. and McEvoy, D. (1984) 'Ethnic advantage and minority business'. In Ward and Jenkins (eds.)

Allen, V. L. (1981) *The Militancy of British Miners*. Shipley, Yorks, The Moor Press

Almond, G. A. (1970) *Political Development: Essays in Heuristic Theory*. Little Brown

Almond, G. A. and Powell, G. (1966) *Comparative Politics: a Development Approach*. Little Brown

Almond, G. and Verba, S. (1963) *The Civic Culture*. Princeton University Press

Alt, J. (1979) *The Politics of Economic Decline*. Cambridge University Press

Amin, S. (1976) *Unequal Development*. The Monthly Review Press

Anderson, Alice H. (ed.) (1980) *The Economics of Women and Work*. Penguin

Anon (1983 a) 'Social habits and health'. In *Social Trends*. HMSO

Anon (1983 b) 'Pattern of household spending in 1982'. *Employment Gazette*. 91, 517–23

Antonella, Picchio del Mercato (1981) 'Social reproduction and the basic structure of labour markets'. In Wilkinson (1981 a)

Anwar, M. (1979) *The Myth of Return: Pakistanis in Britain*. Heinemann

Anwar, M. (1982) *Young People and the Job Market – A Survey*. Commission for Racial Equality

Armor, D. J., Polich, J. M. and Stambul, H. B. (1978) *Alcoholism and Treatment.*
    Wiley
Aron, R. (1962) *Dix-huit lecons sur la societé industrielle.* Gallimard
Aron, R. (1968) *Progress and Disillusion: the Dialectics of Modern Society.* Pall Mall
Ashton, D., Maguire, M. J. and Garland, V. (1982) *Youth in the Labour Market.*
    Research Paper no. 34, Dept of Employment
Auster, E. and Aldrich, H. (1984) 'Small business vulnerability, ethnic enclaves and
    ethnic enterprise'. In Ward, R. and Jenkins, R. (eds.)
Austrin, T. and Beynon, H. (1980 a) *Global output: The working class experience
    of big business in the North East of England.* Durham, Dept of Sociology and
    Social Policy, University of Durham
Austrin, T. and Beynon, H. (1980 b) *Masters and Servants: Paternalism and its Legacy
    on the Durham Coalfield.* Working paper
Bailey, Thomas (1983) *Labor market competition and economic mobility in low-wage
    employment.* Dept of Economics, MIT
Bailey, T. and Waldinger, R. (1983) 'The labor market transition in New York City:
    problems and prospects'. Special Report, Division of Policy Analysis, New York
    City Office of Economic Development
Baker, C. (1981) 'Redundancy, restructuring and the response of the labour move-
    ment: A case study of BSC at Corby'. Working paper no. 26, School for Advanced
    Urban Studies, University of Bristol
Banks, M. H. (1983) 'Validation of the General Health Questionnaire in a young
    community sample'. *Psychological Medicine.* 13, 349–53
Banks, M. H. and Jackson, P. R. (1982) 'Unemployment and risk of minor psychiatric
    disorder in young people: cross sectional and longitudinal evidence' *Psychological
    Medicine.* 12, 789–98
Banks, M. H. *et al.* (1980) 'The use of the General Health Questionnaire as an indicator
    of mental health in occupational studies'. *Journal of Occupational Psychology.*
    52, 187–94
Barbash, J. (1972) *Trade Unions and National Economic Policy.* John Hopkins Press
Barker, D. L. and Allen, S. (eds.) (1976 a) *Sexual Divisions and Society: Process
    and Change.* Tavistock Publications
Barker, D. L. and Allen, S. (eds.) (1976 b) *Dependence and Exploitation in Work
    and Marriage.* Longman
Barkin, S. (1975) *Worker Militancy and its Consequences, 1965–75.* Praeger
Barling, P. W. and Handal, P. J. (1980) 'Incidence of utilization of public mental
    health facilities as a function of short-term economic decline'. *American Journal
    of Community Psychology.* 8, 31–9
Barrett, Michèle and McIntosh, Mary (1982) *The Antisocial Family.* Verso
Barron, R. D. and Norris, E. M. (1978) 'Sexual divisions and the dual labour market'
    in D. Barker and S. Allen (eds.)
Barry, B. (1966) 'The roots of social injustice'. *Oxford Review.* 33–46
Bauman, Z. (1982) *Memories of Class.* Routledge and Kegan Paul
Baxandall, Rosalyn, Ewen, Elizabeth, and Gordon, Linda (1976) 'The working class
    has two sexes', in *Monthly Review.* 28, no. 3
Beavis, D. (1980) *What Price Happiness? My Life from Coal Hewer to Shop Steward.*
    Whitley Bay, Strong Words
Bebbington, P., Hurry, J., Tennant, C., Sturt, E. and Wing, J. K. (1981)
    'Epidemiology of mental disorders in Camberwell'. *Psychological Medicine.*
    11, 561–80
Bechhofer, F. and Elliott, B. (1981) (eds.) *The Petite Bourgeoisie.* Macmillan
Becker, H. S. (1960) 'Notes on the concept of commitment'. *American Journal of
    Sociology.* 66, 32–40

Becker, H. S. and Carper, J. (1970) 'Adjustment of conflicting expectations in the development of identification with an occupation'. In H. S. Becker, *Sociological Work – method and substance.* Aldine

Becker, H. S. and Strauss, A. L. (1956) 'Careers, personality and adult socialisation'. *American Journal of Sociology.* 62, 253–63

Beechey, Veronica (1977 a) 'Some problems in the analyses of female wage labour in the capitalist mode of production'. *Capital and Class.* no. 3

Beechey, Veronica (1977 b) 'Some notes on female wage labour in capitalist production'. *Capital and Class.* no. 3, autumn, 45–66

Beechey, Veronica (1978) 'Women and production: a critical analysis of some sociological theories of women's work' in Annette Kuhn and Ann Marie Wolpe (eds.)

Beechey, Veronica (1979) 'On patriarchy'. *Feminist Review.* no. 3

Beechey, Veronica (1983) 'Reconceptualising women's employment'. Paper presented to British Sociological Association, Sexual Divisions Study Group, Oxford, December

Beechey, V. and Perkins, T. (1982) 'Women's part-time employment in Coventry – a study in the sexual division of labour' (unpublished)

Beetham, D. (1967) *Immigrant School Leavers and the Youth Employment Service.* Institute of Race Relations

Behrend, H. (1964) 'Price and income images and inflation'. *Scottish Journal of Political Economy.* 11, 85–103

Behrend, H. (1966) 'Price images, inflation and national incomes policy'. *Scottish Journal of Political Economy.* 13, 273–96

Behrend, H. (1974) 'The impact of inflation on pay increase expectations and ideas of fair pay'. *Industrial Relations Journal.* 5, 5–10

Behrend, H. (1977) 'Research into inflation and conceptions of earnings'. *Journal of Occupational Psychology.* 50, 169–76

Behrend, H., Davies, J., Paterson, E. and Rose, E. (1971) 'What does the word 'Inflation' mean to you? and What is the connection between wage claims and prices?' *Industrial Relations Journal.* 2, 35–46

Bell, C. (1968) *Middle Class Families.* Routledge and Kegan Paul

Bell, C., McKee, L. and Priestley, K. (1983) *Fathers, Childbirth and Work.* Equal Opportunities Commission

Bell, D. (1973) *The Coming of Post-industrial Society.* Heinemann

Bell, D. (1976) *The Cultural Contradictions of Capitalism.* Basic Books

Benwell Community Development Project (1980) *Adamsez – the story of a factory closure.* Final Report Series no. 8, Newcastle upon Tyne, Benwell Community Project

Berger, B. (1960) *Working Class Suburb: A study of auto workers in suburbia.* University of California Press

Berger, J. and Offe, C. (1982) 'Die Zukunft des Arbeitsmarktes. Zur Ergönzungsbeduerftigkeit eines versagenden Allokationsprinzips'. *Kölner Zeitschrift für Soziologie und Sozialpsychologie.* Sonderheft 24, Materialien zur industriesoziologie. 348–71

Berger, P. (1975) 'The human shape of work'. In G. Esland *et al.* (ed.) *People and Work.* Holmes McDougall

Berger, S. (1981) 'The uses of the traditional sector in Italy: why declining classes survive'. In Bechhofer and Elliott (eds.)

Berger, S. (1981) (ed.) *Organizing Interests in Western Europe.* Cambridge University Press

Berger, S. and Piore, M. J. (1980) *Dualism and Discontinuity in Industrial Societies.* Cambridge University Press

Bergman, J. and Tokunaga, S. (1983) (eds.) *Industrial Relations in Transition.* University of Tokyo Press

Berlin, B. and Kay, P. (1969) *Basic Colour Terms.* Berkeley

Bessel, R. (1982) 'Germany's unemployment and the rise of the Nazis'. *Times Higher Education Supplement.* 4 February 82, 12–13

Birmingham Feminist History Group (1979) 'Feminism as femininity in the nineteen-fifties'. *Feminist Review.* 3, 1979

Blackburn, R. M. and Mann, M. (1979) *The Working Class in the Labour Market.* Macmillan

Blalock, H. (1967) *Toward a Theory of Minority Group Relations.* Wiley

Blauner, R. (1964) *Alienation and Freedom. The factory worker and his industry.* University of Chicago Press

Blaxall, M. and Reagan, B. (1976) (eds.) *Women and the Workplace.* Chicago University Press

Boeke, J. H. (1953) *Economics and Economic Policy of Dual Societies.* George Allen and Unwin

Bohannan, P. (1959) 'The impact of money on African subsistence economy'. *Journal of Economic History.* 19, 491–503

Bohannan, P. and Dalton, G. (eds.) (1965) *Markets in Africa. Eight subsistence economies in transition.* Anchor Books

Bonacich, E. (1973) 'A theory of middleman minorities'. *American Sociological Review.* 38, 583–94

Bonacich, E. and Modell, J. (1980) *The Economic Basis of Ethnic Solidarity.* University of California Press

Booth, Charles (1889–91) *Labour and Life of the People.* Williams and Norgate

Bott, E. (1957) *Family and Social Network.* Tavistock

Bousfield, J. (1979) 'The world seen as a colour chart', in R. F. Ellen and D. Reason (eds.), 195–220

Bowlby, J. *et al.* (1983) 'Urban austerity – the impact on women'. Unpublished paper presented at the SSRC's Conference on Urban Change and Conflict

Bradburn, N. M. (1969) *The Structure of Psychological Well-Being.* Rand McNally

Bradburn, N. M. and Caplovitz, D. (1965) *Reports on Happiness.* Aldine

Brandstatter, H., Davis, J. H. and Stocker-Kreichganer, G. (1982) *Group Decision Making.* Academic Press

Brandt, G. (1983) 'Industrial relations in the Federal Republic of Germany under conditions of economic crisis'. In Bergman and Tokunaga (eds.)

Branson, N. (1981) *Poplarism: 1919–1925.* Lawrence and Wishart

Braverman, H. (1974) *Labor and Monopoly Capital: The Degradation of Work in the Twentieth Century.* Monthly Review Press

Breakwell, G. M. (in press) 'Identity at work'. In H. Beloff (ed.) *Getting into Life.* Methuen

Breakwell, G. M., Collie, A., Harrison, B and Propper, C. (1984) 'Attitudes towards the unemployed: effects of threatened identity'. *British Journal of Social Psychology.* 23, 87–8

Breakwell, G. M., Harrison, B. and Propper, C. (1984) 'Explaining the psychological effects of unemployment for young people: the importance of specific situational factors'. *British Journal of Guidance and Counselling.* 12, 2, 132–40

Brenner, M. H. (1971) 'Economic changes and heart disease mortality'. *American Journal of Public Health.* 61, 606–11

Brenner, M. H. (1973 a) *Mental Illness and the Economy.* Harvard University Press

Brenner, M. H. (1973 b) 'Fetal, infant, and maternal mortality during periods of economic instability'. *International Journal of Health Services.* 3, 145–59

Brenner, M. H. (1976) *Economic Crises and Crime.* UNSDRI

Brenner, M. H. (1979) 'Mortality and the national economy: a review, and the experience of England and Wales'. *The Lancet.* 2, 568–73

Brenner, M. H. (1980 a) 'Industrialization and economic growth: estimates of their effects on the health of populations'. In M. H. Brenner, A. Mooney and T. J. Nagy (eds.) *Assessing the Contributions of the Social Sciences to Health.* American Academy for the Advancement of Science

Brenner, M. H. (1980 b) 'Importance of the economy to the nation's health'. In L. Eisenberg and A. Kleinman (eds.) *The Relevance of Social Science for Medicine.* Reidel

Brenner, M. H. 1983) 'Mortality and economic instability: Detailed analyses for Britain and comparative analyses for selected industrialized countries'. *International Journal of Health Services.* 13, 563–620

Brenner, M. H. and Mooney, A. (1982) 'Economic change and sex-specific cardio-vascular mortality in Britain 1955–1976'. *Social Science and Medicine.* 16, 431–42

Brenner, M. H. and Mooney, A. (1983) 'Unemployment and health in the context of economic change'. *Social Science and Medicine.* 17, 1125–38

Breughel, I. (1979) 'Women as a reserve army of labour: a note on recent British experience'. *Feminist Review.* no. 3, 12–23

Brinkmann, C. (1983) 'Health problems and psychosocial strains of the unemployed'. In J. John, D. Schwefel and H. Zöllner (eds.) *Influence of Economic Instability on Health.* Springer

Brittan, S. (1977) *The Economic Contradictions of Democracy.* Temple Smith

Brody, R. A. and Sniderman, P. M. (1977) 'From life space to polling place: the relevance of personal concerns for voting behaviour'. *British Journal of Political Science.* 7, 337–60

Brown, A. (1983) 'On socialism'. *Solidarity.* 1, 3, 7–11

Brown, C. (1984) *Black and White Britain: The Third PSI Survey.* Heinemann Educational Books/PSI

Brown, R. (1984) 'Work: past, present and future'. In *Work and Society: Sociological Perspectives on Work.* K. Thompson (ed.). Heinemann

Brown, R., Curran, M. and Cousins, J. (1983) *Changing Attitudes to Employment?* Research Paper no. 40, Dept of Employment

Brown, Richard (1976) 'Women as employees: some comments on research in industrial sociology'. In Barker, D. and Allen S. (1976)

Brown, R. K. (1983) 'Work histories and labour market segmentation'. Paper to SSRC symposium on the Use of Work Histories for the Study of Economic Life, University of Surrey, unpublished

Brown, R. K. and Brannen, P. (1970) 'Social relations and social perspectives amongst shipbuilding workers – a preliminary statement'. *Sociology.* 4, 1 and 2, 71–84, 197–211

Brown, R. K., Brannen, P., Cousins, J. M. and Samphier, M. L. (1972) 'The contours of solidarity: social stratification and industrial relations in shipbuilding'. *British Journal of Industrial Relations.* 10, 1, 12–41

Brown, W. (1981) *The Changing Contours of British Industrial Relations.* Basil Blackwell

Browning, H. and Singelmann, J. (1978) 'The Transformation of the US Labor Force: The Interaction of Industry and Occupation'. *Politics and Society.* 3–4, 481–509

Brusco, S. (1982) 'The Emilian model: productive decentralisation and social integration', *Cambridge Journal of Economics.* 6

Brusco, S. and Sabel, C. (1981) 'Artisan production and economic growth'. In Wilkinson (ed.) (1981 a)

Buck, N. H. (1981) *An Admiralty Dockyard in the mid-Nineteenth Century: Aspects of the Social and Economic History of Sheerness.* SSRC Final Report. Grant no.

HR 6939/1

Buck, T. (1979) 'Regional class differences'. *International Journal of Urban and Regional Research*. 3, 516–26

Bulmer, M. (ed.) (1975) *Working Class Images of Society*. Routledge and Kegan Paul

Bulmer, R. (1967) 'Why is the cassowary not a bird? A problem of zoological taxonomy among the Karam of the New Guinea highlands', *Man*. (N.S) 2, 5, 25

Bunker, N. and Dewberry, C. (1983) 'Signing on and staying in'. *Journal of Community Education*. 2, 4, 37–43

Bunn, A. R. (1979) 'Ischaemic heart disease mortality and the business cycle in Australia'. *American Journal of Public Health*. 69, 772–81

Buroway, Michael (1979) *Manufacturing Consent: changes in the labour process under monopoly capitalism*. Chicago University Press

Butler, D. and Rose, R. (1960) *The British General Election of 1959*. Macmillan

Buxton, N. K. and Mackay, D. I. (1977) *British Employment Statistics*. Basil Blackwell

Cagan, P. (1979) *Persistent Inflation: Historical and Policy Essays*. Columbia University Press

Cain, G. G. (1976) 'The challenge of segmented labor market theories to orthodox theory: a survey'. *Journal of Economic Literature*. 14

Cambridge Economic Policy Review 1980. 'Urban and regional policy with provisional regional accounts 1966–78'. CEPR 6, Dept of Applied Economics, University of Cambridge

Campbell, A., Converse, P. E. and Rodgers, W. L. (1976) *The Quality of American Life*. Russell Sage Foundation

Cannon, I. C. (1967) 'Ideology and occupational community: a study of compositors'. *Sociology*. 1, 2, 165–85

Carchedi, G. (1977) *On the Economic Identification of Social Classes*. Edward Arnold

Carr-Hill, R. A. and Stern, N. H. (1979) *Crime, The Police and Criminal Statistics*. Academic Press

Carr-Hill, R. A. and Stern, N. H. (1983 a) 'Crime, unemployment and the police'. Research Note no. 2, SSRC Programme on Taxation, Incentives and the Distribution of Income, International Centre for Economics and Related Disciplines, LSE

Carr-Hill, R. A. and Stern, N. H. (1983 b) 'Unemployment and crime: a comment', *Journal of Social Policy*. 12, 3, 387–94

Carter, M. (1966) *Into Work*. Pelican

Castells, M. (1975) *The Urban Question*. Edward Arnold

Castles, F. G. (ed.) (1982) *The Impact of Parties*. Sage Publication

Castles, S. and Kosack, G. (1973) *Immigrant Workers and Class Structures in Western Europe*. Oxford University Press

Castoriadis, C. (1965) *Modern Capitalism and Revolution*. Solidarity

Catalano, R. and Dooley, C. D. (1977) 'Economic predictors of depressed mood and stressful life events in a metropolitan community'. *Journal of Health and Social Behavior*. 18, 292–307

Catalano, R. and Dooley, C. D. (1979) 'Does economic change provoke or uncover behavioral disorder? A preliminary test'. In L. Ferman and J. Gordus (eds.) *Mental Health and the Economy*. Upjohn Foundation

Catalano, R. and Dooley, C. D. (1983) 'Health effects of economic instability: a test of economic stress hypothesis'. *Journal of Health and Social Behavior*. 24, 46–60

Catalano, R., Dooley, C. D. and Jackson, R. (1981) 'Economic predictors of admissions to mental health facilities in a non-metropolitan community'. *Journal of Health and Social Behavior*. 22, 284–97

Cater, J. (1984) 'Acquiring premises: a case study of Asians in Bradford'. In Ward, R. and Jenkins, R. (eds.)

Cavendish, Ruth (1982) *Women On the Line*. Routledge and Kegan Paul

Central Office of Information (1978) *Chemicals.* HMSO

Central Statistical Office (1983) *Social Trends no. 13.* HMSO

Chaplin, S. (1978) 'Durham mining villages'. In Bulmer, M. (ed.) *Mining and Social Change.* Croom Helm

Chesterman, Colleen (1978) 'Women in part-time employment', unpublished MA thesis, University of Warwick

Childers, T. (1966) 'The social bases of the National Socialist vote'. *Journal of Contemporary History.* 1966, 11, 17–42

Chinoy, E. (1955) *Automobile Workers and the American Dream.* Garden City, Doubleday and Co. Inc.

Chiswick, Barry (1978–9) 'Immigrants and immigration policy'. In William Fellner (ed.) *Contemporary Economic Problems.* American Enterprise Institute

Clark, P. and Rughani, M. (1983) 'Asian entrepreneurs in wholesaling and manufacturing in Leicester'. *New Community.* 11, 23–33

Clarke, R. (1982) *Work in Crisis.* St Andrew Press

Cleary, P. D. and Mechanic, D. (1983) 'Sex differences in psychological distress among married people'. *Journal of Health and Social Behavior.* 24, 111–21

Clegg, H. A. (1960) *A New Approach to Industrial Democracy.* Basil Blackwell

Cleland, Sherrill (1955) *The influence of plant size on industrial relations.* Industrial Relations Section, Princeton University

Clemitson, I. and Rodgers, G. (1981) *A Life to Live: Beyond Full Employment.* Junction Books

Clutterbuck, J. (1982) 'The state of industrial ill-health in the United Kingdom'. *International Journal of Health Services.* 12, 113–40

Coates, K. (1981) *Work-ins, sit-ins and industrial democracy.* Spokesmen Books

Cobb, S. and Kasl, S. V. (1977) *Termination: The Consequences of Job Loss.* NIOSH Research Report, US Dept of Health Education and Welfare

Cochrane, R. and Stopes-Roe, M. (1980) 'Factors affecting the distribution of psychological symptoms in urban areas of England'. *Acta Psychiatrica Scandinavica.* 61, 445–60

Cockburn, C. (1977) *The Local State.* Pluto Press

Cockburn, Cynthia (1983) *Brothers: Male Dominance and Technological Change.* Pluto Press

Codere, H. S. (1968) 'Money exchange systems and a theory of money'. *Man.* (N.S.) 3, 557–77

Coffield, F. (1982) 'Young unemployed in the North East'. Paper presented at the BPS Development Section Conference, September, University of Durham

Coffield, F., Robinson, R. and Sarsby, J. (1980) *A Cycle of Deprivation? a Case Study of Four Families.* Heinemann

Cohn, R. M. (1978) 'The effect of employment status change on self attitudes'. *Social Psychology.* 41, 81–93

Commission for Racial Equality (1978) *Looking for Work: black and white school leavers in Lewisham.* CRE

Commission For Racial Equality (1981) *B L Cars Ltd . . . Report of a Formal Investigation.* CRE

Cook, D. G., Cummins, R. O., Bartley, M. J. and Shaper, A. G. (1982) 'Health of unemployed middle-aged men in Great Britain'. *The Lancet.* 5 June, 1290–4

Cook, J. D., Hepworth, S. J., Wall, T. D. and Warr, P. B. (1981) *The Experience of Work.* Academic Press

Counter Information Services (1974) 'Courtaulds, inside and out'. CIS Report 10, CIS

Courtenay, G. (nd) *Local Labour Force Survey.* Social and Community Planning Research

Courtenay, G. and Hedges, G. (1977) *A Survey of Employers' Recruitment Practices.*

Social and Community Planning Research

Cousins, J. M. and Brown, R. K. (1975) 'Patterns of paradox: shipbuilding workers' images of society'. In M. Bulmer (ed.) (1975)

Cousins, J. M., Curran, M. M. and Brown, R. K. (1982) *Working in the Inner City - a Case Study*. Inner Cities Research Paper no. 8, Dept of the Environment

Cousins, J. M., Curran, M. M. and Brown, R. K. (1983) *Employment in the Inner City - an Extended Report*. Dept of Sociology and Social Policy, University of Durham

Cowling, K. (1980) *Mergers and Economic Performance*. Cambridge University Press

Cragg, A. and Dawson, T. (1984) *Unemployed Women: a Study of Attitudes and Experiences*. Research Paper no. 47, Dept of Employment

Craig, C., Garnsey, E. and Rubery, J. (1983) 'Women's pay in informal payment systems'. *Department of Employment Gazette*. April

Craig, C., Garnsey, E. and Rubery, J. (1984) *Women in Informal Pay Structures*. Research Paper no. 49, Dept of Employment

Craig, C., Garnsey, E. and Rubery, J. (forthcoming) *Pay in Small Firms: Women and Informal Payment Systems*. Research Paper no. 48, Dept of Employment

Craig, C., Tarling, R. and Wilkinson, F. (1982) *Labour Market Structure, Industrial Organisation and Low Pay*. Cambridge University Press

Craig, C. and Wilkinson, F. (forthcoming) *Pay and Employment in Four Retail Trades*. Dept of Employment Research Paper

Crane, Sir J. (1982) *The Guardian*. 9 March

Crewe, I. (1981) 'Why the Conservatives won'. In Penniman, H. R. (ed.) *Britain at the Polls*. American Enterprise Institute for Public Policy Research

Crewe, I. (1983) 'The disturbing truth'. *The Guardian*. 13 June, 5

Crompton, R. (1979) 'Trade unionism and the insurance clerk'. *Sociology*. 13, no. 3

Crompton, R. (1980) 'The double proletarianisation thesis'. *Sociology*. 14, no. 3

Crompton, R. and Jones, G. (1984) *White Collar Proletariat: Gender and Deskilling in the Workplace*. Macmillan

Crompton, R., Jones, G. and Reid, S. (1982) 'Contemporary clerical work: a case study of local government'. In West, J. *Work, Women and the Labour Market*. Routledge and Kegan Paul

Crouch, C. (1979) (ed.) *State and Economy in Contemporary Capitalism*. Croom Helm

Crouch, C. and Pizzorno, A. (1978) (eds.) *The Resurgence of Class Conflict in Western Europe since 1968*. Macmillan

Crum, R. E. and Gudgin, G. (1973) *Nonproduction Activities in the UK Manufacturing Industry*. Brussels: EEC (Regional Policy series) 3

Crum, R. E. and Gudgin, G. (1977) *Non-production Activities in the UK Manufacturing Industry*. Commission of the European Community Regional Policy Series, 3, Brussels

Crump, T. (1978) 'Money and number. The Trojan horse of language'. *Man*. (N.S.) 13, 503–18

Cummings, S. (ed.) (1980) *Self-help in urban America: patterns of minority business enterprise*. NY Kennikat

Curran, M. M. (1982 a) 'Work histories and changes in the economy'. Urban Employment Study Working Paper, Dept of Sociology and Social Policy, University of Durham

Curran, M. M. (1982 b) 'Processes of change in work histories: finding, leaving and losing jobs'. Urban Employment Study Working Paper, Dept of Sociology and Social Policy, University of Durham

Curran, M. M. (1983) 'Internal labour market change in work histories'. Urban Employment Study Working Paper, Dept of Sociology and Social Policy, University of Durham

Czada, R. and Lehmbruch, G. (1981) 'Economic policies and societies consensus mobilization'. University of Konstanz

Daniel, W. W. (1968) *Racial Discrimination in England*. Pelican

Daniel, W. W. (1972) *Whatever Happened to the Workers in Woolwich?* PEP

Daniel, W. W (1974) *A National Survey of the Unemployed*. Political and Economic Planning Institute

Daniel, W. W. (1975) *The PEP Survey on Inflation*. PEP Broadsheet 41, no. 553

Daniel, W. W. (1980) *Maternity Rights: the Experience of Women*. PSI no. 588, Policy Studies Institute

Daniel, W. W. (1981) *The Unemployed Flow. Interim Report. Stage 1*. Policy Studies Institute

Daniel, W. W. (1983) 'How the unemployed fare after they find new jobs'. *Policy Studies*. April 3, 246–60

Daniel, W. W. and Millward, N. (1983) *Workplace Industrial Relations in Britain*. Heinemann

Dauncey, G. (1983) *Nice Work if You Can Get It*. National Extension College, Cambridge

Davidoff, L. *et al.* (1976) 'Landscape with figures: home and community in English society'. In Oakley, A. and Mitchell, J. (eds.) *The Rights and Wrongs of Women*. Pelican Books

Davidoff, L. and Hall, C. (1983) 'The architecture of public and private life: English middle class society in a provincial town 1780 to 1850'. In Frazer, D. and Sutcliff, A. (eds.) *The Pursuit of Urban History*. Edward Arnold

Davies, J. (1972) *The Evangelistic Bureaucrat*. Tavistock

Davis, H. H. (1979) *Beyond Class Images*. Croom Helm

Davis, J. (1972) 'Gifts and the U.K. economy'. *Man*. (N.S.) 7, 408–29

Davis, J. (1975) 'The particular theory of exchange'. *European Journal of Sociology*. XVI, 151–68

De Grazia, R. (1980) 'Clandestine employment: a problem of our times'. *International Labour Review*. 119

Delors, J. (1978) 'The decline of French planning'. In Holland (ed.) *Beyond Capitalist Planning*. Blackwell

Dennis, N., Henriques, F. and Slaughter, C. (1956) *Coal is our Life*. Tavistock

Department of Employment (1971) *British Labour Statistics – Historical Abstract 1886–1968*. HMSO

Department of Employment (1974 a) *Women and Work: a Statistical Survey*. Manpower Paper no. 9, HMSO

Department of Employment (1974 b) *Women and Work: A Review*. Manpower Paper no. 11, HMSO

Department of Employment (1975) *Women and Work: Overseas Practice*. Manpower Paper no. 12, HMSO

Department of Employment (1982) *Employment Gazette*. 92, 1

Department of Employment (1983 a) *Employment Gazette*. 91, 1

Department of Employment (1983 b) 'Labour market data'. *Employment Gazette*. 91, 9, 61–4

Devis, T. (1983) 'People changing address: 1971 and 1981'. *Population Trends*. 32, summer, 15–20

Dex, S. (1978/9) 'Job-search methods and ethnic discrimination'. *New Community*. 7, 1, 31–9

Dex, S. (1982) *Black and White School-leavers: the First Five Years of Work*. Research Paper no. 33. Dept of Employment

Dex, S. (1984 a) *Women's Work Histories: an Analysis of the Women and Employment Survey*. Research Paper no. 46, Dept of Employment

Dex, S. (1984 b) *Women's Work Histories – Part II: an Analysis of Women and Employment Survey.* Part II of a report submitted to the Dept of Employment (unpublished)

Doeringer, Peter and Piore, M. J. (1971) *Internal Labor Markets and Manpower Analysis.* D. C. Heath

Donovan, A. and Oddy, M. (1982) 'Psychological aspects of unemployment: An investigation into the emotional and social adjustment of school leavers'. *Journal of Adolescence.* 5, 15–30

Dooley, C. D., Catalano, R., Jackson, R. and Brownell, A. (1981) 'Economic, life, and symptom changes in a non-metropolitan community'. *Journal of Health and Social Behavior.* 22, 144–54

Dore, R. (1973) *British Factory – Japanese Factory.* Allen and Unwin

Douglas, M. (1966) *Purity and Danger. An Analysis of Concepts of Pollution and Taboo.* Routledge and Kegan Paul

Duke, V. and Edgell, S. (nd) 'Public expenditure cuts in Britain and consumption sectoral cleavages', mimeo, unpublished. University of Salford, Dept of Sociological and Anthropological Sciences

Dunford, M., Geddes, M. and Perrons, D. (1980) 'Regional policy and the crisis in the UK: a long run perspective'. *International Journal of Urban and Regional Research.* 5, 377–411

Dunnell, K. and Head, E. (1973) *Employers and Employment Services.* Office of Population Censuses and Surveys

Échanges et Mouvement (1979) *The Refusal of Work.* BM Box 91, London

Economist Intelligence Unit (1982) *Coping with Unemployment*

Edgell, S. (1967) *Middle Class Couples.* Allen and Unwin

Edwards, P. K. (1983) 'Control compliance and conflict: analysing variations in the capitalist labour process' (unpublished paper)

Edwards, R., Reich, M. and Gordon, R. (1982) *Segmented Work, Divided Workers*

Edwards, R. C. (1979) *Contested Terrain: The Transformation of the Workplace in the Twentieth Century.* Heinemann

Elbaum, R. and Wilkinson, F. (1979) 'Industrial relations and uneven development: a comparative study of the American and British steel industries'. *Cambridge Journal of Economics*, 3, September

Eldridge, J. E. T. (1968) *Industrial Disputes. Essays in the Sociology of Industrial Relations.* Routledge and Kegan Paul

Elias, P. and Maine, B. (1982) *Women's Working Lives.* Institute for Employment Research, University of Warwick

Ellen, R. F. and Reason, D. (eds.) (1979) *Classifications in their social context.* Academic Press

Elliott, B. and McCrone, D. (1982) 'The social world of petty property'. In Hollowell (ed.)

Engels, F. (1958) *The Condition of the Working Class in England.* Basil Blackwell

Erikson, R., Goldthorpe, J. H. and Portocarero, L. (1983) 'Intergenerational class mobility and the convergence thesis'. *British Journal of Sociology.* 34

Erikssen, J., Rognum, T. and Jervell, J. (1979) 'Unemployment and health'. *The Lancet.* no. 1, 1189 (letter)

Estes, R. J. and Wilensky, H. L. (1978) 'Life cycle squeeze and the morale curve'. *Social Problems.* 25, 277–92

Eurostat (1980) *Labour Force Sample Survey: 1973, 1975, 1977.* Office for Official Publications of the European Communities

Eurostat (1981) *Labour Force Sample Survey 1979.* Office for Official Publications of the European Communities

Evans, Mary and Ungerson, Clare (1983) *Sexual Divisions, Patterns and Processes.*

Tavistock

Ewing, A. F. (1972) *Planning and Policies in the Textile Finishing Industry*. Bradford UP with Crosby, Lockwood and Son

Eyer, J. (1977) 'Does unemployment cause the death rate peak in each business cycle?' *International Journal of Health Services*. 7, 625–62

Fagin, L. and Little, M. (1984) *The Forsaken Families: The Effects of Unemployment on Family Life*. Penguin

Falding, H. (1961) 'The family and the idea of a cardinal role', *Human Relations*. 14

Feather, N. T. (1982) 'Unemployment and its psychological correlates: A study of depressive symptoms, self-esteem, Protestant ethic values, attributional style, and apathy'. *Australian Journal of Psychology*. 34, 309–23

Feather, N. T. and Bond, M. J. (1983) 'Time structure and purposeful activity among employed and unemployed university graduates'. *Journal of Occupational Psychology*. 56, 241–54

Feather, N. T. and Davenport, P. R. (1981) 'Unemployment and depressive affect: a motivational analysis'. *Journal of Personality and Social Psychology*. 41, 422–36

Featherman, D. and Hauser, R. M. (1978) *Opportunity and Change*. Academic Press

Fenton, M. (1977) 'Asian households in owner-occupation: a study of the pattern, costs and experiences of households in Greater Manchester'. *Working Papers on Ethnic Relations*. 2 ESRC London Research Unit on Ethnic Relations

Festinger, L. (1954) 'A theory of social comparison processes'. *Human Relations*. 7, 117–40

Fevre, R. (1983) 'Employment and unemployment in Port Talbot – a reference paper'. Working paper, University College, Swansea

Fevre, R. (1984) 'Contract work and the recession'. Paper presented to British Sociological Association Conference, Bradford, 1984

Finlay-Jones, R. A.. and Eckhardt, B. (1981) 'Psychiatric disorder among the young unemployed'. *Australian and New Zealand Journal of Psychiatry*. 15, 265–70

Finley, M. I. (1972) *The Ancient Economy*. Chatto and Windus

Firth, R. (1964) *Essays on Social Organisation and Values*. LSE Monographs on Social Anthropology, Athlone

Foner, N. (1979) 'West Indians in New York City and London: a comparative analysis'. *International Migration Review*. 13, 284–95

Forbes, J. F. and McGregor, A. (1984) 'Unemployment and mortality in post-war Scotland'. *Journal of Health Economics*. In press

Fothergill, S. and Gudgin, G. (1979) 'Regional employment change: a subregional explanation'. *Progress and Planning*. 12, 155–220

Fothergill, S. and Gudgin, G. (1981) *Unequal growth: employment change in British cities and regions*. Heinemann

Fox, A. (1980) 'The meaning of work'. In G. Esland and G. Salaman (eds.) *The Politics of Work and Occupations*. Open University Press

Fox, A. J. and Goldblatt, P. O. (1982) *Sociodemographic Mortality Differentials Longitudinal Study, 1971–1975*. OPCS, LS no. 1, HMSO

Frank, J. A. (1981) 'Economic change and mental health in an uncontaminated setting'. *American Journal of Community Psychology*. 9, 395–410

Fraser, C. (1980) 'The social psychology of unemployment'. In M. Jeeves (ed.) *Psychology Survey*. no. 3, Allen and Unwin

Fraser, C. and Marsh, C. (1984) 'Individuals' political reactions to unemployment'. Paper presented at Annual Conference of Social Psychology Section of British Psychological Society, Oxford

Freeman, G. P. (1979) *Immigrant Labor and Racial Conflict in Industrial Societies*. Princeton University Press

Frese, M. (1979) 'Arbeitslösigkeit, Depressivität und Kontrolle: eine Studie mit

Wiederholungsmessung'. In T. Kieselbach and H. Offe (eds.) *Arbeitslösigkeit*. Steinkopff

Friedman, E. A. and Orbach, H. L. (1974) 'Adjustment to retirement'. In S. Arieti (ed.) *American Handbook of Psychiatry*. 1, Basic

Fröhlich, D. (1983) 'Economic deprivation, work orientation and health: conceptual ideas and some empirical findings'. In J. John, D. Schwefel and H. Zöllner (eds.) *Influence of Economic Instability on Health*. Springer

Fryer, D. and Warr, P. B. (1984) 'Unemployment and cognitive difficulties' *British Journal of Clinical Psychology*. 23, 67–8

Fuchs, V. R. (1968) *The Service Economy*. National Bureau of Economic Research

Fulcher, M. N., Rhodes, J. and Taylor, J. (1966) 'The economy of the Lancaster sub-region'. University of Lancaster Economics Dept Occasional Paper 10

Furnham, A. (1982 a) 'Explanations for unemployment in Britain'. *European Journal of Psychology*. 12, 335–52

Furnham, A. (1982 b) 'Why are the poor always with us? Explanations for poverty in Britain'. *British Journal of Social Psychology*. 21, 311–22

Furnham, A. (1982 c) 'The Protestant work ethic and attitudes towards unemployment'. *Journal of Occupational Psychology*. 55, 27–286

Furnham, A. (1983) 'The Protestant work ethic and attitudes towards taxation'. *Journal of Economic Psychology*. 3, 113–28

Gallie, D. (1978) *In Search of the New Working Class. Automation and Social Integration within the Capitalist Enterprise*. Cambridge University Press

Gallo, C. (1983) 'The construction industry in New York City: immigrants and black entrepreneurs'. Working Paper, Conservation of Human Resources, Columbia University

Gans, H. J. (1967) *The Levittowners – Ways of Life and politics in a new suburban community*. Allen Lane and Penguin Press

Gardiner, T. (1975) 'Women's domestic labour'. *New Left Review*. no. 89, 47–57

Garnsey, E. (1978) 'Women's work and theories of class stratification'. *Sociology*. 12, 2

Garraty, J. A. (1978) *Unemployment in History*. Harper and Row

Gaskell, G. and Smith, P. (1981) ' "Alienated" black youth: an investigation of "conventional wisdom" explanations'. *New Community*. 9, 182–93

Geertz, C. (1963) *Peddlers and Princes*. The University of Chicago Press

Geertz, C. (1979) 'Suq: the bazaar economy in Sefrou'. In Geertz, C., Geertz, H., and Rosen, L., *Meaning and Order in Moroccan Society*. Cambridge University Press

Gershuny, J. I. (1979) 'The informal economy: its role in industrial society'. *Futures*. February, 3–15

Gershuny, J. I. (1983 a) 'Changing use of time in the United Kingdom: 1937–1975 – the self-service era'. *Studies of Broadcasting*. 19

Gershuny, J. I. (1983 b) *Social Innovation and the Division of Labour*. Oxford University Press

Gershuny, J. I. and Miles, I. (1983) *The New Service Economy*. Frances Pinter

Gershuny, J. I. and Pahl, R. E. (1979/80) 'Work outside employment'. *New Universities Quarterly*. 1, 34, 120–35

Gershuny, J. I. and Pahl, R. E. (1980) 'Britain in the decade of the three economies' *New Society*. 3 January 1980, 51, no. 900, 7–9

Gershuny, J. I. and Thomas, G. S. (1982) 'Changing Leisure Patterns in the UK, 1961–1974-5'. In *Leisure Research: Current Findings and Future Challenge*. M. Colling (ed.) Sports Council

Gibbs, J. P. and Poston, D. L. (1975) 'The division of labor: conceptualization and related measures'. *Social Forces*. 53, March, 468–76

Gil, D. (1971) 'Violence against children'. *Journal of Marriage and the Family*. 33, 637-57

Giner, S. and Salcedo, J. (1978) 'Migrant workers in European social structures'. In Giner, S. and Archer, Margaret S. (eds.). *Contemporary Europe: Social Structures and Cultural Patterns*. Weidenfeld and Nicolson

Goffman, E. (1952) 'On cooling the mark out', *Psychiatry* 15, 4, 451-63

Goldberg, D. (1972) *The Detection of Psychiatric Illness by Questionnaire*. Oxford University Press

Goldberg, D. (1978) *Manual for the General Health Questionnaire*. National Foundation for Educational Research

Goldberg, D. (1981) 'Estimating the prevalence of psychiatric disorder from the results of a screening test'. In J. K. Wing, P. Bebbington and L. N. Robins (eds.) *What is a Case?* Grant McIntyre

Goldthorpe, J. H. (1971) 'Theories of industrial society: reflections on the recrudescence of historicism and the future of futurology'. *Archives européennes de sociologie*. 12

Goldthorpe, J. H. (1972) 'Class, status and party in modern Britain: some recent interpretations, Marxist and Marxisant'. *European Journal of Sociology*. 13, 342-72

Goldthorpe, J. H. (1974) 'Social inequality and social integration in modern Britain'. In Wedderburn (ed.) (1974)

Goldthorpe, J. H. (1978) 'The current inflation: towards a sociological account'. In Hirsch, F. and Goldthorpe, J. (eds.) (1978)

Goldthorpe, J. H. (1979) 'Intellectuals and the working class in modern Britain'. Fuller Lecture, Dept of Sociology, University of Essex

Goldthorpe, J. H. (1983 a) 'Social mobility and class formation: on the renewal of a tradition in sociological theory'. Nuffield College, Oxford

Goldthorpe, J. H. (1983 b) 'Social structure, interests and political partisanship'. Nuffield College, Oxford mimeo

Goldthorpe, J. H. (1984) 'Problems of political economy after the end of the post war period'. In Maier (ed.) (forthcoming)

Goldthorpe, J. H. and Lockwood, D. (1963) 'Affluence and the British class structure'. *Sociological Review*. 11, 2

Goldthorpe, J. H. *et al.* (1968) *The Affluent Worker: Industrial attitudes and behaviour*. Cambridge University Press

Goldthorpe, J. H. *et al.* (1969) *The Affluent Worker: Political attitudes and behaviour*. Cambridge University Press

Goldthorpe, J. H. *et al.* (1970) *The Affluent Worker: The Class Structure*. Cambridge University Press

Goodwin, L. (1972) *Do the Poor Want to Work?* The Brookings Institution

Gordon, D. (1972) *Theories of Poverty and Underemployment*. D. C. Heath

Gordon, D. M. (1976) 'Capitalist efficiency and socialist efficiency'. *Monthly Review*. 28, 3, 19-39

Gordon, D. M., Edwards, R. and Reich, M. (1982) *Segmented Work, Divided Workers*. Cambridge University Press

Gordon, M. E. and Scott, R. D. (1972) 'Evaluation of a manpower development project in terms of its effects on the personal lives of its graduates'. *Journal of Vocational Behaviour*. 2, 467-78

Gorz, A. (1983) *Farewell to the Working Class*. Fontana

Grammenos, S. (1982) 'Migrant labour in western Europe'. European Centre for Work and Society Studies and Documents 3. Maastricht

Granovetter, M. (1973) 'The strength of weak ties'. *American Journal of Sociology*. 78, 1360-80

Granovetter, M. (1974) *Getting a Job*. Harvard University Press

✕ Gravelle, H. S. E., Hutchinson, G. and Stern, J. (1981) 'Mortality and unemployment: a critique of Brenner's time-series analysis'. *The Lancet*. 2, 675–9

Gurney, J. N. and Tierney, K. T. (1982) 'Relative deprivation and social movements: a critical look at twenty years of theory and research'. *Sociological Quarterly*. Winter, 23, 33–47

Hahlo, K. (1980) 'Profile of a Gujerati community in Bolton'. *New Community*. 8, 295–307

Hain, P. (1976) *Community Politics*. Calder

Hakim, C. (1979) *Occupational Segregation – Comparative study of the degree and pattern of differentiation between men and women's work in Britain, the United States, and other countries*. Research Paper no. 9, Dept of Employment

Hakim, C. (1981) 'Job segregation: trends in the 1970s'. *Employment Gazette*. 89, 12, 521–9

Hakim, C. (1982) 'The social consequences of high unemployment'. *Journal of Social Policy*. 2, 4, 433–67

Hakim, C. and Dennis, R. (1982) *Homeworking in Wages Council Industries: a study based on Wage Inspectorate records of Pay and Earnings*. Research Paper no. 37, Dept of Employment

Hall, Peter (1964) *The Industries of London*. Hutchinson

Hall, S., Critcher, C., Jefferson, T., Clarke, J. and Roberts, B. (1978) *Policing the Crisis*. Macmillan

Hallaire, Jean (1968) *Part-time Employment, its extent and its problems*. Organisation for Economic Co-operation and Development

Hanisch, T. (1981) 'Markets and politics in wage determination', Institut for Samfunnsforskning, Oslo

Harrison, B. and Sum, A. (1979) 'The theory of "dual" or segmented labor markets'. *Journal of Economic Issues*. 13, 3, 687–706

Harris, C. C. (1969) *The Family*. Allen and Unwin 162–75

Harris, C. C. (1981) 'The idea of a labour market', working paper, University College, Swansea

Harris, C. C. (1982 a) 'The geographical definition of the labour market of west industrial South Wales', working paper, University College, Swansea

Harris, C. C. (1982 b) '"Chequeredness" and the two sides of the labour market', working paper, University College, Swansea

Hart, K. (1973) 'Informal income opportunities and urban employment in Ghana'. *Journal of Modern African Studies*. 11, 61–89

Hartmann, Heidi (1976) 'Capitalism, patriarchy and job seegregation by sex' in M. Blaxall and B. Reagan (1976)

Harvie, C. (1981) *No Gods and Precious Few Heroes: Scotland 1914–1980*. Edward Arnold

Hauser, R. M., Dickinson, P., Travis, H. P. and Koffel, J. N. (1975) 'Structural changes in occupational mobility among men in the United States'. *American Journal of Sociology*. 40 (October): 585–98

Hauser, R. M. and Featherman, D. L. (1977) *The Process of Stratification*. Academic Press

Hauser, R. M., Koffel, J. N., Travis, H. P. and Dickinson, P. (1975) 'Temporal change in occupational mobility: evidence for men in the United States'. *American Sociological Review*. 40 (June): 274–97

Hebden, J. E. (1975) 'Patterns of work identification'. *Sociology of Work and Occupations*. 2 (2), 107–32

Heidbreder, E. M. (1972) 'Factors in retirement adjustment: white collar/blue collar experience'. *Industrial Gerontology*. 12, 69–79

Heinze, R. G. and Olk, T. (1982) 'Development of the informal economy'. *Futures*.

14 (3), 189–204

Henderson, S., Duncan-Jones, P., Byrne, D. G., Scott, R. and Adcock, S. (1979) 'Psychiatric disorder in Canberra: A standardised study of prevalence'. *Acta Psychiatrica Scandinavica.* 60, 335–74

Henry, S. (1978) *The Hidden Economy.* Martin Robertson

Henwood, F. (1983) 'Employment, unemployment and housework' unpublished MSc dissertation, SPRU, University of Sussex

Henwood, F. and Miles, D. (n.d.) 'Unemployment and the sexual division of labour'. SPRU, mimeo (forthcoming)

Hepworth, S. J. (1980) 'Moderating factors of the psychological impact of unemployment'. *Journal of Occupational Psychology.* 53, 139–45

Herman, H. (1979) 'Dishwashers and proprietors: Macedonians in Toronto's restaurant trade'. In Sandra Wallman (ed.) *Ethnicity at Work.* Macmillan

Herron, F. (1975) *The Labour Market in Crisis.* Macmillan

Hill, S. (1981) *Competition and Control at Work.* Heinemann

Hill, S. (1976) *The Dockers. Class and Tradition in London.* Heinemann

Hill, M. J., Harrison, R. M., Sargeant, A. V. and Talbot, V. (1973) *Men Out of Work.* Cambridge University Press

Hirsch, F. (1975) *The Social Limits to Growth.* Routledge and Kegan Paul

Hirsch, F. and Goldthorpe, J. H. (1978) *The Political Economy of Inflation.* Martin Robertson

Hodson, R. and Kaufman, R. L. (1982) 'Economic dualism: a critical review'. *American Sociological Review.* 47

Hoel, B. (1982) 'Contemporary clothing "sweatshops" – Asian female labour and collective organisation'. In West, J. (ed.) *Work, Women and the Labour Market.* Routledge & Kegan Paul

Hoggart, R. (1958) *The Uses of Literature.* Penguin

Holland, S. (1978) *Beyond Capitalist Planning.* Basil Blackwell

Holland, S. (1979) 'Comment' in Blackaby, F. (ed.) *Deindustrialisation.* Heinemann

Hollowell, P. G. (1968) *The Lorry Driver.* Routledge and Kegan Paul

Hollowell, P. G. (1982) (ed.) *Property and Social Relations.* Heinemann

Home Office (1974) *Equality for Women.* Cmnd, HMSO

Hough, M. and Mayhew, M. (1983) *The British Crime Survey.* Home Office Research Study, no. 76, HMSO

House of Commons Select Committee on Social Services (1982) *Age of Retirement.* HC 26, HMSO

House of Lords Select Committee on Unemployment (1982) *Volume 1 – Report.* HL 142, HMSO

Hubbuck, J. and Carter, S. (1980) *Half a Chance? A Report on Job Discrimination Against Young Blacks in Nottingham.* Commission for Racial Equality

Hughes, E. C. (1958) *Men and their Work.* Free Press

Hughes, M. *et al.* (1980) *Nurseries Now.* Penguin Books

Hunt, A. (1968) *A Survey of Women's Employment.* HMSO

Hunt, A. (1975) *Management Attitudes and Practices towards Women at Work.* HMSO

Hurtsfield, Jennifer (1978) *The Part-time Trap.* Low Pay Pamphlet no. 9

Ingham, G. (1970) *Size of Industrial Organization and Worker Behavior.* Cambridge University Press

Jackson, A. A. (1973) *Semi Detached London: Suburban development, life and transport, 1900–1939.* George Allen and Unwin

Jackson, J. S. III (1973) 'Alienation and black political participation'. *Journal of Politics.* 35, 849–85

Jackson, P. R., Stafford, E. M., Banks, M. H. and Warr, P. B. (1983) 'Unemployment and psychological distress in young people: the moderating role of employment commitment'. *Journal of Applied Psychology*. 68, 525–35

Jackson, P. R. and Warr, P. B. (1983) *Age, Length of Unemployment and other Variables Associated with Men's Ill-Health*. SAPU Memo 585

Jackson, P. R. and Warr, P. B. (1984) 'Unemployment and psychological ill-health: The moderating role of duration and age'. *Psychological Medicine*. 14, 605–14

Jaco, E. G. (1960) *The Social Epidemiology of Mental Disorders*. Russell Sage Foundation

Jacobsen, K. (1972) 'Dismissal and morbidity'. *Ugeskrift for Laeger*. 134, 352–4

Jahoda, G. (1979) 'The construction of economic reality by some Glaswegian children'. *European Journal of Social Psychology*. 9, 115–27

Jahoda, M. (1982) *Work, Employment and Unemployment: A Social Psychological Analysis*. Cambridge University Press

Jahoda, M., Lazarsfeld, P. F. and Zeisel, H. (1972) *Marienthal*. Tavistock

Jay, P. (1976) *A General Hypothesis of Employment, Inflation and Politics*. Institute of Economic Affairs

Jenkins, R. (1982) *Managers, Recruitment Procedures and Black Workers*. Working Papers in Ethnic Relations no. 18. Research Unit on Ethnic Relations

Jenkins, R. (1984) 'Classifying people/peopling classes: recruitment into employment and practical production of stratification'. Paper presented to the Annual Conference of the British Sociological Association

Jenkins, R., Bryman, A., Ford, J., Keil, T. and Beardsworth, A. (1983) 'Information in the labour market: the impact of recession'. *Sociology*. 17, 260–7

Jenkins, R. and Troyna, B. (1983) 'Educational myths, labour market realities'. In *Racism, school and the labour market*. B. Troyna and D. I. Smith (eds.), National Youth Bureau, 5–16

Jessop, R. (1975) *Traditionalism, Conservatism and British Political Culture*. Allen and Unwin

Jessop, R. (1978) 'Capitalism and democracy: the best possible political shell?'. In Littlejohn *et al.* (eds.)

John, J. (1983) 'Economic instability and mortality in the Federal Republic of Germany'. In J. John, D. Schwefel and H. Zöllner (eds.) *Influence of Economic Instability on Health*. Springer

Jolly, J., Creigh, S. and Mingay, A. (1980) *Age as a Factor in Employment*. Dept of Employment

Joshi, H. (1984) *Women's Participation in Paid Work: Further Analysis of the Women and Employment Survey*. Research Paper no. 45, Dept of Employment

Kasl, S. V. (1979 a) 'Changes in mental health status associated with job loss and retirement'. In R. M. Rose and G. L. Klerman (eds.) *Stress and Mental Disorder*. Raven Press

Kasl, S. V. (1979 b) 'Mortality and the business cycle: Some questions about research strategies when utilizing macro-social and ecological data' *American Journal of Public Health*. 69, 784–8

Kasl, S. V. (1982) 'Strategies of research on economic instability and health'. *Psychological Medicine*. 12, 637–49

Kasl, S. V. and Cobb, S. (1980) 'The experience of losing a job: Some effects on cardiovascular functioning'. *Psychotherapy and Psychosomatics*. 34, 88–109

Kasl, S. V., Gore, S. and Cobb, S. (1975) 'The experience of losing a job: Reported changes in health, symptoms and illness behavior'. *Psychosomatic Medicine*. 37, 106–22

Keeble, D. (1976) *Industrial Location and Planning in the UK*. Methuen

Keil, T. (1976) *Becoming a Worker*. Leicestershire Committee for Education and Training/Training Services Agency

Kenrick, Jane (1981) 'Politics and the construction of women as second class workers', in Wilkinson (1981 a)

Keohane, R. O. 'Economics, inflation and the role of the state: political implications of the McCracken Report', *World Politics*. 31

Kerr, C., Dunlop, J. T., Harbison, F. H. and Myers, C. A. (1960) *Industrialism and Industrial Man*. Harvard University Press

Kerr, C., Dunlop, J. T., Harbison, F. H. and Myers, C. A. (1973) *Industrialism and Industrial Man*. 2nd edition, Penguin

Kettle, M. and Hodges, L. (1982) *Uprising: the Police, the People and the Riots in Britain's Cities*. Pan Books

Kilpatrick, R. and Trew, K. (1982) 'What unemployed men do: A Belfast sample'. Paper presented to *Understanding Unemployment*. Conference, Belfast

Kim, I. (1981) *The New Urban Immigrants: Korean Immigrants in New York City*. Princeton University Press

Kinder, D. R. and Kiewiet, D. R. (1981) 'Sociotropic politics: The American case'. *British Journal of Political Science*

Kindleberger, C. P. (1967) *Europe's Postwar Growth: the Role of Labor Supply*. Harvard University Press

Kinzzer, R. and Sagarin, E. (1950) *The Negro in American Business: The Conflict between Separatism and Integration*. Greenburg

Klandermans, B. (1980) 'Unemployment and the unemployed movement'. Unpublished ms, Dept of Social Psychology, Free University of Amsterdam

Klausen, H. and Iversen, L. (1981) *The Closing of the Nordhavn Shipyard*. Copenhagen: Institute for Social Medicine

Klein, J. (1965) *Samples from English Cultures*. Routledge & Kegan Paul

Klein, Viola (1965) *Britain's Married Women Workers*. Routledge and Kegan Paul

Knight, A. (1974) *Private Enterprise and Public Intervention: the Courtaulds Experience*. George Allen and Unwin

Komarovsky, M. (1940) *The Unemployed Man and His Family*. Anchor Books

Korazim, J. and Freedman, M. (1983) 'Self-employment and the decision to emigrate: Israelis in New York City'. Working Paper, Conservation of Human Resources, Columbia University

Korpi, W. (1978) *The Working Class in Welfare Capitalism*. Routledge and Kegan Paul

Korpi, W. (1983) *The Democratic Class Struggle*. Routledge and Kegan Paul

Korpi, W. and Shalev, M. (1980) 'Strikes, power and politics in the western nations, 1900-1976', *Political Power and Social Theory*. 1

Kosmin, B. A. (1979) 'J. R. Archer (1863-1932): a Pan-Africanist in the Battersea Labour Movement'. *New Community*. 7, 3

Kuhn, A. and Wolpe, A. M. (eds.) (1978) *Feminism and Materialism*. Routledge and Kegan Paul

Kumar, K. (1978) *Prophecy and Progress*. Penguin Books

Lafargue, P. (1880) *Le Droit à la Paresse*. Paris. First English edition published 1907 by the Charles H. Kerr Coop, under the title, *The Right to be Lazy*.

Lajer, M. (1982) 'Unemployment and hospitalization among bricklayers'. *Scandinavian Journal of Social Medicine*. 10, 3-10

Lancaster City Council (1977) 'Industrial strategy for Lancaster'. Lancaster Town Hall (unpublished)

Land, H. (1976) 'Women: supporters or supported'. In Barker, D. L. and Allen, S. (1976 a)

Land, H. (forthcoming) 'Poverty and gender: The distribution of resources within the family'. In M. Brown (ed.) *The Structure of Disadvantage*. Heinemann

Lange, P. (1979) 'Sindicati, partiti, stato e liberal-corporativismo', *Il Mulino*. 28

Lange, P., Ross, G. and Vannicelli, M. (1982) *Unions, Change and Crisis: French* and Italian Union Strategy and the Political Economy, 1945–1980. Allen and Unwin

Lasch, C. (1979) The Culture of Narcissism. Warner Books

Lauman, E. O. (ed.) (1970) Social Stratification: Research and Theory for the 1970s. Bobbs Merrill

Lawlis, G. F. (1971) 'Motivational factors reflecting employment instability'. Journal of Social Psychology. 84, 215–23

Lee, D. (1981) 'Skill, conflict and class: a theoretical critique and a deviant case', Sociology. 15, 1

Lee, G. and Wrench, J. (1983) Skill seekers – black youth, apprenticeships and disadvantage. National Youth Bureau

Lee, R. M. (1983 a) 'The job-search activity of unemployed redundant steel-workers', working paper, University College Swansea

Lee, R. M. (1983 b) 'The job-acquisition behaviour of redundant steel-workers', working paper, University College Swansea

Lee, R. M. (1983 c) 'Survey of redundant steel-workers: selected results from waves 1 and 2', working paper, University College Swansea

Lee, R. M., Morris, L. D. and Harris, C. C. (1983) 'Aspects of the everyday life of the redundant: the place of informal relations', unpublished paper presented at the Urban Change and Conflict Conference

Leggett, J. C. (1964) 'Economic insecurity and working-class consciousness'. American Sociological Review. 29, 226–34

Lehmbruch, G. (1983) 'Interest, intermediation in capitalist and socialist systems', International Political Science Review. 4

Lehmbruch, G. and Schmitter, P. (1982) (eds.) Patterns of Corporatist Policy-making. Sage Publications

Leighton, P. (1983) Contractual arrangements in selected industries: a study of employment relationships in industry without work. Research Paper no. 39, Dept of Employment

Lester, R. A. (1958) As Unions Mature. Princeton University Press

Leventman, P. G. (1981) Professionals out of Work. Free Press

Lever-Tracy, C. (1983) 'Immigrant workers and post-war capitalism: in reserve or core troops in the front line?', Politics and Society. 12

Lewis, A. (1982 a) The Psychology of Taxation. Martin Robertson

Lewis, A. (1982 b) 'The social psychology of taxation'. British Journal of Social Psychology. 21, 151–8

Lewis, O. (1951) Life in a Mexican Village. University of Illinois Press

Light, Ivan (1972) Ethnic Enterprise in America. University of California Press

Light, R. (1973) 'Abused and neglected children in America'. Harvard Educational Review. 43, 556–98

Liker, J. K. and Elder, G. H. (1983) 'Economic hardship and marital relations in the 1930s'. American Sociological Review. 48, 343–59

Lipset, S. M. (1960) Political Man: the Social Bases of Politics. Heinemann

Lipset, S. M. (1969) Revolution and Counter Revolution. Heinemann

Lipset, S. M. and Bendix, R. (1959) Social Mobility in Industrial Society. Heinemann

Little, C. B. (1976) 'Technical-professional unemployment: middle-class adaptability to personal crisis'. Sociological Quarterly. 17, 262–74

Littlejohn, G., Smart, B., Wakeford, J. and Yuval-Davis, N. (1978) (eds.) Power and the State. Croom Helm

Littler, Craig R. and Salaman, Graeme (1982) 'Bravermania and beyond: recent theories of the labour process'. In Sociology. 11, no. 2, May 1982

Lloyd, P. (1979) Slums of Hope? Penguin

Lockwood, D. (1966) 'The sources of variation in working class images of society', Sociological Review. 14, 3

Lockwood, D. (1974) 'For T. H. Marshall'. *Sociology.* 8

Lockwood, D. (1981) 'The weakest link in the chain? Some comments on the Marxist theory of action'. In Simpson, S. and Simpson, I. (eds.) *Research in the Sociology of Work.* 1. JAI Press

McCrudden, C. (1981) 'Legal remedies for discrimination in employment'. *Current Legal Problems.* 34, 211–33

Macfarlane, A. (1979)

McGeown, P. (1969) 'Steelman'. In Fraser, R. (ed.) *Work 2: Twenty Personal Accounts.* Penguin

McGoldrick, A. and Cooper, C. (1980) 'Voluntary early retirement'

McIntyre, S. (1968) *Little Moscows.* Croom Helm

McIver, J. P. (1982) 'Unemployment and partisanship: A second opinion'. *American Politics Quarterly.* 10, 439–51

Mackay, D. I. and Reid, G. L. (1971) *Men Leaving Steel.* BSC

Mackay, D. I., Boddy, D., Brack, J., Diack, J. A. and Jones, N. (1971) *Labour Markets Under Different Employment Conditions.* George Allen and Unwin

Mackay, R. and Thomson, L. (1979) 'Important trends in regional policy and regional employment – a modified interpretation'. *Scottish Journal of Political Economy.* 2, 233–60

MacKenzie, R. and Silver, A. (1968) *Angels in Marble.* Heinemann

McKibbin, R. I. (1969) 'The myth of the unemployed: who did vote for the Nazis?' *Australian Journal of Politics and History.* 15, 25–40

Madge, N. (1983) 'Unemployment and its effects on children'. *Journal of Child Psychology and Psychiatry.* 24, 311–19

Maier, C. S. (forthcoming) (ed.) *The Changing Boundaries of the Political.* Cambridge University Press

Manley, P. and Sawbridge, D. (1980) 'Women at work'. *Lloyds Bank Review.* 29–40

Mann, M. (1970) 'The social cohesion of liberal democracy', *ASR.* 35, 3

Mann, M. (1973) *Workers on the Move.* Cambridge University Press

Mann, M. (1983) 'Social change and ideological response'. Fabian Society Seminar

Mann, M. (forthcoming) *The Sources of Social Power.*

Manpower Services Commission (1983) *Labour Market Quarterly Report, Great Britain, September 1983*

Marin, B. (1983) 'Organizing interests by interest organizations: associational prerequisites of co-operation in Austria', *International Political Science Review.* 4

Marquand, J. (1980) 'The role of the tertiary sector in regional policy. Commission of the European Communities', *Regional Policy Series.* no. 19, Brussels

Mars, G. (1982) *Cheats at Work: An Anthropology of Workplace Crime.* George Allen and Unwin

Marsden, D. and Duff, E. (1975) *Workless.* Penguin

Marsh, C. (1982) *The Survey Method.* George Allen and Unwin

Marsh, C. (1984) 'Predictions of voting behaviour from a pre-election survey'. Unpublished ms. Social and Political Science Committee, University of Cambridge

Marshall, A. (1952) *Principles of Economics.* Macmillan

Marshall, G. and Rose, D. (1983) 'Stagflation and British society: some background issues examined', University of Essex, Dept of Sociology

Marshall, G. *et al.* (1983) *Social Classes and Distributional Struggles in Contemporary Britain.* University of Essex

Marshall, J. R. and Funch, D. P. (1979) 'Mental illness and the economy: a critique and partial replication'. *Journal of Health and Social Behavior.* 20, 282–9

Marshall, J. R. and Funch, D. P. (1980) 'Reply to Ratcliff'. *Journal of Health and Social Behavior.* 21, 391–3

Marshall, T. H. (1950) *Citizenship and Social Class.* Cambridge University Press

Martin, A. (1979) 'The dynamics of change in Keynesian political economy: the Swedish case and its implications'. In Crouch (ed.) (1979)

Martin, J. and Roberts, C. (1984 a) *Women and Employment: a lifetime perspective.* HMSO

Martin, J. and Roberts, C. (1984 b) *Women and Employment: technical report.* Office of Population Censuses and Surveys

Martin, R. M. (1983) 'Pluralism and the new corporatism'. *Political Studies.* 31

Martin, R. M. and Fryer, R. H. (1973) *Redundancy and Paternalist Capitalism.* George Allen and Unwin

Martin, R. M. and Wallace, J. G. (1983) 'Female Unemployment – Redundancy Studies'. (unpublished ms)

Martin, R. M. and Wallace, J. G. (1984) *Working Women in Recession: Employment, Redundancy, and Unemployment.* Oxford University Press

Marx, Karl (1973) *Grundrisse.* Penguin

Massey, D. (1978) 'Regionalism: some current issues'. *Capital and Class.* 6, 106–25

Massey, D. (1979) 'In what sense a regional problem?'. *Regional Studies.* 13, 233–43

Massey, D. (1982 a) 'Industrial production as class restructuring; production decentralisation and local uniqueness'. *Regional Studies.* 17, 2

Massey, D. (1982 b) 'Industrial restructuring as class restructuring'. Mimeo, 2

Massey, D. (1983) 'The shape of things to come'. *Marxism Today.*

Massey, D. (1984) *Space and Class: Industrial Location, the Regional Problem and British Economic Decline.* Macmillan

Massey, D. and Meagan, R. (1982) *The Anatomy of Job Loss.* Methuen

Mellor, J. R. (1975) 'The British experiment: combined and uneven development'. In M. Harloe (ed.) *Proceedings of the Conference on Urban Change and Conflict.* University of York

Michon, F. (1981) 'Dualism and the French labour market: business strategy, non-standard job forms and secondary jobs'. In Wilkinson (ed.) (1981 a)

Middleton, C. (1979) 'The sexual division of labour under feudalism', *New Left Review.* No. 113–14

Miles, I. D. (1975) *The Poverty of Prediction.* Saxon House

Miles, I. D. (1983 a) 'Work and non-work: Europe in the 1980s and beyond'. *Futures.* December

Miles, I. D. (1983 b) *Adaptation to Unemployment?* SPRU Occasional Paper 20

Milkman, Ruth (1976) 'Women's work and the economic crisis: some lessons of the Great Depression'. *Review of Radical Political Economy.* 8, 1

Millar, J. (1983) *Family Men.* Cohort Study Working Paper no. 4

Miller, M. J. (1981) *Foreign Workers in Western Europe.* Praeger

Mincer, Jacob (1962) 'Labour force participation of married women: a study of labour supply' in National Bureau of Economic Research *Aspects of Labour Economics: A Conference of the Universities-National Bureau Committee for Economic Research.* Princeton University Press

Mincer, Jacob (1966) 'Labour participation and unemployment: a review of recent evidence' in Robert A. Gordon and Margaret S. Gordon (eds.) *Prosperity and Unemployment.* John Wiley and Sons

Modell, J. (1977) *The Economics and Politics of Racial Accommodation.* University of Illinois Press

Moen, P. (1979) 'Family impacts of the 1975 depression: duration of unemployment'. *Journal of Marriage and the Family.* 41, 561–72

Molyneux, M. (1979) 'Beyond the domestic labour debate', *New Left Review.* 116, 3–24

Monopolies Commission (1968) *Man-made cellulosic fibres: a report on the supply of man-made cellulosic fibres.* HMSO

Moore, R. (1977) 'Migrants and the class structure of Western Europe'. In Scase (ed.)

Moore, W. E. (1966) 'Changes in occupational structures'. In N. J. Smelser and S. M. Kipset (eds.), *Social Structure and Mobility in Economic Development*. Aldine. 194–212

Moorehouse, H. R. (1976) 'Attitudes to class and class relationships in Britain'. *Sociology*. 10, 3

Moorehouse, H. R. (1983) 'American automobiles and workers' dreams'. *Sociological Review*. 31, 3

More, C. (1979) *Skill and the English Working Class, 1870–1914*. Croom Helm

Morgan, K. (1983) 'Restructuring steel', *International Journal of Urban and Regional Research*. 7, no. 2

Morrey, C. R. (1976) *1971 Census: Demographic, Social and Economic Indices for Wards in Greater London*. 2, GLC Research Report no. 10

Morris, L. D. (1981) 'Women in poverty'. *Anthro. Quarterly*. July 1981

Morris, L. D. (1983 a) 'Local social networks and post-redundancy labour-market experience'. Working paper, University College Swansea

Morris, L. D. (1983 b) 'Renegotiation of the domestic division of labour in the context of male redundancy'. Paper presented to British Sociological Association Conference

Morris, L. D. (1983 c) 'Redundancy and patterns of household finance'. Working paper, University College Swansea

Morris, L. D. (1983 d) 'Patterns of social activity and domestic organisation – a study of redundant steel-workers and their wives'. Working paper, University College Swansea

Moscovici, S. (1976) *Social Influence and Social Change*. Academic Press

Moser, C. (1978) 'Informal sector or petty commodity production'. *World Development*. 6, 9/10, 1041–64

Moser, C. and Scott, W. (1961) *British Towns*. Oliver and Boyd

Moss, P. and Fonda, N. (1980) *Work and the Family*. Temple Smith

Moylan, S. and Davies, B. (1980) 'The disadvantages of the unemployed'. *Employment Gazette*. August, 830–1

Moylan, S. and Davies, B. (1981) 'The flexibility of the unemployed'. *Employment Gazette*

Moylan, S., Millar, J. and Davies, B. (1982) 'Unemployment – the year after'. *Employment Gazette*. 90, 8, 334–40

Mueller, D. C. (1983) (ed.) *The Political Economy of Growth*. Yale University Press

Mueller-Jentsch, W. and Sperling, H. J. (1978) 'Economic development, labour conflicts and the industrial relations system in West Germany'. In Crouch and Pizzorno (eds.)

Mullins, D. (1979) 'Asian retailing in Croydon'. *New Community*. 7, 403–5

Murgatroyd, L. (1981) 'De-industrialisation in Lancaster: a review of the changing structure of employment in the Lancaster district'. Lancaster Regionalism Group Working Paper 1, University of Lancaster

Murgatroyd, L., Savage, M., Shapiro, D., Urry, J., Walby, S., Warde, A. and Mark-Lawson, J. (1984) *Localities, Class and Gender*. Pion Books

Murgatroyd, L. and Urry, J. (1983) 'The restructuring of a local economy: the case of Lancaster'. In J. Anderson, S. Duncan, R. Hudson, *Redundant Spaces in Cities and Regions*. Academic Press. 67–98

Murgatroyd, L. and Urry, J. (1984) 'The class and gender restructuring of the Lancaster economy, 1950–80'. In L. Murgatroyd *et al.* (1984)

Myrdal, Alva and Klein, Viola (1956) *Women's Two Roles*. Routledge and Kegan Paul

Narendranathan, W., Nickell, S. and Metcalf, D. (1982) *An Investigation into the Incidence and Dynamic Structure of Sickness and Unemployment in Britain,*

1965–1975. Centre for Labour Economics

National Foundation for Educational Research

Neustadt, D. (1980) 'They also serve: waitering a changing union, and Chinatown struggles'. *Village Voice*. 12 May

New Survey of London Life and Labour (1935) 9 vols. King

Newbould, C. D. (1970) *Management and merger activity*. Guthstead

Newby, H. (1977) *The Deferential Worker*. Allen Lane

Newby, H. (1982) 'The state of research into social stratification in Britain', ESRC

Nichols, T. and Armstrong, P. (1979) *Workers Divided*. Fontana

Nichols, T. and Beynon, H. (1977) *Living with Capitalism: Class Relations and the Modern Factory*. Routledge and Kegan Paul

Nisbet, R. (1959) 'The decline and fall of social class'. *Pacific Sociological Review*. 2

Nolan, Peter and Edwards, P. K. (n.d.) 'Homogenise, divide and rule: an essay on segmented work, divided workers'. (Unpublished paper)

Nordlinger, E. A. (1967) *The Working Class Tories*. McGibbon and Kee

Norris, G. (1978) 'Industrial paternalism, capitalism and local labour markets'. *Sociology*. 12, 469–89

Norris, G. (1982) 'Towards a sociology of local labour markets'. In *Bibliographies on Local Labour Markets and the Informal Economy*. (ed.) J. Laite, SSRC

North Tyneside Community Development Project (1978) 'In and out of work: a study of unemployment, low pay and income maintenance services'

Nowikowski, S. (1980) 'The social situation of an Asian community in Manchester'. Unpublished PhD thesis, University of Manchester

Nowikowski, S. (1984) 'Snakes and ladders: Asian business in Britain'. In Ward, R. and Jenkins, R. (eds.)

Nowikowski, S. and Ward, R. (1979) 'Middle class and British? An analysis of South Asians in suburbia'. *New Community*. 7, 1–10

Oakley, A. (1972) *Sex, Gender and Society*. Temple Smith

Oakley, A. (1974) *The Sociology of Housework*. Martin Robertson

OECD (1976) *The 1974–5 Recession and the Employment of Women*. Organisation for Economic Co-operation and Development

OECD (1977) *Towards Full Employment and Price Stability*. Paris

OECD (1982) *Information Activities, Electronics and Telecommunications Technologies, 1*

Offe, C. (1976) *Industry and Inequality*. Edward Arnold

Office of Population Censuses and Surveys (1982) *Labour Force Survey 1981*. OPCS LFS no. 3, HMSO

Olson, M. (1982) *The Rise and Decline of Nations*. Yale University Press

Paci, M. (1973) *Mercato del lavoro e classi sociali in Italia*. Bologna, Il Mulino

Paci, M. (1979) 'Class structure in Italian society', *Archives européennes de sociologie*. 20

Pahl, J. (1983) 'The allocation of money and the structuring of inequality within marriage', *Sociological Review*. 31, 2, May

Pahl, R. E. (1974) 'Instrumentality and community in the process of urbanization', *Sociological Inquiry*

Pahl, R. E. (1980) 'Employment, work and the domestic division of labour', *International Journal of Urban and Regional Research*. 4, 1, 1–20

Pahl, R. E. (1985 a) 'The restructuring of capital, the local political economy and household work strategies: all forms of work in context'. In Urry, J. and Gregory, D. *Social Relations and Spatial Structures*. Macmillan

Pahl, R. E. (1984) *Divisions of Labour*. Basil Blackwell

Pahl, R. E. and Dennett, J. H. (1981) *Industry and Employment on the Isle of Sheppey*. Progress Report to SSRC. Work Strategies Unit, University of Kent

Pahl, R. E. and Gershuny, J. I. (1979) 'Work outside employment: some preliminary speculations'. *New Universities Quarterly.* Winter, 121–35

Pahl, R. E. and Wallace, C. D. (1982) 'The restructuring of capital, the local political economy and household work strategies: all forms of work in context'. Paper prepared for the Xth World Congress of Sociology, Mexico City. Work Strategies Unit, University of Kent

Pahl, R. E. and Wallace, C. D. (1985 b) 'Household work strategies in an economic recession', to be published in *Beyond Employment: Household, Gender and Subsistence.* (eds.) Redclift, N. and Mingione, E. Basil Blackwell

Panitch, L. (1977) 'Profits and politics: labour and the crisis of British corporatism'. *Politics and Society.* 7

Panitch, L. (1981) 'Trade unions and the capitalist state', *New Left Review.* 125

Parker, S. (1980) *Older Workers and Retirement.* HMSO

Parker, S. (1982) *Work and Retirement.* Allen and Unwin

Parker, H. (1982) *The Moral Hazards of Social Benefits.* Institute of Economic Affairs Research Monograph 37

Parkin, F. (1967) 'Working class conservatism: A theory of political deviance'. *British Journal of Sociology.* 18

Parkin, F. (1979) *Marxism and Class Theory. A Bourgeois Critique.* Tavistock

Parkinson, C. H. Northcote and Lancaster, O. (1958) *Parkinson's Law: The Pursuit of Progress.* John Murray

Parsons, T. (1937) *The Structure of Social Action.* Free Press

Parsons, T. (1964) 'Evolutionary universals in society'. *American Sociological Review.* 29

Parsons, T. (1966) *Societies: Evolutionary and Comparative Perspectives.* Prentice Hall

Payne, R. L., Warr, P. B. and Hartley, J. (1984) 'Social class and the experience of unemployment'. *Sociology of Health and Illness.* 6, 152–74

Peach, C. (1968) *West Indian Migration to Britain.* Oxford University Press

Pearlin, L. I. and Lieberman, M. A. (1979) 'Social sources of emotional distress'. *Research in Community and Mental Health.* 1, 217–48

Perkins, Teresa (1983) 'A new form of employment: a case study of women's part-time work in Coventry'. In Evans, M. and Ungerson, C.

Phillipson, C. (1983) *Capitalism and the Construction of Old Age.* Macmillan

Pichelmann, K. and Wagner, M. (1983) 'Full employment at all costs: Trends in employment and labour market policy in Austria 1975–1983'. Institut für Hohere Studien

Piore, M. J. (1973) 'The role of immigration in industrial growth: a case study of the origins and character of Puerto Rican migration to Boston'. Working paper 112, Dept of Economics, MIT

Piore, M. J. (1979) *Birds of Passage: Migrant Labour and Industrial Societies.* Cambridge University Press

Piore, M. J. (1980) 'The technological foundations of dualism and discontinuity'. In Suzanne Berger and Michael Piore *Dualism and Discontinuity in Industrial Society.* Cambridge University Press

Pizzorno, A. (1978) 'Political exchange and collective identity in industrial conflict'. In Crouch and Pizzorno (eds.)

Pizzorno, A. (1981) 'Interests and parties in pluralism'. In Berger (ed.)

Platt, S. (1983) 'Unemployment and parasuicide in Edinburgh 1968–1982'. *Unemployment Unit Bulletin.* 10, 4–5

Platt, S. (1984) 'Unemployment and suicidal behaviour: A review of the literature'. *Social Science and Medicine.* 19, 93–115

Pollard, S. (1959) *A History of Labour in Sheffield.* Liverpool University Press

Pollert, Anna (1981) *Girls, Wives, Factory Lives.* Macmillan

Porat, M. (1977) *The Information Economy.* US Department of Commerce

Poulantzas, N. (1975) *Classes in Contemporary Capitalism.* New Left Books

Pratten, C. F. (1976) *Labour Productivity Differentials within International Companies.* Cambridge University Press

Pye, L. and Verba, S. (eds.) (1965) *Political Culture and Political Development.* Princeton University Press

Pyke, F. (1982) 'The redundant worker: work, skill and security in an engineering city'. Working Paper no. 18, Dept of Sociology and Social Policy, University of Durham

Radloff, L. (1975) 'Sex differences in depression: the effects of occupational and marital status'. *Sex Roles.* 1, 249–65

Rainie, A. L. and Stirling, J. (1981) 'Plant closure: the trade union response'. Occasional paper, Newcastle upon Tyne Polytechnic

Rainwater, L. (1966) 'Fear and the house-as-haven in the lower class'. *Journal of the American Institute of Planners.* 32, 23–31

Rainwater, L. (1974) *Inequality and Justice.* Aldine

Ratcliff, K. S. (1980) 'On Marshall and Funch's critique of "Mental illness and the economy"'. *Journal of Health and Social Behavior.* 21, 389–91

Ratcliffe, P. (1981) *Racism and Reaction.* Routledge and Kegan Paul

Rees, A. (1966) 'Information networks in labour markets'. *American Economic Review.* 56, 559–66

Reeve, C. (1976) 'Refus du travail', *Spartacus.* July/August

Regini, M. (1982) 'Changing relationships between labour and the state in Italy: Towards a neo-corporatist system?'. In Lehmbruch and Schmitter (eds.)

Regini, M. (1983) 'I tentativi Italiani di "Patto Sociale" a Cavallo degli Anni Ottanta: Velleita' da *Late-comer.* o Linea di Tendenza Relistica?'. University of Milan, Dept of Sociology

Reid, G. L. (1972) 'Job search and the effectiveness of job finding methods'. *Industry and Labour Relations Review.* 25, 4, 479–95

Rex, J. and Moore, R. (1967) *Race, Community and Conflict.* Oxford University Press

Rex, J. and Tomlinson, S. (1979) *Colonial Immigrants in a British City.* Routledge and Kegan Paul

Richardson, J. J. and Moon, J. (1984) 'The politics of unemployment in Britain'. *Political Quarterly.* 55, 29–37

Richta, R. *et al.* (1969) *Civilization at the Crossroads.* International Arts and Sciences Press

Rimmer, L. and Popay, J. (1982) 'Employment trends and the family'. Study Commission on the Family

Rist, R. C. (1979) 'Migration and marginality: guestworkers in Germany and France'. *Daedalus.* Spring

Roberts, B. (1973) *Organizing Stranger.* University of Texas Press

Robertson, J. (1982) 'What comes after the welfare state?'. *Futures.* 14 (1), 24–37

Roberts, K. *et al.* (1977) *The Fragmentary Class Structure.* Heinemann

Robinson, O. and Wallace, J. (1984 a) *Part-time Employment and Sex Discrimination Legislation in Great Britain.* Dept of Employment

Robinson, O. and Wallace, J. (1984 b) 'Growth and utilisation of part-time employment in Great Britain'. *Employment Gazette.* 92, 9, 391–7

Robins, L. and Wormwald E. (1979) 'The political attitudes of unemployed teachers'. *Teaching Political Science.* 6, 275–90

Rose, E. J. B. and associates (1969) *Colour and Citizenship: A Report on British Race Relations.* Oxford University Press

Rosenberg, S. (1977) 'The Marxian reserve army of labor and the dual labor market'.

Politics and Society. 7

Rosenstone, S. J. (1982) 'Economic adversity and voter turnout'. *American Journal of Political Science.* 26, 25–46

Ross, A. M. and Hartman, P. T. (1960) *Changing Patterns of Industrial Conflict.* Wiley

Routh, G. (1980) *Occupation and Pay in Great Britain, 1906–1979.* Macmillan

Roy, A. (1981) 'Vulnerability factors and depression in men'. *British Journal of Psychiatry.* 138, 75–7

Rubery, Jill (1978) 'Structured labour markets, worker organisation and low pay'. Cambridge Journal of Economics. 2, March

Rubery, Jill and Tarling, Roger (1982) 'Women in the recession'. *Socialist Economic Review 1982.* Merlin Press

Rubery, J., Tarling, R. and Wilkinson, F. (1983 a) 'Social welfare provision and employment: a case for income maintenance'. In Bekemans, L. (ed.) *Social Security and Employment: New Patterns in Employment*, 5, The Netherlands, Vangarain Essen

Rubery, J., Tarling, R. and Wilkinson, F. (1983 b) 'Inflation, employment and income distribution in the recession'. Report to Directorate General of Social Affairs, EEC, Study no. 830234

Rubery, J., Tarling, R. and Wilkinson, F. (1984 a) 'Industrial relations issues in the 1980s: an economic analysis'. In Poole, M. *et al. Industrial Relations in the Future.* Routledge and Kegan Paul

Rubery, J., Tarling, R. and Wilkinson, F. (1984 b) 'Government policy and the labour market: the case of the UK'. *Federation News.* General Federation of Trade Unions

Rubery, J. and Wilkinson, F. (1981) 'Outwork and segmented labour markets'. In Wilkinson, F. (ed.) (1981 a)

Ruebens, B. (1970) *The Hard-to-Employ: European Programs.* Columbia University Press

Runciman, W. G. (1966) *Relative Deprivation and Social Justice.* Routledge and Kegan Paul

Rushton, P. (1979) 'Marxism, domestic labour and the capitalist economy'. In C. C. Harris (ed.) *The Sociology of the Family.* Sociological Review Monograph 28, 32–48

Sachs, J. D. (1979) 'Wages, profits and macroeconomic adjustment: a comparative study'. *Brookings Papers on Economic Activity 1979.*

Sachs, J. D. (1980) 'The changing cyclical behaviour of wages and prices'. *American Economic Review*

Sahlin, M. (1974) *Stone Age Economics.* Aldine-Atherton

Salaman, G. (1974) *Community and Occupation.* Cambridge University Press

Sarlvik, B. and Crewe, I. (1983) *Decade of Dealignment.* Cambridge University Press

Saunders, P. (1981) *Social Theory and the Urban Question.* Hutchinson

Saunders, P. (1983) *Urban Politics.* Hutchinson

Scase, R. (ed.) (1977) *Industrial Society: Class, Cleavage and Control.* George Allen and Unwin

Scase, R. and Goffee, R. (1980) *The Real World of the Small Business Owner.* Croom Helm

Scharpf, F. (1981) 'The political economy of inflation and unemployment in western Europe: an outline'. Berlin: Internationales Institut für Management und Werwaltung

Schlozman, K. and Verba, S. (1979) *Injury to Insult – Unemployment, Class and Politics.* Harvard University Press

Schmidt, M. G. (1982 a) 'Does corporatism matter? Economic crisis, politics and rates of unemployment in capitalist democracies in the 1970s'. In Lehmbruch and

Schmitter (eds.) (1982)

Schmidt, M. G. (1982 b) 'The role of the parties in shaping macroeconomic policy'. In Castles (ed.) (1982)

Schmitter, P. C. (1974) 'Still the century of corporatism?'. *Review of Politics.* 36

Schmitter, P. C. (1981) 'Interest intermediation and regime governability in contemporary Western Europe and North America'. In Berger (ed.) (1981)

Schmitter, P. C. (1983) ' "Neo-corporatism", "consensus", "governability" and "democracy" in the management of crisis in contemporary advanced industrial/capitalist societies'. Florence European University Institute

Scitovsky, T. (1978) 'Market power and inflation'. *Economica.* 45

Scitovsky, T. (1980) 'Can capitalism survive? – An old question in a new setting'. *American Economic Review.* 70

Scott, J. (1979) *Corporations, Classes and Capitalism.* Hutchinson

Scott, W. H., Banks, J. A., Halsey, A. H. and Lupton, T. (1956) *Technical Change and Industrial Relations.* Liverpool University Press

Seabrook, J. (1982) *Unemployment.* Quartet

Seeley, R. J., Sim, R. A. and Loosley, E. (1956) *Crestwood Heights.* John Wiley

Segenberger, W. (1981) 'Labour market segmentation and the business cycle'. In Wilkinson (ed.) (1981 a)

Segenberger, W. (1983) 'The gradual re-activation of the labour reserve army mechanism'. Institut für Sozialwissenchaftliche Forschung

Sennett, R. (1977) *The Fall of Public Man.* Cambridge University Press

Shalev, M. (1983) 'Strikes and the crisis: industrial conflict and unemployment in the Western nations'. *Economic and Industrial Democracy.* 4

Shepherd, D. M. and Barraclough, B. M. (1980) 'Work and suicide: An empirical investigation'. *British Journal of Psychiatry.* 136, 469–78

Shorter, E. (1976) *The Making of the Modern Family.* Collins

Showler, B. and Sinfield, A. (eds.) (1981) *The Workless State: Studies in Unemployment.* Martin Robertson

Sinfield, A. (1968) *The Long-Term Unemployed.* Organization for Economic Co-operation and Development

Sinfield, A. (1981 a) *What Unemployment Means.* Martin Robertson

Sinfield, A. (1981 b) 'Unemployment in an unequal society'. In B. Showler and A. Sinfield (eds.) 122–66

Singelmann, J. (1978) *From Agriculture to Services: The Transformation of Industrial Employment.* Sage

Singelmann, J. and Browning, H. L. (1980) 'Industrial transformation and occupational change in the US, 1960–70'. *Social Forces.* 59 (September), 246–64

Singelmann, J. and Tienda, M. (1979) 'Changes in industry structure and female employment in Latin America, 1950–70'. *Sociology and Social Research.* 63 (July), 745–69

Smart, R. G. (1979) 'Drinking problems among employed, unemployed and shift workers'. *Journal of Occupational Medicine.* 11, 731–6

Smith, D. J. (1974) *Racial Disadvantage in Employment.* Broadsheet no. 544. Political and Economic Planning

Smith, D. J. (1977) *Racial Disadvantage in Britain.* Pelican

Smith, D. J. (1981) *Unemployment And Racial Minorities.* No. 594. Policy Studies Institute

Snell, M. W., Glucklich, P. and Povall, M. (1981) *Equal Pay and Opportunities.* Research Paper no. 20, Dept of Employment

Solidarity (1983) 1, 3, back page

Sorrentino, C. (1981) 'Unemployment in international perspective'. In B. Showler and A. Sinfield (eds.). 167–214

Sparrow, P. (1983) 'An analysis of British work values'. *Work and Society*. Report no. 8

Spruit, I. P. (1982) 'Unemployment and health in macro-social analysis'. *Social Science and Medicine*. 16, 1903–17

Stafford, E., Jackson, P. and Banks, M. (1980) 'Employment, work involvement and mental health in less qualified young people'. *Journal of Occupational Psychology*. 53, 291–304

Stankiewicz, F. (1982) *Travail noir, productions domestiques et entraide*. Cahiers de l'Observation du Changement Social, CNRS

Steinerg, L. D., Catalano, R. and Dooley, D. (1981) 'Economic antecedents of child abuse and neglect'. *Child Development*. 52, 975–85

Stephens, J. D. (1979) *The Transition from Capitalism to Socialism*. Macmillan

Stewart, A., Prandy, K. and Blackburn, R. M. (1980) *Social Stratification and Occupations*. Macmillan

Stillwell, F. (1968) 'Location of industry and business efficiency'. *Business Ratios*. 2, 5–15

Stokes, G. (1984) 'Work, unemployment and leisure'. *Leisure Studies*. 2, 269–86

Stokes, G. and Cochrane, R. (1984) 'The relationship between national levels of unemployment and the rate of admission to mental hospitals in England and Wales, 1950–1976'. *Social Psychiatry*. (In press)

Stone, K. (1975) 'The origins of job structures in the steel industry'. In R. C. Edwards, M. Reich, and D. Gordon (eds.) *Labour Market Segmentation*. D. C. Heath

Street, D. and Leggett, J. S. (1961) 'Economic deprivation and extremism: A study of unemployed negroes'. *American Journal of Sociology*. 67, 53–7

Tambs-Lyche, H. (1980) *London Patidars: A Case Study in Urban Ethnicity*. Routledge and Kegan Paul

Tarling, R. (1981 a) 'Short-run employment functions: their evolution failure and replacement'. Report to Director-General, V, EEC Study no. 79/15

Tarling, R. (1981 b) 'The relation of employment to output: an alternative view'. In F. Wilkinson (ed.) (1981 a)

Tarling, R. (1982) *Unemployment and Crime*. Home Office Research and Planning Unit, no. 14, HMSO

Tarling, R. and Wilkinson, F. (1977 b) 'The social contract: post-war incomes policies and their inflationary impact'. *Cambridge Journal of Economics*. 1, December

Tarling, R. and Wilkinson, F. (1982 a) 'Changes in the inter-industry structure of earnings in the post-war period', *Cambridge Journal of Economics*. 3, September

Tarling, R. and Wilkinson, F. (1982 b) 'The movement of real wages and the development of collective bargaining in the period 1855 to 1920'. *Contributions to Political Economy*, 1

Tarling, R. and Wilkinson, F. (forthcoming) 'Income distribution, wage income and the role of the State: some policy issues in the Greek labour market'. Report of the Centre of Economic Planning and Research, Athens

Taylor-Gooby, P. (1982) 'Two cheers for the welfare state: public opinion and private welfare'. *Journal of Public Policy*. 2, 4, October, 319–46

Taylor-Gooby, P. (1983) 'Legitimation deficit, public opinion and the welfare state'. *Sociology*. 17, 2 May

Thatcher, H. R. (1979) 'Labour supply and employment trends'. In Blackaby, F. (ed.) *Deindustrialisation*. Heinemann

Thomas, L. E., McCabe, E. and Berry, J. E. (1980) 'Unemployment and family stress: A reassessment'. *Family Relations*. 29, 517–24

Thurow, L. C. (1980) *The Zero-sum Society*. Basic Books

Thurow, L. C. (1983) *Dangerous Currents: The State of Economics*. Oxford University Press

Tiffany, D. W., Cowan, J. R. and Tiffany, P. M. (1970) *The Unemployed: A Social-Psychological Portrait.* Prentice-Hall

Tiggemann, M. and Winefield, A. H. (1980) 'Some psychological effects of unemployment in school-leavers'. *Australian Journal of Social Issues.* 15, 269–76

Tittle, G. R., Villemez, W. J. and Smith, D. A. (1981) 'One step forward, two steps back: more on the class/criminality controversy'. *American Sociological Review.* 47, 3, 435–8

Todd, J. and Butcher, B. (1982) *Electoral registration in 1981.* Office of Population Censuses and Surveys

Touraine, A. (1969) *The Post-industrial Society – Tomorrow's Social History: Classes, Conflict and Culture in the Programmed Society.* Random House

Touraine, A. (1974) *The Post Industrial Society.* Wildwood House

Townsend, P. (1979) *Poverty in the United Kingdom.* Penguin

Townsend, P. and Davidson, N. (1980) *Inequalities in Health.* Penguin

Tracy, M. (1979) *Retirement Age Practices in Ten Industrial Societies, 1960–1976.* Geneva ISSA

Treiman, D. (1970) 'Industrialization and social stratification'. In Lauman (ed.) (1970)

Trew, K. and Kilpatrick, R. (1983) *The Daily Life of Unemployed – Social and Psychological Dimensions.* Final Report to the SSRC

Troyna, B. and Smith, D. I. (eds.) (1983) *Racism, School and the Labour Market.* National Youth Bureau

Turner, C. (1967) 'Conjugal roles and social networks'. *Human Relations.* 20

Turner, R. (1980 a) 'We're a' Jock Tamson's bairns: central lowland Scotland as a culture area'. (Unpublished)

Turner, R. (1980 b) 'An ethnographic study of a Scottish Lowlands village'. SSRC Final Report, British Lending Library, Boston Spa, HR 5571/1

United Nations (1979) *Labour Supply and Migration in Europe: Demographic Dimensions 1950–75 and Prospects.* United Nations

University of Liverpool, Dept of Social Science (1954) *The Dock Worker.* Liverpool University Press

Urry, J. (1980) 'Paternalism, management and localities'. Lancaster Regionalism Group Working Paper 2, University of Lancaster

Urry, J. (1981) 'Localities, regions and social class'. *International Journal of Urban and Regional Research* 5, 455–74

Urry, J. (1983) 'Some notes on realism and the analysis of space'. *International Journal of Urban and Regional Research.* 7, 122–7

Urry, J. (1984 a) 'De-industrialisation, households and politics'. In L. Murgatroyd *et al.*

Urry, J. (1984 b) 'Social relations, space and time'. In Gregory, D. and Urry, J. (eds.) *Social Relations and Spatial Structures.* Macmillan

Useem, B. and Useem, M. (1979) 'Government legitimacy and political stability'. *Social Forces.* 57, 840–52

Verba, S. and Schlozman, K. L. (1950) 'Unemployment, class consciousness, and radical politics: what didn't happen in the thirties'. *Journal of Politics.* 39, 291–323

Verbrugge, L. M. (1983) 'Multiple roles and physical health of women and men'. *Journal of Health and Social Behavior.* 24, 16–30

Vietorisz, T., Mier, R. and Ginlin, J. (1975) 'Subemployment: exclusion and inadequacy indices'. *Monthly Labour Review.* May, 3–11

Villa, P. (1981) 'Labour market segmentation and the construction industry in Italy'. In Wilkinson (ed.) (1981 a)

Walby, S. (1983 a) 'Patriarchal structures: the case of unemployment'. In Eva Gamarnikow and David Morgan (eds.). *Gender, Class and Work.* Heinemann

Walby, S. (1983 b) 'Women's unemployment, patriarchy and capitalism'. *Socialist*

Economic Review 1983. Merlin Press

Walby, S. (1984) 'Gender and unemployment, patriarchal and capitalist relations in the restructuring of gender relations in employment and unemployment'. Unpublished PhD, University of Essex

Walby, S. (1985 a) 'Some spatial and historical variations in women's unemployment'. In L. Murgatroyd, D. Shapiro, J. Urry, S. Walby, A. Warde and J. Mark-Lawson (eds.). *Localities, Class and Gender.* Pion Press

Walby, S. (1985 b) 'Women and unemployment: a review of current theories'. In L. Murgatroyd, D. Shapiro, J. Urry, S. Walby, A. Warde and J. Mark-Lawson (eds.) *Localities, Class and Gender.* Pion Press

Waldinger, R. (1982) 'The integration of the new immigrants'. *Law and Contemporary Problems.* V45, 2

Waldinger, R. (1983) 'Ethnic enterprise and industrial change: a case study of the New York garment industry'. PhD Dissertation, Dept of Sociology, Harvard University

Waldinger, R. (1984 a) 'Immigration and industrial change: a case study of the New York apparel industry'. In Marta Tienda and George Borjas, (eds.) *Hispanic Workers in the US Economy.* Academic Press

Waldinger, R. (1984 b) 'Ethnic enterprise in the garment industry: Latin Americans in New York City'. *Social Problems.* June

Walker, A. (1980) 'The social creation of poverty and dependency in old age'. *Journal of Social Policy.* 9, 1, 49-75

Walker, A. (1981 a) 'South Yorkshire: the economic and social impact of unemployment'. In B. Crick (ed.) *Unemployment.* Methuen, 74-87

Walker, A. (1981 b) 'Towards a political economy of old age'. *Ageing and Society.* 1, 1, 73-94

Walker, A. (1982 a) *Unqualified and Underemployed.* Macmillan

Walker, A. (1982 b) 'The social consequences of early retirement'. *The Political Quarterly.* 53, 1, 61-72

Wall, T. D. and Clegg, C. W. (1981) 'Individual strain and organizational functioning'. *British Journal of Clinical Psychology.* 20, 135-6

Wallace, C. D., Pahl, R. E. and Dennett, J. H. (1981) *Housing and Residential Areas on the Isle of Sheppey.* Progress Report to SSRC. Work Strategies Unit, University of Kent

Wallace, C. (1984) *Informal Work in Two Sheppey Neighbourhoods.* ESRC Final Report. Grant no. G00 230036

Wallman, S. (1978) 'The boundaries of race: processes of ethnicity in England'. *Man.* 13, 2

Wallman, S. (ed.) (1979 a) *Social Anthropology of Work.* Association of Social Anthropologists Monograph 19, Academic Press

Wallman, S. (1979 b) 'The scope for ethnicity'. In *Ethnicity at Work.* (ed.) S. Wallman, Macmillan

Wallman, S. (1984) *Eight London Households.* Tavistock

Wallman, S., Dhooge, Y., Goldman, A. and Kosmin, B. A. (1980) 'Ethnography by proxy: strategies for research in the inner city': *Ethnos.* October 1980, 1-2

Wallman, S. *et al.* (1982) *Living in South London.* Gower Press, LSE

Ward, R. (ed.) (1984) *Race and Residence in Britain.* Monographs on Ethnic Relations 2. ESRC, Research Unit on Ethnic Relations, University of Aston

Ward, R. and Jenkins, R. (eds.) (1984) *Ethnic Communities in Business.* Cambridge University Press

Ward, R. and Nowikowski, S. (1981) 'Settlement in the suburbs: an analysis of Asians in Manchester'. *International Journal of Contemporary Sociology.* 18, 102-34

Ward, R. and Reeves, F. (1980) 'West Indians in business in Britain'. (Memorandum submitted to the Home Affairs Committee Race Relations and Immigration Sub-Committee, Session 1980–1). House of Commons, 15 December

Warren, K. (1971) 'Growth, technical change and planning problems in heavy industry with reference to the chemical industry'. In M. Chisholm and G. Manners (eds.) *Spatial policy problems of the UK economy.* Cambridge University Press

Warr, P. B. (1978) 'A study of psychological well-being'. *British Journal of Psychology.* 69, 111–21

Warr, P. B. (1982) 'A national study of non-financial employment commitment'. *Journal of Occupational Psychology.* 55, 297–312

Warr, P. B. (1983 a) 'Twelve questions about unemployment and health'. Paper presented to Workshop on local labour markets, Manchester, November 1983

Warr, P. B. (1983 b) 'Work, jobs and unemployment'. *Bulletin of the British Psychological Society.* 36, 305–11

Warr, P. B. (1984 a) 'Job loss, unemployment and psychological well-being'. In V. Allen and E. van de Vliert (eds.) *Role Transitions.* Plenum Press

Warr, P. B. (1984 b) 'Work and unemployment'. In P. J. D. Drenth, H. Thierry, P. J. Willems and C. J. de Wolff (eds.) *Handbook of Work and Organization Psychology.* Wiley

Warr, P. B. (1984 c) 'Reported behaviour changes after job loss'. *British Journal of Social Psychology.* 23, 271–5

Warr, P. B. (1984 d) 'Economic recession and mental health: a review of research'. SAPU Memo 609, Sheffield

Warr, P. B., Banks, M. H. and Ullah, P. (1984) 'The experience of unemployment among black and white urban teenagers'. *British Journal of Psychology.* (In press)

Warr, P. B. and Jackson, P. R. (1983 a) 'Self-esteem and unemployment among young workers'. *Le Travail Humain.* 46, 355–66

Warr, P. B. and Jackson, P. R. (1983 b) 'Men without jobs: some correlates of age and length of unemployment'. SAPU Memo 593, Sheffield

Warr, P. B. and Jackson, P. R. (1984) 'Men without jobs: some correlates of age and length of unemployment'. *Journal of Occupational Psychology.* 57, 77–85

Warr, P. B., Jackson, P. R. and Banks, M. H. (1982) 'Duration of unemployment and psychological well-being in young men and women'. *Current Psychological Research.* 2, 207–14

Warr, P. B. and Parry, G. (1982) 'Paid employment and women's psychological well-being'. *Psychological Bulletin.* 91, 498–516

Warr, P. B. and Payne, R. L. (1982) 'Experiences of strain and pleasure among British adults'. *Social Science and Medicine.* 16, 1691–7

Warr, P. B. and Payne, R. L. (1983) 'Social class and reported changes in behaviour after job loss'. *Journal of Applied Social Psychology.* 13, 206–22

Warren, K. (1971) 'Growth, technical change and planning problems in heavy industry with reference to the chemical industry'. In M. Chisholm and G. Manners (eds.) *Spatial Policy Problems of the UK Economy.* Cambridge University Press

Watkins, S. J. (1982) 'Recession and health: the policy implications, paper presented at the WHO Workshop on Health Policy in Relation to Unemployment in the Community, Leeds

Watson, J. (ed.) (1977) *Between Two Cultures: Migrants and Minorities in Britain.* Basil Blackwell

Watson, T. J. (1977) *The Personnel Managers.* Routledge & Kegan Paul

Weber, M. (1930) *The Protestant Ethic and the Spirit of Capitalism.* Unwin University Books

Wedderburn, D. (1974) (ed.) *Poverty, Inequality and Class Structure.* Cambridge University Press

Werbner, P. (1979) 'Avoiding the ghetto: Pakistani migrants and settlement shifts in Manchester'. *New Community.* 7, 376–89

Werbner, P. (1984) 'From rags to riches: Manchester Pakistanis in the textile trade'. In Ward, R. and Jenkins, R. (eds.)

Westergaard, J. (1984) 'Class of '84'. *New Socialist.* Jan/Feb, 30–6

White, Michael (1983) *Long Term Unemployment and Labour Markets.* no. 622, Policy Studies Institute

White, Michael and Goberdhian, A. (1984) *Job Evaluation and the Working of the Equal Pay Act.* Policy Studies Institute

Whyte, W. H. (1960) *The Organisation Man.* Penguin

Wilder, C. S. (1980) *Selected Health Characteristics by Occupation, United States 1975–6.* US Department of Health and Human Services

Wilkinson, F. (ed.) (1981 a) *The Dynamics of Labour Market Segmentation.* Academic Press

Wilkinson, F. (1984) 'Worker organisation, state expenditure and capitalist crises'. *Etudes d'économie politique.* 1

Wilkinson, F. and Turner, H. A. (1972) 'The wage-tax spiral and labour militancy'. In D. Jackson, H. A. Turner and F. Wilkinson, *Do Trade Unions Cause Inflation?* Cambridge University Press

Williams, R. G. A. (1983) 'Kinship migration strategies among settled Londoners. Two responses to population pressure'. *British Journal of Sociology.* 34, 3 September

Williamson, B. (1982) *Class, culture and commodity. A study of social change in Mining through Biography.* Routledge and Kegan Paul

Wilson, K. L. and Portes, A. (1980) 'Immigrant enclaves: an analysis of the labor market experiences of Cubans in Miami'. *American Journal of Sociology.* 5, 86, 295–319

Wilson, K. L., Portes, A. and Martin, W. Allen (1982) 'Ethnic enclaves: a comparison of the Cuban and black economies in Miami'. *American Journal of Sociology.* 5, 88, 135–60

Winter, J. M. (1983) 'Unemployment, nutrition and infant mortality in Britain 1920–1950'. In J. John, D. Schwefel and H. Zöllner (eds.) *Influence of Economic Instability on Health.* Springer

Wong, B. (1979) *A Chinese-American Community.* Chopmen

Wood, D. (1980) 'Managerial reactions to job redundancy through early retirement'. *Sociological Review.* 28, 4, 783–807

Wood, D. (1982) *DHSS, Cohort Study of Unemployment: Men.* Working Paper no. 1

Wood, S. (ed.) (1982) *The Degradation of Work: Skill, Deskilling and the Labour Process.* Hutchinson

Wood, S. and Cohen, J. (1977–8) 'Approaches to the study of redundancy'. *Industry Relations Journal.* 8, 4, 19–27

Woodward, J. L. and Roper, E. (1950) 'Political activity of American citizens'. *American Political Science Review.* 872–85

Wright, E. O. (1978) *Class, Crisis and the State.* New Left Books

Wright, E. O. and Singelmann, J. (1978) 'Proletarianization in advanced capitalist societies: An empirical intervention into the debate between Marxist and post industrial theorists over the transformation of the labour process'. Mimeo, Dept of Sociology, University of Wisconsin

Wright, E. O. and Singelmann, J. (1982) 'Proletarianization in the American class structure'. In M. Buraway and T. Skocpol (eds.) *Marxist Enquiries: Studies of Labour, Class, and States. American Journal of Sociology* 88 (Supplement). University of Chicago Press

Yankelovich, D., Zetterberg, H., Strumpel, B. and Shanks, M. (1983) *Work and Human Values: an International Report on Jobs in 1980s and 1990s.* Aspen Institute for Humanistic Studies

Young, M. and Wilmott, P. (1962) *Family and Kinship in East London.* Penguin

Zeitlin, M. (1966) 'Economic insecurity and the political attitudes of Cuban workers'. *American Sociological Review.* 31, 35–42

Zimbalist, A. (1979) *Case Studies in the Labour Process.* Monthly Review Press

Zweig, F. (1961) *The Worker in an Affluent Society.* Heinemann

Index